KU-406-313

# ROMANTIC BRITAIN

✦

## THE NATIONAL HERITAGE OF BEAUTY
## HISTORY AND LEGEND

✦

EDITED BY
TOM STEPHENSON

ODHAMS PRESS LIMITED
LONG ACRE, LONDON, W.C.2

*Copyright*
*RS538*

*Made and Printed in Great Britain by*
*Odhams (Watford) Ltd., Watford*

# CONTENTS

W. F. TAYLOR

## TUDOR GLORY

*Few places can offer such a beautiful example of Elizabethan England as is to be found at the little village of Chiddingstone, near Tonbridge, in Kent. Here, facing the church, is an ancient inn and a row of delightful old houses timbered and gabled and still retaining the leaded casement windows. Here indeed there lingers the serenity of bygone days, and the mellowed, graceful beauty of forgotten craftsmen.*

# INTRODUCTION

## *by* TOM STEPHENSON

ONE of the most remarkable developments of modern times has been the great awakening to the pleasures of the country-side, and the growing recognition of the treasures with which we have been so lavishly endowed. Poets and writers in the past have paid their tribute, and in every generation there have been a fortunate few conscious of the fair face of Britain. Never before, however, has there been such widespread interest. Never has there been so much general admiration of our peaceful rural scenes, our mountain grandeur, our rivers, lakes and forests, and our numerous time-mellowed villages and pleasing towns, which, beneath their superficial modernity, still retain an air of less hurried times and many an intriguing memento of days that have been.

There was a time when Britain, with all its storied relics of the past, was appreciated more by visitors from abroad than by our own countrymen. Those who had the means would hasten to the Continent or to the far corners of the earth, woefully ignorant of the beauty and grandeur on which they turned their backs. Long ago Bacon remarked that " Travel in the younger sort is part of education ; in the elder a part of experience." This we need not dispute, but if travel is educational it does not follow that learning, like travel, may be measured by the mileage. Yet at one time there appears to have been a general acceptance of this fallacy.

The author of *Tom Brown's Schooldays* made comment on this :

" You have," he said, " seen men and cities, no doubt, and have your opinions, such as they are, about schools of painting, high art and all that ; have seen the pictures of Dresden and the Louvre, and know the taste of sauerkraut. All I say is, you don't know your own lanes and woods and fields . . . not one in twenty of you knows where to find the wood-sorrel, or bee-orchis, which grow in the next wood, or on the down three miles off. . . . And, as for the country legends, the stories of old gable ended farmhouses, the place where the last skirmish was fought in the civil wars, where the parish butts stood, where the last highwayman turned to bay, where the last ghost was laid by the parson, they've gone out of date altogether."

If Judge Hughes was living today, however, he would see how the wheel has turned. In cars, on cycles and on foot, the present generation escapes to the country-side of Britain on every possible occasion. Men and women, young and old, are to be seen following the highways to the far corners of the isle, penetrating lanes, grass-grown and at one time in danger of being forgotten, roaming the field ways and moor-land trails, ever questing for the beauty of the land.

With this new awakening there has arisen an insistent and insatiable demand for information ; a thirst for knowledge of the story behind the scene and all that has gone to the making of the pic-ture. For the artist the beauty may not be enhanced by a know-ledge of how it came into being, but the average man likes to humanize his pictures and to enliven them with visions of the romance, or it may be the tragedy, the toil and strife, and the comings and goings of folk who are now little more than memories, but who in their passing added some detail to the scene. There is a desire for knowledge of the making of mountains and valleys, of the clearing of the forests and the building of homesteads, hamlets and towns. Some seek information of the men who first made the trackways and the roads, of those who dis-covered the fords and built the bridges, of the

STEPHENSON

### A FOAMING RIVER

*Amid the lonely Pennine Moors on the borders of Yorkshire, Durham and Westmorland, the River Tees at Cauldron Snout plunges down these black crags.*

men who raised the earliest churches and conceived the magnificent splendour of the monasteries and cathedrals.

Within the crumbling shell of some feudal stronghold there may come a desire to picture lords and ladies, and knights in resplendent armour, jousting to gain an admiring glance from " beauty's matchless eye." We may seek to visualize the archer on the walls, the warder at the gate, and the feasting in the hall, and, not forgetting the tragic note, perhaps to sigh for the hapless captive in the noisome dungeon.

In the following pages we have sought to relate some of this long and fascinating story, to tell of

STEPHENSON

### THE VILLAGE SHOP

*Close to the yew-shaded churchyard in the Sussex hamlet of Bignor stands this quaint old building with its thatched roof, its diamond-leaded windows, its ancient timbers and walls of flint cobbles and herring-bone brickwork.*

mountains, rivers and forests, and, as far as possible, the history and legends associated with them.

Other chapters tell of the wanderings and workings of the first men, of the Romans conquering, building and civilizing; of the ravages and subsequent settlements of Saxon and Dane, and of the Conquest by the Normans. The making of the roads, the building of the castles, monasteries and cathedrals come under review. The development of the villages and towns and the story of the bridges and inns has also been told. Scenes of history and romance, the country of poet and novelist are included, and altogether, it is hoped, the work presents a readable survey of what has gone to the making of this the " most fairy-like and romantic of all countries."

The beginnings of the story take us far back in the annals of time to a period long before man

had evolved from his lowly ancestors. With the aid of the geologist we might trace from those distant beginnings the changes and chances whereby the land was raised mountain high and carved into giant peaks which through the long æons slowly crumbled and were carried to " sow the dust of continents yet to be." We should see the land sinking beneath the sea, being elevated only to disappear again beneath the waves. By these recurring processes of denudation and periods of deposition were formed the various strata which today are the very bones of our landscape.

Intermittent with the piling up of the great thicknesses of sedimentary rocks, were the periods of volcanic activity. The rare colourful beauty of Borrowdale, the domed brow of Great Gable, and the grand crags of Scafell; the shapely peak of Tryfaen and the cwms and precipices of Snowdon, all had their origin in the ejections of primeval volcanoes. So also at a later period of the earth's history issued forth those great outpourings of lava which subsequently were carved into the jagged fantastic peaks of the Cuillin.

### Coral Seas

The Black Mountains of Brecon and the ruddy loam of Hereford and Devon had their beginnings in lakes and landlocked seas inhabited by weird armour-plated fishes. In later seas where corals flourished was formed the limestone which now provides the soaring cliffs of Cheddar, the delightful dales of Derbyshire, the great rift of Gordale and the stark terraces and numerous waterfalls of the Yorkshire Dales.

In less deep water some uncharted Amazon poured the debris of a vanished continent, the sands which were to become the millstone grits, crowning the weather-worn arch of the Pennines, and forming that long series of edges, cloughs and spacious moorlands where the cotton grass blows, where the curlew cries down the wind, and peaty burns rush over rocky ledges.

The plains of Cheshire, and the gentle undulations spreading with a rosy blush across the Midlands, tell of the making of the new red sandstone in the deserts, the torrential streams and salt lakes of Triassic times. The limestones which sweep across the country from the Dorset coast to the cliffs of Whitby affording the beauty

STEPHENSON

## A MOORLAND ROAD

*Britain has its thronged highways, but it also has many a quiet lane.   Many, now neglected and often grass-grown, are only used by the local people and those seeking the peace of lonely places.   Above is such a moorland road climbing out of Wharfedale and making a graceful sweep with its grass banks and bounding walls.*

STEPHENSON

## A PEACEFUL HAMLET

*At the foot of the Chilterns, in Hertfordshire, is the pretty village of Aldbury.   In the centre of the village opposite the tree-shaded pond are these beautiful Tudor houses of brick and timber and old tiled roofs.   On the left are seen the remains of the old village stocks once used for the chastising of local delinquents. The village church, dating from the thirteenth century, contains the tomb of Sir Robert Whittingham (d. 1471).*

STEPHENSON

### A CHURCH BENEATH THE DOWNS

*Finely placed among venerable trees on a slight eminence at the foot of the North Downs stands the grey old church of Wotton, in Surrey. The name takes us back to pagan times for it is probably derived from Woden. John Evelyn, the seventeenth-century diarist, who attended school in the church porch, is buried here.*

of the Cotswolds and a chain of lovely villages, and providing the stone out of which Wren and others have fashioned many a noble edifice—these materials also were slowly built up out of the remains of corals and molluscs which lived when the unwieldy pterodactyl was pioneering the conquest of the air. In yet later seas there was deposited through countless æons the great thicknesses of chalk which today gives us the wide reaches of Salisbury Plain, the sleek curving downs of Surrey and Sussex, the beech-clad Chilterns and the wolds of Lincolnshire and Yorkshire, Dover's famous cliffs, Beachy Head and the Seven Sisters, the jagged Needles of the Isle of Wight and the lofty white wall of Flamborough Head.

Other strata have a story to tell of subtropical times when palm trees flourished where London now stands. From those sunny days may be traced the decline into conditions of Arctic rigour, when glaciers formed on the mountains and the roar of the avalanche echoed through the hills, and great sheets of ice ploughed across the land.

Today the cwms of Snowdon, the valleys of Lakeland and the glens and corries of the Highlands, are yet eloquent of those frigid times. In Cwm Glas, for instance, above the Pass of Llanberis, the grey hummocks of rock remain smooth and polished from the passage of the ice sweeping down to the valley. At the head of Ennerdale, Greenup and other valleys in the Lake District are numerous mounds of debris left by

the glaciers in retreat, and near the head of Glen Torridon, in Wester Ross, they are so numerous as to have inspired the name of " The Corrie of a Thousand Hills."

One glacier sweeping down from Scotland filled the North Sea and overrode Snae Fell in the Isle of Man, carrying rocks from the Galloway Hills and the Lake District down into Lancashire, and even into the Midlands. Another glacier swept over the Pennines leaving boulders of granite from Shap Fell, in Westmorland, strewn along the Yorkshire coast where they may be seen today, in the neighbourhood of Robin Hood's Bay.

#### Glacier Lakes

The famous Parallel Roads of Glen Roy, in Inverness-shire, also tell of this period. There, like ruled lines along the sides of the glen, are the beaches of a lake formed by the water impounded by a barrier of ice. In similar fashion the valleys of the Cleveland Hills were dammed, and the wide Vale of Pickering, between the wolds and the moors, was once filled with a great lake.

Slowly the land recovered from this visitation and vegetation gradually spread over the barren earth, clothing the bare lowlands and mantling the stark hillsides. The rivers began to flow again in some places filling a glacier-gouged hollow to make a gleaming lake, and elsewhere cutting new channels where their old courses were filled with mud and clay and boulders left

STEPHENSON

### A MOATED MANOR

*There can be few more lovely houses than Ightham Mote, in Kent, which lies surrounded by its moat, and it is almost as secluded as in the days when its masonry was new, six centuries ago. It has been suggested that the word mote refers to its having been the Moot Hall or meeting place for the courts of the manor,*

STEPHENSON

## MELLOW BEAUTY

*In the Wiltshire village of Potterne, south of Devizes, is preserved this lovely Tudor dwelling, now known as the Porch House. In bygone days it has served as the church house and as an inn. It has been carefully restored, and as will be seen in the above view from the garden, it retains an air of dignified old age.*

STEPHENSON

## STONE WALLS OF A YORKSHIRE DALE

*In the hilly districts stone walls often take the place of hedgerows, and they may be seen criss-crossing in the valleys, winding along the slopes and sometimes running over the highest hill-tops. Skilfully built without any cement, many of these walls have stood for generations. Above is a scene near Grassington, in Wharfedale.*

by the ice. Since then our streams have continued to flow unceasingly from the hills to the sea, deepening and widening their valleys, looping and meandering in the lowlands, and adding the finishing graces to the landscape. So have matured the delightful rivers of today, Thames, Severn and Wye ; the sweet placid flowing streams of the south country ; the brawling streams of the Pennines, that " tumble as they run " ; Tees and Tyne, Tweed and Tay and many another river which we now regard as beautifying features of the land.

With the passing of the Ice Age primeval man

Stonehenge, Rollright and Arbor Low, the stones of Callernish and Stennes and numerous other stone temples built to unknown gods.

Round those mysterious monuments there has gathered through subsequent ages a wealth of fascinating legend and mythical explanations of their origin. Curious mixtures of imaginative guesswork, and strange notions of wizardry, devils and druids.

To the land held by those Iron-Age tribes, Julius Cæsar made his flying visit and a century later Britain became part of the great Roman Empire. Time and succeeding invaders have

DIXON-SCOTT

## TUDOR BEAUTY IN SUFFOLK

*The lovely Suffolk village of Lavenham is well endowed with timbered buildings. The village was a centre of the cloth trade in the fifteenth and sixteenth centuries, and to that period it owes its distinctive buildings including a fine Guildhall. The handsome perpendicular church also is indebted to that old industry.*

becomes more in evidence, leading his gregarious life, shaping his flints and eking out a meagre existence. Centuries after him came the better equipped men of the New Stone Age, followed in turn by the people of the Bronze and Iron Ages. Their marks still endure, for it was probably they who first blazed the old tracks along the upland ridges. They made the gentle-domed tumuli, swelling on the skyline of the downs and moorlands, the ramparts and dykes of mighty Maiden Castle and the camps of Dolebury and Hambledon and Uffington. They also left us Avebury and

largely but not entirely effaced the imprint of the legions. Watling Street and the Fosse Way, Ermine Street, Dere Street and Stane Street are memories of the roads they engineered.

Some of their towns are now green fields. Others are revealed as excavated ground plans where the curious may trace the lines of the ancient streets and the foundations of forum and basilica, baths and temples, inns and shops, and the orderly layout of an early town planning.

In many a well-chosen site may be seen the remnants of a Roman villa, with tesselated floors,

STEPHENSON

## GREAT RAMPARTS OF AN ANCIENT VILLAGE

*On a hill-top in Dorset, a few miles from Wimborne, are the earthworks of Badbury Rings. This is one of the many camps or forts, as they were formerly known, of our prehistoric ancestors. It is now considered that the ramparts were the defensive works of towns or villages. Most of them date from the Iron Age, though some, it has been discovered, had their beginnings in Neolithic times. Badbury has three tiers of banks and ditches enclosing fourteen acres, and the middle bank, which is 40 feet high, is a mile in circumference.*

STEPHENSON

## RUGGED PEAKS OF SKYE

*The Black Cuillin of Skye present scenes of mountain grandeur unrivalled in Britain. Here is a view above the clouds across the desolate Coir' a Ghrundda. Directly above the small loch is Sgurr Alasdair (3,251 feet), the highest point of the Cuillin. On the right is the point of Sgurr Thearlaich. On the left is Sgurr Sgumain. Alasdair and Thearlaich are so precipitous from this side that they can only be scaled by the rock-climber.*

STEPHENSON

### SALISBURY'S SOARING SPIRE

*A landmark for miles around is the graceful tapering spire of Salisbury Cathedral which is 404 feet high, and which is the highest in England. Building of the cathedral was begun when Old Sarum was abandoned in 1220, and completed in less than forty years, but it was not until 1320 that this culminating glory was added.*

the ever-present bathrooms and the hypocausts of their central heating arrangements. Hadrian's Wall crowning the crags of Northumberland and reaching from the Tyne to the Solway has been preserved sufficiently to indicate the magnitude of their defensive works.

At Porchester and Pevensey and elsewhere may be seen their ancient forts of the Saxon shore, those defences which failed to keep out the marauders from across the sea, the invaders who, "plundered all the neighbouring cities and country and spread the conflagration from the eastern to the western sea."

of the fascinating origins of the place-names of Britain, often in themselves crystallized history.

Next came the Conqueror, seizing and suppressing and parcelling out the land among his henchmen. Scattered about the land are ruins of the great feudal strongholds which arose out of those times. From those medieval fortresses as comfortless as they were impregnable, grew the more homely mansions, many-gabled manor houses dormered and mullioned, and homes of more florid but not necessarily of more graceful design.

Side by side with the building of the great castles and baronial halls and the walled towns of

STEPHENSON

## SUSSEX GABLES

*At the foot of the South Downs lies the little town of Steyning, a place of ancient houses with grey gables such as those seen above. Edward the Confessor gave land here to the Abbey of Fécamp. Harold the Saxon king seized the property, one of the acts said to have brought the Norman Conqueror to England.*

Here and there a fragment of rudely fashioned architecture may bring to mind the days of the Saxons, of Aethelbert, diffidently receiving St. Augustine, of his daughter wedding the Northumbrian king and taking Paulinus with her to baptize the barbarians of the north. Elsewhere we may recall the saintly Abbess Hilda and the inspired Caedmon at Whitby or the Venerable Bede chronicling the story of the past and working until his last breath in the monastery at Jarrow.

Norsemen and Danes follow in turn, plundering and pillaging like the Saxons before them and eventually settling in peace to earn a hardy living from the soil.

So arose the homesteads, the hams and thwaites and thorpes of persisting villages, reminding us

the Middle Ages, we should see the developing architecture of church and cathedral and monastic splendour; the now mellowed grandeur of Ely and Wells, Canterbury and York, and Durham's stately pile above the Wear "Half church of God, half castle 'gainst the Scot."

So also must be included the stately ruins of Tintern, the splendour of Fountains Abbey, the romantic beauty of Bolton and Rievaulx and ancient Glastonbury steeped in legend, and the picturesque remains of Melrose, Jedburgh and Dryburgh, for these also are treasured features of the scene.

Another long story lies behind the making of the roads from the beginning of the prehistoric downland trails and on through Roman times.

EDGAR WARD

## CLIFFS OF DEVON
*At Seaton, where the River Axe enters the sea an outlier of chalk gives this bold headland rising above the curving shores of shingle in which beryls, jaspers and garnets occur. A theory with little foundation claims Seaton as the Roman Moridunum and the southern termination of the Roman road known as the Fosse Way, which ran diagonally across England by Ilchester, Cirencester, Leicester and Newark to Lincoln.*

The tale would take us through the dark ages of neglect, when road making was a forgotten art and the highways of the legions lay in ruin, and on through the centuries when travel between the towns was an ordeal not lightly to be undertaken.

From the groanings and curses of sorely tried wayfarers we may learn something of the discomfort and misery entailed. The glamour of

W. F. TAYLOR

THE VILLAGE INN

*In many an old-world village the church and the inn are the two chief features and often they are close neighbours. Here is seen the " Barley Mow," at Long Wittenham, a Berkshire village.*

the coaching days fades before the facts of slow and cumbrous motion, and the delays due to the condition of the roads. So also the curious shifts and dodges resorted to for the upkeep of the roads make strange reading in these days.

Along the roads we can also be reminded of many other features recalling the past, including the hundreds of famous and historic inns with memories of by-gone days. Their very names make an interesting commentary from the " Bear " and the " Ragged Staff," symbol of the ancient Earls of Warwick, down to the less imaginative " Railway Tavern " or " Bricklayer's

Arms." Many a picturesque bridge has a tale to tell, and perhaps a fanciful legend of its origin, and here and there may be seen the old toll-houses of the turnpike days.

Throughout all these centuries of development, through all the clash and strife, while others were blustering and plundering, crusading in the Holy Land or ranging the Spanish Main, generation after generation of forgotten serfs, peasant and yeomen, followed more peaceful pursuits.

Their work also must be portrayed for they cleared and tilled the land, and by their sweat and toil made meadow and cornland and sweet pasture out of the tangled forest and swamp and fen.

### Village Hampdens

They dug and ploughed and drained and drove the green of cultivation up the barren hillsides. They planted the hedgerows, the beech clumps and the avenues and glades, and built the stone walls over moor and fell and across the floors of moorland dales.

They built the villages and hamlets of every size and shape, spreading round the green, drawn out in a straggling street or huddled like sheep in a gale, hiding in the vale, or standing boldly on a hill-top.

Built of whatever materials might be at hand, of brick and tile and thatch, or from the doorstep to the chimney top entirely of local stone, their homely architecture is also an integral part of the landscape.

To them also we are indebted for the preservation of many a village green and piece of common land, for many a tale could be told of stouthearted village Hampdens who fought to save from enclosure the lands which were rightly a common heritage.

The shepherd returning from the hill, the ploughman crossing the fields to the village church or inn, the chapman journeying from one farm to the next or from village to village, the drover and the pack-horse man, and all whose business took them about the countryside—they made the footpaths and the winding by-ways, the ox roads and the White Ways and Welsh Ways, the Smuggler's Lanes and the Lovers' Lanes, which are also part of the pattern.

So through the long slow march of time, all these and other innumerable factors have contributed to the making of Britain and all its varied, appealing beauty.

A. A. MACGREGOR

## A ROAD TO THE ISLES

*Along the west coast of Scotland the sea runs far inland among the mountains. All traffic has to be ferried across these inlets. Above is Dornie Ferry on the coast of Wester Ross. Here Loch Alsh divides at its head into two arms, Loch Duich and Loch Long. The latter branch is seen above with Dornie on the far shore.*

STEPHENSON

## LAKELAND BEAUTY

*From the high crags of Ashness, rising sheer above the Borrowdale Road, Derwentwater makes a delightful picture. This lake, almost completely surrounded by hills, is one of the most beautifully placed of the English lakes. In the background is the swelling mass of Skiddaw (3,054 feet) which overlooks the town of Keswick.*

STEPHENSON

## MIGHTY MONUMENT OF THE PAST

*Many theories have been propounded in explanation of Stonehenge and, like other stone circles, it has been ascribed to the Druids. The monument, however, belongs to a much earlier period than that of those Celtic priests or " wise-men." It is thought to have been built in the early days of the Bronze Age, perhaps about 1700 B.C. Most of the stones are of local origin, but some of the smaller ones were brought from Pembrokeshire.*

# BEFORE THE ROMANS CAME

## *by* TOM STEPHENSON

IT is only within recent years that it has been possible for the layman to gain an idea of the life and habits of prehistoric man. Nowadays, however, we may learn something of the long ages that elapsed before Rome was built. Painstaking workers have been patiently digging and sifting the land, collecting innumerable trifles and laboriously piecing together the details of a most intricate mosaic.

One of the first difficulties is to gain an impression of the time scale. About 2000 B.C. the Late Stone Age was merging into the Bronze Age. Beyond that date there is a backward extension into unmeasured time, and it may well be that a million years have passed since the idea of fashioning a piece of flint into a useful tool first dawned in the mind of some sub-human creature.

Of the earliest men in Britain the land today offers little evidence except to the expert who is willing to make a minute scrutiny. We will, therefore, only outline the story in brief, and mention some of the places which have provided interesting clues.

In the little Kentish village of Ightham lived Benjamin Harrison, a village grocer who was also a keen archæologist, and whose discoveries set the experts debating at great length. On the North Downs Harrison found some flints which he believed had been roughly shaped by man. Today, while the authorities are not unanimous, many accept these stones as primitive tools.

These flints, possibly the earliest indication of man as a tool-making animal, are termed *eoliths* from two Greek words meaning " dawn of stone."

In the neighbourhood of Ipswich, beneath a deposit known as the Suffolk Crag, Mr. J. Read Moir discovered flint implements which he considered the connecting link between eoliths and tools undoubtedly shaped by man.

Of these discoveries Mr. T. D. Kendrick has written :

> " Pre-Crag man stands forth suddenly, unheralded and astonishing, revealed, as it were, by the swift drawing aside of a curtain ; his background is the darkness of the immeasurable past and he inhabits a land which was believed to be untenanted by the human race."

From this faintly visualized dawn of tool-making man, we pass to the *Paleolithic* (Greek *palaios* = old, and *lithos* = stone) or Old Stone Age.

Anyone familiar with the Norfolk coast at Cromer will remember the accumulation of flint fragments along the foreshore. Among this shingle have been found orange-coloured flints evidently shaped by primitive man. It has been

W. F. TAYLOR

### A STONE CIRCLE IN LAKELAND

*Scattered about the country there are many stone circles where our prehistoric forefathers carried out unknown rites. None of these ancient temples, not even Stonehenge, is situated in more impressive solitude than the so-called Druid's Circle at Keswick. Here one appears to be completely ringed with high and mighty hills.*

suggested that here was a workshop where those early artificers fashioned their implements. Many of the tools, including huge rough hand axes and scrapers and choppers, are so large that it is considered that the people who made and used them were men of exceptional strength with big and powerful hands.

Subsequent to the coming of the first tool-makers, Britain, in common with Northern Europe, suffered conditions similar to those of the Arctic regions of today, and glaciers ploughed across the land.

In those times Britain was still part of the Continent, unsevered by the English Channel. Therefore the animals, driven southwards by the advancing ice-sheet, or returning northwards in the warmer intervals, had no sea barrier to interrupt their passage. This land bridge would also facilitate the migrations of Paleolithic Man, for he also at times was, no doubt, compelled to retreat to a more endurable climate.

He was, it must be remembered, a hunter depending on the chase for his food, augmenting his larder probably with fish, berries, nuts and roots. He had not discovered the arts of cultivation or domestication of animals, and, at best, his existence could only have been a very lean one. A wanderer, with nothing more permanent as a home than a rude shelter of twigs covered with grass or skins, he had no anchorage, but roamed as he was led by his quest for food. Generally he appears to have lived in the vicinity of rivers, and the most abundant finds of flint implements have been located in such places.

So far, prehistoric man appears to have lived in the open, but towards the middle of Paleolithic times the Ice Age reached its greatest intensity, and the hardy individuals who remained to face its rigours were driven to seek shelter, and this brings us to the period of the Cave Men, perhaps 20,000 years ago.

Probably they inhabited mouths of caves and hollows under overhanging rocks. At Oldbury Hill, near the village of Ightham, previously mentioned, we may see one of these rock shelters. Since it was inhabited some of the overhanging

STEPHENSON

### A STONE-AGE DWELLING

*These overhanging rocks on Oldbury Hill, at Ightham, Kent, provided a home for prehistoric men whose implements have been found nearby. At the time it was inhabited it was no doubt considered a desirable residence, well placed on a hill-side, affording shelter from the weather, with an adjacent water supply.*

W. F. TAYLOR

A COMMUNAL GRAVE

*Communal burial was a practice of the people of the Late Stone Age, and over their dead they raised large mounds of earth, now known as Long Barrows. Some are 300 feet or more in length. Many of them contain stone passages and burial chambers. Above is the Long Barrow of Belas Knapp, in Gloucestershire.*

rock has fallen down the hillside. Sufficient remains, however, for the imaginative mind to picture a family living here; man, the hunter, ranging the adjacent country for his prey, and the woman busy with household life, dressing the food, scraping skins and fashioning them into clumsy garments. Some of their weapons lost and perhaps trampled in the mud, remained buried on the slopes beneath until Benjamin Harrison found them ages later and recognized the story behind them.

Kent's Cavern, near Torquay, was another habitation, and remains have been found there belonging to several distinct periods, and the implements range from the early drift period to the New Stone Age. This does not mean that the cavern was continuously occupied by man through such a lapse of time. In fact, from the bones which were found, it was evident that it had also served as a retreat for animals such as the cave-hyena, rhinoceros, bison, bear, cave lion, wolf, fox and reindeer. Another cave at Brixham provides a similar story, and the limestone caves in the Mendips have also yielded many clues of early habitation.

This Neanderthal Man, as he has been named, appears to have been a most unprepossessing creature. He had a flat receding forehead, with a heavy continuous brow ridge protruding over large eye sockets, a chinless jaw and thick neck,

and a head thrust forward. His arms were long and his thighbones curved, and he probably shuffled along with a stooping gait.

Neanderthal Man completely vanished with the arrival of a superior type known as the Cro-Magnon Man. This newcomer was tall and had a well-developed forehead and a strong chin. The first discovery of Cro-Magnon man in Britain was made at Paviland Cave, near Rhossilly, in South Wales. The skeleton was found associated with a skull and tusk of a hairy mammoth, and his bones had been stained red with oxide of iron which suggests the existence of some ritual connected with burial. Near the thighs were a number of small shells which may have formed a waist girdle, and there were also some small rods of ivory, perhaps the remains of a necklace.

### An Artistic People

Thus we come to the latter stages of Paleolithic times which were eras of remarkable development. A higher standard of tool making is evident and implements fashioned of bone, such as harpoons, are found, and eventually bone needles appear and there is, moreover, an indication of artistic tendencies.

Among these artistic folk there came from the east a horde of invaders, who have been likened to Philistines or prehistoric Huns. For a time

OFFICE OF WORKS                                                                BY PERMISSION H.M. STATIONERY OFFICE

## ANCIENT DWELLINGS

*A Skara Brae, Orkney, there is a remarkable group of prehistoric dwellings. The photograph shows Hut 7, the best preserved of them. In the centre is the rectangular fireplace, and on each side of it is a bed which would be filled with heather. At the back is a stone cupboard or dresser, possibly used for the storing of food.*

these barbarians dominated Western Europe and evidence of their influence has been discovered at Kent's Cavern and in the caves of Creswell Crags, in Derbyshire. With the passing of these people their predecessors rose again and developed a most amazing culture. In France and Spain, caves have been discovered in which are engraved and painted on the rock face pictures of remarkable artistic merit and small statues of ivory and stone have been found.

In Britain, so far, there have been no discoveries of caves decorated by these artists, but the Creswell Caves have yielded carved bone implements of the period.

A process of degeneration appears to mark the close of the Old Stone Age. Man the hunter and the artist passes from the scene and his place is taken by people in some respects his inferiors yet in others marking very definite advances. Thus we pass into the *Neolithic* Period (Greek *neos* = new, and *lithos* = stone) or New Stone Age, a time when Britain was emerging from the final rigours of the Ice Age.

It may have been about 5000 B.C. when these long-headed Neolithic men reached Britain, but some authorities put it as late as 3000 B.C., and suggest that the period may only have lasted about 1,000 years until the beginning of the Bronze Age.

These newcomers may rightly be said to have introduced the first civilization in these islands for they brought with them a communal life not likely to have been known in the Old Stone Age. They had learned something of agriculture, and certainly before the end of the period they were cultivating cereals. Unlike their nomadic predecessors, they were farmers and herdsmen. Pottery they knew how to manufacture, and their stone implements were polished instead of being merely shaped by chipping. Whilst their clothing in the main probably consisted of skins, they had discovered the uses of flax and acquired a knowledge of weaving.

### Early Villages

Their primitive dwellings were often sunk in the ground, and the depression was surrounded by piled stones upholding the walls and roof which consisted of a timber framework, perhaps filled with wattle and daub, or thatched with turf. The huts were generally grouped in villages, sometimes on sites which lent themselves to defence, and where some attempt at fortification was made.

Windmill Hill, near Avebury, in Wiltshire, appears to have been such a site and the camp was surrounded by three oval concentric ditches, the outermost of which had a diameter of about 1,200 feet.

The Trundle, near Goodwood racecourse, in

Sussex, was another site with an inner ditch and two incomplete outer ditches, interrupted by causeways, and it has been suggested that these barriers formed part of a defence with wooden towers. Another theory is that there were probably dwelling places situated between the causeways.

Another aspect of the settled life of those days is the evidence of the organized industry of the flint mines from which the raw materials for implements were obtained. One of these was at the famous Grimes Graves, near Brandon, in Suffolk, where the workings cover about twenty acres. As many as three hundred and sixty-six circular depressions have been counted, marking the spots where shafts were dug down to the level of the flint and then opened out into galleries.

A number of these flint mines have been excavated in Sussex, and one of the most interesting is that of Cissbury Ring on the South Downs, near Worthing. Picks made from the antlers of red deer, shovels fashioned from the shoulder blades of oxen, and fitted with handles made from deer antlers, have been found on this site as well as an interesting specimen of a prehistoric miner's lamp. In one of the galleries, the roof was found still blackened with soot from such a lamp used by a miner who possibly worked there 4,000 years ago.

## "Giants' Graves"

One of the outstanding features of Neolithic times was the practice of communal burial, and the erection of large mounds over the dead. Many of these Long Barrows, as they are termed, still remain and whilst they are of most frequent occurrence in Wessex and the Cotswolds, they may be traced from Lincolnshire to Wales and from Cornwall to the far north of Scotland.

For an illustration we might take the Long Barrow at West Kennet, close to the Bath Road, in Wiltshire. This was excavated in 1860, and then had a length of 336 feet tapering from a width of 75 feet at the east end, where it was 8 feet high, to a width of 40 feet at the western extremity. Near the eastern end some stones

DIXON-SCOTT

### THE DEVIL'S DEN

*Dolmens, or stone tables, such as this one on the downs near Marlborough, in Wiltshire, are probably the remains of Neolithic Long Barrows. The covering mantle of earth has been ploughed away or removed by the action of the weather, leaving exposed some of the stones which formed the burial chamber.*

ORDNANCE SURVEY                                                                    BY PERMISSION H.M. STATIONERY OFFICE

### THE OLDEST MONUMENT IN BRITAIN

*Avebury, in Wiltshire, was an important place in Neolithic times. Towards the close of this period and at the time when bronze implements were coming into fashion, this great temple was built. This view from the air shows the ditch and rampart which surrounded the stone circle from which an avenue of stones led to Overton Hill.*

were found protruding from the soil, and others were lying about on the mound, and from these it was possible to reconstruct the original work.

From the east end a double row of upright stones extended 60 feet into the mound and there terminated in a burial chamber. Both the chamber and the corridor were roofed with large flat stones, some of them a ton in weight. Over this the earth had been heaped in a mound, round the outer edge of which was a ring of standing stones and between these were courses of dry walling.

Another interesting specimen is at Capel Garmon, in Denbighshire. This had a side entrance and a passage leading into a chamber with three divisions. A series of Long Barrows have also been recognized on the Lincolnshire Wolds, some of them having significant names such as " Deadman's Graves," " Hills of the Slain " and " Giants' Graves."

Many other Long Barrows have lost their coverings, and sometimes the stones as well have been removed, and it is probable that the many dolmens (stone tables) as they are termed, are relics of Long Barrows. Such a one is Kit's Coty, between Chatham and Maidstone, in Kent, which

Pepys believed to be the monument of a Saxon king. In plan this is like a broad H with a large cap-stone set across the three upright stones.

Cornwall has several examples, one of the best known being the Lanyon Quoit. Wales is well sprinkled with them, many having interesting legends. Among them may be mentioned the Tinkinswood Dolmen at St. Nicholas, Glamorgan, the Maen Cetti, or Arthur's Stone, in Gower, and the one at Clynnog Fawr, in Caernarvonshire. In Ireland, about nine hundred dolmens have been catalogued and one at Mount Brown, near Carlow, has a cap-stone weighing one hundred tons.

### Temple Builders

The period during which prehistoric man, aided with only the simplest of engineering devices, expended such an enormous amount of labour in erecting these great tombs, has been termed the *Megalithic* Age (*megas* = great, *lithos* = stone). Before considering other relics of this period, it should be mentioned that the Megalithic culture did not terminate with the end of Neolithic times, but was carried forward into the subsequent Bronze Age.

The best known, and most popular, remains of this kind are the numerous stone circles, the Druid's Circles as they are often termed, examples of which are found in many parts of the country from the south of England up to the Orkneys.

It is now generally believed that these served as temples or places of assembly, and were the outcome of some deep-seated feeling which was sufficiently strong to impel men to co-operate in the gigantic labour involved in the erection of structures which still endure as tribute to their endeavours.

The first and foremost of these temples in for about one mile to another stone circle on Overton Hill, known as the Sanctuary. Recent excavations have been made along this line, and some of the stones have been restored to their original position. These can now be seen alongside the lane connecting Avebury with the Bath Road.

Stonehenge, the most famous of all the circles, is probably the latest in date, and is certainly the most elaborate. Avebury and Stonehenge may be regarded as the two extremes of circle architecture, the one the prototype and the other the culminating masterpiece. The former consisted

## TEMPLE OF MYSTERY

*This sketch gives an impression of Stonehenge in its complete state. The outer ring consisted of thirty upright stones carrying horizontal stones. Inside them was a ring of smaller stones. Next were five Trilithons in a horseshoe, then a horseshoe of smaller stones and finally a flat slab now termed the Altar Stone.*

magnitude and in antiquity are the Avebury ruins, in Wiltshire. Of the five hundred great monoliths which comprised the temple, only about two dozen remain, but by excavations and examination of earlier records, it has been possible to create pictures of its former splendour.

Round the modern village may be seen the great ditch and rampart which surrounded the temple, enclosing some twenty-eight acres, and having an average diameter of 1,200 feet. Within the ditch was a large circle of massive unhewn stones, enclosing two smaller double circles. From the temple an avenue of stones extended of rough hewn blocks and the latter of squared and dressed stones arranged in a more complicated plan. At Avebury and in most other circles, the stones are of local origin, but at Stonehenge some of the blocks were brought from the Prescelly Hills, in Pembrokeshire, nearly one hundred and fifty miles away. These stones, it is believed, were brought to Salisbury Plain in the time of the Long Barrow men, and as the monument was not completed in its final form until the Bronze Age, it is possible they were part of an earlier circle which was incorporated in the later work.

Much has been written of Stonehenge, and many speculations have been made regarding its purpose. But the precise object for which it was built is still a subject of conjecture. The fact that at the summer solstice the sun rises over the Hele Stone in a line with the axis of the monument has been used to formulate a theory of sun worship. At the heart of the monument is a flat stone known as the Altar, and outside the ring is another recumbent slab termed the Slaughter Stone, and these have been incorporated in fanciful notions of Druids and sacrificial rites.

Whatever the nature of the ceremonies, there can certainly be no doubt that it was a place of supreme importance in its day; an object of veneration, possibly a place of pilgrimage and, as the number of burial mounds in its vicinity suggest, a desirable and hallowed resting place.

### The Beaker Folk

The Bronze Age, to which we have referred, is believed to have opened in this country about 2000 B.C. or possibly a little later. The first implements of bronze from which the period takes its name were introduced by round-headed stocky people who have been labelled the " Beaker " folk from the beaker-shaped pottery which they brought with them. The main stream of immigrants is believed to have reached our eastern shores from the Rhinelands and to have established themselves among the Long Barrow folk on the Yorkshire Wolds. From there they afterwards spread northwards, westwards into Wales, and southwards to Wiltshire.

For the wayfarer the most obvious relics of the Bronze Age are the innumerable Round Barrows scattered about the countryside. These circular, domed mounds are particularly conspicuous on the smooth turfed downland where they may often be seen as gentle swellings above the general level of the land, and sometimes standing out clearly as rounded elevations on the skyline. In Wiltshire alone there are said to be 2,000 Round Barrows and about three hundred have been enumerated in the vicinity of Stonehenge.

Like the Long Barrows they served the purpose of burial mounds, and have afforded interesting information of their times. The beakers were buried with the dead, and may have held refreshment intended for the departed spirit.

Many of these Bronze-Age folk appear to have been sufficiently wealthy to adorn themselves with numerous ornaments. Fragments of leather garments, and of linen and woollen clothes have been found. Some of the chiefs fastened their tunics with buttons of gold, ivory and amber. Necklaces of jet have been discovered as well as beads of amber, glass, and various gold ornaments.

W. F. TAYLOR

### BRONZE-AGE BURIAL MOUNDS

*In many parts of the country and especially on the chalk uplands, may be seen domed mounds known as Round Barrows. The majority of these are burial mounds of the Bronze Age, and the relics found in them have provided information of that period. Above are some typical examples at East Kennet, in Wiltshire.*

W. F. TAYLOR

### HOME OF BRONZE-AGE MAN

*At one period prehistoric men built themselves dwellings similar to the one above which are known as Beehive Huts. These consist of slabs of stone set in a ring with a horizontal stone over the low doorway, the roof being covered with turf and supported by a centre post. This example is to be seen on Bodmin Moor, Cornwall.*

For a glimpse of a Bronze-Age habitation we may journey to Dartmoor where there are a number of hut circles believed to date from this period. Grimspound, four and a half mile south-west of Moretonhampstead, appears to have been a village of twenty-four huts surrounded by a dry stone wall. These huts consisted of a circle of upright slabs of stone about 3 feet high, backed with turf, a space about 30 inches high being left for a doorway. Near the centre of the circle was a stone on which may have stood a centre-post supporting a roof of boughs covered with turf or bracken.

### Travelling Tinkers

On Bodmin Moor, in Cornwall, are other examples where stone foundations may be seen in walled enclosures and, as on Dartmoor, the fields of the villagers may be traced.

Considerable light has been thrown on the period by the discovery of numerous collections of implements which had been buried by their owners, perhaps during times of crisis and not afterwards recovered. Some of these consist of broken or disused implements collected by travelling tinkers for remelting.

The travelling tinker and the tribal smith, it has been said, stand for hitherto unknown conditions, both social and economic, and there is abundant evidence of the commerce which

developed in these times. At Bologna, in Italy, there were large depots to which were brought for re-smelting old bronze collected from all over Europe including Britain.

Cornish tin was doubtless exported to Ireland, possibly in exchange for Irish gold, but it may be that the gold ornaments found in Cornwall were specimens lost by the Irish traders on their way to the Continent, for these people are assumed to have crossed the peninsula instead of rounding Land's End by sea.

There has been much speculation regarding the antiquity of the Cornish tin trade, and there have been fascinating theories about dark Phœnicians venturing so far for the metal as early as 1200 or 1500 B.C. Imaginative writers have given us pictures of these folk bartering for tin, and carrying it overland by ancient tracks to the Isle of Wight, or even to the Straits of Dover before they took to the sea for their home voyage.

Pytheas, the Greek explorer, appears to have reached these shores about 325 B.C. From Land's End, he says, the natives carried ingots of tin to an island called Ictis, which at low tide was left dry, and there they sold the metal to the merchants. Ictis is considered to be the little island of St. Michael's Mount, in Mount's Bay, although the Isle of Wight has been claimed as the site, largely on the basis of the similarity of its own name Vectis, to Ictis. This commerce had no doubt been in existence for some time before the voyage of Pytheas, but for how long we must leave in conjecture.

For fifteen centuries the Bronze Age developed and matured in Britain before the coming of iron. This metal which had been in use for some time on the Continent is believed to have reached England about 500 B.C., and with its coming a new era opened.

### Skilled Craftsmen

Bronze still remained in use during the Iron Age, and was fashioned into various articles including helmets, shields, mirrors and other objects. Iron, however, was used where its greater hardness and durability was advantageous. Beautiful specimens of the artistic work of this period, including some excellent enamel work, have been found. These testify to the skill of the early British craftsmen who were unsurpassed by any of their continental contemporaries.

Iron-Age villages and towns have been located in various parts of the country. At Chysauster, in Cornwall, may be seen the remains of a typical village. This consisted of eight large houses, four on each side of a street. One of the houses is an oval enclosure 90 feet long with masonry still standing in places to a height of 6 feet. A passage led into a central chamber which apparently was not roofed. On each side of this were rooms built into the thickness of the walls. Excavation revealed paving, hearths, ashes, a

granite basin and a drain along the west side of the house. Behind the houses were artificially terraced garden plots surrounded by stone walls.

At Carn Euny, four and a half miles southwest of Penzance, are traces of a village similar to that at Chysauster, and in one of the houses a doorway in the wall afforded entry into a fogou or underground dwelling. This was a stone-lined tunnel about 60 feet long and 6 feet high. Near the eastern end a side passage leads into a circular chamber 16 feet in diameter. This room was partly paved and under the flagstones was a drain extended along the passage. Another fogou at Halligye, near Trelowarren, is well preserved and may be explored with the aid of a torch or candle. In the tunnel of this one there is a ridge of rock across the passage, evidently intended as a booby trap or stumbling block to give warning of the approach of a stranger.

For the layman the most impressive remains of the Iron Age are the great earthworks which crown many a hill-top and which, with their mighty swelling ramparts and deep ditches contouring the flanks of the hills, present an air of permanence and of enduring harmony with the landscape.

There are more of these structures than we could include even in a bare catalogue, and mention of a few must suffice. Along the Berkshire and Wiltshire Ridgeway there are several outstanding examples, one of the finest being Uffington Castle. This stands on the edge of

W. F. TAYLOR

PRE-ROMAN EARTHWORKS
*On many a hill-top may be seen the earthworks of prehistoric men. Most of these were probably built in the five hundred years before the Roman Conquest, but some are considered to have had their beginnings in the Late Stone Age. The photograph shows the ramparts of the British Camp on the Herefordshire Beacon.*

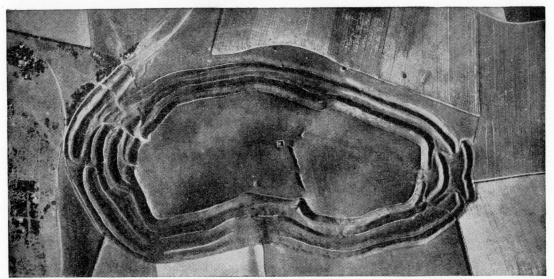

ORDNANCE SURVEY BY PERMISSION H.M. STATIONERY OFFICE

## THE GREAT RAMPARTS OF MAIDEN CASTLE

*This aerial view of Maiden Castle, near Dorchester, affords some idea of this great earthwork which is by far the largest in Britain. In late Stone-Age times there was a town here. For 1,500 years it appears to have been deserted, and then from about the fifth century* B.C. *it was again occupied until Roman times.*

the downs overlooking the spreading Vale of the White Horse. That famous animal, in fact, is carved in the chalk slopes beneath the ramparts. He would be dull indeed who could pace that great circling bank and look down on the outer ditch and the gateway leading to the camp without wondering by whom, and for what purpose, such a place was constructed by the forgotten inhabitants of the downs.

From that vantage point, nearly 900 feet above sea-level, we may gaze to westward along the line of the Ridgeway and pick out the ramparts of Liddington Castle, a similar structure where Richard Jefferies loved to bask and daydream on the smooth grassy walls of the camp. A few miles westwards again and we reach Barbury Castle, with double ditch and rampart encircling about twelve acres.

Salisbury Plain has several of these great earthworks, including Bratton Castle overlooking the vale of Pewsey, and the great upstanding camps of Battlesbury and Scratchbury, near Warminster, and the lonely camp of Yarnbury with triple ditches and double ramparts and complicated entrances as if designed to baffle unwanted visitors.

On the western edge of the Mendips stands Dolebury, with stone-faced ramparts, and west of this, overlooking Weston-super-Mare, is the similarly engineered Worlebury. In Dorset, at the eastern end of the vale of Blackmore, the twin heights of Hod Hill and Hambledon Hill are each crowned with a conspicuous camp.

Some of these may have had an earlier origin, and in some instances there is evidence of Bronze

Age and even Neolithic occupation, prior to the building of the ramparts, but generally these works are believed to date from the Iron Age. Although in the past they have been referred to as camps, this term is now considered misleading and it is suggested that " hill-forts " or " hill-towns " would be a more accurate appellation, for the earthworks were the walls of villages or towns.

### A Prehistoric Town

By far the greatest and most imposing of all these earthworks are those of Maiden Castle, near Dorchester. Recent excavations have established that here, 4,000 years ago, was a town covering about fifteen acres and enclosed within triple entrenchments. This Neolithic settlement was apparently raided about 1,900 B.C. Then for fifteen centuries the site was abandoned. Towards the end of the fifth century B.C. it was again occupied and developed into a town with upwards of 4,000 inhabitants. The innermost rampart was given a stone parapet and entrance was gained through a passage between massive stone walls. Inside the great gateway there was a sentry-box on each side. Nearby was a pit containing thousands of sling stones stored ready for defence. Only in Roman times was the place finally abandoned for a site now occupied by modern Dorchester.

Here, perhaps more than anywhere else in Britain, is evidence of the long drawn out centuries and of the labour and life of our prehistoric forefathers.

HADRIAN'S WALL

Torwood Moor
BLATOBVLGIVM (Birrens)
Gilnockie
CASTRA EXPLORATORVM (Netherby)
Newcastle
HABITANCVM (Risingham)
AMBOGLANNA (Birdoswald)
BORCOVICVM (Housesteads)
AESICA (Great Chesters)
RVDANVM
VINDOBALA (Rudchester)
SEGEDVNVM (Wallsend)
South Shields
LITTON
Bowness
Drumburgh
Stanwix
MAGNIS (Carvoran)
PROCOLITIA (Carrawburgh)
CILVRNVM (Chesters)
CORSTOPITVM (Corbridge)
VINDOMORA (Ebchester)
PONS AELII (Newcastle)
Chester-le-Street
Beckfoot
Burgh by Sands
Castlesteads
LONGOVICIVM (Lanchester)
Whitley Castle
LVGVVALLIVM (Carlisle)
PETRIANAE (Old Carlisle)

REFERENCE

| TOWNS | | | VILLAGES |
|---|---|---|---|
| MVNICIPIVM AND COLONIE | | | |
| FINDS INDICATING PERMANENT SETTLEMENTS | POTTERIES | | MINING SITES |
| LARGE TEMPORARY MARCHING CAMPS | LEGIONARY FORTRESSES | | FORTS |
| | SIGNAL STATIONS | | MILESTONES |

ROADS, COURSE CERTAIN
COURSE UNCERTAIN

HADRIAN'S WALL

NORTH SEA

IRISH SEA

HIBERNIA

NORTH CHANNEL

ST. GEORGE'S CHANNEL

BRISTOL CHANNEL

ENGLISH CHANNEL

GALLIA

Raedykes
Battledykes, Keithock
Inchtuthill
Kirkbuddo
Lintrose
Dalginross
Bertha
Grassy Walls, Scone
Strathgeath
Ardoch
Camelon
Bridgeness
Old Kilpatrick
Cramond
Inveresk
Castle Greg
Cleghorn
Castledykes
Channelkirk
Lyne
TRIMONTIVM (Newstead)
SELGOVÆ
Cappuck
Pennymuir
Makendon
Clyde Burn
Featherwood
BREMENTIVM (High Rochester)
Torwood Moor
CASTRA EXPLORATORVM (Netherby)
BLATOBVLGIVM (Birrens)
HABITANCVM (Risingham)
NOVANTÆ
HADRIAN'S WALL
EPIDIVM PROM. (Mull of Kintyre)
CORSTOPITVM (Corbridge)
SEGEDVNVM (Wallsend)
VXELLODVNVM (Maryport)
LVGVVALLIVM (Carlisle)
LONGOVICIVM (Lanchester)
BROCAVVM
ABALLAVA (Papcastle)
Moresby
VINOVIA (Binchester)
Huntcliff
VERTERÆ (Brough)
LAVATRÆ (Bowes)
Goldsborough
GALAVA (Ambleside)
ALONE (Watercrook)
Ravenscar
MONA INS. (Isle of Man)
CLANOVENTA (Ravenglass)
CATARACTONIVM (Catterick)
Scarborough
Cawthorn
Filey
BRIGANTES
Lancaster
Lead Mines
Malton
ISVRIVM BRIGANTVM (Aldborough)
EBVRACVM (York)
EDRVS INS. (Isle of Howth)
Elslack
OLICANA (Ilkley)
Newton Kyme
Brough
BREMETENNACVM (Ribchester)
LEGIOLIVM (Castleford)
Holyhead
VARÆ St. Asaph
Slack
Castleshaw
DANVM (Doncaster)
Caistor on the Wolds
MONA INS. (Anglesey)
COCCIVM (Wigan)
Melandra
Templeborough
SEGELOCVM (Littleborough)
SEGONTIVM (Carnarvon)
KANOVIVM (Carnarvon)
MAMVCIVM (Manchester)
NAVIO (Brough)
LINDVM (Lincoln)
Horncastle
Burgh Marsh
DECEANGLI
AQVAE (Buxton)
Caer Gai
DEVA (Chester)
AD PONTEM (East Stoke)
CROCOCALANA (Brough)
BRANODVNVM (Brancaster)
Tomen-y-mur
CORNOVII
Littlechester
CAVSENNAE (Ancaster)
METARIS ÆST. (the Wash)
VERNEMETVM (Willoughby)
VIROCONIVM CORNOVIORVM (Wroxeter)
VXACONA (Oakengates)
MARGIDVNVM (Castle Hill)
Pennal
Caer Flos
LETOCETVM (Wall)
RATE CORITANORVM (Leicester)
DVROBRIVÆ (Castor)
VENTA ICENORVM (Caistor by Norwich)
GARIANNONVM (Burgh Castle)
Caer Sws
PENNOCRVCIVM (Penkridge)
CORITANI
ICENI
ORDOVICES
BRAVONIVM (Leintwardine)
MANDVESSEDVM (Mancetter)
VERONÆ (High Cross)
TRIPONTIVM (Caves Inn Farm)
Godmanchester
Dunwich
Castell Collen
Worcester
Alcester
Chesterton
BANNAVENTA (Whilton Lodge)
Cambridge
Gt. Chesterford
Stonham
Llanio
MAGNIS (Kenchester)
ARICONIVM (Weston-under-Penyard)
LACTODORVM (Towcester)
MAGIOVINIVM (Little Brickhill)
Grantchester
Walton Castle
TRINOVANTES
Y Pigwn
MARIDVNVM (Carmarthen)
Y Gaer
GLEVVM (Gloucester)
DVROCOBRIVÆ (Dunstable)
DEMETÆ
Llandovery
GOBANNIVM (Abergavenny)
CORINIVM DOBVNORVM (Cirencester)
VERVLAMIVM (St. Albans)
CÆSAROMAGVS (Chelmsford)
CAMVLODVNVM (Colchester)
SILVRES
NIDVM (Neath)
BVRRIVM
DOBVNI
Alchester
Dorchester
SVLLONIACÆ (Brockley Hill)
OTHONA (Bradwell)
LEVCARVM (Loughor)
VENTA SILVRVM (Caerwent)
CYNETIO (Mildenhall)
PONTES (Staines)
LONDINIVM (London)
REGVLBIVM (Reculver)
ISCA (Caerleon)
ABONE (Sea Mills)
AQVÆ SVLIS (Bath)
VERLVCIO (Sandy Lane)
CALLEVA ATREBATVM (Silchester)
DVROBRIVÆ (Rochester)
DVROVERNVM CANTIACORVM (Canterbury)
RVTVPIÆ (Richborough)
Cardiff
ATREBATES
BELGÆ
CANTII
DVBRIS (Dover)
Old Barrow
SORBIODVNVM (Old Sarum)
VENTA BELGARVM (Winchester)
Alfoldean
LEMANIS (Lympne)
Iron Mines
Hastings
HERCVLIS PROM. (Hartland Point)
Ilchester
VINDOGLADIA (Woodyates)
CLAVSENTVM (Bitterne)
REGNI
DVROTRIGES
Yeovil
PORTVS ADVRNI (Portchester)
REGNVM (Chichester)
ANDERIDA (Pevensey)
ISCA DVMNONIORVM (Exeter)
DVRNOVARIA (Dorchester)
Hengistbury
MAGNVS PORTVS (Portsmouth Harbour)
BONONIA (Boulogne)
DVMNONII
VECTIS INS. (Isle of Wight)
FRETVM GALLICVM
STRAIT OF DOVER
BOLERIVM or ANTIVESTÆVM PROM. (Land's End)
DAMNONIVM or OCRINVM PROM. (Lizard Point)
TIN MINES

10 5 0    10    20    30    40    50   English Miles

Based on Ordnance Survey Map by permission H.M. Stationery Office

# BRITAIN OF THE ROMANS

## by TOM STEPHENSON

THROUGHOUT Britain there yet remains many an interesting memento of those three and a half centuries during which this country was a part of the great Roman Empire, enjoying the advantages of that amazing civilization, and developing under its rule to an extent not generally realized.

In many places we see relics of the days when soldiers and merchants from the far corners of a wide-spread empire wandered through the land, of the days when the toga was worn, when Latin was the recognized tongue and Roman culture prevailed, and men congregated at the baths, or worshipped strange gods in Roman temples.

Confronted with a straight stretch of road, we immediately hazard a guess as to its Roman origin, and frequently we are not mistaken. Camps and forts where the Legions stayed are not difficult to recognize. Here and there we may discern the bare outlines of a town, perhaps only faint markings in the soil or a few fragments of masonry tell the tale of vanished glory.

Along the moors and basalt crags of Northumberland we may walk the ramparts of Hadrian's Wall, the greatest of all our Roman relics. There we may linger within the confines of a fort or town whose lowly foundations tell of the mighty past. There we may trace the plans of barracks and granary, the commandant's quarters and the regimental chapel ; the forum and the temple, the shops and houses and baths, and, beyond the fort, the village where dwelt the soldiers' native wives and the various camp followers.

Elsewhere we may stand amid the ruins of Roman villas where mosaic floors, the elaborate

### ROMAN BATH
W. F. TAYLOR

*According to legend the warm mineral springs at Bath were discovered by Bladud, father of King Lear. The waters were appreciated by the Romans, who erected bath houses and made the place a spa.*

arrangements for the all-important baths, the central heating systems and other details may tell of the domestic arrangements of a wealthy citizen of the Empire.

On the Ordnance Survey maps are indicated Romano-British villages where the native population lived and worked, and where excavations have revealed the shards and weapons and tools of the common people.

Before Cæsar made his hurried invasions in 55 and 54 B.C., arts, industry and commerce had been developed in Britain. Kings or tribal chieftains governed from their respective capitals, and they had close connections with kindred tribes across the Channel.

Cunobelinus (Shakespeare's Cymbeline) who reigned until A.D. 43, gained some ascendancy over his rivals and was regarded by Rome prior to the conquest, as king of England and Camulodunum, the Colchester of today, where he had a mint, was considered the virtual capital of England.

In A.D. 43, during the reign of Claudius, it was decided the time was opportune for bringing Britain within the Roman Empire. Four Legions with auxiliary troops landed on the Kentish coast, possibly at Dover, Richborough and Lympne. After defeating the native forces commanded by two sons of Cunobelinus, they advanced to the Thames. There Claudius joined the Legions with additional troops, including the impressive elephant corps. Although Claudius was only in the country sixteen days, within that time the Thames had been crossed, Camulodunum seized and south-eastern England was under Roman rule.

Colchester has many reminders of its early days. Even the modern by-pass named in one

PHOTOCHROM

## NEWPORT ARCH, LINCOLN

*Once used by the legionaries and citizens of the Roman city of Lindum Colonia, this gateway which has stood for nearly nineteen centuries was the northern gate of the city and is still an exit from modern Lincoln.    This was probably the inner gateway, the outer having disappeared.    From here Ermine Street continued northwards.*

portion Cymbeline's Way, recalls Cunobelinus, whose capital was most likely at Lexden, two miles west of Colchester. A mound there, traditionally known as Cunobelinus's circus is thought to have been his tomb.

The existing city has grown on the site of the town founded by Claudius as the first Colonia or Roman colony in Britain. There the retired legionaries were comfortably settled with grants of land, and in the centre of the town was erected a temple dedicated to the deified Claudius. Beneath the Norman castle may be seen the vaulted crypt of this temple which, according to Tacitus, was regarded with hatred by the Britons as " a stronghold of eternal tyranny."

At first the town was unfortified, but after the disastrous events in A.D. 61, it was surrounded by a massive wall 10 feet thick and 30 feet high, and making a circuit of nearly two miles. One well-preserved length of the wall may be followed from the cattle market to the Balkerne Gate, the main gateway of the Roman town. The gate towers, the guard room, the arches over the stone-paved carriage ways and the smaller arches for pedestrians, stand as an imposing memento of the days when within the wall, warriors from distant lands bowed to strange

deities including the invincible Sun-God Mithras.

Other remains in the Castle Park include ruins of houses with mosaic floors. These dwellings were part of a street 300 feet of which was uncovered in 1920, when it was found that the houses had been built about A.D. 75 over the ruins of an earlier street which had probably been burnt down when Boudicca sacked the town.

### Advance of the Legions

With a base securely established at Colchester, the Romans set out to overcome the rest of the country, and dividing their forces they pushed outwards on radiating lines, one section advancing to the south-west, another to the west, and the third northwards. After four years' campaigning they had advanced as far as the line now represented by the Fosse Way, the Roman road running from Lincoln by way of Leicester, Cirencester and Bath to Axminster, in Devon.

Leicester, the Ratae of Roman times, has a number of mosaic pavements which suggests that the town had some affluent citizens. The Church of St. Nicholas is partly built of Roman materials, and recent excavations have established that the Jewry Wall, a large mass of masonry, was part of the entrance from the Roman basilica, or town hall, to the forum.

Lincoln, whence the Ninth Legion advanced from Leicester, was first established as a military centre, but later developed into Lindum Colonia, a privileged colony of retired Legionaries similar to that at Colchester. Except for a few fragments the defensive walls have disappeared, but in the street now known as Bail Gate, circles in the roadway mark the sites of the pillars of a colonnade which fronted a building nearly 300 feet long, and which is believed to have been the basilica, a usual feature in the forum of a Roman town.

### Slaughter of the Druids

Before continuing the westward advance the Romans deemed it advisable to turn about and subdue the Iceni or East Anglia rather than proceed with such a warlike tribe in their rear. This accomplished, a campaign was opened which was to last for thirty years before the intractable tribes of Wales led by Caractacus were finally conquered.

By A.D. 61 the legions had advanced through North Wales to the shores of the Menai Straits. Tacitus tells of the Druids and their followers gathered on the Anglesey shore, the women with dishevelled hair carrying flaming torches and dashing through the ranks like furies, while the priests poured forth curses on the invaders.

While the luckless Celts of Anglesey were being exterminated there came news that sent the Roman general hastening back to England. In the interval since the coming of Claudius wealthy towns had sprung up at Verulamium (St. Albans), Colchester and London, and these were now threatened by the rebelling Iceni, led by the redoubtable Queen Boudicca, the Boadicea commemorated by the chariot memorial near Westminster Bridge.

"Mighty in stature, terrible in aspect; her voice was harsh and her countenance savage," says the historian, Dion Cassius, of this fierce amazon who wreaked terrible vengeance for her wrongs before she poisoned herself in despair.

At Colchester strange omens and portents foretold her coming and a statue of Victory fell to the ground with its back to the enemy. With fire and sword Colonia was reduced to ruins, its inhabitants slaughtered, and the altar and temple to the deified Claudius were razed to the ground. London and Verulamium suffered a similar fate before this devastating revolt was quelled.

Each of these towns, however, rose again out of its ashes. London doubled its size and became the largest town in Britain, a city well planned and complete with adequate drainage and water supply.

Verulamium, near St. Albans, still offers

STEPHENSON

### ROMAN THEATRE AT ST. ALBANS

*On the edge of St. Albans are many evidences of the Roman town of Verulamium. Most interesting of them all is this second-century theatre which stood by Watling Street. Excavation of the site revealed striking evidence of the decline of Roman civilization. In the fourth century the theatre became a municipal refuse dump.*

VALENTINE

MULTANGULAR TOWER, YORK
*The lower portion of this tower consists of Roman masonry and is part of the legionary fortress of York which was surrounded by a wall with towers and gates.*

evidence of its historic and prehistoric past. The original town of the British Catuvellauni occupied the brow of the hill at Prae Wood, south of the present town. The town which Boudicca sacked stood a little lower down the hill near the River Ver. In the second century Verulamium became a walled city standing on the ancient Watling Street, and rose to considerable importance. It was, in fact, the only Roman town in Britain to be constituted a self-governing *municipium*.

Portions of the Roman Wall may be seen, and excavations are each year revealing more of the ruins including the lines of the streets, and the buildings with beautiful tesselated floors.

By far the most interesting feature is the Roman theatre built about A.D. 141, and so far the only building of its kind discovered in Britain.

There one may walk round the smooth grassy banks of the auditorium and look down on the circular orchestra, the gangways and the foundations and piers of the stage, the green room and dressing rooms, and the slot into which the curtain was lowered. Confronted with these ruins no great amount of imagination is required to picture the Roman citizens of Verulamium, perhaps joined by a merchant or soldier on his way north, sitting here and witnessing Greek dramas or pantomimes and burlesques.

The famous Agricola, who took a prominent part in the conquest of Britain, arrived in A.D. 77 or 78, and after completing the conquest of

Wales, he set out to subdue the north of England and eventually to advance into Scotland.

Chester, Agricola's starting-point for the north, had already been established as a fortress on a bluff of red sandstone by the Dee, then a broad arm of the sea, up which the Roman galleys came to moor beneath the fortress on a site now silted up by the sands of Dee to form the level ground known as the Roodee.

Deva, as this fortress was termed, from the River Dee, was one of the three legionary fortresses in Britain, a distinction it shared with York and Caerleon on Usk.

The existing medieval walls of Chester follow the lines of the earlier walls of the east and north sides. Roman masonry has been exposed in several places and the foundations of a Roman tower may be seen at the New Gate. The main streets in the centre of the city evidently coincide with the Roman streets and the picturesque Rows, of which Chester is proud, are built over the ruins of second- and third-century buildings.

In some of the shops in these thoroughfares may be seen odd remnants of this erstwhile city of the legions.

Agricola, in A.D. 79, overcame the Brigantes, and in the following year made his headquarters at York as being better suited for his further campaigns.

Ultimately he overran the north of England, and consolidated his position with roads and chains of forts. One of these may have been at

STEPHENSON

ROMAN MASONRY IN VILLAGE SCHOOL
*Schoolchildren at High Rochester have a reminder of Rome's departed glory. The school porch is built of stones from the adjacent fort of Bremenium.*

Ribchester on the banks of the Ribble, in Lancashire, where the ancient time-worn parish church stands on the site of a temple dedicated to Minerva.

From here one road was driven up the west side of the Ribble Valley across the vale of the Hodder and through the moorland country of Bowland on its way to Overborough. Another road ran on the other side of Ribblesdale to Elslack, in Yorkshire, and through the Aire gap at Skipton. Beyond there the road divided, one branch continuing across the Wharfe and over Blubberhouses Moor where a straight length of seven miles is still termed Watling Street, and on to Aldborough. The other branch proceeded to Ilkley and on to York. Agricola is believed to have established forts at Ilkley which would guard the route through the low Pennine Pass of the Aire gap.

Farther north another road was driven over the Stainmore Pass with forts at Greta Bridge and Bowes, and at Rey Cross on a commanding site overlooking the wide vale of the Eden, whilst another was located on the western side of the Pennines at Brough under Stainmore. These roads and forts are considered part of a strategic plan to encompass the great block of hilly country between the Aire Valley and Stainmore, the two natural routes through the Pennines.

When Agricola went to York, or Eboracum, as it was known, a military base was already established there with the Ninth Legion in occupation. In later years York developed into the chief military centre of Roman Britain, the " Altera Roma," or other Rome. Four emperors are known to have visited it. Hadrian was there in A.D. 121 or 122, and he it was who made it the naval headquarters. Severus stayed there, and there he died. Outside the walls, according to legend, his body was burnt and his ashes were carried to Rome in an urn, to which before his death he had addressed the words, " You are about to contain a man for whom the world was too small."

York's most prominent relic of Roman days is the Multangular Tower which formed the south-west bastion of the city wall. In the museum, as might be expected, are numerous objects, including altars to Mars, Hercules, Jove and Britannia, and a touching inscription " To the gods, the Shades ; for Simplicia Florentine,

**VICTOR AND VANQUISHED**
*In Hexham Abbey may be seen this tombstone of Flavinus, a standard-bearer of the Ala Petriana, a cavalry regiment stationed on the wall. It depicts a mounted Roman kicking a naked Briton, who is crouching on the ground and looking rather woe-begone.*

a most innocent being who lived ten months. Her father Felicius Simplex, of the VI Legion, dedicated this."

About sixteen miles north-west of York, the village of Aldborough occupies the site of Isurium Brigantium, the Romanized capital of the Brigantes where many mosaic pavements have been discovered. Aldborough stands on the road which remains to mark the line followed by Agricola in his advance into Scotland.

On the north banks of the Tyne, near the present-day village of Corbridge, Agricola founded the fort of Corstopitium, which later grew into an important military town and a base for the soldiers who were later stationed on the wall.

Excavations have unearthed the foundations of a forum and huge granaries as well as temples, shops and houses. One building, evidently a pottery shop, had its wares arranged in rows, and in the floor were found coins, perhaps dropped by the shopkeeper or intending purchasers in the second century.

Corstopitium knew some troublous days and was sacked on at least three occasions, and each time was rebuilt before being finally left to decay about A.D. 395.

From there Agricola drove his line into the wild and hilly country of the North Tyne and the barren solitudes of the Cheviots. At West Woodburn the fort of Habitancium is to be seen, and at High Rochester are the more imposing remains of Bremenium. This site has yielded a number of inscribed stones and altars which tell something of its story. Here were installed great catapults or stone-throwing machines and a number of stone balls used as projectiles, some of them weighing more than a hundredweight, have been unearthed.

On the roadside near the fort stands the base of a circular tomb believed to be that of Severus Alexander, a third-century governor of the fort.

High amid the Cheviots on the lonely heights at the head of the Coquet Valley, stands Chew Green Camp or Camps, which have been described as " the most perfect group of Roman earthworks that exist, not merely in this kingdom, but perhaps anywhere in the Roman Empire." From this desolate spot Dere Street crossed the Scottish Border and ran down to the Tweed and on towards the upstanding Eildon Hills. Those triple peaks suggested the name of Trimontium for the great fort which Agricola established at Newstead, near Melrose. Unfortunately no signs of this are visible today, but excavations in the past have yielded innumerable relics of the days when centurions of the Twentieth Legion dedicated altars to Silvanus and other gods.

### A Scottish Frontier

Still northwards Agricola thrust his way to Stirling, on to Perth and as far north as Inchtuthill, where another of his forts was established. Somewhere in the Highlands in A.D. 84, and after he had constructed a chain of forts from the Forth to the Clyde he fought the famous unlocated battle of Mons Graupius.

After Agricola's recall to Rome, there were frequent revolts which eventually compelled the Romans to consider the establishment of a definite frontier. In A.D. 121 or 122 the Emperor Hadrian visited Britain, and to him is ascribed

W. F. TAYLOR

RUINS OF CILURNIUM ON HADRIAN'S WALL

*At Chesters on the North Tyne near Chollerford are the remains of one of the most interesting forts on the Roman Wall. The photograph shows a street of the fort with bases of pillars and remains of buildings. From burnt debris found during excavations, it is surmised the fort was burnt on three occasions by the Picts.*

D. MCLEISH

## ROMAN WALL AT HOUSESTEADS

*Along the heights of Northumberland runs Hadrian's Wall, the greatest and most spectacular of Roman frontier works, extending from the mouth of the Tyne to the Solway Firth. The builders took advantage of the natural features by taking the wall along the highest ground which presents a steep escarpment towards the north.*

the famous wall which was built across England from the mouth of the Tyne to the Solway, and which is now known as Hadrian's Wall.

This mighty piece of engineering, the grandest of all our Roman remains, and the one most likely to rouse the imagination and bring to mind visions of the Legions, the Tungrians, the Asturians, the Thracians, Dalmatians and Batavians, is even yet a splendid witness of the power and infinite resources of Imperial Rome.

### Hadrian's Wall

Recent work has established that the wall, with its chain of forts, mile castles and turrets, extending for seventy-three miles from sea to sea, was completed within a period of five years. The borough of Wallsend, as its name implies, was the eastward termination of the wall. Newcastle took its Roman name of Pons Aelius from the bridge built across the Tyne in Hadrian's reign, Aelius being the family name of the Emperor.

Westwards from Newcastle for about twenty-seven miles, the line of the wall is now covered by an eighteenth-century road, and we may start our brief survey at the point where the

wall crossed the North Tyne at Chollerford.

There was situated the fort of Cilurnium, occupied by Asturian cavalry. This site on the private estate at Chesters, has been carefully excavated and in the adjacent museum is a splendid collection of inscribed stones, votive offerings and jewellery, and a reproduction of a bronze tablet, the " discharge certificate " of a time-expired legionary. Within the grounds may be seen the foundations and lower walls of the buildings, including barracks and remains of a colonnade, and the regimental chapel from which a stairway led down to the strong room which housed the pay chest. The commandant's house with hypocaust for central heating may be recognized, and near the river stands the regimental bath-house with seven small recesses which may have been lockers for the bathers' clothes. On the opposite bank of the Tyne is the abutment of the bridge which crossed the river, and three stone piers are sometimes visible in the water.

About six miles west of Chesters there begins the best preserved length of the wall, and from Sewingshields as we walk the wall along those heights, and gaze northwards across the brown waste of moors towards the distant Cheviots, we may well wonder what were the effects of such a bleak and cheerless prospect on the minds of legionaries from Spain and other southern climes. Did they with native oaths curse the bogs and sombre moorlands, and grey weeping skies of this northern frontier?

On this length there is sufficient to indicate the nature of the wall, and it has been discovered that the Second, the Sixth and the Twentieth Legions were engaged in its construction, aided no doubt by auxiliaries and native slaves.

### Building of the Wall

Stone was quarried in the locality, dressed and shaped and carried to the required site. At first the wall was intended to be 10 feet thick, but later this was altered to 8 feet. North of the wall a V-shaped ditch about 30 feet wide and 10 feet deep was excavated.

South of the wall runs the Vallum, a ditch which was crossed at intervals by roadways spanned by ornamental arches. This work is considered earlier than the wall, and may have marked the frontier in the reign of Trajan (A.D. 98-117). Throughout its length the wall was guarded by a chain of forts, and at each Roman mile stood a milecastle, providing quarters for the men on sentry duty. Between each milecastle two turrets divided the wall into three equal lengths, and it is supposed these turrets were used for signalling by fire or smoke.

From Sewingshields we follow the wall to Housesteads, the ruins of Borcovicium. This famous fort, now owned by the National Trust, is one of the most fascinating ruins on the wall. Careful exploration has brought to light the structure of the fort, and there we may wander in and out of the various buildings all neatly labelled. Here was stationed the First Cohort of the Tungrians (from Tungres, Belgium), one thousand strong and housed in ten long, narrow barracks. Three other similarly-placed buildings were probably workshops and stables. In the centre of the fort stood the commandant's quarters with courtyard and colonnade. North of this were two granaries, their floors raised to keep the grain dry. Some of the masonry of the four gateways remains, and in the south entrance the pivot holes of the gates may be seen and the central stone against which the doors closed. On each side of this stone are grooves worn by Roman wheels, seventeen or eighteen centuries ago.

Outside the fort were other buildings, and on the south slopes was a considerable settlement of civilians. Some of the houses there have been uncovered, and one is known as " the Murder House," from the fact that the skeletons of a man and woman were found beneath the floor. The broken end of a sword was found between the man's ribs, and, as by Roman law, burial was forbidden within the town, these two victims had evidently been concealed by the unknown assassin.

Westwards along the wall from Borcovicium is one of the best illustrations of a milecastle

STEPHENSON

### A MILECASTLE ON THE WALL

*At intervals of a Roman mile these buildings are found along the wall. About 20 yards square, these structures served as quarters for those on sentry duty. The gate of this milecastle near the fort of Borcovicus has evidently been narrowed at some period. On each side may be seen the beginnings of the arch of the gateway.*

By permission of H.M. Stationery Office                    H.M. OFFICE OF WORKS

## A ROMAN AMPHITHEATRE

*At Caerleon-on-Usk, once an important fortress of the legions, this amphitheatre has been excavated.  It was probably constructed before the end of the first century.   The arena, 184 feet long and 136 feet wide, was hollowed out of the hillside and was lined with smooth masonry 12 feet high to prevent the hunted animals from escaping.*

with walls and gateways still standing. Onwards we might still follow the wall on over Winshields, its highest point (1,230 feet), and on by the Nine Nicks of Thirlwall, by Great Chesters, and on to Birdoswald and close by the ruined Priory of Lanercost, built in the main of stones from the wall, and finally by Carlisle and out to the Solway at Bowness.

### Antonine's Wall

Less than twenty years after the completion of this enormous work, it was decided to establish a frontier farther north along the line of Agricola's forts from the Forth to the Clyde. This was built of turf instead of stone, and the forts were much closer together. Today Antonine's Wall, as it is known, is not so conspicuous a feature as Hadrian's frontier. A few meagre evidences may be seen at Mumrills, near Falkirk, at Bar Hill, near Kirkintilloch, at Castle Carey and on Ferguston Moor.

By the time the Antonine's Wall was completed Britain had known a century of Roman rule, and great strides had been made in the Romanization of the country, and a number of towns had developed into important centres. York and Chester have been referred to as legionary fortresses, and the third place of this type was Caerleon-on-Usk, known to the Romans as Isca

Silurium. Very little of the walls of the fortress which once held 5,000 soldiers is now visible. Although barracks and baths, temples and shrines have tumbled down, there remains an interesting feature in the Roman amphitheatre, long associated with later fables and legends.

Where once the officers and men of the second August Legion gathered to witness gladiators in combat, the baiting of animals and possibly the torture of prisoners, we may walk the grass-grown banks and gaze upon the arena and the masonry of the entrances, and see the inscriptions still in position recording by whom the walls were built.

Another town of considerable importance though never of military or commercial eminence was Bath, the Aqua Sulis, so named from the British goddess of the waters, Sol or Sulis. Even in those days this was a place of widespread fame, where strangers came from overseas to take the waters. The "great bath," partly restored, indicated the grandeur of the original structure, which covered more than one and a half acres, and included in addition to the swimming baths, vapour baths, hot chambers and other rooms.

A number of small towns served as tribal capitals in the same way as Aldborough, to which reference has already been made. Silchester, on the northern edge of Hampshire, was, as its name, Calleva Atrebatum, implies, the Calleva of the Atrebates. This, the most completely excavated Roman town, has unfortunately been covered over again, and instead of beholding the ground-work of its methodical town planning, its streets of shops and houses, its inns and forum, and baths and temples, only a crumbling section of the town wall is now on view.

Chichester, which was linked with London by the Stane Street, was called Regnum, and served as a tribal town of the Regni. There, in the middle of the first century, the British chief, Cogidubunus, ruled by Roman authority. An inscribed slab preserved in the walls of the council house at Chichester, records that on a piece of ground given by one Pudens, King Tiberius Claudius Cogidubunus, dedicated a temple to Neptune and Minerva.

Cirencester, that picturesque old town on the southern edge of the Cotswolds, was "Corinium of the Dobuni," the second largest town in Roman Britain, rich and prosperous and standing at the junction of several important thoroughfares. One more town which must be mentioned is Uriconium, which stood on Watling Street, near its crossing of the Severn, and not far from the Wrekin, in Shropshire. Much of this site is now

exposed, to reveal the bases of the pillars of the colonnade which formed one side of the great forum. One of the finest Roman inscriptions yet discovered came from here. This was a slab of stone, 12 feet wide and 4 feet high, which was placed over the main entrance of the forum, recording its erection by the "Cornovii," the local tribe, in honour of the Emperor Hadrian in A.D. 130.

Besides the evidences of town life there are many indications of life in the country under Roman rule, the most interesting features being the Roman villas, of which about five hundred have been discovered.

### Luxurious Villas

These villas, it is now considered, were not the homes of Roman officers or settlers, but domiciles of native landowners who had adopted Roman fashions and ways of living. Many of these gentry would have learned the Latin tongue, and some maybe read Latin authors.

One of the best preserved of these houses is at Chedworth, in the Cotswolds. There may be seen the general plan of the house and its associated buildings; its courtyard with a corridor on three sides, the dining-room with mosaic floor, and the bath-house with hot room and warm

STEPHENSON

### CRUMBLING WALLS OF A ROMAN TOWN

*On Watling Street, near Wroxeter, stood the Roman Uriconium which may have had its beginnings in A.D. 47 as a base from which to quell the native tribes of Wales. Eventually the town covered 170 acres and was surrounded by a wall three miles long. The photograph shows the remains of the basilica, or public hall.*

STEPHENSON

### HOME OF WEALTHY CITIZEN

*Numerous villas of wealthy Roman-Britons have been discovered, and one of the finest examples is that of Chedworth in the Cotswolds. The photograph shows the bases of two pillars of a colonnade, and remains of the buildings of the north wing. The dining-room has a mosaic floor with representations of the four seasons.*

room, and a plunge bath with outlet and drain pipe complete.

On the north side of the courtyard was the blacksmith's forge, and blooms of iron are preserved in the museum on the site. Along this side also was a fulling establishment for the cleaning of cloth, the manufacture of which may have been the source of the owner's wealth. Adjoining this building was the bakehouse, and next came the servants' quarters. At Bignor, in Sussex, the largest villa in the country has been unearthed, exposing some excellent mosaic work. Folkestone possesses a fine example, and others may be visited at Brading in the Isle of Wight, at Darenth in Kent, at Spoonleywood in the Cotswolds, North Leigh in Oxfordshire, and many other places.

The Roman Occupation, however, was by no means a period of unbroken peace and prosperity, and there are many evidences of uprisings of the local tribes, of invasions of the barbarian Picts and Scots who stormed Hadrian's Wall, and who burned and plundered as far as they could reach.

More serious dangers arose when Saxon raiders from overseas began to harass our eastern shores, and to meet this danger a series of forts was erected from the Wash to the Solent, and placed under the control of an officer known as Count of the Saxon Shore.

### Forts of Saxon Shore

In several places there are relics of this phase of Roman Britain. Burgh Castle, near Great Yarmouth, still displays portions of the walls and bastions of one of these forts.

Richborough, already mentioned as a landing-place of the Romans in A.D. 47, subsequently developed into Rutupiae, the chief port of the period, although the receding sea has since left it amid the marshes. Here also a Saxon shore

fort was built, and its ruins are sufficiently substantial to indicate the magnitude of the work.
Long lengths of the wall are standing, in places
to a height of 25 feet, and defended by external
ditches. The entrances and lower portions of
the towers or turrets on the wall are also exposed,
and various buildings, including the inevitable
baths, have been unearthed.

### A Roman Lighthouse

Dover was another fort, and tiles which have
been found inscribed CL.BR. indicate it was a
station of the Classis Britannica, the Roman
" Channel Fleet." Like Richborough it was
fortified against the Saxons, though its fort has
vanished. On Castle Hill, however, there is a
relic, the only one of its kind in Britain. This
is the pharos or Roman lighthouse, which must
have been 80 feet high when, with its companion
on the opposite headland, it served to guide the
Roman vessels to the harbour of Portis Dubrae.
The existing structure is 62 feet high, but only
the lower 40 feet consist of Roman masonry, and
this portion has been faced with later work.

At Pevensey, the walls of Anderida, another
fort of the Saxon shore, are still standing. Portchester, near Portsmouth, was yet another of these
forts, and there, as at Pevensey, a Norman castle
was later built within the fortifications.

Despite these elaborate precautions, Britain

proved insecure, and in A.D. 367 it suffered
severely from a disastrous raid by the Picts and
the Scots, who swept across Hadrian's Wall while
simultaneously Saxon raiders landed on the east
coast. Together they ravaged and thieved and
destroyed what they could not pillage. The
forces of the Duke of Britain and the Count of
the Saxon Shore were put to flight, and their
leaders fell in battle, and when Count Theodosius
arrived to put matters right he found the invaders
hammering at the gates of London.

It was after these foes had been driven out and
order restored that a series of signal stations were
erected along the Yorkshire coast, where their
remains may be seen at Castle Hill, Scarborough,
and at Hunt Cliffe, near Saltburn. The purpose
of these structures was to give warning of the
approach of hostile fleets, but Rome's power was
waning, and her rule in Britain was drawing to
its close. Today these ruined stations afford
tragic evidence of the final days of Roman
Britain for they disclose that they were overrun, their watch towers burnt, and the inhabitants
slaughtered, the corpses of men, women, children
and dogs being flung unceremoniously into the
wells of the forts.

So Rome's glory departed. Her troops were
gradually recalled, and in the fifth century Britain
was left to her fate, to lapse from a high standard
of civilization to a state little less than barbarian.

*by permission of H.M. Stationery Office*                                                          H.M. OFFICE OF WORKS

### RICHBOROUGH CASTLE

*Richborough, the Roman port of Rutupiae, bears witness to the decline of Rome. In the above photograph
are seen the ditches and the massive walls of a fort of the Saxon shore, one of the strongholds raised to
withstand the raids of pirates from across the North Sea. The walls have an average width of eleven feet.*

# LANDMARKS OF SAXON AND DANE

## *by* TOM STEPHENSON

SAXON England arose from the ashes and ruins of Roman Britain. During the period of the Roman occupation our eastern shores had suffered raids by fierce pirates from across the North Sea. But after the withdrawal of the Legions " a flock of cubs burst forth from the lair of the barbaric lioness " and the land was at the mercy of the relentless Saxons, Angles and Jutes.

It would be easy to present a picture of the period as one of continuous destruction, of sacking, burning and slaughtering and for this the early Chronicles would provide many lurid details. The Romano-British civilization, we know, was swept aside. Towns, temples and villas were overthrown, priests, we are told, were slain before the altars and the people cruelly slaughtered.

Even a race of warriors, barbarians as they may be, cannot, however, live entirely by the sword. If they were pirates and vandals, these invaders were also farmers and husbandmen. They soon began to cultivate the land, to build homes for themselves, not of stones such as those they found in existence, but of wood from the forests. Split logs of oak, like those to be seen in Greensted Church in Essex, served for the walls of the humble dwellings of the people, and also for the hall of the lord. Clearings were made and townships established and in later days a little church, at first also of wood, but afterwards of stone, became the centre of the village. Gradually the land was divided into parishes, each with its church and priest, and many of our existing churches stand on the sites of Saxon structures, though nothing may remain of the original foundation. Some retain odd fragments of the early masonry, and in a few places an ancient edifice has weathered the storm and neglect of centuries.

These primitive little buildings and odd remnants, a window or door or crypt incorporated in a medieval church or cathedral; hog-backed tombstones and weather-worn crosses, with ancient carvings and strange runes—these are some of the clues to the days when the land hitherto known as Britain was beginning to be known as England.

Such relics enlivened with stories from the Chroniclers may recall for us the times of the possibly mythical Hengist and Horsa, the days of ealdormen, thegns and ceorls, who worshipped Woden and Thor ; of St. Augustine converting an English king or Paulinus baptizing the pagans in the cold rivers of Northumbria ; of Penda and Offa, the fighting kings of Mercia or Alfred confronting the ruthless Norsemen.

Of the two centuries between the abandoning of England by Rome and the coming of St. Augustine in A.D. 597, we have but vague notions, and it is not always possible to discriminate between the facts of history and the fancies of legend and tradition.

Kent was the gateway for the Saxons, just as it had been for the Romans and for prehistoric

D. MCLEISH

**ALFRED THE GREAT**

*Winchester was Alfred's capital and at the foot of the High Street stands this imposing statue inscribed, " To the founder of the Kingdom and the Nation."*

STEPHENSON

### GREENSTED CHURCH

*The nave of this little church near Chipping Ongar, Essex, is probably 1,200 years old. The walls consist of split logs of oak placed close together in upright position. In 1013 the remains of King Edmund were deposited in the chapel for the night whilst on the difficult journey from London to Bury St. Edmunds.*

adventurers long before Cæsar came. Between Sandwich and Ramsgate, within sight of the Roman fort at Richborough, lies Ebbsfleet. Today this place is a mile from the sea, but in A.D. 449 according to the Anglo-Saxon Chronicles, it afforded landing for three shiploads of Jutes under the brothers Hengist and Horsa. Vortigern, the British king, accepted these people as allies, and, for their services, allowed them to settle in the Isle of Thanet. Soon, however, the newcomers turned on their host and fought against Vortigern at a ford over the Medway, at the place now known as Aylesford. There, it is said, Horsa was slain and Hengist with his son Esc or Oisc, afterwards ruled the kingdom.

#### Founding of Sussex

Sussex, or the kingdom of the South Saxons, had its reputed beginnings in A.D. 477, when Ella came to Britain with his three sons, Cymen, Wlenking and Cissa. Cymens-shore, the place of their landing, is supposed to have been near Selsey Bill, and from there they first advanced eastwards and captured the fortified town of Regnum, which may have taken its new name of Chichester from Cissa, just as Lancing

may commemorate his brother Wlenking.

Cerdic and his son Cynric are two other chiefs who, according to the Chronicles, came with five ships and landed at Cerdic's-Ore. This may have been in the vicinity of Totton at the head of Southampton Water, whence, it has been suggested, they advanced northwards along the ancient track known as the Cloven Way.

A little north of Salisbury, and overlooking the valley of the Avon, there stands a prominent landmark long famous as Old Sarum. This was the Searoburh where Cynric defeated the Britons in A.D. 552. From prehistoric time onwards Sarum was an important site. In Saxon days Alfred is said to have repaired the fortifications. The Danes, under Sweyn Forkbeard, found it worth sacking, and later both Canute and Edward the Confessor had royal mints there. In Norman times it became a fortified city complete with castle and cathedral, and today the most obvious features are the ruins of those buildings standing grey and forlorn within the great earthworks.

At Barbury, a few miles south of Swindon, and at Durdham, near Bristol, the British were also defeated and so the kingdom of Wessex was established from the English Channel to the Severn, and the upper valley of the Thames.

This is the version of the Chronicles, but in recent years suggestions have been put forward that Wessex was overcome by an advance from the east coast which followed the line of the Icknield Way, along the foot of the Chilterns and on to the upper reaches of the Thames.

Meanwhile, similar developments had taken place elsewhere. The immigration had continued and thousands of Anglo-Saxons had landed along the east side of Britain, slaughtered or driven westwards the native tribes, and established new kingdoms in the land they found full of promise. East Anglia was the home of the East Angles, and Norfolk and Suffolk the divisions of the north and south men of the kingdom. Essex and Middlesex were occupied by the East and Mid-Saxons respectively, and in the valley of the Trent was founded the kingdom of Mercia which later spread over the whole of the midlands, westwards to the borders of Wales, and then northwards to the Humber.

Beyond that river other tribes had founded the kingdom of Deira reaching up to the Tees, and Bernicia extending northwards again beyond the Tees.

About this time Rome once again exerted its influence, sending on this occasion instead of the conquering legions, a small band of missionaries to convert the pagan Saxons. When Augustine and his monks arrived in Thanet in A.D. 597, Aethelbert was King of Kent and also recognized as overlord of Britain. He had married a Christian wife, Bertha, daughter of the king of the Franks, and she practised her religion at Canterbury under the guidance of a French bishop Luidhard.

A few days after the arrival of Augustine, Aethelbert went to hear his message. This the king apparently did with some diffidence. Sitting in the open air, he ordered Augustine and his companions to be brought into his presence, " for he had taken precaution that they should not come to him in any house lest, according to an ancient superstition, if they practised any magical arts, they might impose upon him and so get the better of him."

### Historic Canterbury

Although Aethelbert did not at once accept the new religion, he gave the monks lodging in the city of Canterbury and licensed them to preach, and win as many as they could unto their profession.

Equally cautious was the king's reply to the address of Augustine : " You give us very fair words and promises ; but yet for that they are strange and unknown to me, I cannot rightly assent unto them, forsaking that ancient religion which this long time both I and all English men have observed."

Canterbury, among all its memories of later days, has many indications of its religious beginnings. Most famous is the Church of St. Martin where the Christian legionaries once worshipped, for, as Bede says, it had been built whilst the Romans were still in the island. There eventually Aethelbert was baptized perhaps with water from the font still preserved.

In the same historic city are the ruins of the

FELTON

### OLD SARUM
*Surrounded by ditches and ramparts this famous landmark above the Wiltshire Avon, was probably occupied in pre-Roman days. Throughout Saxon and Norman times it was a place of note and grew into a city with castle and cathedral before it was abandoned in the thirteenth century for the present site of Salisbury.*

VALENTINE

## A CHURCH ON A PAGAN SITE

*The Yorkshire village of Goodmanham was the Godmundingham where the pagan priest of Edwin, after hearing Paulinus preach, profaned and destroyed the altars and temples of his old gods.*

Church of St. Pancras which is believed to have served Aethelbert as a pagan temple before being dedicated by St. Augustine. The remains of a Norman Abbey occupy the site of the monastery founded by Augustine. There Aethelbert and his queen were buried and four empty tombs, which are preserved in the grounds, are believed to be those of Augustus and his successors.

Among Augustine's monks was one described by Bede as "tall of stature, a little stooping, his hair black, his visage meagre, his nose slender and aquiline, his aspect both venerable and majestic." This was Paulinus destined to take a prominent part in the conversion of the north.

### Pagan Northumbria

When Edwin, King of Northumbria, married Aethelberga, the daughter of Aethelbert, it was stipulated that she should retain her Christian faith, and that she should be allowed to take her priests with her, and for this purpose Paulinus was made bishop in A.D. 625 and accompanied the bride into pagan Northumbria.

Edwin, like his father-in-law, was no impulsive proselyte, and for two years he clung to his old gods, but in A.D. 627 he called a Witan or Council of his wise men and asked them what they thought of the new doctrine. At that meeting was made the famous speech, "The present life of man, O King, seems to be in comparison of that time which is unknown to us, like to the swift flight of a sparrow through the room wherein you sit at supper in winter, with your commanders and ministers, and a good fire in the midst, whilst the storms of rain and snow prevail abroad ; the sparrow, I say, flying in at one door, and immediately out at another, whilst he is within, is safe from the wintry storm ; but after a short space of fair weather, he immediately vanishes out of your sight, into the dark winter from which he had emerged. So this life of man appears for a short space, but of what went before, or what is to follow, we are utterly ignorant. If, therefore, this new doctrine contains something more certain, it seems justly to deserve to be followed."

Paulinus then addressed the assembly and after his exhortation Coifi, chief priest of the king, was first to cry for the destruction of the old temples and altars.

Edwin and his court were baptized at York and the king, under the direction of Paulinus, began the building of a larger and nobler church of stone in place of the previous wooden structure. So were laid the foundations of the forerunner of York's present-day glorious Minster.

W. F. TAYLOR

## ST. PETER ON THE WALLS

*Since Saxon days this church near Bradwell, Essex, has served various uses, but was restored in 1920.   Built of stone, it remains as a landmark overlooking the low-lying fields and mud flats of Essex.*

W. F. TAYLOR

### A THOUSAND-YEARS-OLD CHURCH

*The Saxon church of St. Lawrence at Bradford-on-Avon, described as " the most ancient unaltered church in England," probably dates from the tenth century and may have replaced an earlier wooden structure. For years the nave and porch served as a charity school and the chancel was used as a dwelling place.*

To continue the story of Northumbria, we might journey to Bamburgh, where a modernized castle crowns a rocky eminence overlooking the North Sea. On that craggy height Ida, the Flamebearer, first Anglian king of Bernicia, founded a stronghold in A.D. 547. A later castle there was occupied by Queen Bebba, wife of Ida's grandson. So the place became known as Bebbanburh, or Bebba's Burh, and later as Bamburgh.

#### Holy Isle of Lindisfarne

From Bamburgh we may gaze across to the Holy Isle of Lindisfarne, which for centuries was a great religious centre of the north. There, Aidan, who became Bishop of Northumbria, founded a monastery in the seventh century. Many stories are told of Aidan's piety and abstinence and his supposed divine powers. From one of the Farne Isles during the reign of Oswy, he beheld Bamburgh being attacked

by Penda and his Mercian army. When Aidan saw the flames of fire and smoke carried by the boisterous wind above the city walls, he lifted his hands to heaven and cried, " Behold, Lord, how great mischief Penda does," which words were hardly uttered, says Bede, " when the wind immediately turning from the city, drove back the flames upon those who had kindled them," and they forebore any further attempts against the city.

With a successor of St. Aidan, the Bishop Colman, we might travel to Whitby where, on a headland overlooking the sea, and high above the red roofs of the town, stand bare and forlorn the ruins of a medieval monastery.

Beneath those ruins have been found stone foundations of the Anglo-Saxon monastery established by the Abbess Hilda in A.D. 657. There, as a modern cross reminds us, Cædmon, a tongue-tied lay brother, received heavenly inspiration, and he who had hitherto been dumb at the feast, found himself gifted with the eloquence of the poet.

It was in A.D. 664 that Colman came to Whitby for a great religious gathering, the Synod of Streonshalh, for so Whitby was then known. Among the noted churchmen there assembled was Wilfrid, Abbot of Ripon, a stormy restless soul, frequently in trouble. Twice he was deposed from the Bishopric of York and eventually he was excommunicated. But despite his varied life Wilfrid was a great builder, and is said to have travelled his diocese always accompanied by a number of skilled masons. Some remains of his work may be seen in the crypt beneath Ripon Minster, but the best example of his skill is to be found in the church and monastery he established at Hexham, in Northumberland, in the year A.D. 673.

The dominant feature of this picturesque old town by the Tyne is the Abbey Church standing on the site of the structure built by Wilfrid. Of the original building it was said that " of all others throughout England, this church was deemed the first for workmanship, design and unequalled beauty ; and lastly, that in those days nothing equal to it existed on this side of the Alps."

Underneath the church is preserved the crypt of Wilfrid's edifice into which we may descend by the same stone steps used by the pilgrims who centuries ago came to visit the holy relics of St. Andrew.

### Seat of Sanctuary

Above ground is Wilfrid's font, made from the inverted base of a Roman column. Another interesting relic is his episcopal chair carved out of a block of stone and still adorned with scrolls. This is known as the Frith Stool or Seat of Sanctuary, a reminder of the Saxon custom of sanctuary which gave protection to the fugitive from his pursuers.

Cedd, Bishop of East Anglia, who was also at the Synod of Whitby, had his centres in Essex at Tilaburg, the modern Tilbury, and at Ythanceaster, this being the Saxon name for the Roman fortress of Othona at the mouth of the River Blackwell. Tilbury offers no clues of Cedd, but near the village of Bradwell there stands the rude Saxon church known as St. Peter on the Walls.

Cedd also had a monastery among " craggy and distant mountains, which look more like lurking places for robbers, and retreats for wild beasts, than habitations for men." Thus does Bede describe Lastingham, now a pleasant moorland village, seven miles north-west of Pickering in Yorkshire. There Cedd died and a few remnants of his monastery may be seen in the crypt beneath the village church. Two wells in the village commemorate St. Cedd and his brother, St. Chad, who became Bishop of Lichfield.

The Saxon villages have endured in name only and it would be fruitless to search for the homes of our early forefathers, the wooden dwellings, or the painted halls where the mead cup went round, and the gleeman's song echoed among the smoked rafters. These have gone, but here and there may be seen crudely-built churches where the priest preached of Christ

W. F. TAYLOR

**A SAXON TOWER AT SOMPTING**

*The little village of Sompting, at the foot of the downs near Worthing, has an ancient church with a curiously gabled tower which is generally believed to have been built prior to A.D. 1000.*

STEPHENSON

## EARLS BARTON

*On a grassy height above the Northamptonshire village of Earls Barton, stands this medieval church with its impressive Saxon tower rising some seventy feet above the ground, and which is said to be " the most noteworthy architectural monument of the Saxon period." The mound was probably a prehistoric stronghold.*

to people who would not have completely forgotten the pagan gods of their ancestors.

One of the most notable of these buildings is the small church at Bradford-on-Avon, which is said to have been founded by St. Aldhelm, a Bishop of Sherborne, who died in A.D. 709. The village of Wing, near Leighton Buzzard, has a church dating from the eighth century with a crypt beneath the chancel.

### Saxon Churches

Northamptonshire offers some interesting illustrations as at Earls Barton where the church tower still stands as a splendid monument of Saxon craftsmanship. Barnack also has a Saxon tower and Brixworth, between Northampton and Market Harborough, has a church which was built of Roman masonry about the end of the seventh century.

Roman ruins often served as a quarry for these buildings, and the mining village of Escombe, in Durham, has an eighth-century church built of stones from the Roman fortress of Vinovia, and

the chancel arch appears to have been rebuilt from one of the gateways of the fort.

The churches of Jarrow and Monkwearmouth in the same county also contain Saxon work and are of especial interest for their associations with Bede.

The Venerable Bede, the learned monk, whose *Ecclesiastical History of the English Nation* is our chief source of knowledge of Anglo-Saxon times down to A.D. 731, died at Jarrow where he had laboured so long, and there he was buried in A.D. 735. The monastery of Jarrow has gone, but the church of St. Paul possesses a chancel founded in A.D. 685. Within those ancient walls which the boy Bede saw being built nearly thirteen centuries ago, there is preserved a straight-backed chair which is said to have belonged to him.

Another phase of Saxon sculpture is expressed in the stone crosses many of which are still in existence, some of them elaborately decorated with interlacing scrolls or adorned with carvings of birds, beasts and human figures. One excellent specimen is preserved at Bewcastle, a little

Cumberland village north of the Roman wall. An inscription on this cross records that it was erected by Hwætred and Wothgær in honour of King Alcfrith, son of Oswy.

At Gosforth and at Irton, also in Cumberland, are other fine crosses, and at Ruthwell, in Dumfriesshire, a remarkable specimen is now preserved in the church. In the market place at Sandbach, in Cheshire, two restored crosses standing in the market place are said to have been raised by the seventh-century Peada, King of Mercia.

In the latter half of the eighth century the central kingdom of Mercia was ruled by the warlike Offa who established himself as overlord of England. The closing years of Offa's reign saw the coming of the first Danish marauders. Three ships came to the Dorset coast in A.D. 789 and the reeve, or sheriff, as he would be termed in later days, " rode thereto and wished to drive them to the king's town, because he knew not what they were ; and they slew him ; and those were the first ships of Danish men that sought the land of England."

W. F. TAYLOR

### A SEVENTH-CENTURY CRYPT
*The Church of St. Wystan at Repton, Derbyshire, has a Saxon chancel beneath which is this interesting crypt. Here the Bishopric of Mercia was established.*

Dread prodigies, we read, appeared over Northumbria in A.D. 793. There were whirlwinds beyond measure and lightnings ; and fiery dragons were seen flying in the sky, and in the same year, " the heathen men miserably destroyed God's church at Lindisfarne through robbery and slaughter."

Those first despoilers of the monasteries returned to their fjords and creeks across the sea, carrying with them, in addition to their loot, stories of the wealth they had found ready for the taking. So began the long series of raids and bloody conflicts equalling if not surpassing the ferocity with which three centuries previously the Anglo-Saxons had ravaged the land.

Bury St. Edmunds, in name at least, commemorates an incident of those troubled times, for it takes its name from the last Saxon king of East Anglia. The Danes, after sacking the monasteries at Peterborough and Ely in A.D. 870, took up winter quarters at Thetford, in Norfolk, and there in the same year came in conflict with Edmund's army. At Snareshill, some mounds on the heath are said to mark the graves of those who fell in this battle.

PHOTOCHROM

### ANGLIAN CROSSES AT ILKLEY
*The Saxons after their conversion to Christianity erected many elaborate crosses. On the tallest of those at Ilkley the four evangelists are represented.*

There Edmund was slain, having been, according to tradition, tied to a tree to serve as a target for the Danish archers who afterwards cut off his head. At Hoxne, a stone cross is reputed to mark the site of the tree to which he was bound. Thirty years later the dead king was revered as a saint and a martyr and his remains acquired miraculous propensities. A church was built to house his shrine at Beodricsworth, which later became known as St. Edmunds Burh, and eventually as Bury St. Edmunds ; now the seat of the Diocese of St. Edmundsbury.

### Alfred the Great

It was the famous King of Wessex, Alfred the Great, who ultimately checked the inroads of the Danes and laid the foundations of a united England. Wantage, a little town in the vale of the White Horse, prides itself on being the birthplace of Alfred, and a statue of him overlooks the market place. Somewhere on the Berkshire Downs, south of the town, was fought the battle of Ashdown in A.D. 871, when the Danes were invading Wessex.

The Chronicles tell how four nights after a battle at Reading, King Aethelred and Alfred his brother fought with the whole body of Danes at Ashdown. Aethelred fought against the host in which were the heathen kings Bagsecg and Healfden, and Alfred fought against the host of the earls, and both of the hosts were routed ; and there were many thousands slain and they were fighting till night.

The curious White Horse carved in the chalk near Uffington, though now considered a prehistoric work, was formerly held to commemorate this defeat of the Danes, and about three miles to the south-west, the name Ashdown still persists and a nearby mound is known as King Alfred's Castle.

Healfden and his army spent the following winter in London and some of the coins he struck there may be seen in the British Museum.

Four years later the same king fixed his winter quarters by the Tyne, and in A.D. 876 he dealt out the lands of the Northumbrians. So the Danes were established in Yorkshire, and subsequently the ancient kingdom of Deira was divided into thridings or ridings.

York, which Healfden made his capital, was for nearly a century ruled by Scandinavian kings. Today the venerable city offers no tangible evidence of its Viking times when fleets from Norway and Denmark anchored in the Ouse, but the names of some of its quaint streets commemorate the times of Ragnvald and Sigtryg and Eric Bloodaxe. Goodramgate takes its name from one Gothomr, Fishergate was the street of the

W. F. TAYLOR

### SCENE OF MARTYRDOM

*Near the attractive Suffolk village of Hoxne, Edmund, the Anglian king, was martyred by the Danes in*
A.D. 870, *because, it is said, he steadfastly refused to renounce his faith or hold his kingdom as a vassal from the heathen overlords. A stone cross marks the site of the tree to which he was bound by his captors.*

PHOTOCHROM

## SAXON EARTHWORKS AT WAREHAM

*The " Green Walls " of Wareham, in Dorset, served as the earthworks of the Wessex fortress of King Alfred, but their origin may be Roman or prehistoric.   In the parish church lies the marble coffin of Edward the Martyr, who, at the age of thirteen, was murdered at Corfe Castle in A.D. 978 by his stepmother's retainers.*

W. F. TAYLOR

## SITE OF DANISH DEFEAT

*The picturesque little village of Edington by the northern edge of Salisbury Plain is believed to be the Ethandun, where Alfred overcame the Danes in A.D. 878.   After the conflict the Danes swore that they would withdraw from Alfred's kingdom in the south and west and the Danish king, Guthrum became a Christian.*

Fiskare, or fisherman, and Skeldergate, the street of the Skjaldari, or shieldmaker.

In the same year that Healfden shared out the land of Yorkshire, the Danes entered Wareham, in Dorset. There Alfred made peace with them, but the truce did not last long, and in A.D. 878 the Danes seized Chippenham, in Wiltshire, and Alfred and his chiefs fled to Athelney, in Somerset. There for some months they stayed in the marshes by the River Parret. It was there that the legendary incident of the burnt cakes is supposed to have occurred, and from there that Alfred is said to have visited the camp of the Danes disguised as a harpist. A farmhouse now

was baptized and afterwards signed the famous Treaty of Wedmore which defined the boundaries of the Danelaw or Danish territory and provided that Guthrum should withdraw from Wessex.

Alfred's further campaigns, his taking of London from the Danes in A.D. 885, his raising of the siege of Exeter and his diversion of the River Lea to leave the Viking ships high and dry and easy to capture, we cannot attempt to describe. Mention must, however, be made of Winchester, the historic city which for long served as the capital of Wessex kings.

There Alfred founded the Abbey of St. Mary, and built the new Minster, both of which were

W. F. TAYLOR

WHERE ALFRED MADE PEACE WITH THE DANES

*In the Somerset village of Wedmore, Alfred and Guthrum the Danish king came to terms after the battle of Ethandun. There they agreed to the famous Treaty of Wedmore, whereby the boundaries of the Danelaw were defined, and after which Guthrum retired from Wessex and settled in East Anglia in comparative peace.*

stands on the site where Alfred founded Athelney Abbey and a monument is all that marks his refuge.

From this retreat Alfred rallied his men, and the banner of the golden dragon, the emblem of Wessex, was unfurled for a decisive onslaught on the Danes at Ethandun. The attractive village of Edington, which lies beneath the Wiltshire Downs, near Westbury, is believed to have been the site of this conflict, where Alfred fought with the whole force of the Danes and put them to flight.

Three weeks after this battle the Danish king, Guthrum, was lavishly entertained by Alfred at Aller, a Somerset village near Athelney. Guthrum

destroyed at the Reformation. There also he initiated the recording of the Anglo-Saxon Chronicle and the compilation of books for the education of his people.

Edward the Elder and his sister Ethelflaed continued the work initiated by their father Alfred by fortifying the English burghs, restoring the crumbling fortifications of the Romans or erecting new earthworks where necessary.

Tamworth, the old capital of Mercia, was so fortified by Ethelflaed and in A.D. 907 she restored the Roman city of Chester. Runcorn and Eddisbury, in Cheshire, and Shrewsbury and Bridgnorth, in Shropshire, were other places strengthened by this lady. Under Edward the Danelaw was brought under English rule and the Danish burghs became the centres of the shires named after them as in Lincoln, Derby, Leicester and Nottingham, and for each shire of the Danelaw a Danish earl was responsible to the English king.

Aethelstan succeeded his father, Edward, and according to the Anglo-Saxon Chronicle he was crowned at Kingston-on-Thames. An interesting relic of those days is a stone preserved in the market place, where seven Saxon kings are reputed to have been crowned.

### Battle of Brunanburgh

Somewhere in the north, Athelstan fought the unlocated Battle of Brunanburgh, where five kings lay on the field of battle in the bloom of youth, as well as seven of the earls of Anlaf. Before this conflict Athelstan is said to have visited Beverley Minster and to have placed on the altar the sword given to him by his grandfather, Alfred, and there the weapon lies in the tomb of St. John of Beverley.

The interesting old town of Malmesbury, in Wiltshire, also claims association with this monarch, for there he restored an ancient monastery and in the parish church, itself part of a medieval abbey, Athelstan's tomb may be seen.

Towards the end of the tenth century the

Danes were again on the warpath, reckless and ruthless as ever. The pleasant little Berkshire town of Wallingford, which, like Wareham, still preserves its old earthworks, was one of the many places to suffer in these later campaigns. On the downs south of Wallingford stands the burial mound of Cuichelme, a Wessex king. This was supposed to be an ominous spot for the Danes, for it was foretold that if they ever came there they would never get back to the sea. But the plunderers scorned the old wives' tale, and in defiance went to Cuichelme's Low, or Cuckamsley Hill, and after a battle at Kennet, returned to the coast by Winchester where the people might see the rank and iniquitous foe as they passed by their gates carrying their meat and plunder to the sea.

Ten years after this episode England was ruled by the Danish king, Canute. In 1013, his doughty father, Sweyn Forkbeard, had been accepted king, but his reign was brief and after his death an attempt was made to reinstate an English monarch.

At Ashingdon, in Essex, Canute battled with Edmund Ironside, and Canute, we are told, had the victory, though all England fought against him. Edmund thereupon fled to the village of Deerhurst, south of Tewkesbury.

Two centuries previously a monastery had been founded in Deerhurst, and the Abbey

HUMPHREY AND VERA JOEL

### A STREET IN SHAFTESBURY
" One of the queerest and quaintest spots in England " was Thomas Hardy's description of this ancient Dorset town which overlooks the picturesque vale of Blackmore. Here Alfred founded an abbey on the site of a pagan temple and this was probably the nucleus of the town. Canute is said to have died here in 1035.

Church, restored, of course, in subsequent ages, now serves as the Parish Church and is a beautiful and interesting structure. Not far from the church is another Saxon building, known as Odda's Chapel, which according to an inscription found in an adjacent orchard, was built by Earl Odda in the reign of Edward the Confessor.

South of the village, in a meadow now known as the "Naight," but then termed "Olney," an island in the Severn marshes, Edmund Ironside and Canute met in 1016. There they became allies and sworn brothers, and it was agreed Edmund should rule Wessex, and Canute Mercia and the north.

Only a few months after this Edmund died and was buried with his grandfather, Edgar, at Glastonbury. Canute thereupon became King of England, and for a time he also ruled Norway and Denmark.

### Palace of Canute

The charming village of Bosham, near Chichester, also has memories of Canute. Whether he ever rebuked the waves may be questionable, but Bosham, like Southampton, claims to have been the scene of that incident. There he had a palace, and through the centuries there was handed down a tradition that his infant daughter had been buried in the church. During restorations in 1865 a stone coffin and some bones of a child were found on the legendary site, and this spot is now marked by a tile bearing the Danish raven.

Bosham also serves as a reminder of the closing days of Saxon England, for its little church is figured in the famous Bayeux tapestry. In Bosham, it is said, there was of old a palace belonging to Harold Godwinson, the ill-fated monarch who in his brief reign made that famous march from Sussex to Yorkshire, there to overcome at Stamford Bridge the Norsemen under Tostig, his brother, and Harold Hardrada of Norway.

HUMPHREY AND VERA JOEL

#### BOSHAM HARBOUR
*The church of this Sussex hamlet dates from early Saxon times. In the seventh century Bishop Wilfrid found a colony of Irish monks there. Tradition makes it a home of Canute, and Harold had a palace there.*

The Saxon Chronicle in its usual terse style tells of one brave Norwegian who held the bridge over the Derwent. "An Englishman aimed at him with a javelin, but it availed nothing. Then came another under the bridge and pierced him terribly inwards under the coat of mail. And Harold, king of the English, then came over the bridge followed by his army." Both the king's brother and Harold Hardrada of Norway were killed in the battle.

These foes conquered we may picture Harold hastening southwards again to that battle on the outskirts of Hastings where he was to meet his death and the era of Saxon England was to come to its close.

W. F. TAYLOR

## TINTAGEL

*" Wild Tintagel by the Cornish seas " figures in legends of Uther Pendragon and Ygerne, the parents of Arthur, of the wizard Merlin and the romance of Tristram and Iseult. It was the supposed birthplace of Arthur, and, according to the old tales, he still haunts the scene in the shape of a bird—the Cornish chough. The castle was most likely a Norman building and was once a stronghold of the Earls of Cornwall.*

# KING ARTHUR AND HIS KNIGHTS

## *by* TOM STEPHENSON

ARTHUR of Britain, however insubstantial a figure he may be in history, is commemorated in folk lore and legend throughout the land. This mysterious, perhaps mythical hero of romance and fable, this champion of many wondrous exploits, the favoured of the fairies and most glamorous of kings, yet lives in the tales that are told of Tintagel and Glastonbury and " many towered Camelot." In place-names and stories his name occurs from Cornwall to Caerleon and Carlisle, and even beyond the Border, for has not Edinburgh its Arthur's Seat and Argyll its Ben Arthur?

Whether Arthur ever lived has long been debated. Caxton stated " that diverse men hold opinion that there was no such Arthur, and that all such books as be made of him be but feigned and fables."

The ninth century Welsh Nennius makes Arthur a " Dux bellorum " or war leader who led the Britons against the Saxons in twelve battles, the last of which was fought at Mount Badon, possibly near Bath. Gildas, another historian, says this battle was fought at the time of his nativity, about A.D. 516. Gildas, however, makes no mention of Arthur.

Allusions to Arthur occur in the songs of the earliest Welsh bards, some of whom lived in the sixth and seventh centuries, but it is in the twelfth century that he attains his full heroic prominence with the appearance of Geoffrey Monmouth's *History of the Kings of Britain*. In 1485 Caxton printed Mallory's *La Morte d'Arthur*, and by that time innumerable legends had gathered round the supposed erstwhile British king. Arthur had become a phantom monarch and leader of a goodly array of noble knights, and fairy tales and notions of intervening ages had been taken to embellish the tale.

One of the best known of Arthur's haunts is the Castle of Tintagel on the Cornish coast. It matters not that the masonry is of Norman or perhaps later date. The legends assert that Arthur, with Lancelot and Gawaine, came to a little chasm in the combe and saw that the enclosure of the castle was fallen down into an

PHOTOCHROM

### SLAUGHTER BRIDGE

*This bridge near Camelford, in Cornwall, is claimed to be the scene of Arthur's last battle when he was mortally wounded by his rebel nephew, Mordred. According to one version, the stricken king was borne to Tintagel and all the time he lay dying the sea and winds moaned unceasingly until the hero was buried at Glastonbury.*

abysm. A priest told them it was the great Tintagel, and when they asked how it was the ground was caved in, he gave the following explanation.

"King Uther Pendragon, that was father to King Arthur, held a great court and summoned all his barons. The king of this castle that then was here was called Gorlois. He went to the court and took his wife with him that was named Ygerne, and she was the fairest dame in any kingdom.

"Gorlois liking not Uther's overtures to

it was not for himself but for his uncle. On the voyage home, however, Tristram and Iseult drank a love potion which had been prepared by Iseult's mother, and which was to have been given to King Mark and his bride on the nuptial night. By the virtues of that drink, ' happed the love first betwixt Sir Tristram and La Beale Isoud, the which love never departed the days of their life.'

"Iseult, nevertheless, married the Cornish king, and there is a long story of the lovers' intrigues and escapes until they are caught in guilt. Tristram

EDGAR WARD

### GLASTONBURY AND ITS FAMOUS TOR

*This ancient town is the supposed Avalon, the fairyland or paradise to which the dying Arthur was borne by fair maidens. There Arthur and his Queen Guenevere were said to have been buried. On the Tor, seen in the background, was buried, according to tradition, the Holy Grail brought by Joseph of Arimathea.*

Ygerne, left unceremoniously and brought her back to Tintagel. Uther demanded that she should be returned to the court, and, on being defied, came and besieged the castle. Now Uther had with him the crafty Merlin who changed the king into the semblance of Gorlois and so he gained access to Ygerne and ' begat King Arthur in the Great Hall that was next to the enclosure where this abysm is. And for this sin hath the ground sunk in this wise.'

#### Tristram and Iseult

" ' Tyntagel, on its surge-beat hill,' also figures in the romance of Tristram and Iseult. Tristram was the son of a British prince and nephew of King Mark of Cornwall, who had a stronghold at Tintagel. In early life Tristram proved his prowess by overcoming an Irish giant and shortly afterwards he journeyed to Ireland and met Iseult, La Beale Isoud as Mallory names her.

" Of all earthly men Iseult loved Tristram most, but when the knight asked for her hand

subsequently withdrew to Brittany, where, believing himself forgotten by his uncle's wife, he wed the Iseult of the White Hands, who, however, was but wife in name. In the end, dying of a poisoned wound, Tristram sent for Iseult. If she came the ship was to bear a white sail, but if she refused then a black sail was to be shown.

"Tristram is falsely told by his wife that the ship is returning with a black sail, and his hope departs. Iseult arrives too late to save him and dies by his side, and so in a ship they bore those lovers cold and

" ' In Cornwall Tristram and Queen Iseult lay ;
In King Marc's chapel in Tyntagel old.' "

Camelford, a few miles inland from Tintagel, has been claimed as the original Camelot, where " the joyous court of knights and beauteous ladies of Arthur's day, held high revelry." But there is little ground for the assumption, and Cadbury, in Somerset, is a more likely locality.

Near Camelford, however, is Slaughter Bridge, with its tradition of being so named from the site of Arthur's last conflict. Four miles from Camelford, amid the shaggy brown moors, is Dozmary Pool. There exists the general belief that this was the mere in which the dying Arthur bid Sir Bedivere fling the brand Excalibur, the famous weapon bestowed on Arthur by the Lady of the Lake.

This story, however, is also localized in the ancient city of Glastonbury. There the River Brue is spanned by a bridge known as " Pomparles." The meaning of the name is said to be the " Bridge Perilous." Leland, the king's antiquary, about 1542, refers to the bridge of his day as " Pont Perlus, wher men fable that Arture cast in his Swerd."

For seven centuries at least Glastonbury has been supposedly the island valley of Avilion, or Avalon, the vague and shadowy Celtic paradise,
" Where falls not hail, or rain, or any snow,
Nor ever wind blows loudly ; but it lies
Deep meadowed, happy, fair with orchard-
    lawns
And bowery hollows crown'd with summer
    sea."
And that last battle where " there were slain all the brave ones, Arthur's warriors, high and low, and all the Britons of Arthur's board," Arthur declared he would " fare to Avalon, to the fairest of all maidens, to Argante, the Queen, an elf most fair, and she shall make my wounds all sound ; make me all whole with healing draughts, and afterwards I will come again to my kingdom and dwell with the Britons with mickle joy."

### The Passing of Arthur

Even as he spoke, " there came from the sea a short boat, borne on the waves, and two women therein, wondrously arrayed and they took Arthur anon, and bare him quickly and softly laid him down and fared forth away. Then was brought to pass that which Merlin whilom said, that there should be sorrow untold at Arthur's forthfaring." This is Layamon's version and Mallory tells much the same story with a few additional details.

Amid Glastonbury's monastic ruins may be seen the reputed grave of Arthur, for, although his burial place had for centuries been considered beyond human ken, the monks who claimed Joseph of Arimathea as their founder, did not find it beyond their ability to locate the grave

STEPHENSON

### WHERE ARTHUR SLEEPS
*Snowdon figures in Arthurian legend, and in a cave on the peaks of Lliwedd, seen in the above photograph, Arthur and his knights lie in magic sleep awaiting recall. On the right of Lliwedd, between that peak and the highest point of Snowdon, is Bwlch y Saethau, the Pass of the Arrows, where Arthur is said to have fallen in battle.*

of the legendary monarch within their walls. At the command of Henry II they sought the burial place as indicated by Welsh tradition.

First they found a leaden cross, recording the interment of Arthur and his queen. Next they unearthed a stone coffin containing the bones of a woman with beautiful golden locks which crumbled to dust at the touch of a monk. Beneath this was found a coffin of hollowed oak containing the remains of a huge man with an enormous head bearing twelve wounds, all of which had healed save one. But there are other places where Arthur is supposed to rest, not dead but lying in enchanted sleep.

Glastonbury links Arthur with a yet earlier figure, and on Weary-All Hill, a stone marks the spot where Joseph of Arimathea is said to have planted his staff which thereupon took root and flourished. In the Abbey grounds, and in St. John's churchyard, are preserved offshoots of this Holy Thorn which blossoms at Christmastime.

Joseph brought with him the chalice or Holy Grail used at the Last Supper and in which he collected the blood of Christ from the Cross.

It was at the Vigil of Pentecost, when all the fellowship of the Round Table were come unto Camelot, that the Quest of the Holy Grail was inaugurated. To the court was brought "a young knight, the which is of Kings lineage and of the kindred of Joseph of Arimathea,

whereby the marvels of this court and of strange realms shall be fully accomplished." This was Sir Galahad, son of the fair Elaine and Sir Lancelot.

After the tournaments in which Sir Galahad proved himself, and surmounted all other knights save Sir Lancelot and Sir Percevale, the Holy Grail passed through the hall but none might see it and "then was all the hall fulfilled with good odours and every knight had such meats and drinks as he best loved in the world."

Then the knights pledged themselves to labour in quest of the grail, and one hundred and fifty of them, to Arthur's sorrow, mounted upon their horses and rode through the streets of Camelot.

### Many Towered Camelot

The site of Camelot has long been considered to be the ancient camp of Cadbury about four and a half miles south of Castle Cary, in Somerset.

An old track from Camelot is still known as King Arthur's Lane, and the village of South Cadbury has a King Arthur's Well.

Camelot today presents no evidence of the "dim rich city" with "tower after tower, spire beyond spire" climbing to the mighty hall that Merlin built. Nor shall we find St. Stephen's Church where Arthur wedded Guenevere, despite

W. F. TAYLOR

### BAMBURGH CASTLE

*This restored castle on the Northumbrian coast stands on the site said to have been first fortified by the Anglian king, Ida the Flamebearer, in A.D. 547. Possibly this was the "Joyous Garde," the castle from which Sir Lancelot of the Lake, "flower of all knighthood," rode to Carlisle to return Queen Guenevere.*

DIXON-SCOTT

### RICHMOND CASTLE

*The romantic Yorkshire Richmond, with its mighty castle standing high above the River Swale, is another reputed burial place of Arthur with its story of a luckless wight who discovered the sleeping warriors but failed to break the magic spell. Had he done so, he would have been " the greatest man that ever was born."*

the warnings of Merlin that she would prove unfaithful and would love Sir Lancelot. But beneath the grassy slopes Arthur and his mail-clad knights are sleeping still, and, according to tradition, when the moon is full, the ghostly company still ride the ramparts on horses shod with silver.

### Fair City of Caerleon

Arthur's Court was not permanently fixed at Camelot, and frequent mention is made of Caerleon-on-Usk, near Newport, in Monmouthshire. "In those days," says Layamon, "no burgh so fair was in any land, nor so widely known, as Caerleon by Usk, unless it were the rich burgh that is named Rome." Thither came many kings and earls of noble cities to see Arthur crowned, and as he was led to the church four kings "went before him, bearing before him, as was their right, four golden swords."

The hollow in a field at Caerleon, which in recent years has been excavated to reveal the remains of a Roman amphitheatre, has long been known as the Round Table. Many other sites

are similarly named, but in the Great Hall at Winchester, there hangs on the wall a table top long claimed as " Arthur's Board." This table, eighteen feet in diameter, is divided into sectors for the king and twenty-four knights, but the Round Table of the legends was a far larger piece of furniture.

At one of Arthur's feasts there had been a great slaughter of knights arising from disputes as to precedence. Afterwards there came to the king a Cornish craftsman who said he would make a table at which sixteen hundred or more might sit, "and then thou needest never fear, to the world's end, that ever any moody knight may make fight, for there shall the high be even with the low."

Throughout Wales, Arthur's memory is maintained by place-names and features with associated legends. Gower was the Gore of which the sorceress, Morgan le Fay, was queen in her own right. On Cefn Bryn, near Swansea, is a dolmen known as Arthur's Stone and Guenevere has her monument at Llantilern, near Cardiff. Between the peaks of the Brecon Beacons is

R. M. ADAM

### THE EILDON HILLS, MELROSE

*A cavern in these hills is another supposed resting place of Arthur, where the monarch and his retinue await one who will sound the horn " that bids the charmed sleep of ages fly " and " rolls the long sound through Eildon's caverns vast."   According to another legend, these hills were cleft in three by the wizard Michael Scott.*

Arthur's Chair and on Cefn Carn Cavall, near Builth, is the footprint of Cavall, " Arthur's hound of deepest mouth."

Snowdon, formerly known as Caer Eryri, has numerous legends. One of them localizes Arthur's death on Snowdon. Up the valley of Cwm Llan, Arthur and his knights drove the enemy, up to the dip between Y Wyddfa and Lliwedd, two of the peaks of Snowdon. There, Arthur fell before a shower of arrows and so the place is named Bwlch y Saethau, or the Pass of the Arrows. Then Arthur's knights carried his body over Lliwedd and interred it in a vast cavern, " The Cave of the Young Men of Snowdon." In this undiscovered recess the warriors still sleep in their armour awaiting Arthur's re-awakening.

In the far north of England we are still in Arthur's country, and there are many references to Carlisle and its neighbourhood. The ballad of " The Marriage of Sir Gawaine " tells that,

" King Arthur lives in merry Carleile,
    And seemly is to see ;
    And there with him Queene Guenever
    That bride so bright of blee."

In the Castle of Carlisle Sir Mordred and Sir Agravaine and twelve other knights surprised Sir Lancelot in the chamber of Guenevere. Sir Agravaine and the twelve knights were slain, but Sir Mordred, sore wounded and smitten, fled to Arthur and told him the news. So the king ordained that Guenevere should be burnt to death for her sins.

### Rescue of Guenevere

" Then the queen was led forth without Carlisle and there she was despoiled into her smock," and there was " weeping and wailing and wringing of hands." But Lancelot came to the rescue, slew another batch of knights, had a kirtle and gown cast about the queen, and so rode away with her to his castle of Joyous Gard " and there he kept her as a noble knight should do."

Of Joyous Gard, according to Mallory, " Some men say it was Alnwick and some men say it was Bamburgh," both in Northumberland. Whichever it was, Arthur ventured there ; but was unhorsed by Lancelot, and only by the compassionate nature of the knight was Arthur's party permitted to withdraw. After that the Pope intervened, and Lancelot and Guenevere returned and Lancelot " rode throughout Carlisle, and so in the castle that all men might behold; and wit you well there was many a weeping eye." So was Guenevere returned to Arthur.

Between Carlisle and Penrith, in Cumberland, is the region of Inglewood Forest, where in the vicinity of the village of Upper Hesket has been located the Tarn Wadling, or, as it is sometimes called, Tarn Wathelayne, which is mentioned in the Ballad of Sir Gawaine, son of Loth and nephew of Arthur.

### Castle of the Grim Baron

On an island in this tarn stood the castle of "The Grim Baron, a churlish knight, whom Arthur was only able to overcome by the aid of a 'foul ladye.'" For her services Arthur was to find her a fair and courtly knight for husband. Gawaine alone of all the knights would undertake to wed the repulsive hag to absolve Arthur of his pledge. But Gawaine had the reward of discovering on the wedding night that instead of the loathly dame, he had for wife "a young ladye faire,"

"Her eyen was black as sloe ;
The ripening cherry swellde her lippe,
And all her neck was snow."

From Carlisle we may journey into Northumberland, and there, near Housesteads on the Roman Wall, is the lonely farm of Sewingshields.

"Immemorial tradition has asserted that King Arthur, his Queen Guenevere, his court of lords and ladies and his hounds were enchanted in some cave of the crags or in a hall below the castle of Sewingshields." There they will continue entranced until someone first blows a bugle and then with the sword of stone cuts a garter to be found in the hall.

A shepherd, so the story goes, found his way into the place and withdrew the sword from the scabbard. Thereupon the sleepers awoke and sat upright. He then cut the garter, but as he sheathed the sword the enchanted ones fell back in slumber, but not before Arthur had cried,

"O, woe betide that evil day
On which this witless wight was born,
Who drew the sword, the garter cut,
But never blew the bugle horn."

Across the Scottish border we find the same story, for in the Eildon Hills, the triple peaks that rise above Melrose, the sleepers await one who shall peal

"proud Arthur's march from fairyland."

There, with much left unsaid, with no mention of the luckless maid of Astolat or Sir Gawaine's encounters with the Greene Knight, with many a strange adventure and many a pleasing story not even hinted at, we must say farewell to Arthur and his fellowship of famous knights.

VIOLET BANKS

### ARTHUR'S SEAT, EDINBURGH

*Overlooking the Scottish capital, this famous landmark which has been likened to a couchant lion, is a remnant of an extinct volcano. It is said to take its name from the legendary monarch. According to the story, Arthur stood on the summit of the hill, watching the tide of battle as his followers overcame the opposing Picts.*

EDGAR WARD

## IMPRESSIVE RUINS OF CASTLE HEDINGHAM

*This great Norman keep, with walls twelve feet thick and archway thirty-two feet across, was built by Alberic de Vere in the twelfth century. Queen Maud, wife of King Stephen, died there and the castle also figures in the wars of King John. Henry VII was sumptuously entertained there, and for centuries it was a seat of the Earls of Oxford. With the exception of the keep the castle was reduced to ruins in 1666.*

# SCENES OF NORMAN TIMES

## *by* HAROLD SHELTON

THE walls of Anderida, looking out over the waters of Pevensey Bay, recall the first event in the occupation of Britain by the Normans, for it was here in September of 1066 that William landed on the shore of Sussex and inaugurated an era of change which was to prove the most complete upheaval of custom and tradition that the island had witnessed since the coming of the Romans under the Emperor Claudius, almost exactly a thousand years before.

If we make Pevensey Bay our starting-point we can follow the course taken by William on his first victorious progress to London. We follow him first to the hill of Senlac overlooking the Hastings plain. On this exposed plateau we see him in conflict with Harold, last of the Wessex kings, who had raised an army in London and marched southward to meet the invader. Harold's infantry armed with scythes, sticks and battle-axes proved but a poor match for the cavalry and bow-men of the Normans. Harold fell, pierced by an arrow in the eye, and his troops retreated in disorder. The splendid pile of Battle Abbey which today dominates the village, marks for us the place where tradition relates the battle was fought. It is said that, faithful to a vow which he made before the battle, William founded an abbey to commemorate his victory.

Next we follow William as he marches directly to London, first over the tumbled hills of the Forest Ridge, then across the Weald of Surrey, finally breasting the steep slopes of the North Downs. With Sussex, Kent and Surrey owing allegiance to him, he found no opposition until he attempted to cross the river at London Bridge.

DIXON-SCOTT

### A BEAUTIFUL NORMAN DOOR
*The late Norman church of Kilpeck, near Hereford, possesses this richly sculptured doorway, one of the finest specimens of Norman moulding in the country.*

Here the citizens of Saxon London, built north of the river on the twin summits of Cornhill and Ludgate Hill, met him in battle and drove him back.

So with William we must retrace our steps and leave the smouldering ruins of Southwark (which was then a flourishing town independent of London). We follow the south bank of the river to Wallingford, which is the first place where it could be forded, and then re-approach London from the north. We must imagine the Normans once more meeting the Saxons in battle, this time a few miles to the west of London in the open fields where Hammersmith and Wandsworth now stand. Resistance soon ceased and Edgar, who had acceded to the crown of Wessex on the death of Harold, abdicated. Our journey ends at Westminster Abbey, where on Christmas Day of 1066 William was crowned.

The first stage of the Norman Conquest was over. Yet it was not a conquest of alien wresting the throne from its rightful holder, for William had been nominated to the crown of England by Edward the Confessor, and Harold had promised William his support.

It is a sardonic fact that the Normans who brought unity to an England which had not been united since the departure of the Romans should come of the same stock as the Norsemen or Danes who had spread desolation throughout the land at the time when the Saxons had been building a new civilization in the seventh century ; for the word Norman is a corruption of Northman—the Viking stock of Scandinavia and Denmark.

The White Tower of the Tower of London,

W. F. TAYLOR

### ANCIENT WALLS OF PEVENSEY

*Pevensey has a long and stirring history. There the Romans built their great fortress of Anderida which was later overrun by the Saxons who " slew all that dwelt therein." William the Conqueror landed in Pevensey Bay and within the Roman walls his half-brother built the Norman castle which was frequently besieged.*

DIXON-SCOTT

### CASTLE RUINS AT HASTINGS

*This shattered stronghold, possibly founded by the Conqueror not long after the Battle of Hastings, is said to have been built for the purpose of obtaining unrestricted passage across the Channel for the royal messengers. The first tourney ever held in Britain is supposed to have taken place there in the presence of King John.*

rising majestically above the broad waterway of the Thames, the great bulk of Castle Hedingham, most impressive landmark in Northern Essex, the still more solid though more battered ruins of Colchester Castle—all recall the efforts which William made to hold the country in check. All three are early Norman fortresses where garrisons were established to hold the conquered Saxons in subjection.

William utilized and enlarged the Saxon earthworks where these existed, as at Corfe Castle. The grand position of the mound commanding the whole of the Isle of Purbeck shows how well the Saxons chose their sites. Sometimes, as at Pevensey, William built within the confines of a Roman fort. Where new sites were chosen he constructed the rectangular Norman keeps of which the Tower of London was one of the first and one of the largest, as befitted a place which was the only considerable town of the Saxons and the only one which resisted his progress.

If we journey northward from Castle Hedingham along the boundary of East Anglia we shall come ultimately to the fen country, which covers more than half of Cambridgeshire and Huntingdonshire. Today it is level pasture, well drained and fertile. But in Norman times before the dykes were cut and the rivers persuaded into their present channels the whole district was an impenetrable swamp, above which only the Isle of Ely emerged as dry land. It was here that Hereward the Wake, immortalized in the work of Charles Kingsley, led a rebellion which has assumed a significance as great as the rising of Boudicca against the Romans. In 1071 Hereward, at the head of several hundreds of the oppressed, established himself in the island and defied the Normans for nearly a year. When at last he was forced to submit, his courage won him a place in the army of William the Conqueror, who declared Hereward was "a man of noble soul and a most distinguished warrior."

The New Forest, most gracious of England's

woodland country, owes its origin to an act of the first Norman king. Hunting was the chief sport of the Norman nobles as it had been of the Saxons. A great part of England was set apart as royal preserves where the red deer and wild boar continued undisturbed and woe betide the impetuous serf who dared to loose an arrow at the king's deer.

PHOTOCHROM

CRUMBLING RUINS OF CORFE CASTLE

*In a commanding position overlooking a gap in the Purbeck Hills this ruin founded by William the Conqueror was for centuries an impregnable stronghold. King Edward was murdered by his stepmother at Corfe.*

Within a hundred years of the Conquest about seventy royal forests had been established, and special courts were instituted where the harsh forest laws of Normandy were rigorously applied. Of the Conqueror the Anglo-Saxon Chronicle says, "He made many deer-parks; and he established laws therewith; so that whosoever slew a hart or hind, should be deprived of his eyesight. As he forbade men to kill the harts, so also the boars; and he loved the tall deer as if he were their father. Likewise he decreed by the hares, that they should go free. His rich men bemoaned it, and the poor men shuddered at it. But he was so stern that he recked not the hatred of them all; for they must follow withal the king's will, if they would live, or have land or possessions, or even his peace."

### Barons in Revolt

The square bulk of Rochester Castle, overlooking a broad reach of the Medway recalls the troubled reign of William II, surnamed Rufus from his red complexion, which suspicious historians have hinted might spring from too great an attachment to the red wine of Normandy. It was at Rochester that Baron Odo flew his flag for six months in open rebellion against the king, who from the beginning of his reign met with more resistance from his own nobles than from his subjects at large—a state of affairs which was characteristic of the later Norman days. Bamburgh too is the scene of another siege in which the Earl of Northumberland held out manfully against the king's men until Rufus built another castle mound, overlooking Bamburgh, and there laid wait until Northumberland sallied forth for provisions. The traces of this second mound, a kind of counter castle, are a unique monument of Norman warfare.

In the Welsh Marches we shall find a more lasting reminder of Rufus in the temper of the countrymen and the tales that are still told of the stern Norman rule. As he was unable to subdue the indomitable spirit which has always marked the hill men of Britain, he laid a charge on his barons to conquer what land they could on the borderland of Wales and hold it for their own. Thus arose the rule of the Marcher Lords who, removed as they were from the centre of government, gained for themselves a great measure of independence, so that each became virtual king in his own right. They built castles at Gloucester, Pembroke and Chester, and, descending from them upon the villages and settlements, slew the men and violated their women folk, returning always to their strongholds as soon as the news came of an organized resistance. Hamelin de Baladun held sway over Breconshire and Monmouthshire from the castle of Abergavenny. Fitzhamon, Earl of Gloucester, Fitz Osborne of Chepstow, Roger de Montgomery of Shrewsbury—all did irretrievable damage which has lived on in tradition and which has tended to make the peasants of the Welsh Marches more insular and more race conscious than the subjects of "wildest" Wales.

Abergavenny, a little town on the Usk, and overlooked by the Sugar Loaf, was later held by William de Braose of whom a tale is told which well illustrates the spirit of the times. This de Braose, during one of his expeditions, was captured by the Welsh and later ransomed by his own people. With an admirable gesture

D. MCLEISH

### COLCHESTER'S MIGHTY KEEP

*The massive keep of Colchester Castle, by far the largest in Britain and about twice the size of the White Tower of London, is built partly of Roman materials. Perhaps because of its tremendous strength it never experienced a serious siege, although it was defended by the Royalists for three months during the Civil War.*

W. F. TAYLOR

## DEATH SCENE OF A MONARCH

*The arrow shot by Sir William Tyrell is said to have glanced from a tree and mortally wounded the king, William Rufus. Near Stoney Cross the Rufus Stone marks the traditional site of the tree. According to another version, Rufus was killed by a discontented Saxon for, it is said, Rufus was loathed by the people.*

he invited the Chief who had held him to ransom, and the leading men of his clan, to a feast. In the midst of the banquet soldiers entered the hall and slew every guest except one who escaped to perpetuate the story.

The effigies of the crusaders, of which there are several in the cathedrals and in some of the parish churches too, show better than anything else how Norman knights went into battle swathed in armour from head to foot and armed with the destructive battle-axe. They recall the time when the Norman nobles answered the call of the first religious war. Though many of the unorganized armies, which at the invitation of the Pope and the Emperor of the Eastern Roman Empire set out to rescue Jerusalem from the Mohammedans, never reached the scene of their activities, it was still the first attempt on the part of Britain since Roman days to take part in continental wars.

The Rufus Stone, halfway between the bleak crossroads at Stoney Cross and Cadnam, in the midst of the most desolate part of the New Forest, where the woodlands begin to thin out and their place is taken by mile after mile of windswept heather-covered heath, marks the spot where Rufus fell. An inscription on the stone tells us that he was mortally wounded by a stray arrow from the bow of one of his companions, Sir Walter Tyrell, when hunting in the forest.

His tomb is in Winchester Cathedral where he was buried without ceremony. He was unloved at his death as he had been unpopular in his life, owing to the severity which he showed in the exaction of the utmost farthing from his subjects and in the prosecution of the Forest Laws.

The castles of Arundel and Shrewsbury, the former constantly rebuilt in later centuries and today a palatial residence rather than a fortress, are remembered for the part they played in the struggle between Henry I and Robert of Bellême, pretender to the throne. For it was at Arundel that Robert was besieged for nearly a year before making good his escape, whilst at Shrewsbury he finally took refuge and surrendered.

### Siege of a Castle

We can easily imagine the stern struggle before one of these early castles was captured. No siege passed without hand to hand battles and the employment of every available means of offence and defence. When Rochester Castle was besieged in 1215 the besiegers tunnelled under the castle, filled the tunnel with brushwood and set a light to it, so that when the beams that supported the tunnel were burnt, one corner of the keep subsided into the tunnel and fell in ruins.

The battering-ram was used also. This was crashed against the sides of the castle until a

W. F. TAYLOR

## GUILDFORD CASTLE KEEP

*This ancient keep, now a picturesque ruin, is almost all that remains of the castle built in the reign of Henry II. It was a residence of Henry who converted the adjacent caverns into wine cellars.   On one occasion the castle fell into the hands of Louis of France.    It also served as the county gaol and is now the property of the town.*

breach was made in the walls. Catapults hurled rocks into the ward and moving towers were brought up to the gates so that the attackers could reach the walls. During all these operations defenders and attackers alike kept up a continuous fire of arrows and the besieged replied also by dropping heavy missiles, boiling water, or molten lead on the heads of those intrepid soldiers who came too near the walls, and by catching up as many of the attackers as they could with the assistance of grappling irons.

How well the castle could be defended against a formal siege is shown by the fact that Exeter Castle, a fortress of no great strength, was held for five months against King Stephen. Even then it was only a failure of the well with which every castle was provided that hastened the final surrender. When, as sometimes happened, the infuriated peasants made a more or less organized attack on one of the castles, it was fatally easy for the defenders, standing on the ramparts of the walls and protected by the embrasures, to pick them off with arrows as they advanced.

The Norman House of Christchurch, which was built inside the outer wall of the castle, shows how towards the middle of the twelfth century, when the danger of revolt from the peasants was growing less, the Norman nobles began to change their mode of living. They started to build manors and granges which had greater comfort than the stonework of the castles, and which were modelled rather on the lines of the Anglo-Saxon Hall which had been constructed of timber after the style of the later medieval barns. In much the same way the abbot of the monastery frequently built himself a separate residence outside the confines of the convent.

The Jew's House at Lincoln belongs to the twelfth century, and with its windows of two lights on the first floor shows the growing tendency to comfort rather than defence. The Old Hall at Ower Moigne, in Dorset, illustrates how this tendency developed still further in the course of the next century.

### Great Architects

When we come to consider the life of the poorer people we are on less sure ground. Towns were still small and few in number, and the townsmen were forced to become servants to the baron in his castle. In town and country alike they lived in wooden houses with thatched

roofs, consisting of a hall with alcoves which served for kitchens, and drawing-rooms, and of a loft built over the hall.

The Normans were great architects. They re-introduced into England the art of carving in stone, and we can trace their handiwork in the ruins of abbeys, in cathedrals and in parish churches, for as in every age of architecture the greatest works were the monuments which were raised for religious devotion.

No single Norman church has been preserved

D. MCLEISH

JEW'S HOUSE, LINCOLN

*One of the oldest inhabited dwellings in Britain is the twelfth-century house at Lincoln. In the reign of John it was occupied by a Jewess named Belaset, who was hanged in 1290 for debasing coins.*

intact. There is no church in England so characteristic of the Norman style as the Church of Greensted, in Essex, or the Church of St. Lawrence at Bradford-on-Avon is of the Saxon. But what they lack in completeness they amply compensate for in number and in the beauty of the fragments which survive. If we go to Barfreston, in Kent—a tiny village set at the foot of the rolling country, where the downs reach to the edge of the Thanet marshes—we shall find a church which shows much of their artistry and craftsmanship. Here in a small circular window we shall see the beginnings of the stone tracery which was to prove the most fascinating attraction of the later Gothic style.

Barfreston shows, too, the tendency to

subdivision which gave all Norman building its great symmetry, and, at the same time, rendered it a style which can easily be distinguished from any other. So in Chichester Cathedral the wall above the main arcade is divided into several arches, and they in turn into smaller arches, each dependent on the other, and each contributing to the beauty of the whole. We can see this subdivision carried out even in the stone vaults with which the Normans roofed the nave.

The little Church of Walsoken, in Norfolk, shows well how the chancel arch is broken up and supported on columns in the same way as the great vault of St. Albans is supported on the vast square columns which rise from the aisles of the nave. The very mass and solidity of these columns, so perfectly proportioned to the

magnificence of the abbey is an integral part of the beauty of Norman building. We need only go to Waltham Abbey or the Cathedral of Durham to see how much is added by the great circular piers whose only resemblance to the classical column is that they have the same base and capital.

### Imaginative Sculptors

So long as they were concerned with construction in detail, and until they had mastered the principles of vaulting, the Normans gave little attention to decoration. Even so, if we look at the Norman font in Lincoln Cathedral, we cannot fail to marvel at the technique and delicacy with which the figures moulded upon it are picked out. Still more, if we visit Ely Cathedral and find the Prior's Doorway, with its beautifully carved tympana set in the ornamented semicircle of the Norman arch, we shall realize the full imaginative capacity of the Norman sculptors.

How beautiful even the simplest arch can be is shown by the chancel arch of Rainham Church, in Essex, which throws an interesting light, also, on how the people worshipped in Norman times. For the chancel was the place of devotion for the priests, where the altar was set against the east end, whilst the lay brethren in the monasteries, and the country people in the parish church must needs be content with sitting in the nave and watching the Elevation of the Host through the chancel arch.

It would take many months to visit all the sacred buildings which show Norman workmanship, either in the general plan of the church or perhaps in a single rounded arch, or perhaps in the narrow windows of two lights set high in the church wall which were so typical of their art. Especially worthy of a visit, however, is the Church of St. Cross, Winchester, where the nave is almost entirely Norman and shows the generous proportions of which the builders were capable.

We must also see the splendid arcade and the rounded porch of the priory church at Castle Acre, the splendid arch of the porchway to Selby Abbey, and the grand Norman tower of St. Albans, built before the end of the eleventh century from Roman tiles stripped from the ruins of Verulamium. Even at Canterbury,

W. F. TAYLOR

SOUTHWELL MINSTER

*The beautiful austere nave of Southwell presents an excellent example of Norman church architecture, with the massive piers of the nave arcade surmounted by the lofty triforium and clerestory.*

FELTON

## HISTORIC HALL OF WESTMINSTER

*This famous Hall, built by William Rufus, was completed in 1099. The beautiful timber roof dates from the end of the fourteenth century when the Hall was restored by Richard II. Westminster Hall served for centuries as the chief law court of England, being abandoned for this purpose when the present Law Courts were built in the Strand.*

though the splendour of the Gothic Cathedral will enthral us most, we shall remember that it was originally the church of a Norman monastery of which the round arches of the ruins to the north-east of the cathedral are our sole reminder.

It was perhaps natural that the Normans should build more and more monasteries, for they offered the only profession which gentlemen could follow, apart from that of the soldier. So one county alone can show four such monasteries which were founded before the last of the Norman kings. Yorkshire will reveal the illustrious ruins of Rievaulx, Roche, Fountains and Kirkstall, all founded by one Order—the Cistercian. We must remember when we visit them that the first buildings were of wood, and that most of the majestic ruins date from the end of the twelfth and the thirteenth centuries.

STEPHENSON

NORMAN GATEWAY, CASTLE ACRE

*The Conqueror granted the Norfolk Manor of Castle Acre to William de Warenne, who built a castle on a mound flanked by earthworks. This gateway, which afforded access to the stronghold, spans the village street.*

### Domesday Book

Our chief link with the life of the people is the Domesday Book, the minute survey of the land and its resources which William initiated in 1086. The Anglo-Saxon Chronicle says he sent his men all over England into each shire. " So very narrowly, indeed, did he commission them to trace it out, that there was not one single hide, nor a rood of land, nay, moreover (it is shameful to tell, though he thought it no shame to do it) not even an ox, nor a cow, nor a swine was there left, that was not set down in his writ. And all the recorded particulars were afterwards brought to him."

The whole country was divided into counties, the counties into Hundreds and the Hundreds into manors. Only in a few cases have the Hundreds been preserved on the modern map— the Three Hundreds of Aylesbury, the Chiltern Hundreds and the Hundred of Hoo, in Kent, are instances where the titles have survived even though the political significance has disappeared. Everything in the manor belonged to the lord of the manor, held in trust by him for the king. Apart from the land which he ploughed himself, most of the manor was granted by him to his followers in return for their services.

The Domesday Book shows several classes among the retainers of the lord of the manor including the villeins who held about thirty acres, the cottars who held about five acres as well as a number of bondsmen who held no land and were, in fact, slaves or serfs who worked in return for board and lodging, and were never allowed to possess property of any kind, but had their freedom.

Probably the life of the villein or cottar was no harder than that of the modern labourer. As today he depended for his prosperity on the goodwill of the landowner, but, he had his house, he ploughed his own land and raised his own vegetables, and, in return for these privileges, he ploughed the land of his lord and was plighted to follow him into battle. Even though he had no money with which to buy pleasures, in a simple age there were no pleasures to be bought and he enjoyed the protection without which life would have been impossible. Nor must we take too seriously the dire tales of rape and oppression which are perpetuated in legend and story. It is certainly true that the Norman lords brooked no opposition. To have done so would probably have cost them their lives ; for the countrymen, as ever conservative, looked on them as interlopers and continued to do so even though their life under them may have been easier than under the Saxons. In any case, we must remember that the Feudal System effected a vital change towards unity and co-operation which would have been impossible in a purely individualistic manner of life.

A drive along the byways of Central Essex, or in the Vale of Blackmore, or the Valley of the Ouse, in Bedfordshire, reveals a curious link

DIXON-SCOTT

## ESSEX MEMORIES OF CANUTE

*Said to have developed from a church founded by a standard-bearer of Canute, Waltham became an Augustinian Abbey in Norman times. The parish church seen in the background formed the nave of the abbey church. Waltham also has Saxon associations, and King Harold, who fell at Hastings, is said to be buried there.*

W. F. TAYLOR

## GREY RUINS OF OLD SARUM

*In Norman times this ancient site near Salisbury grew into a walled city and was an episcopal see from 1072. After disagreement between the castellans and the clergy the site was abandoned and the cathedral was pulled down in 1331, the materials being used again in the building of Salisbury Cathedral.*

with Feudal England. The villeins tilled their land in long, narrow strips, and there was always a Right of Way at the sides and ends of the strips. These Rights of Way in later times were turned into roads which so took on the typical appearance of an English country lane—straight for a quarter of a mile down the side of one strip, turning through a right-angle bend along the bottom of the strip for perhaps a hundred yards or so, and straight for another quarter of a mile down the next strip.

During the closing years of the Norman era, there was a great increase in trade. In Saxon days England had been self-supporting, and even under the Normans the manor required little that was not raised within its confines. But gradually markets were established in the towns where goods were bartered, and market crosses, with roofs to protect the buyers and sellers, were raised.

DIXON-SCOTT

WHITE TOWER OF LONDON

*Within the south-east angle of the Roman walls the Conqueror raised the great edifice of the Tower of London  The White Tower, seen above, was designed by Gundulf, Bishop of Rochester.*

Foreign trade was developed and London, we are told, was a city to which " merchants rejoice to bring their trade in ships," and " ships and merchandise of foreign merchants " were present at Boston Fair in 1196.

Annual fairs were established and granted royal charters. All ports and roads William " ordered to be open to merchants, and no injury to be done to them." In one charter the king says, " I will and ordain that all who come to the fair, remain at it, and return from it have my firm peace."

Winchester had its St. Giles Fair, licence for which was granted to Bishop Walkelin by the Conqueror. Cambridge had its widely famous fair of Stourbridge which flourished through the Middle Ages, and only dwindled in comparatively recent days. In Defoe's day it was a tremendous gathering, a " prodigious resort of the trading people of all parts of England, with streets of booths and tents."

Such was the life in Norman times. Even with men's thoughts turning naturally to warfare, life may have been on the whole more peaceful, more leisured and (who shall say otherwise?) happier than it is today.

FELTON

ROCHESTER'S MASSIVE KEEP

*This impressive Norman keep, 120 feet high and overlooking the Medway, is an illustration of the military architecture of the period. Built in 1125 the walls at the base are 12 feet thick.*

# THE STORY OF THE CASTLES

## *by* HAROLD SHELTON

OF the many contributing factors to the beauty and splendour of Britain, the remains of the castles and ancient strongholds are among the most popular features. Frequently, because of their well-chosen position they remain, even in ruin, a dominant note in the landscape. Their weathered and perhaps decaying masonry, their embattled towers and walls and remnants of barbican, drawbridge and portcullis may still conjure from the past visions of pomp and pageantry, and of tales of tyranny and feudal subjection.

The evolution of the castle is part of the great struggle between the means of offence and those of defence. Each stage of development represents a further effort to overcome the available means of attack, from the puny earthworks of Neolithic man to the culminating strongholds—the concentric castles of the Edwardian period. By that time defence had become stronger than offence, so that the castle could withstand a siege of many months, and was virtually immune to the engines of warfare.

The modern castle is no longer a stronghold, but a dwelling-place, whose battlements are an idle show which could not withstand a determined siege for a day. Steel has taken the place of masonry, and the mobile tank which can spread destruction as it goes and yet afford protection to the destroyers has more in common with the castle than any other means of warfare.

The castle ruins have much in common with those of the monasteries. Just as the latter epitomize the art of religious architecture, so, from Roman times onwards, castles are the sum total of military architecture. The civil life of the Early Middle Ages centred round the convent; so the military life centred round the castle. The monasteries later attracted townships because the abbot was the principal buyer of the district and labour was wanted to work the monastic land. So towns often arose near the castles because the castle was the home of the lord of the manor, and there was protection in living under the castle walls. To complete our comparison, just as the monasteries were allowed to fall into decay through the avarice of one man, Henry VIII, so the hand of man—Oliver Cromwell—was responsible for the decay of the castles when, at the close of the great Civil War, they were slighted at his command, which means that their roofs were stripped, their battlements destroyed, and the fabric made unfit for future defence.

Those which at first glance seem to have survived miraculously, such as Windsor and Arundel, to name only two of the finest, closer inspection shows to have been rebuilt again and

DIXON-SCOTT

### HENRY VIII GATE AND ROUND TOWER, WINDSOR
*Overlooking the Thames, Windsor Castle, which down through the centuries has served as a royal residence, was founded by William the Conqueror. Parts of the structure date from the reign of Henry III.*

DIXON-SCOTT

### FORMIDABLE GATEWAY OF LEWES CASTLE

*One of the earliest of Norman castles, this Sussex stronghold, on a height in the middle of the town, was built by William de Warenne, the first Earl of Surrey, who died in 1088. The inner gate is part of the original work, but the outer gate is Edwardian. De Warenne and his wife, Gundrada, daughter of the Conqueror, also founded the priory at Lewes. Their coffins, found in the ruins, are preserved in St. John's Church, Southover.*

again, so that little of the original building can be discerned. Even so, the massive ruins that remain are a testimony to the skill of the Roman and Norman builders who constructed buildings of a solidity which has withstood the ravages of weather and men for a period of six hundred to sixteen hundred years.

The hilltop fortresses of Prehistoric Britain are the earliest attempts at castle building. The second era was begun with the advent of the Romans. The Romans inherited the traditions of the great castle builders of Asia Minor, of Troy and Tiryns and of Phœnicia. They brought to Britain an art which was already fully developed. Their own great contribution lay

the Stour and the Thames, that the Romans turned of necessity to defend the coast and appointed a Count of the Saxon Shore, who was responsible for the line of citadels which extended from the Wash on the east coast to the Solent on the south.

In the north and north-west the position was very different. Here the country was never Romanized, but was held with more or less success in face of constant opposition from the Picts and Scots and from the Celtic tribes of Wales. The walls of Hadrian and Constantine were efforts to define the Roman boundary for close on two hundred years. Along the former castella were constructed at intervals which

DIXON SCOTT

## SPLENDOUR OF WARWICK CASTLE
" *The fairest monument of ancient and chivalrous splendour* " *was Scott's description of this noble structure with its embattled walls and stately towers. Probably replacing a Saxon stronghold, the foundations were laid by Earl Turchil in the days of the Conqueror, but the fortifications are chiefly fourteenth century.*

in the construction of walled cities with defensive turrets at intervals rather than in the erection of single fortresses. The multi-angular tower on the Roman wall at York is more significant than even Richborough.

The history of the Roman occupation, too, is reflected in the distribution of castles. The south of England was quickly won over by a peaceful, rather than a military, occupation. Hence in the south there was no need for fortresses to quell the spirit of the insurgents. It was not until the fourth century, when marauding tribes of Saxons were beginning to sail up the eastern estuaries and penetrate into the country by the Blackwater,

constituted the largest and most important scheme of Roman castle building.

With the weakening of the Roman influence the second period of castle building came to an end. The Saxon invaders burned and pillaged the Roman castles with the same ruthlessness as they overthrew their towns and houses. Perhaps they even manned once more the deserted earthworks of the downs. The Vikings, who in turn came to harry the Saxon chieftains, were just as ignorant of the art of castle building as the Teutonic tribes.

The Norse tribes who settled in Normandy developed a new art of fortification. Their

W. F. TAYLOR

## FEUDAL FORTRESS OF THE PERCYS

*The restored Alnwick Castle in Northumberland was founded by Ivo de Vescy, the Norman Baron of Alnwick, about 1096. After frequent assaults by marauding Scots, it was rebuilt by the famous Percys between 1310 and 1350. It once ranked as one of the most formidable strongholds in the North of England.*

influence impelled the Saxon chieftains in the tenth century to strengthen naturally strong positions with artificial aids, nearly a hundred years before William of Normandy led his army to victory at Senlac. The method adopted in those last years of the Saxon Kingdoms was to raise a mound and surround it with a deep moat, further strengthening the top of the mound with a wooden palisade. Probably the earthen mound and timber stockade was the only type of castle known in this country before the Norman Conquest.

### Norman Strongholds

The landing of William and his rapid conquest of the country heralded the third and greatest period of castle building, continuing intermittently until the reign of Henry VIII. William had two problems to solve. He needed garrisons to be the headquarters of his soldiers and he needed some visible strength to overawe the countryside. The Norman castle satisfied both these needs. Under the government of one of the Norman barons it held undisputed sway over the rural population. William de Braose ruled Sussex from Bramber—a great man who won the name of "Just" because he did not kill everyone who chanced to stand in his way, and refrained from pillaging the homes of the old and infirm. If we journey to Bramber today we shall still

find the castle ruins dominating the quiet village. Raised high on a grassy mound from which there is a long view over the Sussex Weald they command the river where in medieval days there was an important ford and so stand guard over the gap between the two spurs of the South Downs which stretch eastward towards Lewes and westward to Chanctonbury Ring and Washington.

Two distinct types of early Norman fortress survive in most parts of Britain, one distinguished by a " shell " keep, the other by a " rectangular " keep. The shell keep was by far the more numerous. Where William or his lieutenants found Saxon mounds, they reoccupied them and strengthened the palisades which surmounted them, digging a wide bank and ditch to protect the earthwork and a considerable portion of land as well. The wooden structure on the top of the mound became known as the keep, the rest of the enclosure as the ward. Within the ward dwelling-places of wood were built for the knights, and enclosures made for cattle and stores. So within a couple of days William could devise a rough-and-ready fortification which could resist unexpected attacks.

Thirty or more years afterwards, when their position was stronger, the Normans started to replace the timber palisades and buildings with masonry, constructing a roughly circular building

DIXON-SCOTT

## CARISBROOKE CASTLE.   PRISON OF A KING

"*I do not think I shall ever see a ruin to surpass Carisbrooke Castle,*" *remarked the poet Keats of this Norman stronghold in the Isle of Wight.   Charles I was held a prisoner here during the Civil War and twice attempted to escape.   The photograph shows the formidable gatehouse with the battlemented towers.*

on the summit of the mound, and the living accommodation in the ward. The keep on the mound was only a last line of defence in which the garrison could take refuge when the outer ward had fallen before the enemy. But so strong did the timber palisade prove that the Normans showed no haste to build the structure of masonry. Hence these shell keeps are often a little later in date than the rectangular keeps which were not preceded by timber defences. Corfe Castle, which dominates the gap in the Purbeck Hills in just the same way as does Bramber the gap in the South Downs, must have been one of the earliest. If we approach it along the main road from the direction of Wareham

by treachery from within, was it reduced to its shattered state.

Although more numerous at the date of construction, the shell keep has not survived so frequently. This is partly because the construction was less massive, but chiefly because this type, like the Saxon mound, was practically confined to towns. So when the castles were dismantled after the Civil Wars, the ruins were not allowed to occupy for long what was obviously a fine building site. First they were used as quarries—it is said that the Seaford Road is built from the stones of Lewes Castle. Then, if they escaped that fate, they were rebuilt to form prisons or courts of justice, so perpetuating

W. F. TAYLOR

### HISTORIC KENILWORTH
*Founded about 1120 by Geoffrey de Clinton, Kenilworth was granted to Simon de Montfort in 1234. John of Gaunt made additions, including the banqueting hall and two towers, one of which bears his name. Elizabeth granted it to her favourite, the Earl of Leicester. The oldest part is the Norman keep of 1180.*

its gaunt ruined outline stands out clear against the sky. From its mound we look over the sandy wastes of Dorset's heathlands with the same sweeping views as at Bramber we look over the Sussex Weald.

Solidly built by the Conqueror and well placed on a height, Corfe proved unconquerable to Stephen. King John who used it as a residence considered it offered safe storage for his regalia during his dispute with the barons, and he also decided it was a useful prison, for there he is said to have starved to death twenty-two French prisoners. Down to the days of Cromwell it stood intact. Then, only after it had been taken

the custom by which the Lord of the Manor was both the dispenser of justice and the jailer of the local folk. Even when the castle remained a castle until modern times, it became first and foremost a prison.

The Tower of London, for instance, has in turn been fortress, royal palace and prison house. Stephen was the first king to reside in it. Henry III and the three Edwards all held court there. Richard II was in residence when he abdicated. Henry VI died there, put to death, so tradition relates, by the Duke of Gloucester. Another regal victim was the child King Edward V, slain side by side with his brother. Anne Boleyn and

PHOTOCHROM

### KINGMAKER'S YORKSHIRE FORTRESS

*This imposing ruin in Wensleydale, probably founded about 1170, came into the Neville family in 1270 and was a stronghold of Warwick the Kingmaker. His daughter, Anne, married Richard III and their only son was born and died at Middleham. In 1539 it was reported that there was at Middleham a castle highly decayed and in ruin and thereunto adjoining six Parks and six Chases otherwise called Forest or dales.*

DIXON-SCOTT

### CONWAY'S ROMANTIC RUINS

*As part of his plan for the subjugation of Wales, Edward I completed this embattled pile in 1284 on the site of an early fortress built by Hugh Lupus, Earl of Chester, in the reign of the Conqueror. When the Welsh Prince Llewelyn was slain, Edward is said to have received the head of his foe in the banqueting hall of Conway.*

Katherine Howard lived here in solitary confinement before being executed. In later days a long line of distinguished prisoners came to know its walls only too well—Sir Thomas More, Sir Walter Raleigh, Perkin Warbeck, Lady Jane Grey, Guy Fawkes, and many others.

Windsor and Arundel were both originally castles of the shell type. Their chequered history is typical of every type. Windsor was founded by William the Conqueror, and has been the royal palace of almost every king since that time. It was rebuilt entirely by Edward III, and again by the architect Wyatville in the early Victorian era. Even his " cruel " restoration was unable to spoil its magnificence; seen from the river it appears the veritable prototype of all castles.

Arundel, too, has suffered many vicissitudes. There are still considerable portions of the Norman keep intact, and of the Edwardian defences, though the imposing pile of the present castle—all that can be seen from the road—was constructed in the nineteenth century. Here it was that Robert of Montgomery won such an unenviable name for cruelty and rapaciousness.

In 1102 it was besieged by Henry I. Thirty-seven years later King Stephen beleaguered it, but it bravely withstood his onslaught. It was only at the end of the great Civil War that it surrendered to the Roundheads, and was " slighted " after the manner of all the other medieval strongholds. Tradition relates that the circular hole in the keep was the entrance to a secret passage leading to the banks of the Arun. Alas for tradition ! It is more probably the entrance to the Norman dungeons which have since been filled in.

### A Magnificent Palace

The magnificent palace of the Earls of Warwick, which stands upon a cliff almost overhanging the Avon, is yet another of this type of Norman fortress which has lived through the stirring history of all the castles, declined and then risen again to become one of Britain's most splendid castle mansions. The gatehouse which bears the crest of the Warwick family, a bear and a ragged staff, is a worthy entrance to the warm grey pile of the castle itself. A road hewn out of the

PHOTOCHROM

**COURTYARD, SKIPTON CASTLE**

*This Yorkshire stronghold occupies a strategic position in the gap carved in the Pennines by the River Aire. Founded in the eleventh century by the Norman, Robert de Romille, it later became the homes of the warlike Cliffords, Earls of Cumberland. Of the original structure, only the western doorway of the inner castle remains.*

living rock leads into the outer court, where the two great towers, Cæsar's and Guy's, dominate the whole building. The mansion is unique if only because it is raised on a wonderfully vaulted undercroft beneath which are the vast cellars, these too being hewn from the rock on which the castle stands. It was Thomas Beauchamp who rebuilt the Norman fortress and so laid the foundations for the present edifice, which is surely the most splendid example of Gothic domestic architecture in the country.

There are many lesser castles which fall into this group. Leeds, in Kent, is unique because instead of the artificial mound we find a natural island in a lake doing justice for it. The later medieval mansion which stands on its site, whether we view it from the main Ashford-Maidstone road or approach it by the footpath which runs through the park, has the same air of an island fortress which the Norman castle must have had. It is only when we reach the very fringe of the lake that we discern the art of the later builder, the large windows and spacious rooms which belong to an age when attack was no longer feared. Alnwick, Carisbrooke, and Berkeley Castle, in Gloucestershire, though these, too, have been reconstructed, all retain the shell keep. Perhaps it was because this type combined the functions of palace and fortress and was thus the forerunner of the castellated manor house that where it has survived it has never survived without reconstruction.

Thus Alnwick was the medieval home of the Percy family who were permitted to fortify the town in the fifteenth century, as witnessed by the Bond Gate which bears the armorial lion of the Percys. Prior to the fourteenth century the castle was held by the de Vescys, descended from the great Ivo de Vescy who was Baron of Alnwick at the beginning of the twelfth century. It passed into the Percy family by chance; for it was bequeathed by the last of the de Vescys to the Bishop of Durham to hold in trust for de Vescy's bastard son, William. Perhaps it was moral disapproval which led the bishop to sell the estate to Henry de Percy and apply the proceeds to his privy purse!

### A Royal Prisoner

Carisbrooke (where the sombre ruins of the old are in marked contrast with the later mansion, yet each throws into relief the beauty of the other) became the seat of the Governors of the Isle of Wight when it had ceased to be necessary as a fortress. It was here that Charles I was imprisoned for a time in 1647, and here, too, that his daughter Elizabeth met her death three years later. Berkeley again has been the manorial seat of the Earls of Berkeley ever since it was granted to Roger de Berkeley by William of

STEPHENSON

**FOURTEENTH-CENTURY CASTLE**
*Bodiam, near Robertsbridge in Sussex, was one of the latest of the great fortified houses. Among the defences were drawbridges, barbican and portcullis.*

Normandy. Even in the Civil Wars the tenure was not broken, for the castle was given back by Cromwell to the eighth baron on condition that the battlements were destroyed. In history it is remembered as the place where Edward II was murdered in 1307. The blackest deeds always seem to win most fame.

The castles with rectangular keeps were military strongholds primarily and dwelling-places only when need arose. They were built on sites where no previous fortifications existed, often in a commanding position in a thinly populated part of the countryside. Awe-inspiring, spectacular, magnificently constructed, they stand today as a supreme memorial to the Norman masons' work. Although they, too, were surrounded by an encircling wall, they differed from the castles with " shell " keeps in that residence was taken up in the keep itself instead of in the outer ward. The entrance was guarded by a strong forebuilding, presenting an almost insuperable obstacle to any foolhardy enemy who hazarded to attack it. The White Tower of the Tower of London and the keeps of Rochester and Colchester, and lofty Castle Hedingham are

HUMPHREY AND VERA JOEL

## PICTURESQUE CASTLE OF HURSTMONCEAUX

*This restored fortified manor on the edge of the Pevensey Levels in Sussex, built of warm red brick, was founded by Sir Roger Fiennes in the fifteenth century and dismantled in 1777. The castle, recently restored, is two hundred feet square and has four corner towers. The photograph shows the lofty gate towers with machicolated parapet through the openings of which missiles could be dropped on the enemy at the gates.*

EDGAR WARD

### ENGLAND'S OLDEST MOATED MANOR

*Stokesay Castle, in Shropshire, dating from the thirteenth century and the oldest fortified manor in Britain, has a romantic, fairy-like charm. It was probably built as a moated dwelling by John de Verdon about 1270. Seventy years later it was fortified and embattled by Lawrence, a merchant of Ludlow who then owned it.*

a few of the most beautiful. Each shows a thickness of wall twenty or more feet in places which seems incredible in an era of jerry-built residences. How mighty they were we can well judge from the fact that all Norfolk was held in subjection by three great fortresses—Castle Rising, Castle Acre, and Norwich.

Kenilworth, too, was originally a rectangular Norman keep, and the most vital stronghold of the later Norman period in the midlands. John of Gaunt and Simon de Montfort both held it for a time; the work of the former being perpetuated in the range of buildings known as Lancaster's Buildings. But it is due to the genius of Sir Walter Scott that Kenilworth springs to the mind among the foremost of English castles. In *Kenilworth* we read of the magnificent entertainment which was offered Queen Elizabeth by Robert Dudley, a degenerate descendant

of John of Gaunt. In Scott's pages the splendour and pomp of castle life live again.

Farther north, amid the characteristic scenery of the Yorkshire dales, Middleham in the valley of the Ure, better known as Wensleydale, was for centuries the home of the Neville family, and once one of the strongholds of the Earl of Warwick, nicknamed the Kingmaker. Here is a castle which has never been rebuilt since the thirteenth century. Raised on a plateau which overlooks the valley, it is the most conspicuous feature of the landscape. Its rough stone architecture is typical of northern strongholds. No trace of ornament relieves the grim outline. The keep, of which the outer faces of two stories are nearly intact, rises from the centre of a great ward seventy yards long and sixty yards broad, itself surrounded by a wall nearly thirty feet high. As if to emphasize its great bulk flanking towers protect the outer wall, and vast buttresses project from the corners of the keep. There is no more forbidding edifice in England, nor one which allies so much beauty with its strength.

Towards the end of the Norman period a new type of castle appeared. It was found that when once the outer wall of the shell keep castle had been overthrown, the keep itself offered but a poor further defence. By the reign of Henry II, too, there was less need of such impregnable fortresses as Rochester or Hedingham. Accordingly the shell keep was discarded and the rectangular keep was replaced by a circular one with walls much less thick, which could be roofed in by masonry instead of by the timber roofs which were the only ones possible in the rectangular shape. The cost of raising such a castle was less than half the cost of raising a rectangular keep and its defensible strength nearly as great. So we find castles like Pembroke and Conisborough and Orford which mark a distinct step in the evolution of design.

Yet no one would judge them insignificant despite their less massive construction. The castle of Pembroke stands over the town with just as much majesty as does Rochester. Conisborough seems no less impressive than Hedingham. Orford is still the most striking feature of the decaying coastal town which came into being when it was built and declined as soon as it fell into ruins.

The great era of building in central and southern England soon came to an end. The country was more settled, and the king found that it was not an unmixed blessing to have powerful nobles esconced in fortresses which could not be subdued without a six months' siege.

### Conquest of Wales

Richard I and Henry III discouraged further building, and it is only in the north of England and on the borders of Wales that we find progress maintained. Throughout the thirteenth century systematic attempts were made to complete the conquest of Wales, and, to this end, lines of castles were built to keep open the means of communication as well as to serve the prime purpose of sheltering the barons and their retainers. New influences were at work in determining design. A greater standard of comfort

DIXON-SCOTT

SUPERB RUINS OF RAGLAN CASTLE

*On the site of an earlier structure, William Herbert, Earl of Pembroke, erected this picturesque stronghold in Monmouthshire, completing it shortly before his execution in 1469. Converted into a mansion in Tudor times, it was still strong enough in the Civil War to withstand for ten weeks the Parliamentary forces under Fairfax.*

DIXON-SCOTT

## DECAYING GLORY OF NUNNEY

*In the Somerset village of Nunney may be seen the picturesque ruins of this moated medieval castle which was completed about 1373. Rectangular, with a round tower at each angle, it was a compact and well fortified manor, and even in ruins is invested with dignity and grandeur. It was besieged by Cromwell's forces.*

was expected than had been possible in the earlier Norman castles. Great strides were being made in manufacturing engines of attack so that fresh means of defence were required. The result was that the keep was discarded entirely and the main line of defence provided by a far stronger outer wall flanked by mural towers and embrasures which commanded the attackers who brought battering rams or scaling ladders to bear upon the walls. The moat was still a vital part of the fortifications and often natural hills were cut away so as to fall with the steepness of a precipice.

### Welsh Fortresses

A number of these fortresses in the Marcher Country have survived, Skenfrith and Grosmont on the Monnow, Kidwelly, and Lougharne overlooking the Pendine Sands ; Caerphilly and Carric Cennen each adding immensely to the charm of the scenery in which it is set.

The concentric castles of Edward I are in the same tradition and represent the highest pinnacle to which medieval military architecture attained. They, too, are built without keeps and depend for their might on the strength of the encircling walls, but instead of these being protected merely by the mural towers, they are surrounded by other complete walls, these too being defended with

embrasures and turrets. How well they served their purpose we may judge from the contemporary record that Harlech Castle was held by no more than twenty-five men and held successfully. Many of the castles built in the preceding reign were rebuilt or enlarged as at Caerphilly ; others, as Beaumaris and Conway, were built on fresh sites. Perhaps the most remarkable feature to be noted in these Edwardian fortresses is the gatehouse which, as the ruins of Harlech testify, was a veritable castle in itself.

Caernarvon Castle, by far the most spectacular and most complete of the medieval ruins in Wales, was built in the reign of Edward I on a different plan and defended by a single encircling wall of immense strength. But even this single wall was proved adequate when, in 1403, the castle was besieged in the Welsh rising under Owen Glyndwr, and, though manned only by a few loyalists, held out magnificently until the siege was raised. Right through that period of revolt Caernarvon and Conway remained loyal in the face of an almost united Welsh nation. It was at Caernarvon that the first Prince of Wales was born in 1284.

All that comes after is anti-climax. A licence from the king was necessary before fortified residences could be erected, and so carefully was

DIXON-SCOTT

A GATEWAY OF ENGLAND
*Dover has long been the " Key of England." The Norman castle,
built by Henry II, was strengthened in later Norman days. The
Constable's Gate seen above was added in the fourteenth century.*

masonry. Tongue ferns grow on the ledges, a few trails of ivy serve as tapestry, and moss and lichen pattern the walls of hall and kitchen alike, and a thorn tree grows in what was the Lady's Bower.

Half the south side of the castle was taken up with the great hall. At the eastern end of this would be the dais with the lord's table and at the opposite end are the doorways through which food and drink would be brought from butlery and kitchen.

The kitchens with their huge fireplaces a dozen feet across and arched like pack-horse bridges ; the flues still black with the grime of ancient fires, the butlery and pantry and cellars may help to give some idea of the domestic side of the establishment.

In the north, Bolton Castle, in Wensleydale, where in later years Mary Queen of Scots was held captive, was built about the same time. Though its beauty cannot vie with that of Bodiam it is imposing enough and in the general style of northern castles, rougher and less ornate than those of the south. So strongly was Bolton fortified that every gate, even those in the outer courtyard, was protected by a portcullis.

By the end of the fifteenth century the visible means of defence were only to give a show of magnificence, and the timbered banqueting-hall with minstrels' gallery, like that of Penshurst Place, was far more important than the guard room or the dungeons.

Bodiam in the south and Bolton in the north were the last of the purely military strongholds. The brick-built castle, manor house of Hurstmonceaux—the first house to be built of brick since Roman days—was erected in the same century. Its genial grace in contrast with the grim splendour of the earlier fortresses is testimony enough to the changing times and man's growing taste for comfort and spaciousness.

Our story is completed by a passing reference to the line of castles which were built by Henry VIII to defend the coast against the attacks of the French. Walmer, Deal, Sandown and Camber form just such an epilogue to the third era of castle building as did Richborough and the others raised by the Count of the Saxon Shore to the second era. Once again it was to ward off attacks from the other side of the Channel that recourse was had to an art which had almost been discarded and was never revived.

the licence reserved that only those families received it whose loyalty was assured.

Sir Edward Dalyngrigge, who had fought at Crécy and Poitiers, and who was a favourite of Richard II, was in 1386 given licence to crenellate and make into a castle his manor house of Bodiam. From a lily-decked moat Dalyngrigge's masonry still rises sheer and smooth, presenting at once an aspect of stern and yet graceful beauty, and an air of unassailable strength. It stands on a slight eminence above the valley of the Rother. As we approach it from the village no other building can be seen, and thus its apparent size is magnified.

So complete are its walls that, until we are on the very edge of the moat, we might believe it still inhabited. Once we have passed the fragment of the barbican and beneath the iron teeth of the portcullis, and through the gatehouse, we find, however, that we have entered an empty shell.

In the grass-grown court are fragments of

# FOLK LORE AND LEGEND

## *by* TOM STEPHENSON

BY no means the least fascinating of our national heirlooms are the romantic myths and curious legends which have been handed down the generations through countless centuries, tales that were told by the ancient bards, epics that were sung by the Saxon gleemen, and the Danish scalds' ballads recited by medieval minstrels and curious narratives which doubtless whiled away many a winter's night.

So captivating stories have been preserved, strange accounts of fairies, pixies and goblins, the doings of giants and pagan gods, and the exploits of legendary heroes such as the bold Robin Hood and the brave William of Cloudesley.

Some of these myths were probably the outcome of the vivid imagination of early people who sought to explain the world around them by crediting inanimate objects with attributes of the living. Mountains, rivers and forests had their spirits and were conscious beings. Rivers in flood, thunder and lightning, falling branches or boulders rolling down the hillsides were ascribed to the activities of invisible beings. Other beguiling stories were born in the imaginative minds of early romancers and gained further colour and imagery with their subsequent re-telling.

In Ireland and Scotland many features of the landscape were created by giantesses, and one of the most hardworking of these mythical beings appears to have been Cailleach Bheara, the old Woman or Hag of Beare. Near Oldcastle, in Meath, is the Hag's Mountain. On this and neighbouring hills she built three great piles of stones which she carried in her apron. In building a fourth cairn, which would have brought her greater power, she slipped and broke her neck.

In Highland folk-tales she was described as one-eyed with a blue-black face and hair like frosted twigs. Ben Nevis was her principal abode and there she kept a beautiful maid imprisoned. It was this same hag who built the tumbled mountains of Ross and piled up Ben Wyvis with rocks from her creel, Little Wyvis being formed by a load of boulders she accidentally dropped in passing.

The Wrekin in Shropshire, the domed height near Wellington, overlooking the site of the Roman Uriconium, and the green vale of the Severn, is another hill of legendary origin. According to one story it was built by two giants to serve as a citadel, and the Severn Valley was formed by their excavation. During a quarrel, one of the monsters threw a spade at his colleague. The spade missed its mark, but, in falling, cleft the rock and made the Needle's Eye.

Another version tells of a wicked giant from Wales with a grievance against the town of Shrewsbury. He came with a tremendous spadeful of earth intent on damming the Severn and flooding the town. At Wellington he was met by a wise cobbler, who, having no wish to lose his customers in Shrewsbury, decided to outwit the malevolent monster. The cobbler was carrying a sack of shoes at the time, and told the giant he had worn them out walking from Shrewsbury. Thereupon

**DRAGON'S HILL**

*The flat-topped hill on the left of the road has long been known as Dragon's Hill in the Vale of the White Horse. Some have linked the name with Uther Pendragon, Arthur's father. Legend makes it the site of St. George's conflict with the dragon.*

A. A. MACGREGOR

93

R. M. ADAM

## MOUNTAIN BUILT BY A GODDESS

*Ben Wyvis, a mountain in Ross and Cromarty, here seen from near Strathpeffer, was, according to Highland folk lore, formed by a fall of rocks from the basket of an ancient goddess who was passing overhead. This fabulous being who was said to ride on the clouds, sought to keep the world barren and troubled with storm.*

the giant, believing his goal so distant and being wearied of his load, he threw it down in disgust and so made the Wrekin.

Cornwall was another notorious haunt of giants, and today there are so many Giant's Chairs, Cradles, Graves, Castles and Pulpits as to suggest the whole peninsula was once thickly populated with mighty men.

### A One-eyed Monster

St. Michael's Mount was the home of Cormelian or Cormoran, an evil, one-eyed monster, who, when the tide was low, would walk across to Marazion, seize the best cow in sight and, slinging it over his shoulders, return to the island.

Morvah has its Giants Field, Giants House and Giants Cradle, relics of a prolific monster, the first settler in the district, who had twenty sons whom he planted round the coast. On August 1 he was wont to gather his family together. So arose the Morvah Fair, once a popular festival when " a quarter of an acre would not hold the horses ridden to the fair."

From the gigantic folk we may turn to the tiny sprightly people, the fairies, elves, pixies, brownies and goblins, the mischievous frolicking or more benign sprites, legends of whom are common throughout the land.

These elfin folk worked wonders in the night, mowing a field or threshing the corn, spinning yarn or doing other useful labour. Typical is the story of the farmer at Washington, beneath the Sussex Downs. Often he had found heaps of corn which had been threshed by unseen hands. Peering through a crack in the barn door one night he saw two " Piskies " wielding their flails. " Well done, my little men," he cried and thereupon the sprites vanished and never came again.

Wales has several stories of humans marrying fairy folk. One of these is located at Mydfai, near the Carmarthen Vans. In the little lake of Llyn y Fan Fach the son of a widow beheld a beautiful maiden. Eventually he persuaded her to become his bride and she brought with her from the lake a goodly dowry of cattle, sheep, goats and horses.

A condition of the marriage was that should the husband ever strike his wife three times without cause, then she would return to the lake. Thrice he tapped her on the shoulder—once at a christening, then at a wedding, and thirdly at a funeral. On the third occasion she reminded him that the contract was broken, and, calling her cattle after her, and leaving husband and sons behind, she disappeared in the lake. On a later occasion she confronted her eldest son and told him he was to become a physician and healer of mankind. For this purpose she furnished him with prescriptions and indicated the habitat of healing herbs, and so Mydfai became renowned for its wonder-working physicians.

Llangorse Lake, near Talgarth in Breconshire, has a legend of a princess who refused to marry her lover unless he acquired wealth by fair means or foul. This he did by robbery and murder. For long they lived in affluence, so long that they saw nine generations of descendants, and then came retribution. The evil pair and their offspring, whilst feasting, were overwhelmed and their town was buried beneath the flood of water which now forms the lake.

### Fate of a Proud City

Wensleydale, in Yorkshire, has another of these stories of submerged cities. In a fold of the hills near Bainbridge is the little lake of Semerwater, of which the late Sir William Watson has told the story in his *Ballad of Semerwater*. To the now vanished city came a beggar who was turned unfed from the doors of the wealthy. But at a humble cottage he was given oatcake and ale. Then he cursed the proud city and bid the waters rise and drown all save that one cottage. So the town with king's tower and queen's bower now lies buried "Deep asleep till doom."

Rivers also had their legendary sprites, probably memories of ancient river deities for the sixth century Gildas refers to "mountains, wells, hills and rivers" which were given divine

honour "by a people who were then blind."

Children in Teesdale used to be warned from playing on the banks of the river, especially on Sundays, by the threat that Peg Powler would drag them into the water. The Ribble had a sprite known as Peg O'Nell, though the name was probably a comparatively modern appellation given to a much more ancient goddess. Before the building of Brungerley Bridge, near Clitheroe, the river had to be crossed by a ford or stepping stones. Peg O'Nell had been a servant at the adjacent Waddow Hall, and her ghost haunted the spot, demanding every seven years a sacrifice in the waters of the Ribble. If by the end of the period a bird, cat or dog had not been drowned there, then a human being would assuredly be the victim.

The idea of sacrifice is linked with many other rivers and there is a grim note in the dialogue:

"Tweed said to Till
'What gars ye rin sae still?'
Till said to Tweed,
'Though ye rin wi' speed,
An' I rin slaw,—
Yet whar ye droon ae man,
I droon twa.'"

Round the ancient standing stones of vanished races, the dolmens and cromlechs and stone-circles of prehistoric man, a remarkable collection

EDGAR WARD

### THE DOMED HEIGHT OF THE WREKIN

*This hill near Wellington in Shropshire, is one of the many features of the landscape which were anciently believed to be the work of giants or other fabulous beings. The Wrekin is a prominent landmark in the midlands and itself commands wide views extending southwards to the Cotswolds and the Malvern Hills.*

of legends have persisted down the ages. Long after their original purpose had been forgotten these monuments were still regarded with fear and reverence, credited with supernatural powers and weird origins, and frequently recognized as objects of worship or sacrifice.

### Story of Stonehenge

Geoffrey of Monmouth brings in the Wizard Merlin to explain the origin of Stonehenge, and the magician tells that giants of old carried the stones from the furthest ends of Africa and set them on a mountain in Ireland where they were known as the Dance of the Giants. Hearing of the marvellous properties of these stones the Britons decided to acquire them and, for this purpose sent 15,000 men under Uther Pendragon, and with Merlin as Chief Engineer and Clerk of Works. So the stones were brought to England, and set upon the site where Aurelius had defeated Hengest, and there Aurelius was buried as was also Uther Pendragon.

In Cornwall and elsewhere the circles are explained as evidence of divine displeasure. The "Hurlers," the "Merry Maidens," the "Nine Maidens" and other circles were explained as sinners (usually Sabbath-breakers) who had been turned into stones.

Of many of these ancient monuments there is a legend that their individual stones cannot be counted, and there is a tale told of the Rollright Stones in Oxfordshire, and of the Countless Stones in Kent. In each place a persistent baker endeavoured to count them by placing a loaf on each stone, but as fast as he did so the "evil one" removed the loaves.

Amid a clump of beech trees on the Berkshire Downs stands Wayland's Smithy. Actually these stones are the remains of a long barrow or Neolithic burial mound, possibly erected 4,000 years ago. For centuries, however, the site has been associated with Wayland or Weland, a mighty smith and monarch of the metal workers of mythology. Of him many tales are told, and he is a prominent figure in the folk lore of German and Scandinavian countries.

Wayland was an invisible smith, and if a wayfarer required his horse shoeing he had to leave the steed by the cave, place a groat on the stone and then retire. On returning a few minutes later, provided he had not attempted to pry into the mystery, he would find his horse reshod. Sir Walter Scott, it will be remembered, introduces this legend in *Kenilworth*.

Not far from Wayland's Smithy is another legendary site, the flat-topped Dragon's Hill beneath the famous White Horse. Here we have a reminder of the days when fire-breathing monsters stalked the land and valiant knights went out to battle with them, perhaps to rescue

### ST. MICHAEL'S MOUNT FROM MARAZION

*This rocky islet in Mounts Bay near Penzance, is accessible by a causeway from the mainland at low tide. It has many legendary associations, and has been claimed as a fragment of the submerged Lyonesse. There the ancient Phœnician traders are said to have bartered for tin with the native Britons of Cornwall.*

STEPHENSON

### LONELY WILDS OF TEESDALE
*The Tees here seen in the wild moorland country below Cauldron Snout on the Durham-Yorkshire border, had a sprite known as Peg Powler, described as " a sort of Lorelei, with green tresses and an insatiable desire for human life." The frothy foam on the water was known as " Peg Powler's suds " or " Peg Powler's cream."*

a beautiful maiden or free the land of a voracious beast. This curiously shaped hill near Uffington is by tradition the site of the most famous of all these combats, for there, according to local legend, St. George of England battled with and overcame the dragon.

Such stories are associated with a number of places. At St. Osyth, in Essex, there appeared in 1170 " a dragon of marvellous bigness, which, by moving, set fire to houses."

St. Leonard's Forest, near Worth, in Sussex, takes its name from the hermit, St. Leonard, who battled with a dragon. When Leonard first retired to the forest he found nothing more harmful than the nightingales. Their singing, however, disturbed him, and he bade them begone, and so to this day the forest is shunned by those songsters.

Then there appeared a ferocious dragon with which Leonard had many struggles, and wherever the blood of the saint was shed, lilies of the valley have flourished ever since his day. Finally, the beast was overcome and crawled feebly into the undergrowth, presumably to die.

Early in the seventeenth century, however, it

was believed the dragon was still at large. It " was oft-times seen at a place called Faygate, and it hath been seen within a mile of Horsham, a wonder, no doubt most terrible and noisome to the inhabitants thereof."

In the north of England there are several legends of these creatures where they were known as worms, a term said to be derived from the Norse *Ormr*—a serpent or worm.

### A Fiery, Flying Serpent

A custom which is said to date from Richard I, and which was maintained for centuries, was the presentation of a falchion to the Bishop of Durham on his first entry into the diocese.

On Croft Bridge over the Tees near Darlington, the bishop was met by the Lord of the Manor of Sockburn who tendered the weapon with these words : " My Lord Bishop, I here present you with the falchion wherewith the champion Conyers slew the worm, dragon, or fiery flying serpent, which destroyed man, woman, and child ; in memory of which the king then reigning gave him the manor of Sockburn."

The Laidley (loathsome) Worm of Spindlestone

R.B.—D

A. A. MACGREGOR

**RIVER SPEY AT CRAIGELLACHIE**

*The River Spey is usually referred to as "she" and has been likened to "a woman dangerous, sometimes fickle, but always winsome." It was supposed to have a sprite which demanded at least one victim a year.*

Heugh was originally a maiden of Bamburgh Castle.
"Excelling all of woman kind
In beauty and in worth."
Because of her beauty she was transformed by her jealous stepmother into a fearsome monster, so poisonous that for seven miles around it laid the country waste. News of this was carried overseas to Childe Wynde, the maiden's brother, and he hastened homewards. As the boat bringing him to the rescue came in sight, the wicked queen mother sent out her witch wives to sink the ship. But they were powerless against the charm of rowan wood. The hero came ashore

in Budle Bay, and drawing his sword went forth to meet the worm. There was no conflict, however, for the monster bid him give it kisses three. This broke the spell and the worm crept into its hole and reappeared as a lady.

To Bamburgh Castle Childe Wynde then bore his sister, and pronounced the doom of the wicked stepmother. For evermore she was to wander round the castle in the shape of a toad.

### Bold Robin Hood

More credible than these supernatural exploits, though perhaps just as mythical, are the renowned adventures of Robin Hood and his "merry men." Whether Robin ever actually lived or not does not matter much. The fact remains that he survives in ballad and story as the most popular and romantic of our legendary heroes.

Robin is said to have lived in the days of Richard I, and Sir Walter Scott in *Ivanhoe* brings about a meeting between the monarch and the outlaw.

In those days we are told there " were many robbers and outlaws, among the which Robin Hood and Little John, renowned thieves, continued in woods despoiling and robbing the goods of the rich."

Robin " entertained a hundred tall men and good archers with such spoils and thefts as he got—he suffered no woman to be oppressed . . . poor men's goods he spared, abundantly relieving them with that which by theft he got from abbeys and the houses of rich old carles." Of all thieves, he was affirmed to be " the prince, and the most gentle theefe."

The glades and recesses of the far-spreading Sherwood Forest were, of course, his favourite haunts, but his name is commemorated farther afield. Derbyshire has several features named after him. At Birchover two blocks of sandstone mark Robin Hood's Stride. Two monoliths near Glossop are known as Robin Hood's Picking Rods, and there is also a Robin Hood's Well. Of these wells there are, in fact, several about the country. In Yorkshire a group of tumuli on the Cleveland Moors are termed Robin Hood's Butts, and on the coast a little north of Whitby is the picturesque Robin Hood's Bay.

At Fountains Abbey there was in Robin's day a " curtal friar," and Robin took a solemn oath that he would neither eat nor drink " Till that friar he did see." Coming into Fountains Dale he saw the friar walking by the water side.

" Robin Hood lighted off his horse
And tied him to a thorn :
' Carry me over, thou curtal friar,
Or else thy life's forlorne.' "

With surprising meekness the friar did so, and then addressed the outlaw :

" Carry me over the water thou fine fellow
Or it shall breed thee paine."

### Friar Tuck

So Robin in turn was steed. Another trip across the stream was begun with Robin in the saddle, but in mid-stream the friar flung him in the water. On regaining the shore the outlaw took bow and arrow and

" To the friar he did let fly,
The curtal friar with his steel buckler
He put that arrow by."

The ballad runs on telling how they fought till Robin craved the boon of a blast on his horn. This granted " He blew out blasts three," and half a hundred bowmen came hurrying over the lea. The friar in turn whistled thrice and half a hundred bandogs came at his call. The bowmen shot at the bandogs but the dogs caught the arrows in their mouths.

Eventually, however, a truce was called and the curtal friar of Fountains became Friar Tuck of Robin Hood's company, a colleague of Little John, Will Scarlet and Allan-a-dale, and assuredly as jovial a rascal as any in the notorious band.

It was at another religious house in Yorkshire that Robin Hood met his end and at Kirklees Priory is his supposed grave.

The day came when Robin sadly remarked to Little John he could not shoot any more and his arrows would not fly. From the Prioress of Kirklees he sought aid, asking her to let his blood. That she did with a vengeance for

" There he did bleed all the
livelong day
Until the next day at noon."

When he would be gone he found himself too spent, but on his horn he " blew out weak blastes three." Said Little John on hearing the sounds :

" I fear my master is near
dead
He blows so wearily."

Suspecting treachery Little John burst in the place, and would have burned the priory to the ground, but Robin would not have it so. Instead he called for his bow and arrow, saying :

" And where this arrow is taken up,
There shall my grave digged be."

So there where the arrow fell Little John opened the earth and lined the grave with green sods that men may say " Here lies bold Robin Hood."

Another popular hero was William of Cloudesley who with Adam Bell and Clym of the Clough dwelt in the forest of Inglewood, near Carlisle. Cloudesley, the English William Tell, was, it is suggested, quite a mythical person, but a lengthy ballad tells of his rescue from Carlisle by Adam and Clym, and of their journey to London to plead for pardon from the king. " Ye shall be hanged all three," was the king's reply, but the queen obtained their freedom as a boon, but only just in time. For from the north came messengers to the king saying how these outlaws had slain three hundred men and more, the justice, the sheriff, and the mayor of Carlisle town, constables and bailies, and serjeants of the law.

The king was sore and called for his best archers and he would see how these fellows could shoot, who in the north had wrought such woe. William of Cloudesley scorned their butts and instead loosed his arrow at an hazel wand and cleft it in two. Next he brought forth his seven-year-old son and led him to a stake and placed an apple on his head. The apple he

STEPHENSON

### LLYN IDWAL AMID THE HILLS

*In a rock-girt hollow of the hills above the Welsh pass of Nant Ffrancon, lies this little lake which takes its name from the legendary prince Idwal who was drowned in its waters by his foster-father Nefyddy the Handsome. Because of that crime, it was said, no bird would fly over the lake.*

said he would cleave in two with an arrow at six score paces.

Should the child be touched by the arrow then the king vowed by the saints in heaven that William and his colleagues should hang. But Cloudesley cleft the apple without mishap and " God forbid " said the king " that thou shouldst shoot at me,

" I give thee eighteen pence a day
And my bow shalt thou bear."

So the outlaws came to dwell with the king " And died good men all three."

There are numerous legends dealing with the

attracted the attention of a shopkeeper to whom he told his story.

The shopkeeper thereupon remarked " Alas ! good friend, should I have heeded dreams, I might have proved myself as very a fool as thou hast ; for not long since I dreamt that at a place called Swaffham Market, in Norfolk, dwells one John Chapman, a pedlar, who hath a tree at the back of his house under which is buried a pot of money. Now, therefore, if I should have made a journey thither to dig for such hidden treasure, judge for yourself whether I should not have been counted a fool."

EDGAR WARD

STONE CIRCLE OF STANTON DREW

*This prehistoric stone circle near Pensford in Somerset is locally known as the " Fiddlers and the Maids " or " Wedding Stones."   A young couple were married on a Sunday and some guests so far forgot themselves as to dance on the green.   For this misdemeanour they were turned into stone and there they have since stood.*

quest for buried treasure, and one of the most definite of these stories is that associated with the little Norfolk town of Swaffham, though variations of the tale are told elsewhere.

In Swaffham there lived in the reign of Henry VII, John Chapman, a tinker or pedlar, and the *Black Book of Swaffham*, a compilation dating from 1454, and preserved in the parish church, records that the north aisle of the church was built by this John Chapman " the Swaffham Pedlar." So, whatever we may think of the story it would seem the pedlar was an authentic being.

Chapman dreamt that if he went to London and stood on London Bridge he would meet a man bringing him good news. On the strength of this the pedlar took up his pack and, with his dog at heel, he walked to London. For some time he stood on the bridge, and in doing so

The tinker readily agreed with this wisdom, and, concealing his impatience, added he would take himself home and pay no heed to such dreams.

Once home, however, he lost no time in digging beneath the tree indicated. Soon he discovered a pot filled with money, and on the lid of the pot was inscribed in Latin

" Under me doth lie
Another much richer than I."

Whether the tinker was sufficiently learned or not to transcribe this, he continued digging until he unearthed the second pot which contained twice as much wealth as the first.

In gratitude for his good fortune Chapman dedicated some of his wealth to the improvement of Swaffham Church in which was preserved for a long time a statue of the pedlar with his pack on his back.

STEPHENSON

### WAYLAND'S SMITHY
*Close to the Ridgeway, an ancient track on the Berkshire Downs, are these stones, the burial chamber of a Neolithic tumulus. From Saxon days the site has been known as Wayland's Smithy or Forge. Wayland or Weland was said to be son of the giant Wada and was lamed by the king of the Niars and set to work at the forge.*

STEPHENSON

### THE CHARM OF ROBIN HOOD'S BAY
*This fishing hamlet on the Yorkshire coast, south of Whitby, owes its name to the famous outlaw. Robin Hood was given to plundering rich abbots and perhaps the monastery at Whitby brought him so far afield. Another story says he had a secret landing place in the bay whereby he could put to sea when hard pressed.*

STEPHENSON

### NIGHTFALL AT STONEHENGE

*This greatest and best known of our stone circles has several legends about its origin.   According to one the Devil brought them from Ireland where he had tricked an old woman into selling them to him for a few pence. While she was counting the coppers the Devil lashed the stones together and flew with them to Salisbury Plain.*

DIXON-SCOTT

### A SUNLIT RIDE IN SHERWOOD FOREST

*This ancient forest, now but a shrunken remnant of its former expanse, was the supposed haunt of Robin Hood and his Merrie Men.   Even if Robin be an imaginary hero, there is no doubt that the forest was in ancient days the abode of outlaws living precariously and defying even the very harsh forest laws of the Normans.*

Another method of acquiring wealth by no means so innocent as that of the Swaffham Pedlar relied on the supposed magical properties of the " Hand of Glory," and superstitions regarding this gruesome aid to fortune were common in several European countries.

## Strange Doings at an Inn

The "Hand of Glory" was a hand taken from a gallows corpse and prepared by an elaborate recipe. In the hand was placed a lighted candle and " wherever one goes with this contrivance those it approaches are rendered incapable of motion as though they were dead."

High on Stainmore, where a lonely moorland road crosses the Pennines, stands the Old Spital, now a farm but once an inn where the coaches changed horses. In the closing years of the eighteenth century there arrived one night an old woman who asked to be allowed to stay the night. As it was her intention to leave early in the morning a servant girl was left to sit by the fire and see the traveller off the premises.

FELTON

### THE PEDLAR OF SWAFFHAM

*This attractive sign at Swaffham in Norfolk recalls the story of the Pedlar who dreamed that if he went and stood on London Bridge the profits of his journey would be equal to his pains. He did so and learned of the treasure buried in his garden. Nothing doubting, he returned home and found his faith amply rewarded.*

The servant caught a glimpse of a man's trousers beneath the old woman's gown and became suspicious. Feigning sleep she closed her eyes and pretended to snore. Thereupon the traveller produced a dead man's hand and attached a lighted candle to it saying, " Let those who are asleep be asleep and let those who are awake be awake."

This done he placed the hand on the table and went out to call his fellow robbers. Immediately the supposed sleeper jumped up, banged the door and locked it, and ran to awaken the family.

They, however, were in magic sleep and not until she had extinguished the candle with a bowl of milk was she able to rouse them. From the window the landlord's son asked the intruders what they wanted. They replied that if they were given the dead man's hand they would depart. Instead of the hand, however, they got a charge of shot from the family blunderbuss, and next morning stains of blood could be traced across the moor.

This concluding tale illustrates how recently such stories were steadfastly believed. For years, it is said, the brown, withered hand was kept in the house. In 1861 the story was related to an inquirer by an old woman in the neighbourhood, the daughter of the servant girl who outwitted the thieves.

W. A. CALL

## THE STATELY RUINS OF TINTERN

*Beautifully situated in the valley of the Wye below Monmouth, and surrounded by wooded hills, Tintern today is one of our most romantic ruins. Founded in 1131, it was not completed until one and a half centuries later. In 1900 the Duke of Beaufort presented the estate to the nation, and extensive repairs were carried out.*

# THE BEAUTIFUL ABBEYS
# OF BRITAIN

### *by* HAROLD SHELTON

THE monastic ruins of Britain are a vital part of the heritage which the Middle Ages have handed down to the present. If only because we find in them a beauty of architecture allied with beauty of situation, they have a double claim on our appreciation. So Tintern Abbey in the Valley of the Wye, Bolton in Wharfedale, Strata Florida in Cardiganshire and Llanthony in the Black Mountains add enormously to the beauty of the scene. Rievaulx, Abbey Dore, Fountains or Mount Grace, to name only four out of very many, are as important as the annals of contemporary chroniclers in helping us to understand the life of the monks and the difficult times in which they lived.

The beginnings of monasticism are to be found in the rebellion against the false values of an age when Christianity was beginning to spread a humanizing influence over the western world, but Paganism still held undisputed sway over the people at large. The solitary hermits are the first sign of such a rebellion. They lived a solitary life, existing on the bare necessities, devoting their lives to reflection on God and seeking peace in the midst of strife. The transition from the state of these solitary hermits to organized communities of devout men is a simple one and inevitable.

Towards the end of the fifth century, when most of the civilized Romano-British inhabitants had been driven into Wales or Ireland, many communities were founded with the object of providing missionaries to reintroduce Christianity into Saxon England. Names such as St. Columb and St. Patrick associated with these earliest monastic foundations bulk more largely in the annals of Irish legend than does our own St. Augustine in English history. It was the missionaries sent out from Ireland who founded the first houses in England. Whitby, among several others in the north, is a conspicuous example. In the south of England their influence extended to one place only—Glastonbury—our sole link in the southern counties between the old and the new monasticism. St. Hilda was the first abbess of Whitby, and Cædmon, the father of English poetry, one of the earliest monks.

Once more religious consciousness received a serious set-back, for, just when the inspired work of the Irish missions bade fair to convert thousands of country folk, a new peril appeared in the persons of the Vikings, and the new seats of religion and learning, where the Saxon monks had begun to write and preach, were swept from the land.

It was not until the country was resettled after the Treaty of Wedmore that an opening was found for a revival of monasticism. Then arose the first of the great orders—the Benedictines—who swore allegiance to the rule of St. Benedict and vowed to observe chastity and poverty. That order, like most of those which followed it, had its origin in Normandy. It was from that source after the Conquest, when the great era of abbey building began, that most of the monks were drawn.

Gradually the wealth of the Benedictines increased to enormous proportions, and with it the temptation to disregard the simplicity which had first bound them together. The abbots ultimately became the richest in the land and travelled from country to country with large

STEPHENSON

### PAST BEAUTIES OF WHITBY ABBEY
*Overlooking the North Sea the Saxon abbess, Hilda, built an abbey which was sacked by the Danes in A.D. 867. The existing ruins are those of a Benedictine monastery built in Norman times.*

D. MCLEISH

### FAN-VAULTED CLOISTERS, GLOUCESTER CATHEDRAL

*These exquisitely vaulted cloisters were part of the abbey which formerly occupied the site of Gloucester Cathedral, and they probably date from 1351. On the left are the carrels, or recesses, used by the monks.*

was the focal point of the other orders, and giving to each monk his own cell in which he lived a life of meditation and study in complete asceticism. Although only nine such abbeys were founded in Britain, they retained the ideals for which they were founded until the Dissolution.

The abbey ruins are mainly fragments dating from the Dissolution in the reign of King Henry VIII when the monastic orders had reached the height of their wealth. Consequently their buildings attained an unprecedented magnificence.

The earlier foundations of the Benedictine Order are less ornate than those of the Cistercians or Cluniacs. Without exception, too, they are the only ones which can trace an origin before the Conquest. The cloisters of Norwich stand out as the most extensive monastic cloisters in the country. Nearly 200 feet square, with walks 12 feet broad, they show all the magnificence which we associate with fourteenth-century architecture. The tracery of the windows, the carved bosses (more than four hundred in number) which give added beauty to the vaulted roof, and the columns of the monastic infirmary to the east of the cloisters combine to make this one of the most beautiful and the most living reminders of the monks' life. Tradition relates that in 1272 the citizens of Norwich, incensed by the unjust treatment meted out to them by the abbot as Lord of the Manor, set fire to the church and damaged it extensively, an incident which can be paralleled in the history of many of the abbeys.

### A Cradle of Christianity

The ruins of Lindisfarne, in Northumberland, and of Tynemouth are substantial and unusually beautiful. The red sandstone from which the former is built and its romantic situation outweigh for many the superior architecture of the latter, its magnificence dimmed by the grime of nearby industry. The severe lines of the abbey church, its grand Norman doorway, and the unadorned beauty of the claustral ruins make a

retinues of attendants and something of the pomp of kings. Their lives became political as well as religious, and their wealth was reflected in a higher standard of living for the monks and the consequent disappearance of the ideals of simplicity. So new orders were founded by those who deplored the growing indulgence and laxity of the older orders.

Before the end of the eleventh century a number of Benedictine monks founded a new settlement for themselves. This they did at a place called Citeaux in Burgundy, from which is derived the name of the Cistercian order which ultimately rivalled the wealth and influence of the Benedictines. In the course of the next two hundred years more than six hundred Cistercian abbeys were founded in England alone.

The same cause was responsible for the founding of the Cluniac order by Abbot Odo of Cluny, and of the Carthusian order which re-established the principle of the solitary hermit, setting its face against the principles of communal life which

deep and lasting impression even on the casual wayfarer.

Lindisfarne can justly claim to be one of the cradles of Christianity; it was founded in A.D. 635 by St. Aidan who became first abbot and first bishop of the See of Northumberland. The illustrious St. Cuthbert was the sixth abbot; when the abbey was laid waste by the Norsemen the monks took the coffin of St. Cuthbert and moved it from town to town until they founded a new See at Durham, which is thus derived directly from Lindisfarne. It was during this time, before finally settling at Durham, that the bishop's See was set up for more than a hundred years at the village of Chester-le-Street.

St. Albans was a Benedictine House, though only the foundation of the cloisters remains of the conventual buildings. But St. Albans illustrates how great was the influence of monastic life on religious history in the Middle Ages, for the cathedral today is the direct descendant of the original abbey church.

There is a legend that Albanus, a citizen of the Romano-British town of Verulamium, served as was usual in the legions of the emperor, and in his travels on the Continent was converted to the Christian faith. Returning, he tried to convert his fellow citizens, and paid the penalty of so many in advance of their times, and was put to death on a hill overlooking the town. Four hundred years later the Saxon King Offa laid the first stone of an abbey to be the lasting memorial of the martyred Albanus. In the course of time the town of St. Albans grew up around the abbey, and the abbey church became the place of worship for the burgesses. The abbot was one of the wealthiest men of his age, and travelled with a retinue of more than a hundred.

## Royal Patronage

Several others of the cathedral churches have their origin in Benedictine abbeys, and, though the ruins seem less spectacular under the more imposing shadow of the cathedral, they are still full of interest. The abbey of Canterbury, where the ruined round arches show the work of the Norman craftsman, had a long history of prosperity and royal patronage, entertaining King Edward I and Richard II, as well as Henry VIII before that merry monarch overthrew the house which had given him shelter. The church which was to become Canterbury Cathedral, the most magnificent example of Gothic architecture in Britain, was originally the church of the monastery. Westminster Abbey and the cathedrals of Peterborough, Rochester, Winchester and Gloucester, Ely, Chester and Worcester, all show more or less of their monastic beginnings. The remains of three of these—Chester, Gloucester and Worcester—are wonderfully preserved, though they have been reconstructed from time to time. At Gloucester we shall see the " carrels,"

DIXON-SCOTT

### THE MELLOW BEAUTY OF FOUNTAINS ABBEY
*To the valley of the Skell, near Ripon, there came in 1132 a little band of monks from York. In what was then a desolate dale they laid the foundations of Fountains Abbey, which was to become the greatest and richest religious house in the north. In their sylvan setting, these ruins still testify to their original grandeur.*

the stone reading-desks at which the monks worked in the cloisters; at Chester the Norman undercroft which adjoins the west walk is the finest of its kind in England. We shall linger, too, over the refectory, a beautiful specimen of the early English style, with its reader's pulpit, where the priest would read lessons and say grace before and after meals. For the rest, the magnificent gateway of Bury St. Edmunds, the fine nave of Blyth and the picturesque ruins of Monk Bretton are all derived from the Benedictines.

Cluniac Houses are fewer in number, but none

of the rich sculpture which distinguished later work—the thirteenth-century choir and refectory which must have been, like that of Chester, typical of the best which that great age of architecture could produce. Fountains is no less impressive. Does the early English elegance of the Chapel of the Nine Altars take pride of place? Certainly its lofty, gracefully pointed arches, its generous windows, its perfect proportions call to the imagination a picture of supreme beauty, even though the glory of its roof has perished. But it is only one of many triumphs. We shall admire the symmetry of the lofty

STEPHENSON

### A MONASTERY WITH A TRAGIC STORY

*On the banks of the Calder, at Whalley in Lancashire, this Cistercian Abbey was established in 1296. John Paslew, the last abbot, and a leader of the Pilgrimage of Grace, was hanged as a rebel in 1537.*

will carp at the artistry and brilliance of Much Wenlock or Castle Acre.

A tour of Yorkshire will demonstrate the wealth and magnificence of the Cistercians. No other county can show such splendour as the combined elegance and interest of Kirkstall, Jervaulx, Fountains, Byland, Rievaulx, Roche and Sawley. Yet all these are within the one county and all belong to the same order. The ruins of Fountains are the most complete of their kind; those of Rievaulx the most picturesque in architecture and situation alike. Rievaulx was the first of the Cistercian abbeys to be founded in the north—it survived to become the wealthiest in the whole country. That perhaps explains the splendour of the ruins, the late Norman nave and cloister, already showing traces

square tower, added a century after the rest of the buildings were complete. We shall pause at the noble piers which support the vaulted roof of the warming room, and at the serene and dignified outline of the refectory. We shall carry away the impression of a unique experience.

When we visit Fountains we shall be at once impressed by the beauty of the abbey's surroundings, for it is set in park-like undulating country, well wooded and fertile. It was not always so. When twelve monks set out in 1132 to found a cell from the abbey of York, they found a desolate wilderness covered in tangled forest and rank undergrowth wherein they had to make a small clearing in which to build their first wooden church. The handiwork of the monks was the

W. F. TAYLOR

## THE GREY WALLS OF BYLAND

*In a green recess of the Hambledon Hills, near Coxwold in Yorkshire, stand the time-shattered fragments of Byland Abbey, another Cistercian house which was begun in 1177. The photograph shows the remains of the abbey church with the base of a massive pillar and all that is left of an impressive circular window.*

DIXON-SCOTT

ABBEY OF COUNTLESS MEMORIES

*Glastonbury's ruins recall many incidents of legend and history.   Joseph of Arimathea is said to have brought Christianity there, and to have planted the famous thorn that bloomed on Christmas Day.   St. Patrick was another supposed visitor.   Beneath its altar the reputed remains of King Arthur and his queen were reinterred.*

DIXON-SCOTT

A BORDER MONASTERY

*Charmingly placed on a bend of the Tweed, Dryburgh Abbey was established by David I in 1150 on the site of a sixth-century sanctuary and became a wealthy institution.   The abbey suffered in border warfare and was sacked on several occasions.   Sir Walter Scott is buried in one of the aisles and Earl Haig rests nearby.*

first step in reclaiming the valley from the harsh hand of Nature.

In the neighbouring county of Lancashire the most splendid ruins are of a Cistercian House—Furness—where the red sandstone has mellowed and become an integral part of the landscape. Tintern, too, immortalized by Wordsworth's poetry, was built by the same order—the ultimate consummation of Art and Nature combined, taking tone from the horse-shoe bend of the Wye in which it lies, yet, adding as much to its beauty as it derives from it. Curiously, today it looks as much a work of Nature as the other features of an incomparable landscape. Netley and Beaulieu, in Hampshire (in the second of which the monks' refectory is used as a church); Calder Abbey, in Cumberland; Waverley Abbey, in Surrey, which like Tintern is set in a horse-shoe bend of the river; Cleeve Abbey, in Somerset, and Valle Crucis, in Denbighshire, are a few of the others which claim our special notice.

In southern Scotland, Sweetheart or New Abbey was a Cistercian House. Its gaunt beauty is part and parcel of the scene, its weather-beaten ruins toning perfectly with the country's stone walls. Mystery surrounds its foundation. According to popular legend, it was founded in 1275 by Devorguilla, wife of John de Baliol, who also founded Balliol College, Oxford, in memory of her husband. In New Abbey she was buried, and John de Baliol's embalmed heart was buried with her.

Whilst we are in the border country there are several spectacular ruins which invite us to visit them. A mile and a half from Dumfries we shall find Lincluden—in the words of the poet Burns, " an old ruin in a sweet situation "; at Jedburgh an abbey which still shows the full beauty of thirteenth-century art; at Melrose the charming fragments which inspired Scott's *Lay of the Last Minstrel*. Here in the monastery, which was founded by David I, tradition relates that the heart of Robert the Bruce is buried.

### Beauty of Cistercian Ruins

Finally, there are Dryburgh and Kelso, both of which were destroyed in the wars between England and Scotland. The church of the former is the last resting place of Sir Walter Scott and of Earl Haig; but of the monastic buildings only insignificant fragments remain, except of the chapter house, which is more richly decorated than any other in Scotland.

It is not surprising that the Cistercian ruins are generally more extensive and more beautifully situated than those of the other orders, for it was the Cistercian custom to build in the countryside, whilst the Benedictines chose places that were already inhabited. Thus, after the dissolution, the ruins which adjoined or formed part of growing townships, were not allowed to stand, but were either pulled down to be replaced by churches or incorporated in modern houses. In the open country, however, when the sites

EDGAR WARD

### ROMANTIC RUINS OF FURNESS

*In the Furness district of Lancashire, in the " Vale of Deadly Nightshade," Benedictine monks from Normandy settled in 1127 and began the building of a splendid monastery which later adopted the rules of the Cistercians. Built of warm red sandstone, the ruins present a wealth of beauty and architectural detail.*

EDGAR WARD

ABBEY OF THE FLOWERY VALLEY

*Cleeve Abbey, near Washford, Somerset, founded for Cistercian monks in 1188 by William de Romara was dedicated to " Our Blessed Lady of the Cliff." On the left is the Chapter House with the dormitory above. At right angles to this is the beautiful building with domestic rooms below and the refectory above.*

were of less value, the abbey buildings were left to decay, at the mercy only of local road builders who looked upon them as valuable quarries.

It is hard to think of Tintern or Rievaulx being built by unskilled workmen, yet the modern grace of Buckfast will convince the doubtful of what can be achieved by willing, if unpracticed, hands. Medieval chronicles describe the building of several abbeys. Generally a small working party was despatched from one of the powerful abbeys, with a meagre supply of food and water, to found a new house. When they were sent to a town their task was relatively easy, but when, as in the case of the Cistercians, new monasteries were established in the midst of the country, their task was always an Odyssey of toil and patience. We must imagine a party of some twenty or thirty seeking a suitable site for the new foundation, exposed to the dangers of man and Nature alike, for the land was infested with robbers and there was no shelter for the infirm.

### How the Abbeys were Built

A valley site was always chosen, for the monks must needs have water. How necessary it was for them to build near the banks of a river is aptly illustrated by the story of William the Conqueror and the Benedictine monks whom he commanded to build a monastery on the site of the Battle of Hastings. The monks started to build in the valley immediately to the south of Senlac; but when William heard of it, he commanded them to destroy their work and make a fresh start on the hill where Battle Abbey stands today. So disturbed were the builders that they feared God would visit a curse upon the abbey for the Conqueror's impiousness in daring to build where no water flowed.

When at last the site was found, the monks started to clear the ground and build themselves rude huts of wood for protection, utilizing what shelter they could, and hewing the trees to provide them with timber. Then they would till the ground to provide themselves with the necessities of life, and at the same time started to build a church of timber. When this was completed their own temporary dwelling places were rebuilt, still on a modest scale, and the abbey was truly founded. More and more monks were attracted to the new centre, and a start was made on rebuilding the church in stone, the work proceeding either by the hands of the monks themselves or by hired bands of workmen who travelled the country seeking work where they could find it, generally under a Norman master mason.

After the building of the church had been finished the monks' lodgings and other conventual buildings were rebuilt in stone. But this

DIXON-SCOTT

## BEAUTIFUL REMAINS OF BEAULIEU ABBEY

*The refectory of this once wealthy Cistercian monastery founded by King John in 1204 now serves as the parish church. Other remains include part of the chapter house, dormitory and cloisters. After the Battle of Barnet, in 1471, Queen Margaret and her son sought refuge in Beaulieu, which had the privilege of sanctuary.*

great task was rarely completed without disappointments, or without part of the building collapsing through faulty construction, or through the force of tempest and storm. In the early days funds were often lacking, and it was left to the bounty of the king to complete the building. Eighty years was no long time from the choice of the site to the laying of the last stone of the conventual buildings, and, though the wages paid to the hired workers were often no more than sixpence per day, many thousands of pounds were necessary to complete a building for such an exalted purpose, and to embellish it with the engravings and frescoes which are such a valuable part of Britain's medieval heritage.

The church was the centre of the monastic buildings, and, in its construction, the choir was built before the nave, the former being reserved for the devotions of the monks, the latter being sometimes thrown open to the local people. The monastic buildings were raised round three sides of a square, the fourth side being against the church. Between the buildings and the square were the cloisters which was where the monks walked and talked and studied. At first, after the Italian fashion, the cloisters were left unprotected; but, alas! the monks found the

English climate more draughty than that of the Mediterranean countries, so that in all the later monasteries the sides of the cloisters facing the central square were built up and windows provided. Often the cloisters were divided into studies on the side facing south so as to draw warmth from the sun.

In reconstructing the life of the monks we must remember that they were allowed no heating except in the sick room, and that the climate was at least not materially warmer than it is now. Even so, the life of the average citizen in Norman, or even later, times was unprotected in a way that could not be tolerated today. There must have been far fewer invalids if only because the weak rarely survived to man's estate. Perhaps what we regard as undue hardship in the life of the monks was accepted by them without thought. The absence of artificial heating, the stone floors and the abundance of fresh air in which they worked may well have led to greater health and greater vitality.

## Well Planned Buildings

Chester, Fountains and Rievaulx show well how the monks' buildings were planned. On the side facing the church was the dining-room or refectory, with the monks' washing-place or lavatory—which had a religious as well as a utilitarian significance, seeing that the washing of hands before and after meals was an integral part of the ritual. On the western side were ranges of store-houses and minor buildings, while on the east was the Chapter House where the officers of the monastery met to transact their daily business, and which, after the church itself, was the most richly ornamented and the most sacred part of the buildings. The rest of the eastern side was occupied by the dormitories and other common rooms of the monks. In the earlier, more austere, days of monastic life the abbots slept with the monks, but, as their wealth and position increased, they had separate lodgings built for them, so that in many ruins the abbot's lodging often rivals the elegance and size of the conventual buildings.

So far we have dealt only with the monkish orders in which the lay brethren outnumbered the priests; but there were also Orders of Canons regular, all of whose members were ordained, and whose chief contribution to the legacy of monasticism consisted in church building. Chief

D. MCLEISH

FAIR MELROSE
*Sir Walter Scott wrote eloquently of the beauty of " St. David's ruin'd pile " at Melrose. Like Dryburgh, this monastery suffered in war. Robert Bruce restored it on one occasion, and beneath the window of the stately choir seen above his heart was buried.*

STEPHENSON

## THE STATELY PILE OF LANERCOST PRIORY

*Near Brampton, in Cumberland and eleven miles from Carlisle, this priory for Austin Canons was established by the Norman, Robert de Vaux, in 1169, and is built largely of stones from the Roman Wall. In 1346 the Priory was plundered by the Scots under David Bruce. The ruins contain some very old and interesting tombs.*

among these were the Augustinians whose first house was founded in this country near the beginning of the twelfth century, and who are better known to posterity as the Black Canons from the black vestments which they adopted. The only Augustinian church which attained cathedral rank was that of Carlisle where we can still observe traces of the monks' life in the refectory. Lanercost Priory in Cumberland, Bolton in Yorkshire, Llanthony in Monmouthshire and Walsingham in Norfolk are a few of the distinguished ruins belonging to this order. The last named became very famous during the late Middle Ages owing to the great number of pilgrims who visited annually the reputed shrine of the Virgin Mary—the Shrine of Our Lady of Walsingham.

### Holy Shrine of Walsingham

It is related that in 1661 a widow, praying that she might be able to spread devotion, was transported in a dream to Nazareth where God showed her the Sancta Casa, the home where the Holy Family had lived, and bade her build another like it at Walsingham. Angels helped her in her task, and when it was finished, its fame and the story of the miracles performed there spread all over England.

Many were the kings and nobles who came to do homage at the shrine in which it was thought the Holy Virgin herself had taken up her abode. Edward I of England, David of Scotland, and King Henry VIII all made the pilgrimage; but this did not prevent the last-named monarch enriching himself from Walsingham's coffers at the dissolution. The way these pilgrims travelled was by the Palmers' Way through Newmarket, Brandon and Fakenham; its name means Pilgrims' Way, for it was the custom for pilgrims to Jerusalem to carry palms as a sign of devotion. So the words Palmer and Pilgrim came to have the same meaning.

Bolton, too, which like Tintern owes much to Wordsworth's poetry is rich in legend; for it is related that it was founded in honour of the boy Egremont who was drowned in the Wharfe, near where the famous stepping-stones now span the river. Cold fact discredits the legend, for the priory was originally founded at Embsay in 1121 and transferred to its present site thirty years later.

Scarcely less powerful than the Augustinians were the Premonstratensians, better known as the White Canons, taking their name, as the Augustinians, from the colour of their vestments. Priories belonging to this order were fewer—Torre Abbey in Devon, Bayham Abbey in Sussex, and Shap Abbey in Westmorland are the only ones of which there are remains.

Finally, we must not overlook the Orders of

STEPHENSON

### AN IMPOSING FRAGMENT AT GUISBOROUGH

*Robert Bruce, of Skelton, an ancestor of the more famous Bruce, endowed this Augustinian priory in 1119. The lofty east window is a beautiful example of Decorated architecture and still bears the lion of Bruce and arms of other local families. In front of the window are bases of pillars of the nave arcades.*

Friars who were trained to become wandering preachers, and did more than other orders to spread the Gospel through the countryside. They were introduced into England in the thirteenth century, and for two hundred years acted as missionaries in a still unfriendly land, earning high praise for their care of the sick as well as for their preaching of the Gospel. Like the canons they too were generally known by the colour of their vestments. So the Dominicans are better known as Black Friars, and the Carmelites as White Friars.

The monks' life started at midnight when they were roused and filed into the church for the longest service of the day. After a second sleep they arose at daybreak and literally spent the time until sundown in devotion, study and eating. Almost every movement was governed by order—the manner in which they took their food, the order of the services, the pews in which they worshipped. There were breaks for talk in the cloisters and in the afternoon for recreation and work, though their games seem to have been limited to draughts and skittles. Even the vestments in which they retired for the night were fixed.

The influence of the church builders on architecture is obvious ; the English styles became second to none in the world. Because the monks were almost the only class who could read or write, they kept alive the spirit of literature and made possible the beginnings of learning which never became extinct in the centuries which followed the dissolution. More, they brought education into existence, for the monastic schools were the earliest in the country and set an example of discipline and scholarship which otherwise would have been impossible. They re-established, too, the dignity of the worker on the land by doing themselves the work which the Norman landowner thought fit for inferior classes only, and they set a high standard of hospitality by throwing open the convent to the wayfarer in search of a night's lodging.

As the orders became more and more powerful they too became great landowners and shared in the faults of the barons. They began to employ outside labour and rewarded their workers with no better treatment than they received from the squires ; nor did they use their wealth always to alleviate distress among the people who dwelt under the protection of their goodwill. So they displeased the countrymen, and the villages which had sprung up around the monasteries, now grown into towns, rebelled against their pride and prejudice. Instead of a home of peace and learning they became a centre of strife, so that when Henry VIII enriched himself at their expense and dissolved all the monasteries, they had long ceased to be useful institutions.

### Founded by Canute

Even after the dissolution the ideal of monastic life survived. The history of Buckfast Abbey is proof enough of that. We know that it was founded in the reign of Canute ; then it disappears from the annals of history. In the twelfth century it was refounded by the Cistercians. Dissolved by Henry VIII its ruins were turned into a Gothic mansion, then in 1882 the site was purchased by the Benedictines who in the course of forty years have raised the immortal structure which stands today as a wonderful monument to their devotion.

W. F. TAYLOR

## MONASTIC SPLENDOUR IN A YORKSHIRE DALE
*Wordsworth and Ruskin wrote of Bolton and its romantic situation by the banks of the Wharfe.   The Priory Church, built in 1170, escaped destruction during the dissolution of the monasteries and is still is use.*

EDGAR WARD

## TREE-CLAD WALLS OF BUILDWAS ABBEY
*The ruins of this Shropshire monastery founded in the twelfth century consist mainly of remains of the chapter house and the nave and chancel of the church.   The Abbot's House, dating from the following century, has been restored.   The seven massive pillars of the nave were said to represent the Seven Pillars of Wisdom.*

D. MCLEISH

## WESTERN TOWERS OF ENGLAND'S PREMIER CATHEDRAL

*Canterbury, England's premier cathedral, takes us back to the days of St. Augustine, the Roman missionary who converted Ethelbert, King of Kent, and who was the first " bishop of the English." The oldest remaining fragments date from Archbishop Lanfranc (1070-1089), but most of the structure is due to subsequent builders, including William of Sens the famous French master mason, who began building in 1175.*

# THE CATHEDRALS OF ENGLAND

## *by* CHARLES FRY

THE history, if not the fabric, of most of our cathedrals has its origin towards the close of the Dark Ages. Its background is that half-primeval England of the swamps and forests, in which a scattered population was settling down to husbandry in huddled little hamlets and clearings, still much at the mercy of warring chiefs and raiders, while the weeds grew thick over the foundations of the Roman settlements. It was a shaggy England still, brooding, as it were, in a dangerous early light, to which Christianity was to bring the first promise of a dawn.

The story of St. Augustine's great mission has often been recounted. We owe to it our three earliest cathedral foundations, Rochester, London and Canterbury; while three more, Lincoln, Southwell and York, in part or in whole owe their inception to the greatest of his followers, Paulinus, one of that eager band sent out from Rome by St. Gregory to further Augustine's task. While Augustine, with his English converts and Roman followers, spread the doctrine of Christ through the southern provinces, to Paulinus and his successors belonged the task of gathering the wilder north into the Catholic fold.

It was a task made delicate at first by the labours of another missionary group, simple men who had already in these parts made many converts to a primitive Celtic Church. The influence of this church had spread from Ireland to Iona, a little island off the west coast of Scotland, a forcing-house of faith, whence a devoted band had set forth to preach and baptize in the wilds of Scotland and Northumbria.

Chief among the Celtic missionaries was St. Cuthbert, who, after a youth spent as a shepherd boy near Melrose, joined the fraternity of Iona and made his way to Lindisfarne, the Holy Island off the Northumberland coast from which this evangelization of Northern England was largely effected. Here he died and was buried in A.D. 687. But with the growing terror of the Danish and Norse raids, it soon became necessary to remove his relics, with the treasure of the little church, to more secure surroundings, and so the Lindisfarne brotherhood set out on a remarkable pilgrimage of several hundred years' duration. Each place of halt was commemorated by a church dedicated to the saint, but it was not until A.D. 997 that the brothers " with great joy arrived with his body at Dunholme," where, attracted by the security of that hill-fortress surrounded on three sides by the Wear, they built " a little church of wands and branches " on the site where Durham Cathedral now stands.

Such was the origin of one of the most splendid of our cathedral churches. Many another can tell a story equally fraught with danger and devotion. Some owe their inception to Saxon or Roman missionary bishops, as Lichfield to St. Chad, Winchester to St. Swithun, Ripon to St. Wilfred—men whose tombs were to develop into some of the most popular shrines of the Middle Ages, the offerings at which went largely to endow the costly fabrics and fitments of later cathedrals. Some again were due to the piety of Saxon rulers; the first cathedral of Peterborough commemorated the conversion of Peada, King of the Mercians, about A.D. 665 ; that at Hereford

**NORWICH CATHEDRAL**
W. F. TAYLOR
*Norwich became a cathedral city in 1094, and the Norman tower surmounted by a fifteenth-century spire makes a landmark, rising above the historic town.*

DIXON-SCOTT

**THE LOVELY WESTERN TOWER OF ELY CATHEDRAL**

*On the site of a Benedictine abbey, established by a seventh-century Queen of Northumbria, stands the magnificent Cathedral of Ely. The building of the present structure was begun in 1083 by Abbot Simeon, and after the collapse of the tower in 1322 was completed with a wealth of fourteenth-century carving by William of Walsingham. Far and wide across the low levels of the fens its lofty towers are seen soaring heavenwards.*

was originally raised about A.D. 825 over the tomb of Ethelbert, King of the East Angles, who was lured to his death by the great Offa of Mercia ; while that at Ely was founded in A.D. 673 by Ethelreda, princess of East Anglia, who built a religious house on her own lands and assigned to it her absolute principality of the surrounding " Isle of Ely "—a bequest that was to form the nucleus of the wealth accruing to one of the proudest monasteries of the Middle Ages.

The early days of some of these rude little churches were often stormy. The establishment at Ely, for instance, was sacked and gutted by the Danes less than a hundred years after its foundation. But a handful of survivors escaped, creeping back a few years later to effect a partial restoration of the church, which, surviving the fury of Hereward's last stand at the nearby " Camp of Refuge," was to continue in active use until 1080, when its rebuilding was begun in the present form. The church at Peterborough suffered a rather similar fate, having been sacked by the Danes in A.D. 870 and rehabilitated, very sumptuously for the time, a hundred years later. At the Conquest the abbey passed into Norman hands, but was stormed by Hereward, who destroyed all but the church where he himself had taken the vows of knighthood.

W. F. TAYLOR

### WEST FRONT, PETERBOROUGH CATHEDRAL

*Peada, a Saxon King of Mercia, founded a monastery at Peterborough in the seventh century. This suffered many vicissitudes, being destroyed by the Danes in A.D. 870 and after rebuilding being burnt down in 1116.*

### Danish Plunders

Even in the west the sacred places were not immune from the Danish terror, and we find the church built by St. Oswald for the Worcester Benedictines plundered and burnt as late as 1041, though only a few years were to elapse before a greater building rose from the ashes at the hands of the famous Wulstan, who alone among English prelates retained his position after the Conquest.

The earlier churches were, for the most part, rough and ready affairs of timber, easy to destroy and not so difficult to rebuild. But with the more settled conditions of the tenth century, and the establishment of rudimentary connections with the Continent, came a wave of rebuilding in stone, in a style that may be recognized as a primitive but none the less effective version of the Anglo-Norman Romanesque that was to succeed it. These churches and their surrounding buildings formed little oases of thought and devotion in the crude life of a barely united people. They might be served by colleges of secular canons, as was the case with nine of the pre-Conquest sees—Chichester, Exeter, Hereford, Lichfield, Lincoln, London, Sarum, Wells and York—or by communities of monks or nuns, communities who were just beginning to sort

DIXON-SCOTT

### WORCESTER CATHEDRAL

*From Saxon times Worcester has been the seat of a bishop.  St. Oswald rebuilt the original church in* A.D. 964.
*His work was destroyed by the Danes to be built again on a grander scale by Wulstan, the only Saxon bishop
to retain his seat after the Conquest.  Today the Cathedral makes a fine picture with the Severn in the foreground.*

themselves out among newly rising monastic
orders.  Chief among these orders was the Benedictines, whose growing prestige and wealth did
much to enhance the progress of the Romanesque
style, and had by the time of the Conquest clothed
Northern France in its "white robe of churches."

#### Norman Builders

But it is from the Conquest that the history of
the English cathedrals as we know them today
begins.  With the consolidation of Norman rule
began that remarkable outburst of building
vigour—*furor Normanorum* it has been called—
that has left its permanent mark upon so many
of our cathedral churches.

To the pre-Conquest sees were added at this
time the abbey churches of Canterbury, Durham,
Ely, Norwich, Rochester, Winchester and Worcester, each still with its establishment of Benedictine
monks, but containing, by an arrangement little
known outside England, the throne of a bishop.
They were bishops of a new type, these Norman
prelate-princes—active, ambitious men who com-
peted with one another in the grandeur of their
building schemes, the speed of their realization.

De St. Carileph at Durham, De Losinga at
Norwich, Walkelin at Winchester, and many
others, filled the little cities where they ruled
with swarms of untrained workmen, and scoured
the country for that rare phenomenon of those

days, the skilled craftsman.  Considering the
speed at which they arose, and the frequent
haphazardness of the methods employed, it is
indeed a wonder that some of these buildings
have endured at all.

But what splendid churches they were!
Norwich, Ely, Peterborough, Rochester, and,
in supreme measure, Durham, furnish unforgettable instances of the solid strength and dignity
of the Anglo-Norman manner at its best, though
now stripped of the external covering of thin,
white plaster that must have given them a radiance
that their present severity belies.

Similarly, within, one can only visualize from
the worn traces that survive here and there upon
their walls the former richness of their frescoed
decorations, forming a glowing background to
the glitter of myriad candles.  But deeply impressive as are the ranges of vast internal piers, their
appearance is often deceptive, for in many cases
they constitute no more than a casing of ashlar
masonry filled with loose rubble, occasionally
in itself insufficient to support the weight of the
squat central towers that crowned the crossings.
Thus it was at Norwich, where the collapse of
part of the tower, necessitated the building of
the beautiful fourteenth-century substitute surviving today, and the reconstruction of the quire
clerestory to form one of the most perfect eastern
terminations of any English church.

Impressive, too, are the cavernous triforium arcades of round-headed arches, the tiers of inter-woven arcading such as adorn the great tower at Ely, and the sculptured portals that may be seen at the same cathedral, at Rochester, and elsewhere. If there is sometimes an almost cliff-like severity in the external elevations, with their successive strata-bands of arches, arcading and windows, the whole style breathes a virility and grandeur which, I think, expresses itself as well in a very concise manner in a handful of English cathedrals as in any contemporary productions to be found on the Continent.

### Cruciform Churches

Planned and arranged on remarkably consistent lines, each of these churches took the form of a vast cross—though the theory that this was ever based symbolically upon the Cross of Christ has proved a fallacy. In the case of those that also served a monastic purpose, the quire that formed the eastern limb contained the stalls of the monks and the sanctuary of the high altar, ending eastward either in a trio of chapel-apses or a continuous semi-circular processional path with small chapels radiating from it. Beneath the quire was usually a vaulted crypt to house the sacred relics in the possession of the community. Quire and transept were separated from the nave by a stone *pulpitum* or screen. East of this screen was the domain of the community, who served the church in a ceaseless rotation of ritual and worship, while the nave west of it was reserved for the services of the lay congregation.

The subject of the conventual buildings attached to these churches is beyond the scope of this chapter. Nevertheless, two outstanding features demand brief mention, for throughout the Middle Ages they were often to persist in cathedral churches of non-monastic foundation. They were the cloister, or vaulted quadrangular walk which formed the centre of communal life and activity in every monastery, and was usually placed on the south side of the church between nave and transept, and the Chapter House, where the brethren met in conference and for the administration of justice. It is certainly cause for rejoicing that their appearance became almost a convention of later cathedral architecture, for the vaults and open arcades of

the cloisters, giving on to the green lawns of their garths, were to see the development of some of the loveliest stonework of English Gothic, while the Chapter House, taking as its prototype the decagonal thirteenth-century structure at Lincoln, with its great areas of glazing and intricate scheme of vaulting from a central pier, was to develop into a rich and individual national feature, and produce the superb examples at Wells, Salisbury, Southwell, York and elsewhere.

If the eleventh and twelfth centuries were *par excellence* the period of monastic building in this country, with the thirteenth came a change of heart. The population was growing and the lay congregation beginning to assert itself. The flow of subscriptions and bequests from the faithful now began to be diverted to other ends, and the new century witnessed what was perhaps

HUMPHREY AND VERA JOEL

### TRIPLE SPIRES AND WEST FRONT OF LICHFIELD

*St. Chad moved the Saxon bishopric of Mercia from Repton to Lichfield, but the first church was built by Bishop Hedda (A.D. 700). The oldest portions of the existing structure date from about 1200.*

the most spectacular wave of cathedral building in our history—one that was to produce in their original entirety the great fabrics of Salisbury, Lincoln and Wells, and leave its mark upon many another of our cathedrals.

Perhaps this tendency was due in part to the growing arrogance and unpopularity of the monastic houses. Thirteenth-century records contain many accounts of clashes between monks and townsmen, clashes which must have reached a climax in the pitched battle fought out at Norwich in 1271, lasting for several days, in which many were killed and the cathedral gutted down to its walls.

But the new period, like the old, owed its measure to its "building bishops." Grosseteste, who carried on the work begun by St. Hugh at Lincoln; Poore, who transferred the see of Sarum from the little hill-fortress to its present Salisbury site, and was afterwards to add the splendid Chapel of the Nine Altars to the east end of Durham; and Jocelyn, who at Wells

completed the great task begun by Reginald de Bohun as early as 1174—to these men, and there were others, belongs credit for fostering the enterprises of a school of masoncraft that was to produce the first achievements of a dawning national Gothic.

### William of Sens

We know that a French master mason, William of Sens, was employed by the Canterbury monks for the rebuilding of their quire, one of its earliest experiments; but we know, too, that after the fall from the scaffolding that incapacitated him from further work the task was taken over by one William the Englishman, while at Wells, at least, west country masons had already begun to formulate, in the new nave, a precocious and highly successful experiment in Gothic before its time.

We know that at Durham, by 1133, English masons had completed the task of roofing the entire cathedral with ribbed stone vaulting—

EDGAR WARD

### GLOUCESTER CATHEDRAL

*Founded in* A.D. 681 *as an abbey for monks and nuns, Gloucester later became a college for secular priests. These were expelled by Canute in 1022 for evil living and their place was taken by Benedictine monks. The Norman work dates from Abbot Serlo 1089. The beautiful Central Tower was erected in 1450.*

DIXON-SCOTT

## THE NOBLE BEAUTY OF WELLS

*This beautiful cathedral at the foot of the Mendips has been described as " the best example to be found in the whole world of a secular church with its subordinate buildings." According to tradition, the first church was founded by King Ine in A.D. 705. The present structure dates from the days of Bishop Reginald de Bohun.*

possibly the first achievement of its kind in Europe—and how largely it was from this constructional innovation that the pointed fashion emerged. It would, of course, be absurd to suggest that the first phase of English Gothic— " Early English," to use the time-honoured, if rather unsatisfactory, label—did not originate in the main from the experiment that had already filled the Ile de France with its cathedral constellation. It may even be admitted that such a cathedral as Salisbury represents little more than a minor provincial variation on that prodigious theme. Nevertheless, there is much in the development of this style, and in its ornament, that breathes an English air, and that, to me at least, makes these great churches of the thirteenth century a dearer possession than the mightier achievement of France.

Their planning marked a definite innovation on English precedent, involving a considerable enlargement of the eastern limb to provide more altar accommodation for the canons who now swarmed the cathedral precincts. Beyond the

high altar, a processional path generally gave access to an eastern extension, or retro-quire, often with its own eastern transept, sumptuously built to contain the relics and treasure brought above ground from the crypt.

### Lady Chapels

With the rising cult of Our Lady, a Lady Chapel of lower elevation came to be considered the most fitting eastern termination to these *congeries*, with the effect of largely abolishing the original apse-scheme and substituting the square ends always so characteristic of English Gothic. These innovations were not only applied to new buildings ; in varying degrees they were carried out, now and hereafter, on existing structures. Thus it was at Canterbury, Ely, Beverley, to name only three ; while as a compromise to the lay congregation, the nave might be lengthened westward by a few bays, and one of those majestically sculptured screen-fronts in which the thirteenth century delighted added as a frontispiece, as at Peterborough, Wells and Lincoln.

W. F. TAYLOR

## SALISBURY'S SPLENDID NAVE

*This cathedral was begun in 1220 by Bishop Poore and was consecrated thirty-eight years later in the presence of Henry III. It was ruthlessly restored in 1798 and later, and many fine features were destroyed. The long narrow and lofty nave is divided into ten bays by smooth grey piers and slender pillars of Purbeck marble.*

This last great church, crowning its steep little hill above the Witham, does, in fact, represent an almost complete epitome of the progress of the thirteenth-century style in this country. The severity of St. Hugh's own quire (1186-1200) shades into the solemn beauty of Grosseteste's nave and transept (1209-1235), with their tall clustered piers and ranges of lancet windows and arcading, just rescued from sternness by the sculptural relief of mouldings and foliated capitals. From here one must move eastward to realize the rich culmination of this art during the later years of the century. The so-called " Angel Choir " was built as a presbytery to contain the relics of the canonized builder-bishop, St. Hugh, and its consecration about 1280, attended by most of the crowned heads of Europe, was one of the most glittering ceremonies in the history of our cathedrals. It is a work exquisite in proportion and rich in sculptured detail, culminating in the carved angel orchestra from which it takes its name, filling the spandrels of a sumptuous triforium arcade which displays the stone cuspings and circles of the " geometrical " tracery on which the transition from Early English to the " Decorated " of the next century so largely centred.

W. F. TAYLOR

ANGEL CHOIR, LINCOLN

*Magnificently placed on a hill above the city, Lincoln Cathedral is a landmark. The exquisite Angel Choir was built in the thirteenth century and takes its name from the thirty figures of angels carved on the spandrels.*

Just as Lincoln forms an epitome of thirteenth-century development, so Exeter, in supreme measure, exemplifies the transient beauty of the style that succeeded it during the earlier part of the next century, to receive its quietus from the epidemic of the Black Death which was to paralyse church building for over a generation. The Cathedral of the West owes much of its peculiar radiance to a line of bishops with whom the work of enlargement and adornment was nearer to a passion than a duty. The earlier work of Bronscombe, Quivil and Bytton was brought to a conclusion under Stapledon and Grandison, from whom the quire received its furnishing and the whole church its rich covering of vaulting. It is hard to give any impression in words of the warmth and exuberance of the finished effect. " A luxurious, spendthrift art," Professor Prior characterized the almost pagan profusion of its close-clustered shafting and restless curvilinear tracery, its elaborate screenwork and soaring bishop's throne.

EDGAR WARD

### YORK MINSTER'S SPLENDOUR IN STONE

*York's great and glorious minster had its humble beginnings in a little wooden church where Paulinus, first Bishop of York, baptised Edwin, the Northumbrian king, in A.D. 627. The present structure was begun about 1227 while the massive central tower, the largest in England, was completed early in the fifteenth century.*

It was an art that found similar expression among the cathedrals in the perhaps slightly overloaded west front of York Minster, in the splendid free carving of the Southwell Chapter House and the Ely Lady Chapel, in the tower and slender spire of St. Mary's at Salisbury, and in great curvilinear windows at Carlisle and York, with their movement "as of a flickering of wings."

### Pilgrims' Shrines

This period marks the culmination of perhaps the most lavish phase of English cathedral building. The church was now at the summit of its power and activity. The cathedral shrines were flocked with pilgrims, each bearing his offering, however modest, to add to the sums expended on the developing fabrics. It was not only to the older shrines that the pilgrims journeyed; the cult of some latter-day saints had grown to prodigious proportions, and Chaucer, in *The Canterbury Tales*, which dates from about this time, has left a picture of the varied companies, drawn from all classes, that would wend their way, on horseback or on foot, over the green Kentish country, to sink one and all to their knees on first sight of the gilded " Angel Steeple " from the crest of Harbledown Hill.

A steady stream of bequests also went to the building of the chantry chapels that so enrich our cathedrals, each with its resident priest and endowment for the saying of masses " in perpetuity " for the soul of the faithful departed. Some of the finest craftsmanship was bestowed on these little chapels, and on the costly tombs of nobles, bishops and burgesses that crowded the available spaces. Masoncraft had by now reached its highest peak of skill and organization. It had travelled far from the haphazard, speculative days of Anglo-Norman construction, and represented a mature guild of artisans, working under masters in collaboration with a variety of dependent crafts such as those of the carpenters, glaziers and metalworkers, supplemented by local supplies of labourers, hewers and carriers.

Here it may be mentioned that the theory that the religious themselves were ever responsible in any large degree for the fabrics of their churches has been discarded. The bishops, priors and sacrists to whom so many famous works have been loosely attributed acted in the majority of cases as little more than " business organizers " of the projects, though they were often responsible for the provision of building materials—no light task when one remembers the appalling state of communications throughout the Middle

Ages. If the famous sacrist, Alan of Walsingham, can no longer be credited with the design of that unique and lovely fourteenth-century feature, the Ely Octagon, it is at least to be remembered that its great timbers, of a scantling prodigious for modern times, were transported under his direction over the soggy marshes that surrounded the cathedral by roads and bridges specially built for their carriage.

It was to the cult of pilgrimages that, in some degree at least, we owe the last and greatest revolution in English medieval building. After the murder of Edward II at Berkeley Castle in 1327, none of the great churches of the West had been willing to receive his body until it was brought to Gloucester, whose monks gave it a fitting burial and later set up a shrine to the newly-canonized martyr which began to attract pilgrims from all over England.

So greatly did the flow of offerings increase into the Gloucester coffers that it was decided, with the proceeds, to reconstruct the old Norman choir as a splendid mortuary chapel to the profitable saint. To this end Abbot Wygmore, a man of singular artistic perception, employed the " clever and rather eccentric " masons who had formed a school in the Severn Valley which had already devised the curious open-work vaulting in the Bristol aisles. Their work at Gloucester, begun less than halfway through the fourteenth century, brought about an almost overnight revolution in building methods, a revolution that was to be perpetuated through the remaining Middle Ages and beyond in the so-called " Perpendicular " style—the last, the most enduring and perhaps the greatest of the phases of our national Gothic.

### Fan-vaulted Roofs

Broadly speaking, it was a style of open, airy spaces, lighted by sheets of radiant " silver-stain " glazing ; a style of light rectilinear stone panelling and lofty slender shafting, that was to evolve as a covering the most individual of our forms of stone roofing, the fan vault. It was a style that, for its economy and effectiveness in those depleted days, found almost instant acceptation ; already, by 1379, the Canterbury monks had adopted it for their new nave, while under William of Wykeham the immense Norman nave of Winchester was recased with brilliant effect in the same manner.

It was a style that went hand in hand with the remarkable reflorescence of woodwork in stalls, roofs and screens, during the fifteenth century, when English carpenters first adopted to their uses the slender pinnacled conceptions of mason-craft, and was to evolve in its time the lofty aisleless fabrics of a great preaching age, best exemplified in the chapels of St. George at

DIXON-SCOTT

### WINCHESTER FROM THE CLOSE

*Winchester, the ancient capital of Saxon kings, became a bishopric about* A.D. 670, *and St. Swithun of the rain legend was bishop* A.D. 852-862. *Alfred, Canute and others were crowned in the old minster. The present cathedral was begun by Bishop Walkelin in* 1079, *additions and alterations being made later.*

Windsor, King's College at Cambridge and Henry VII at Westminster. And lastly it was a style to which we owe some of the stateliest of our cathedral towers—splendid structures such as arose over the central spaces at York, Gloucester, Worcester, and, perhaps most strikingly, Canterbury, to fill England with the music of bells and form the focal points of what are still some of our loveliest landscapes.

The events of the Reformation belong as much to political as to cathedral history, but it is perhaps not always realized what a spoil awaited the fingers of Henry's commissioners as they

W. F. TAYLOR

ST. DAVID'S FROM THE NORTH-WEST
*St. David's, in Pembrokeshire, is the smallest of our cathedral cities. Traditionally the see was founded by the patron saint of Wales about A.D. 550. Peter de Leia, the third Norman bishop, began the present edifice in 1180.*

went about their task of suppression and eradication. The cathedrals were by now treasure houses of craftsmanship of every kind, and the riches of their shrines, despite a slowly waning popularity, were enough to dazzle the eyes of the stranger privileged to inspect them in their completeness, as the eyes of Erasmus were dazzled by the jewelled hoard of St. Thomas.

These national shrines were accorded the same ruthless treatment as the conventual riches. In 1538 Henry issued his posthumous writ against Thomas Becket for "treason, contumacy and rebellion," which was in due course read at Canterbury before the saint's tomb. The suit was tried at Westminster, and had its sequel in the removal of twenty-six cartloads of gold and jewels into the royal treasury. But at least this bleak ecclesiastical reorganization made its public

gifts, for at this time the great Benedictine churches of Peterborough, Gloucester and Chester were saved from otherwise inevitable decay or destruction by their conversion into cathedrals, as was also the case with the Augustinian churches of Bristol and Oxford.

The seventeenth century marked the leanest and saddest years in our cathedral history. Those of the greater churches that had been afforded a status in the post-Reformation scheme had remained largely intact in fabric and fitting, and it was left to the factional zeal of extreme parties at this later time to work a thoroughgoing vengeance on all vestiges of the old ecclesiastical dignity. Much of the glories of English stained glass, for instance, that had survived the Reformation, was destroyed by Puritan fanaticism at the time of the Civil War. Certain fabrics were singled out for particular violence, as Peterborough, where every interior fitment was smashed to pieces by Cromwell's troops and even the walls shaken to their foundations, and Rochester, where Puritan soldiers " so far profaned this place as to make use of it in the quality of a tippling place, as well as dug several saw-pits, and the chief joyners made frames for houses in it." The embattled close at Lichfield was subjected to a fierce siege, and the cathedral shelled by artillery ; at Exeter the cathedral was divided into two preaching-houses, the " East and West Peters," while at St. Albans a public passageway was driven through the exquisite little Saint's Chapel of the immense and mouldering abbey church, since restored as a cathedral. Many another case of violation could be instanced. It is little wonder that, after the long laxity and neglect of the eighteenth century, the cathedrals presented a shameful and woebegone spectacle that roused a fury in the younger Pugin. " I have been at the Cathedral all the morning," he wrote from Ely in 1834. " How I am delighted ! How I am pained ! Here is a church, magnificent in every respect, falling into decay through gross neglect. Would you believe it possible? There is no person appointed to attend to the repairs of the building, and the only person who has been employed during the last sixty years is a bricklayer. Not even common precautions are taken to keep the building dry," While at another cathedral the bishop, who had refused to subscribe to the re-erection of his own throne, had lost £7,000 on the Derby !

It is easy to be over critical of the hand of the nineteenth century on the cathedrals. It is true that Wyatt, the first and therefore the least informed of the restorers, worked much havoc on the ancient fabrics, such as the demolition of the splendid Beauchamp and Hungerford chantries at Salisbury, though he was fortunately thwarted in his attempt to demolish the unique late-Norman " Galilee " at Durham to make a carriage-drive to the west front.

Nevertheless, though they sometimes over-stepped their powers, it must be conceded that the Victorian church architects accomplished a magnificent structural feat in saving many crumbling edifices from otherwise inevitable decay. If such buildings as Worcester and Chester now represent little more than mid-Victorian reconstructions, it is doubtful whether any less drastic treatment would have been efficacious, for long years of neglect of their soft friable stonework had probably left them past repair. But in their work on the interiors the Victorians were guilty of some appalling lapses. It would be hard to envisage a more hideous object than Scott's screen at Hereford—the last touch of humiliation to that humiliated fabric—or a more unhappy scheme of decoration than that which left Salisbury in its present state of " encaustic floors, varnished marble and a quire bepainted and bedizened."

Only three new cathedrals have been built on English soil since the Reformation, though a number of churches intended for collegiate or parochial uses have, with the growth of the population and the multiplication of its centres, been of recent years raised to cathedral status. St. Paul's, Wren's great monument to Renaissance craftsmanship, humanism and churchmanship, stands in a class by itself. Truro Cathedral, completed almost a couple of centuries later to Pearson's designs, incorporate some of the structure of the old Perpendicular parish church on the south-east and so add a third aisle to the choir. Like the half-completed Liverpool Cathedral, it marks successful if somewhat over-literal essays in revived Gothic, though almost as I write the foundation stone has been laid of a new cathedral at Guildford which will unite modern structural developments with traditional English forms.

It is clear, therefore, that the cathedral achievement in this country is almost overwhelmingly a medieval one. It was an achievement so fertile, so various and withal so characteristically English that it is almost impossible to condense its

W. F. TAYLOR

### TRURO CATHEDRAL

*This beautiful modern cathedral begun in 1880, was the first one to be built in England after the Reformation. Cruciform in structure and built in the Early English style, it has a handsome central tower.*

appreciation into a brief preroration. Serenity, I think, is the most befitting word for the sum effect of these great churches, despite the grandeur of a Durham, the glory of a Lincoln. Their very inconsistency—that patchwork quality that is the despair of the foreign purist—lend them an intimate and English quality that is enhanced by the almost invariable beauty of their settings among smooth lawns and quiet old houses. Their piecemeal evolution seems, in fact, almost one with that of the English people, striving through splendour, humiliation and danger towards that peaceful maturity that has always been their better goal. To the aura of dignity and veneration that surrounds them has been added a gentleness that seems to emanate from the affection of Englishmen through many centuries. It is not the least part of our national duty to preserve them, reverently and solicitously, in the twilight beauty of their last phase.

W. A. CALL

### AUSTERE NORMAN WORK AT ROCHESTER

*This photograph of Rochester Cathedral shows the Norman nave arcade, the triforium (middle storey) and the clerestory (upper storey). Observe the typical scalloped capitals on top of the pillars and the chevron (zig-zag) ornament round the arches. The cathedral was built on the site of a Saxon church.*

# ARCHITECTURE THROUGH THE AGES

## *by* EDMUND VALE

IT was Linnæus who first opened the eyes of the world to the beauty of flowers. He did so by founding a system whereby every different flower could have a name of its own. His work was greater than that of an explorer for by its means the Old World was able to discover a new world in its very midst. What Linnæus did for botany, Rickman (1776-1841) did for architecture. He recognized certain differences of style in buildings of the Middle Ages, named them, and thus conferred individuality upon them. A thing without a label cannot exist except vaguely in the consciousness, and people had been quite blind to the beauty of old English buildings until Rickman produced his system of named styles ranged in a chronological order. After the eyes of archæologist and laymen alike had been opened in this manner the scientific architect began to expound on the logic of the styles—why and how they came into being, a process still far from exhausted.

The principal styles can be placed under four main architectural and five historical headings.

| Historical | Architectural | Centuries |
|---|---|---|
| Pre-Conquest and Pre-Reformation | Romanesque | Saxon 7th to 11th |
| Post-Conquest and Pre-Reformation | | Norman 11th to 13th |
| | Gothic | |
| | | Early English 13th |
| | | Decorated 14th |
| | | Perpendicular 15th |
| Post-Reformation | Renaissance | |
| | | Tudor 16th |
| | | Jacobean 17th |
| | | Hanoverian 18th |
| | Mixed | |
| Pre-War | | Victorian 19th |
| Post-War | | Ferro-concrete 20th |

These are the characteristics of the styles. Under the Romanesque division come imitations of the building methods of the ancient Romans, of which the principal sign is that of the round-headed arch.

The Saxon style is only imperfectly understood, as most of the examples which remain are late in character, the Normans having ruthlessly restored all the greater churches. The double-belfry window divided by a stout baluster placed halfway in the thickness of the wall is a typical feature of the Saxon tower. The Normans built a similar window but placed the central support forward so as to be flush with the outside wall. Another Saxon characteristic is the building of quoins (corner-stones) and wall-pilasters in a

W. A. CALL

### ST. BENET'S TOWER, CAMBRIDGE

*A Saxon tower in three stages. Notice the lathe-turned balusters in belfry windows. They are set midway in the wall. Long-and-short work is plainly seen on the near corner of the tower.*

DIXON-SCOTT

### CASTLE ACRE PRIORY, WEST FRONT

*A beautiful Norman façade. The doorway is a typical one in three orders. The interlaced arcade surrounding it would be picked out in paint and gilt. Two small windows on right are transitional Norman-Early English. The large window is a Perpendicular addition similar to that at Southwell, Rochester and Durham.*

manner known as long-and-short. Stones are placed so as to appear alternately vertical and horizontal—the method was evidently regarded as highly decorative and copied from Carolignian sources.

The openings of doors and windows are round-headed with a few exceptions where a pointed head has been produced by flat slabs of stone leaned together as in the central structure of a house of cards.

### Norman Building

The Normans did not use this last method, otherwise they also imitated the architecture of ancient Rome by building round-headed doorways and windows. Their arcades are supported on massive round columns, yet their buttresses are mere thin pilasters, more for ornament than anything else, for as supports to the thick heavy walls which the Normans delighted in they were ridiculously inadequate.

The Early English style has a narrow-pointed arch likened to the point of a lancet, a simile belonging to the days of the barber-surgeon—

torpedo-headed would be a more up-to-date description. The dog-tooth ornament belongs to this style exclusively.

The Decorated style has a wider arch into which an equilateral triangle would fit. The ball-flower is its exclusive ornament.

The Perpendicular style has a wider arch still. Door-heads of four-centred arches have the shape of Cupid's bow. It is called Perpendicular from the vertical bars (super-mullions) in the heads of the windows.

Under the label Renaissance comes another hark-back to the classical styles. So long as the church remained powerful classical writers had been regarded as pagan authors. But the power of the church was relaxed in the sixteenth century and classical authors, classical allusions, and classical architecture all came into vogue irresistibly. This "movement" was called the New-learning or Renaissance. The Tudor (which covers the Elizabethan period) style was a mixture of Gothic and Classical forms. The Jacobean was less Gothic and more Classical. The Hanoverian was as Classical as an Englishman was able to make it—even the statues of contemporary men of eminence were dressed in Roman togas. The Victorians had no architectural scruples of any sort. Behold the three principal railway stations of London, all adjoining—Classical Euston, Early English St. Pancras, Hanoverian King's Cross !

The two principal types of building in the Middle Ages were the hall and the tower. The hall was a barn-like building with or without side aisles. It served as a house, a church, a court of justice. In the hall of the great man the household slept as well as ate. Only the great man had a small room apart. A feature of the hall was that one end of it was regarded as being more important than the other and called the upper end. Here the owner of the house took his meals while the domestics and dependants fed in the lower part. Halls (though only for eating purposes) still survive at the universities and inns of court. The plan of a church with its upper end (chancel) for the Lord's Table and the clergy, and the lower end for the laity is a survival of the hall idea.

The hall idea was that of an open house but the tower idea had developed as a dwelling of defence. This was probably true even in the case of the church towers. The first castles were introduced in the eleventh century by the Normans. At first they consisted of a simple tower made of wood built on a special emplacement called a *motte*. This was a flat-topped mound shaped like a pudding-basin. As soon as the invaders, and also the mounds of earth they had raised, became consolidated, they built a tower of stone in place of a wooden one.

### Defensive Dwellings

The advantage of the tower idea in a defensive dwelling is quickly seen. By having several small floors raised one above another instead of one large one on the ground level you reduce the wall space that can be attacked. At the same time you place your wall tops above the reach of scaling ladders, you gain a splendid look-out and also, as a fighting-top, that gives you an unquestionable advantage over all besiegers.

Thus the first castles which, as I have said, were a Norman invention, consisted of a tower raised on a mound and a double enclosure in the form of a wide-waisted figure 8, known as the outer and inner bailey (or ward). This was fenced in with a strong palisade.

The next stage (thirteenth century) was to

W. F. TAYLOR

DECORATED WINDOWS, LEOMINSTER CHURCH

*A Saxon monastery was founded here in the seventh century and later gave place to a Benedictine Priory. The church is said to illustrate every style of architecture from Norman to Perpendicular. These early fourteenth-century windows of geometric tracery are encrusted with the typical ball-flower ornament.*

W. F. TAYLOR

THE CHOIR, WORCESTER CATHEDRAL

*The style here is Early English (thirteenth century).   Being before the date of the invention of tracery the
east window is made of five separate lancets.   Note the clustered shafts of Purbeck marble surrounding
the columns, and the stone groined roof of Early English type.   On the left, above the pulpit, a window of
the clerestory is just visible over the openings of the triforium gallery which stands above the nave arcade.*

replace the palisade with stone curtain walls set with half-round flanking towers, while the entrance was defended with a gate-house. The original tower was now regarded merely as a last resort should the defences of the two wards be pierced, consequently it was called a keep.

### Edwardian Castles

The next step in evolution (late thirteenth century) was the Edwardian castle. In this the keep disappears. The flanking towers are made into living-towers with proper floors and sanitary arrangements so that each one can be occupied by a complete household. Another important difference is that the two wards instead of being outside each other (as in the wide-waisted figure 8) are placed one inside the other. A castle built on such a plan is called concentric.

The tower will thus be seen to have evolved from a simple to a complex form, but it has not gone on independently of the hall. True, one of the rooms of the keep was called a hall, but the Great Hall, a church-like building in one of the wards, was always the centre of the castle's social life.

The merger of the tower and hall idea came in the fourteenth century. The country was now more settled so that the extra complication of concentric wards was thought unnecessary. One quadrangle surrounded by the moat was deemed sufficient defence. A tower was placed at each corner of this quadrangle. But these towers were only secondary and not primary abodes. Instead of a number of different buildings under separate roofs all were now assembled under one roof between the main curtain-wall and an immense hall. The hall was included in this arrangement, and the space left vacant was called no longer a ward or bailey but a *court-yard*.

So if you go to see an old castle these stages of evolution should all be borne in mind. The types are roughly as follows :

W. F. TAYLOR

**CHRIST CHURCH CATHEDRAL, OXFORD**
*There was a Saxon monastery at Oxford, and a church was built there by Ethelred the Unready in 1004. The photograph shows the fan-vaulted roof of the Perpendicular period built on top of a Norman arcade.*

Motte-and-bailey — Earthen mound with wooden tower and figure 8 palisaded wards, eleventh century.

Tower converted to stone—twelfth century.

Wooden palisades converted to stone walls with towers at salient points—thirteenth century.

Edwardian castle — keep abolished. Large household towers—defences sometimes concentric—late thirteenth and early fourteenth century.

The courtyard castle—late fourteenth and fifteenth centuries.

In going over an old castle you always begin at the gate-house (if such a thing is still standing).

This is often the most interesting feature of the castle. The architect has generally done his best to make the entrance look as impressive and as formidable as possible. Often special architectural features are displayed here—the statue of a king under a canopy, a coat of arms, etc. The mechanical arrangements are of great interest too—the means of raising the drawbridge and dropping the portcullis.

No complete medieval drawbridge is to be found in Great Britain, and there are only five relics of portcullises. But the clues to the whereabouts and workings of both are generally in evidence—a circular chase cut in the stone where the trunnion of the drawbridge pivoted, grooves indicating where the portcullis slid down, a slot in

W. F. TAYLOR

**RELICS OF ROMAN AND NORMAN**

*In this photograph of Portchester Castle the barbican and the gate-house are seen in the foreground beyond the moat. In the background rises the Norman keep which is dovetailed into the walls of the Roman fort.*

the portcullis chamber above the gate where the grating was wedged in the upper position. Some gate-houses have three portcullis ways. In addition, the passage under the gate-house generally shows the hinge-pins of the gates and rebates for rearing a timber barricade in the last resort, while, overhead, appear the gaps called *meurtrieres* or *murder-holes* through which romance tells us that boiling oil, pitch, or lead was dashed down on the heads of the enemy—more likely boiling water or dry quick-lime would be used.

It was under the gate-house that the dungeon (meaning the castle prison) was situated. The upper part of the building was often the residence of the constable of the castle and fitted with state apartments including an oratory. Then there is the moat to examine, and sometimes there is a specially-continued passage or screen on the outer side of the gate-house called a barbican, making an extra hazard for the besiegers to storm before they could attack the gate-house. Sometimes the barbican is found on the far side of the moat. Occasionally the outer ward has two gate-houses, and often there is one between the outer and the inner wards. At Warkworth Castle the keep itself is defended by a pit-fall. It appears to have consisted of a false floor which gave way on the withdrawal of a bolt and let the intruders down into a stone pit fifteen feet deep.

The foundations of the great hall (seldom in a complete state) should be looked for, and the chapel. This last and the gate-house are

W. F. TAYLOR

**THE NAVE, WELLS CATHEDRAL**

*Wells Cathedral provides a very good illustration of Early English work, the stiff-stalked foliage on the capitals of the piers being typical of this period.*

often the only parts of a castle which have had architectural flourishes bestowed on them.

Castles vary far more in plan and construction than monasteries. You can always find your way about a ruined monastery quite easily whereas a castle needs to be " discovered." The reason for this is that a monastery always conformed to the plan of the particular order which built it, but the castle was designed to meet local conditions.

### Where Monks Worked

The centre of the monastery was the cloister— an open quadrangle with a lean-to passage built all round it lighted with large windows to admit light to the monks at work on their tasks of copying and illuminating manuscripts. When going over an old monastery you should seek out the site of the cloister first.

usually on the north side so that the cloister could be lit and warmed with the maximum amount of sunlight. If the ground site did not admit of this it had to be placed on the south side—but the other case is far more common.

The North Walk, then, is placed against the nave wall of the church and a doorway will be found in the north-east angle of the cloister which takes you into the eastern arm (transept) of the church. Beside this doorway is the sacristy, a rather more important room than the modern vestry, as besides containing robes and vestments it often held the treasures and precious vessels of the abbey. If we do not enter the church for the moment but go to the next door in the eastern walk we shall probably find it highly ornamented. It leads into the Chapter House. This is the administrative centre of the monastery. Here, every day, the

W. F. TAYLOR

### PRISON OF MARY QUEEN OF SCOTS

*Bolton Castle, a grim-looking structure in Wensleydale, Yorkshire, was a stronghold of the Scrope family and is typical of the courtyard type of castle built in the fourteenth century. The unhappy Scottish queen was imprisoned there for six months and during the Civil War the castle was held by the followers of Charles.*

The most regular plan of all was that of the Cistercian monastery, and it was the one in which space was most economized, as the community was virtually a double one, consisting of regular monks and lay brothers who lived in separate quarters and worshipped in separate parts of the conventual church.

Let us go over a ruined Cistercian house together. Here is the cloister with its four walks giving access to four distinct ranges of buildings. The church (which was the most important feature of every monastery) was

abbot presided over the assembled community to direct matters of procedure and discipline.

The next door will open on a staircase (the day stairs) leading up to the monks' dormitory. This upper room reaches the whole length of the eastern range and usually projects beyond, terminating in the rere-dorter (sanitary convenience). The undercroft below the dormitory may be occupied by the monks' parlour and the warming room, though these are sometimes in the southern range. At the corner where the eastern walk turns to become the southern walk

W. F. TAYLOR

**WHERE NORMAN BARONS FEASTED**
*Winchester Great Hall is part of the castle begun by William the Conqueror and completed by Henry III. It is a typical hall of the thirteenth century. At the western end are the remains of the royal dais and above this is the reputed Round Table of King Arthur.*

their own dormitory, warming-room, and refectory. But the remains of this range are always very scanty. It can only be seen in anything like its fullness at Fountains Abbey, in Yorkshire.

The public, unless they were guests of the monastery, were not admitted to the abbey church. The lay brothers worshipped in the western part of the nave below a screen called the *pulpitum.* Eastward of that was the choir of the regular monks.

Benedictine and Cluniac houses and those of the Augustinian fathers (who were not monks but priests living in a community under a rule of conduct) are all made on a very similar plan. The houses of the Carthusians (Charterhouses) are the great exception. These monks lived a solitary and not a communal life ; but there is only one ruin in England which is anything like intact, namely the monastery of Mount Grace, near Northallerton.

### Chaste Restraint

An appreciation of the architectural styles is more necessary for the enjoyment of a monastic ruin than a castle, for all monastic communities vied with each other in beautifying their houses. The early Cistercians were as severely plain as the early Puritans but they soon found means for evading the austere precepts of their founder in matters of architecture. Nevertheless there is a chaste restraint about the Cistercian buildings which, together with the wild situation in which they are always found, give them a distinction above all other monastic houses.

The parish church though, to all appearances, a simple building is the most complex of ancient monuments which we possess. There is endless variety in its planning, in its architecture and decoration and in the sentimental associations which permeate it.

Before entering the building the *steeple* should be noted. Is it a plain tower or a tower carrying a spire? Note its position, western or central (the Saxons favoured the former, the Normans the latter).

Walk round the church before entering and notice the stone tracery in all the windows which not only gives clues as to date but is a study in itself in mute poetry. Note the line of the eaves where gargoyles and interesting carvings are often to be seen.

there is a passage which goes right through the eastern range, under the dormitory. This is called the *slype.* It leads to the monks' cemetery and also to the infirmary buildings.

The principal building in the southern range is the hall. Its use has already become restricted to a dining-room. It is called the *refectory* or *frater.* Entrance is at the lower end adjacent to the cloister. At the far end there has been a raised dais for the " high table " where sat the abbot and his guests. If the walls are still standing there will be seen a small pulpit reached by steps in the thickness of the wall from which one of the brethren read aloud during meal-times. Opposite the refectory door there is often the remains of the *lavatory* where the brethren washed their hands before meals. The kitchen is adjacent.

The western range was given up to the quarters of the lay brothers who did most of the manual labour on the land (the Cistercians being an agricultural community). The lay brothers had

The south porch is usually the principal entrance. The holy-water stoup sometimes remains here. This doorway is generally an architectural feature. Having entered, it is a good rule to make sure of seeing the font; it is often the oldest thing in the church. If the nave of the church has two aisles the north arcade will frequently be found to be older than the south, as when the church was first enlarged it interfered with the graveyard less to build on this side.

The chancel arch is a principal feature and often goes back to Norman times. On the western side of it stood the rood-loft. If this has been destroyed the stair and door leading up to it may generally be either seen or traced. Other architectural features are sedilia (stone seats for the priests), piscinæ (where the washings of the sacred vessels were poured away), and the aumbry (the cupboard where the communion vessels were kept). All these are to be found in most old chancels. A piscina in the nave marks the site of a chapel. In each part of the church you should raise your eyes to the roof to note its structure and whether it is enriched with carvings.

The cathedral is something more than an extra large church containing the seat of a bishop. It is a collegiate church, served, that is, by a chapter of canons under the rule of a dean. It has accordingly the extra appointments of stalls for them to sit in, a Chapter House to meet in and a cloister through which they may walk dry-shod to their living quarters. Most of our great cathedrals are monastic churches which at the Reformation were converted to the simpler uses of Dean and Chapter. These churches were originally made of a great size to accommodate the quantities of pilgrims who came to worship at the shrines of special saints. To this also we owe two peculiar features seldom seen in the parish church—an ambulatory or walk on either side the choir and behind the high altar, and a Lady Chapel. The latter is almost invariably a thirteenth-century addition built in the Early English style.

PHOTOCHROM

MASONRY OF FORGOTTEN MONKS

*Fountains Abbey, even in its ruined state is an impressive building. The photograph shows the vaulted undercroft of the dormitory of the lay brothers, with arches springing from a central row of eighteen pillars. The abbey contains the most complete remains of the lay brothers' quarters to be seen in Great Britain.*

EDGAR WARD

### AN ANCIENT STREET IN YORK

*This delightful city has many fascinating reminders of its long and varied past. There is a remarkable suggestion of the Middle Ages in the Shambles, a narrow winding street flanked with old houses and shops and overhanging upper storeys from which one may shake hands with a neighbour across the street. Formerly known as High Mangergate it takes its present name from the fact that in olden days cattle were slaughtered there.*

# SOME MEDIEVAL TOWNS

## *by* HAROLD SHELTON

TO the Romans belongs the distinction of introducing the walled town to Britain. It was they who encircled cities such as Canterbury, Rochester and York many years before the first castle was built. The medieval walled town is in the same tradition, for in many cases the medieval walls were constructed in the form of, and from the fragments of, the Roman defences.

Only Colchester, Chester, York and Southampton retain their walled girdle in any degree of perfection. But there are very many others where parts of the wall, or perhaps a gate-house remains, and in which we can trace the narrow, crooked streets of the medieval, or like as at Wareham, the straight intersecting thoroughfares of the Roman town. It is, in fact, surprising how often the ancient town survives as the core of the modern city, sometimes being characteristically raised above its surroundings, and generally lying within a circumference of between one and two miles. At Bristol the course of the old wall is marked by a lane which was originally the alley-way between the wall and the houses. It encloses a space less than nineteen acres in extent, but the circuit of the walls of York is nearly three miles. Most of the existing walls are derived from the Norman builders, though they were reconstructed as occasion arose down to the fourteenth and fifteenth centuries. Walled towns like Conway and Caernarvon, and others in Wales and the Welsh Marches owe their mural defences to Edward I.

We can trace in nearly every case the reasons which led to the growth of a town. A frequent cause was the existence of a ford or bridge where an important road crossed a wide river. Again, many towns arose round the castles and the abbeys when these began to offer an assured market, bringing trade and employment with them. A good natural harbour was reason enough for the rise of a port. The place where two roads intersected naturally drew an increasing population as men travelled more and trade became greater. In fact, a moment's reflection will show that all the towns which we shall describe

sprang from economic or military causes except those which were founded again and again on the site of previous centres of population.

Canterbury is perhaps the most interesting of all the cities of England. In turn an early British settlement, Roman walled city, the capital of the Saxon kingdom of Kent, it became the See of St. Augustine whom Ethelbert, King of Kent, invited to the English shore. St. Augustine's Abbey, where the saint was buried, was founded in A.D. 613. Thereafter the history of the cathedral became the history of the town. Burnt by the Danes it was rebuilt by King Canute. It was burnt again in a great fire which destroyed

W. F. TAYLOR

## BRISTOL'S BEAUTIFUL ABBEY GATE

*This structure which now serves as an entrance to the Cathedral Close was the gateway of the abbey which was founded in 1142 and which flourished through medieval times. After the Reformation the abbey church became the cathedral of Bristol.*

PHOTOCHROM

**CHEPSTOW'S CRUMBLING RUINS**
*On the high ground by the banks of the Wye, William Fitzosbern raised a fortress in Norman days which was known as the Castle of Striguil. Except for the keep, the structure dates from the fourteenth century.*

half the town, but a new cathedral was consecrated by the Normans in 1130, destined to become the perfect example of Gothic architecture in England, and dominating the city from whatever angle it is approached. The martyrdom of St. Thomas made Canterbury the mecca of countless pilgrims who brought prosperity and trade to the medieval city, increased by the migration of the Flemish weavers whose quaint houses overhang the Stour. The fourteenth-century walls are about half intact, and contain within them not only the cathedral and the abbey ruins, but the great Dane John also, the mound which may well be a prehistoric fortress, the church of St. Martin which is certainly of Saxon foundation, and was probably the church from which St. Augustine first preached, and the ruins of the Norman castle. One gate only survives—the West Gate—though this barely escaped demolition at the end of the last century when rumour has it that the City Fathers decided by a single vote against removing it as an obstruction to traffic.

York has much in common with Canterbury. Like Canterbury Cathedral, York Minster has grown from a Saxon church where King Edwin was baptized in the seventh century. Like Canterbury Cathedral, too, the Minster dominates the town, with its great central tower which is more massive than any other in England. The Roman walls and the multangular tower stand cheek by jowl with the later walls, and four of the main gateways are standing, so making York unique among English cities. But it is the ancient gabled houses of the Shambles, where the upper storeys almost meet each other across the narrow lane which lend the city its chief enchantment.

York was the Roman outpost city of the north-east, Chester of the north-west, and, like York, Chester has the air of a walled town within the modern city. If we enter by the East Gate we are confronted by dozens of half-timbered houses with overhanging fronts. A medley of ancient dwellings reaches its greatest distinction in The Rows—a double row of shops, one above the other, the upper ones being fronted by a covered footway to which access is gained by steps leading up at frequent intervals from the ground

HUMPHREY AND VERA JOEL

**THE LANDGATE, RYE**
*Rye, now two miles from the sea, became one of the Cinque Ports in the twelfth century. Despite its mural defences dating from Edward III, the town was burnt by French invaders in 1377 and in 1448.*

VALENTINE

### CITY WALLS OF SOUTHAMPTON

*Southampton is said to have been surrounded by a defensive wall in Saxon times. The Normans shortly after the Conquest enclosed it with ramparts of masonry thirty to forty feet high, and making a circuit of one and a quarter miles. Three gates remain. On two sides the River Test was utilized as a moat.*

PHOTOCHROM

### POTTERGATE, LINCOLN

*Lincoln had its beginnings in Roman times, if not earlier, and in the thirteenth century was the fourth seaport in Britain. This fourteenth-century gateway of the medieval defences is said to take its name from the supposed existence of a Roman pottery near the spot. In the background are the imposing towers of the cathedral.*

FELTON

## A PICTURESQUE STREET IN HISTORIC CHESTER

*In Eastgate Street, Chester's principal thoroughfare, are some of the famous Rows. These galleries or arcades along the first floor level are a unique feature of the city. They are possibly built over the ruins of Roman Chester, and had the advantage of being above the ill-kept streets. Shops were later opened on the ground level, thus giving the double tiers. In the basement of No. 28 is a finely preserved medieval crypt.*

level. The seventeenth-century "God's Providence House" and the "Bear and Billet" are two of many black and white houses which are so characteristic of the Marcher country. Side by side with the red brick of many of the other houses, toned to a depth of mellowness almost unbelievable, they stand out in startling but wonderfully effective contrast. Though the exterior of the cathedral is not so impressive as those of Canterbury and York, the early English architecture of the choir and the carved woodwork of the choir screen contain beauty enough to make a journey to Chester well worth while if only on that account.

As at York the best views of the town are obtained from the parapet walk along the wall. The Phoenix Tower, which we reach at the northern corner, is a reminder of the troublous times of the seventeenth century ; for it was here that Charles I watched the dwindling of his hopes as his troops were defeated at Rowton Moor. On the opposite side of the circuit in the south-east corner we shall find the wishing steps where, in order to have our wish fulfilled, we must run up and down seven times with one breath. It is from the parapet, too, that the red sandstone of the cathedral walls gives such a warm colouring to the whole city.

### Border Cockpit

Berwick-on-Tweed is another northern town which has lived through many wars and rumours of wars. It was the cockpit of all the fighting between England and Scotland, and was in the hands of first one and then the other country, a problem which was solved in 1551 by declaring it a neutral town after it had changed hands, it is said, no less than thirteen times. Here, too, no inconsiderable fragments of the walls survive, more than usually interesting because the fortifications, dating only from the sixteenth century, show the modifications in design which were thought necessary to combat the invention of artillery. Perhaps it is by its three noble bridges that Berwick impresses itself most upon the imagination, where the medieval stands side by side with the modern. The most recent is a three-span bridge opened in 1928, designed to take the place of the seventeenth-century stone bridge of fifteen arches, whilst the

third is the high railway viaduct designed by Stephenson in the middle of the last century.

It has been said by one shrewd observer that the more turbulent the history of a town, the quieter the dignity which it presents to the modern world. Certainly Chichester bears out that statement, for this is a city which has been British settlement, Roman town, Saxon capital and cathedral city. It was destroyed in turn by the Romans, the Saxons and the Norsemen, yet, when once the Saxon bishopric had been transferred from Selsey in the eleventh century, it led a life of peace and quietness. Apart from the cathedral there is the medieval hospital of St. Mary and the sixteenth-century market cross to remind us of past times—the only cross remaining in Sussex apart from the

W. A. CALL

### MEDIEVAL GATE AT MONMOUTH
*On the bridge spanning the River Monnow stands this thirteenth-century gateway, the only instance in England of a defensive gateway situated on a bridge. Formerly known as Welsh Gate it was one of the five gates in the town walls of Monmouth.*

FELTON

## GATEWAY OF A CORNISH TOWN

*Launceston has a long historic past, and became a royal borough in the days of William the Conqueror who built a castle there. In the Middle Ages it was a walled city, and some fragments of the walls are still standing. The photograph shows the South Gate of the city wall, a solidly built fourteenth-century structure. Above the town stands the ruined Norman castle where the Quaker, George Fox, was imprisoned in 1655.*

stump at Alfriston. A legend is remembered in Chichester that if the church steeple were to fall, there would be no king in England—a legend which was given the stamp of truth when the steeple fell in 1861 when there was no king, but a queen on the throne of England.

Although Chichester has exchanged turbulence for peace its near neighbour, Southampton, belies the statement. As the most strategic point along the Channel coast, it has through history been a place which invading forces have tried to capture, but in the modern era it has increased rather than diminished in activity, and is today a bustling centre of trade. Its medieval character is almost lost except in the walls which are almost as complete as those of York and Chester, and at least as impressive as either. Its three gates, the North, the West and the Spur are intact. Near the West Gate the *Mayflower* memorial was raised to the memory of the Pilgrim Fathers who sailed from the port in 1620, and the High Street, which runs to the Bar Gate, surmounted by the Guildhall, still retains the aspect of a very ancient thoroughfare.

### Border Castles

Chepstow is another walled town which was an important medieval port. In the struggles with Wales it played almost as great a part as Berwick in the struggles with Scotland. Indeed the whole of the Marcher country is rich in medieval fortified towns. Monmouth is unique in that its ancient bridge of stone which spans the Monnow is surmounted by a stone gateway which was the main entrance to the town, and withstood for some time the siege of Simon de Montfort in the reign of Henry III, and another siege in the Civil Wars when Cromwell in person marched to subdue it.

Ludlow, too, was a border town which was often attacked, but protected as it was by its two rivers on three sides its position was well nigh impregnable. On the north, by the church, the wall rises nearly twenty feet above the ground. The Edwardian Broad Gate, the Elizabethan Feathers Inn, the timbered houses which rival those of Chester, and the dignified Georgian dwelling-places combine to make it in appearance the perfect ancient town. Aptly was the manuscript of " Comus," first produced in the castle

VALENTINE

QUAINT OLD SHREWSBURY

*This attractive city almost encircled by the Severn, and from its situation near the Welsh border a place of historical importance, has many interesting old streets with quaint names. One of these is Fish Street, seen above, with its ancient timbered houses.*

which is the ancestral home of the Mortimer family.

Hereford is another picturesque and historical city with remains of its old walls and a few scanty fragments of its Norman castle which was of old "high and stronge and full of great towres." Within the cathedral which had its beginnings in the days of Offa, the seventh-century Mercian king, there is preserved the famous " Mappa Mundi." This map of the world, one of the earliest attempts of its kind, was drawn on vellum by a monk about 1300, and illustrates the medieval conception of geography. Jerusalem occupies the centre of the map, and Paradise is located at the top. Today a peaceful old town, Hereford has known turbulence and tumult. That fierce Welsh chieftain Owen Glyndwr seized the city on one occasion, and it was there, after the battle of Mortimer Cross, that Owen Tudor was beheaded.

W. F. TAYLOR

### A FIFTEENTH-CENTURY INN

*This interesting old hostelry most inappropriately named, was probably built about 1450, and may have served as a hostel for pilgrims. In its fascinating galleried courtyard seen in the photograph, the ill-fated Lady Jane Grey was proclaimed queen in 1553.*

have an ancient and outlandish ring. Castle Street, Pride Hill and Shoplatch may not be unusual, but what of Mardol and Dogpole, of Wyle Cop and Murivance, of Grope Lane and Leopard Passage?

Hidden in these narrow streets and medieval alleys are many strikingly antique buildings including the Old House which lodged Mary Tudor; the house, now a shop, where Henry VII stayed on his way to Bosworth Field, and the Council House, partly modernized, which served as a meeting place for the Council of the Welsh Marches.

#### Royal Saxon City

Gloucester, seat of the Norman Earl Fitzhamon, like Shrewsbury, stands guard over the Severn. Its traditions of independence date from the time when Glevum was a self-governing Roman town, and from the Saxon days when the kings of Mercia had a royal palace there. Henry III was crowned in the cathedral and two kings, Richard II and Henry IV held parliament in the city. Apart from the cathedral, whose cloisters are the most magnificent in the country, there is little of the medieval left except the " New Inn " (what an anachronism!) which boasts timber work of the fifteenth century.

Among the ancient and attractive towns of England, Shrewsbury must be given honourable mention. In the ground almost encircled by the Severn there stood the British town of Pengwern. On the same site grew the Saxon Scrobbesbyrig. The Normans saw the advantages of the place, and the Conqueror made Roger de Montgomery overlord of the surrounding country. Roger added to the natural strength of the place by erecting a castle on the narrow neck of land, thus guarding the only dry approach.

In subsequent centuries the town developed, and much of its old architecture still stands as evidence of the past. The very street names

FELTON

### MEDIEVAL HOUSE AT COLCHESTER

*This well preserved fifteenth-century, timbered dwelling is an interesting relic of ancient Colchester. It is known as the Siege House, and its woodwork bears many bullet marks received during the Civil War when the Royalist forces held out for twelve weeks against Fairfax's soldiers.*

East Anglia is almost as rich in ancient towns as the border country of Wales. Like the Welsh Marches too it is singularly apart from the rest of England, in history and tradition alike. Until a comparatively recent date it was to all intents and purposes cut off from communication with central England, and has the history of an island within an island. The Wash, the North Sea and the estuary of the Thames formed effective barriers on three sides, and on the fourth, Fenland, before it was drained, acted as a complete barrier between Norfolk and the country to the west. The cities even now reflect this insular position. They have a character akin to the independence of outlook which the typical East Anglian retains in the face of growing uniformity.

Norwich is the true capital of East Anglia. The Boom Towers and St. Martin's Gate belong to that period in the city's history when it was one of the largest of the walled towns. The Norman cathedral with its magnificent tapering spire, the castle of Robert Bigod, the Strangers' Hall (a fifteenth-century house which is now used as a museum), the Erpingham Gate which

is nearly a century later than the walls, and the queerly-named Sampson and Hercules House, which is a perfect example of sixteenth-century architecture, are a few of the other links with the past which the wayfarer will find in modern Norwich.

Two other towns in Norfolk—Yarmouth and King's Lynn—were illustrious in the Middle Ages, both ports of the first magnitude, though they have suffered unequal fates in the intervening centuries. Yarmouth has grown apace, and, in its growing, has lost its former charm, whilst Lynn has declined, but testifies by its many fine seventeenth-century merchants' houses how great was its former prosperity.

Colchester is another city of East Anglia which allies historic interest with modern prosperity. Here, as at Canterbury and Norwich, the Flemish established a weaving industry perpetuated in the cloth manufacture of today. There are records that flour-milling, another staple industry, has been carried on since Saxon days. The Normans have bequeathed the ruins of the prior of St. Botolph, and the castle which is on the lines of

EDGAR WARD

## A BEAUTIFUL RELIC OF THE OLD GUILDS

*The Merchant Guilds arose in the eleventh century and developed during the Middle Ages, playing a prominent part in the development of the town. Royal Charters were granted to the guilds, and Guildhalls were created to conduct their business. This example at Lavenham, in Suffolk, served a Cloth Guild.*

FELTON

## A MONASTIC FRAGMENT

*The Dorset town of Sherborne had its beginnings in Saxon times. A Benedictine monastery was founded there in A.D. 998. Parts of the abbey, which was rebuilt in the thirteenth and fourteenth centuries, now serve as Sherborne School. The photograph shows the Conduit which once stood in the cloisters. Behind it are some beautiful timber framed houses, and in the background the tower of the abbey church.*

those at Rochester and London. It has much in common with Bath, which, though its chief claim to interest is its Roman remains, and in appearance is a typical nineteenth-century town, yet was an important walled city in the Middle Ages.

The cathedral cities of the older foundation were without exception towns of antiquity. Six of these, Exeter, Durham, Salisbury, Winchester, Carlisle and Lincoln, have not so far been mentioned. All except Salisbury were walled cities; all have become the county towns of their respective counties. Exeter has flourished under every civilization. The castle of Rougemont was built by the Normans, besieged by Perkin Warbeck, by the religious insurgents of the Western Rebellion, and again by Prince Maurice. Its ruins are small but picturesque, whilst the Elizabethan Guildhall is a reminder of the town's later wealth. Durham is best seen from the hills to the south. The square block of the cathedral looms over the whole town, and the three bridges that span the Wear give it added grace.

Carlisle, like Berwick, is still essentially a border town as it has been since Hadrian's Wall was built where its northern suburbs now stand. Lincoln has many ancient monuments. The High Bridge is one of the very few in England which still bears houses, as did the Old London Bridge. The Jew's House, a Norman dwelling-place, is claimed to be the oldest in the country. The bishop's chair in the cathedral Chapter House is the throne on which Edward I sat when he convened his parliament in Durham.

### City of Peace

Salisbury, dominated by the four hundred feet of the cathedral spire, is rather Georgian in appearance, though the Hall of John Halle, and the Poultry Cross are of the fifteenth century, and there is the Joiners' Hall, a very ancient house which is now the property of the National Trust. Unlike so many towns we have described, the history of Salisbury has been one of peace. It always has been, and probably always will be a cathedral city and little else. Not so Winchester, which was the Venta Belgarum of the Romans, the capital of United England under King Canute and, with London, joint capital of William the Conqueror. Yet here, too, after the cathedral was founded, peace reigned.

Our search for Britain's medieval towns must end with a passing reference to the Cinque Ports —Hastings, Romney, Hythe, Dover and Sandwich, to which were added Winchelsea and Rye, all of which throughout the Middle Ages enjoyed many privileges of independence in return for supplying ships for the navy. The latter three retain much of their medieval appearance. Sandwich, with its barbican; Winchelsea, with one gate a full half mile from the present village; and Rye, with its cobbled streets, live more really in the past than any of the great cities.

DIXON-SCOTT

## A CORNER OF ANCIENT NORWICH

*This old dwelling stands in Tombland Alley, a passage taking its name from a piece of open ground long known as Tombland. There medieval fairs were held, and often proved occasions for conflict between the citizens and the monks of the adjacent monastery.*

STEPHENSON

### EVENTIDE IN A HIGHLAND GLEN

*Glen Affric in western Ross is perhaps the wildest and most beautiful of Scottish glens. In the lower portions of the glen ancient pine forests fringe the dark flowing stream and the lonely lochs, but these are eventually left behind and the glen leads into the scarcely tenanted and little frequented mountainous country between the heights of Mam Soul and Ben Attow, through which a right of way leads to the sea at the head of Loch Duich.*

# SCOTLAND, LAND OF ROMANCE

## by A. A. THOMSON

SCOTLAND is a land steeped in beauty and drenched in romance. This romance lies deeper than what is called scenery—a rather theatrical word which suggests " set pieces " and perfunctorily praised views. It is something that breathes in Scotland's caller air and is impregnated in the very soil itself. It is a romance of sharp-edged contrast and bewildering variety, of grim peaks and smiling green straths, of foaming mountain torrents and rippling silver streams, of gently sloping meadows and rolling moorlands where the wild wind skirls like a pibroch.

It is a romance of history, of a people battling fiercely for liberty and independence. The Scots, true to their emblem of the thistle, have always been a turbulent race. Even from the days of the fierce Picts who surged round Hadrian's Wall, they have had in their veins the fighting blood of mountain men. Under Wallace and Bruce they struggled indomitably to national freedom against the English invader. But they never fought in a mean cause. The story of the Jacobite rebellions is a tale of deathless heroism and unstinted loyalty for a cause that could not succeed. And even now, wherever a Scot plants his foot at the uttermost bounds of empire, there stands something of the old Scotland. He carries its spirit with him to the ends of the earth.

It is a romance of character—character that comes from the land ; the free winds of the mountains, the salty tang of the rugged east coast, the misty airs of the rainbow west, the breezes that blow over the sturdy lowland hills— all these things have gone to weld the character of the Scots. Dreamy Celt and sturdy Lowlander alike owe their character to the land they live in. Romance is Scotland and Scotland is romance, but you cannot tell why this should be so, unless you see the country for yourself.

To cross the border at Carter Bar amid the Cheviots is to plunge headlong into history. By that road the old freebooters—steel-capped, bearded men on shaggy horses—rode down under a misty moon to rob the English of their cattle. The Border rievers were a fierce race, and found raiding easier than farming. All the old stories and ballads tell of their wild exploits, sometimes with a grim humour and sometimes with moving and tragic pathos. There is the story of the lady of Yarrow, who placed a pair of spurs upon the great meat-dish, as a hint to her husband that cattle were needed (from English farms) to replenish honest Scots larders ; there is the rattling tale of Kinmont Willie's escape from Carlisle Castle ; and there are exquisite fairy stories, such as those of Thomas the Rhymer, or of Janet of Carterhaugh. But most moving of all are the tales of stark tragedy, like that of the *Border Widow's Lament* or the *Dowie Dens of Yarrow*. " Nae living man I'll love again,

Since that my lovely Knight was slain,
Wi' ae lock of his yellow hair
I'll chain my heart for evermair."

Women must weep.

W. F. TAYLOR

" TANTALLON'S DIZZY STEEP "

*This fourteenth-century stronghold overlooking the North Sea, figures in Scott's classic " Marmion."*

. . . That is the burden of many a song of those wild days, and even now something of that air of pensive sadness hangs over the Borderland, by the streams of Yarrow and Ettrick, and along the moorland, still dotted with grim grey peel towers, sentinels that kept silent ward against the raider.

Men, alas, were harsh and cruel, but, oh, they were brave. The Border is rich in ruined castles, the skeletons of far-off feuds and battles long ago—Hermitage, home of the ruthless Bothwell, Lochmaben, reputed home of Robert Bruce, Newark, where the last minstrel sang his lay, and red Tantallon, where Marmion bearded
" the lion in his den,
The Douglas in his hall."

There are peaceful fields, too, where once swords flashed and musketry rattled; Dunbar, where "the Lord delivered the Scottish army into Cromwell's hands," and red Philiphaugh, where Leslie defeated the gallant Montrose.

The Border was wealthier in lovely abbeys than any other part of Scotland—Jedburgh, Kelso, Melrose, where the heart of Robert Bruce lies buried, and Dryburgh looped in a silver bend of the chiming Tweed, where sleep Sir Walter Scott and Earl Haig. The abbeys tell their own tale, first of the piety of the kindly monks, then of the ferocity of English harryings and then of the still crueller hands of decay and neglect. But now, in happier times, their ruins are preserved and carefully tended, and the tranquil peace of the old monastic life in some measure returns.

Nor are all the tales of Border history shadowed by the wastage of strife. Great poets have sung to the ripple of the Tweed. The Vale of Ettrick enshrines the life and exquisite lyrics of James Hogg, the shepherd-poet, who sang of the birds and trees of his own sweet valley, and rollicked by the ingle of Tibbie Shiels' Inn. But if one spirit more than another can be said to call the Border its home, it is the serene and gallant spirit of Sir Walter Scott. The Border saw his boyhood, it inspired his grandest work. It watched his success, his financial disaster through another's fault and his ultimate triumph through Herculean labours and strength of spirit.

Many places are rich in memories of him: Sandy Knowe, Smailholm Tower, Selkirk with its memorial to the men of Flodden and to Scott's brave explorer-friend, Mungo Park, Eildon, Bemersyde, Ashiestiel and Abbotsford, the home he loved, and which he built as part of the romance of his eager life, and Dryburgh, where he now lies sleeping. All these names are enshrined in the one name, Tweed, that silver river which rippled past his home, where he fished with the devoted, cantankerous Tam Purdie, and where his footsteps ever strayed, in sickness and health, in sorrow or contentment.

### Gaunt Peel Towers

Many are the romantic pictures which the traveller may carry away from the Border: the soft green of low hills where the curlew pipes and the sheep wander at will, leafy woods of birch and beech that run down to wimpling streams; grey abbey ruins and gaunt peel towers, the silent waters of Our Lady's Lake. These are such stuff that dreams are made of; the warp and woof of Border history, tragedy and life. Yet there is one more picture which the traveller must not miss. Before the War Memorial in Galashiels, that little grey town which lies at the foot of sturdy green hills, where Tweed and

R. M. ADAM

### LONELY BORDER COUNTRY

*Out of Redesdale, in Northumberland, a road climbs to the border at Carter Bar, 1371 feet above the sea level. On the Scottish side there is a splendid prospect including the Cheviots, the vales of Tweed and Teviot, and the fine upstanding Eildon Hills. The Cheviot, 2676 feet, is seen in the background.*

R. M. ADAM

## A POET'S STREAM

*Many of the old Border Ballads mention the River Yarrow, here seen near St. Mary's Loch. Later poets, including Wordsworth and Scott, also sung its charms. From the banks of Yarrow came James Hogg, the "Ettrick Shepherd," "after Burns the greatest poet that ever sprang from the bosom of the common people."*

Gala meet, stands the figure of the Border Horseman, a bearded warrior, morion on head and lance at saddle-bow. Here is the true spirit of the Border, the epitome of Border story—a long tale of not ignoble strife, of eternal vigilance and, above all, of matchless courage.

The country of the western Border may not, at first sight, have the same romantic appeal as the immediate east, but the hurrying traveller, did he but know it, would find in Galloway, lochs as enchanting and mountains as wild as ever he would hope to find in the Highlands. Grey Galloway . . . So runs the ancient name, but the grey is neither dull nor drab.

Galloway, like Fife, is an ancient kingdom, and it preserves all that craggy individuality of scenery and character which is an ancient kingdom's right. It has a widely varied coast; the long low line of the Solway and the western sea-board with its myriad caves and inlets, and these two stretches culminate where wild seas roll around the mighty cliffs of the Mull of Galloway. Away from the sea, the land rises, sometimes gently and sometimes sharply, towards highlands of almost incredible wildness.

Many are the enchanted corners of Galloway, and better roads have made them less inaccessible than once they were. The coast roads are full of fascination; either along the south by Heston Island (the Isle Rathon of Crockett's *The Raiders*), and the ruined abbey of Dundrennan, where Mary, tragic Queen of Scots, said her last farewell to Scotland; or by the west, past Turnberry, early home of the Bruce, and Gamesloup, scene of the ancient ballad of May Collean.

If you take the hill-road inland from Newton Stewart—the road where the old Free Traders drove their pack-horses—you will come to one of the fairest lochs in all Scotland, Loch Trool. Here is a mirror of cool, clear water, encircled by silent hills and wooded to the shore. Even now, he is an intrepid traveller who penetrates to the inmost recesses of the Gallovidian hinterland; towards the Wolf's Slock and the Dungeon of Buchan and dark Loch Neldricken, with its legendary Murder Hole. There lies the real secret of Grey Galloway.

Galloway lives in literature by the extraordinary grip which it has always held on the imaginations of great writers. R. L. Stevenson wrote of the grim cliffs of the Mull in his rousing ballad, *The Secret of the Heather Ale*.

" The King in the red moorland
    Rode on a summer's day ;
  And the bees hummed, and the curlews
    Cried beside the way. . . ."

A. DURRANT

### ABBEY OF THE SWEET HEART

*This abbey, near Dumfries, was built in the thirteenth century by Devorgilla, who ordered that the heart of her husband, John Baliol, founder of Balliol College, Oxford, should be buried in her tomb; hence the name. Only the south transept has a roof, but the central tower and arches of the nave are well preserved.*

Borgue, that home of ancient smugglers, is the original setting of that gripping romance *The Master of Ballantrae*, with its sinister, but enthralling hero-villain.

Scott, too, found romance here. Much of the action of Redgauntlet takes place upon the Solway coast, while near Gatehouse of Fleet, which Scott in *Guy Mannering* calls Kippletringan, you may still see the reputed cave of Dirck Hatteraick, the book's doughty smuggler-villain.

#### Rugged Galloway

But of all the names in Gallovidian literature that of S. R. Crockett shines the brightest. He knew every inch of Galloway, and in many romantic novels has vividly painted both its ruggedness and its gentler charms. If you want a breathless story of the old smuggling days, read *The Raiders*, and take it with you on your journey, for it pictures this wild countryside as no other book has ever done.

The history of this south-western corner of Scotland is a stormy chronicle of civil and religious strife. It has at least one lovely abbey—red Sweetheart—which lies under the shadow of blue Criffel—and its many castles—among them, Caerlaverock, Lochmaben and the grim keep of Thrieve—tell of desperate fights and fierce

encounters. The old free-traders haunted the caves and sea-roads of the Solway, singing their rough song:

" There's brandy at the Abbeyburn, there's rum at Heston Bay,
   And we will go a-smuggling afore the break o'day."

The darkest and yet the bravest page in this land's story concerns the religious persecutions of "the killing time." The Scottish Covenanters were the bravest of the brave; in the rocky glens they held their conventicles in defiance of cruel laws. Hundreds died for their faith; their blood stained the heather and the moss-hags. At Wigton you will see the spot where two brave women suffered for the Covenant,

" Within the sea, tied to a stake,
   They suffered for Christ Jesus' sake."

The rough stones that are found in the heather mark the graves of the martyrs who were shot for their faith by Claverhouse's dragoons, and it was the man whom Scott calls " Old Mortality " who sought out and restored as many as he could find, wandering among the lonely moors, " where about the graves of the martyrs the whaups are crying . . ."

Moving northward on this western side we come to the gentler shires of Dumfries and Ayr.

Less wild than Galloway they may be but they are not without their romance, for they hold within their borders the life-story of Robert Burns. It is no great distance from the auld clay biggin at Alloway, near the banks of bonnie Doon, where he was born, to Dumfries, where he died young. Place-name after place-name in this district tells of his brave, tragic life; Kirkoswald, where he went to learn surveying, Mauchline, where the flower of his genius blossomed, Ayr, where the Tam o' Shanter's Inn still stands, Kilmarnock, where his "little beuk for Scotland's sake" was first published, Ellisland on the banks of lovely Nith, and Dumfries, douce country town, with its old inns and sturdy Mid-Steeple, where he lies sleeping in St. Michael's Kirkyard.

This is a pleasant countryside, greenly meadowed and wooded, and watered by the streams he loved so well: the Doon, of which he wrote one of his saddest love songs; the Ayr, where he wandered, singing his song of farewell to Scotland and the Nith, which ran behind his little farm at Ellisland and on whose bank he strode up and down, joyously shouting aloud the immortal couplets of "Tam o' Shanter."

To see this land as he saw it, with its fields and woods and rippling streams, is to see Burns as he himself was, ploughman, patriot and immortal singer of life's simpler joys and sorrows. Nor must you miss, in this south-western section the enchanting village of Moniaive, with its white cottages and rambler roses, nor Maxwelton House, near Dunscore, where dwelt Bonnie Annie Laurie of the song, nor Craigenputtock, where Carlyle wrote *Sartor Resartus*, nor Irongray, where in the old churchyard, sleeps Helen Walker, real-life prototype of Scott's sweetest heroine, Jeanie Deans. Almost every cottage and every by-road is alive with romantic history.

## The Busy Clyde

Central Scotland is almost cut in half by two deep river valleys, the Clyde on the west and the Forth on the east. The Clyde flows through the most thickly-populated industrial districts of Scotland. On its banks lies Glasgow, second city of the Empire, and from its clanging yards the great ships go out to the seven seas. The building and launching of the mighty ship, the *Queen Mary*, in times of industrial depression, is one of the most romantic episodes of our time. No tale of ancient chivalry can match the gallant hope and dauntless courage that went to the making of that brave ship.

But the Clyde is not wholly shrouded by chimney smoke or deafened by the clang of riveters' hammers; you may sail down past the yards of Greenock towards the open waters of

R. M. ADAM

### A GALLOWAY GLEN

*Amid the desolation of the Galloway Hills lies Glen Trool with its beautiful loch reaching almost to the head of the glen. It was in this glen that Robert the Bruce overcame an English force in 1307, and began the campaign of independence which was brought to a decisive close at Bannockburn seven years later.*

A. A. MACGREGOR

## BY THE BANKS OF LOCH LOMOND

*Loch Lomond is the largest, and to many people also the most beautiful of Scottish lochs. Its surroundings have not the rugged grandeur of Loch Coruisk, and it depends rather for its charm on the harmonious combination of green curving shores, picturesque isles and mountains sweeping rather than soaring upwards. The photograph shows the loch at Rowardennan, near where the track starts to climb the famous Ben Lomond.*

A. A. MACGREGOR

## SNOW-CLAD HILLS

*Winter at the base of Rest-and-be-Thankful, the name given by General Wade and his road-making soldiers to the highest point attained by their military road running westward up Glen Croe, from the shores of Loch Long, and then descending through Glen Kinglass to Loch Fyne, at Cairndow, on its way to Inveraray, the ancestral home of MacCallum Mhor, the Duke of Argyll and chief of the Campbell Clan.*

the Firth, where sunshine and dappled shadow play among the fairy islands of the Kyles of Bute. And not very far to the north-west of Glasgow lie the bonnie, bonnie banks of Loch Lomond. Here you may see not merely one of the world's most dazzling beauty spots, but one which has survived the handicap of a hundred years' praise. The beauty of Loch Lomond captures the imagination of even the most hardened sightseer; its wooded banks, its gleaming waters and its jewelled islands blend in a picture of unforgettable colour and charm. You feel that you are in a fairy world. And above the north-eastern corner towers the mighty shadow of Ben Lomond, the mountain-guardian of the lake.

Westward you might go, in sunshine or shadow, by Inversnaid, where Wordsworth saw his "Highland Girl," towards wilder country by the shores of Loch Long, where Magnus, the Manx pirate king, once rowed his raiding galleys, and over the pass of Rest-and-be-Thankful to Inveraray, ancient home of the great Clan Campbell.

In Inveraray you may consider the living romance of the brave fisher folk who bring the "Caller Herrin'" from Loch Fyne, or you may ponder on the ancient feuds and fights of the Campbells, who gained an undeservedly evil reputation for treachery and cowardice, because their chiefs were sometimes on the side of the English. The most delightful portrayer of this wild west country was Neil Munro, who, in such novels as *Doom Castle* and *John Splendid* depicted scenes and doughty deeds.

A. A. MACGREGOR

### DOOM CASTLE
*Near the shores of Loch Fyne in Argyll stands the tall, grey, turreted Dundarave Castle, the Doom Castle of Neil Munro's book, "John Splendid."*

### Rob Roy's Country

If you go eastward from Loch Lomond, you come to the Trossachs and the enchanted country which Scott has immortalized in *The Lady of the Lake* and *Rob Roy*; Loch Katrine from whose clear waters rises Ellen's Isle, home of The Lady of the Lake; the gorge of the Trossachs, where Fitz-James fell with his "gallant grey" under him; Loch Achray, with its thickly-wooded shores—all these are part of what Scott called "the scenery of a fairy dream." Everywhere

you will find pictures, which your mind's eye can carry away to typify this magical land; stretches of glittering water, fringed with larch and silvery birch; guardian hills whose slopes are stained wine red with heather, and fairy glens where the wild hyacinths, the purple foxglove and the scarlet rowanberry colour the seasons as they come and go. And over all these beauties lies a kind of luminous haze, as though this land were under a magic spell. A fairy dream indeed.

The eastern side has less of this purely enchanted quality, but it is none the less alive with beauty and interest. In whichever direction you go from Edinburgh, with its castled rock and quiet Georgian squares, you are never far from romance. The short road down from Edinburgh to Queensferry, where the great Forth Bridge spans a mile and a quarter of water, tells us many tales: of Margaret, gracious Queen of Malcolm Canmore, who encouraged the peaceful arts among a turbulent people, and of the famous Jock Howieson who saved his king's life from robbers at Cramond Bridge. Pict and Roman, Saxon and Norman, Whig and Jacobite have trodden this road, from ship to capital and capital to ship.

If you cross the Firth by railway bridge or ferry boat, you are in the ancient kingdom of Fife, that compact peninsula which lies between the long arms of Forth and Tay. A king once described Fife as a "grey cloth mantle with a fringe of gold." The grey mantle is now represented by the smoke of modern factory and mine, but the golden fringe remains as bright and shining as in the old days. All along the Fife coast you will find little sandy bays of the purest gold, and here the "grey" North Sea is, as often as not, a beautiful blue.

The fishing villages of the Fife coast are among the most fascinating little places in the whole of these islands: Elie, St. Monans, Crail—these make a series of unforgettable pictures, with their rocky harbours, their winding streets and their gaily-painted fishing boats. There is hardly a village on this coast which does not preserve some link with the past: Kirkcaldy, where

VIOLET BANKS

### LOCH KATRINE AND ELLEN'S ISLE

*Loch Katrine owes much of its fame to Sir Walter Scott who called it Loch Cateran, or the Lake of the Robbers, and is part of the famous Trossachs country, once a wild and inaccessible region but now one of the most frequented of Highland beauty spots. Ellen's Isle, mentioned in " The Lady of the Lake," was the refuge of the banished Douglas, and still retains the " blighted tree " against which the harper reclined.*

Carlyle was a schoolmaster, Largo where lived Alexander Selkirk, from whose real adventures the story of Robinson Crusoe was taken, and Anstruther, where certain ships of the Spanish Armada drifted to destruction. And so, by many a quaint " auld-farrant " fishing town, and many a tiny golden bay, the coast winds round to the venerable university city,

" . . . the little town,
    The drifting surf, the wintry sea,
    The college of the scarlet gown,
    St. Andrews by the Northern
      Sea. . . ."

Inland, where the conformation of the country is so deeply indented, the traffic of history has passed, perforce, through a narrow channel. Linlithgow, Falkirk, Stirling. Here are names that, by battle, siege and sortie, live in history's page. Stirling, with its castle set on a high rock, has been from time immemorial " the gateway of the south, the bulwark of the north," and it has looked down on battles from Wallace to Prince Charlie.

### To the Highlands

But now the traveller is impatient to be away to the Highlands, to the land of the mountain and glen. Shall he go eastward from the fair city of Perth, by the rich Carse of Gowrie and over the Devil's Elbow to Braemar, whence the road winds onward through our greatest queen's own Balmoral country toward Aberdeen, city of granite and of " Bon Accord "?

W. F. TAYLOR

A NOBLE NORMAN NAVE

*Dunfermline Abbey, among later and less worthy features, retains its impressive nave, one of the finest illustrations of Norman architecture in Scotland. Robert Bruce is buried in the church.*

Shall he take the middle road, that magnificent highway, which pierces the heart of the Highlands, and sweeps up under the shadow of the towering mountains, by Pitlochry and Blair Athol toward Inverness? Or again, shall he follow a westward route over the sinister pass of Glencoe to Fort William and thence farther westward still, to the misty sea-lochs, whose outer waters wash the islands of the Hebrides?

He can go farther; by the east coast road to Scotland's most northerly point, where John o' Groat's eight-sided house looks out towards the Orkneys, or, westward, by rough roads, to where the Atlantic breakers lash and roar around the lighthouse of Cape Wrath.

The soul of the Highlands lies in the mist-capped mountains, high above the ordinary haunts of men. The very names of some of them have a quality of godlike mystery and grandeur, even of terror. Schiehallion, Stobinian,

dark Lochnagar. . . . No wonder some mountain legends are tales of witches and warlocks, of nameless spectres that haunt the dark rocky glens. But not all the Highland legends are dark and fearful; many of them concern the *sith*, or fairy folk, who live underground, in green knowes or in the pleasant hollows of the hills. These fairies were fairly friendly people, and would do no more harm than a puckish trick or two or, perhaps, the stealing of a crofter's cow. But if, in a Highland valley, you should see a patch of a vivider green than the surrounding grass, you must walk softly, for the fairies dwell below. Or so the old Highland folk will tell you.

There is no beauty like the beauty of a Highland loch, hemmed in by immemorial hills. Sunlight glints on the water, which is clear as a mirror, except where the mountain shadow falls darkly across it. Green woods, starry with

VIOLET BANKS

## A PICTURESQUE FISHING VILLAGE

*On the Fife coast, at the mouth of the Firth of Forth, and about ten miles south of St. Andrews is the village of St. Monans, or St. Monance as it was originally known. In addition to its quaint charm St. Monans is also of historical interest. It possesses a little church founded by the Scottish king, David II, about 1362.*

wild anemones, roll down to the water's edge, and over all silence and tranquillity lie, like the mantle of peace.

" By Tummel and Loch Rannoch and Lochaber
    I will go
By heather-hills with heaven in their wiles. . . ."

Loch Rannoch is lovely, but Loch Tummel is lovelier still. High above its waters, you can stand upon a little wooded eminence and see the view which Queen Victoria so often delighted to look upon : richly wooded slopes, purple hills melting into blue sky, river-loop glittering like

treacherously slain ; the Great Glen, Wade's men stolidly toiling on the new road that was to conquer the Highlands more surely than English muskets ; Glenmoriston, a fugitive prince, hiding among the heather ; Balmoral, the tiny figure of a great queen, riding in her carriage, attended by the stalwart John Brown.

Mountains, tumbling torrents, silent moorlands.
" Lo ! for there, among the flowers and grasses,
    Only the mightier movement sounds and passes ;
    Only winds and rivers,
    Life and death. . . ."

R. M. ADAM

RIVER TUMMEL AND SCHIEHALLION'S GRACEFUL CREST

*Above the River Tummel, in Perthshire, rises the splendid pyramid of Schiehallion (3,547 feet), one of the most beautiful of Scottish mountains. From the summit the view extends westwards across the desolate Moor of Rannoch to the peaks at the head of Glencoe. The name is said to mean a dwelling-place of fairies.*

a diamond necklace, and the still sheen upon the bosom of the loch. Truly a view for a queen.

The romantic names of the Highlands are legion. They recall the rushing rivers, where the salmon leaps—Garry, Spey, Don and Dee ; they tell of magic glens where the wild deer roams—Shirra, Cannich and Affric, loveliest glen of all ; of Glengarry and Glen Quoich, of Glen Moriston and the lonely Glen Shiel reaching down to the sea.

You have only to close your eyes to see the pictures that a few Highland names, taken at random, may evoke : Killiecrankie, the cataract-charge of kilted clansmen, hurtling down the gorge ; Glencoe, the glen of weeping—weeping amid desolate snows for sons and fathers,

There are a dozen ways in which the traveller may drink delight from the glamour of Scotland. Book in hand, he may study the romantic topography of his favourite authors : the Scotland of Sir Walter Scott, not merely the beloved borderland that was his home, but the ancient city of *The Fair Maid of Perth*, the Arbroath of *The Antiquary*, the Covenanting country of *Old Mortality*, the southern Highlands of *Rob Roy* and many another real place which gave pleasure under fictional guise. He may seek out the Ayrshire farmsteads and Dumfriesshire streams of Robert Burns, or wander round the little Angus town of Kirriemuir that was Barrie's *Thrums*.

He may follow, in the Appin country, near the

shores of Loch Linnhe, all the thrilling adventures of the hero of Stevenson's *Kidnapped*, with his friend, the "bonnie fechter," Alan Breck, and, in the western highlands and along the Great Glen, he may see the places he has read of in the breathless tales of Neil Munro and the exquisite Jacobite romances of D. K. Broster. And if he is one of those happy old-fashioned folk who once revelled in *Beside the Bonnie Brier Bush*, he will find the original Drumtochty, which is really the Perthshire village of Logiealmond.

defended Dunbar Castle against the English, Catherine Douglas who, in the old Blackfriars Monastery at Perth, thrust her arm through the bolt-staples of the door in a vain attempt to save her king from the assassin's dagger, and Flora Macdonald, more lovable heroine than any other. Everywhere he will find places and memories connected with these great names; and he will learn, too, how it was something in the spirit of the land itself which inspired great deeds and high endeavours. He will feel in his

R. M. ADAM

### THE GLEN OF WEEPING

*For Macaulay, Glencoe was the most dreary and melancholy of all the Scottish passes—the very valley of the Shadow of Death. As the valley of historic tragedy it is still remembered, but the visitor today sees in it more than gloom and desolation, and is able to appreciate its wild beauty and its long and lonely reaches.*

Or he may seek to see Scotland in terms of the lives of heroes, and here he will be on rich, fruitful ground, for Scotland has ever been a land of strong individual character, of men who were great *as* men, but who drew much from their national environment. Carlyle, himself something of a crotchety hero, might well have written of them: fighting heroes, like Wallace-wight and Bruce, the warrior king; zealot-heroes, like Wishart and Knox and the unknown martyrs of the moss-hags, soldier-statesmen, like the noble Marquis of Montrose and, most lovable hero of all, the gallant Bonnie Prince Charlie. There are heroines, too; Black Agnes, who

bones the atmosphere of certain places: the peace of the old abbeys, the bravery of Bannockburn, and the infinite sadness that broods for ever over Culloden Moor.

But, being a traveller, he may see Scotland as a land of journeyings, for history itself is, in a sense, a series of journeys, brave, gay, adventurous or sad. He may think of the journeys of the early saints, of Ninian, who, landing on the Isle of Whithorn, first brought Christianity to the rough Picts of Galloway; or of Columba, who founded the monastery of Iona and sailed up Loch Ness to beard the heathen kings. He may stand upon the battlefields of Bruce or gaze

STEPHENSON

### SUNLIT BEAUTY OF A HIGHLAND RIVER

*Amid the lovely and little known mountains of Ross, the River Beauly has its several beginnings, and three of Scotland's finest glens pay it tribute. Farthest from the sea are the head waters of the stream which flows down Glen Affric. Another branch runs on the north side of the great bulk of Mam Soul and flows down Glen Cannich. Yet another tributary issues from the Loch Morar and runs through Glen Farrar.*

upon the grey walls of the many castles which that dauntless warrior stormed, despite their reputed impregnability. The places of his birth, of his exiled wandering, of his brave victories and of his death are still to be seen.

And what of the sad journeys of Mary Queen of Scots? The places and the roads are still there: Linlithgow Castle, where she was born; Holyrood Palace, where she was browbeaten by the stern Knox and witnessed Rizzio's murder; Carberry Hill, where the Lords of the Congregation defeated her; Lochleven's island castle, scene of one of the most thrilling escapes in

waukin' yet? ") After this smashing victory there were tragic delays, and when the prince finally marched by Carlisle into England, it was too late. He would even have gone on from Derby, if his commanders had supported him, but from that turning-point, his story is a tale of retreat. On Scottish soil again, he won a barren victory at Falkirk, but the relentless pursuit of the English armies forced him farther and farther northward, and in the bitter fight of Culloden Moor, his last hopes of victory were ruthlessly shattered. Even then, his wanderings were not at an end. In Glenmoriston he lived

STEPHENSON

### RUGGED PEAKS OF SKYE

*The Black Cuillin of Skye, those gaunt, bare hills, weathered and splintered into slender peaks, narrow ridges and soaring crags, have no rivals in Britain for sheer splendour and diversity of form. In this view from the flanks of Sgurr Sgumain, we see Gars-bheinn (pronounced Gars-ven), the southernmost peak of the Cuillin.*

history, and Dundrennan, from whence she set out upon the journey that was to lead to her imprisonment, betrayal and death.

But every Scottish road follows or crosses at some point the most romantic road of all, the path of the 'forty-five, down which Prince Charles Edward marched, upon a forlorn hope which came within an ace of success. He landed with seven men at Moidart in the west, and unfurled his standard in Glenfinnan. The chieftains of the clans, reluctant at first, were won by his gallant bearing and flocked to his banner. With a rapidly growing army he swept down on Perth and then took Edinburgh with scarce the firing of a shot. From the capital he sallied out to Prestonpans and cut to ribbons Sir John Cope's army. ("Hi, Johnnie Cope, are ye

amid the rocks and caves, sheltered with selfless loyalty by impoverished men who knew that there was a price of £30,000 upon his head, and in the Isle of Skye he was aided, in one hairbreadth escape after another, by the fidelity of Flora Macdonald. A brave, tragic journey, paved with the dead hopes of loyal men and women.

So we have seen Scotland as a land of glamour and enchantment, an enchantment that touches its hills and its glens, its songs and its stories, its battlefields and its romantic journeys. A journey still remains the most romantic of human enterprises, and it is not for nothing that the ancient Gaelic wisdom gave a special blessing to the traveller: "Blessings go with you; may a straight path be before you, and a happy end to your journey!"

W. K. R. NEILSON

### THE LANTHORN OF THE NORTH

*So Elgin Cathedral was termed. Founded in 1224 by Andrew, Bishop of Moray, the cathedral, in its entirety, was said to be " a building of Gothic architecture inferior to few in Europe." After the Reformation the cathedral was allowed to fall in ruin " as a piece of Romish vanity too expensive to keep in repair."*

EDGAR WARD

### HISTORIC PALACE OF HOLYROOD HOUSE

*Holyrood had its beginnings as a monastery built by David I and later became a royal residence. Of all its regal occupants none has left more tragic memories than Mary Queen of Scots. There she was married to Bothwell within three months of Darnley's death, and there her favourite, Rizzio, was foully assassinated.*

Based on Ordnance Survey Map by permission H.M. Stationery Office.

# MEMORIES OF TUDOR AND STUART DAYS

## by G. BAKER

THE sixteenth and seventeenth centuries saw the beginnings of Britain overseas. In Tudor and Stuart times Bristol and Barnstaple, Bideford and Plymouth played their parts in the romance of the Empire's making.

Bristol, in 1497, then the second largest city in England, saw John and Sebastian Cabot with eighteen Bristol sailor-men set out on the voyage which ended in the discovery of the North American mainland—an historic feat of which Cabot Tower on Brandon Hill commemorates the fourth centenary. The Cabots were members of the Company of Merchant Venturers—one of the oldest guilds in England—whose fine hall stands in Marsh Street. Sebastian Cabot was still alive when, in 1554, the Merchant Venturers erected the almshouses to be found near their hall ; on three sides of a stone paved courtyard are the yellow cottages which today house a score of old sailors and a dozen sailors' wives.

**OLD SURREY HALL**

*In a little hidden valley near Lingfield lies this timber-fronted moated building with its unusually elaborate façade. Probably built in the fifteenth century, it had a Great Hall which is now divided into two rooms.*

STEPHENSON

In Corn Street is the Exchange before which are four bronze tables rather like immense mushrooms, known as the " Nails." Upon these the Bristol merchants of Tudor and Stuart times used to pay those accounts which they settled in cash— a custom from which comes the phrase " to pay on the nail." At the end of Corn Street stands the Old Dutch House, tall and timbered, which was brought from Holland in parts, and erected in 1676.

From Bideford and Barnstaple came many of the famous sea-captains of Elizabeth's reign. Bideford has an interesting relic of their daring. In the Victoria Park are to be seen Spanish guns of the sixteenth century which were captured from the Armada. In Barnstaple seafaring descendants of the great Elizabethans ended their days in the Penrose Almshouses in Litchdon Street, notable for their seventeenth century colonnade of granite pillars.

At Plymouth, New Street, Castle Street, and neighbouring thoroughfares are much as they were when in 1577 Sir Francis Drake brought back the *Golden Hind* into Plymouth Harbour, after that famous voyage which had given him the title of the first Englishman to circumnavigate the world ; and when in July, 1588, after the Armada had been sighted off the Lizard, he sailed out of the Sound with the greater part of the English Fleet. Today Drake's statue looks out to sea from the Hoe. Near the Barbican on the edge of Sutton Pool—Plymouth's first harbour which is now the fishermen's port—are a memorial arch and a tablet commemorating the sailing of the *Mayflower* from Plymouth on September 5, 1620.

In the latter years of Elizabeth and in the reign of James I England was prosperous and comparatively at peace. In the villages, especially, " Merrie England " was more than a mere term. Improved agricultural methods, and the high price of corn improved the lot of the country worker and the farmer alike. This improvement was reflected in the feasts and festivals which centred round the seasons and events of the farmer's year. The first of these was Plough Monday, the Monday following Epiphany, when sword dancers, their white shirts sewn with fluttering ribbons, went dancing across the fields, cracking the whips they carried. They were led by fantastically dressed men having tails, and wearing wigs and masks to make them look like old women. Before any house where their demand for money was refused, they ploughed up the soil. The

EDGAR WARD

## A FAMOUS ELIZABETHAN PORT

*The Devonshire town of Bideford was given a charter by Elizabeth in 1574, and was long a famous port. Spanning the River Torridge is a fine bridge of twenty-four arches, built in 1550 but considerably modified since.*

EDGAR WARD

## MILTON'S PARADISE

*At Chalfont St. Giles, about 1665, Thomas Ellwood, John Milton's pupil and secretary, bought " a pretty box " in which the blind poet and his family might live in safety from the plague then spreading in London.*

May Day games were followed by the Lamb Feast at Whitsun; while Midsummer's Eve was celebrated with wrestling matches and the lighting of a great bonfire in the village street, round which there was dancing at midnight. Plays were still mummed, and prancing on hobby-horses was still the amusement of grown men and women. From time to time wandering showmen brought bull-running, cock-fighting, and bear-baiting to the villages; and at the country fairs—Stourbridge, near Cambridge, was the most famous of them all—the great attractions were the jugglers, fire-eaters, performing apes and girl stilt-walkers.

### Merry England

Such merry-making was general throughout England. There were local variations, of course. Normally, each parish organized its own festivities and frowned upon "foreigners" living a mile away in the next village who might attempt to join in. At times, however, there was co-operation. Thus in the Reading district as early as 1511 no fewer than twenty-seven villages joined to produce the Bassingbourne Play. Again, a number of parishes would join in athletic contests. To Barton-on-the-Heath, Cotswold villages for many miles around sent their young men to compete at leaping, cudgel-playing, fighting with sword and buckler, tossing the pike and pitching the bar.

There was a reverse side to this particular medal. Small mercy was shown to the nomad or the vagrant, the scold or the alleged witch. For these, stocks and whipping-posts, pillories, ducking-stools and branks (a kind of iron bridle with a gag attached) were kept and constantly used. On scores of village greens today stocks, with or without their central whipping-post are still to be seen. Some of these take unusual forms. The stocks of Much Wenlock (now in the Town Hall) are mounted on wheels; those of Ashby de la Zouch are made to imprison the fingers and not the feet. Coleshill, Warwickshire, is one of the few places in which today a pillory can be seen standing in its old position,

STEPHENSON

### A LINK WITH CROMWELL

*On the River Hodder, which joins the Ribble on the borders of Lancashire and Yorkshire, stand the Lower Hodder Bridges. The nearer bridge in the photograph, now disused, is an old pack-horse bridge dating from the sixteenth century. Cromwell is said to have crossed it with his army before the Battle of Preston in 1643.*

EDGAR WARD

### HAUNT OF FAMOUS ELIZABETHANS

*This quaint old structure in the Cathedral Close, Exeter, was formerly known as Mol's Coffee House. It is said to have been built in 1596 and contains an Elizabethan oak-panelled room with some fine carving. In the armorial bearings on the frieze are those of Drake, Raleigh and Gilbert.    According to the notice over the door it was " The meeting place of our naval and military generals who fought with the Spanish Armada."*

At Hungerford and Barkham (Berkshire) are still preserved the whips with which the parish constables of the period whipped the tramps caught wandering in their town or village. Melton Mowbray has a record of the twopences which it was customary for the constable to give to a tramp after the whipping.

The fighting of the troubled years of Charles I's reign took place north, south, east and west. Some of the remotest corners of the country

cloth as a sign of their mourning when Charles I was executed in 1649.

In the south it was Rupert who achieved the first considerable success of the Civil War at the Battle of Chalgrove Field, in Oxfordshire—against that great protagonist of the Parliamentarian side, John Hampden. Only a few miles from the battlefield upon which Hampden received his death wound is the country town of Thame where he was educated. Here, in the sixteenth

PHOTOCHROM

HEREFORD'S BEAUTIFUL OLD HOUSE

*Three centuries ago Hereford must have presented a most attractive appearance for it possessed many buildings like this with massive oak beams and gabled roofs. The Old House, as it is known, was one of many built by a famous architect, John Abel, the King's Carpenter. It was the Guild House of the Butchers' Company.*

were affected. Even Lindisfarne, the Holy Isle of St. Cuthbert, saw the royalist garrison of the castle—built only a century earlier on foundations made from the stones of the old priory—besieged and driven out by the Parliamentarians in 1644, immediately before the Battle of Marston Moor.

In the west, Exeter declared for the king. Over a bookshop in the High Street there is a low room with uneven floor, oak-panelled walls, and small leaded windows, which was once the headquarters of Prince Rupert, the impetuous cavalry leader who was his royal uncle's most successful general. Exeter Guildhall still has the sword which local loyalists covered in black

century grammar school, may be seen the wooden bed on wheels in which he slept.

In the eastern counties there was strong support for the Parliamentarians. It was Cromwell's own countryside. The valley of the Great Ouse is picturesque with thatched cottages now as then ; Huntingdon with its tranquil grey brick houses, its Shire Hall, and its low-fronted Falcon Inn was the Protector's birthplace. The entry of his baptism is to be found in the registers of All Saints' Church. Godmanchester is little changed since Cromwell's day. It has many timbered houses and a delightful Elizabethan grammar school in old red brick. Five miles to the east is St. Ives, where, as a young man, Cromwell had his farm. " Cromwell's Barn " with its magnificent timber roof is there today. In the market place is a bronze statue of the Protector.

In 1651 Cromwell made the Commonwealth safe by his victory at Worcester. This old cathedral town is rich in fine specimens of Tudor timbered houses, many of them four storeys high,

EDGAR WARD
THE HANGING CHAPEL OF LANGPORT
*This gateway at Langport, in Somerset, is said to have gained its name from Judge Jeffreys having hanged three men there in 1685 for participation in the Monmouth Rebellion.*

overhanging the street. The most remarkable among these is the Commandery, a sixteenth-century hostel for travellers, with which the Elizabethans re-established the former Norman rest-house for pilgrims. It was from Worcester that the defeated Charles II took flight into Dorset. He was resting at the George Inn after his arrival at Bridport when a party of Roundheads came to look for him. When the Parliamentarians trooped into the inn yard—part of which exists today—Charles in his disguise of a servant, picked his way casually through them, and reached his horse. He had been recognized,

however, and the Roundheads were quickly after him. Leaving the Dorchester road on which he had started, Charles turned down a lane not far from Bridport, while the pursuers rode on. At the corner of Lee Lane stands a stone inscribed with an account of this incident.

At Taunton in June, 1685, Charles's son Monmouth—who had landed at the old stone harbour-pier of Lyme Regis—put up his standard and was proclaimed king. A band of Taunton's most beautiful young girls with garlands on their heads welcomed him as Protestant Defender of the country—a welcome for which the town was to pay heavily. When the rising failed, over a hundred Taunton men were brought before the Bloody Assize held by Judge Jeffreys in the Castle, and sentenced to death. Colonel Kirke, who escorted Jeffreys to the west, declared martial law on the day he reached Taunton, and hanged nineteen men without trial. In the market place today there is a grocer's shop which in that tragic September, 1685, was an inn. In its upper room, the day after his arrival Kirke and a party of his officers drank toasts. By Kirke's orders thirty Taunton men were hanged in batches of ten in the square below : the first batch as a health to the king, the second as a health to the queen, and the third as a health to Jeffreys.

### A Pathetic Army

Bridgwater also has links with the Duke of Monmouth. From the tall octagonal spire of its church, he and his officers watched James II's troops take up their position near the hamlet of Weston Zoyland on Sedgemoor. The Duke decided to make a surprise attack. At midnight, therefore, on July 5, 1685, Monmouth's pathetic force, consisting chiefly of peasants armed with pikes and pitchforks and scythes, marched by narrow lanes to North Moor, where the royal army was encamped. The accidental discharge of a pistol by one of Monmouth's men robbed the attack of its element of surprise, and the issue of the last battle to be fought on English soil was settled before it was begun.

The village church of Weston Zoyland was made the temporary prison of the five hundred men taken by the royal army : on its ancient stones can still be seen the marks made by the pikemen as they sharpened their weapons in preparation for the battle.

W. A. CALL

### A STATELY MANSION

*A dozen miles from Stratford-on-Avon stands Compton Wynyates, built by William Compton in the reign of Henry VIII. Built round a square courtyard, it is an excellent example of the Tudor manor house.*

STEPHENSON

### AN ANCIENT KENTISH MANOR

*This charming moated hall known as Ightham Mote dates from about 1340. The gate-house was built towards the end of the fifteenth century, and the beautiful domestic chapel with its painted ceiling belongs to the early sixteenth century. Another fine feature of the hall is the library, a low-ceilinged, timbered room.*

STEPHENSON

### A TUDOR BARONIAL HALL

*The mansion of Knole, near Sevenoaks, Kent, stands in a park of six miles circumference. Originally built in the thirteenth century, it was partly rebuilt in the fifteenth century, and belonged to the Archbishops of Canterbury until Cranmer gave it to Henry VIII. Elizabeth presented it to her cousin, Thomas Sackville.*

In the sixteenth century and until the time of the Civil War a great amount of building went on in England. The forests began to disappear —the Elizabethans used nothing but oak for their timber houses.

The village started to take on the appearance which we know today in such picturesque survivals as Elstow, in Bedfordshire, where Bunyan was born in 1628. In most parts of the country cottages with thatched roofs were grouped round the village green; there were high gables, and projecting boards carved with tracery. The Elizabethans finished off the ends of the gables at the eaves with pendants. A corner post curved outward to carry the angle posts of the upper story. Large uprights and horizontal beams made squares of framework, divided into smaller squares. Manor houses were often E-shaped with high, twisted chimney stacks, red tiled roofs, and heavy buttresses flanking the gateway.

One of the architectural glories of this period is Compton Wynyates. This picturesque old mansion, rebuilt in Henry VIII's reign, stands on the Oxfordshire border of Warwickshire in a fold of the Edgehill ridge, overshadowed by hanging woods. With its half-timbered gables, its stone towers and turrets, its noble porch, this great quadrangular building set round a wide courtyard is one of the finest Tudor mansions

extant. Its magnificent hall, as high as the house itself, has a notable timbered roof and a fine minstrels' gallery. This great manor house was besieged and captured by the Parliamentarians in 1644.

The love story of one of its owners, Sir William Compton, is as romantic as the old house itself. Sir William loved Elizabeth, daughter of Sir John Spencer, a very wealthy merchant who strongly opposed the match. Disguised as a baker's man (the story goes) Sir William secured admittance to his lover's house, carried her off in his basket and straightway married her. When the girl's father disinherited her, Queen Elizabeth intervened. She invited the merchant to be godfather to a child in whom she was interested. Pleased at the Queen's condescension, he made the infant heir to the property of which he had deprived his daughter—only to discover that it was that daughter's child who benefited.

### A Cardinal's Palace

Contemporary with Compton Wynyates is Hampton Court Palace begun by Cardinal Wolsey in 1514. Eleven years later the Cardinal, who intended it to be the most splendid private dwelling in England, was forced to surrender his palace to Henry VIII. Henry added the chapel, the Great Hall with its magnificent hammer-beam roof, and that fine bridge which crosses the moat in front of Wolsey's Great Gatehouse. Thus completed, the palace consisted of three principal quadrangles with various smaller courts, round which the dignified red-brick buildings rise, to which the passing of four hundred years has added a mellow loveliness. A favourite royal residence for over two centuries, Hampton Court was the birthplace of Edward VI in 1537.

A little later in date and more modest in size than these two palaces, such manors as Ightham Mote, near Sevenoaks, Kent, and Great Tangley Manor, near Wonersh, Surrey, illustrate other features of Tudor architecture. The square walls of Ightham Mote rise out of the water; while its gateway, tower, hall, chapel

STEPHENSON

### A QUEEN'S HOUSE

*This old manor house in Southover High Street, Lewes, is traditionally known as the House of Anne of Cleves, who is said to have lived there after her divorce from Henry VIII. It was granted to her in 1541.*

DIXON-SCOTT

### A QUAINT OLD GUILDHALL

*Totnes, one of the oldest boroughs in England, has a list of mayors from 1377 onwards. The Guildhall is a fragment of the abbey founded by Judhael de Totenais, who is mentioned in the Domesday Book. Inside the hall are preserved the old stocks, the bull ring and a man trap. The Council Chamber has a frieze dated 1624.*

W. A. CALL

### IN A CHARMING COTSWOLD TOWN

*Chipping Campden, a delightful old-world town, once the principal centre of the Cotswold wool trade, has many attractive buildings reminiscent of its prosperous days, and preserves to a remarkable degree the beauty and dignity expressed by its thriving citizens in their buildings of stone, now given added grace by the mellowing hand of time. The photograph shows the arched and gabled seventeenth-century Market Hall.*

D. MCLEISH

## A CORNER OF TUDOR WARWICK

*The main gate of Leycester's Hospital. This picturesque old building, a splendid example of half-timbered architecture was, in 1571, converted by Robert Dudley, Earl of Leicester, into a home for twelve poor brethren. Over the doorway is the bear and ragged staff, the emblem of the once powerful Earls of Warwick.*

and timbered Elizabethan out-buildings all go to justify its reputation as one of the finest moated granges in the country. Great Tangley Manor is a moated timbered house, whose timbering takes the form of gracious panels with strong curved braces. Two other moated houses, each having the E-shaped design favoured in Elizabeth's reign, are Rushbrooke Hall and Kentwell Hall, both in Suffolk. The mitred turrets and embayed windows of Melford Hall in the same county are evidence of the Elizabethans' desire for architectural grace, and of their love of light which led Bacon to write grumblingly of "houses so full of glass that we cannot tell where to come to be out of the sun or the cold." Later, in 1696, a window tax was devised, and today old farm-houses of this period may be seen with their windows bricked up—a relic of this hated tax.

Suffolk is rich in smaller Tudor dwellings also. The village of Lavenham has many timbered houses which date from the fifteenth and sixteenth centuries when Lavenham was a thriving centre of the cloth trade. Some of these were occupied by Flemish weavers, who decorated English timberwork with the emblematic fleur-de-lys. The ancient Guildhall in the market-place is a beautiful specimen of a timber-framed building, and was originally the hall of one of the cloth guilds—the Guild of Corpus Christi.

### Elizabethan Kent

The same timbered graciousness marks the Kentish village of Chiddingstone, which is near Penshurst, where Sir Philip Sydney lived, and where Edmund Spenser, his friend, wrote the *Shepherd's Calendar.* The neighbouring Hever Castle was the home of Anne Boleyn. The village public-house, now named the " Henry the Eighth," at one time bore the sign of the "Boleyn Butchered "—a bold indication of local feeling. The village takes its name from the Chiding Stone, a natural pulpit formed by a mass of sandstone from which, in the time of the Puritans, itinerant preachers harangued the people.

In Cheshire both towns and villages are remarkable for the number of their half-timbered houses belonging to the Tudor and Stuart period. In the famous Rows of Chester itself, many of the houses and shops are of Tudor timberwork whose carving is particularly rich. Brereton in its " Bear's Head " and Sandbach in its Old Hall possess two of the most superb black and white timbered inns in the country.

Shropshire also has a wealth of " magpie " houses. Those of Shrewsbury are especially picturesque with their gables, king-posts and carvings; while the old market house standing on its open arcade is typically Elizabethan. So too is Ludlow's very beautiful Feathers Inn, which has the additional interest that its carved ceilings and panels belong to Stuart times. With its many half-timbered buildings, its Reader's House and its Butter Cross, Ludlow is architecturally a lovely place.

Where stone was available locally, Elizabethan and Stuart builders made use of it in preference to timber. Thus the Cotswold villages are built of stone from the quarries in the hills. Their manor houses are some of the loveliest in England. The grey stone of their roofs and walls glows with a tinge of ochre. The line of their dormers and oriels is very beautiful.

As with such lovely villages as Guiting Power, Temple Guiting, Broadway, Stanton and Stanway, Willersley and Mickleton, so with the towns. Chipping Campden's main street is full of stately sixteenth- and early seventeenth-century houses with fine mullioned windows and shapely gables. Carved doorheads; ancient mural sundials; a picturesque Market Hall; old stone-tiled roofs, and, crowning them, chimneys beautiful in their grouping: all these make up a picture memorable for its mellow beauty.

The marked changes in English architecture which took place in the sixteenth and seventeenth centuries were symbolic of a social change. Feudalism had ended. The massive walls and battlements of the medieval castle had lost favour with a people that asked for more light and more comfort—for the social equivalent of the grace of an Elizabethan hall.

Politically Charles I and James II stood for the medieval castle. The one lost his head and the other his throne. By their follies they helped to further English political freedom. From the anonymous carpenters, carvers, joiners and stone-cutters whose skilled craftsmanship was responsible for the Elizabethan hall, our own age has that other legacy—a legacy of beauty in timber and in stone.

STEPHENSON

**BEAUTIFUL BLACK AND WHITE WORK IN WILTSHIRE**
*The little village of Potterne, near Devizes, displays in its main street these picturesque old buildings which have endured for centuries. The house on the left is now known as the Porch House, and in bygone days may have been the Pack Horse Inn. It has been most carefully restored, and has a beautiful dining-room.*

# THE STORY OF PLACE-NAMES

## by P. H. REANEY

BEHIND our place-names lies many an interesting story, and many a curious fragment of history and evidence of the various peoples who have overrun these isles. Most of our village names are English; some carry us back to the Romans and their predecessors the Celts, and others are Scandinavian or French.

Place-names are simply words. They were formed in accordance with the normal habits of speech of those who gave them and they must be interpreted according to the known laws of the grammar of the particular language concerned.

Very rarely, indeed, is the modern spelling of a place-name a guide to its etymology. Oxford, it is true, was the place where oxen forded the river, and most Newtons and Newingtons were " new farms," but it is a safe rule that the earliest spellings of the name must be known before any attempt is made at an explanation. Langham usually means " the long village or homestead," but the place of that name in Lincolnshire was *Langholm*, " the long island," whilst Langham, in Essex, was earlier *Lawingeham* and *Leingeham*. Langton is normally " the long *tun*, farm or village," but Langton, in Durham, was *Langadun* in 1050, " the long *dun* or hill," whilst Tur Langton (Leicestershire) is written Terlintone in Domesday Book, " the village of Tyrhtel's or Tyrli's people." Place-names often contain personal-names, and these have frequently undergone considerable simplification. Chelmsford was formerly *Celmeresfort* " Ceolmær's ford," Isleworth was *Gislheresuuyrth* in A.D. 695 " the *worth* or homestead of Gislhere."

When Cæsar invaded Britain he found the island occupied by Celtic tribes akin to those of Belgium and northern France. The only names of places he mentions are Thames and Kent, both of Celtic origin. For other names we have to wait nearly a hundred years, for the Roman Conquest and occupation, but many of the Celtic names, which we find latinized in Roman history, must have been in existence before the time of Cæsar.

Many of the river-names still survive, e.g., Thames, " dark river," Lea, either " the bright river " or " the river dedicated to the god Lugus," Esk, Axe and Exe " water," Darent, Dart and

### CASTLE OF PEVERIL OF THE PEAK

*The pleasing little village of Castleton, in Derbyshire, takes its name from the famous castle of Peveril of the Peak, which is finely placed on a precipitous limestone crag a little south of the village. Today the small Norman keep is almost all that remains of the castle which was originally built by William Peveril in 1068.*

PHOTOCHROM

STEPHENSON

### A QUIET HAMLET IN SURREY

*Leigh, or Lye, as it is locally known, a village in the valley of the Mole, near Reigate, takes its name from an old English word meaning an open place in a wood.   The village today consists of not much more than the fifteenth-century church, a school, an inn and a few houses pleasantly arranged round the green.*

Derwent " oak stream," Tyne " water, river," etc.  Most of these names are difficult to interpret and quite a number seem to mean simply "water." But some rivers have English names, e.g. Wensum and Wantsum " the winding one," Sheaf " the boundary " between Yorkshire and Derbyshire, whilst still others, like the Cumbrian Greta " the stony one," are Scandinavian.

#### Boar-village

Perhaps the most interesting example of the transformations undergone by a Celtic name is that of York.  The Celtic name, probably associated with yew trees, was latinized as *Eboracum*. This was modified by Saxon lips into *Eoforwic*, which looks like a good English compound " boar-village."   Then came the Danes who adopted the name, but with their own pronunciation.  Just as they pronounced *eorl* " earl " as " jarl," so they turned the name into *Iorvik*. This came to be pronounced *Yorick*, and was later written Iork, pronounced very much like the modern York.  Thus the name is a history of the district in miniature.

It has long been recognized that the oldest type of Saxon place-name ended in *-ingas* (now *-ing*) a plural ending usually added to the name of a man to denote his sons, then by a natural extension, his descendants, and later, all those dependent on him, his followers.  A name such

as *Readingas* (Reading) was originally not the name of a place but of a number of individuals, the sons or descendants or followers of *Reada*. Later, the name of the people was given to the place where they lived.  Similarly Hastings meant either the sons or descendants or followers of *Hæsta*.  But we know that the *Hæstingas* were a tribe of some importance occupying a district much more extensive than the modern Hastings, and including Hastingford, in Hadlow Down, in Sussex, and probably Hastingleigh, in Kent. Clearly we cannot regard the whole of the tribe as Hæsta's descendants, and names of this kind point clearly to early communities of Saxon invaders, sometimes, perhaps, of a ship's company or of larger groups who remained with their victorious leader and settled together on the land they had conquered.  A further indication that we are concerned with groups of settlers rather than with a hero's family is given by such names as Epping " the upland dwellers," Blything " the dwellers on the banks of the River Blyth," and Nazeing " the dwellers on the *ness* or spur of land."

Names of this type are most frequent in the east and south-east of England, and are rare or absent in the west.  We have thus a clear indication that in the first tide of invasion the Saxon conquerors settled in communities under their leaders on the lands they had won.  After they had consolidated their victory, the colonization of the country farther west was of a different kind, the steady penetration of enemy or unoccupied country by adventurous pioneers or settlement under the protection of victorious kings steadily extending their territory. And here names of a different type occur.

Perhaps only a little later than names in -ing are those in -ingham. They occur generally in the same districts, are situated in easily accessible river valleys or on Roman roads, and as a rule are names of old villages and parishes. They too, point to a settlement by groups of communities and possess the same two types as names in -ing : Walsingham (Norfolk) and Immingham (Lincs) " home or village of the followers of Wæls and Imma " respectively ; and Uppingham " village of the upland dwellers," Greetingham (Suffolk) " village of the dwellers in a sandy or gravelly district."

Another very common Saxon suffix was -tun " enclosure, homestead, village," but it is difficult to draw safe general conclusions from its occurrence. Names ending in -tun were formed throughout the Anglo-Saxon period, and this element is no safe criterion of early settlement. That it was in very early use is proved by the case of Nottingham, and the not far distant Sneinton. These were originally Snotingaham and Snotingatun respectively " the ham and the tun of Snot's people." Sneinton was originally an -ingtun name and must date from about the same period as Nottingham.

Many -tun names denoted farms belonging to an individual, e.g., Balderston (Lancs) "Baldhere's farm" Elston (Notts), " Ælfwig's farm." Some point to women as land owners, e.g., Abberton (Essex) " Eadburg's farm," Harvington (Worc.) " Herewynn's farm." Some of these names are late, and the individual after whom the farm was named can be identified. East Garston (Berks), for example, was formerly Esegareston " the farm of Esgar," a Berkshire landholder in 1066. Castleton (Derbyshire) is even later, for it was named after Peveril of the Peak, builder of the castle, and in Domesday Book is called simply castellum Willelmi Peveril.

### The Farm on the Lea

Not all names in -ham are as early as those in -ingham. We have the same types as for names in -ton, e.g., individual owners, Petersham (Surrey) " Peohtric's homestead," women owners, Babraham (Cambs) " Beaduburg's farm," etc., and also others in which the first element is a descriptive or topographical term. Just as we find Leyton " the farm on the Lea," numerous Nortons and Middletons, so we have Farnhams and Highams, named from the bracken in the neighbourhood or from their high position. But here a further difficulty arises as the modern -ham corresponds to two Anglo-Saxon words, ham " village, estate, homestead," our " home," and hamm " meadow, especially a flat, low-lying meadow on the banks of a stream " and also " an enclosure," so that Higham may mean either " the high village " or " the high enclosure."

These names ending in -ing, -ham and -ton give

EDGAR WARD

A PICTURESQUE CORNER IN AN OXFORDSHIRE VILLAGE

*Many places gained their names from the nature of the country or from the kind of crops they produced. The village of Wheatley, on the old coach road from London to Oxford, is an obvious reference to the fact that wheat was grown in the ley, or open country among the many woods that are around the village.*

us, then on the whole, a good general idea of the oldest sites occupied by the Saxons. Terminations such as *-field*, *-hay*, *-leigh* or *-ley*, on the other hand, throw some light on the nature of the country in the days of the Saxons, and how they gradually pushed out from their earliest settlements and, as the population increased, gradually occupied the less desirable sites and cleared away much of the dense forest with which the land was covered. The old English *-feld* meant " open country, land free from wood," and is particularly common in old forest districts. The first element may be descriptive, Benfield or Bentfield " open country covered with bent-grass," Clanfield " clean open country," denoting an absence of thorn-bushes and thick under-growth or may refer to the pasturing of sheep or cattle as in Sheffield and Rotherfield. Occasionally, through French influence, the term appears as *-ville*, Enville (Staffs) " smooth *feld*," Caville (Yorks) " jackdaw *feld*," and Clanville (Hants) identical with Clanfield.

Lea, Lee, Leigh and the terminations *-ley*, *-lay*, all derive from old English *leah*, meaning originally " an open place in a wood," " a glade," as in Farley and Farnley " fern," Farsley " furze," etc. Graveley, Groveley and Woodleigh point clearly to the meaning " glade in a grove or wood," and the kind of tree most common in the district is often indicated as in Acle and Ockley (oaks), Bartley and Birchley (birches), etc. In these glades horses were pastured (at Horseleigh and Studley), calves at Callaly, and Chawleigh, goats at Gatley and Raleigh, and pigs at Loseley. Wilder animals were often found in the wood : wild cats (Catley), wild boars (Barley, Borley, Everley, Eversley), and wolves (Woolley, Woolfly) ; deer were common (Hartley, Darley, Durleigh), and dogs (Whelpley). This stretch of open country in the wood often came to be cultivated and produced crops of wheat (Wheatley) flax (Linley) and barley, whilst from the surrounding wood were cut staves, poles and stocks which were used for the construction of bridges, houses and churches (Staveley, Stockleigh, Yardley).

### Heathen Gods

Another term commonly found in old wood-land areas is *hay* " an enclosure," and names containing this element help us to trace the gradual clearing of the forest and the establishment of a settled agriculture. Many of these names are descriptive of the early state of the enclosure : Tryndehayes (circular), Likely and Lilly (small), Roffey, Rolphy, Roughway and Rowney (rough), or of the animals kept there : Cownhayne (cows), Chalvey, Chaffhay (calves), Yorney (ewes), and Fairy (pigs).

Centuries of Christianity have failed to oust from our daily vocabulary the names of heathen

STEPHENSON

BEAUTIFUL VILLAGE WITH PAGAN NAME

*In a glade draped with lofty pine trees lies the lovely Surrey hamlet of Friday Street. The still pond reflecting the trees and the few houses which comprise the village harmonize in a delightful picture. It takes its name from the Anglo-Saxon deity Frig or Frea. Other places of the same name occur in Lancashire and Suffolk.*

EDGAR WARD

### A VILLAGE IN THE CHILTERNS

*Stokenchurch, a village in the Chilterns where an annual horse fair is still held, and where gipsies frequently congregate on the green, is an old-time place, the inhabitants of which are chiefly engaged in the local chair industry. It probably takes its name from its original church being built of stocks or planks.*

gods worshipped by the Saxons on their first coming to this island. Tig, Woden, Thunor and Frig we still commemorate in Tuesday, Wednesday, Thursday and Friday. Thunor, god of thunder, who governed thunder and lightning, winds and rains, fair weather and crops, was once worshipped at Thundersley, in Essex, Thursley, in Surrey, and Tig, god of war, at Tysoe in Warwickshire, and Tuesley, in Surrey, and Woden, at Wednesfield.

Places such as Harrow-on-the-Hill, Harrowbank (Durham), and Peper Harrow (Surrey), were often sites of heathen temples, whilst sacred groves or clearings containing either idols or a shrine once existed at Weyhill (Hants), Patchway (Sussex), and Willey (Surrey). These and similar names must date back to a very early period of the settlement before the introduction of Christianity to this country, when heathen beliefs were strong and flourishing.

An interesting group of names ending in -*head*, preceded by the name of an animal, where " head " can only rarely be associated with a topographical feature, may very probably be relics of the time when the place was the site of bloody sacrifice in which the head of some man or animal was offered to a heathen deity. Such names are Manshead, Farcet (bull), Gateshead (goat), Swineshead, Ramshead, Rampside (ram's head), Broxted and Broxhead (badger).

But Christianity has itself left its mark on our place-names. Many places take their name from their church, and some of these names throw light on the appearance and architecture of Saxon churches. The various Whitchurches were probably so called because built of stone. Bradkirk, in Lancashire, and Berechurch, in Essex, were made of *bredes* or planks and Stokenchurch, in Oxfordshire, of stocks, perhaps half-oak timbers similar to those still to be found at Greensted, in Essex, whilst Felkirk in the West Riding is a Scandinavian name of the same meaning. Frome Vauchurch, in Dorsetshire, and Vowchurch, in Herefordshire, like the Scottish Falkirk, were speckled or variegated churches, perhaps half-timbered black and white buildings such as still exist in Cheshire.

#### Church Owners

The Saxon church was often regarded as a profit-making appurtenance to an estate, and the " owner " could grant it to a clerk in terms similar to those used in granting a mill. This one-time owner's name sometimes persists as part of the name of the place. Offchurch, in Warwickshire, is " Offa's church," and Buckminster, in Leicestershire, is " Bucca's minster." Alvechurch, in Worcestershire, was owned by a woman, Ælfgyth, whilst in Layston (Herts), originally " Leofstan's church," the " church "

EDGAR WARD

### VILLAGE OF CELTIC ORIGIN
*The Oxfordshire village of Dorchester in Saxon times was the centre of a bishopric. Its name, however, takes us much farther back. It is probably derived from the Celtic " Doric," meaning " the bright or splendid place." As there was a Roman station there the Saxons added " ceaster," so the name became Dorceceaster.*

has been lost, and we are left solely with the owner's name.

Means of communication have always been of importance, and in days of political instability and of powerful and lawless landowners, travel was often a thrilling and perilous adventure. The importance of the Roman roads is clearly shewn by the numerous place-names containing Old English *stræt*, a loan-word from Latin (*via*) *strata* "a paved road," in its various forms, Stradbrook, Stratton, Stretton and Sturton, Stratford and Stretford, and in the less common Trafford, Startforth and Strefford.

Numerous names of importance ending in *-ford* call to mind one of the difficulties of travel. The building of bridges was a mark of progress, and *ford* is much more frequent than *bridge* in names of places. These fords were often named from the animals that used them (Oxford, Shefford, Swinford). At Stapleford the crossing was marked by a post or posts ; at Bamford there was a beam or footbridge by the side of the ford as there still is in some parts of the country today ; often we have reference to the trees growing by the ford (Alderford, Widford " willow ") and frequently the name enshrines that of a former owner who charged toll for crossing.

On the much debated question of the extermination of the Britons by the Saxons, place-names can throw some interesting light. In Old English,

*Wealas* meant in the first place " Britons," but was also used of serfs. The word undoubtedly occurs in a number of place-names, and whether these refer to serfs or Britons matters little, for such Celts as survived would be slaves. Wales in the West Riding, near which is Waleswood, like names in *-ing*, was originally the name of the people which later became that of the place.

#### Surviving Britons

There can be little doubt that groups of Britons survived in most parts of the country, usually in the less attractive parts, and many of their habitations can be traced in such names as Walcot, Walton and Walden, and in the less frequent Walmer, Walworth and Wallasey. But not all such names belong here. Many, like the Cumbrian Walby, owe their names to their position near some wall, here the Roman Wall, sometimes sea-walls or other defences. Villages of Britons also existed among the neighbouring Scandinavians at Birkby in the North Riding, and at two places of the same name in Cumberland.

The invaders from the Continent who overwhelmed the Britons are usually said to have consisted of Angles, Saxons and Jutes. But there is evidence on the map for the inclusion of Frisians and Swabians among them. Freston and Friston, in Suffolk, the two Friestons and Friesthorpe, in Lincolnshire, and Frisby, in

Leicestershire, were all villages of the Frisians, whilst the Swabians settled at Swaffham in Cambridgeshire and Norfolk.

Of the Vikings and the Danelaw we all know, but much interesting information can be derived from place-names which has not yet reached the school history books. Not all the Scandinavian invaders were Danes. Many were Norsemen or Norwegians, and many of these invaded the north-western counties from Ireland where they had lived long enough to be half-Celticized. They adopted Celtic words and names and formed their patronymics by the use of the Celtic *Mac* instead of the Norse *-son* (e.g., Thorfynn MacThore). Dovenby, in Cumberland, Melkinthorpe, in Westmorland, Becconsall, in Lancashire, Commondale, in Yorkshire and Corsenside, in Northumberland, are all Scandinavian names containing a Celtic personal-name.

### Celtic and Norse

They had adopted Celtic habits of speech, too, and formed many of their compounds in the Celtic way, e.g., Aspatria, earlier *Ascpatric* "Patrick's ash-tree," Kirkoswald and Kirkandrews, "St. Oswald's and St. Andrew's church," Setmurthey "Murdac's shieling" (all in Cumberland), Brigsteer (Westmorland) "Styr's bridge," in all of which we have the Celtic order, the reverse of the Norse and the English. Note,

too, that Patrick and Murdac are Celtic personal-names, whilst in all, the first element is Scandinavian.

These Norwegians spread to other districts, and we can trace their settlements among Danes and Anglians by places named after Irishmen and Northmen. Such a name as "village of the Irish," or of the Norwegians would have no meaning unless the majority of the inhabitants of the district were of another race, and so we find their scattered settlements at Irby, Ireleth, Irton, and Normanby.

Settlements of Danes among a preponderatingly Anglian community can similarly be traced by such names as Danby, Danthorpe, Denaby, Denby and Denny. Many names, however, beginning with *Dan-* or *Den-* have other origins. Ingleby and Ingleton were isolated colonies of Englishmen in a thoroughly Scandinavianized district.

The Scandinavian element is particularly strong in Yorkshire, Lincolnshire, Leicestershire, Nottinghamshire, Rutland and the Lake District, also in Norfolk, parts of Derbyshire, Northamptonshire, Durham and Cheshire. Elsewhere it is on the whole slight. Names of Danish origin are those containing *thorp* "hamlet," *both* "booth" and *hulm* "holm." Norwegian testwords are *breck* "hill, hillside," *buth* "booth," *gill, slack* "valley," *scale* "hut." Other common

STEPHENSON

#### A YORKSHIRE ABBEY WITH NORMAN NAME

*In the green vale of the Rye in north-east Yorkshire was founded in 1131 a Cistercian abbey, the ruins of which are " so exquisitely graceful, so humble, silent and deathlike—the very image of a bygone age." Instead of the English name the monks used a Norman-French one and today the place is known as Rievaulx.*

DIXON-SCOTT

BIRTHPLACE OF JOHN BUNYAN

*The little village of Elstow was the birthplace of the famous author of " Pilgrim's Progress," and it was on the village green he had the vision which led to his conversion. The ancient Moot Hall, seen above, was for many years used by his followers. The name Elstow is said to mean the " place where alder trees grow."*

Scandinavian elements, common to both Danes and Norsemen, are *by* " village," *toft* " home stead," *thwaite* " clearing," *garth* " enclosure," *fell* " hill," *lund* " grove," *beck, tarn, gate,* " road, street."

The interpretation of Scandinavian place-names in England is not an easy task. Some of the names are purely Scandinavian, containing Scandinavian inflexions, others were English names adapted to Scandinavian habits of speech ; some are hybrids. Amounderness, Beckermet, etc., contain the Scandinavian genitive in -*ar*, Skelton and Skipton are Scandinavianized forms of the English Shelton and Shipton, Keswick and Kildwick of Chiswick and Childwick.

### Norman Influence

The influence on our place-names of the last great cataclysm in our history—the Norman Conquest—was of a different kind. The Romano-British civilization had been swept away in the dark days of the Saxon invasions. England became Teutonic instead of Celtic. Danes and Norsemen were Teutonic too. They were akin to the Saxons ; their language was akin. In the districts where they settled they imposed their customs, and for a time their language, but gradually a mixed Anglo-Scandinavian dialect arose which ultimately gave way to English with a strong Scandinavian admixture.

The two races fused, but there is still a marked difference between Saxon and Scandinavian England. The dialects of the north have borrowed much from the conquerors. There we still have ridings, wapentakes and bierlows, Scandinavian institutions and administrative divisions and agricultural terms. This Scandinavian settlement was a lasting contribution to the development of English life, but its influence affected only part of the country.

The Norman Conquest, on the other hand, imposed Norman rule on the whole country. Apart from the harrying of the north, there was no great devastation. The peasant suffered a change of master, and in turn compelled his conqueror to become English. By a wise stroke of genius the shires, hundreds and parishes were left untouched and, in spite of manifold changes, the impression left on the modern map by the Normans is much less than that of the Scandinavian names. Occasionally a French name has ousted the English as at Beaumont, in Essex, where the English *Fulepet* " the filthy hollow " was replaced by the more pleasant French " beautiful hill." Or as at Virley in the same county, where the Saxon Salcott had attached to it the name of its Domesday Lord, Robert de Verli, and from Salcott Virley came to be called simply Virley.

Apart from such changes, Norman influence is

to be seen in the names of castles and monasteries founded by Normans who frequently transferred to them names with which they had been familiar in France. Of the four great fortresses on the Welsh border, two, Montgomery and Caus, were named from places in Normandy. The others, Mold (*Mons Altus*, *Mo haut*) " the lofty mount," and Grosmont " the big mount " were descriptive of their sites. The monasteries of Jervaulx and Rievaulx were named from the valleys of the rivers in which they were situated, the Ure and the Rye ; Vaudey is " the valley dedicated to God," Kirmond " goat hill " the equivalent of the French Chevremont and Quevremont.

The intensive feudalization of the country led to the need for new names for new holdings, and in the north and south-west we find the English *tun* and the Scandinavian *by* still in use, but now compounded with Norman names. Aglionby (Cumb.) was held by Lawrence, son of Agyllun, in the twelfth century, Ponsonby (Cumb.) by John, son of Puncun, in 1177 ; in the North Riding Jolby owes its name to a Joel living about 1170, and Halnaby to one Halnath about 1200. In the south-western counties we find such names as Forston, in Dorset, earlier *Forsardeston* from William Forsard 1285, Quarlston from William Quarel 1303, and in Devon, Chenson from Thomas Cheygny 1346 and Corstone from Peter Corbin 1240.

In the south-east Norman influence around London was particularly strong. In Essex some dozen Saxon names were ousted by those of their Norman holders. *Alfereston* became Bigods and *Richeham* Culvert's Farm. Thirteen names, too, such as Fowe's Farm, Pointwell Mill and Spain's Hall, are derived from Domesday landholders, and numerous others from later feudal lords.

But perhaps the most obvious result of Norman influence is that class of picturesque compound names in which a Norman family name, often much changed, is added to an English village-name in such delightful combinations as Huish Champflower, Layer de la Haye, Sampford Courtenay, Norton Curlieu and Stoke Bliss.

### Wonderful Collection of Names

And so we must leave this study of our place-names. Celt, Roman, Saxon, Dane, Norwegian, Norman—all have contributed to that wonderful collection of names that have become as much a part of our heritage as the countryside they adorn. But much has been left unsaid. Flemings and Huguenots have made their contribution. Baldock, in Hertfordshire, is the French name for Bagdad, brought from the east by the Knights Templars. And what of those places within our shores with such names as Antioch, Egypt, Jerusalem and Jericho? The map of England is, indeed, the most wonderful of all palimpsests.

EDGAR WARD

### LOVELY RIVER WITH ANCIENT NAME

*It is principally in the names of natural features that the old Celtic place-names have survived. Rivers such as the Darent, the numerous Derwents and the Dart, seen in the picture, are believed to derive their names from the Celtic* dwr, *meaning water. The photograph depicts the River Dart at Dartmeet Bridge, Devon.*

DIXON-SCOTT

## CATHEDRAL OF AN ANCIENT SEE

*Llandaff Cathedral, near Cardiff, claims to serve the oldest see in the kingdom, which was founded, according to tradition, in A.D. 547 by St. Teilo. The present building, of twelfth- to thirteenth-century origin, is unique in that it has no transepts. The triforium, a feature of the thirteenth-century design, is also missing.*

# WILD WALES

## by I. O. EVANS

WESTWARDS of England lies the mountainous, valley-pierced, wave-beaten land of Wales. Though small in size it is unequalled in its beauty and charm. Its mountains are higher than any that England can show, its valleys more beautiful, its coastline more rugged. Round its shores are islands, one a county in itself, others bare rocks just peeping above the tide. It is a land older than its larger neighbour to the east—it is without doubt literally true that the mountains of Wales were immeasurably old when the chalk that forms the Downs and Salisbury Plain was a mere ooze on the bed of the ocean.

If the land itself is older, so equally are its people. The original inhabitants of the British Isles, the swarthy Iberians from the Mediterranean, have left their descendants among them. So, too, have the conquering Celts and the Gaels. Its people traded with the sea-farers of far Phœnicia, exchanging for the products of civilization tin and the spoils of the chase. Its people built the great monuments found all over the land, from great Stonehenge and Avebury to the smaller dolmen and menhir, the Druid's Circle of Keswick and Kit's Coty House of Kent. Its people for a time held at bay even the might of Rome, and were only conquered after a fierce resistance. Its people, later, resisted no less fiercely the Saxon invaders, the Danish pirates, and the raiding Irish bands. When all England was subject to Norman rule, the inhabitants of Wales still for many years remained free.

The " Ancient Britons," as we are accustomed to call them, were by no means the uncouth barbarians whom Cæsar describes, clad only in a coat of blue paint and burning their prisoners alive. We know nowadays just how much faith can be placed in the narrative of a military commander, anxious to " civilize " outlying tribes at the sword's point ! The people who could transport and build Stonehenge, who could cover the countryside with a system of well-surveyed straight tracks, who could hold at bay the Roman legions, were certainly not backward in the arts of life. None the less the Britons learned much from the Romans who conquered them ; when the legions departed they took over something of the tradition of Roman rule, striving to keep at bay the hordes of English who were invading their land.

Fiercely fighting, the Britons were pressed into the highlands of the west and north. At last the *Cymry* (" comrades ") were cut off by the English of Wales, first from those of Cornwall, and then from those of Strathclyde. Yet they were not subdued; Offa's Dyke remains to tell us of the efforts that were made by the rulers of England to keep in bounds the race whose country they had seized. Even the Normans could only hold them at bay by a chain of stern and forbidding strongholds.

Valiant in war, the Cymry were not unskilled in the arts of peace. Their bards had devised elaborate poetic forms, had composed works that would certainly attract attention had they been written not in Welsh but in English. Their Druids formed a mystical priesthood, the secrets of which have not been revealed ; their lore, it

W. F. TAYLOR

### AN EDWARDIAN CASTLE

*Beaumaris Castle, Anglesey, founded by Edward I in 1293, is now a picturesque ruin with fragments of the gatehouses, the Great Hall and oratory still standing. In 1646 it was surrendered to the Parliament forces.*

has been claimed, challenges comparison both in age and in depth with that of ancient Egypt.

Not a county in Wales but is associated with what is romantic—with some gallant episode of history or some imaginative piece of legendary lore. Richest perhaps in such memories is *Môn Mam Cymri*, " Mon the Mother of Wales," which the Romans called Mona and the English Anglesey. It earned its title of the Motherland of Wales, perhaps because of its fertility, feeding with its crops the folk of the barren mountain regions on the mainland, perhaps because it was the Sacred Island, the centre of bardic tradition. Only when the Romans had conquered it did

mighty bounds. . . . Returned from the wars he found that his wife, supposing him dead, had married one of his rivals. Einion first, in the guise of a harper, composed a song reproaching her for her forgetfulness, and then ejected his rival and claimed her for his own.

If Anglesey was the stronghold of Wales, one of its warlike outposts is Lleyn, the peninsula which juts out westwards from North Wales into the Irish Sea. It was easily invaded by the Irish, who conquered it and who have left the remains of their camps to show how they dominated the folk of the land. Here died Vortigern, whom tradition holds responsible for the invasion of

W. F. TAYLOR

### AN ANCIENT PRIORY

*Penmon Priory, in the north-eastern corner of Anglesey, is said to have been founded in the seventh century. Later it became an Augustinian monastery, and the nave and transept of the cruciform church are Norman. The Prior's Lodging is now a farmhouse, and other remains include the refectory and a dovecot.*

they feel their hold on Wales was secure. Many are the cromlechs and menhirs to be found on its surface, monuments whose purpose we can only guess. It was the sacred land of the Druids and when they had departed it was no less sacred to the Holy Men of the Christian church ; so numerous are their bones in the soil of their burial place, Puffin Island, that the rabbits turn them up.

Yet there are lighter associations to Mona's Isle. Three stones near Red Wharf Bay mark the Three Leaps by which Einion, Lord of Trefeilir, won his bride. So many were her suitors that they had to *leap* for her—and the victor was Einion, who covered fifty feet in three

Britain by the Angles and Saxons and Jutes. He asked their help to drive away the Picts and Scots —and then discovered too late that they had come to stay. The disgusted Britons turned against him, and he was burned in the Irish fort of Tre'r Ceiri where he had sought refuge.

Of another ruler of Lleyn, King March, it is related that he had horse's ears ! To silence his barbers, he used to kill them and bury their bodies in a marsh, but as soon as a pipe was made from its reeds its notes broadcasted his affliction to the world. This monarch was none other than the husband of Iseult, who eloped with Tristram in a manner familiar to all opera-goers. More fortunate was his grandson, who made a

STEPHENSON

### SUNSET OVER SNOWDON

*From Capel Curig the narrow moorland road to Pen-y-Gwryd runs alongside these lakes in which are often mirrored the splendid peaks of Snowdon. The mountain as seen from this side appears as a group of individual heights arranged around the great " Horse-shoe " of Cwm Dyli. In the centre of the photograph is the double crest of Lliwedd. Y Wyddfa, the highest point (3,560 feet) is hidden in the clouds on the right.*

VALENTINE

### CAERNARVON'S HISTORIC STRONGHOLD

*Most elaborate of Welsh fortresses, this famous castle was begun in 1285 by Edward I. It was not completed until 1322 in the reign of Edward II. This monarch was born at Caernarvon where, it will be remembered, as an infant he was presented to the Welsh, in 1284, as a Prince of Wales who could speak no English.*

friend of the birds, feeding them with scraps of meat out of his hand. When a prisoner in the Holy Land, the legend goes, he called to the birds and in gratitude they flew away with him and carried him home to the land of the Cymry.

Not merely the highest and most beautiful part of Wales, but its stronghold and fastness is the mountain-pass of Eryri—or, as the Saxons call it, Snowdonia. Pressed by the invader, the fierce mountain warriors could retreat into its recesses ; the pressure released, they could sweep from the ravines to descend upon some undefended castle or unwary camp. It was here that Llewelyn, the last native Prince of Wales, held out against Edward I, here that he rallied his forces in readiness for the final battle he never lived to lead. No longer stronghold or fortress, no longer, with its threefold peak, the sacred mountain of the Druid, Snowdon still draws through its beauty and grandeur travellers from all over the world. The summit, by tradition, is never completely free from cloud ; and sometimes the wayfarer may see, thrown by the sunlight on the mists below, his own shadow, magnified and enhaloed like the spectres of Germany's Brocken.

The difficulty the English felt in subduing the region is shown by the castles that surround it ; Conway and Harlech may with some reason be claimed as the finest in the world. " Every schoolboy knows" the story of Caernarvon Castle, whether it be historical or not, how Edward I promised to the assembled chieftains of Wales that he would give them a prince born in their own country who could not speak a word of English—and then how he fulfilled his word by triumphantly producing his baby son, cradled inside a shield. According to the early chroniclers, the chiefs received the harmless joke in good spirit, feeling that the young king born among them would wish them well ; and, indeed, until his tragic end he showed sympathy with " his countrymen," strove to remedy their grievances and gave them their own law.

### Greatest of Welsh Bards

Conway lives in Welsh story not so much for its castles as for the stream on which it stands. On its waters, 1,500 years ago, was found floating a leather-covered coracle, and in the coracle was a young child. This was no other than Taliesin, the greatest of the Welsh bards. For the bards of old were indeed great ; they were held as of equal rank to a king, of equal holiness to a priest, and among their tunes were traditional

STEPHENSON

### CLOUDS ON THE CARNEDDS
*Carnedd Dafydd and Carnedd Llewelyn, the bulky round heights rising from the vale of the Llugwy, are second only in height to Snowdon, Llewelyn being 3,484 feet. The photograph was taken above the Devil's Kitchen, near Ogwen, looking across Nant Ffrancon Pass to Pen yr Olwen, a southern spur of the Carnedds.*

DIXON-SCOTT

### HOME OF LOST CAUSES
*Harlech Castle was the last fortress in Britain to hold out for the House of Lancaster in 1468, and the last in Wales to surrender to the Cromwellians over two hundred years later. In the early fifteenth century, Owen Glendower reigned for four years as Prince of Wales before Harry of Monmouth captured Harlech.*

"triads," threefold sentences of mystic meaning from the Druid lore. They strung their harps with human hair, and played them with their sharpened finger-nails.

The harp, so the Triads tell us, was the invention of a giant of old, Idris Gawr, himself a bard and skilled in the knowledge of the stars. His chair, or throne, is the mountain of Cader Idris, steeply rising to the south of the Snowdon range. Whoever sleeps in his chair will awake next morning either a madman or else an inspired bard.

Cader Idris overlooks Cardigan Bay, the site of one of those lost lands of which Welsh legend is rich. Off the north coast are other regions said to have been fertile land, with towns and valleys, where the sea now flows, and more than one of the beautiful Welsh lakes is believed to cover with its waters a township now lost. To catch a glimpse of the city plunged beneath Llangorse Lake is a sign of impending death, but no such grim warning attaches to the *Cantref y Gwaelod*, the "lost hundred" hidden by the waves of Cardigan Bay. The bells of Aberdovey, immortalized in a well-known song, give a message not of destruction but of peace.

Idris Gawr, Idris the Great, is not the only legendary figure whose name is associated with the shores of Cardigan Bay. At the Twr (tower) Bronwen, where Harlech Castle stands today, dwelt Bran the Blessed, the hero of a poem by

Taliesin the Bard. To him was given, by a giant, a witch, and a dwarf, a bowl or caldron, with strange and wonderful powers. Its touch healed every ill and restored the dead to life—but left them dumb, lest they should reveal the secrets of the other world. Moreover it bestowed poetic genius, with wisdom and knowledge of the arts and sciences. Bardic lore is full of stories of this mysterious vessel, one of the Thirteen Wonders of Britain's isle.

### A Turbulent Hero
Bran the Blessed led the Welsh against their foes the Irish, and Harlech Castle figured both in those wars and in those which later ravaged the land. Here was summoned one of the last Welsh parliaments, those of Owen Glendower, the turbulent hero of Cymric freedom. Here was fierce fighting during the Wars of the Roses, and here Margaret of Anjou took refuge. Only after a blockade and after great slaughter did Harlech Castle fall to Edward IV, and to this period is attributed that stirring battle song the *March of the Men of Harlech*.

That Owen Glendower, who summoned his Parliament at Harlech, raised his insurrection not idly but in protest against the injustice of English rule. A common which lay near his home at Glyndyfrdwy was unjustly seized by his Norman neighbour, Reginald de Grey of Ruthin Castle.

PHOTOCHROM

### CHAIR OF A MIGHTY GIANT

*Cader Idris, the impressive height near Dolgelly, is the legendary chair of a giant who was even greater in mind than stature.   Composed of volcano rocks, it runs in a long ridge culminating in the precipitous face of Pen-y-Gader (2,927 feet).   The view shows the rocky flanks of the north face and the lake, Lln-y-Gader lying at the foot of the crags.   The Foxes' Path descends the steep screes on the far side of the lake.*

More than that, he was denounced to the king as disobedient and sentenced to be deprived of his lands, and de Grey treacherously tried to capture him during a friendly talk.   Ruined, dispossessed, and outlawed, Glendower proclaimed himself Prince of Wales, and his countrymen flocked to his standard, the Golden Dragon.   He showed himself a skilled and daring leader and a statesman able to negotiate with barons and kings. The common people spread tales of his supernatural powers, and when the camp of the English king was overthrown by a sudden squall, they held that this was the work of the " spirits " his magic could command.   Before he was finally conquered Glendower had made himself the ruler of almost the whole of Wales ; and, suppressed though it was, the revolt showed that the spirit of Welsh freedom was not yet dead.

Although it gave birth to that fiery hero Glendower, the valley of the Dee is one of beauty and peace.   It is a region one would wish not merely to visit but to live in, and two of its inhabitants over a century ago attained almost a national reputation.   These were the " Ladies of Llangollen," who shunned society and scorned married life ; they made their home in this quiet vale, which they barely quitted for

fifty years.   Every traveller of repute who passed through North Wales made a point of visiting them, and they are described in the memoirs of the period as formal and rather mannish in attire, and looking " exactly like the respectable superannuated old clergymen."

To the everyday Englishman Wales means North Wales, the high mountains that centre on Snowdon.   Certainly, with its mountains and with Anglesey, it has some claim to be the most romantic as well as the most beautiful region of Wales, but it by no means forms the whole of the principality.   The districts to its south have charms of their own.

### Bleak Plynlimon

Very different from the craggy heights of Snowdon and Cader Idris, and yet not without appeal in its bleak austere lowliness is Plynlimon. Pumplummon, as it should be called, " the Five Heads," gets its name because it has five summits (beside another supplementary one, Bryn y Llo, " the Hill of the Calf ") ; also from it lead off five rivers, two to travel far afield eastwards and to flow through England before they reach the sea, and the other three to plunge more swiftly westwards to Cardigan Bay.   As Borrow in *Wild*

*Wales* translates for us a Welsh *pennill* (rhyme):
" Oh pleasantly do glide along the Severn and
 the Wye ;
 But Rheidol's rough, and yet he's held by all
 in honour high."

Certainly Rheidol is worthy of honour, for its
course is spanned by a famous ancient monument
of Wales. Built probably by the residents of
Strata Florida, Pont ar Mynach, " the Monk's
Bridge," has a curious legend attached to it. A
Welsh countrywoman was distressed to find that
a ravine had opened in the ground, separating
her from her cattle and her home. A person in
monkish-looking garb suddenly appeared and
offered to span it with a bridge for her, provided
she would give him the first living thing that
crossed it. Of course she accepted, and the
bridge was built—then in the nick of time she
noticed a cloven hoof peeping out from under
his monkish robe. So instead of crossing it herself she threw a crust of bread over the bridge.
Her little dog dashed over it, and the devil
angrily disappeared, no doubt muttering the
Welsh equivalent of " foiled again ! " That gulf
is the gorge of the Rheidol, a place of impressive
beauty that deservedly draws hosts of visitors to
see it ; that bridge is the arch that spans it, Pont
ar Mynach, still sometimes spoken of as " the
Devil's Bridge."

Farther south, in this Ystwyth Valley, lies
Strata Florida, which Baring Gould calls the
Westminster Abbey of Wales. Here were buried
the most noble of the Welsh princes, the most
eloquent of the Welsh bards; here were preserved
the most precious of the Welsh records. Here
was a church over 200 feet long, greater than any
of Cambria's cathedrals—and now reduced to a
mere shattered ruin.

Two historic battles took place in Radnorshire.
At Caer Caradog the British king Caratacus
made his last stand, heroic though vain, against
the Roman conquerors—even the official military
historian, Tacitus, admits that the deciding factor
was the heavy armour of the legionaries compared
with the uncovered bodies and heads of the
" natives." At Pilleth Owen Glendower inflicted
a crushing defeat on the English forces of Sir
Edmund Mortimer.

### A Vanished City

Curious indeed is Llangorse Lake, Llyn
Safaddan, of Breconshire. Not merely is there
beneath its waters one of the vanished cities of
Wales, but its very birds had a magic insight.
On the approach of the rightful Prince of Wales,
so Giraldus Cambrensis informs us, they would
clap their wings and burst into song.

This Giraldus Cambrensis was born, nearly
800 years ago, in Manorbier, Pembrokeshire,
" the fairest spot," he tells us, of the fairest county
of the fairest region of all the lands of Wales.
When Baldwin, Archbishop of Canterbury,

W. F. TAYLOR

" OLD CONWAY'S FOAMING FLOOD "

*So Thomas Gray described the River Conway, here seen in a typical setting near Bettws-y-Coed. Since then
the river and its surroundings have had many admirers. Borrow speaks of " the celebrated Vale of Conway
to which in summer time the fashionable gentry from all parts of Britain resort for shade and relaxation."*

the low-lying lands of Holland to form the Zuyder Zee, a number of the Flemish refugees sought a home in England. Henry I, as a Welsh chronicler nastily puts it, " being very liberal with that which was not his own," gave them southern Pembrokeshire ; and in southern Pembrokeshire their descendants remain even to this day.

This change of population in a rich area may be the theme of a strange Welsh legend. A prince saw one day that all the people of his land had vanished, and that a horde of field-mice was raiding his wheat. He caught one of the mice and erected a gallows to hang it. A scholar, a priest, and a bishop strove to ransom the mouse, and the prince realized that they were no other than the enchanter who had laid the country waste. In return for the mouse his country was re-populated, but not, it seems, with its original inhabitants.

### St. David's

Right in the extreme west of Pembrokeshire stands St. David's, surrounded by the sea on three of its sides, and the only cathedral town in Britain not served by a railway. By tradition it is here that the patron saint of Wales

**STRATA FLORIDA ABBEY**

W. F. TAYLOR

*Founded and endowed by the Lord Rhys in 1164, this Cistercian monastery was for two hundred years the Westminster Abbey of Wales. Today its ruins give but faint indication of its former grandeur, but the ornamentation of the western doorway (above) is said to be architecturally unique.*

travelled through Wales not merely preaching the Crusade but seeking to get the supremacy of Canterbury acknowledged by all four dioceses of Wales, Gerald the Welshman went with him. Part of his job was to be the first to volunteer for crusading if the nobles were slow in coming forward, so as to shame them into " doing their bit " ! This journey he has described in his *Itinerary*, a most interesting book, full not only of strange legends but of descriptions of the scenes and the people among which he passed.

Pembrokeshire, where he was born, is " the Little England beyond Wales. The place-names are English ; the speech is English ; the accent is English ; the appearance of the people is English—throughout almost the whole of south Pembrokeshire (the north and extreme west are Welsh enough). When the sea overwhelmed

was born, and here was one of the earliest centres of British Christianity. For the Gospel was preached and accepted by the British inhabitants of these islands before the coming of the Saxons. Is there not a tradition that it was preached by persons no less than Joseph of Arimathea and St. Paul themselves, the one in the west on the Tor of Glastonbury, the other in the east on the Hill of Ludd? For centuries the Welsh Church was independent of the English, and only very reluctantly did it acknowledge Canterbury's rule.

A curious military episode marks the history of northern Pembrokeshire. During the Napoleonic Wars a thousand odd Frenchmen landed on its coast and advanced on Fishguard, living on the country as they came. The British forces rallied against them, and at the same time a party of Welshwomen gallantly shouldered

VALENTINE

## HOMELAND OF A WELSH HERO

*The Dee Valley at Glyndyfrdwy, seen above, was the birthplace of the famous Welsh hero, Owen Glyndyr or Glendower as he was known to the English. In the neighbourhood is Glendower's Mount, another memento of the valiant, fifteenth-century rebel who overcame several of the great castles and called Welsh parliaments at Machynlleth and Dolgelly. Of where Glendower died or where he was buried no record remains.*

W. F. TAYLOR

## HILLS AND THE SEA

*The peaks known as The Rivals, here seen across Caernarvon Bay from Nevin, are prominent hills, curiously isolated from the main group of mountains of Snowdonia. On the right-hand summit is Tre'r Ceiri (Giants' Town), the most extensive prehistoric remains in Wales, with fragments of the ancient walls and dwellings. According to legend the British king, Vortigern, fled to these hills after betraying his people to the Saxons.*

their broomsticks and marched about on the hill-tops. The French saw them with the red petticoats, their tall hats, and shouldered brooms, mistook them for a hostile army, and surrendered on the spot. In this comic-opera style ended the last invasion of the British Isles.

Parts of South Wales, if not as widely known as the high mountains of the north, are justifiably popular among lovers of fine scenery. Other regions though less frequented are no less attractive. Much of Carmarthenshire is "off the beaten track" and unknown to the holiday-maker, yet its hills and the Towy Valley are beautiful indeed, and the country is full of the oddest legends. At

was Rees Pritchard, a Church of England clergyman of the seventeenth century. In his early life he was an inveterate drunkard ; to the scandal of his parishioners he used to be wheeled home from the inn in a barrow. When one day a billy-goat wandered into the inn, it amused the parson to make the creature drunk with a saucer of beer and to watch it staggering about and finally collapsing on the floor. Next evening, when he tried to repeat his little joke, the goat disdainfully turned its back on the drink and walked away. So the vicar realized that the brute beast was wiser than he, and from that time forward he was a reformed man, earnest in

W. F. TAYLOR

### RIVER OF BEAUTY
*Rising on the slopes of gaunt Plynlimon, the River Wye descends from the lonely moorlands and winds across Wales through scenery of rare beauty, through meadowland, green pastures, and wooded country. The photograph shows the view below Erwood, in Breconshire and the Black Mountains of Brecon beyond.*

Llanfihangel Abercowin are the "Graves of the Five Pilgrims"; so long as their graves are respected the village will be free from poisonous snakes.

At Llandilo is a castle built by Rhodri Mawr, Roderick the Great, one of the few kings who ruled over all Wales—for its different peoples, when not fighting against Roman or Saxon, were too often fighting among themselves, and to this day there is rivalry between the Welsh of the north and those of the south. His grandson, Howel Dda, Howell the Good, drew up a code of laws, based on the customs of the people, to have force over all the land.

Well known among Carmarthenshire characters

the performance of his parochial duties, and leaving the people a book of religious verse known as the *Welshman's Candle*.

Carmarthenshire was the centre, ninety years ago, of some most curious riots. The government had run over the land some excellent highways, liberally embellished with tollgates by which their cost was to be repaid. The tolls aroused much indignation, and a strange new movement appeared, gangs of men disguising themselves as women, tearing down the gates, wrecking the toll-houses, and turning their tenants adrift into the bleak night. In one of these onslaughts a poor old woman was slain, yet the authorities could get no information as to their

W. A. CALL.

## PICTURESQUE COAST OF PEMBROKE
*On either side of the limestone cliffs of Tenby lie the North and South Sands. The South Sands illustrated above extend for a distance of nearly two miles. One of the routes to the Sands, the Merlin Walk, passes over a cave of that name terminating close to its entrance, now almost obscured with sand. Hoyle's Mouth, another cave 100 feet long, is divided in three chambers. From Tenby start the famous Pendine Sands.*

**ROMAN STEPS**

W. F. TAYLOR

*In the hills east of Harlech are these so-called Roman steps which, according to tradition, were built for the use of Roman sentries patrolling the pass known as Bwlch Tyddiad. Only in modern times have the steps been termed Roman, and it is more probable that they date from the Middle Ages.*

away, Gowerland is a favourite resort for visitors. For the rest Glamorganshire rather scares travellers away. They think of it only as a vast coalfield, where the streams are polluted from the mineral workings and the hills are slag, yet there is romance even in these scarred and ravished hills.

### King Arthur

In the mountains of Glamorganshire sleep the minerals that give the county its trade. Yet in them sleep too, so the story runs, King Arthur and his Knights, waiting till the day shall come when they are to rise to rule Britain, to inaugurate a reign of justice and peace. On the Craig-y-Dinas is a cave which leads to the hall where they repose. Whoever enters that cave may bring away from their treasures as much gold as he can carry; but if he touches the bell that hangs within the cave they will awake and ask: "Is it yet day?" To this the intruder must reply "Sleep on; it is still night," whereupon they will return to rest. A villager who was too flustered to think of this watchword was beaten by the knights and thrust treasure-less out; and never again did he discover the entrance to the cave.

instigator. "Rebecca," their male leader, got "her" name merely from the verse of Genesis which says that the seed of Rebekah should possess the gate of their adversaries. The rioters attempted to wreck a workhouse; they succeeded in destroying a salmon weir thought to injure the upper waters of the stream. Then, as suddenly as they had begun, the "Rebecca Riots" came to an end.

The Gower Peninsula of Glamorgan has a general resemblance in shape to Pembrokeshire south of Milford Haven; and it also is "a little England," being largely peopled not by the Welsh but by the Flemings. With its magnificent castle at Oystermouth and its blowhole at Rhosilly, the roaring of which as the waves drive the air through its aperture can be heard seven miles

Monmouthshire, from the strict political point of view, is not a county of Wales but part of the Welsh Marches. Yet it is certainly part of the principality in everything except political convention. Guarding the pass into South Wales, a pass used by invading Roman, Saxon and Norman, is Abergavenny. Its castle has a most unsavoury reputation of being dishonoured by treachery more often than any other in Wales. After Henry II had forced the Norman Marcher Lords and the Welsh princes of the region into apparent amity, its ruler William de Braose invited them to a feast to celebrate. Suddenly he commanded all the Welsh guests to swear to abandon the right of wearing arms; and when they hesitated he had his men-at-arms cut them down. Afterwards he sent emissaries to murder the wife and infant child of his most influential victim. Acts such as these drove the Welsh into a frenzy of revolt, until at last they stormed the wicked castle and razed it to the ground.

In contrast with this scene of treachery and strife is a neighbouring place of peace, Llanthony Abbey. Its site in the Vale of Ewias, high up in the hills, so forcibly impressed a noble of William II by its solitude that at once he abandoned his military career and turned hermit. In the monastery he founded St. David had a cell; hence its name, which is short for Llanddewi nant Honddu, "David's Church by Honddu stream." Not far from Llanthony is another church in a situation as romantic, Partrishow, with a magnificent rood-screen and a holy well.

From the scenic point of view, Monmouth is famous chiefly because its boundary is formed by the River Wye, with its unequalled scenery, and with many places of note on its banks. Here stand Monmouth, which lent its name to Geoffrey of Monmouth, author of a quite incredible *History of the British Kings*, and which was the birthplace of Henry V—his cradle, and the sword he used at Agincourt, are still preserved; Chepstow, once " the stockaded market " where Saxons and Welsh, when not at war, used warily to barter; Trellech, with its three blocks of red stone supposed to be erected by King Harold. Grandest of all is Tintern Abbey, beautiful even in its decay.

The conquering English spoke of the Cymry as the Welsh, the " strangers," ridiculed their

STEPHENSON

## A CHURCH IN THE HILLS
*In the Black Mountains of Brecon, at Partrishow, near Crickhowell, is this little church founded in the eleventh century and rebuilt in the days of Henry VIII. It possesses a beautiful rood-loft and a font.*

language, lampooned them in a nursery rhyme. Yet they have not destroyed their culture, have not merged the Welsh into themselves. The Cymry of today still keep their ancient language, cherish their ancient tradition, honour the ancient bards and heroes, know themselves as distinct from the Englishmen. But they are not narrowly contemptuous of the " Saxons." Dispossessed from England they yet have their motherland, Wales, where every place-name has its meaning, where every hill and valley has its association or its legend. Here the Welsh still live; and thus they fulfil the prophecy of Taliesin the Bard:

" And British men
Shall be captives then
To strangers from Saxonia's
strand;
They shall praise their
God, and hold
Their language, as of old,
But except Wild Wales they
shall lose their land."

STEPHENSON

## RIVER OF LEGEND
*One of the most beautiful of Welsh rivers, the Usk, rises in Carmarthen and flows for sixty miles to the sea passing Brecon, an ancient borough and now a cathedral city. In the background of the photograph are the Brecon Beacons (2,907 feet), the highest hills in South Wales.*

STEPHENSON

### THE SUBLIME CLEFT OF GORDALE

*This magnificent limestone gorge at Malham, in Yorkshire, has impressed many poets and artists.   For Wordsworth it was " one of the grandest objects in nature," and he wrote, though not in his best style, of " Gordale chasm, terrific as the lair*
*Where the young lions crouch."*

# POETS' COUNTRY

## *by* IVOR BROWN

DESPITE various foreign conceptions of the British citizen as a mean-spirited shop-keeper or a beevish blockhead, conceptions which the British themselves have patiently accepted with a smile, our country has probably bred more and better poets and more varied schools of verse than any other. To this happy state our small and our various landscape, so quick in its changes of mood, crops, colour, architecture and altitude and so blessed in its temperate quality of climate, has notably contributed and it is my purpose to examine the relation of the singer to the scene. While the countryside has provided the minstrel with his matter, the poet has been pastoral guide and rural philosopher to his fellows. So, when we wander across Britain, his words may linger in our minds to enhance that beauty of land and water which evoked the beauty of his words and music.

In this brief study of Poets' Country it seems simplest to begin at the bottom, territorially speaking. England, like Gaul of old, can be roughly divided into three parts : downland, arable, and heather. First, starting from the south, comes the dominion of the downs, the land of chalk and mutton and, in Somerset, of chalk and cheese. Immediately we see

" Along the sky the line of the Downs
  So noble and so bare."

That is from Belloc's poem *The South Country*, which assures us that

" The men that live in the South
  Country
  Are the kindest and most wise,"

a sentiment echoed by many, for Sussex and Kent, hills and the sea, have been rich in admirers from Chaucer in the fourteenth century to Kipling in the twentieth. Chaucer wrote more of humanity than of landscape, but what a lover he was of spring, of the green field and the nimble air, of " fresshe May " and " smale fowles " that " maken melodie." Nobody should go to Canterbury without giving Chaucer the practical compliment and themselves the pleasure of a new glance at the old Pilgrims' Tales. On a spring morning in Kent on " every holt and heath " and among " tendre croppes " the lines of Chaucer sing themselves, a quality which

Kipling attributed to our English flowers and their tripping, melodious names.

Kipling, too, must be on our lips as we stand on the sweet, crisp turf of the South Downs and look across the rich, agricultural plain to the northern scarps which were London's old defence, once George Meredith's breezy paradise, and now have become the healthy suburban dormitories and " Surrey Highlands " of the modern house agent. No summary of the bare and windy hill and the lush prospect northward on a summer day could be better than Kipling's.
" No tender-hearted garden crowns,
  No bosomed woods adorn
  Our blunt, bow-headed, whale-backed Downs
  But gnarled and writhen thorn—
  Bare slopes where chasing shadows skim,

DIXON-SCOTT

### MARY ARDEN'S COTTAGE

*In the Warwickshire village of Wilmcote, near Stratford-on-Avon, is preserved this attractive timbered house dating from Tudor times with modifications belonging to the reign of Elizabeth. In this house lived Mary Arden, Shakespeare's mother.*

And, through the gaps revealed,
Belt upon belt, the wooded, dim,
Blue goodness of the Weald."

Proceeding northward we shall pass by Meredith's Box Hill, with its surge of the south-west wind, which was the great music of his soul, and the combing breaker of the downs, which was the great music of his eye. Away to the west is similar country; Dorset has downland grass for the sheep by the sea's verge while inland it offers fine soft pasture for the cattle in the green, rich vales where Tess worked out her fate. Since this is the domain of Hardy, the novelist, I shall only quote

" Sweet cyder is a great thing,
    A great thing to me,
  Spinning down to Weymouth town
    By Ridgway thirstily."

There is no more rewarding journey for the traveller with a feeling for places and for poetry than to follow the ridgways of the Dorset Downs into the bare, rolling splendour of Wiltshire with its magnificent tracks, tombs, avenues and circles of the earliest English civilization. Here are " the grassy barrows of the happier dead." The contours of these gentle pyramids run with the rhythm of the hills while their often beech-clad knolls give a point of rest among the rolling seas of turf. It is always a surprise that Wilt-shire, which has evoked some of the noblest

English prose from Jeffries, Hudson, and many another lover of our landscape and its natural life, has not been greatly celebrated in verse, while so much poetry has come from the less romantic scenery of the midlands and East Anglia.

### St. Paul's above the City

London I shall have, for reasons of space, to flit over with a speedy glance; but it certainly cannot be omitted, since all the centre and almost every suburb have been poets' country. The skyscapes of the town might move any man to song and nobody had a happier eye for them than sad John Davidson.

" The clouds on viewless columns bloomed
  Like smouldering lilies unconsumed "
while,

  " Afloat upon ethereal tides
    St. Paul's above the city rides."

The truth of that majestic metaphor I realize on any summer day when I stand upon my own doorstep in Hampstead. But whether we can

EDGAR WARD

### A SHEPHERD OF THE SOUTH DOWNS
" Gives not the hawthorn bush a sweeter shade
To shepherds looking on their silly sheep,
Than doth a rich embroidered canopy
To kings that fear their subjects' treachery."—SHAKESPEARE.

still sing of the capital with the ecstasy of Scottish Dunbar, that entranced excursionist of the fifteenth century,

"Gemme of all joy, jaspre of jocunditie."

and proclaim it "the flour of cities all," I somewhat doubt. Still, whether in its Elizabethan taverns or in its leafy suburbs, in Hampstead of Keats or in Swinburnian Putney, it has ever been with "bricky towers" and softly running Thames "merry London, my most kyndly Nurse" to many a poet beside Spenser, who so nobly praised the London water-front of his time. As late as Keats's period Hampstead was almost "Home County" in its separation from the city. On the Heath he saw his friend Dilke shoot partridges by the ponds where Mr. Pickwick studied the origins and habits of the tittlebat. Here in his garden he heard that nightingale whose song will last for ever.

"Thy plaintive anthem fades
Past the near meadows, over the still stream,
Up the hill-side."

### Hampstead Heath

But not, thanks to Keats, out of the world's affection. The stream, I think, must be the River Fleet which rises in the Vale of Health, flows across Hampstead Heath and on (now underground) to join the Thames at Blackfriars, thus giving to the eastern end of the Strand the name of Fleet Street. It was on the Vale of Health pond that Shelley was said to sail paper boats with Leigh Hunt's children.

But there is no time to linger, not even by Coleridge's niche in Highgate Village or Marvell's haunt upon that famous hill. Working north of London we should carry John Clare in our pockets or our minds as the quiet songster of the plain east-midland scene. "Give me no high-flown fangled things," sighed Clare in a poem of nostalgia for the simplicities of level England.

"I miss the heath, its yellow furze,
Molehills and rabbit tracks that lead
Through beesom, ling, and teazel burrs
That spread a wilderness indeed :
The woodland oaks and all below
That their white-powdered branches shield,
The mossy paths ; the very crow
Croaks music in my native field."

Clare, so happy in the ordinary sights and sounds of any field or farm or hedge, is typically English, like the charming but never sensational views which his serene, utilitarian, countryside affords with its mixture of arable, woodland, grass, and heath. Cowper on the Ouse,

"This glassy stream, the spreading pine,
Those alders quivering to the breeze."

and Crabbe at Aldeborough supplement the tranquil picture of an England whose life abides unchanging by its quiet rivers and on the

DIXON-SCOTT

### SHELLEY'S COTTAGE AT LYNMOUTH
*In this house the poet is believed to have stayed in 1812, and to have written poems and pamphlets there. Some of his writings were considered seditious, and to avoid arrest he went to Wales.*

"stolchy" ploughlands of the eastern plain. The modern singer of these lands has been Mr. Edmund Blunden, who knows their wintry frown as well as the basking mildness of a summer look,

"Black ponds and boughs of clay and sulky
sedge."

as well as

"Some bell-like evening when the May's in
bloom."

If we had turned westerly out of London we should have passed Stoke Poges whose churchyard has inspired a poem so well known that I propose, like the lowing herd, to wind slowly o'er the lea, making without comment for the Chiltern chalk, with a memory of Milton at Chalfont St. Giles, and so onward to Oxford and

"The stripling Thames at Bablock Hythe."

This is the country of a score of poets since Matthew Arnold sang of the Scholar Gipsy upon Cumnor Hurst. Robert Bridges lived and died close to Cumnor. The Upper Thames Valley, still strangely lonely once Oxford is passed, contains the scene of William Morris's happy labours in art and poetry at Kelmscott, and abounds in exquisite solitude, reaching up to the sheeplands of Cotswold where the early English wool trade so prospered as to build for its grandees the loveliest of English towns, Burford, Chipping Campden, and many another. The names of the rivers Windrush and Evenlode are poetry in themselves, like the grey-stone High Streets of that enchanting region. Listen here to Mr. Belloc, who has caught the very genus of the land where Gloucester's hills drop down to the Oxford plain.

" The quiet evening kept her tryst :
    Beneath an open sky we rode,
And passed into a wandering mist
    Along the perfect Evenlode.

Shakespeare's town was close enough to " Cotsall " or Cotswold for the poet to see on his journeys the misty splendour of a hilly horizon. " And far-off mountains turned into clouds," while the river scene (Queen Gertrude gives it when describing Ophelia's death) offered slanting willows, crow-flowers, daisies and long-purples. Spring was (and still is) the time for Stratford. Late spring, after the daffodils have ceased to " take the winds of March with beauty " is the safer time.

" When daisies pied and violets blue
    And lady-smocks all silver-white

STEPHENSON

### "HIGH WHITBY'S CLOISTERED PILE"

*In the abbey founded by St. Hilda, there was an unlettered cowherd who was wont to retire from the feast when it came his turn to sing. This was Caedmon who, so the story runs, received inspiration in a dream and found himself singing of the beginning of creation and thereafter wrote many religious poems.*

The tender Evenlode that makes
    Her meadows hush to hear the sound
Of waters mingling in the brakes,
    And binds my heart to English ground.
A lovely river, all alone,
    She lingers in the hills and holds
A hundred little towns of stones,
    Forgotten in the western wolds."

And now we are getting across to the Severn and the Severn's tributary, Avon, which meanders through the orchard counties from Stratford to Tewkesbury ; in " proud-pied April " that journey is blossom all the way. Stratford-on-Avon is essential England, its water-meadows so miry in winter and offering in return the glorious greenery of spring which only inundation can produce.

And cuckoo-buds of yellow hue
    Do paint the meadows with delight."

The town itself, though growing rapidly, has great fascination. To follow the sweep of the river from the theatre to the church, to saunter past the true Tudor houses with their well-preserved timbering, and to rest awhile in the garden where Shakespeare's house once stood will bring you far closer to Shakespeare's vision of England than poring over the bits and pieces under glass cases in the museums. His vision, as true to " furious winter's rages " as to the heat of the sun, has the vigilance and the verity of his outlook on mankind. Shakespeare, supreme in depicting Nature as well as human nature, had abundant scope because his local

STEPHENSON

## WHERE SHAKESPEARE MADE MERRY

*On the River Avon, a few miles below Stratford-on-Avon, is the village of Bidford, with a little grey church by the riverside. There is a tradition that Shakespeare and some friends had a drinking contest here with a convivial company known as the " Bidford Society of Sippers," so the place was designated " Drunken Bidford."*

DIXON-SCOTT

## THE MALVERN HILLS WHICH RISE ABOVE THE SEVERN VALE

*On these hills tradition has it Caratacus, the British chieftain, was defeated by the Romans, and here, according to John Masefield,*

" *Savage and taciturn the Roman*
*Hewed upwards in the Roman way.*"

W. F. TAYLOR

### LUDLOW'S CASTLE ABOVE THE TEME

*This Norman castle was once a stronghold of the Lords President of the Marches. In its Council Hall, Milton's " Comus " was presented in 1634. Thirty years later, in the rooms over the gateway to the Castle Green, Samuel Butler wrote much of his " Hudibras."*

scene was so various, thus epitomizing the infinite variety of England as a whole. Forest of Arden, River of Avon, orchard, water-meadow, tilth, the neighbouring pastoral life of " Cotsall " and its sheep-folds, the great castles of Warwick and Kenilworth, and the cloistered scholarship of Oxford—such inheritance for the senses was as generous as the use made of it was majestic.

Moving up through the north-west midlands past Bredon Hill we come, by way of " the coloured counties " and the Malvern Beacons where Piers Plowman sang, to the Welsh Marches and certainly we shall halt at Ludlow, in whose keep Milton's *Comus* was first performed, and whose unspoiled beauty retains the quality of a medieval missal.

No county has owed more to a poet than Shropshire, as the death of A. E. Housman reminded us. It is threaded by the noble Severn, a river robbed of just praise and honour by the prominence of the Thames but remembered in Milton's *Sabrina Fair* with her " rushy-fringed bank " and " glassie cool, translucent wave."

The shire soars to the noble hills of Clee and the muscular ridges which guard the road to Wales. It is murmurous with battles long ago, raids and revenges, and now it echoes for us the sorrows of the ploughboy and the soldier and their lasses. Not sorrows only linger in this Shropshire air but laughter too, for Housman's poetry contains as well as the sadness of the *Last Post* the glitter of lights in tavern windows, the roaring banter of market-merry men, and the whisper of lovers in the copse. Springs can be harsh there,

" The chestnut casts his flambeaux
    and the flowers
  Stream from the hawthorn on the
    wind away,"

and call for the comfort of the tavern and the can. Spring, too, can be soft there and consoling,

" Star and coronal and bell
  April underfoot renews
  And the hope of man as well
  Flowers among the morning dews."

The " coloured counties " seen from Bredon Hill when the music of church bells vies with that of larks in the sky or the glorious vespers of a summer day in the Shropshire Hills are equally well described.

" Wenlock Edge was umbered,
    And bright was Abdon Burf,
    And warm between them slumbered

The smooth green miles of turf ;
  Until from grass and clover
  The upshot beam would fade,
  And England over
  Advanced the lofty shade."

Housman was particularly happy in his response to evening in the western valleys, beside his " brooks too broad for leaping."

" I see the air benighted
  And all the dusking dales
  And lamps in England lighted
  And evenings wrecked in Wales."

The whole glory of an English sunset as well as of the diverse Shropshire landscape is in those lines.

Though Thomas Gray could honour " Old Conway's foaming flood " we must leave Wales to its own language, as no doubt the Welsh nationalists would prefer, and strike up into that third part of England, which has coal in its plains and heather on its hills. The Pennine range, apt to be under-rated for solitude and splendour owing to the fame and glory of the Lake District, has had its sternness honoured in prose and verse by the Brontë sisters, who, half Irish and half Cornish, never seem to me to have got the true feel of Yorkshire, whatever may be said of their power in other directions. Still, the wild Decembers on the brown hills are portrayed as passionately as the calmer advent of

" Western winds, with evening's wandering airs,
    With that clear dusk of heaven which brings
        the thickest stars."

Scott's *Rokeby* gives a vigorous survey of Teesdale and the spare grand hills round Greta Bridge. Perhaps the best Pennine poems are to be found, suitably, in dialect. Anyhow Ilkla' Moor has given the nation its own authentic example of the Northern Muse.

With a left turn we come into Westmorland and Cumberland, romantic land and home of the romantic revival. Undeniably the mountains and lakes of Cumbria, though they might pass for normal in the Scottish Highlands, are unique in England both for the sharpness and the jaggedness of the hills. The Pennines usually create a smooth outline, noble, but tranquil, whereas the Cumbrian peaks fret the sky-line and stab at heaven. So these angry peaks may stir emotions more deeply and rouse more poetic fancy than the suave contours to the west. Wordsworth was the child, the lover, and the poet of this land and to mention Grasmere is

to think at once of him and of his circle. Scarcely a fell or force or mere of this region has not some tribute of affection or of awe within the volume of his verse. To him most of all men Nature was an ethical, even a political force. The vernal wood gave him the moral impulse, the mountains proclaimed the splendours of liberty. Here

" the earth
And common face of Nature spoke to me
    Remarkable things."

Here he reflected on the sublimity of England's landscape and on those doings of mankind which, missing the sublime, approach the ridiculous.

The Lake District is thickly beset by echoes and memories of the romantic revival. That revival was a revolt against urban artifice in verse and an assertion of simple and eternal values. The common round as theme, the common man as hero, the common speech as medium, Nature naturally honoured, these were the new ideals, so different from the fashionable notions of the eighteenth century which regarded mountains and desolation as barbarous, uncivil things. What better place for the revival of romantic values and elemental modes than England's most romantic counties, where the elements may most easily be met in their fury as in their serenity, now stinging with the gale, now soothing with the breeze? That is Wordsworth's message, a message endorsed by brilliant description of his

DIXON-SCOTT

## THE LOVELY LAKE OF WINDERMERE

*Wordsworth, Scott and other poets were charmed with Windermere. Christopher North wrote, perhaps with exaggeration, " There is to be seen thence the widest breadth of water, the richest foreground of wood, and the most magnificent background of mountains, not only of Westmorland, but, believe me, in all the world."*

meres and fells and by many a moral drawn therefrom.

Wordsworth, who wrote so well of Scotland, leads us to the Border, great land of ballad and of song. The hills are not so sharp, but on the broad heathery and grassland surge of Pennine, Cheviot, and the Scottish Lowlands the keen and hungry winds touched the singers of the people to irony, humour, pathos, and the capture of strange beauty. The ballads are narrative, sheer story-telling in first intention, full of tragic suspense, but often acquiring the lyrical beauty of a carol as well as the pounding force of stern tragedy. Here in the country of the Border chieftains, the Percys and the Douglases, barren and cruel wastes on the summits but with fertile and merciful straths below, flowered the bitter-sweet genius of balladry, red rose with sharpest thorn. Typical is that song of Douglas and Lady Margaret, coming by the light of the moon to " a wan water,"

" They lighted down
    to take a drink
O' the spring that
    ran so clear,
But down the stream
    ran his red heart's
    blood
And she began to
    fear."

The essence of ballad fancy is in that quatrain. It is more comfortable to work upwards to St. Mary's Loch and the land of Hogg, the Ettrick Shepherd, wit and minstrel of the Lowland Moors or to cross over into Ayrshire and share a cottar's Saturday night with Robert Burns.

There is in Burns the hungry Scotland of the upland farms and untameable moors which are so often ill-described as " Lowland."

" Oh wert thou in the cauld blast,
    On yonder lea, on yonder lea,
    My plaidie to the angry airt
    I'd shelter thee, I'd shelter thee."

Of highland scenery the poetry is not large. Byron saluted the Deeside of his boyhood and that majestic mountain which makes the setting for Balmoral " dark Lochnagarr." It was Scott, naturally, who responded most to the Grampians with their mass of peaks rising well above the 3,000-foot level, their trackless desolation, their nestling lochs, and long thrust of the intruding sea. The west he most pictured in *The Lord of the Isles* : the central Grampian mass and especially the Trossachs in *The Lady of the Lake*.

" One burnished sheet of living gold
    Loch Katrine lay beneath him roll'd.
High on the south huge Benvenue
    Down to the lake
        in masses threw
    Crags, knolls and
        mounds, con-
        fusedly hurl'd,
    The fragments of
        an earlier world."

Scott would hardly now be judged a sensitive poet, but he was a great descriptive versifier and he had a great country for his theme.

A trip to Ireland immediately suggests to the average English reader the bean-rows and the bee-loud glades of Innisfree, a land where

" The mid-night's all
    a glimmer and
    noon a purple
    glow
And evening full
    of the linnet's
    wings."

But Ireland is a bare land very often with great winds, damp and warm, shouting across it, and you get closer to the Atlantic sea-board in the verse of Eva Gore-Booth who knows " wet winds that roam the country-side " and sees " Great waves of the Atlantic go storming on their way." Poets of Ireland are honest about the climate. Moira O'Neill cried in exile for

" Sweet Corrymeela an' the same soft rain."

But Ireland, after all, is a nation and a province, too large a piece of geography for much discussion here. The nation, too, has its own tongue, and in that, no doubt, the poet has done his customary task of recording in beauty of phrase the beauty of scene which stirred him to expression.

A. A. MACGREGOR

THE OLD VICARAGE, GRANTCHESTER

*In Grantchester, wrote Rupert Brooke, you may lie and :*
*" Hear the cool lapse of hours pass*
*Until the centuries blend and blur."*

STEPHENSON

## LOCH CORUISK, ISLE OF SKYE

*" A scene so rude, so wild as this,*
*Yet so sublime in barrenness*
*Ne'er did my wandering footsteps press."*
*[" The Lord of the Isles."]*

STEPHENSON

## LONELY HOMESTEAD IN THE CHEVIOTS

*A shepherd's cottage at the head of Coquetdale among the bare hills of the Scottish Border. This is the country of the old ballads such as the famous "Chevy Chase" which sings of Percy of Northumberland and of the doughty Douglas who burned the dales of Tyne and parts of Bamburghshire and left them all on fire.*

FELTON

## SUPERB TUDOR GOTHIC
*Built in 1503-1519 the beautiful chapel of Henry VII in Westminster Abbey is the most exquisite example in England of Tudor Gothic. On each side of the chapel are the stalls and banners of Knights of the Bath.*

# THE STORY OF LONDON

## *by* MARTIN R. HOLMES

LONDON today is one of the world's greatest ports, and in that fact lies the clue to its origin. In the first place, the Thames estuary, facing the Continent, gave easy access by water into the interior of the island; and in the second place the site of London is the lowest point at which the river can be crossed with comparative ease. Indeed, as late as the twelfth century the Thames was occasionally fordable at London Bridge, and the presence of a hard gravel subsoil on both banks at this point facilitated the construction of the bridge itself. On the other hand, the site of London was largely hemmed in by dense oak forest, of which the forests of Epping and Hainault are time-worn fragments. It was not therefore until the arrival of the Romans in A.D 43, with their overseas interests on the one hand and their engineering skill on the other, that the ford assumed permanent importance as a focus of maritime and overland traffic. The erection of the bridge and of the extensive bridgehead settlements on the sites of the city and of Southwark may be regarded as the outcome of that great event.

The new London or Londinium grew rapidly as a commercial centre, and within a few years of the Roman invasion was already one of the five largest cities north of the Alps. But in A.D. 61 this prosperity received a sudden sharp check. In that year the Iceni, taking advantage of the absence of the bulk of the army in the north, marched on Colchester, and thence proceeded to London where they indulged in massacre and destruction.

The Romans were thus faced with the necessity of rebuilding London. The city was laid out on the usual Roman grid-iron plan, and doubtless on a more monumental scale than had been possible in the first flush of conquest. As in the case of the Great Fire of 1666, the catastrophe of A.D. 61 probably proved, in the long run, beneficial to progress of the city, which now extended from the Fleet river in the west to the site of the present Tower of London in the east.

In the second century, probably in the time of the great empire-builder Hadrian, whose colossal bronze statue once stood in Roman London, the city was girt with three miles of wall and ditch, of which fragments (notably in the courtyard of the General Post Office, St. Martin's-le-Grand) can still be seen.

Our knowledge of the buildings of the new town is limited by the disintegrating effects of post-Roman neglect and medieval or modern reconstruction, which, in succession, have helped in a large measure to obliterate the original Roman street-plan. It is, however, clear that in the lay-out of the main features of the town, consideration was given first to the provision of a forum and the basilica as representing the commercial and administrative aspects of urban

ORIGINAL SIGN 1668

FELTON

**A PICTURESQUE SIGN**

*Outside a rope and sailmaker's shop in Fish Street Hill may be seen this quaint old sign of a "Peterboat and Doublet."*

life. This important group of buildings stood on the present site of Leadenhall Market and St. Peter's, Cornhill. The basilica, a long rectangular hall some 500 feet in length, served the combined purpose of Town Hall, Law Court and Exchange. Other public buildings included temples and baths, and a fragment of one of these baths may still be seen under the Coal Exchange in Lower Thames Street.

### Roman Housing Problem

Industrial development naturally tended to keep pace with the growth of the city. Building materials were urgently required to house the increasing population; tiles and bricks were manufactured on the spot, and freestone was imported from western England. A vigorous demand for earthenware for domestic purposes led to the use of native wares such as those from Castor and the New Forest, in addition to the imported " Samian " ware of Gaulish origin. This last, with its familiar red glazed surface, has been found in great quantities on London sites, and is well represented in our museums. So also are the large two-handled vessels or " amphorae " in which wine and oil were imported from Gaul and Italy. Equivalent exports were metal, corn, slaves, and probably wool.

With the arrival of the Roman general, Theodosius, in A.D. 368 for the purpose of reorganizing the province after a period of disturbance, the written history of Roman London comes to an end. In A.D. 410, with a hostile army besieging the gates of Rome, the Emperor, Honorius, sent to the " Cities in Britain " a message of despair, advising them to take measures for their own safety. The ensuing period, in respect of civic life, was one of stagnation and decay, due on the one hand to the rupture of economic relations with the Roman world and on the other hand to the chaos resulting from the invasions of the Picts and Scots in the north and the Teutonic incursions in the south and east.

Between the years A.D. 400 and 500 very little is known of the history of London. Excluding a reference in an official Roman list of disputed date, the first mention of London after the fourth century is a reference in A.D. 457 in the

D. MCLEISH

### REMAINS OF A ROMAN BATH

*Outside the wall of Roman London, on a slight eminence overlooking the Thames, once stood the second-century villa of some wealthy citizen of the ancient empire. On the south side of the Strand, at 5, Strand Lane, may be seen this bath, which is still fed by a spring as it was in the days when the villa was inhabited.*

FELTON

## LONDON'S HISTORIC FORTRESS

*On the north bank of the Thames, at the south-east angle of the Roman fortifications, William the Conqueror founded the Tower of London, and the Keep, or White Tower, dates from his reign. It has served as fortress, palace and gaol and held many illustrious prisoners, most of whom only escaped by way of the executioner's block.*

Anglo-Saxon Chronicle according to which, after a fight between the forces of Hengist and the Britons, the latter left Kent and fled to London.

At the end of the sixth century the city was dependent upon Kent, and Augustine's foundation of a bishopric at Canterbury was accordingly followed by the establishment of others at London and Rochester. The site of St. Paul's was consecrated in A.D. 604, the year of Augustine's death, and the continuation of Kentish supremacy is indicated by the fact that Canterbury, and not, as Pope Gregory had intended, London, became the southern headquarters of Christianity in Britain.

The cathedral of St. Paul occupied the summit of the western hill of the city. Close to the cathedral we find the churches of St. Gregory at the west end and St. Augustine at the east end. It is possible that this group of churches stood in alignment from west to east, forming an imposing façade to anyone ascending the hill. It has also been said that not far from the cathedral Ethelred II, in later years, built himself a palace. In Westcheap the folkmote, an assembly of the freemen of London, was held on a site north-east of St. Paul's. This evidence, coupled with discoveries which have taken place in this part of the town tend to show that the " west end " of London had then already established its prestige.

During the eighth and ninth centuries, the London Wall was repaired and strengthened to withstand the Danish attacks which during the latter part of this period became a frequent occurrence in the neighbourhood. But in spite of this ever-present danger, London continued to develop apace, aided no doubt by the paternal rule of Alfred. Under his successors, the town passed largely unscathed through the ravages of the Danes, until, in 1017, together with the rest of England, it finally submitted to them. Of the struggles of this phase, Viking weapons recovered from London sites, and particularly from the foreshore of the river, are eloquent witness.

### Tower of London

But throughout these vicissitudes, the city had risen from strength to strength, and the fearless independence which it showed at the time of the Norman Conquest in 1066 it retained throughout its later history. Indeed, the first structure erected by the Normans was designed as a check upon this insubordinate spirit and is today a token of it. The Tower of London, built by King William within the south-eastern angle of the old town wall, and known from its ancient coats of whitewash as the " White Tower," is and has always been outside the civic administration. In the modern system of local government

FELTON

### OLDEST CHURCH IN LONDON

*St. John's Chapel in the Tower of London, a fine example of Norman architecture, built about 1080, is situated in the White Tower. Edward VI destroyed its many rare and beautiful ornaments.*

given to that bridge which was the real nucleus of London. It was during the reign of Henry II that the old timber bridge across the Thames was first rebuilt in stone. The new London Bridge had twenty pointed arches, and the roadway was flanked on either side by shops which in some places were joined above it, completely shutting out the sky. It was considered superior to the Pont Nôtre Dame at Paris and the Rialto at Venice, and an Elizabethan writer named it as "worthily to be numbered among the miracles of the world." On the central and largest pier, a chapel was built and dedicated to a famous Londoner—St. Thomas of Canterbury.

Just outside London, also, lay the important Court suburb of Westminster. Until the disastrous fire of 1834, a considerable part of the medieval Palace of Westminster was still standing, including the famous Painted Chamber, with its elaborate mural decoration. Now, however, almost the only surviving portion is Westminster Hall, built originally by William II and altered under Richard II into its present form. Contemporary with this alteration is the greater part of the nave of the Abbey Church of Westminster, near by. The builders, instead of following the architectural fashion of their own time, designed a nave in the style of a hundred years before, to harmonize with the remainder of the building, as set up by Henry III, and it takes careful observation to tell where the work of the thirteenth century ends and that of the late fourteenth begins.

### Abbey of Westminster

The actual Benedictine Abbey of Westminster, which guarded the relics of St. Edward the Confessor, was finally dissolved by Elizabeth, but enough of the buildings remained in the reconstituted Deanery and School to illustrate even in our own day the layout of a great medieval monastery; and the walls of the Chapter House still retain, in some degree, their bright paintings of angels and scenes from the Apocalypse.

It is perhaps only fair to outline very briefly the other side of the picture. The London of those years would appal the sanitary authority of today. Early in the Middle Ages it had easily afforded a home to a semi-pastoral population. The city itself was small, the open country lay

it forms a remarkable and significant enclave of the external Borough of Stepney into the natural territory of the City of London.

Further building in the early years following the Norman Conquest was stimulated by a succession of fires, which destroyed many churches, St. Paul's among them. After this disaster, the citizens set to work to erect the finest church in England—a new St. Paul's, which dominated the city for some 600 years to follow. In 1090 the Church of St. Giles was constructed in the vicinity of Cripplegate, and at about the same date the archiepiscopal palace at Lambeth was begun. Thirty years later there arose just outside the city walls the monastery of St. Bartholomew the Great, founded by Rahere. Today the monastic buildings are gone, and of the church attached to them only the eastern end remains to symbolize the grandeur of the vanished monastic architecture of London.

Amongst secular buildings, priority may be

D. MCLEISH

### QUIET PRECINCTS OF THE TEMPLE

*Pump Court, seen above, was built shortly after the Great Fire of London. The Temple was originally the seat of the famous Order of Knights Templars. When this order was dissolved the property passed to the Knights Hospitallers of St. John, who leased it in the fourteenth century to professors of the common law.*

in easy reach, and it was possible for the Londoner to keep his cattle and pigs within the city and have them driven out every morning to pasture. With the increase in building, however, the pasture land became further and further removed from the heart of the city, and the change had its reactions upon the aspect of the London streets.

The foreign merchant, coming to London on business, would find in it many unexpected savours of the farmyard, and the measures passed again and again to regulate the cleanliness of the streets and the proper housing of cattle, and to check the practice of allowing pigs to feed at random in the gutters, show that the authorities were well awake to the necessity of keeping the

pastoral element of the city under due restraint. Regulations exist, moreover, prescribing the digging of cesspools, stone-lined or otherwise, and reprehending the practice of emptying filth indiscriminately into the brooks and streams which still ran uncovered through the city. Notwithstanding these insanitary conditions, it has been roughly estimated that the population of London stood close upon 40,000.

But no description of medieval London would be complete without some mention of that important feature of civic life—the City Company. Gilds, comparable to the modern friendly societies, had existed in Saxon times. It was not, however, until the twelfth century that they became predominantly mercantile. Briefly, the Craft Gilds aimed at establishing a monopoly in each industry by regulating production and distribution for the ultimate benefit of their members. Their position had originally rested on the somewhat unstable footing of an annual rent paid to the Crown, but the granting of a charter of incorporation to the Weavers' Company by Henry II established a precedent of which other companies were quick to take advantage. When this degree of security had been reached, the next step was usually the erection of a permanent meeting place for purposes of business and social intercourse. Of the actual appearance of these city halls, very little is known, since the Great Fire swept away most of them, but they doubtless resembled the old Guildhall.

The chief disadvantage of the gilds in later years lay in the restrictions they imposed upon new industries arising within the city, and their prohibition of any change in wages at a time when economic conditions were altering rapidly. Some of their functions have now become the work of the trades unions, but their social and charitable work is still continued by the Livery Companies of the City of London. These bodies retain their courts, their officers and their customs,

FELTON

RICHARD COEUR DE LION

*Within the shadow of the Houses of Parliament stands this statue of Richard I (1189-1199), the crusading monarch whose adventures in the Holy Land and elsewhere have provided themes for many a romantic story.*

D. MCLEISH

### CHURCH OF THE DANES
*In the middle of the Strand is the Church of St.*
*Clement Danes, named from its being the traditional*
*burial place of Harold Harefoot and other Danes.*

re-grant of them to his nominees, helped to fill London with unemployed men who had formerly worked on the monastic estates. These were now in part diverted to the use of palatial residences, as when Henry VIII built St. James's Palace on the site of a leper hospital. Elsewhere to meet the needs of the swarming population, more and more houses were erected, and the streets were rapidly darkening on account of the overhanging upper storeys. Sanitation was at its worst, and disease was rife throughout the whole area.

It is impossible to say how long this state of affairs might have continued had not the Great Fire of 1666 provided an effective, if drastic, remedy. After it, little remained of medieval London, and, for the first time for many centuries, there was opportunity for a complete remodelling of the street plan. Wren, full of the ideals of the Renaissance movement, was appointed assistant surveyor by Charles II, and prepared a plan for the town which, owing to the nearsightedness of the authorities, was not adopted. Much of the genius of Wren remains today in his immortal buildings, the cathedral of St. Paul's, and in no fewer than thirty-nine of the city churches, of which St. Stephen Walbrook may be quoted as one of the best examples.

From this time onward London entered into its greater glory. Such buildings as Wren's churches, the additions to the Palace of Hampton Court, and the hospitals of Chelsea and Greenwich,

and some of them, but not all, have their halls. The formal dinners of these companies are survivals of the old social gatherings of craftsmen, and many grammar schools and almshouses, in and about London, have been founded and endowed by the Livery Companies just as the old gilds made provision for educating the children of deceased members, or housing craftsmen overtaken by old age.

A great economic change of early Tudor times was the drift of population from the village to the town, which is reflected in London's town planning, or lack of it. So overcrowded did the city become during the fifteenth and sixteenth centuries, that even the encircling ditch was filled in and built over. The confiscation of monastic lands by Henry VIII, and his

D. MCLEISH

### TUDOR BUILDINGS IN HOLBORN
*In Holborn may be seen this picturesque façade of Staple Inn, a quaint relic*
*of the streets of old London. This inn is believed to have been a hostel of*
*wool-staplers in the fourteenth century and later became an Inn of Chancery.*

EDGAR WARD

## THE GREAT DOME OF ST. PAUL'S

*The dominant note in this London panorama is St. Paul's Cathedral, Wren's famous masterpiece.   In the seventh century there is said to have been a church on this site.   This was followed by a Norman structure which, with later additions, was the old St. Paul's.   After the Great Fire, Wren planned the present building which was begun in 1675, the last stone being laid in 1710.   Many of England's greatest men are buried in St. Paul's.*

EDGAR WARD

## THE SILVER-DAPPLED POOL

*That reach of the Thames on each side of the Tower Bridge has long been famous as the Pool of London.   Of old it was the city's shipping centre, but since the building of the Tower Bridge only vessels of moderate dimensions reach the upper portion.   Below the bridge begins London dockland, although all except the Surrey Commercial Docks are on the north side, London now handles one-third of Britain's overseas trade.*

all grace London today, and afford us an insight into the appearance of the city and its environs in the years of the seventeenth-century Renaissance. The new learning was not solely confined to architecture, but embraced all branches of the arts. Books were published on the town, and from such famous diarists as Pepys and Evelyn we get intriguing sketches and descriptions of the period. From now until the end of the century, London saw a succession of fine new buildings which continued into the early nineteenth century under the skilled hands of such architects as Hawkesmoor, Gibbs, Soane, Dance, Wilkins and Nash.

### Fashionable Soho

With the establishment of a more or less permanent court at Westminster, London had become the permanent residential city for fashionable society. The city itself was, and is still, devoted to the merchants—the real aboriginal citizens of London—but residential quarters began to rise towards the west. First Soho was fashionable, as many fine late seventeenth-century houses remain to show us ; then, in the first quarter of the eighteenth century, a new residential district sprang up outside London, about the Oxford Road, and between that road and St. James's the West End came into being. Here was no gradual expansion, but a complete scheme for a new quarter, laid out and planned round its fashionable squares, and in due course, when it was completed, London Society entered and took possession.

By the eighteenth century London had reached a position such as it had never before attained as a centre of the brilliant world of folk and fashion. The clothes of the *ton*, silks and satins, periwigs and lorgnettes, the gay livery of the servants, and above all the interest of the common throng—everything indeed tended to make life colourful. The apparent lightheartedness of the times is shown by the number of amusements which increased each year. It was at this time that the famous pleasure resorts of Vauxhall

and Ranelagh were opened and attended by all who were considered, or considered themselves, to be of the élite. Scenes of excess were not infrequent at both these gardens, and, according to both Fielding and Walpole, they were mostly responsible for numerous quarrels and duels.

Even the architecture took on a lighter vein, and the brothers Adam engaged pipers to cheer the Scottish builders of the Adelphi, now unfortunately mainly demolished to make room for

D. MCLEISH

**WHERE THE FIRE OF LONDON BEGAN**
*Fish Street Hill, seen above, is adjacent to Billingsgate. On the left is the base of the Monument, commemorating the Great Fire of 1666. In the background is the Church of St. Magnus the Martyr, rebuilt by Wren.*

the growing needs of the metropolis. The Adelphi must have been a pleasant place in the eighteenth century, with the streets leading down to the foreshore through that little architectural gem, the York Water Gate. Furniture too changed in these years, and examples in public and private collections remain to show how the work of Chippendale, Hepplewhite and Sheraton was used to adorn the fashionable London houses.

Many of the famous London clubs owe their

EDGAR WARD

### LIONS OF TRAFALGAR SQUARE

*On the south side of Trafalgar Square, described as " the finest site in London," stands the lofty Nelson's column surmounted by the huge monument of the famous admiral. Round the base of the column are four bronze lions, designed by Sir Edwin Landseer and erected in 1868 some months after the completion of the column.*

inception to the bucks of those days, and their lives are reflected in the delightful caricatures by Rowlandson. The later style of the Adam brothers may be seen to advantage in a number of beautiful door-cases still in existence in the remaining part of the Adelphi, Chelsea and the back streets of Westminster. Their later work, however, tended to over-elaboration and, as is only natural, reaction set in during the early nineteenth century and was reflected in the fashions of the time as well as in the architecture. Such " upstart " places as Kensington, which only fifty years before had been a distinct and separate village, were gradually joined to the West End by a chain of heavy pseudo-Renaissance palaces or by overdone Gothic mansions.

#### Carlton House Terrace

A redeeming feature of this later period was the work of John Nash which may be seen today in Carlton House Terrace in the Mall. Of the eighteenth century we still have the fine examples of the outer wall of the Bank of England (1733), Somerset House, and many churches including St. Martin's-in-the-Fields and St. Mary-le-Strand by Gibbs. Little need here be said of the nineteenth-century rebuilding of a great part of London, save perhaps to mention the buildings

by Wilkins—the National Gallery and University College, London. For the rest, the century witnessed what may best be called the gradual " mechanization " of architecture : the use, for example, of machine-made terra-cotta tiles, and of concrete apologetically disguised by façades in the traditional fashion. It has been a common plaint that the fine independent quality of the buildings prior to the introduction of machinery is gone, and the individuality of the streets, except for occasional buildings, is lost.

Many people still remember with amusement the first horse-tram, a very rickety affair on which only the young and foolhardy would risk their lives. The London hansom-cab, growlers, drain-pipe trousers and bustles, would seem strange to us even after so few years. Gone today are the crossing-sweepers and fly-posters of Dickens's day, and with them the picturesque streets which have given way to stately avenues of stone and concrete. Yet change is a symptom of vitality and carries with it its own compensations. The Londoner today, looking at his new London based on steel rather than on stone, is able to find a new beauty in his city both comparable with, and at the same time wholly different from, that of the medieval and Georgian cities which have now so nearly vanished.

# THE ENGLISH FOREST

## *by* H. E. BATES

WHEN it comes to a question of assessing the beauties of his country, the English-man is in a delicate position. Is he to be true to that tradition of sturdy honesty which for no apparent reason time has pinned on him, and honestly call most of his mountains simply hills and most of his hills simply molehills, and most of his rivers simply brooks? or is he to be true to that tradition of dishonesty which glorifies and magnifies anything English, good or bad, simply because it is English, and dishonestly pretend that in the richness and grandeur of her natural scenic beauties England is second to none?

Whichever course he takes —and in typically English fashion he is not likely to take any course at all until the beauties in question have been lost to him for ever, when he will be very appre-ciative of what he has lost and very angry, and will write to the press about it —there is one aspect of his English scenery which will bother him a lot. This is the question of English forests. It will bother him for two reasons. First, because he will have to make an extra hard choice here between honesty and dis-honesty, for although it is all very fine and attractive to talk of English forests it is an altogether different matter to face the fact that they are, with one or two exceptions, not forests any longer. And second, it will bother him because he will, generally speaking, know nothing about them.

Ask him to name half a dozen English forests and he may tell you Sherwood, Dart-moor, Exmoor, Ashdown, Epping and the New Forest. Ask him for another half-dozen and he will look at you with truly English sus-picion, as though there were a catch in it and you were trying to make a fool of him. He may even tell you that there are no more. And he will, in a sense, be right.

For the forests of England are gone. It is true that we may still count them, very surpris-ingly, in scores and in the most unexpected places, on maps that still mark them for us. We know that the State provides a Forestry Com-mission, and that the work of afforestation goes on. But forests? Except for the New Forest, Dartmoor, Exmoor, Dean, Epping, Savernake,

W. F. TAYLOR

### ROYAL FOREST OF DEAN

*Most interesting of English woodlands. The Court of Verderers, founded under the Forest Laws of Canute, grant mining rights to those born of a "free father" and who have worked in a mine for a year and a day.*

DIXON-SCOTT

### SILVER BIRCHES IN SHERWOOD FOREST
*" Birches, frail whispering company are these?*
*Or lovely women rooted into trees?*
*Daughters of Norsemen, on a foreign shore."*—V. Sackville West.

Sherwood, the name is a mockery. The rest are the ghosts of forests; these places are merely woods. We have nothing to compare with the Black Forest of Germany, still less the Black Forest of Russia; and when we begin to think of, say, the forests of Brazil and Bolivia our biggest forest, with its 90,000 almost prim acres, begins to seem as significant as a drop of spittle on the face of an ocean.

What is a forest? How does it come into being, magnificent and huge as the forests of Russia and Bolivia still are and as the forest—note the *but in some certaine and meet for that purpose, and hereupon a forrest hath the name, as one would say, Feresta, that is, a station of wild beasts."*

This description is very English, rather homely in its civilized gentleness. Apply it to the forest so well described by Mr. Julian Duguid in *Green Hell*, and it seems a little comic. Only in England, where the forests were so long subordinate to the pleasures of kings, could wild beasts and a safe harbour have gone together.

That brings us not only to what a forest was but what, in England at any rate, it contained in

A. DURRANT

### MORNING IN EPPING FOREST

*A delightful study of spreading shafts of sunlight in a cool glade, where morning mists still linger. Epping provides a variety of pleasing walks through copse and thicket and beneath the shade of hornbeam, beech and oak. This beautiful sanctuary was saved for the nation by the Corporation of the City of London.*

singular—of Britain once was? Of many descriptions I like best that which appears in Camden. It has poetry and aims to describe, I think, only the specifically English forest, the chase, the royal domain as England once knew it. It has nothing to do with the primeval, the huge virginity of uncharted places. What Camden describes is very English indeed: " What a Forrest is, and the reason of that name, if you desire to know (but see you laugh not thereat) take it heere out of the blacke booke of the Exchequer. *A Forrest is a safe harbor, and abiding place of deere or beasts, not of any whatsoever, but of wilde, and such as delight in woods : not in every place,*

the way of savagery. There are, or were, five beasts which were properly beasts of forest, or venery; they were hart, hind, hare, boar and wolf. It is curious that the hare is there but not the fox. It may seem curious, in fact, that the hare is there at all, since hares are not creatures of the woodland, but of open country.

This brings us to something else, to the necessity of revising that poetical definition of Camden, to add that a forest is not necessarily a piece of woodland but, according to John Manwood, " a certain territory or circuit of woody grounds or pastures, known in its bonds and privileges . . . to be under the Kings protection for his princely delight." This holds good for the forest of today, for Dartmoor and Exmoor especially, and for the New Forest, in all of which woodland is much broken up by pasture and heath and by villages and private land.

But there was a time, and authorities hold it to have been not so very far distant, before princely delight had its day, when almost the whole of England was forest. Cæsar found it so : the land with any settled agricultural life all being confined to the south coast, the interior being a single great forest, with clearings for habitation.

### Born Hunters

It was the Saxons, and not the Romans, who did so much to change all that. Nothing could have delighted them more, as born hunters and lovers of the sword, than those vast and almost barbaric territories abounding with beast and game, and it is in their time that the first records of the enactment of forest laws are to be found, laws which were passed in 1016, in the reign of Canute the Great. They were inexorably cruel and inspired by sadistic savagery. I quote again from Camden, who is in turn quoting *Polycraticon* by John of Salisburie :

". . . that which you may marvell more at, to lay gins for birds, to let snares to allure them with nooze or pipe, or by any waies laying whatever to entrap or take them, is oftentimes by vertue of an Edict, made a crime, and either answered with forfeiture of goods, or punished with losse of limbe or life . . . Husbandmen are debarred their fallow fields which Deeres have libertie to stray abroad, and that their pasture may be augmented, the poor farmer is abridged, and cut short of his grounds. What is sowne, planted, or grassed, they keep for the husbandmen that bee tenants : both pasturage for heardmen, drovers and graziers, and Bee-hives they exclude from floury plots : yea, the very bees themselves are scarcely permitted to use their natural libertie."

These laws, enforced right down to the reign of Henry III, touched not only commoners, but clergy and nobles, and it was the nobles who, fed up at last, drew up the Charta de Forresta, got it signed and brought it into force. That began the most amazingly complex system of forest government, altogether too cluttered up with obsolete legalities and phraseology for the layman of today, with its system of visiting justices, courts of attachment, courts of regard

DIXON-SCOTT

### SWAN GREEN IN THE FOREST
*Swan Green is a typical hamlet in the New Forest near Lyndhurst. Two miles away the Knightwood Oak is a splendid example of the trees which provided the wood for the ships of Queen Elizabeth's navy. Ruthless cutting three centuries ago, depleted the forest, though some twenty thousand trees still remain.*

EDGAR WARD

## THE UPPER POND AT BURNHAM BEECHES

*This splendid tract of mixed woodland, extending over nearly 500 acres, is part of East Burnham Common, south of Beaconsfield. It was a favourite haunt of the poet Gray, and it was his letters which first brought it into notice. The woods were purchased by the City of London Corporation and dedicated to the public in 1883.*

and so on which enquired into offences and complaints against the forest laws.

All this went on for a long time. It serves to show how important a part of English life the forest was, and also how important it was not only for kings, for the princely delight, but for the people. William the Conqueror, in order to create the New Forest and to ensure himself a little sport, could demolish thirty-six mother churches, innumerable towns and villages and appropriate an area of something like fifty miles compass and then enforce his wishes with a tyrannical lopping off of disobedient limbs; but later we get laws, by the demand of the people, which are not only less harsh but also enforced by a proper system of judicial circuit and inquiry. That seems to me one of the most interesting of early English movement towards democracy.

Only a country of very considerable forest area could have needed such a system of government. If you look at the map of England today and draw an imaginary line across it from Rutland to Nottinghamshire and the Isle of Anglesey, you will find that, excluding Scotland, almost all the forests are south of it: Dartmoor, Exmoor, Dean, Epping, Ashdown, the New, Savernake; and the most famous of the lesser, Rockingham and Salcey, in Northamptonshire, St. Leonards and Wolmer and Alice Holt, in Sussex, and so on.

Yet once, north of that line, there were forests which made the New Forest itself look very small beer. Cumberland and Westmorland contain great forests, with an appropriate conflict of outlaws. Yorkshire had great forests: the forests of Whitby and Knaresborough and, in the West Riding, Hatfield Chase, containing at least 180,000 acres, and, in the centre of the county, the forest of Gaultries, and still others. Lancashire and Cheshire had wild and desolate forests: the forests of Macclesfield, Delamere, Wirrall, of which the last is said to have covered the land between the estuaries of Mersey and Dee.

### Legendary Forest of Anderida

South of the line the former extent of forests seems, now, incredible. The whole of Northamptonshire is said to have been forest; Windsor Forest, of which we now have only Windsor Great Park, was 120 miles in length and thirty miles wide; the great and almost legendary forest of Anderida, of which we now have Ashdown and a bunch of minor names, stretched for about the same distance right across Sussex; London is said to have been surrounded by forest; in Essex there were two great names, Epping and Hainault, of which the last is now a ghost; in Leicestershire lay the forest of Charnwood, of an antiquity, according to a nineteenth-century authority, " higher than authentic history will carry us," and in turn part of a still greater forest, the forest of Arden, which is said to have once stretched across the whole of middle England; in Oxfordshire there was Wychwood Forest, over 3,000 acres, disafforested in the nineteenth century; in Staffordshire the royal forest of Needwood was, in 1658, roughly the size of what the New Forest is at the present day, 92,000 acres, and in 1684 contained almost 50,000 trees, not counting holly and underwood.

According to an early nineteenth-century observer England then had (c. 1801) sixty-nine forests, thirteen chases, and something like 750 parks.

Such an extent of woodland must have been a wonderful thing. The strange thing is that literature, even the literature of the romantic revival, has given us very little in the way of a pictorial record of it. Today, that lovely heritage of woodland would have sent a hundred writers bounding about with an excess of delight. Yet

DIXON-SCOTT

### THE SPREADING FOREST OF SAVERNAKE

*Some sixteen miles in circumference, Savernake Forest, in Wiltshire, is probably the finest expanse of ancient woodland in England. Mighty oaks of venerable age, tall beeches making lovely Gothic aisles, thickets of thorn and many delightful glades give it the true appearance of a forest as it is generally imagined.*

In the reign of Elizabeth a list of nearly eighty forests was compiled, with reasonable accuracy, by Sir Henry Spelman, and of these more than half lay in the south, only fifteen counties and those mostly on the east coast, having no forest at all. There were always, too, a great number of parks and chases, many of large extent. A park was an enclosure, in a general way, for deer, the name lapsing if all deer were destroyed. A chase was of the same liberty as a park, but not enclosed and much more like a forest, but having no courts and no judicial machinery at all for the infliction of punishment. Every forest was a chase, but every chase was not, however, a forest.

the famous novelists and poets of a hundred years back offer us very little in the way of a picture of rural England. From this I except Crabbe and Clare and Emily Brontë and Hazlitt. Of the rest Keats and Shelley and Byron were more celestially and sensuously occupied; Dickens and Thackeray were devoted, almost entirely, to an exposition of the social life of the day; and it was left to a gentleman—some said *not* a gentleman—named William Cobbett to tour the country on a nag's back and give us such a vivid, downright and forthright picture of rural England in general and some remarks on forests in particular, as had not been done since early times.

H. FELTON

## A CROWN FOREST

*Delamere Forest, in Cheshire, now Crown Property, is a relic of the ancient spreading Forest of Mara and Mondrum. Much of it has been cleared of timber, but there are still some tracts of woodland, mainly consisting of conifers. Oakmere and Hatchmere are two meres which may have suggested the present name.*

DIXON-SCOTT

## THE LONG WALK, WINDSOR

*Windsor Great Park, traversed by the famous Long Walk, although it covers about 1,800 acres is but a fragment of the ancient Royal Forest of Windsor. In its glades roamed the ghost of Herne the Hunter, who, according to tradition, having incurred the wrath of Elizabeth, hanged himself on a tree by which she would pass,*

Later, Tennyson made a most abortive attempt to put the English countryside on paper in terms of shadowy romance and rose leaves and that special splendour that falls on castle walls. Then, still later, after Hardy had also done something, came a trio of writers who gave us, together, the picture of rural and especially woodland England that we had lacked. W. H. Hudson, Richard Jefferies and Edward Thomas filled in that large and hungry gap in our literature with sumptuous and bountiful generosity, and in Hudson we have, to my mind, the loveliest descriptions of the New Forest that have ever been done or are, in fact, ever likely to be done in English.

The New Forest is still our largest, most popular and perhaps most precious forest. It is in some ways an ironical survival. Created out of a viciously selfish demand for royal pleasure,

REMNANT OF AN EXTENSIVE FOREST

DIXON-SCOTT

*Ashdown Forest is a shrunken remnant of the Forest of Anderida, which extended from Kent to Hampshire. It was the hunting ground of John of Gaunt to whom it was granted by Edward III.*

at the cost of a living and pulsating limb of the land, then governed by the harshest possible system of laws at the cost, paid by the offenders, by living and pulsating limbs in reality, it became, much later, the source of supply for staggering quantities of oak for the ships of the Royal Navy and has become, in our day, the haunt of gipsies and naturalists, cricketers playing in the grass glades and a million cars on summer Sundays. An odd fate for a royal domain and a still odder memorial to a piece of royal barbarism. It is difficult to know whether to praise or damn that Conqueror.

### Secret Places

I have seen the forest in May, when the oaks are in flower and the immense pink clouds of rhododendron are in blossom and when, in secret places, great bushes of wild yellow azalea bloom with almost exotic look and fragrance, and the cotton-grass is like blowing cocoons in the dark heathland; and I have also seen it again in July and February. But I am not sure that it is not seen at its best, at any time, from a distance and from some considerable height. From the hills beyond Romsey the vast extent of trees, in May of all colours from olive and yellow to bottle and emerald, is very impressive. From here you get the effect, as you never get lower down and among the trees, of both width and density, the true impression of a forest, the effect of looking down on something at once beautiful and great and, strangely, quite virgin and unspoilt. In the forest itself the sense of inertia is very great; the trees sap up the air and leave the body and soul limp, with a curious sleepy dejection. The stretches of raw, brown gorse-broken heath have more vigour of life and, to me, a special beauty of their own and a sense of primeval wildness. Cobbett hated them; but then, Cobbett hated potatoes. I feel in them a sense of release, of width and light, after the soporific airs under too many trees.

The closeness of sea to forest here is wonderfully attractive, too. On a misty May morning I went once, with horse and caravan, from Beaulieu up to Southampton, and in a very still world of mist-gloomed spring trees and heath I heard the boom of ships in Southampton Water. It created a strange sense of solitude, some feeling that the forest was really vast,

"DAILY HERALD"

## GNARLED OLD TIMBER IN EPPING FOREST

*For a thousand years this Essex woodland has retained its forest character. In Saxon times Edward the Confessor " made Ranger of my forest of Chelmsford Hundred and Deering Hundred, Ralph Peverell, for him and his heirs for ever; With both the red and fallow deer, hare and fox, otter and badger; wild fowl of all sorts, partridges and pheasants, timber and underwood, roots and tops, with power to preserve the Forest."*

EDGAR WARD

## THE NEW FOREST

*A forest in the widest meaning of the word, covering 62,746 acres of land in its wild natural state, uncultivated and unenclosed. A delightful variety of scenery is to be found here and a feature of the forest are its shaggy and semi-wild ponies which roam its glades and cross its highways with little regard for passing traffic.*

primitive, cut off from all worlds except the world of sea and sea-sounds. It was a romantic notion, but in some way impressive and, as I think of it now, unreal.

But if the New Forest is the most popular of present-day English forests, there is no doubt at all which is the most romantic. Sherwood has 700 years start in the race of romanticism. No other piece of country in England, except perhaps the country of Hereward the Wake, has ever had such power over the common imagination. Robin Hood is the arch type of all romantic outlaw heroes, and there is no chance of his ever being usurped. The forest in Hood's day must have been immense, stretching over Nottinghamshire, and extending into Yorkshire and Derbyshire. According to Camden it " overshadowed all the Country over with greene leaved branches, and boughs and armes of trees twisted one within another, so implicated the woods together that a man could scarcely goe alone in the beaten pathes : But now the trees grow not so thicke, yet hath it an infinite number of fallow Deere, yea and Stagges with their stately branching heads feeding within it."

Take a map, and look. It is one of the most fascinating forms of stand-still travel to search the map of England for the word forest. It crops up with surprising frequency and in surprising places. It never indicates much more than a large wood or a group of woods, and

it may even indicate more heath than wood, and in that sense it is a mockery ; but it indicates, at least, the situation of the treasure we have lost.

Not that all of it has been lost. In Northamptonshire, now much industrialized, it is surprising to find three forests, Salcey and Whittlewood in the south, and Rockingham, once very large, overlooking the great green width of the Welland valley in the north-east. In Sussex the remnants of the great Anderida appear in great and small names : Wolmer, St. Leonards, Alice Holt ; Worth, Tilgate, Sheffield, Pease Pottage and so on. In Hampshire, the forest of Bere, and in Worcestershire the Wyre Forest are still considerable names. Kent still has its forests. Windsor has gone, leaving only the Great Park, but Savernake remains, glorious with beeches. Hainault has gone, but Epping remains.

### Departed Glory

And so on. The giants have gone ; the ghosts remain. It seems strange, now, to think of an almost wholly afforested England in the past, and stranger still to imagine an afforested England of the future, a world of lost by-passes and ruined filling stations being replaced by a world of trees so thick " that a man could scarcely goe alone in the beaten paths," a world of outlaw and deer and fox and boar and adder and silence. Yet many stranger things than that have happened in the evolution of this island.

# THE VARIED COAST OF BRITAIN

## *by* E. A. BAKER

A GROUP of islands west of a continent, facing the great ocean currents, and thus exposed to the maximum of erosion by the sea and the maximum of weathering, are bound to be particularly rich in coastal scenery. When, as is the case of the British Isles, they are composed of a very large variety of rock, hard and soft, ancient and comparatively recent, reacting in different ways to forces of denudation, the maximum picturesqueness inevitably results. And then, these islands of ours lie not very far from the edge of the Arctic, and some æons ago went through the sculpturing process of the Great Ice Age.

The higher portions were at that time ranges of lofty peaks, snow-covered and seamed with glaciers, which for long periods cut and undermined the rocks, and produced both the summits which we now see and the abrupt cliffs which overhang the Atlantic. The present highest ranges tower chiefly above the coast—the Lake Mountains, the peaks of Snowdonia, Macgillicuddy's Reeks by the Lakes of Killarney, the Mountains of Mourne, and the most rugged of the Highland bens. They " roll " as the song writer puts it, or tumble or plunge, down to the sea, or beetle along and overhang the foam, often for many miles.

The Rockies and the Cordilleras of America remind us of this tendency of mountains to group themselves along the coast, and nearly always the western coast. Some of the tips of old submerged peaks are now islets, Ailsa Craig, for instance, which is such an astonishing and beautiful object in the Firth of Clyde. In fact, the British Isles are an almost countless archipelago of big islands and little, Great Britain and Ireland being simply the biggest of the lot.

For diversity of contour and general picturesqueness they can vie with the Greek or any other Archipelago. And though our climate is not always smiling, its continual changes of expression, nay, its very frowns, are an essential element of their beauty where land and sea mingle. Take any famous example of scenic beauty abroad, such as the view of the Alps at the head of the Adriatic, or of the Cyclades and other Greek isles just mentioned, or of the Pyrenees or the Sierra Nevada glimpsed from the sea, and you will find something to compare with it somewhere in our isles, for the simple reason that the peaks crowd closer to the sea—they are in and of the coast-line.

No one would underrate the grandeur of the west coast of Norway. But there is many a sea-loch in the highlands not less impressive than the finest Norwegian fjord ; and the rest of them, though not so colossally grim, are more enchanting in their blend of the sublime and the beautiful. Take any headland, from the North Cape to Gibraltar or from Finisterre to Matapan, and you will find plenty of British promontories as grand, as rugged, and as famous in mariners' lore. For it is notable that our very language shows how our forefathers have been struck by the characteristic features of our coasts. Look on the map for the number of words for a cape or headland—foreland, head, point, bill, butt, ness, mull—not to mention individual names, such as Lizard, or Hangman, or simply Land's End. Look at the words for inlets, straits and estuaries —sound, bay, cove, firth, haven, channel, and, in Scotland, minch and loch. All this has a very obvious significance.

It is usually the hardest rock that makes the

STEPHENSON

### LOVELY CLOVELLY

*The picturesque herring-fishing village of Clovelly, in Devonshire, is distinguished by a main street descending in a series of steps to the cove here illustrated.*

STEPHENSON

### THE SENTINEL OF THE SOUTH DOWNS

*Forming one of the highest points of the South Downs, Beachy Head, in Sussex, is a landmark to Channel navigation.   For over 100 years a lighthouse has marked this spot, the present station being erected on the rocks below the Head.   The view from the summit is one of the most varied in the south of England.*

W. F. TAYLOR

### THE BOLD CLIFFS OF FLAMBOROUGH

*These lofty chalk cliffs, 400 feet high, are a famous sanctuary for sea-birds.   This length of coast with little opportunities for landing was once frequented by French and Flemish pirates.   It was off Flamborough Head in 1779 that the renowned Paul Jones captured the British ship, " Serapis," after a fierce encounter.*

most rugged coast. Yet some of the finest sea-cliffs in Britain are composed of chalk, one of the softest of rocks. The legend is that Cæsar called this country Albion on account of the white walls which were the first thing to heave into sight when he crossed the Channel. It is not only the Cliffs of Dover, or Beachy Head, or the splintered and richly-coloured chalk cliffs of the Isle of Wight, that are our standing memorial of that classic legend. For the very finest, the most sheer and forbidding of the chalk cliffs are those of Flamborough Head and the Bempton and

Other rocks emerge, and the coast changes its outline farther north, growing more varied, and in parts rugged and romantic in the extreme, towards Northumberland and the Border.

Southwards, the East Coast is comparatively tame till the chalk cliffs of Kent are reached. These shall be the starting-point of our perambulation, west along the shores of the Channel, up the indented margin of the Irish Sea, on to Scotland, over to Ireland, and then home again.

Under quiet conditions, the white walls of cliff along the English Channel are beautiful in

STEPHENSON

### GOLDEN CAP ON THE DORSET COAST

*Above the tiny hamlet of Sea Town, east of Lyme Regis, like a miniature Table Mountain, rises the beautiful headland of Golden Cap. Its multi-coloured strata, its smooth green turf and golden gorse enhance its bold outlines. From its summit there is a wide view from Portland Bill to the white cliffs of Beer, in Devon.*

Speeton cliffs north of it, in the East Riding of Yorkshire. The terrific plunge straight down to the water takes one's breath away ; from above, the wall looks smooth and sheer. And yet from below, in a boat or at low tide, you find great caves have been scooped out at the base, and here and there groups of arches have been pierced in the massive chalk.

The picturesqueness below rivals the wonder of the view from the top of the cliffs, over Bridlington Bay to the south, and in the other direction to Filey and Filey Brig, with Scarborough Castle and the coast about Robin Hood's Bay, barely caught sight of in the remoter distance.

themselves ; but at close quarters they also form a vast screen against which the phenomena of the sea in stormy weather appear magnified and glorified. Turner, and how many other artists, appreciated this when they painted Beachy Head and other great white headlands, with surf and cloudwrack flying across and half shrouding their enormous faces.

The Needles look their best in a storm. But the Isle of Wight has a whole gamut of beauties all its own. It is a microcosm of complicated geology, as a sail round its coast-line brings out tellingly. Between it and the mainland stretch the Solent and Spithead, with Southampton

PHOTOCHROM

### THE JAGGED NEEDLES

*Where the chalk downs thrust into the sea on the western extremity of the Isle of Wight, the waves have battered the rocks into three isolated stacks.   A fourth and more slender pinnacle, which fell in 1764, probably inspired the name of the Needles.   A lighthouse at the end of the rocks warns Channel shipping of these cruel teeth.*

Water running deep into the land : three of those majestic firths, inlets, and havens, like Plymouth Sound and Milford Haven, which are peculiarities of the British coast.

All along one side of the Solent stretches the fringe of the New Forest. Along the other extends the Isle, with its heathery downs and wooded bays, and then the chalk cliffs of Freshwater, Totland Bay, the upturned strata of Alum Bay, banded with vivid colour, and finally the Needles. It is hard to say whether they look in between. There are endless temptations to linger, before we put in at Plymouth Sound or find ourselves skirting the promontory of the Lizard. The rocks are harder here ; the Lizard is composed of serpentine, which is at least as durable as granite, and has moreover the colour of a precious stone.

One of my oldest and most exhilarating memories is of coming down one morning for a bathe in Kynance Cove, when the sea was gently foaming in over smoothest sands, between

A. DURRANT

A POPULAR CORNISH BAY

*The picturesque sweep of Bedruthan Bay, with its sands studded with isolated masses of rock, curiously weathered, is reached from St. Columb Minor by a series of 123 steps cut in the cliff. One of the rock towers is known locally as the Queen Bess Rock and is said to present a full-length picture of the Virgin Queen.*

best from the sea or from the high downs towering above, with the farther coast in the distance. To see the Chines, which are such a striking feature of the east and south-west flanks of the Isle, it is also necessary to make a tour both by land and by water.

Westward, right away to the Lizard and Land's End, it is a continual succession of beauties ; but the arresting objects are St. Alban's Head, the Isle of Portland, and Start Point, with the strange configurations of Lulworth Cove and the Durdles, the Chesil Bank and the cliffs of Lyme Regis, and the magnificent drowned valleys of the Dart, the Salcombe river, and the Yealm, enormous blocks of serpentine, wet and glistening in the sunshine. This and Mullion Cove open out on Mount's Bay, another of our finest inlets, dominated by the granite mass of St. Michael's Mount, a peninsula at low water, and the rugged heights of the uttermost corner of England frowning behind. I have stood on Dunmore Head, in Ireland, the westernmost point of Europe ; and I have stood on Finisterre. Both are high and rugged, and look out over scarped rocks and islets to the Atlantic. But Land's End is, or was when I used to know it, the most imposing of these three terminations of a country.

The walk along the cliff-top, past the Logan Rock to Land's End itself, and then up the other side to Gurnard Head, is like going along the edge of a mighty castellated rampart, shattered and breached by ages of strife, but still formidable, still defiant. The reef surmounted by the Longships Lighthouse, everlastingly swept by the surf, is the final bit of Old England, reminding one irresistibly of the tossing plume in a warrior's helm.

The long sail up the coast of Cornwall and

All along both sides of the Channel, the impressive feature is the hills of Somerset, or of South Wales crowding forward above the green country between them and the sea. But if our course is round St. David's Head and up the Welsh coast, the hills rise into mountains. The far-stretching bulk of Plynlimon is the dominating feature of Cardiganshire, till, after passing Aberystwyth and Aberdovey, we have the lordlier mass of Cader Idris towering a few miles from the shore. North of that rise the peaks of Snowdonia, with

FRITH

### THE WAVE-WORN ARCH OF LYDSTEP CAVERN

*The limestone strata which reach the sea along the Pembroke coast provide a number of interesting scenic features, including several picturesque caverns.  Lydstep Point, south-west of Tenby, is typical.  This precipitous, level-crested promontory, overlooking Skrinkle Bay, has several great caverns similar to the one seen above.*

Devon to Barnstaple Bay and the entrance to the Bristol Channel is not a whit less interesting. Heathery forelands and the heights of Exmoor and then the Quantocks tower over cliff and sandy bay. Some of the big grassy hills rise straight from the water as imposingly as Countisbury Foreland itself. Once, on the Great Hangman, I remember two of us saw an incipient Brocken spectre, our shadows outlined on the bank of mist floating between us and the sea, with shreds of a rainbow, or glory, trying as if to encircle them.

a long spine extending between Cardigan Bay and Caernarvon Bay and culminating in the gracious saddleback of the Rivals. So we pass the wave-washed stacks of Holyhead, round into the Irish Sea.

Nothing would be pleasanter than to coast along the southern margin of the great bight between North Wales and the low-lying edges of Lancashire ; the Welsh mountains are in full view behind a picturesque coast-line, and then in reasonably clear weather, the hills of the Pennine redeem the dullness of the flats, and

W. F. TAYLOR

### THE TOE OF ENGLAND

*At the end of the Cornish peninsula, England dips a granite toe in the breakers of the Atlantic. Other parts of the coast may present more rugged grandeur, but the magic words " Land's End " invest this spot with exceptional appeal. Beyond the headland and beneath the waves is said to be the lost land of Lyonesse.*

R. M. ADAM

## SUNSET ON A HIGHLAND LOCH

*Between the Isle of Skye and the mainland runs Loch Alsh. One of the most beautiful of Scottish sea lochs, it presents a delightful combination of mountains and sea. Loch Alsh divides into Loch Long and Loch Duich, which penetrate farther into the hills. In the right-hand corner may be seen the castle of Eilean Donan.*

everywhere there are gleaming sands and wildernesses of sand-hills near the sea. But let us steer due north, till the Lake Mountains are in sight. They, too, come almost down to the sea. Black Combe is a far-seen headland, the narrow margin between its steep sides and the water disappearing in the wider perspective. It is all but 2,000 feet high, and a famous view-point— a noble corner-stone to the cluster of peaks encircling Scafell.

### The Mull of Galloway

All along the coast of Galloway, it is the same thing, but in rich variety, rocky headlands, deep bays, and stretches of sand, with the naked moorlands rising to gaunt summits behind. Then at last we round the Mull of Galloway, and steering north between Scotland and Ireland enter the busy, ship-strewn waters of the Firth of Clyde, majestic approach to one of the foremost seats of commerce in the world. As the map shows, Scotland is almost cut in two halves by the enormous indentations of the Firth of Forth on one side and the Firth of Clyde on the other, just as again farther north it is bisected by the Great Glen, almost a continuous string of lakes, with the Moray Firth at the north-east end and the Firth of Lorne at the south-west. The isolated monolith, the Bass Rock, sentinels the approach to Edinburgh, as Ailsa Craig, on

our starboard bow, does the great portal to Glasgow.

The finest view I ever had of this marvellous scene was, not from the air, nor from shipboard, but many years ago from the cliffs above the Giant's Causeway, over there in Antrim, on one of those halcyon days of spring that store up images for a lifetime. Everyone knows the Causeway. A great flow of lava has solidified in a countless multitude of basaltic columns, which stretches down and into the sea. Hard by, in the Amphitheatre, the wall of a deep bay is lined with the same columnar formation, which breaks out here and there into such fantastic objects as have been nicknamed the " giant's organ," the " giant's cannon," the " lady's fan," and so on. On that day the ledges between the cliffs, and every cranny holding a handful of earth, were garlanded with primroses. These and the beetling cliffs, ridges cut into arches, and the foaming skerries 400 feet below the cliff-top, were more fascinating than the Causeway itself. But what took the breath away was the panorama of the Scottish mainland and the isles environing the Firth of Clyde, across the scarcely wrinkled azure.

At first I took the block of land, apparently a few miles out, for Irish Rathlin Island. Then I began to recognize old familiar friends. This was not Rathlin, but Kintyre. There to the left was Islay, with the Paps of Jura sticking up to the right. Right in front was Arran, with Goatfell and the appendant ridges thrusting down to the sea. And farther still to the right, Ailsa Craig raised its head like some ocean monster peering above the waves. Hundreds of peaks were visible behind, part of the great host of the Grampians that look west towards the Hebrides.

The west coast of Scotland is so deeply and plentifully indented that freshwater loch seems to blend with sea loch, and the far-stretching forelands and peninsulas are inextricably mingled with the islands. A cruise north from Glasgow gets exciting when the Crinan Canal or the Mull of Kintyre is passed, and the boat is threading the Inner Hebrides. If one had sailed up Loch Long or Loch Fyne, it would have brought one ultimately almost as far inland as the head of Loch Lomond. Loch Linnhe has the charms of an arm of the sea and of a great inland lake ; and it sends out limbs to right and left, Loch Etive, Loch Leven and Loch Eil, which reach far in to the very foot of the mountains. The two ranges of lofty peaks enclosing Glencoe have western abutments, in Ben Vair and the Pap of Glencoe, that rise straight from the shore ; and the buttresses of Ben Nevis and Mamore Forest tower over the coast-line of Loch Linnhe.

### A Giant's Footprint

On a clear day, from the top of Ben Nevis, the view extends to the isles ; the summits of Arran and of Jura, of Mull and Rum and Eigg, and even the red peak of Blaven in Skye can be seen. Mull should be circumnavigated, if all its points of interest are to be seen. Rounding the Ross of Mull leads to Staffa and Iona, both unique in different ways. Fingal's Cave, on Staffa, is hollowed out by the sea in the same columnar basalt as gave us the Giant's Causeway : according to legend, the same giant left his footprint here. The basalt may be tracked by way of the Treshnish Isles to the Shiant Isles, north of Skye. Bleak Iona is nothing much to look at in comparison ; but the hoary old cathedral is a memorial of the oldest spiritual movement in Scotland and England, and homage must be paid to St. Columba who landed there about A.D. 563.

W. F. TAYLOR

## A REMOTE FISHING VILLAGE

*On the shores of Loch Broom, in the north-western edge of Ross-shire and more than 30 miles from a railway, is the isolated village of Ullapool. It was established in 1788 by the British Fisheries' Association, but in recent years has gained some popularity as a holiday resort. At the mouth of Loch Broom are the Summer Isles.*

Along the north of the Ross of Mull lies Loch Scridain, with Ben More, lava-built, towering behind. Then a deep bay forks into a pair of sea lochs, half-encircling Ulva's Isle, and looking west across the Passage of Coll to Coll and Tiree and the Outer Isles. Loch Sunart, to the north of Mull, runs so deep inland that it almost cuts through to Loch Linnhe. But the ordinary route from Oban to the Hebrides and the Isle of Skye is through the Sound of Mull, a beautiful strait winding like a river between the hills of Morven and the island.

It is a sail that must not be missed at any price. It brings you out to Loch Sunart; and then, doubling Ardnamurchan Point, you have before you one of the most astonishing views that this or the other hemisphere can show. Ahead, Eigg lifts its huge, outlandish tower of basalt, the Scuir, high into the heavens. A little to the left and almost behind it rises the long, serrated crest of Rum. Green islands, rocky islets, and odd bits of porphyry and trap, stud the watery expanse here and there. Beyond is Skye, with the Red Hills and Blaven at the nearer end and the Black Cuillin farther to the left scraping the clouds with their teeth.

This is the seascape, but the procession of dark inlets to Loch Morar, Loch Aylort, and then Loch Nevis and Loch Hourn, the loch of heaven and the loch of hell, is not less

entrancing, with the big peaks in between, from Ben Resipol to Larven and Ben Screel, two mountains that I have longed in vain to climb, so far are they from human hotel or so strictly guarded by the deer-forest owners.

At Lochalsh, where Skye and the mainland almost touch, Loch Duich opens to the right, and must on no account be left unexplored. It runs up between the hills to the lower end of two famous glens, with the enormous mass of Ben Attow to the extreme left, Scour Ouran and the Five Sisters of Kintail in the middle, and the long range of the Saddle to the south. The lofty and savage pass of Glen Lichd on one side rivals Glencoe in grandeur; Glen Shiel on the other is wildly romantic in character, though it is a natural highway to the other side of Scotland and has a good road down it.

### Black Cuillin of Skye

The great route for traffic is through the broad firth or sound between the coast of western Ross and Skye; it leads to Portree, and on to Stornoway. Coming out into it through the narrows of Loch Alsh is almost as great a sensation as the entry to the open sea beyond grim Ardnamurchan. On one hand tower the Red and Black Cuillin of Skye, with the long, barren islands of Scalpay and Raasay forming a breakwater off shore; on the other, behind the actual

FOX PHOTOS

CASTLE OF SCOTLAND'S PATRON SAINT

*Perched on a rocky height on the Fife coast stand the ruins of the Castle of St. Andrews. Founded in 1200 it has witnessed many stirring events. There, Cardinal Beaten was assassinated by the followers of George Wishart who had been burnt for heresy, and the murderers, joined by Knox, defended themselves within its walls.*

R. M. ADAM

## WHERE THE LAMMERMUIRS MEET THE SEA

*From Berwick to the Firth of Forth runs an attractive length of coast with rocky headlands and little bays. One of the most prominent features is St. Abb's Head, named after the Saxon, Saint Ebba. Here the high range of rough grassy hills, known as the Lammermuirs, terminate abruptly in a bold high promontory.*

coast-line, which is still the bare rocky terrace, with rare strips of sand or sandy coves, that has been our close companion all the way, the mountains of western Ross just up from a vast elevated platform of the oldest British rock— a barren wilderness, with picturesque glens and gorges cleaving it however in places, for the benefit of those who venture on a tramp into such an inhospitable interior.

It is the same thing farther north, and more so, as we get nearer to Sutherland and Cape Wrath. The coast of the Minch, between Lewis and the mainland, has several openings into lovely sea lochs hardly inferior to Loch Duich. Loch Torridon, for instance, which has an inner section, Upper Loch Torridon, stretches along the base of Ben Alligin up to the foot of huge, black Liathach, behind which frown the cliffs, of Torridonian gritstone, of Ben Eighe. Swinburne had a night walk here, and in one of his most musical poems, sings of the glory of this intermingling of mountain and sea—the portal that opens

" On the world unconfined of the mountains, the reign of the sea supreme."

That is what gives such enchantment to the Gairloch and Poolewe, from which it is but a step over to Loch Maree and Ben Slioch; and still more to little Loch Broom, at the head of which, round the lone hostelry of Dundonnell,

are grouped the incomparable Challich Hills, or An Teallach, as the Gael uncompromisingly spells the name.

Here we have another colossal mass of the purple Torridon grit, rising in dark precipices round a sombre lake to a serrated knife-edge. From the summits, you look over the Sutherland coast and bare and forbidding interior, with the weird mountain-shapes of Canisp, Suilven, Stack Polly and her sisters, raising their heads above the waste.

### Old Man of Hoy

It has not been my luck, personally, to get farther north, but the cliffs of Sutherland and Caithness, with their old red sandstone stacks cut off from the land, and such things as the precipices of Orkney, with the Old Man of Hoy, a stack of the same resistant stuff, soaring 600 feet out of the water, are too famous to need description. These are paralleled, however, by the scenery on the west coast of Skye, where the volcanic foundations of the isle are exposed and face the Atlantic in the lofty cliffs of Talisker, and in the group of basaltic stacks extending into the sea, known as Macleod's Maidens.

There is nothing like so much of scenic importance on the east coast of Britain as on the west, though almost everywhere sea and land are continually creating those symphonies of colour and

EDGAR WARD

### A SMUGGLER'S RETREAT

*The little fishing village and holiday resort of Eyemouth, on the Berwickshire coast, was once notorious for its smugglers who augmented their more legitimate earnings by evading the excisemen. It was said to have so many subterranean passages and hiding places that there was as much of the village below ground as above.*

atmosphere which are not surpassed in ethereal beauty even among the mountains. Here and there some striking feature is a landmark; a crag of old red sandstone, with blow-holes and isolated stacks, a limestone cliff or a solid wall of conglomerate, a battered bulwark against the assaults of the North Sea in winter.

There are also deep land-locked inlets and harbours, more like our southern havens than the wild sea lochs of the west, finest among them the Dornoch Firth, the deep and winding Cromarty Firth, and the wide Moray Firth, with Beauly Firth opening into a deeper recess at the head of it. Lofty Ben Wyvis gazes down on the head of the Cromarty Firth, the gateway to which is a narrow gorge between the two rocky peaks called the Sutors. Of the blow-holes, the Buller of Buchan, in Aberdeenshire, is certainly the finest. Seen from inland, this is a huge pot-hole half-filled with sea-water, which is fed by the tides through a cave-like hole to the sea.

### Wave-beaten Cliffs

The cliffs of Kincardineshire are among the noblest in Britain; those of Berwickshire are among the more picturesque, hewn out of hard, contorted Silurian rock. And all along the Northumbrian coast, many a bold headland or line of wave-beaten cliffs will give us pause, a goodly number of them crowned from time

immemorial with fortresses built against foes from the sea or from across the Border. So old they are, they seem part of the geology of the region. Dunstanburgh Castle, on its basaltic sea-cliff, is a ruin; Warkworth, looking down on the Coquet and Coquet Island, is better preserved; Bamburgh Castle has been only too well restored, and is now a palatial residence.

It is a very pleasant excursion at low water to tramp over the sands to Lindisfarne, or Holy Island, where the abbey of St. Aidan and St. Cuthbert is in ruins, but the gallant little castle of Beblowe, perched on a jutting rock, is now in a perfect state of habitation. This and the Farne Islands in general are almost as rich in early Christian legend as Iona, from which monastery St. Aidan originally came.

Scanned on the map, England, it will be noticed, appears almost cut in two by the Thames estuary and the Bristol Channel, just as Scotland is by the Firths of Forth and Clyde; and, again like Scotland, it has a sort of waist where a great cantle of the Irish Sea on one side is balanced by the Wash and the Humber on the other. Ireland on the map presents a much more buxom figure. She is solidly built, without a pronounced waist anywhere. On the west, however, the Atlantic side is deeply frilled and indented, and shows the far-projecting capes and the narrow inlets that abound on the west coast of Scotland;

but they are not so many, and there is not the same multitude of islands of every size and shape.

From the Giant's Causeway, we looked westward to Malin Head. Between the two points opens one of the finest of those great landlocked havens, Lough Foyle, with Londonderry at its head. And, hidden by the Inishowen Peninsula, another comes up from the west almost to meet it, in Lough Swilly. All down the Irish shore of the Irish Sea, great bays and estuaries and winding havens rival those of England, and mark the natural sites for great sea ports: Belfast Lough, Strangford Lough, Dundrum Bay, Dundalk Bay, and Dublin Bay, and Wexford and Carlingford Harbours.

## Magnificent Harbours

The Irish havens or sounds have the best of it for picturesqueness, with the Mourne Mountains and the Wicklows and many another fine hill towering behind, steep slopes of green slashed with purple heather or golden gorse and tipped with rock. The south has Waterford Harbour, Youghal Harbour, and the magnificent harbours of Cork and Kinsale. Westward of these it begins to be rugged and indented; and after rounding Cape Clear and Mizen Head we come to a series of majestic inlets, Bantry Bay, the Kenmare River, and Dingle Bay, which can only be rivalled, certainly not outdone, by the great sea lochs of Scotland. For these are really drowned mountain-valleys, sloping down from the Macgillicuddy Rocks and neighbouring ridges, and the geological architecture is on a large scale.

Curious to say, though I have been on the summit of every one of these Killarney peaks, even including isolated Brandon, on the far side of the Dingle Peninsula, I have never had a view from them. Pellucid as the day may be at the outset, by the time halfway to the summit is reached, it seems as if the demons believed to inhabit the upper regions wrapped themselves and their abode in a pea-soup atmosphere, needless to add, accompanied with oceans of wet. At my first visit to the Cliffs of Moher, three decades ago, the luck was almost the same: we saw the cliffs, but the return journey was one of

STEPHENSON

### SCENE OF CAPTAIN COOK'S BOYHOOD

*The Yorkshire hamlet of Staithes which lies hidden in a creek north of Whitby is one of the quaintest fishing villages in the country. In a little shop in Staithes, the Cleveland lad James Cook was apprenticed. From there he ran away to Whitby and the sea, and eventually earned fame as the " Circumnavigator of the world."*

W. F. TAYLOR

### A DELIGHTFUL BAY IN DONEGAL

*Except on the east, Ireland's coast-line is broken into multitudinous inlets, not the least charming of which is Mulroy Bay, seen above, with its fir and pine-clad peninsulas and wooded islets that dot its surface. At its southern end, near Milford, is famous Bunlin Glen, through whose secluded shades the little Bunlin River makes its way.*

the wettest in my memory. Those cliffs are unique. They rise straight from the sea, and at the top a wide shelf of gritstone overhangs for miles. If you drop a stone through a chink, it is seven seconds before it hits the water, a height that is, of 650 feet sheer.

### Barren Isles

The limestone forming a basement to a long section of the cliffs is pierced with caves, into which a boat can be rowed if the surf is not running. One cave has a great hole in the roof, through which in normal rough weather water and foam spout high in the air with the explosion of each breaker. The Aran Isles lie nearly a score of miles off this coast—a group of bare limestone slabs, without a tree and very nearly bare of vegetation. Sea and land are beautiful enough in fine weather ; but it is an austere and inhospitable beauty—naked rock, water, and sky —which inspires one with profound commiseration for those condemned to live upon it. But, after all, this and the wilderness that stretches away from Galway Bay to Donegal Bay are

almost identically the same thing as you have in Sutherland and Caithness and the sterner parts of western Ross. Mainland and islands are bare and grim if regarded as a possible home for man ; as a spare bit of the earth's surface left in the beauty of its pristine savagery, it all has its uses for minds tired of overmuch " civilization."

There are a thousand other objects of the sea-shore that one is tempted to dwell upon ; but to finish up nothing better in the way of a seamark is to be found anywhere in the British Isles than the cliffs which rise to the proportions of a mountain in Slieve League, at the south-west end of Donegal. The road to it from Donegal town and Killibegs is through vegetation as sub-tropical, and as ravishing a series of seascapes and landscapes, as Glengarriff itself could furnish. But that is only by the way. This mighty ridge, supported by a vast complication of cliffs and screes, the base of which is in the sea, more grandly even than the Cliffs of Moher in County Clare, is a great westerly land's end, a matchless finis terra, to a great continent and a great country fronting the deep.

# MELLOW BEAUTY OF OXFORD AND CAMBRIDGE

## *by* S. E. GUNN

AN American visitor to Oxford is said to have asked a gardener how the lovely college lawns were brought to such a pitch of perfection. " Well," was the reply, " you mows 'em and you rolls 'em, and you mows 'em and you rolls 'em, and you keeps on doing it for about five hundred years, and, well, there you are."

The supreme charm of Oxford and Cambridge is in their mellowness. The historic buildings of seven centuries constitute their glory; their attractiveness is to be found in the atmosphere of rare and dignified maturity which each university has gathered unto itself during the slow passage of unnumbered years. There are more beautiful cities in Britain ; more ancient and more interesting antiquities ; but nowhere so many venerable institutions which for so long have been devoted continuously to the same cause. In the colleges of these two old towns the life of learning has gone on for 700 years. Today, developed, reformed, and brought up to date though it may be, the same life goes on, in essentials exactly as it did in medieval times. Changes and upheavals there have been, periods of dullness and depression, but the lamp of scholarship has never been extinguished, and today, within walls raised to protect it centuries ago it burns more brightly than ever.

In the earlier Middle Ages Paris was the greatest centre of learning in Europe. Its University styled itself the " first school of the

OXFORD'S CURFEW TOWER
*Tom Tower, of Christ Church, houses Great Tom, a bell which sounds the curfew every night as a warning that all college gates will shortly be closed.*

D. MCLEISH

Church," and from every European country scholars flocked thither to sit at the feet of its famous teachers.

Many came from England. But wars with France and disputes with the Pope arose to hinder English students from crossing to Paris. This, and the development of a national patriotism, led to the assembling, as early as the beginning of the twelfth century, of small groups of scholars at both Oxford and Cambridge.

Oxford, standing on ground protected by the Thames and the Cherwell, commanding an important ford— hence the name—and situated on the borders of the great rival kingdoms of Mercia and Wessex, was a stronghold in Saxon times. Part of the masonry of St. Martin's tower dates from these days, and in the cathedral is the Shrine of St. Frideswide, who founded a priory on the site in the eighth century. Later the town became a point of defence against the Danes, who sailed up the Thames in their long boats.

The royal hunting lodge at Woodstock, only eight miles away, brought the Norman monarchs frequently to Oxford. Under their influence the town flourished and became a centre of court life. A castle arose. Here the Empress Matilda was besieged by Stephen : and from here one wintry night she made her escape, travelling in white across the snowclad ground.

Cambridge too had its Norman castle, though it lacked a priory. It was early an important centre in the fenlands. Like Oxford, it stood

H. FELTON

### THE NOBLE TOWER OF MAGDALEN

*This imposing structure, 145 feet high, was built between the years 1492 and 1507 at a time when Wolsey was junior bursar at the college. Because of its carefully chosen architectural proportions, it achieves an unusual elegance of form, and in the result this graceful tower has become one of the supreme glories of that beautiful old university city of Oxford. Every May morning a ceremony to the dawn is held on Magdalen Tower.*

astride a ford. The main route from East Anglia to the midlands passed through the town. Three great animal fairs were held there, and sea-going ships came up to its wharves, which lined the river along the stretch now bordered by the famous " backs."

Oxford was the first to achieve fame as a university town. Throughout the twelfth century students gathered there, and ere long it was able to boast that it contained the " second school of the Church." It has never been fully

St. Martin's, once the townsmen's church. Its bell summoned the town to fight the scholars, who swarmed out of their lodgings at the sound of the bell of St. Mary's, the University church. At Cambridge the Church of St. Mary the Greater has served both town and gown. Its two organs and moveable pulpit are reminders of its dual purpose.

In 1209 a scholar killed a woman in the streets of Oxford, and the rivalry between town and gown flared up into days of terror and bloodshed.

H. FELTON

KING'S COLLEGE CHAPEL, CAMBRIDGE

*Described by Wordsworth as " this immense and glorious work of fine intelligence," Henry VI's Chapel took a century to build, being completed in 1545. Its exquisite roof is undoubtedly the most impressive of its kind. On the right is the Fellows' Building, erected from plans partly prepared by Wren.*

understood why scholars were attracted to Cambridge, but by 1209 the schools there were sufficiently developed to receive a large migration from Oxford.

In their earlier days the universities of Oxford and Cambridge were strictly ecclesiastical institutions. The students who thronged the streets wore the clerical gown and hood, and enjoyed the protection of the Church. For the most part they were poor. They indulged in gaming and riotous living, and on occasion played the highwayman to eke out their scanty means. Such conduct led to frequent brawls between " town and gown."

Carfax Tower, at Oxford, is all that remains of

King John, always on the losing side, supported the citizens, the Pope the students. Lectures were suspended, and a papal interdict was placed upon the city. A large band of scholars crossed to Cambridge. There is no reason to believe, as has been suggested, that this migration marks the origin of the latter university.

On St. Scholastica's Day, 1354, Oxford beheld further disastrous riots. The university won, though its halls were ravaged ; and from that date it has possessed powers rendering it independent of the town authorities. For centuries, indeed, the latter were held in almost feudal subjection. Until 1824 the Mayor and Corporation went every year to the University Church—for

D. MCLEISH

## OLD COURT OF CORPUS CHRISTI, CAMBRIDGE

*The dignified frontage of Corpus Christi College is nineteenth century, but the old court, seen above, with its picturesque eaves overhanging the low-pitched chambers, dates from the fourteenth century when the college was founded. The buttresses were added to strengthen the walls in the late fifteenth or early sixteenth century. A mural tablet on the right is a reminder that Kit Marlowe, the famous dramatist, lived here.*

many years clad in sackcloth—to do penance for the riots of 1354.

For long after the rise of the universities there were no colleges. The students lived in lodgings or hostels, or, if they were members of a religious order, in monasteries or friaries. Colleges arose to give lay students a community life like that enjoyed by those resident in religious houses.

Though University College, Oxford, claims to be the oldest foundation, Merton College, Oxford, is generally regarded as the pioneer of the college system which distinguishes Oxford and Cambridge from other universities. Founded in 1264, it was, according to its founder, to be a community of poor scholars living frugally on bread and beer, with flesh or fish once a day. It developed into a residential college, and its organization supplied a pattern generally followed by subsequent foundations. In brief, each college is independent as regards internal administration, yet forms part of the university as a whole.

Merton has retained much of its medieval buildings. The lovely Mob Quad, dominated by the Chapel, takes one right into the heart of early Oxford. From this college John Wyclif was banished to his rectory at Lutterworth, where he organized the movement which gained him a place among the early Reformers.

Peterhouse (properly St. Peter's College), Cambridge, was founded within ten years of Merton; it, too, has still some of its earliest buildings in use.

### A Miserable Benefaction

Balliol, another of the earliest Oxford colleges, is named after John de Baliol, who having " unjustly vexed and enormously damnified " the Church was in 1263 ordered by the Bishop of Durham to make provision for poor scholars at Oxford. It is said that all the provision he made was the miserable sum of twopence, and that it was his wife, fearful for the welfare of his soul, who in 1282 decided to endow the college adequately.

Oriel College, Oxford, is said to have been the result of a vow made by Edward II that he would endow a college if he escaped from the field of Bannockburn. All Souls, Oxford, was endowed by Archbishop Chichele. Saddened by the loss of so many lives in the French wars of Henry VI, he established a college which was also a Chantry in which masses were said for the souls of the dead.

New College, Oxford, was founded in the fourteenth century by William of Wykeham to maintain seventy scholarships for boys coming up from his school at Winchester. About a hundred years later King's College, Cambridge, was similarly created by Henry VI to receive boys from Eton. For centuries King's remained exclusively a college of Etonians; it stood aloof from the rest of the university, and claimed the privilege of examining its own candidates for degrees.

Both these colleges stand as magnificent monuments to the vision of their founders. The lovely chapel at King's, begun in 1446, but not completed until 1515, with its gorgeous pinnacles reared high above lawns that slope gently down to the river, is perhaps the most impressive and beautiful sight in Cambridge.

"Tax not the royal Saint with vain expense," cried Wordsworth, and one can well agree, for this "glorious work of fine intelligence" is a gem that could hardly be spared. The glorious great windows of painted glass and the fan tracery of the roof are almost unique in England. Henry projected a college on a like scale of magnificence, but, alas, only the chapel materialized.

New College, like King's, possesses the same superb ecclesiastical atmosphere; its dining-hall has the lines and dignity of a chapel, and the entire college breathes the spirit of the days of Edward III. Its founder was a close friend of the Black Prince.

Corpus Christi College, Cambridge, endowed by the Guild of Corpus Christi, is unique in being the only college founded by the "town." Its Old Court, built in 1377, two centuries later, received Christopher Marlowe, greatest of English dramatic poets before Shakespeare.

### A Cardinal's Scheme

One result of the suppression of the monasteries by Henry VIII was a great harvest of college building. In the days of his power Wolsey planned, with the revenues received from a number of suppressed religious houses, to erect a magnificent college at Oxford, to be called Cardinal College. When the downfall and death of the arrogant churchman threatened to interrupt the project, Henry VIII took it up; and Christ Church, grandest of the Oxford colleges, arose as evidence of the monarch's solicitude for learning. "I tell you," he said, "that I grudge no land in England better bestowed than that which is given to our universities. For by their maintenance our realm shall be well governed when we are dead and rotten."

A portrait of Henry VIII hangs in the Great

D. MCLEISH

OXFORD'S RENOWNED HIGH STREET

*From Magdalen Tower is obtained this fine panoramic view of Oxford, in which the High Street, thought by many to be the most beautiful in the world, winds its way through the city. In the right-hand corner is Magdalen College, while a little farther up, on the same side, a glimpse can be seen of Queen's College.*

H. FELTON

PUMP COURT, QUEENS' COLLEGE, CAMBRIDGE

*Queens' College, founded in 1446, with its warm red brick buildings, has somehow more the air of a country home than the severe semblance of a seat of learning. Pump Court is often called Erasmus Quad after the writer.*

Both universities grew strong during the age of the New Learning, and produced many great figures during the unquiet days of the English Reformation. Oxford pioneered the teaching of Greek, not without opposition. Greek, its opponents said, was the language of heresy : and a warden of New College, Oxford, wrote indignantly to Wolsey, " Do you really know that you have given studentships at Christ Church to men who go about teaching Greek ? Pray let them be dismissed."

### Great Scholars

They were not dismissed. Men like Colet, founder of St. Paul's School, Grocyn, Lily and Linacre, under the patronage of Lady Margaret Beaufort — grandmother of Henry VIII, and founder of Christ's College and St. John's — and Sir Thomas More, expounded the Greek philosophers at Oxford, while Erasmus, the greatest scholar of his day, lived in turn at each university.

At Oxford the famous Dutchman was Professor of Divinity : at Cambridge he lodged for three years at Queens' College, holding the appointment of Professor of Greek. He was not altogether enthralled by the charms of this river-side college which rears its walls sheer out of the water. Times were bad, and he disliked the college ale. From his rooms in the corner of the first court he wrote to a friend that " he had lived like a cockle shut up in a shell. . . . Cambridge was deserted because of the plague. The expense was intolerable, the profits not a brass farthing."

Among the pupils of Erasmus were John Tyndale and Miles Coverdale, translators of the Bible, and Hugh Latimer. In the ancient church of St. Edward, hard by King's College, Cambridge, Latimer, then attached to Clare, delivered two celebrated sermons in 1529. Twenty-six years later, Latimer and Ridley were burned at Oxford, where the Martyrs' Memorial now stands. Archbishop Cranmer, soon to follow them to the stake, watched from the tower of St. Michael's Church.

Hall at Trinity College, Cambridge, for he granted a charter to this college in 1546. Trinity, now the largest and richest foundation in either university, began as an amalgamation of several of the older halls. In the Great Court, notable for two lovely gateways, is a seventeenth-century fountain at which the college bedmakers used to fill their pitchers in the days before bathrooms and water-taps.

At Cambridge, Queens' College and St. John's, both built of homely brick, and Jesus with its exquisite chapel, originally that of the nunnery on which the college was founded, are all redolent of the age of the Tudors. Trinity and St. John's at Oxford were founded on suppressed religious houses and endowed by men of the new nobility of commerce.

D. MCLEISH

## ST. JOHN'S AND THE "BACKS"

*Six of the colleges of Cambridge back on to the River Cam, and the " backs " form a continuous park where lovely trees reach down to smooth green lawns and bridges and college buildings complete the picture.   In the foreground of the photograph the picturesque building of St. John's and the tower of the chapel rise above the River Cam.   On the left are some of the crocuses that turn the " Backs " into a blaze of colour every spring.*

R.B.—I

The trial of Cranmer took place at the University Church of Oxford, St. Mary's in the High Street, where for centuries the business affairs of the university were conducted. Its fourteenth-century tower, one of the city's landmarks, has looked down on many historic events.

When Archbishop Laud was brought to trial by the Puritans, the figure of the Virgin Mary over the door of St. Mary's was used as evidence of his " Popish " tendencies. John Henry Newman, later to become a Cardinal of the Roman Catholic Church, was Rector of St. Mary's from 1828 to 1843. In 1833 was delivered in this church Keble's " Assize Sermon," generally regarded as the starting point of the Oxford Movement.

The reign of Elizabeth was a happy period for both Oxford and Cambridge. The queen saw plays performed at Cambridge in King's College Chapel, and twice displayed her learning by joking with Oxford students in Latin.

In the year of the Armada was founded Sidney Sussex College, Cambridge. To it came some twenty-five years later one Oliver Cromwell, to find it a nursery of Puritanism. During the Civil War he returned to his university town,

this time to occupy it with troops. He prevented the colleges from presenting their valuable plate to King Charles, and restrained his over-zealous followers from doing too much damage.

Later a certain Mr. Dowsing was sent by the Puritans to examine the Cambridge chapels. In all except those of Emmanuel and Sidney Sussex he found statues to be broken, texts to be removed or " Papist " windows to be destroyed.

### Cavalier Oxford

Oxford was strongly loyalist. It was full of Cavaliers : the king lodged at Christ Church, and was made free of the college plate. All Souls surrendered all but one piece.

Magdalen College, Oxford, the famous tower of which is said to have been designed by Wolsey, having fought for Charles I and sheltered Prince Rupert, later turned against James II when he attempted to make Anthony Farmer, a Roman Catholic, president of the college.

To Christ's College, Cambridge, came in 1625 John Milton, a youth of such beauty that he was nicknamed " The Lady of Christ's." While in residence he wrote an epitaph on Hobson the carrier, from whose methods arose the phrase

H. FELTON

### ST. JOHN'S COLLEGE, OXFORD

*A college for Cistercian monks, founded in 1437 and dedicated to St. Bernard, formerly occupied this site. It was in the sixteenth century, however, that owing to the generosity of Sir Thomas White, twice Lord Mayor of London, St. John's College was founded for the Study of Sacred Theology, Philosophy and the Good Arts.*

"Hobson's Choice," and who had his stable where now St. Catharine's College stands.

In the books of Magdalene College it is recorded that in 1653 Samuel Pepys was rebuked for "having been scandalously over-served with drink ye night before." The diarist later presented his books to his old college, and the Pepysian Library at Magdalene treasures the manuscript of his famous diary, written in the quaint shorthand invented by its author.

If founding halted during the troubles of the seventeenth century, building went on. Queen's and Wadham at Oxford, Clare and St. Catharine's at Cambridge reflect the orderly dignity of the architecture of these days. Sir Christopher Wren left the mark of his genius on both universities; some of Nevile's Court at Trinity, Cambridge, probably the bridge next the Bridge of Sighs at St. John's, the Sheldonian Theatre and parts of Queen's, Oxford, were designed by him.

H. FELTON

CORNER OF A FAMOUS QUAD

*Christ Church, Oxford, known as the "House," was founded by Cardinal Wolsey and refounded in 1532 under the name of Henry VIII's College. The photograph shows a corner of the Tom Quad, the largest in Oxford, showing the entrance to the dining hall, one of the finest in the country.*

During the eighteenth century the universities fell asleep. The professors, "old sinners who drank and dozed in the College Common Rooms," lived a life of leisured laziness, drawing their incomes from college livings they rarely if ever visited. The Fellow Commoners, for the most part wealthy scions of nobility, bedecked themselves in gold-trimmed gowns and velvet caps, and spent their time in fashionably elegant pursuits. Almost the only mental activity which interested them was politics. Oxford was strongly Tory, Cambridge equally strongly Whig.

In 1750, Gibbon, author of the *Decline and Fall of the Roman Empire*, wrote, "In the University of Oxford, the greater part of the public professors have for these many years given up even the pretence of teaching . . . the Fellows of Magdalen were decent, easy men who supinely enjoyed the gifts of the founder . . . from the toil of reading, or thinking, or writing, they had absolved their consciences."

Yet scholarship did not die. The poor student existed as a Sizar or Servitor, paid his college dues by waiting at table and performing menial duties, and furnished many a name of eminence. In the seventeenth century Sir Isaac Newton was a Sizar of Trinity, Cambridge. Later he was made a fellow of his college—and in his rooms near the Great Gate did much of the work which led to his formulating the theory of gravity.

Forty years later Samuel Johnson, the great lexicographer, became a Servitor at Oxford, but was not able to complete his course owing to poverty. Unlike Gibbon, Johnson in later life defended his university. "That the rules are sometimes ill observed may be true," he said, "but there is nothing against the system."

### Religious Movements

During the late eighteenth and early nineteenth centuries the life of the universities was shaken by three great religious movements. Methodism was born when Charles Wesley and a few friends, nicknamed the "Holy Club," began to meet together in Christ Church, Oxford. At Cambridge Charles Simeon of King's, Vicar of Holy Trinity Church from 1783 to 1836, inspired the Evangelical Movement in the Church of England. Oxford, always given to ritualism, was the birthplace of the Tractarian Movement of the 1830's, when Newman, Pusey and Keble attempted to revive the spirit of the medieval church in religious affairs.

Religious revival led to secular reform. During the nineteenth century Royal and Statutory Commissions discussed the affairs of both Oxford and Cambridge. Reforms instituted as a result of

VALENTINE

### THE GREAT COURT, TRINITY COLLEGE, CAMBRIDGE

*A corner of the spacious quadrangle or Great Court. On the left is King Edward's Gateway. This, the
original college entrance, was built in 1427 and then stood near the Fountain. It was removed to its present
position in the seventeenth century. On the right is the Great Gateway and between these is the College Chapel.*

their reports left the universities as they stand
today, in possession of all their historic dignity
and rights, fulfilling the same destiny for
centuries, but with a far wider range of studies,
an efficient examination system, and as at their
inception, a large proportion of poor students.

In 1858 Cambridge was thrown open to Non-
conformists, and in 1871 all religious tests were
abolished. In 1873 and 1875 respectively the
famous women's colleges of Girton and Newn-
ham were founded. In 1877 the university made
provision for the study of natural science—and
within a few years the number of its students had
doubled.

Three years previously the Cavendish Laboratory, today the home of advanced physics and the
scene of astonishing experiments on the atom
and the electron, had been opened. In 1887 came
the chemical laboratory, and the progress of
Cambridge science has since been marked by
such steps as the building of the Psychological
Laboratory in 1913, and of the Biochemical and
Biophysical Laboratory in 1922, the founding of
the Sir William Dunn School of Biochemistry
in 1924, and the opening of the Pathological
Laboratory in 1928.

The scientific block in Downing Street is surrounded on all sides by centuries-old buildings,
yet it does not seem out of place, for the magic
of the university dwells not entirely in its age
but rather in its serene and imperishable vitality.
The spirit of Oxford or of Cambridge is not
caught in books and lectures and examinations.
It is discovered in a walk down High Street,
Oxford, or King's Parade, Cambridge, in a stroll
through the gardens of Magdalen, Oxford, or a
leisurely drifting in a punt along the "backs"
at Cambridge.

#### Wordsworth's Reverence

Rupert Brooke conveys that spirit in his poem
on Grantchester, once a haunt of Byron. It is
seen in the affection felt by so many great men
for their university. Wordsworth sang almost
reverently of Cambridge; Newman loved Oxford
all his life. When on his death-bed Gladstone
received a message of sympathy from his old
university. Much moved, the aged statesman
exclaimed, " There is no expression of sympathy that I value more than that of . . . the
God-fearing and God-sustaining University of
Oxford."

# THE ANCIENT CROSSES
# OF ENGLAND

## *by* G. BAKER

IN some English country churchyards the churchyard cross is older than the church itself. Often nothing remains of the cross but the steps on which it stood; sometimes the stump of the ancient shaft is left; occasionally that stump has been made the base of a sundial. In the opinion of many antiquaries these crosses mark the spot where the first missionaries set up their preaching stations. Many years before a church was built and a regular priest appointed, such a cross was erected, and around this sacred symbol of their faith, the early converts were buried. In such cases, like its cross, the churchyard came before the church. Blackwell, in Derbyshire, is one example: in its churchyard, the old Holy Place, a fragment of the cross is preserved.

The primary purpose of wayside crosses is stated very succinctly in a treatise printed by Wynkyn de Worde in 1496: "for this reason ben Crosses by ye waye that whan folke passynge see the Crosse, they sholde thynke on Hym that deyed on the Crosse, and worshypp Hym above all thynge."

These crosses often served more secular ends. In medieval times when signposts were unknown, travellers in wild and lonely districts like that of the Peak often had as their only landmarks such wayside crosses as Whibbersley Cross on Chesterfield Moors, Edale Cross on Kinderscout, or Robin Hood's Cross on Abney Moor. Or a cross would mark a ford, as does that still to be found a little below Wilton Castle, Herefordshire, where the old Roman ford leads across the Wye.

In Norman days crosses were erected to define the bounds of a place of sanctuary. Within the radius of a mile around St. Wilfrid's Shrine, Ripon, a man was safe, whatever wrong he had committed. Hence stone crosses were put up on each of the five roads leading to Ripon, to show the sanctuary limits. Only the stump of Sharow Cross remains.

Similarly, crosses marked the boundaries of a church's or abbey's lands, or the limits of its judicial *soke*, i.e., its right to the fines imposed for offences committed within that area. The limestone cross at Thrybergh, Yorkshire, is an example. Local legend, it is true, accounts for this cross much more picturesquely. The lovely heiress of Thrybergh (the story goes) married a Reresby who went on the Crusades. He was reported to be killed in the Holy Land, and the lady promised to marry another. On the day the marriage was to take place, from the Saracen

DIXON-SCOTT

### A MARKET CROSS AND STOCKS
*This ruined market cross at Ripley, Yorkshire, is typical of scores of others distributed over practically the whole of England. Great skill and labour were expended upon carving these crosses especially in the fifteenth century, and many are amazing in detail.*

DIXON-SCOTT

### AN OLD CROSS IN A DELIGHTFUL SETTING

*The square stone pedestal of this ancient market cross in the village of Castle Combe, Wiltshire, is ornamented with sunk quatrefoiled panels, showing alternately roses and shields.   The great stone piers at the angles of the platform are six feet high.   On them rest the wooden lintels of the pyramid-shaped, tile-covered roof.*

DIXON-SCOTT

### IN A BERKSHIRE VILLAGE

*On this old cross at East Hagbourne the stone cube at the top of the shaft has sundials on three of its sides and an almost obliterated inscription on the fourth.   At its base are two niches, one above the other, with traces of a canopy.   Remains of a second cross may be seen at the Travellers' Welcome Inn, nearby.*

camp where he was a prisoner, the missing husband, his gyves and fetters still about him, was transported miraculously to East Hill, Thrybergh, where the cross now stands in commemoration of this miracle.

Other crosses have somewhat similar traditions. Dame Mabel Bradshaigh was much less lucky than the lady of Thrybergh. No fortunate miracle prevented her second marriage. Ten years afterwards, her absent spouse returned, and killed his successor. As her punishment, Dame Mabel was made to walk barefoot once a week to do penance at the cross which still stands in Standishgate, Wigan, and which to this day is known as "Mab's Cross." Scott makes use of this story in *The Betrothed*.

Crosses were made places of secular punishment as well as of ecclesiastical penance. Poulton-le-Fylde Cross, Lancashire, is but one of many market crosses at the foot of which old-fashioned stocks are to be found. It was left to the notorious Judge Jeffreys to put a village cross to its grimmest use. At Wedmore, in Somerset, near the house where Jeffreys himself lodged during the Bloody Assize, still stands the village cross upon which he hanged one of Monmouth's followers in 1685.

### Proclamations at the Cross

When Monmouth proclaimed himself king from the crosses of Taunton and Bridgwater he was following an ancient custom. For centuries the cross was the place chosen for public proclamations, made usually at the conclusion of the chief Sunday morning service. Again it was often the centre of municipal life. To Folkestone Churchyard Cross (fragments of which remain) and to Ripon Market Cross (only its obelisk is left) the mayor and electors came at the end of the civic year, to elect the mayor's successor.

In the Middle Ages churchyard crosses figured prominently in Palm Sunday ceremonial. The procession held on that day halted at the cross, wreathed with boughs and flowers for the

STEPHENSON

"A RIGHT FAIRE PIECE OF WORK"
*So did Leland describe this cross at Malmesbury which was erected in the reign of Henry VII. Its canopied pinnacle is decorated with a number of statues.*

occasion; in the niche hollowed in the socket of the cross the pyx containing the Host was deposited while the Gospel was read. Some crosses—Tredington, in Gloucestershire, is an example—have holes drilled downward in the shaft, into which the boughs and flowers were put. At other times these holes took the pegs from which small wooden memorial crosses, crucifixes, or holy pictures were suspended.

Many crosses were themselves memorials, as their inscriptions show. The most notable of these are the famous Eleanor Crosses of which more will be said later. By the side of the Retford Road at Doncaster is a cross in the form of a Norman pillar which bears the inscription in Norman-French: "This is the cross of Ote de Tilli, on whose soul God have mercy. Amen." De Tilli was Seneschal of Conisborough in the reigns of Stephen and Henry II. Five slender iron crosses, which were torn down by the Roundheads in 1644, crowned the original cross: the latter was itself taken down in 1792, and the present copy later erected.

Still other crosses commemorate events. The village of Ferryhill, near Durham, has the remains of Cleve's Cross, set up to celebrate the bravery of Roger de Ferry in killing a huge wild boar which had terrorized the countryside. At Hedon, in Yorkshire, is a cross which was originally erected to commemorate the landing of Henry IV in 1339 at the then flourishing seaport of Ravenspur, near Spurn Head. Ravenspur is now under the sea: its cross was removed first to the shore at Kilnsea, and from there, in 1818, to Hedon. Percy Cross, near Redesdale, in Northumberland, commemorates the Battle of Otterburn, 1388, immortalized in the *Ballad of Chevy Chase*. Not to be confused with it is Percy's Cross, near Wooler, a memorial to a later Percy, Sir Ralph, killed in 1464 at the Battle of Hedgeley Moor when Queen Margaret was attempting to regain for her husband, Henry VI, the English throne which he had lost to

D. MCLEISH

### CHICHESTER'S STATELY CROSS

*Although badly mutilated by some of Cromwell's adherents, this edifice yet remains a fine specimen of the late Gothic style and ranks among the most perfect of its kind. Built in the fifteenth century, it for long served as a centre where poor people could market their produce free of toll. The belfry on top of the structure is an incongruous addition, dating from 1724. On the east side of the cross is a bronze bust of Charles I.*

STEPHENSON

**SALISBURY'S HEXAGONAL CROSS**
*This fourteenth-century cross with six arches built round a central pier is known as the Poultry Cross, possibly an allusion to the goods once sold there.*

Edward IV. Round this cross in 1536 the Pilgrims of Grace rallied under their Banner of the Five Wounds.

Fragments of a cross unique in its origin are preserved in St. Frideswide's Church, Oxford. In 1268, as the Ascension Day procession of Oxford scholars and townsmen passed the Jewish synagogue in Fish Street, a Jew rushed out, snatched the crucifix from its bearer, hurled it to the ground, and trampled it underfoot. For this sacrilege the Oxford Jews were sentenced to erect a cross in the city at their own expense— the Jews' Cross, as it was afterwards known. The socket, which alone remains, is carved with Old Testament subjects on three sides. On the fourth, two ape-like creatures turn away from a middle figure, while beneath them is a dragon— a piece of symbolism which baffles the antiquaries. After the Reformation public sentiment in regard to crosses changed so greatly that they were often put to very strange uses. In Wales it was still customary to give a reward for the capture of wolves and foxes. A condition was that the heads should be hung upon the church-yard cross during three church services, after

which they were valued. The reward for a wolf's head was the same as that given for the capture of a robber; for dog foxes 2s. 6d. and for vixens 1s. 6d. was paid. Eglwyscummin, Carmarthenshire, and Amroth, Pembrokeshire, still have such a cross. Parts of others exist at Llansandurnen· and Marrôs : to Marrôs Cross foxes' heads were attached as late as the middle of the nineteenth century.

A number of churchyard crosses—Bishop's Lydeard, Somersetshire, possesses one of them— have hollows scooped out of their base or steps to take the offerings of the faithful. The bigger basin-like cavities in some village and roadside crosses were filled with vinegar in times of plague. Thus, when Newcastle was plague-stricken in the sixteenth century, its citizens would come to the old cross still standing near Ravensworth Castle ; take the butter, eggs and vegetables which the countryfolk had deposited near the cross ; and leave coins in the vinegar that they might be disinfected. In both the Plague of 1665 and the cholera epidemic of 1833 the people of York and the villagers of Fulford used the medieval cross lying midway between their home places for the same purpose.

STEPHENSON

**A FOURTEENTH-CENTURY CROSS**
*This ancient cross at Leighton Buzzard has suffered at the hands of the restorer. The original statues have been removed and inferior copies substituted.*

**WYMONDHAM CROSS**

*In the centre of the little Norfolk town of Wymondham stands this curious octagonal market cross which was built in 1618. Round the cross are carved representations of various articles used in turnery, which was once an important local industry.*

DIXON-SCOTT

be found in Bisley Churchyard, Gloucestershire; 12 feet high and hexagonal in shape, it once held the lamp which shed the "poor souls' light" through the trefoil-headed openings on each of its six sides. Very few of these lantern pillars, common enough in medieval times, remain in Europe.

In Sherburn Church, Yorkshire, are what appear to be two identical cross-heads, each bearing a figure of Christ crucified between Mary and John, with a gable above the figures and delicate Gothic tracery between them. Their history is extraordinary. In the nineteenth century men digging among the ruins of a chantry chapel in the churchyard found the head of the vanished churchyard cross. Both the churchwardens and the owners of the chantry claimed it. A local Solomon settled the dispute by sawing the cross-head down the middle. For some years one half stood against the church wall, while the other was built into the stable wall of a local farmhouse. In 1887 they were set up side by side in the church's south aisle.

The existing socket of the churchyard cross at Ripley, Yorkshire, has eight cavities of a different kind, scooped vertically in its sides. Into these, it is thought, penitents set their knees when begging for forgiveness. Some authorities, however, scout this explanation, declaring that the *weeping cross*, whether of Ripley or elsewhere, is no more than a pretty fancy.

A pretty fancy, which to the men of the Middle Ages was far more than fancy, is connected with the lantern pillar, once cross-crowned, still to

Preaching crosses, from which open-air sermons were delivered, came with the friars in the early thirteenth century. The most famous preaching cross in Europe was Paul's Cross, London, erected before 1240 near the wall of old St. Paul's. Before it was pulled down in 1641, it had been the scene of many historic events. Folk-moots were called at it by both Henry III, who attended in person, and Edward I; papal bulls were read beneath it; Mayors of London were elected in its shadow. Heretics were excommunicated at it, as in 1382: in that year it was damaged by an earthquake. In 1483 Jane Shore was one of the many who did public penance at the cross: the usual practice was for the penitent with a faggot round his neck to stand before the preacher while the sermon was delivered. In 1588 it was from Paul's Cross that the first news of the Armada's defeat was given to the public.

Today only two preaching crosses remain in England—at Iron Acton, Gloucestershire, and at Hereford. The former, dating from the early fifteenth century, has four piers, each with a buttress, rising from the second of three brick steps of an octagonal base. The ribbed and vaulted ceiling has bosses sculptured in the shape of acorns and oak leaves. The shaft of the cross springs from above its arches, but the one-time pinnacles and statues have disappeared.

The Black Friars' Preaching Cross in Widemarsh Street, Hereford, is almost all that remains of the Dominican monastery. Six arches and a central shaft bear the vaulted roof with its battlemented cornice.

Perhaps the most famous, and certainly architecturally the most elaborate, crosses in England are the Eleanor Crosses. In 1290 Queen Eleanor, to whom Edward I was devoted, died at Harby, in Nottinghamshire. Edward directed that stone crosses should be set up at or near each spot where the funeral procession stopped on its way to Westminster. The route taken was through Lincoln, Grantham, Stamford, Geddington, Northampton, Stony Stratford, Woburn, Dunstable, St. Albans, Waltham, London—the body rested in old St. Paul's for the night—and Charing village, the last stopping place before Westminster Abbey was reached. At each halt the office for the dead was celebrated.

Of the twelve crosses erected between 1291 and 1294 only three remain—at Geddington, Northampton and Waltham. All three are spire-shaped, rising in three diminishing storeys. The bottom storey has each side carved with Gothic tracery dividing it into two panels, sculptured with armorial shields. Each niche of the second storey is occupied by a statue of Eleanor.

Over 40 feet high and triangular in shape, Geddington Cross stands in the centre of a Northamptonshire village, in which, according to tradition, squirrel-baiting was once a favourite pastime. Wild squirrels were caught, let loose near the cross, and hunted by the shouting crowd until they took refuge in the carved pinnacles. They were then pelted with stones, driven out and killed. This may account for the damage which so much of the diamond-patterned surface of the cross has suffered.

Most beautiful of the Eleanor Crosses, Northampton's octagonal cross with its nine octagonal steps stands on a roadside bank with a background of trees. The four sundials of the top storey were added when the cross was restored in 1713. The present broken shaft on the summit was erected in 1840 to replace the cross which disappeared centuries earlier.

Waltham Cross, at Cheshunt, Hertfordshire, is

STEPHENSON

### GEDDINGTON CROSS
*Unlike any of the other Eleanor Crosses, that at Geddington, Northants, has three sides. It was built over a spring and from under its ancient foundations water still pours forth.*

hexagonal, has three statues of the queen instead of four, but in other respects it resembles Northampton Cross. In successive restoration, much of the original Caen stone has been replaced.

Of the vanished Eleanor Crosses, Cheapside Cross at the bottom of Wood Street figured picturesquely in the pageant held to celebrate the birth of Edward II's son, afterwards Edward III. A pavilion was set up in front of it, where any who passed might drink from a tun of wine. The rebuilt cross of 1486 had its statues of the queen replaced by figures of saints and of the Virgin. For the latter in 1600 a figure of a half-naked Diana was substituted. Evelyn in his *Diary* records how in May, 1643, he saw a furious Puritan mob destroy the third cross built on the same site.

STEPHENSON

NORTHAMPTON CROSS

*This Eleanor Cross bears a close resemblance to that at Waltham. All of the twelve originally built had certain features in common —they were lofty, tapering structures with pinnacles and gables.*

It was in 1643 that Parliament passed an act ordering all crosses in churches, chapels and churchyards to be taken away and defaced as " Monuments of Superstition and Idolatry." The act was operated only too faithfully. All over the country, crosses of every type and period were demolished or mutilated. The monolith or pillar cross of the Anglo-Saxons, with its elaborate knotwork patterns and its not infrequent combination (as at Gosforth, Cumberland, and Bakewell, Derbyshire) in symbolic carving of Teutonic and Christian beliefs—this Saxon type of cross shared the fate of the shaft-on-steps or calvary cross of the Normans, as of the preaching cross of the friars and of a number of the Eleanor Crosses. Often their material was put to strange uses : stones from old Charing Cross made the pavement in front of Whitehall Palace ; while others, cut up and polished, were converted into the handles of knives sold as souvenirs.

### The Market Cross

Even the market crosses suffered, despite the secular purpose they served. The origin of the market cross was the village cross around which the market was held. Later, at a number of places—Norwich and Bingley among others—a penthouse roof was built round the lower part of the cross to give shelter from rain. From this the specially built market cross was a natural development. As early as 1337 the first market cross at Norwich was large enough to hold a chapel and four shops. In it the standard weights and measures of the city were kept.

Of the existing market crosses one of the finest is at Chichester. Built by Bishop Storey in about 1500 and endowed by him with land at Amberley, the cross was intended " to shelter the poor cottagers who came to sell their produce and to relieve them of the usual market tolls." Octagonal in shape, it has eight flying buttresses forming as many arches, above which the pinnacled roof tapers into a graceful lantern spire.

With their flying buttresses and ring of pinnacles, Malmesbury Market Cross and Salisbury Poultry Cross resemble Chichester Cross and are roughly of the same date, although some ascribe the Poultry Cross to 1388. In that year a Lollard named

Sundays. Like the fine pentagonal market cross at Leighton Buzzard, it is spire-shaped and has four life-sized statues. At Winchester these represent Alfred the Great, William of Wykeham, a city mayor, and St. John the Evangelist.

Market crosses of the seventeenth century include the lovely Yarn-Market Cross at Dunster with its fine sweep of pyramidal roof, pierced by dormer windows ; Oakham Butter Cross, with its stone seats for market women ; the Market Cross at Wymondham (Norfolk) with its outdoor stairway leading to the timbered upper storey, and its carvings of tops, spoons and spindles alluding to the wares for which the town was once famous ; and the Market Cross of now marketless Lymm, in Cheshire, built on a huge boulder and reached by steps cut in the rock.

Although Banbury's ancient cross—possibly a market cross—was destroyed to make a Puritan holiday, the famous nursery rhyme ensures its immortality. For babes and sucklings, those proverbially wise ones, are wiser than the Puritans, to whom all crosses were impure.

STEPHENSON

### WALTHAM CROSS
*One of the only three crosses that now remain of the dozen erected by command of the grief-stricken Edward I, in memory of his Queen, Eleanor.*

Lawrence, as penance for irreverence towards the Host, was made to build a cross in Salisbury, before which he was sentenced to kneel barefoot and bareheaded, every Saturday for the rest of his days.

The fifteenth-century Butter Cross at Winchester is beautifully proportioned and particularly graceful with its double tier of flying buttresses. It was used as a preaching cross on

EDGAR WARD

### GRACEFUL CROSS AT SHEPTON MALLET
*First erected in 1500 and built in the Gothic style, this picturesque cross has a spire fifty-one feet high, built in three tiers. The upper portion was rebuilt in 1841.*

EDGAR WARD

## A WINTER'S TALE

*Such scenes as the above may be witnessed on a winter's evening in countless English inns. This picture was taken at " The White Horse," Eaton Socon, the fine old inn on the Great North Road, originally built in the fifteenth century, but refronted about the middle of the eighteenth century. It was possibly the house at which Mr. Nicholas Nickleby and Mr. Squeers partook of a " good coach dinner " on their way north.*

# THE STORY OF THE INN

## by MICHAEL GEELAN

THE brotherhood of the open road, the lure of light and warmth and food, the precious gift of good companionship, and the magic of welcome—these are things that are inseparable from the story of the inn.

It is a long and captivating story, aglow with legend and tradition, winding its way through hundreds of years of history, through times that were brave and gay, and through times that were brutal, drab and menace-ridden. It is a very human story, very near and dear to the heart of the people and to the soul of these islands.

Seen through romantic eyes, the inn has endured as the sanctuary of the weary, the lonely and the hungry. It has been the rich man's haven and the poor man's solace. Time and time again it has harboured the oppressed and the hounded. Here kings and priests and politicians have found shelter. Here runaway lovers have known the benediction of a host's kindly heart. There lingers still around many of the inns of the countryside the rich and romantic atmosphere of rattling and jingling stage-coaches, of prancing horses and shouting ostlers, of halberd, pike and blunderbuss, of ruff and jerkin and powdered wig, of lace-capped serving maid, of candle-light glinting on fine old brass, of boar's head, sucking pig and cheese-cakes, of jovial, pot-bellied host, waiting, arms akimbo, at the ever-open door.

Through more prosaic eyes another picture is mirrored. A picture of dark and squalid taverns, hot-beds of plotting and corruption, the resorts of rogues and smugglers and highwaymen, where blood flowed with the bad wine, where the price of welcome was gold, and death the penalty of a word out of season. But even these sinister dens had their glamour. Their memories make romance of a different order. Time has woven around them a halo of colour and story.

One aspect of the inns is that they do not decay into empty shells like the castles and the abbeys. They refuse to be merely relics of the past. The march of time cannot trample down their animation. They still serve. They are alive and vital and intensely human. They are next only to the home in permanency and intimacy, keeping pace with progress while still preserving the character and personality engraven on them by the years. Many have still their flagged courtyards and timbered gables ; Canterbury bells and candytuft, columbines and snapdragons, larkspurs and love-in-idleness glorify their walled-in gardens ; amid the cosiness within there is brass and pewter and copper, oaken beams of great age, old prints and horse-pistols hanging on walls as they have done for centuries, and sometimes dark, damp stairways leading to secret passages and mysterious chambers.

From pack-horse to stage-coach, from railway to charabanc, from floors of rushes, sand and sawdust to Turkey carpets, from cakes and ale to cocktails and cherries, the inns have gone, and go their happy, friendly way with a background of charm and tradition that helps to make the study of Romantic Britain more than ever fascinating.

Much of the literature of the land is closely linked with the inns. From Chaucer's time until the present day the great writers have found them places for pleasure, work and inspiration. Shakespeare himself was more than once in merry mood at the " Mermaid," and Ben Jonson drank at the " Devil," in Fleet Street. The name of Burns will be for ever associated with the " Tam o' Shanter," at Ayr. The interior of

STEPHENSON

### "YE OLD FIGHTING COCKS"

*Built on the site of an abbey gateway and close to the Roman city of Verulamium, this octagonal-shaped inn claims to be one of the oldest in the country.*

this inn remains much the same as it was in the days of the poet, and is a place of constant pilgrimage among Burns lovers. It was from here, it will be remembered, that Tam set out, " weel mounted on his grey mare, Meg," on his stormy, witch-haunted ride.

Doctor Johnson, who frequented the " Cheshire Cheese," in London, was equally at home in the hostelries of the countryside. At the inn at Burford Bridge, by the silent stream under Box Hill, poor Keats wrote some of his grandest poetry. At the " White Hart," at Whitchurch,

and other of his works there are incomparable pictures of pleasant and fascinating hostelries. Some of them, including the famous " Golden Cross," in Charing Cross, have since been demolished, but many still remain almost as he knew them.

The " Leather Bottle," at Cobham, Kent, displays a hanging sign bearing a portrait of Mr. Pickwick addressing the cronies of his club, with the inscription, " Dickens's Old Pickwick Leather Bottle." The inn's original sign hangs inside, in one of the quaintest little bars in England.

FHOTOCHROM

THE "CAT AND FIDDLE" AT HINTON ADMIRAL

*This delightful wayside alehouse is only one of the many interesting inns to be found in Hampshire, and is redolent of an age when the small country inn was content to cater for a purely local need. With low-ceilinged rooms, and quaint windows looking out on the tree-shaded road, it retains its rustic atmosphere.*

Newman began his *Lyra Apostolica*. The " Mortal Man," at Troutbeck, has memories of Wordsworth, Coleridge and Southey. Hazlitt nursed his genius and penned many of his greatest essays at the " Winterslow Hut " on the Exeter road. Part of *Robinson Crusoe* was written by Defoe at the " Rose and Crown," at Halifax. Pepys complained bitterly that the " Castle and Ball," at Hungerford, had been " modernized." At the " Royal," at Bideford, Kingsley wrote *Westward Ho!* Addison, Steele and Swift gave vent to their acidity at the " George and Vulture," near Lombard Street, in London. De Quincey writes of the " Lion," at Shrewsbury, in his *Opium Eater*.

Dickens, of course, was a great lover and student of the inns. He knew them in the flourishing coaching days—and in *Pickwick Papers*

The " low-roofed room," of which the great novelist wrote, is still preserved, complete with grandfather clock and antique furniture. Upstairs is the room in which he often slept.

Another inn that is steeped in the Dickensian tradition is the " Great White Horse," at Ipswich. Although the present building dates only from the eighteenth century, the site has been occupied by a hostelry of the same name since 1518. Dickens stayed there when, as a young reporter on the *Morning Chronicle*, he arrived to describe a Parliamentary election. The " Angel," at Bury St. Edmunds, has also been immortalized by Dickens. It was here that Mr. Pickwick heard to **his** alarm that Mrs. Bardell had issued her writ for breach of promise, here also that Sam Weller had his " halfpenny shower bath " under the pump.

Dickens, like many before and after him, was entranced by the names of the English inns. And they do, indeed, make a strange medley of fact and fancy. Who, with a spark of imagination, can fail to be thrilled and intrigued by such subtle and swinging titles as the " Case is Altered," the " Green Man," the " Quiet Wife," the " Cat and Bagpipes," the " Speech House," the " Rover's Return," the " Bell and Mackerel," or " You Might as Well."

### Armorial Signs

Others, less romantic, are more easily explained. The " Lord Nelson," the " Shakespeare," the " Palmerston," the " British Grenadier "— these and their kind were obviously inspired by events and personalities in history, just as the many varieties of " Arms " owe their origin to the armorial bearings of the ground landlords, and the many " Lions," " Bulls " and " Feathers " to heraldic crests. Others, such as the " Wagon and Horses " and the " Pick and Shovel," were undoubtedly based on the trades and callings of the people.

The inn sign itself is often a jolly mixture of the quaint and picturesque. The pity is that so many of the really old and genuine have vanished, ruined by the ravages of the weather, stolen, sold to collectors, forgotten or lost. One of the most remarkable signs ever known in the history of the inn was that of the " White Hart," at Scole. It stretched right across the road and bore twenty-five life-size figures of men and animals fashioned in oak. It is said that its original cost was over £1,000.

The inn sign, of course, has emerged from the days when the people were, in the main, unable to read, when the surgeon-barber, for instance, displayed a striped pole suggestive of a bandaged limb, and traders generally used some manner of symbol to call attention to the nature of their business. The " Bush " was the first of the inn signs, an acceptable explanation being that this

PHOTOCHROM

### AN ORNATE ELIZABETHAN INN

*The Feathers Inn, a beautiful black and white timbered building with its exquisitely-carved front and fine moulded plaster ceiling is one of the architectural glories of the lovely Welsh border town of Ludlow. Granted a licence in 1521, this inn continues to offer a welcome to the wayfarer.*

represented a clump of vine-leaves symbolical of Bacchus.

How old are the oldest existing inns? Many claims are made, but some are so ancient in their origin that documentary evidence is practically non-existent. The " Fountain," at Canterbury, however, must be one of the oldest of all, for inscribed in one of the first visitor's books ever known is the following glowing testimonial from a German visitor—an ambassador—who stayed there in 1129 : " The inns of England are the best in Europe, those in Canterbury are the best in England, and the ' Fountain,' in which I am now lodged as handsomely as I were in a king's palace, the best in Canterbury."

Dating back to the thirteenth century are such

W. F. TAYLOR

### THE "SONDES ARMS," ROCKINGHAM

*This unpretentious but charming hotel is situated at the foot of a hill about nine miles from Market Harborough, in the middle of what was once the Forest of Rockingham. In front of it is a fragment of the old market cross. Standing on the height above it is an historic castle, parts of which date from the thirteenth century.*

EDGAR WARD

### A FAMOUS INN OF SOMERSET

*This beautiful, half-timbered inn, the " George," at Norton St. Philip, erected early in the fifteenth century, has witnessed many historic scenes. The Duke of Monmouth slept there shortly before the fateful Battle of Sedgemoor. While there he was fired at by a man hoping to gain the £1,000 reward on the Duke's head.*

inns as the " George and Dragon," at Speldhurst, the " Angel," at Blyth, and the " Maid's Head," Norwich. The fourteenth century knew the " Green Man," Erdington, the " George," Salisbury, the " Seven Stars," Manchester, and the " Crown," Chiddingfold. From the days of the fifteenth century date hostelries of such age and distinction as the " New Inn," Gloucester, the " Spread Eagle," Midhurst, the " King's Head," Aylesbury, the " Red Lion," Colchester, and the " George," Glastonbury, and from the sixteenth century the " George," Southwark, the " Bull," Long Melford, and the " George," Winchcombe. All of these retain some part, however modest, of their antiquity.

One thing is certain : the inn began with the roads. The Romans knew its hospitality. Next came the Saxon ale-houses, probably crude timber buildings of which no trace remains. That they did exist, however, is a certainty, for there is record of the Saxon rulers making orders for their proper conduct between the years A.D. 600 and 730.

In the early days of travel personages of rank, when moving from place to place, relied upon the hospitality of friendly lords, or arrogantly commandeered the cleanest and most comfortable houses in the towns or villages through which they passed. Those with a less exalted position in life were dependent for food and shelter upon religious establishments which considered it a bounden duty to succour the traveller. To this day such hostels still exist, at least in name. At the " Hospital of St. Cross," outside Winchester, for instance, the traveller may still ask for the " Wayfarer's Dole "—a piece of bread and a drink of beer.

### Religious Hostels

As more and more roads were built, as travel increased and there was an unceasing demand for hospitality, a change in the system was inevitable. Many of the religious hostels became inns, and have remained as such ever since. Guest houses which had been erected by lords and gentry underwent a similar transformation. So did the common ale-houses. Thus, in its true and proper sense, was the inn business born.

They were far from elegant, these early inns, and often far from clean. Rough mattress beds

W. F. TAYLOR

### THE GALLERIED YARD OF THE "GEORGE" AT HUNTINGDON

*When the first inn was erected on this site no one can say. The present edifice modestly displays a mid-Victorian front, but behind this is hidden a courtyard surrounded by buildings which Oliver Cromwell, who lived nearby, must have known as a boy, and the records tell us that the house was even then no longer young.*

EDGAR WARD

## GALLERY OF THE "BULL" AT LONG MELFORD

*For a century prior to 1935, this inn presented a stolid Georgian front to the pretty Suffolk village in which it stands, but in that year a nine-inch brick wall was pulled down revealing a half-timbered façade dating from the fifteenth century. It possesses some noteworthy internal features including exquisitely-carved oak beams, an ancient hearthplace and this picturesque gallery with its uneven roof and long line of windows.*

were laid on rush-strewn floors, and it was an ambitious bill of fare that went much beyond bread, beer and soup, and sometimes a little fish. Still, they were cheap. A bed in 1331, for instance, cost only a halfpenny, and good-class travelling expenses would not much exceed a shilling a day for food and accommodation.

Early steps were taken to guard the traveller against imposition; in fact, in 1349, in the reign of Edward III—a very capable administrator as well as a dauntless warrior—a law was passed whereby the inn-keeper who overcharged a guest could be ordered to repay double the amount he had extracted. On the whole, however, the growth of competition had the result, then as now, of keeping prices within much more reasonable limits.

### Corruption

In those days, any one could open and conduct an inn, subject only to the casual control of the local justices, whose duty it was to stamp out flagrant abuses. Not until 1550 did the licensing system begin to function, and ever since the inn-keeper has been hedged around by a diversity of laws and restrictions, many of which have not failed to evoke criticism and dislike through the years.

STEPHENSON

THE "FOX AND HOUNDS," BARLEY
*This remarkable sign spans the Old North Road in a Hertfordshire village three miles south-west of Royston. Note also the old-fashioned lantern.*

In the days of Elizabeth and James I "mine host" was the victim of a brazen and insidious swindle. Those entrusted with the duty of granting licences and collecting the licensing dues contrived to make a handsome profit for themselves. They fixed their own fees, withheld a considerable percentage of their collections from the State and demanded from the inn-keepers what would be known today as "protection" money. One of these scoundrels, Sir Giles Overreach, did literally overreach himself, with the result that he was brought to the Bar of the House of Commons, deprived of his knighthood and banished.

There was a vast difference in the sixteenth century, between the inn and the tavern. The keeper of the first was prohibited from allowing his house to be used essentially as a drinking place, and the keeper of the second from providing sleeping accommodation. But there were many law breakers who risked severe penalties to gain guilty profits. Many an inn had its " bottle parties " long into the night, and many a tavern sheltered low company, and was the scene of dark plottings for robbery and even murder. Those who may rail at that survival of the war-days, " Dora," will be amused to know, by the way, that the closing hour for intoxicating liquor in those days was eight o'clock in the winter and nine o'clock in the summer.

By the seventeenth century both the inn and the tavern had developed on sound and pleasant lines. Stern supervision was exercised. Offenders were flogged and imprisoned. As a result, most of the unlicensed houses and thieves dens —on the highways, at any rate—were stamped out, and there evolved a splendid code of conduct and hospitality for hosts.

For nearly three hundred years after they were licensed the inns remained without bars or dining-rooms. The " quality " dined and wined in splendid— more or less—privacy, or joined the host and other travellers at a common table. The servants and the common people made the best of things in the kitchen, although, in some ways, this was the most pleasant and friendly place in the house.

The golden age of the inn came with the coaching days. With the beginning of the nineteenth century the inn-keeper assumed a greater dignity and importance. Inns won new reputations for courtesy and service. Both food and accommodation improved. In towns and villages everywhere, as well as on the open road, the inn became a hub of activity by day and by night. The highest in the land stayed there. Lord and squire and clergy were habitués. The bar, the coffee-room and the dining-room were born, and by 1850 the hotel idea was taking shape. Business impetus brought about the Commercial Hotel and the coming of the railroad the " Railway Tavern." These developments were a sorry and crippling blow at the old-time inn, and the wonder is that so many survived it at all. It was generally believed that the railway train would destroy road travel for ever, yet the present century has witnessed a revival of staggering dimensions. The inn is reborn.

What an amazing part the licensed house has played in the public and private lives of the people. Even the modern theatre, with its balconies and boxes, has been modelled on that early courtyard in which strolling players won applause and pennies from the gentry seated at their bedroom windows. The inn has been used as a court for trials and inquests, even as a prison. Politicians have made it their headquarters, and prize-fighters their training camp. To commercial travellers it has been a second home. Even today it is a centre of sporting and social activity, from darts to pigeon racing, from dancing to the slate and loan club. The motorist, the cyclist and the walker alike seek out the best of them for food and shelter.

The stories that can be told of the inns are legion. They come from the forests and the mountains and the lonely sea coasts, from placid villages and thriving cities. There are stories of kings and princes, merchants and paupers, cut-throats and knights-at-arms, scholars and vagabonds. One and all, they mirror the romance that is history.

There is the "Bell," at Barnby Moor, where Dick Turpin is said to have halted to water Black Bess on his notorious ride to York. There is the old Pilchard Inn, on Burgh Island, dating back to 1395, where Tom Crocker, smuggler and pirate, made his headquarters and plotted many a desperate escapade. In the "Pilchard" you can see Crocker's own skull-and-crossbones flag, said to be the only genuine pirate's emblem in existence. A curious feature of this now modern inn is that the timbers of a famous old wooden ship of the line, H.M.S. *Ganges*, have been incorporated into its fabric.

### Some Curious Inns

Another hostelry which once echoed with the oaths and hoarse laughter of pirates and smugglers is the old "Lobster Smack," on Canvey Island, now a favourite rendezvous of yachtsmen from Southend and visitors from London. Almost hidden behind a sea wall, with low-beamed ceilings, it is one of the most glorious examples of its kind in the land.

The "Castle," at Taunton is one of the most curious inns in the west. It is actually a real castle, dating back to Norman times, complete

A. DURRANT

THE "MERMAID," RYE
*Not least of the architectural treasures of the ancient Cinque Port of Rye is this sixteenth-century inn, situated in a narrow, cobbled street of picturesque red-roofed houses. The "Mermaid," with its gables and timbered walls, is reckoned among the finest specimens of the medieval domestic style in the country.*

EDGAR WARD

## COURTYARD OF AN OLD COACHING INN

*In the old coaching days the courtyard was an essential feature of the inns, and was a scene of bustle and strife when the coach arrived and the horses were changed while the weary passengers sought refreshment, and an opportunity to stretch their cramped limbs. The photograph shows the courtyard of the " Greyhound," at Wincanton, in Somerset, a little town on one of the routes from London to Exeter.*

W. F. TAYLOR

AN EXMOOR INN

*The " Royal Oak," a rambling old thatched inn, is charmingly situated in the village of Winsford on the River Exe. Winsford, which boasts seven bridges, is a favourite haunt of anglers.*

with massive stone walls, battlements, great gate-house and arrow slots. The skill with which this medieval fortress has been converted into an up-to-date hotel must really be seen to be believed.

The names of great men and women and of colourful characters in history are inseparable from the story of the inn. For two hundred and fifty years the " George," at Portsmouth, has been linked with the heroes of naval history. Nelson often stayed there. It was here that he spent his last hours ashore before joining his flagship, the *Victory*, on the eve of Trafalgar. He arrived at six o'clock in the evening, but the public would not let their idol rest until he had shown himself and spoken from an upstair window. Later, when he attempted to escape unnoticed by the back door, he was again mobbed. The shouting throng surged around him, " pressing forward," as Southey tells us, " to obtain sight of his face : many were in tears, and many knelt down before him and blessed

him as he passed." Thus, through the back door of an English inn, through an avenue of English patriots, Nelson went forth to his last encounter.

The " George " is a delightful old house. It has charming two-storey bow windows, and a jumble of out-buildings telling of the coaching days. Inside there is a maze of fascinating stairways, a coffee-room hung with old prints of naval battles and heroes, cellars with cat doors, and a kitchen with an old bake oven.

At the " Talbot," Oundle, there is a staircase which was once a part of Fotheringhay Castle, and is believed to have been trodden by Mary Stuart. Jerome K. Jerome, author of the unforgettable *Three Men in a Boat*, was a lover of the " Bull," at Sonning. It is one of the most picturesque inns in the country, a favourite supper haunt of celebrities.

### Death Warrant of a Duke

In 1483, in a room at the " Angel," Grantham, Richard III—who apparently preferred an inn to a palace—signed the death warrant of the Duke of Buckingham. The " Angel " is one of the most spectacular houses on the Great North Road. Its fine stone front dates from the Wars of the Roses, and the gateway is at least a century older. There is a legend that in 1213—two years before the signing of Magna Charta—King John and his nobles rested there. There is also a legend of comedy. In 1706, it is said, the landlord, Michael Soloman, left in his will a legacy of £2 to be paid for the preaching of an annual sermon against drunkenness each Michaelmas Day. And it is still preached !

The " Angel " is one of the three remaining medieval hostels in England, and has been a landmark to millions of travellers along the Great North Road. During the eighteenth century it became a great coaching station. The Royal Mail both to and from London pulled up at the famous fourteenth-century archway, and travellers took their refreshment, as they still do today, in that same room which witnessed the signing of the Duke of Buckingham's death warrant. The rooms below the King's Room, or to give it its modern title, Coffee Room, are distinguished by carved stone ceilings over the windows.

It was from the " Blue Boar," Leicester, that Richard left to die on Bosworth Field, where he

fought to the end. At the " Greyhound,"
Maidenhead, Charles I saw his children for the
last time before his execution. In striking contrast was the first meeting, almost a furtive one,
of Henry VIII and Anne of Cleves—the " mare
of Flanders "—at the " Crown," Rochester. It
was then, probably, if he ever did say it, that
Henry, taking a long, painful look at this queer
woman, exclaimed, " The things I've done for
England ! "

Rich in sporting associations is the " George,"
at Crawley, near Copthorne Common
and Crawley Downs, the scenes of
some of the greatest prize fights in
history. When the Prince Regent had
popularized Brighton, as many as
fifty coaches changed horses within
the space of twenty-four hours. Once,
when her carriage broke down, the
young Queen Victoria, slender and
demure, was an unexpected guest, and
the royal crest now adorns the hotel
staircase. Built from fine old timbers from surrounding forests, the
" George " has existed since at least
1615. Even the bathroom and billiard-
room are richly panelled. The huge,
lofty coffee-room was originally built
as an assembly room, complete with
stage.

### A Famous Fight

Conan Doyle immortalized this
famous hotel in his novel *Rodney
Stone*. It was at the " George " that
Belcher trained Boy Jim for the fight
with Crab Wilson on Crawley Down.
Crowds came from far and wide to
see that contest, and horsemen,
vehicles and pedestrians filled the
roads. " At Kimberham Bridge the
carriage lamps were all lit and it was
wonderful, as the road curved down-
ward before us, to see this writhing serpent with
the golden scales crawling before us in the darkness. And then at last we saw the formless mass
of the huge Crawley elm looming before us in
the gloom . . . and the high front of the old
George Inn glowing from every door, and pane,
and crevice in honour of the noble company
who were to sleep within that night."

From the " Red Lion," Colchester, one of the
pioneer stage-coaches started as early as in 1756,
when one James Unwin advertised that ". . . on
Tuesday, 9th March, he sets out from the Red
Lion Inn, Colchester, with a stage cart and able
horses to be at the Bull Inn, Leadenhall Street,
London, on Wednesday, one o'clock," which was
exceptionally speedy travel for a wheeled vehicle
in those days.

Some idea of the spirit of hospitality—and the
human appetite—of the " good old days " is
afforded by the following hand-written notice
which hangs in the " White Horse," Romsey :
" This day's Bill of Fare will contain
   Turbot and Fried Soles, Lobster sauce
   Leg of Mutton. 6 Tooth wether
   Swanston Lea Lamb and Sparagrass
   Grass Fed Beef
   And all varieties to satisfy
   Inner man."

W. F. TAYLOR

### AN OLD GABLED INN

*" The Chequers," at Tonbridge, is a reminder of how the Eliza-
bethan craftsmen designed their houses, and is luckily not the
only one of its kind in this old Kentish town on the Medway.*

The massive timber work in this ancient house
is very outstanding, and there is not much doubt
that the " White Horse," as an inn, dates back
to at least the early sixteenth century, an earlier
building having been pulled down in the time of
Henry VII.

It is impossible, within the compass of a single
article, to explore anything but the fringe of
those " realms of gold " that are the " inn-"
land. Those hostelries that are mentioned can
be picked only at random. Many, many more
that are worthy of a place here must be passed
by. It is astounding how many inns there are
abounding in romance, beauty and story.

There is the " King's Head," at Chigwell,
Essex, which Dickens described as " delicious."
It has " more gable-ends than a lazy man would

WALTER SCOTT

## ENGLAND'S HIGHEST INN

*From the hamlet of Keld at the head of Swaledale, in Yorkshire, a narrow moorland road winds over the bare desolate hills of the Pennines. At the highest point of the road, 1,732 feet above sea level, there stands a solitary unpretentious whitewashed house. This is Tan Hill, the highest licensed house in England.*

STEPHENSON

## AN OLD SURREY HOSTELRY

*Opposite the church in the charming Surrey village of Witley, stands the White Hart Inn, an ancient hostelry with tiled roof and tile-hung walls typical of local architecture. Many famous artists and writers have lived in the neighbourhood, including the painters J. C. Hook and Birkett Foster and the author of " Mill on the Floss " who dwelt at Witley Heights. In the " White Hart " may still be seen " George Eliot's Corner."*

TRUST HOUSES, LTD.

### THE "BLACK SWAN" AT HELMSLEY

*In the spacious Market Place of the little Yorkshire town of Helmsley stands the Black Swan Hotel, its bold sign of a silhouetted swan being at once noticeable. From its quaint interior and old beams it is evidently an ancient establishment. In the lounge are some fine old pewter plates and dishes and some curious lead weights.*

care to count on a sunny day . . . over-hanging storeys, drowsy little panes of glass, and front bulging out and projecting over the pathway." It is old enough for the Court of Attachments to have been held there in 1713. "Very good diet, but very dear," wrote Pepys, after he had spent a night at the "Old George," Salisbury. Here Cromwell stayed on his way to join his army. The records of the "Old George" show that in 1453 a bay window was added at a cost of twenty shillings! The "Angel," at Henley-on-Thames, was originally a monastic rest-house for travellers, and the "Bear and Billet," at Chester, with its half-timbered frontage, richly carved woodwork and leaded windows—it was built in 1664—was once the private mansion of the Earls of Shrewsbury.

#### A Ponderous Roof

Believe it or not, but there are those who declare that it was at the "Star," Alfriston, on the South Downs, that King Alfred burned the cakes! It is a fine old house, one of its most curious characteristics being that it is roofed with slabs of stone, some of them weighing nearly two hundredweight. In the ballroom of the "White Lion," at Eye, Suffolk, you will find the musician's gallery that is a memory of the old Assembly Hall. Of the "White Lion" it was written a hundred years ago that "dinner was provided at 2s. 6d. a head, including as much wine and punch as each man could swallow." In a loft over the coaching stables at the "Ship," Alveston, there are two ancient machines, an oat-crusher and a bean-kibbler, used to prepare fodder for the coaching horses. The cellars of this inn were undoubtedly used by smugglers.

Standing in solitude in the very centre of the Forest of Dean is one of the most curious inns in England. It is set at the junction of two roads, one of which is of Roman origin and covers a site whereon the ancient Foresters of Dean met to settle their disputes. The name of this inn is "Speech House," and to this day it perpetuates the reason for which it was built some 250 years ago in the reign of Charles II, for the Forest Courts are held there ten times a year.

The meetings are held in the dining-room or courtroom, which contains a raised dais with a railed-off bench for the officers of the court. A notice states when the "Court of Attachment," as it is termed, "will be holden in the Speech House in the said forest at half-past three in the afternoon."

Among the cellars below is to be found a tiny room said to be a cell for offenders against the law, while in an upstairs room a strange octagonal post is claimed to be a whipping post.

There is no end to this story. Windows with sheets of horn in place of glass; bunk-holes for the political refugees of long ago; beer-warmers; an inn where no one can be served more than once each half-hour; a hostelry hollowed out of the solid rock; underground rooms and passages; Roman paving and Dutch tiles—there is surprise and mystery and romance to be experienced by all who choose to explore the inns of other days with which Britain is so richly endowed.

VIOLET BANKS

### THE FAMOUS FORTH BRIDGE

*By this great feat of engineering, Edinburgh gained a more direct link with north-eastern Scotland.  Spanning the Firth of Forth, it was opened in 1890.  With the approaches, the total length of the bridge is nearly 1½ miles.  The three huge cantilevers provide two main spans of 1,710 feet each and two side spans of 690 feet.  The railway runs 157 feet above the river and the top of the bridge is 361 feet above high-water level.*

# THE CHARM OF EDINBURGH

## by ALASDAIR ALPIN MacGREGOR

IF there be in the world any city other than Jerusalem that men might describe as " beautiful for situation," that city surely is Edinburgh, the Scottish capital—a romantic city which has urged the pen of many a poet and ballad-writer ; a city through the streets of which innumerable writers have followed the history of an ancient and romantic kingdom ; a city along whose flag-stoned wynds and closes pass the ghosts of kings and queens, of princes and noblemen, and of the most illustrious of the ordinary common folk, who did so much to make Scotland great.

" By universal judgment," remarked Sir Henry Campbell-Bannerman, " Edinburgh has a place, possibly the highest place, in the small group of the great towns of Europe conspicuous for romance and physical charm." By every Scotsman who knows her, she is regarded as the most picturesque and romantic city in the world — a reputation duly admitted by travellers from every part of the globe. Like Rome, she is a city built on seven hills. Northward, these hills sweep down toward Leith, her ancient seaport, by the shores of the Firth of Forth. Her background is that fine range of green hills known as the Pentlands, a name familiar to all readers and lovers of Robert Louis Stevenson, who spent much of his childhood in the secluded community of Swanston, lying in the shadow of their northern range.

Edinburgh is dominated by that great volcanic mass known as the Castle Rock, which is crowned by the castle itself, and is so precipitous on three sides that, throughout the centuries of warfare between England and Scotland, its summit remained inaccessible to attacking forces except on two occasions.

It is approached by the spacious Esplanade, upon which many of Scotland's great ones were judicially murdered during the Middle Ages. In July, 1538, Lady Jane Douglas, having been convicted of attempting to encompass the king's death, was there consigned to the flames in the presence of her husband and her son.

But not only the well-born and the once-powerful suffered : numerous poor women suspected of being witches were burned there at the stake. So late as the middle of the seventeenth century this custom was still in vogue ; and in 1659 five women were brutally done to death for " dancing with the devil."

From the strictly legal point of view the Esplanade is part of Nova Scotia in Canada : it was declared to be so in the reign of Charles I in order that Nova Scotian baronets created in Scotland might be able to " take seisin " of their new territories. It is now adorned with military monuments, including an equestrian statue of Earl Haig.

Within the 15 feet thick walls of the State

D. MCLEISH

### JOHN KNOX'S HOUSE

*This old building in the Canongate contains many relics of the great reformer. In one room he is said to have worked until shortly before his death. Before Knox's days the house is believed to have been occupied by the last Abbot of Dunfermline.*

VALENTINE

### THE CANONGATE, TOLBOOTH

*In the Canongate, once a fashionable quarter of Edinburgh, stands the Tolbooth. Built in a French style and dating from 1591, it served as a jail and courthouse. There the " Bailies of the Canongate " delivered their verdicts, and it was also a meeting place for the councillors of the burgh.*

the short and narrow street known as the Castle Hill, on the left of which stands the quaint cluster of buildings called Ramsay Gardens, built on the site of Allan Ramsay's country house, and on the right of which is situated the south-west house of Castle Hill. Embedded in the masonry of the latter is a cannon ball which was fired from the castle's bastions when, in 1745, Prince Charles Edward's arrival in the city sent a shudder through the Hanoverians and their garrison. Immediately below lies the town house of the Duchess of Gordon, a house which, at a later date, came into the possession of the Bairds of Newbyth. The mother of Sir David Baird, who distinguished himself at Seringapatan, in India, was living here when the news was brought to her that her son was one of the many prisoners chained two-and-two in the gaol at Mysore. " God help the chiel'," she exclaimed, " that's chained tae oor Davie."

### *St. Giles's Cathedral*

After the castle, perhaps the two best-known objects of romantic Edinburgh are St. Giles's Cathedral and Holyrood Palace, the former standing by the Parliament Buildings and the Municipal Offices on the ancient High

Prison, over the Portcullis Gate more than one Scottish nobleman suffered the agonies of imprisonment. It is sometimes known as Argyll's Tower, since the two Covenanting members of that family languished there before going to face the headsman. The legend-shrouded figure of the noble Montrose also darkened its grim portals.

The Citadel, 384 feet above sea level, is on the site of the palace of Malcolm Canmore, the obstinate defier of England's William Rufus. To Canmore's queen the Castle owes St. Margaret's Chapel, a very fine Early Norman edifice.

The view from the castle itself is uncommonly picturesque and romantic. Looking eastward, and downhill, across the Esplanade, one sees

Street, not very far from the castle itself, the latter situated on level ground at the foot of the Royal Mile, overshadowed by the great igneous masses of Arthur's Seat and the Salisbury Crags. Although to Englishmen, accustomed to cathedrals of great size and extravagance, St. Giles's may appear diminutive, and even unimportant, it must not be forgotten that it is the stage upon which many dramatic scenes in the troublous religious history of a nation, continually at variance on matters spiritual, were enacted. Moreover, few possessing any idea of romantic beauty could fail to be inspired by the graceful lantern tower with its airy crown of stone. Though we have no authentic record of the date at which it was founded, we do know that in the year A.D. 854

D. MCLEISH

### EDINBURGH'S FAMOUS THOROUGHFARE

*Often spoken of as the finest thoroughfare in Europe, Princes Street, running from Shadwick Place to the Register House, is about a mile long. One side is lined with municipal buildings, shops and restaurants while the other is flanked by laid-out gardens from which a fine view of the Castle may be obtained.*

VIOLET BANKS

### WINTER OVER THE CITY

*This view from the castle ramparts shows the spire of St. Giles's Cathedral, between Tolbooth and Greyfriars. Beneath its shade are buried the regent Moray, Napier of Merchiston, the Marquess of Montrose and John Knox. Until recently the General Assembly of the Church of Scotland was held in Tolbooth Church.*

minor alterations were carried out a few years later. Finally, between 1871 and 1883, very great improvements were made, so that the edifice now looks much as it did in pre-Reformation times. The choir (restored in 1873) is a fine example of the fifteenth-century architecture.

### A Lively Episode

Of all the episodes associated with this historic and romantic pile, perhaps the one that sticks most tenaciously in the mind of the Scottish schoolboy is that which describes how, on the introduction of Laud's Prayer Book, on July 23, 1637, an old Edinburgh apple-wife named Jenny Geddes interrupted Dean Hannay during the service by seizing her stool and pitching it at his head, exclaiming in so doing : " Out, thou false thief : Dost thou say Mass at my lug?" History records that the Dean " dooked " just in time, and thus escaped injury. Among the many interesting features of the interior of the cathedral is a brass tablet commemorating Jenny Geddes's act.

In the west wall of the cathedral there is a bronze memorial of Robert Louis Stevenson, to which is added *Requiem*, that haunting poem written by him in warm, Pacific seas, when pining for Edinburgh and the Pentland Hills of Home :

" Under the wide and starry sky,
  Dig the grave and let me lie :
  Glad did I live and gladly die ;
      And I lay me down with a will.
  This be the verse you grave for me,
  ' Here he lies where he longed to be :
  Home is the sailor, home from the sea,
      And the hunter home from the hill.' "

The author of *Treasure Island* was born at 8, Howard Place, in the old town of Edinburgh. The house itself has now been converted into a museum containing much of literary and romantic interest to those who know Scotland, and perhaps Edinburgh in particular. Among the

DIXON-SCOTT

**EDINBURGH CASTLE FROM THE GRASSMARKET**
*On this rock, Edwin, the seventh-century king of Northumbria, probably had a fortress. Several times the site was held by the English. Bruce dismantled the castle, but Edward III, of England restored it in 1337.*

there stood upon this very site an ancient place of worship, serving the people of " Edwin's burg," attached to Lindisfarne, and dedicated to the " guid Sanct Geille."

With the Reformation—which, as everyone knows, went to much greater lengths in Scotland than in England—much of the pristine glory of St. Giles's Cathedral departed ; and for well-nigh two hundred years it stood in a forlorn and ruinous condition.

In 1829 the work of " restoration " was begun by an architect who must have lacked all feeling for the beauty of the ancient pile, since he destroyed some of its finest features. Further

VIOLET BANKS

## ST. GILES'S CATHEDRAL, EDINBURGH

*This, the oldest church in the city, was erected in the twelfth century and partly rebuilt after a fire in 1385. It has experienced many vicissitudes. After the Reformation it lost its forty-four altars and a statue of St. Giles was removed and thrown into the Nor' Loch. During the sixteenth century it was at one and the same time a court of justice, a prison, a school, a workshop, the town clerk's office and a storehouse for the gallows.*

exhibits is a fragment of oak that once formed part of the Spanish galleon, *Florida*, lying deep at the bottom of Tobermory Bay. This fragment recalls *The Merry Men*, Stevenson's fascinating story of the storm-kelpies haunting that romantic tideway, the Sound of Mull.

The phrase, romantic Edinburgh, immediately conjures up pictures of her castle, of St. Giles's, of the High Street, which is called the Royal Mile, and, not least, the Palace of Holyrood. From the days of Robert the Bruce, and to all intents and purposes until the Parliamentary

It included the Duchess of Argyll, the Master of the Household, and a few others, not forgetting, of course, Rizzio. As dusk fell, a band of armed men closed in upon Holyrood, since a plot had been arranged between the Earls of Ruthven and Morton and others to murder the queen's favourite. As the guests sat talking and drinking at the supper table, Darnley and his accomplices crept up the narrow staircase leading to the queen's boudoir, where they seized Rizzio. Out of the boudoir they dragged him, and stabbed him to death. The warm body of their

VIOLET BANKS

PANORAMA OF EDINBURGH

*From the castle ramparts a fine view is obtained of the city which is declared to be the most beautiful and picturesque in these islands. In the foreground, over the railway line, is the National Gallery, left of which is the Royal Scottish Academy. The isolated Gothic spire is the Scott memorial in Princes Street Gardens.*

Union with England in 1707, Holyrood remained the intimate residence of the Stewart kings and their courts. Some were born here : others crowned, married, or buried within its walls. And it was to this palace that, as a symbol of the fact that the Scottish monarch had become King of England, Sir Robert Carey brought a ring for the finger of King James VI.

But of all the romantic associations of this hallowed and storied place, none has the poignancy of those that concern the hapless Mary Queen of Scots.

In one of the several apartments shown to visitors, there occurred on March 9, 1566, a tragedy that had repercussions more serious than were ever anticipated at the time. A little supper party had assembled in the queen's apartments.

victim they are believed to have cast down at the door of the apartment where now may be seen a brass tablet let into the floor. Later Rizzio's corpse was carried downstairs and into Holyrood Abbey. It is said to have been interred there, under the last step. Before long, the burghers and citizens of Edinburgh were clamouring outside the walls of Holyrood, intent on vengeance for their sorrowing queen. Matters were not to be permitted to rest there, however : within a year, Darnley himself was killed in the Provost's House at the fateful Kirk-o'-Field.

Whereas it cannot be proved that Mary herself had anything to do with the planning of this murder, there seems every justification for assuming that she knew her husband's life was in danger. Three months after Darnley's death, and in the very chapel at Holyrood, in which she had married him in 1565, she took Bothwell as her husband.

One of the most romantic apartments visitors to Edinburgh are permitted to see is Queen Mary's bedroom at the Palace of Holyrood, with the door leading to the supper-room just as it was on that evening of ill omen.

In the time of Mary Queen of Scots, Edinburgh and its environs became very French. Evidences of Mary's association with France, and of her employment of French people about her court, are to be found in such names as Picardy Place. Then, on the outskirts of the city, there is a small village called Burdiehouse, which is simply a corruption of Bordeaux House. Here resided many of Mary's French vassals. At this period, sanitation was so little known in Edinburgh that it was customary for its citizens to dispose of their slops and garbage by flinging them out of their windows into the gutters below. This ancient custom was so well established at the time when French influence in Edinburgh was at its zenith, that it gave rise to the familiar street cry, Gardyloo, which is simply a corruption of the French phrase *Gardez l'eau*—mind the water!

Though perhaps one of Edinburgh's least romantic streets, because of its comparative newness, Princes Street is claimed to be one of the finest public thoroughfares in the world. View it from the Castle Rock, or from the slopes of the Mound, backed by the gables and spires of much of the Old Town, with the Firth of Forth

and the Hills of Fife beyond, bordered by its exquisite gardens and its fine monuments, balanced so beautifully by the columns of the Scottish National Gallery, and you readily will realize how Edinburgh won the name, "the modern Athens." Most conspicuous among the many monuments in Princes Street Gardens is that to Sir Walter Scott—a fitting tribute to that giant among Scotland's writers of romance.

It was during the latter half of the eighteenth century, and the opening years of the nineteenth, that there took place in Edinburgh the intellectual revival that did so much to win for her a place among the most celebrated cities in the world. In those days her roofs gave shelter to such men as Smollett, David Hume, Lord Elibank, Dr. Gregory, James Boswell, Adam Ferguson, Adam Smith, Jeffrey, Brougham, and the immortal Sir Walter. We must not fail to mention also two great women, Lady Anne Lindsay, who wrote that beautiful song, *Auld Robin Gray*; and Jean Elliot who, reflecting on the fate that, on Flodden Field, befell the chivalry of Scotland in 1513, wrote her ballad *Flowers o' the Forest*, of imperishable memory and which, played at times of sadness, is one of the most heart-rending melodies.

Edinburgh's peculiar reputation is in no small measure due to Sir Walter Scott. She has had her vicissitudes—her political ups and downs; but in the pages of the Wizard of the North her citizens must ever remain the descendants of an imaginative and a virile race, heritors of a brave and romantic past.

W. F. TAYLOR

**A FAMOUS ALLEY**

*Typical of Edinburgh's many narrow alleys is Advocates' Close, seen above, which gained its name from Sir James Stewart of Goodtrees, who was Lord Advocate of Scotland from 1692-1713.*

R. M. ADAM

### HIGHEST IN BRITAIN
*Above Fort William, in Inverness-shire, rises the bulky broad-shouldered mass of Ben Nevis (4,406 feet), the highest of British mountains. The ascent by the path from Fort William by Glen Nevis presents no difficulty, but on the north-east the mountain falls in magnificent precipices only attempted by expert cragsmen.*

# THE HIGHLANDS OF BRITAIN

## by J. E. B. WRIGHT

THERE is a prevalent belief among the villagers of the Alps that Britain has no mountains. True, we have no giants; but our highlands after ages of erosion and denudation are modest, shapely hills and have a beauty which more than compensates for lack of stature.

Although our highlands are fragments, and are either the worn relics of ancient plateaux with a uniformity of shape and height, or blunt masses of rock which have resisted weathering to some extent, yet, Lilliputian as they may be, under the play of light and shadow, under cloud, snow and rain, they oftimes may assume something of the grandeur of Alpine peaks. Colour and form combine to give unending delight. The green downs of the south curve smoothly up from their ploughed field fringe; Stack Polly rises delicately from the bogs of Sutherland, seeming to hang poised above the black peat; from Wastwater a broad sweep runs up to the smooth grey head of Great Gable.

Often after a strenuous day on the hills I have sat and watched the mountains slowly losing detail as night approached and gradually softening into vague and shadowy forms, colourful, and without exaggeration, mystic and wonderful. From Capel Curig I have seen Snowdon with Crib Goch and Y Wyddfa upstanding like steel blue spears around which played crimson tinted cloud banners. More times than I can remember I have walked slowly down from Sty Head in the Lake District and seen Borrowdale, that beautiful unsurpassable dale, all aglow with crimson and gold and Skiddaw's triple crests transfused into quivering purple peaks. The far Cuillin of Skye I have seen in all weathers sun-baked and snow-clad, wreathed in soft swirling mist or swept with driving rain. From such experience, and from a hoard of ineffaceable memories, I would say without hesitation that in the Highlands of Britain there is encompassed more beauty and grandeur than can be fully comprehended in one brief lifetime.

Legends relate how much the devil had a hand in making these mountains and gorges, while journeys of difficulty were taken among them by the early Britons for the highly moral purpose

STEPHENSON

### CHANCTONBURY RING

*On the Sussex Downs, near Steyning, is Chanctonbury Ring, the most conspicuous landmark in that delightful range of rolling downland. Within the ramparts of an ancient camp grows a compact group of beeches. From the Ring there is a wide prospect over the " checkerwork of woods, the Sussex Weald."*

EDGAR WARD

## THE FRINGE OF DARTMOOR

*In this view from Sheepstor one gets an impression of the cultivated lower lands reaching to the edge of the bare moorlands. In the middle distance is the village of Sheepstor, with its little granite church. Sheepstor was a reputed haunt of pixies, and has a Pixie's Cave in which a local squire hid from Cromwell's troops.*

of being proved a worthy member of the tribe.

At the time of the '45 Rebellion, when soldiers from the south marched up to the border and beyond, the mountains were recorded as fearful and dangerous places. This was the prevalent feeling in the eighteenth century. When Boswell had persuaded Dr. Johnson to make the hazardous journey into the Highlands and the far loneliness of Skye, he mentioned the project to Voltaire, " He looked at me," says Boswell, " as if I talked of going to the North Pole, and said, ' You do not insist on my accompanying you ? ' ' No, sir.' ' Then I am very willing you should go.' "

The poet Gray, among the first to appreciate mountain scenery, tells how he had to draw down the blinds in horror, as his carriage passed at the foot of the steep slopes of Skiddaw, a harmless mass of a hill which today would not raise the least tremor in the most nervous visitor.

Gray, however, wrote with enthusiasm of Lakeland beauty—" Green and smiling fields embosomed in the dark cliffs ; to the left the jaws of Borrowdale, with that turbulent chaos of mountain behind mountain, rolled in confusion ; beneath you and stretching far away to the right the shining purity of the lake reflecting rocks, woods, fields and inverted tops of hills just ruffled by the breeze, enough to show it is alive, with the white buildings of Keswick, Crosthwaite Church, and Skiddaw for a background at a distance."

The outlook of the day is revealed in the poet's further remarks : " The dale opens about four miles higher till you come to Sea-whaite (where lies the way, mounting the hills to the right that leads to the Wadd-mines) ; all farther access is here barred to prying mortals, only there is a little path winding over the fells, and for some weeks in the year passable to the dalesmen ; but the mountains know well that these innocent people will not reveal the mysteries of their ancient kingdom, ' the reign of Chaos and old Night.' "

### Coming of the Mountaineer

By this time, however, there were signs of change in the tastes of leisured people, and soon there was a turning from formal gardens, grottoes and such artificialities. Touring was becoming a fashionable pursuit, and visits to " outlandish " places were also encouraged by the growing interest in science. Poets and philosophers began to seek inspiration in mountains, as a relief from the disillusionment of the industrial age lately come upon them. It was not, however, until the Victorian age that mountaineering as a sport came into being, spreading from the Alps to the British Isles. At first this was just walking in unfamiliar places, but very soon the mountaineer became distinct from the ordinary pedestrian, and at the popular holiday seasons, our crags are now festooned with parties of climbers.

Prehistoric man made good use of the chalk hills of the south. On the South Downs, the Wiltshire and Berkshire Downs and the beech-draped Chilterns, he raised his earthworks and burial mounds and scored the turf with his tracks.

Although these hills only rise to 700 and 800 feet, they are far away from the life of the valleys, and one can share the feeling of Gilbert White, the homely, observant naturalist of Selborne, who wrote " though I have now travelled the Sussex Downs upwards of thirty years, yet I still investigate that chain of majestic mountains with fresh admiration year by year, and I think I see new beauties every time I traverse it."

Away in the west are the limestone hills of the Mendips, riven by the Gorge of Cheddar, and riddled with underground caverns, which provide muddy routes for speliologists (sometimes called " pot-holers ") who seek to trace the ramifications of the caves and the subterranean courses of the streams. These enthusiastic cavemen have been known to colour the water supply of a Somerset village during their investigations, and, on one never to be forgotten occasion, when forcing their way into a cavern by means of explosives, they actually set a church rocking immediately above them when the minister was in the midst of his sermon, and stories of an earth tremor were noised abroad.

From the Mendips we may gaze across the lush green levels of Somerset to the gentle heights of the Quantocks, and beyond them to the heathery uplands of Exmoor. There many of us first journeyed imaginatively in the company of Girt Jan Ridd and the winsome Lorna Doone. Although in reality this country may lack the grandeur with which it was invested by the author, the wide reaches of moorlands and the sudden valleys and hastening streams have a way of winning the heart of countless folk who come to seek Lorna's Bower, the Doone Valley or the Waterslide, and one who has stood on the heathery heights of Dunkery Beacon will ever afterwards long to be—

" Upon the rolling moorlands high above the
    Severn Sea."

### Granite Tors of Dartmoor

Devon also gives us Dartmoor with its upstanding granite tors, its wide reaches of purple heather, its peaty pools and rushing streams and squelchy patches with white tufts of cotton-grass—Nature's way of saying " 'Ware bog." Dartmoor, for south country people at least, probably more than any other region in Britain, typifies the wild and lonely places.

Compared with these shaggy heights the Cotswolds are but a softly carpeted upland, and today they are more famed for their villages than for

W. F. TAYLOR

### THE BRECON BEACONS
*Above the valley of the Usk, and overlooking the little cathedral city of Brecon, rise these attractive sandstone hills, the highest mountains in South Wales (2,907 feet). Near Pen-y-Fan is a great hollow known as Cadair Arthur (King Arthur's Chair). From the summit the view northwards embraces most of mid-Wales.*

their inherent features. Modest hills they may be, and yet there are far greater heights that cannot offer a prospect so fair as that splendid view from the western escarpment of the Cotswolds. Away beyond the vales of Severn and Wye may be seen the long barrier of the Black Mountains of Brecon, lonely heights running north and south like giants' fingers, with deep-set valleys between, and terminating in an abrupt wall overlooking the mid-reaches of the Wye.

North of the Cotswolds are the boldly carved Malverns crowned with ancient earthworks and with Hereford Beacon and Worcester Beacon indicating one of the purposes they have served.

From the Malverns it is no distant step to the Clee Hills, another fine vantage point whence we may trace the scarped Wenlock Edge running across Shropshire, the dark wall of the Longmynd and the long ridge of the Stiperstones, and, by no means least, the solitary height of the Wrekin, gaining added prominence by its isolation.

As we stand on the Wrekin our eyes are drawn westward to Mary Webb's country, "the country that lies between the dimpled lands of England and the gaunt purple steeps of Wales." Yonder are the shapely hills of Breidden in Montgomery and beyond them, if the day be clear, we shall see the more distant Berwyns, the

bulky mass of Plynlimon and the great brow of Cader Idris.

The round, smooth-shouldered Berwyns above the valley of the Dee, pleasant rolling heights as they are, suffer in popularity from their location and are regarded as stepping stones to higher things—the mountains of Snowdonia.

George Borrow, who visited Wales with his wife and daughter, and pursued poets and legends so keenly (having first carefully sent his women folk off to church or on a gentle stroll) may be quoted, in his best informative style, to introduce these mountains.

### Home of Eagles

" Snowdon or Eryri is no single hill, but a mountainous region, the loftiest part of which, called Y Wyddfa, nearly 4,000 feet above the level of the sea, is generally considered to be the highest point of southern Britain. The name Snowdon was bestowed upon this region by the early English on account of its snowy appearance in winter ; Eryri by the Britons, because in the old time it abounded with eagles, Eryri in the ancient British language signifying an eyrie or breeding place of eagles."

As we approach this region from the east, mounting the vale of Llugwy from Bettws-y-Coed,

STEPHENSON

### RUGGED PINNACLES OF SNOWDON
*Snowdon is not a single height, but a group of peaks including Crib Goch, Carnedd Ugain, Y Wyddfa (the highest, 3,560 feet), Lliwedd and Yr Aran. The photograph shows the upstanding pinnacles of Crib Goch. Beyond these is the narrow ridge of Crib-y-ddysgyl, leading to Carnedd Ugain. In the background is Y Wyddfa.*

STEPHENSON

## ON WINTRY HILLS

*Only strenuous and enthusiastic mountaineers gain the summits of the hills in mid-winter when the ascent may call for considerable skill and endurance. The ice-axe may have to be used to cut steps in the frozen snow and ice. This view on the Welsh mountains shows the snow-covered hills as seen from the summit of Tryfaen.*

we are confronted by the graceful peak of Moel Siabod, a mountain which fails to fulfil its promise for on the west it tails off as a featureless expanse of moorland. But beyond Siabod lie the peaks of Snowdon. There they stand in tempting array, the sharp-pointed Crib Goch with its narrow edge leading to Carnedd Ugain, and frowning on the rocky wilderness of Cwm Glas and the deep bowl of Cwm Dyli with its lakes Llydaw and Glaslyn. From the colourful waters of Glaslyn soar the crags of Y Wyddfa, the highest point of the Snowdon Range, falling steeply to Bwlch y Saethau and rising again to the double peaks of Lliwedd.

North of Snowdon are the twins Glyder Fawr and Glyder Fach, not unduly impressive from this side but approached from Ogwen they tell a different story. There they sweep upwards with great rock walls and riven crags and hidden hollows. On that side too stands Tryfaen, surely one of the most shapely of British mountains tapering like a great pyramid and streaked across its eastern face with a thin white line—the Heather Terrace, a mountain track which traverses the hillside, across the gullies, and by the bases of the buttresses beloved by the rock climber.

From this side too we behold the rounded swelling uplands of the Carnedds only little inferior in height to Snowdon but lacking its rugged eminence, yet none the less worthy of exploration.

The mountains of Snowdonia are formed mainly of igneous (volcanic) rocks, and the outlines of the crags are correspondingly varied. Sometimes the bare rock is quite red in colour, elsewhere it is green or grey. There are many moraines, too, left by the ancient glaciers of Snowdon, and the whole area is remarkably diverse and interesting. Not the least of the attractions are the numerous lakes, blue under a summer sky, whipped to fury by the gales of winter, when the whiteness of the blown spray rivals the deep drifted snow, or gleaming with that peculiar indigo blue that comes with a storm sky and catches the breath with its mysterious unreality.

### The Far-reaching Pennines

The Pennines form a long barrier from the Peak to the Cheviots, with the two natural gaps of Aire and Stainmore cutting through them. When Daniel Defoe passed through the Peak District, the southern end of the Pennines, he quite definitely refused to be impressed with the various show places, and went out of his way to ridicule Poole's Hole and Mam Tor (the Mother Rock). He described the Peak as being " the lower rounds of a ladder " and then,

STEPHENSON

### THE BARE HEIGHTS OF DERBYSHIRE

*The Pennine moors, capped with sandstone and their lower slopes consisting of crumbling shale, usually present long ridges or " Edges " such as Stanedge, Blackstone Edge and Mallerstang Edge.  They are generally bare hills of coarse wiry grass and heather given over to sheep and grouse.  Above are seen the moors near Buxton.*

proceeding northwards, says " but the continuance of these mountains is such, that we know no bounds set to them, but they run on in a continued ridge or ledge of mountains from one to another, till they are lost in the southern parts of Scotland, and even through that to the Highlands, so that they may be said to divide Britain, as the Appennine Mountains divide Italy."   He was, however, impressed with the northern Pennines, and quotes the old, and topographically incorrect, couplet :
" Inglebrough, Pendle-hill and Penigent,
  Are the highest hills between Scotland and
      Trent,"
going on to say, " Indeed, they were, in my thoughts, monstrous high ; but in a country all mountains and full of innumerable high hills, it was not easy for a traveller to judge which was highest."

The Pennines in fact provide some of the wildest and most desolate moorland country we possess south of the Scottish border.   They offer no pyramidal heights such as Tryfaen or anything approaching the grandeur of Snowdon or the crags of Scafell.   Yet they have a strong appeal to all lovers of the hills.   Moreover they have the advantage, particularly in the northern portion of long stretches of upland where one may roam mile after mile at an altitude round about 2,000 feet.   Unfortunately much of this country

is preserved for grouse-shooting and Kinderscout, that grand mass of a hill sweeping upwards out of Edale, is forbidden ground without a right of way over its shaggy crest.

Farther north, on the edge of Lancashire, and a little out of the main line of the Pennines, stands the bluff mass of Pendle Hill where of old the Lancashire witches held their unholy revels.   From Pendle we see the dark moors where the Brontës lived and away to the north the twin heights of Ingleborough and Penyghent, probably the most beautiful hills in the whole range.

#### Haunts of Curlew

Still northwards we might continue crossing daleheads and ranging the uplands where the curlew cries down the wind and plover wheel and wail overhead.   On by the narrow defile of Mallerstang beneath Wild Boar Fell ; on over Nine Standards Rigg and across " Stainmoor's shapeless swell " so we eventually reach Cross Fell (2,930 feet), the highest point of this long line of moor and fell.

Over the Eden Valley from Cross Fell rise the Cumbrian Hills, with valleys radiating from the main hub of Great Gable, Scafell Pike, Glaramara and the Langdale Pikes.   This wheel formation is what has made the Lake District so comparatively inaccessible.   Routes lead up the valleys past the lakes to the hills, not through them ;

and what curse is put upon man that he would blast his way straight through, destroying the solitudes, merely to satisfy his lust for speed?

Britain has higher and more rugged mountains than these, lakes that are longer, valleys that are deeper and greater, but nowhere does she offer such an exquisite combination of the three, or present more beautiful harmony of form, colour and design.

There is that grand prospect of the Langdale Pikes at the head of Windermere, the circling fells round Ullswater, and that glorious array of mountains closing round the uppermost reaches of Borrowdale. The glacier-shorn buttresses of Blencathra (as lovely as its name), the hummocky crests of Glaramara, the dark, soaring crags of Scafell, the sheer Napes ridges of Gable and the splendid mass of Pillar Rock rising in solitary splendour above the wilds of Ennerdale—these are a few details of this superb corner of Britain to which men and women, young and old, strollers and tried mountaineers return again and again.

The mountains with Scafell Pike (3,210 feet) smoothly out-topping them all, gain in loveliness as they stand above the winding lakes and wooded valleys, and here, as in Wales, little tarns high in the hills take the sky and the wind to them. Up on Striding Edge on a sunny day, with Red Tarn shining down below, you are above the world, with the wind your companion and Helvellyn a sleepy neighbour. When you have trudged up Blencathra through rain, wondering why you are out at all, you suddenly come above the clouds which fill the combes and all the valleys. white and shining in the sun, and you greet distant Gable as an equal and stand as still as she, to fix it all in your memory for ever.

### John Peel's Country

Lakeland, of course, was John Peel's country and below Blencathra on the north, in Caldbeck Churchyard, is the grave of the famous lakeland huntsman. On the south side of the mountain lies Threlkeld, where today the John Peel hounds, now known as the Blencathra Foxhounds are kennelled. "D'ye ken John Peel" is sung wherever the English language is spoken, but the tune of today is not the original. The old tune is still alive in the north country, and many a Cumberland man has been thrilled to hear its

STEPHENSON

### A MOORLAND PASS
*On the edge of Lancashire and Yorkshire lies the ancient Forest of Bowland, a beautiful tract of moorland once described as the least-known hill country in England. In its valleys are lonely farms, some of them a dozen miles from a railway. Here is a wintry impression of the Trough of Bowland, a pass through the hills.*

STEPHENSON

### A PENNINE PEAK

*Between Ribblesdale and Littondale, a side valley of Wharfedale, in Yorkshire, rises Penyghent (2,273 feet), one of the most shapely hills in the long length of the Pennines. From Horton-in-Ribblesdale it is seen with a bold profile sweeping upwards from a limestone plateau in which are many caverns and underground streams. Note the stone walls on each side of the lane and also in the fields on the hillside in the background.*

STEPHENSON

### CLOUD-SHADOWED HILLS

*A typical Lake District scene is this northward view from the slopes of Glaramara. Beneath is Borrowdale, a valley of varied and appealing beauty through which flows the crystal-clear Derwent. In the distance is the oval mirror of Derwentwater which the stream reaches through the narrows known as the " Jaws of Borrowdale." Beyond the lake rises the great mass of Skiddaw (3,054 feet) with its neighbour Blencathra on the right.*

strains floating over the wireless from that famous male choir known as the Keswick Mountain Singers.

North of the Pennines and the Cumbrian Hills lie the Cheviots, smooth-topped hills, almost devoid of crops, with deep winding glens. Here is the famous Border country, that has borne the passage of invaders and defenders from the time of the Roman invasion of Scotland, right through the troublous times of King Kenneth MacAlpin, Macbeth, Robert the Bruce, and down to the last flare of the '45 Rebellion.

notably Broad Law (2,754 feet) with their sides deeply cut into corries, but for the most part they show a smooth and treeless outline, and contain very few lakes.

In the Middle Valley of Scotland there are several outcrops of volcanic rock which rise steeply from the plain as the Ochil and Pentland Hills. It is not, however, until we have reached the south-west to north-east line of the edge of the Highlands, that the glory of the Scottish mountains begins to show itself. Ben Vorlich and Ben Lomond stand conspicuously, in immediate

STEPHENSON

### THE LINGERING TOUCH OF WINTER

*St. Sunday Crag (2,756 feet) is one of the most distinctive hills round the head of Ullswater. It is here viewed from Grisedale. At the head of this valley, about 2,000 feet above sea level, is Grisedale Tarn, where, according to tradition, lies the crown of Dunmail, the ancient Cumbrian king from whom Dunmail Raise is named.*

In these Cheviot dales lived a wild and reckless people, little given to discriminating between " mine " and " thine," and there is many a tale of lawless doings, of thieving and skirmishing and sallying over the Border on plunder bent. In 1564 the Incorporated Merchant Adventurers of Newcastle laid down that none born in the valleys of Tyne and Reed should be admitted as apprentices. The inhabitants of the upper reaches of those dales were said to be so given to rapine that no faith should be placed in the offspring of " such lewde and wicked progenitors."

The Southern Uplands of Scotland have several large flat-topped remnants of a once high plateau,

contrast to the lowland. The Arrochar Highlands rise above Loch Lomond and the huge mass of Ben More dominates country described in the pages of Sir Walter Scott.

These are the prelude to mountains yet more wild. To the north-east are the magnificent granite blocks of the Cairngorms and the dark mass of Lochnagar, scarred and rounded by glacial erosion and even today oft retaining winter snow far into summer months. Gloomy lakes lie in the corries, and the very names of the peaks tell of their loneliness and dignity. Cairn Gorm (Blue Mountain), Stob Bac an Fhurain (Peak of the Springs), Meur Gorm (Blue Finger).

STEPHENSON

## A DELICATE STEP

*Instead of regarding mountains as terrifying features, many now seek to climb them by the most difficult routes that can be found. The photograph shows a Lakeland Mountain Guide on the initial traverse of Kern Knotts Crack on Great Gable. This climb on an almost vertical wall calls for perfect balance and careful movement.*

All kinds of legends and stories are told of the Cairngorms. There is the water kelpie of Loch Avon who would appear as a beautiful horse, allow a man to mount her, and then dash the rider to his doom in the lonely loch beneath Ben Macdhui. A hollow on the Cairn Gorm, often holding snow until late in the season, is called Ciste Mhairearaid or Margaret's Coffin, the tradition being that Margaret, jilted by Mackintosh of Moy, cursed his family to sterility and died here after mad wanderings.

There are many groups of mountains in the Central Highlands, and these great masses are far removed indeed from the gentle hills of southern England. Here are picturesque peaks, long, narrow ridges and deep lakes. Ben Cruachan (the Mountain of Peaks) famous in Scottish history and song; Ben Alder, where Prince Charlie took shelter for a time after Culloden; and Sgor na Ciche, or the Pap of Glencoe, a shapely cone rising above the fateful Glen of Weeping, the scene of that dreadful slaughter.

STEPHENSON

### EVENING IN A CAIRNGORM GLEN
*Among the most inaccessible hills of Britain are the massive hills of the Cairngorms, most of their summits only being attainable through uninhabited wilds. Above is the view up Glen Lui.*

So we come to the Ben Nevis *massif*, not a solitary peak, but a group of summits so closely joined that they appear like buttresses of the whole. This is a savage, grand pile of steep ridges and pinnacles, that bears a cap of snow far into the summer, and often gathers to itself dark clouds like a volcano, as though in memory of its origin. From the summit in clear weather Inverness is visible fifty miles away, and the dim coast of Ireland, one hundred and twenty miles to the south, and out to the west the jagged Cuillin. When the clouds are up, the grey-white mass parts now and then to give tantalizing glimpses of a steep rock face on the left, or perhaps a brief view of the Caledonian Canal, apparently flowing uphill to Inverness.

Beyond Ben Nevis, into the remote Western Highlands, Prince Charlie wandered after Culloden. One night he climbed to the top of Meall an Spardain to spy out the enemy's camps. Another night, near to the summit of Sgurr nan Conbhairean he was "wet to the skin and devoured by midges." In this sort of country, if anywhere, he could remain at liberty, where the mountains are steep and pointed, the valleys very deep and the sea lochs run into the heart of the mountains. Even today there are few roads and the real traveller follows on foot ancient tracks once used by the clansmen and cattle-drovers.

So we can go right to the north of Scotland, through the regions of Torridonian sandstone, to the rugged mass of Slioch and the terraced heights of Liathach above the shining levels of Loch Maree and on to the black, fantastic peaks of An Teallach. Yet farther north is the Grey Castle of Suilven, a strangely shaped obelisk, and the great sloping bulk of Arkle, whose shining quartzite gleams mistily above Loch Stack. All these are mountains of distinction, often lonely, with only the setting sun to gild them, and the quiet inland lochs and restless winding sea-lochs lapping at their feet.

The sea is never far from the Red and Black Cuillin in Skye, divided by Glen Sligachan, but otherwise a continuous chain of high summits, linked by broken, naked ridges. They are enormous and austere, yet have at all times the mystery of the sea and the mist, sunshine and rain working upon them. Witches have, of course, played a great part in their past, sailing on the sea in baskets, transforming themselves into cats or ravens, and putting terror into the hearts of simple folk. Witches are believed in to this day in Skye, and many stories remain of water-horses and Spanish pirates, of whom the villagers went in dread for many years.

### Unnamed Heights

When the time came for Skye to come within the scope of travellers, notably Dr. Johnson, it was found that several of the peaks and corries had no names. Sgurr Alasdair, the highest peak, was named in 1873, when it was first climbed by Sheriff Alexander Nicolson, a native of Skye. The meaning and origin of the old names is disputed in many cases. The Cuillin have been spelled variously Cuilluelum, Culluelun, Gulluin, Quillin, Cullin, Quillen and Cuchullin. Some say they were named after a Prince of Antrim, Cuchullin; others mention " hollies " and point either to the trees in Glen Brittle or to the prickly nature of the skyline. Sgurr a'Ghread-aidh is supposed to be a Norse name, and despite its Gaelic disguise, is pronounced like its English equivalent, " Greta."

### Rock-girt Corries

The Cuillin Hills are the rock climbers' para-dise. In fact there are but few of the summits which are easily accessible to the walker. Sgurr Alasdair can only be scaled by one route without rock-climbing, and this involves the toilsome scramble up the Great Stone Shoot, 1,300 feet of boulders of all shapes and sizes reaching up to the gap between Alasdair and Sgurr Thearlaich. But once on the tapered summit of Alasdair none will begrudge the energy expended. Splintered ridges and bold and strangely fashioned peaks casting weird shadows across the silent rock-girt corries, the little blue lochans far below, and over the spreading sea, the vision of the Outer Hebrides on the one hand, and the mountains of the mainland on the other—these are the reward of it all and no man could desire more.

Since the days when Dr. Johnson beheld the Cuillin, when he drank innumerable cups of tea and talked as sententiously as if he had been in a Fleet Street tavern, there has been a great change in our attitude to mountains. Nowadays men scale those peaks of Skye by routes the learned doctor would have emphatically termed beyond human capacity.

One beginning of the new attitude is to be found in the daring exploits of a group of Lake District shepherds who made the first ascent of the precipitous west face of Pillar Rock in 1826. This was the actual birth of British rock climbing and it is a remarkable fact that it occurred on the giant wall of one of the most inaccessible of English mountains.

The first recorded tourist ascent was made in 1848, and during the next ten years several ascents were made by the short East Face route. The fame of the " Pillar Stane " began to spread and in 1882 three mountaineers, Slingsby, Hastings and Haskett-Smith, who had some experience of climbing in the Alps decided to attempt the long and difficult North Face. These men found that they derived " great pleasure " in trying to find a way up this steep face of rock and after three attempts made a route which is now known as the North Climb.

About the south face of Great Gable stories were told by shepherds of a great steeple-like rock which later became known as the Napes Needle. Haskett-Smith spent days in trying to

STEPHENSON

### THE FIVE SISTERS OF KINTAIL

*In Western Ross, where the sea winds far inland among the hills, the range of peaks known as the Five Sisters of Kintail rise in full glory at the head of Loch Duich. Sgurr Fhuaran, or Ouran (3,505 feet), the highest point, is the cloudless summit in the scene above, which was photographed from the slopes of Mam Ratagan.*

STEPHENSON

## THE WILDS OF SUTHERLAND
*From the rugged height of Ben More Assynt (3,273 feet) there is a splendid northward view over the long reach of Loch Assynt and out to the Atlantic beyond Lochinver. By Loch Assynt are the ruins of Ardvreck Castle, where the Marquess of Montrose was confined in 1650. In the background is the jagged mass of Quinaig.*

locate it without success until, one day in 1886 he watched the wreathing mists floating about on the precipice of the Great Napes, and saw a pinnacle which the mists showed to be detached from the main mass of the mountain. He climbed the Needle and left his handkerchief on the top as proof of his conquest.

Towards the end of the nineteenth century many ascents were recorded in Scotland and Wales and peaks and precipices, hitherto regarded as unclimbable, fell before assaults launched at them by Owen Glynne Jones, John Mackenzie, the Abraham brothers and many others.

At the beginning of the present century climbers began to record their experiences, and today we have eighteen volumes of guide-books setting out in complete detail the routes up many hundreds of rock climbs all over Britain.

A bibliography of climbing nowadays would catalogue several thousands of books in which men and women have written of the many joys discovered in climbing mountains.

Unlike most other forms of human activity and adventure, mountaineering does not lend itself to ceremonial, and climbers endeavour to avoid rather than court publicity. Nevertheless,

some light has been shed on the dangers of mountain climbing, and the bravery of men who have gone forth to conquer the heights, but countless deeds of heroism remain unrecorded.

The hills are no longer objects of fear, but places for happy leisure hours, with tried companions or alone. There is a satisfaction in pitting human strength and endurance against physical forces that no other form of striving can give. In the wide, unspoiled view of our hills, in the colour of flowers and the secret life of birds and beasts, we find particular delight, but the effort made to reach the high places is what we really feel and enjoy. Because we have forced our bodies up grassy slopes or rock faces, against all adverse weather conditions, using up our foot-pounds of energy, adjusting our minds to the laws of Nature, we have earned the right to call the hills our own. The view of the sheer, steep precipices falling away into nothing, the tiny lakes fringed with golden sand, the rough moorland track by which we have come, blue hills fading into the distance, and right ahead the glinting expanse that we know to be the sea—this is our heritage for ever, ours by right of birth and by right of conquest.

DIXON-SCOTT

### THE LONG MAN OF WILMINGTON

*Carved in the chalk of the Sussex Downs near Wilmington is this huge figure measuring 230 feet from head to toes. Once thought to be the work of the monks of a nearby priory, it is now considered of a much greater antiquity. It has also been suggested it represents a sun god pushing open the doors of darkness.*

# SOME ANCIENT LANDMARKS

## *by* HAROLD SHELTON

HAVE you ever travelled along the little road which hugs the northern slopes of the Berkshire Downs westward of Wantage? If you have not, you have missed one of England's most romantic journeys. The road drops into a wooded combe, then rises again to a low shelf which overlooks the fertile Vale of the White Horse, for all the world like a chessboard of trim hedge and cultivated field, dotted with tiny copses and a wealth of hedgerow timber. On the other hand the abrupt face of the downs rises imminently to the long line of smooth green hills which stretch east and west as far as eye can reach.

A mile or two farther along the road a fantastic scar appears near the summit of the hill where the ridge is clearly defined against the skyline. As we proceed the scar is transformed into the shape of a galloping horse, elongated and attenuated as though it were the very spirit of motion. This, the famous White Horse of Uffington, is one of the ancient but still undated hill figures of England, about which much has been written of late years, but yet so little is actually known.

Who were the men who fashioned this gigantic figure and for what purpose? Tradition, as ever, is a deceiving wench. It relates that the horse is a monument to King Alfred, who was certainly born at Wantage. It says that the great Battle of Ashdown, in A.D. 871, when the Danes were utterly defeated was fought somewhere in this neighbourhood, whereupon Alfred commanded that a figure of himself upon his charger should be cut in the chalk downs as a permanent memorial of the victory.

If only there were the figure of a man upon the horse we might with greater confidence accept tradition, but there is not the slightest evidence to support it. Rather everything tends to other views. It is more likely that Alfred's horse belongs to the dim period in Britain's prehistory.

There are other facts to support the theory. Along the top of the downs runs the Ridgeway, a prehistoric track which branches off the Icknield Way at the chalk gorge of the Thames and so forms a link in the great chain of ancient roads stretching from the Wash to Salisbury Plain,

W. F. TAYLOR

### THE SAXON BOUNDARY OF WALES

*Offa's Dyke, which takes its name from the eighth-century Saxon king, once extended from the mouth of the Dee to the estuary of the Severn, a distance of 130 miles. In the twelfth century any Welshman found on the English side of the dyke was liable to lose a foot. The photograph shows a section of the dyke at Montgomery.*

the metropolis of the New Stone and Bronze Age civilizations. At the foot of the hill too, lies the Icknield Way itself, also used like the Ridgeway, to communicate with Salisbury Plain. Again, it would seem that this part of Berkshire was a centre of habitation second only to Salisbury Plain. The crest of White Horse Hill is crowned by the double ramparts and ditches of an Iron Age camp. Weyland's Smithy is all that remains of a long barrow of the New Stone Age from which the land has been ploughed or washed away. To the south on the Lambourn Downs only a few miles away, are a group of nearly twenty round burial mounds, whilst stone and bronze implements and ornaments have been found in abundance all over the downland country.

### A Prehistoric Monument

Thus with greater confidence we can infer that the White Horse is a monument raised by prehistoric man. If this is so we may conclude that, like almost all the monuments of stone, it was raised in the course of religious devotion. When to that is added the fact that the horse is a sacred sign to many primitive nature worshippers of the east, we see that there is reason to

believe that in this lies the origin of the White Horse.

In historic times the horse has still been associated with traditional observance of a semi-religious kind. The cleaning of the figure took on in medieval days the semblance of a local festival. From the middle of the eighteenth to the middle of the nineteenth century it was cleaned every seven years. There was an old custom by which a cheese called locally the " Manger," was rolled down the precipitous slopes of the hill and chased by the local people. As at the Maypole Festival at Cranham, in Gloucestershire, where also a cheese is rolled down the hill, the winner of the race was regarded as a favourite of the gods.

If we clamber up the steep hillside we shall find ridges immediately below the horse, seven in number with six banks on the south side of a steep ravine, all discernible to the naked eye, which cannot conceivably have been cut for cultivation, for the slope of the hill is much too steep. We can only judge therefore, that these too, had a religious significance.

Evidence of excavation points to the same result, or at least by a process of elimination shows that the figure is unlikely to have been

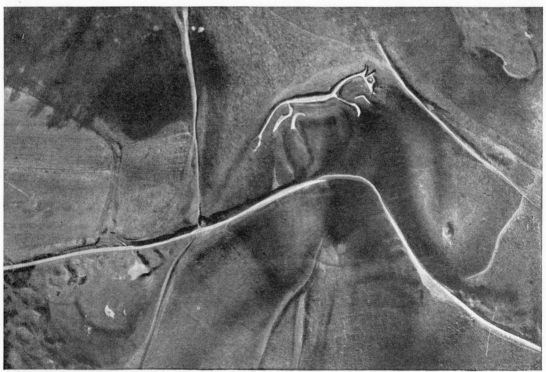

CROWN COPYRIGHT RESERVED                                        BY PERMISSION H.M. STATIONERY OFFICE AND ORDNANCE SURVEY

### BERKSHIRE'S WEIRD WHITE HORSE

*Beneath the earthworks of Uffington Castle on the Berkshire Downs is carved this curious figure of unknown antiquity. It is probably the oldest example of such figures in Britain and is considered much more ancient than the days of Alfred the Great, though local legend ascribes it to that monarch's victory over the Danes.*

STEPHENSON

## WHERE ALFRED DEFEATED THE DANES

*Like the Berkshire White Horse, this figure near Westbury, in Wiltshire, is said to celebrate a victory of Alfred over the Danes. Here, in 878, he is believed to have defeated Guthrum. As the horse was modified towards the end of the eighteenth century and again in 1873, it is difficult to ascertain the real age of the work.*

cut at any time later than the Bronze Age, which was the age of the round barrows and of the greatest use of the hilltop trackways. There is not the slightest evidence to connect it with the Romans, whilst the horses which appear on some of the pre-Roman Celtic coins are quite unlike the attenuated form of the Berkshire White Horse.

None other of the several horses cut in the chalk downs is ancient. In almost every case the date of their origin is known. In every case too, the horse is picked out in the turf without the symbolical attenuation of the Berkshire figure. So the horse, clearly visible from the main road near Westbury on the northern fringe of the chalk belt, had, records show, been made within living memory, in 1742. The horse at Marlborough was cut about 1804; that at Alton Barnes, in 1812; that at Winterbourne Bassett, in 1835; whilst the one at Wootton Bassett is assigned with certainty to 1864. All these, except the one at Westbury, which for long was thought to be as ancient as the White Horse of White Horse Hill, and attached to itself the same legends about Alfred and the Danes, have been allowed to decay, so that the grass is springing on the bare chalk and may soon cause them to disappear entirely.

The figure of a man mounted on a horse on the side of White Horse Hill overlooking Weymouth Bay just above the village of Sutton

Poyntz, depicts the illustrious George III. In the Cuckmere Valley, a mile or so below Litlington on the Seaford side, we can trace from the other bank the vague figure of a horse, but this, like the crown on the hill above Wye overlooking the Valley of the Stour, in Kent, is very recent. Perhaps the most modern of all are the two crosses cut in the Kentish Downs, one above Lenham, the other beneath the hanging woods of Shoreham Place, over the Valley of the Darent, both of which are War Memorials cut about 1920.

So the tradition of the hill figures seems to go on without pause through the centuries from the period of prehistoric man to the present day. But though the Kent crosses are modern there are two others which may be as ancient as the White Horse of Berkshire.

### A Chiltern Landmark

The traveller who crosses the Vale of Aylesbury and approaches the steep escarpment of the Chiltern Hills, near Risborough, cannot fail to see on the hillside the bold, white cross, cut deeply into the green turf and thrown into relief by the dark blur of the beech woods which cover the slopes of the Chilterns southward towards Watlington. The lower part of the cross merges into the huge white scar of a chalk pit, giving a weird effect as though the whole hillside had fallen away under the cross. Four

W. F. TAYLOR

### THE MIGHTY GIANT OF CERNE ABBAS

*On a Dorset hillside is carved this huge figure with club raised on high. Legend asserts he was an ogre who, after glutting himself with fat sheep from the Vale of Blackmore, lay down in torpor and while he slept the peasants slew him. As an everlasting memorial of their valour, they traced his outline in the hillside turf.*

miles away, a bare half-mile from Chinnor Church, is another more regular cross known locally as the Bledlow Cross. Certainly early manuscripts testify that they were not cut within the living memory of any writer. Tradition with curious persistence would have it that they are monuments to more of Alfred's legendary victories.

#### Pagan Crosses

The measurements of the two crosses have been compared with the result that, allowing for denudation and wear and tear, they seem to have been cut in multiples of a unit of about 58 inches, a unit which applies to the Long Man of Wilmington, to which we shall refer later, and which appears in the measurements of Stonehenge. Can anyone suppose that these are coincidences? Is it not more reasonable to think that the unit is in fact an ancient measure of length which is today unknown.

It might be attractive to suppose that the crosses are of Christian origin, but even that is not plausible, for the cross was reverenced during the Bronze Age of Crete, long before Christianity was known to the world. We must remember that these crosses, like all the ancient monuments, lie near one of the early trackways, in this case the Icknield Way, which seems to point almost conclusively to that same shadowy era known as the Bronze Age.

A well attested legend relates that the White-leaf Cross marks the spot where a medieval road crossed the Chilterns, a theory made more likely by the fact that in the Middle Ages the Chiltern country was a wild countryside with perhaps only this one road crossing it. But we must reject it, along with the legend of the battle between the Danes and the Saxons, if only because the cross is not visible from north or east, but only to a traveller approaching it directly over the vale.

There are two other ancient hill figures in England, the Giant of Cerne Abbas and the Long Man of Wilmington. Their antiquity is as certain as that of the White Horse of White Horse Hill and the Crosses of Whiteleaf and Bledlow.

The Giant of Cerne Abbas is an enormous figure of a man, perhaps with the Long Man of Wilmington one of the largest representations of the human form in the world. He overlooks the pleasant vale in which lies Cerne Abbas, threatening the peaceful countryside with the mighty club which he holds aloft. Of what does he remind you as he frowns down on you? Does he not bring to mind visions of strength beyond human power, and achievements beyond the might of man? If he does, his appearance suggests the same idea that the most learned research can reveal.

A trackway long-lost across the hills belonging to the Bronze or early Iron Age of Britain's civilization leads directly to the Giant. That is the only trace of ancient man that the calcareous uplands of this part of Dorset can show. We cannot be far wrong if we suppose that the Giant's form was cut in the chalk of the down by these peoples. If we look at the manifest signs of his virility we cannot err if we think that he was worshipped as a God of Fertility, before whom young men bowed down and offered prayers to grant them the procreation of many and mighty children to carry on the traditions of their struggling race.

Of the Long Man of Wilmington, in Sussex, there is more legend, but little more fact. As we move up the road which begins by the tree-hung cottages of Wilmington village and climb to a spur of the downs overlooking the Cuckmere Gap he looms above us on the hillside holding two staves, one in either hand. Tradition relates that he was cut by the monks of Wilmington Priory in the Middle Ages, but it seems incredible that in the Middle Ages naked figures should be cut in the downs, still less that the monks of a single priory should offer this strange sign of their devotion. Much more strongly do we incline to the other legend that in ancient days the Long Man was, like the Giant of Cerne Abbas, a God of Fertility, but that the monks of Wilmington were shocked at the manifest marks of his virile nature and set out one night to remove from his form the obscenity which

shocked their consciences, so that today, in the words of the ancient Greek proverb, " He is a man, yet not a man."

This too, is supported by another legend that the form was cut in the downs by the devil who wished to tempt the monks of the priory and remind them of the vigour which they were squandering, but that they in their piety recognized the devil's work and forthwith rendered it a mere mockery.

Many ingenious theories have been evolved to give other accounts of its origin. Sir Flinders Petrie diligently measured the points of the figure and found that the length of the staves was equal to double the distance between them and that the height of the figure was of similar, though not exact, proportion. From this it might be deduced that the staves were set up as a measure of length, but more reasonably we may say that they were cut to a forgotten standard of measurement like the Crosses of Whiteleaf and Bledlow.

### Skilful Sculpture

The skill with which the work was done is shown by the fact that from the level of the road the Giant's proportions seem perfectly in accordance with the proportions of man. Yet, in fact, he is almost square. Such is the effect of fore-shortening—an effect which its constructors must have had in mind.

Yet another interpretation suggests that the Long Man's purpose was to mark the longest

STEPHENSON

THE GREAT MOUNT OF SILBURY

*A prominent landmark on the Bath Road near Beckhampton is the great mound of Silbury Hill. With a circumference at the base of nearly 1,700 feet and an altitude of 550 feet, it is by far the greatest artificial mound in the country. Several attempts at excavation have produced no clues to its possible origin.*

day, for it is only about the middle of June that the sun's rays fall directly on the figure. Before it was defined by white bricks in 1874, it could only then have been visible to an observer in the plain.

The hill figures are by no means the only ancient landmarks undated save by inference. Silbury Hill is another fascinating riddle. It rises abruptly beside the high road from Marlborough to Devizes. At first sight it might well seem a natural hill like one of the tors of Somerset which rise so abruptly and so unexpectedly from the plain. Yet in truth it is wholly artificial—the largest artificial mound in Europe.

An old story similar to one told of the Wrekin, in Shropshire, tells how the devil was walking along the road to Devizes with a sack of earth which he proposed uncharitably to dump on the town, for the devil had a grudge against it on account of its holiness. He chanced, however, to meet a tramp carrying fourteen pairs of old shoes. He inquired of the tramp how far it was to Devizes and the tramp, suspecting his fell design (for he was a holy tramp), told him that he had worn out all the fourteen pairs of shoes since leaving Devizes. In despair the devil (who it would appear was easily deterred from his purpose) emptied his sack there and then, and the mound of earth so formed was thenceforth known as Silbury Hill.

The more critical perhaps will accept this legend no more willingly than the legend of the monks and the Long Man of Wilmington. If so, we must rely once more on inference. Silbury was at first thought to be a gigantic round barrow, a theory supported by the fact that it is near the centre of Bronze-Age civilization and the thousands of round barrows which are found in Wiltshire. Unfortunately there is no sign of interment, nor does it conform to any of the known shapes of burial mounds.

### Mound of Mystery

It might be the mound of a Saxon or Norman castle, but alas ! there is no record of one in this district. A more recent suggestion is that it is a Roman burial mound, for a Roman road runs nearby and the Roman mounds are certainly larger than any others, as evidenced by the Bartlow Hills, near Ashdon in northern Essex, which excavation has shown definitely to be of Roman origin. In fact, only a complete upheaval of the site could solve the problem, but, to remove such a mass of earth and chalk would require more time and money than any are likely to expend, even in the cause of archæological research.

The various dykes and banks of southern England offer a problem nearly as intriguing. Always they have much the same form, a single bank fronted by a trench, the total height of ditch and dyke combined varying today from a

DIXON-SCOTT

### THE WHITE HORSE OF CHERHILL

*On Cherhill Down, a few miles west of Silbury and also visible from the Bath Road, is this White Horse which was cut in 1780 by a Dr. Alsop of Calne and which measures 160 feet from head to tail. It stands, however, on ancient ground beneath the ramparts of Oldbury Camp, a prehistoric feature with double banks and ditches.*

mere two or three feet to thirty or forty. But before the levelling effect of time and weather when the sides of the ditch and bank were vertical they must have presented a formidable easily-manned defence.

In many places every vestige of the dykes has disappeared. Even so we can trace four main systems of ramparts. Grim's Dyke extends over almost the whole length of the Chiltern Hills. From the Thames it runs in a nearly straight line in the direction of Nettlebed, then taking a zigzag course it passes by Lacey Green and Redland End where a footpath is astride the bank for nearly a mile giving us a splendid view of the now levelled rampart and the ditch facing in the direction of the Thames basin. And so on by Great Hampden and over Berkhamsted Common.

### Ancient Boundaries

In the west Offa's Dyke stretches from the Bristol Channel to the Cheshire coast sometimes in Wales, sometimes in England, showing by its very uniformity the hand of a single engineering genius. Where it crosses the high land of Shropshire by Clun it is seen in its finest and most impressive aspect. The Wansdyke extends across southern England for eighty miles from Inkpen Beacon in a more or less straight line into Somerset, through Spye Park and over the Wiltshire Downs. South of the Wansdyke where it passes through Wiltshire we shall find the four mile long stretch of Bokerley Dyke and the less well marked but roughly parallel stretch of Combe Bank.

Finally, in East Anglia athwart the Icknield Way beyond the point where it fords the Cam, we find three parallel lines of dykes, the first traditionally known as the Roman Way, the second the Fleam Dyke and the third the Devil's Dyke which extends from Wood Ditton to Burwell Fen.

Probably there are other similar earthworks, though none which are so clearly marked. It is at least probable that these four systems are of similar date and had a similar purpose. Their traditional names tell us little. The Grim of Grim's Dyke seems to refer to no specific person : he may be the devil ; for it has ever been the habit of country people to ascribe to the devil or Cæsar what they could not explain. Or perhaps Grim's Dyke means no more than strong wall, just as the title Graham's Wall is

STEPHENSON

#### A RELIC OF THE STONE AGE
*On a hillside overlooking the Medway between Chatham and Maidstone stands Kit's Coty. Traditionally it is the tomb of Katigern, who was slain in battle, but it is of much greater antiquity.*

given to the Roman wall of Antonine, not as some suppose in commemoration of a certain Graham who breached it but rather using the name Graham as typical of a strong man.

In the case of Offa's Dyke tradition is so fixed in attributing the work to Offa, King of Mercia, whilst references to such a work are so numerous that we can perhaps with safety conclude that this was in fact a boundary line dividing the Saxon Kingdoms of England from the Britons of Wales, and raised by King Offa himself. Thus too, we may suppose that Grim's Dyke divided the Saxon villages of the Icknield Way (we know there were many settlements beneath the Chilterns) from the kingdom of the East Saxons whilst the Cambridgeshire dykes may have separated East Anglia from Mercia, and the Wansdyke determined the boundaries of Wessex.

Whether the dykes are Saxon, or as is most improbable Roman, or Celtic, they make a perfect goal for a weekend or a week's walking holiday ; for tracing their course and reconstructing it where it has disappeared is as fascinating as any hobby of the countryside.

FELTON

## CHANTRY BRIDGE, BRADFORD-ON-AVON

*A grant of pontage was issued in 1350 to " the bailiffs and good-men of Bradeford Co. Wilts " for the repair of this picturesque bridge which was then broken. The curious building on the parapet which served as a lock-up in the nineteenth century probably replaced the chantry or chapel from which the bridge has gained its name.*

# THE ROMANCE OF BRIDGES

## *by* MICHAEL GEELAN

THERE must be few with such poverty of recollection that they cannot associate at least one vivid and happy remembrance with a bridge. Indeed, of all man's creations in wood and stone and iron and steel and concrete, the bridge is the most animated, always so intensely alive with movement, from the stir of traffic across its back in the big city to the lyrical ripple of the stream beneath its arches in the green heart of the country.

There are bridges we have romped across and paddled under as children; bridges we have lingered on as lovers; bridges where we have fished and day-dreamed; bridges we have gone miles to see, to marvel at the splendour of their settings and the nobility of their lines, to hear told of them stories and legends that reincarnate the magic of dead centuries; bridges that we have come upon suddenly in lonely and unexpected places, so lovely in their simple dignity that we have held our breath.

Bridges are the stepping-stones of time. The restless years bound across them, peopling them with ghosts, and impressing them with memories of days that have been. Here, for those with eyes to see, is history almost ageless in its romance, as near to the immortal as the hand of man can ever make it.

"The bridge, even more, I think, than the road," John Buchan has written, "is a symbol of man's conquest of nature. It is concerned with the most beautiful of natural things, running water. A river has a unifying power since it provides continuity of life for the dwellers on its banks; but it is also a dividing influence, and a bridge overcomes the barriers. From the most primitive times it has been a dominant factor in the life of each community. A bridge rules the lines of traffic. There might be a dozen roads of travel, but they all draw to a point at the river crossings. Cities grew up around them and castles were built to command them. Battles were fought for their possession, and schools of strategy were based on them. History, social, economic and military, clusters more thickly about bridges than about towns and citadels."

These islands, so rich in many aspects of beauty and romance, are again fortunate so far as the legacy of their bridges are concerned. We have little hump-backed bridges, narrow pack-horse bridges, and structures of lofty graceful arches, work of the nameless master masons of the Middle Ages who built better than they knew. The great rivers, the reedy, lowland streams, and the waters of the lonely moorlands, all these have been bridged according to man's needs.

From the sentimental point of view, perhaps, the past hundred years of progress has not been kind to many of the bridges that carried the message of the past in their stones. They have been widened and reconstructed. Many have been destroyed completely, others altered beyond recognition. The volume, weight and speed of modern traffic, the claims of modern materials and modern ideas of construction, have had the inevitable result. But æsthetic values have been by no means outlawed. A wealth of bridge-beauty remains. An increasing number of the most historic and entrancing structures are being saved for the nation as ancient monuments. Others are retained, closed to traffic while new bridges erected nearby shoulder the burden of modern transport.

A bridge is always at work, worn down by traffic above and its piers and arches always

Λ. DURRANT

**A GRASS-GROWN BRIDGE**

*At Pont-y-Pandy, near Bettws-y-Coed, is this so-called Roman bridge spanning the Machno, a tributary of the Conway. Many experts declare that it is not Roman and do not believe it is of any great antiquity.*

threatened by the water below. Many of the oldest—weak, narrow and dangerous—may still have to go. Others may be saved by the " bridge-doctors." A typical example of what can be done in this direction is the fine Abingdon Bridge over the Thames, linking Berkshire and Oxfordshire. Built in 1416, it was widened in 1790 and reconstructed in 1926-27 with reinforced concrete and local stone from the demolished structure, and still retains its dignity.

The Romans built bridges in Britain, but many of the so-called Roman bridges are of doubtful parentage. In the Tyne, at Corbridge, fragments of a genuine Roman bridge may sometimes be seen and at Chollerford, a few miles westwards,

before he turned and hastened south to meet his doom at Hastings.

Harold had banished his brutal brother, Tostig, Earl of Northumberland. Tostig, seeking revenge, allied himself with Harold Hardrada, King of Norway, and fiercest of the Vikings. After ravaging Cleveland and the coast, the Norsemen sailed up the Humber and, after defeating the English and entering York in triumph, they withdrew to Stamford Bridge.

Meanwhile the Saxon Harold pressed forward from the south and fell upon the invaders unawares. At the bridge they closed and continued long in the day fighting severely, says the Anglo-Saxon Chronicle. There was slain Harold

FELTON

LONDON BRIDGE IN THE EARLY EIGHTEENTH CENTURY
*After standing for nearly six hundred years, old London Bridge was demolished in 1832, the greater part of its historic fabric being thrown into the river. No one knows when the houses were first built; they were removed about 1757. The first bridge here was erected about A.D. 65, when the Romans rebuilt the city.*

where Hadrian's Wall crossed the river, may be seen masonry of another Roman bridge. Until the Middle Ages the ford or water-splash was the accepted method of crossing all but the deepest streams and rivers. Over a long period of history many of the bridges that were built were the special care of the church. Monks and clergy joined in the work. Indulgences were granted to laymen who assisted in their maintenance and repair. Chapels, prayer-towers and shrines graced many of these bridges, and travellers believed that the cross that so often rose from a parapet midway across a stream or river prevented evil spirits from crossing the water.

It was at Stamford Bridge over the Derwent that there occurred one of the most dramatic episodes in English history. There Harold, the last of the Saxon kings, overcame the Vikings

the Fair-haired, King of Norway, and Earl Tostig and a multitude of people with them.

The English, we read, gained possession of the field but there was one of the Norwegians who withstood the English folk, so that they could not pass over the bridge nor complete the victory. An Englishman aimed at him with a javelin, but it availed nothing. Then came another under the bridge, who pierced him terribly inwards under the coat of mail. And Harold, King of the English, then came over the bridge, followed by his triumphant army ; and there they made a great slaughter, both of the Norwegians and of the Flemings.

The fourteenth century witnessed the beginning of bridge-building on a progressive scale. The work was paid for by wealthy landowners, those who sought the favours of the church and by " pontage " or bridge-toll levied by royal

STEPHENSON

## A DARTMOOR CLAPPER BRIDGE

*On the Devon and Cornish moors there are many primitive-looking bridges similar to this one at Postbridge. They consist of slabs of unworked stone lying on roughly built pillars. It has been suggested they are the work of prehistoric men, but they are now considered much more likely to be the work of the Middle Ages.*

STEPHENSON

## DANBY DUCK BRIDGE

*This curiously named pack-horse bridge over the River Esk, in Cleveland, was originally known as Danby Castle Bridge. In the eighteenth century it was repaired by one George Duck, of Danby. The bridge dates from the fourteenth century and bears the arms of the Nevilles, one-time owners of the nearby Danby Castle.*

FELTON

### A LOW-ARCHED BRIDGE IN SURREY

*The cut-waters of most bridges are pointed or triangular on both sides, but those of six medieval bridges on the River Wey between Tilford and Guildford are pointed on the upstream side and semi-circular on the other. It is thought that they date from the thirteenth century.   The photograph is of Tilford East Bridge.*

licence.  Pontage, however, was sometimes mis-appropriated by unscrupulous administrators of the period, and it is on record that, in October, 1328, six months after a grant had been made to " the mayor, bailiffs and good men of Oxford," a commission was appointed to inquire into " the irregularities in the accounts of pontage recently granted."

### Statute of Bridges

The building of bridges and their repair were two different things, and the responsibility of maintenance was generally shirked.  In this con-nection it may be mentioned that a clause in Magna Charta declared that : " No village or individual shall be compelled to make bridges at river banks except those who from of old were legally bound to do so."  Not until the Statute of Bridges was passed in 1530-31 was the responsibility allocated.  Individual districts were made to answer for the bridges within their confines, and Justices of the Peace were given authority to collect " such reasonable aid and sum of money as they shall think by their discre-tions convenient and sufficient for the repairing, rectifying and amendment of such bridges."

A Roman writer of the third century declares that there was a bridge across the Thames in A.D. 43.  Whether it was near the site of the present London Bridge or whether it even existed is problematical, but discoveries prove that there was eventually a Roman bridge at this point, probably of timber.  A Saxon structure followed which was mentioned in a tenth-century record of a woman being sentenced to death for witch-craft by drowning from London Bridge.  Here, too, the English fought the Danes.

London Bridge, of course, has a story about which there is teeming romance.  In 1136 it was damaged by fire and repaired.  In 1162 it was rebuilt of timber by Peter of Colechurch, priest and chaplain, who, thirteen years later, began the building of a stone bridge, a little to the westward.  He was buried in the chapel of St. Thomas à Becket, on its central pier, in 1205, before he had seen the completion of his work.

In addition to this chapel, the buildings on London Bridge in the thirteenth and fourteenth centuries included the Stone Gate, near the Southwark end, and the Drawbridge Gate, on which the heads of traitors were displayed to the populace. Among those whose heads thus adorned the gate were Wat Tyler, Jack Straw, Jack Cade, Sir Thomas More and Guy Fawkes.  In later years houses, vaults and cellars were built on the bridge, giving it every appearance of a street.  In 1632 the houses were burned down.  By the irony of fate, the Thames was frozen over at the time, and there was no water with which to fight the flames.  Less than half a century later came the devastations of the Great Fire, but Old London Bridge remained until 1832. The present London Bridge was designed by Sir John Rennie, and completed in 1831 at a cost of £1,500,000.

One of the most interesting of the surviving medieval bridges is the Monnow Bridge, Monmouth, which was built in 1272, and is now scheduled as an ancient monument. Over its three stone arches is its famous fortified gate tower, erected about 1296, for the purpose of collecting tolls. There was a toll of a farthing on " 1,000 nails for the tops of houses," threepence on every " ship coming to the said town by water," and fourpence " on every bag of wool." During the days of the Civil War the tower was occupied in turn by Royalists and Parliamentarians.

One of the most fascinating of all memories in stone is the chantry chapel which was built on many of the medieval bridges. There are probably only four now in existence. One is at St. Ives, where, until 1384, the River Ouse was crossed by a wooden bridge, reconstructed in stone about 1414. Built on the middle pier on the south side, its chantry was dedicated to St. Leger, the altar being consecrated in 1426. Today the chapel is a museum.

### A Memorial Bridge

Then there is the chantry bridge at Wakefield, which Defoe described as a stately stone bridge of twelve arches with a chapel of Edward IV " in memory of the fatal battle of Wakefield, wherein his father, Duke of York, was killed by the Lancastrian Army." Defoe added that " it is now made use of for civil affairs, for we do not now pray for the souls of those slain in battle, and so the intent of that building ceases." Built about the middle of the fourteenth century, the bridge is now preserved as an ancient monument.

The chantry bridge at Rotherham, spanning the Don, dates from 1483. Its chantry, believed to have been founded by Thomas Scott (or Rotherham), Archbishop of York from 1480 to

STEPHENSON
### A GREY OLD BRIDGE AT STOPHAM
*Said to be the most beautiful in Sussex, this bridge over the Arun probably dates from the reign of Elizabeth. There was a bridge at this point in 1347, and in 1399 a grant was made to the good-men of Pulberghe, Stopeham, Fileworth, Bury and Petteworth in aid of the repair of the bridge between Pulberghe and Stopeham.*

1500, has descended in its time from the sublime to the commercial. After Elizabeth's accession it became an almshouse, and, in 1779, " a dwelling house for ye deputy constable and secure jail for the reception of prisoners." Later still it became a tobacco shop, but it was eventually restored to something approaching its former dignity, and is now once again used for religious devotions.

Bradford-on-Avon claims the fourth chantry bridge, a stone structure dating from the fourteenth century. It ceased to be used for religious

early road book referred to the bridge as having been " built on piles like Venice (if we may make ye comparison) consisting of 3 streets which have a communication by a triangular bridge ; it is so remote from Pasture that ye inhabitants are obliged to goe milking by water in little boats called skerrys wch carry 2 or 3 persons at a time."

Twizel Bridge, Northumberland, which existed in 1513, bathes in the historical twilight. In the year mentioned it gave passage to the Earl of Surrey and his English troops, enabling them to cut off the Scots and force them to give battle

STEPHENSON

### DEVORGILLA'S BRIDGE AT DUMFRIES
*Built about 1283 by the wife of John de Baliol, this bridge was repaired between 1453 and 1460, but was again in ruins in 1609. In 1426, Margaret, Duchess of Touraine, confirmed the grant of the customs and tolls to " God Almighty, the Blessed Virgin Mary, St. Francis and the Warden and Friars-Minors of Dumfries."*

purposes at the time of the Reformation, and has served both as a prison and as a powder magazine. On the domed roof is a wind vane bearing the gudgeon, the emblem of St. Nicholas, and for this reason the prisoners within were often said to be " under the fish and over the river."

One of the most curious of the oldest bridges is the Trinity Bridge, Crowland. No water runs under it now, but once it spanned the Welland Stream, long since vanished. It stands now, " high and dry," at the junction of three roads. Built in 1360-90, the bridge replaced a former structure referred to in records of A.D. 943. Its thoroughfare, designed for foot passengers and pack animals, is only 8 feet wide. A 6-foot stone statue is believed to be representative either of the Deity or King Ethelbald of Mercia. An

at Flodden Field. It has, incidentally, the longest span of any medieval bridge in England—90 feet, with a rise of 43 feet.

The " Auld Brig " of Stirling, which carried the road between the north and south of Scotland, was of great significance in early times, and was known as " the key to the Highlands." Its predecessor, which stood some little distance upstream, was the scene of the Battle of Stirling Bridge in 1297. So narrow was the bridge that the men of the English Army could march across only two abreast. Sir William Wallace waited until half of his enemies had crossed the river, and then ordered his spearmen to dash in and seize the bridge-head. The English forces were thus cut in two. The existing bridge dates from 1400, but for traffic purposes there is an auxiliary

DIXON-SCOTT

## AN ANCIENT BRIDGE ON THE OUSE

*St. Ives, Huntingdonshire, possesses one of the five remaining bridges adorned with a chapel.   In 1259 there was a bridge here, which probably was of wood, until 1384.   The Chapel of St. Leger on the central pier, and now a museum, was consecrated in 1426 and four of the arches are thought to belong to the same period.*

DIXON-SCOTT

## A DERBYSHIRE PACK-HORSE BRIDGE

*Spanning the River Wye, at Bakewell, is this attractive structure known as Holme Bridge.   The width between the parapets is less than four feet and it was obviously not meant for vehicles.   Note the V-shaped recesses into which pedestrians could retreat to let the horses pass, and the parapets, built low to afford clearance.*

bridge—designed by the grandfather of Robert Louis Stevenson.

There are many fine bridges in Scotland, the romance of which gleams down through the years. Invercauld Bridge, built in 1752, is maintained by His Majesty the King, as part of the Balmoral Estate. With its " rapids " and pines and distant hills, it looks for all the world like a slice of Canada. The Brig o' Balgownie, Aberdeen, is believed to have been built about 1320 to the orders of Robert the Bruce. One of the oldest and most picturesque in Scotland, it consists of a single Gothic arch implanted on rock.

### Tam o' Shanter

Lovely beyond compare is the Auld Brig o' Doon, a single span of fifteenth-century stone. Now classified as an ancient monument, it is immortal as the scene of an incident in Burns's *Tam o' Shanter*, when Tam, riding home from Ayr, passes a haunted church where the warlocks and witches are dancing. His presence is discovered, and, chased by the " hellish legion," he races for " the keystone o' the brig," where safety lies, since witches dare not cross water !

Near the Falls of Dochart is Killin Bridge, near Perthshire, a structure of stone and lime built in 1760. The piers and one of the arches rest on little rocky islands, one of them being the ancient burying place of the Clan McNab. Anyone claiming direct descent from the clan may be buried there.

Devon and Cornwall boast some lovely old bridges. There is the Lostwithiel Bridge, over the Fowey, built in 1437. The Wadebridge, across the Camel, a gem in local stone, described even in 1602 as " the longest, strongest and fairest the shire can muster." During the Civil War it was occupied by Cromwell's men. Once seen, the beautiful sweep of the Gunnislake Bridge (1500), over the Tamar can never be forgotten. And Bideford Bridge is as wonderful as the dream of Sir Theobald Grenville, the parish priest, which is said to have inspired its building.

Old Elvet Bridge, Durham, is in many ways unique. Begun in 1160 by the Bishop of Durham, it was not completed until 1225. In the thirteenth century two chapels were built upon it, and by 1400 there was a row of shops on either side of the structure, some of the land arches being used as cellars. The houses vanished and one of the chapels became a blacksmith's shop.

Bridge-lore is packed with surprises. Did you know, for instance, that there is a bridge across the Atlantic? Clachan Bridge, Argyll, connects the island of Seil with the mainland, and the waters of the ocean flow beneath it !

A remarkable story is told about Croft Bridge,

STEPHENSON

### THE BEGGAR'S BRIDGE
*This pleasing structure over the Yorkshire Esk at Glaisdale is said to have been built in 1619 by Thomas Ferris, Mayor of Hull. According to the story, Ferris was in love with a girl whose father vowed she should never marry a beggar. In consequence of many wettings at this spot when secretly meeting his lover, Ferris vowed to erect a bridge if ever he were rich. Fortune smiled on him. He claimed his bride and built the bridge.*

G. P. ABRAHAM KESWICK

## A HIGHLAND BRIDGE OF ROMANCE

*Between Duncraggan and Loch Achray, in the Trossachs district of the Highlands, is Brig o' Turk immortalized by Sir Walter Scott in " The Lady of the Lake."   Here it was that the hunt became so spread out by a desperate run after the stag that " when the Brig o' Turk was won, the headmost horseman rode alone."*

PHOTOCHROM

## A BRIDGE WITHOUT A RIVER

*Trinity Bridge, Crowland, Lincolnshire, was erected between
1360 and 1390 over two streams which have since disappeared,
leaving the bridge high and dry. An old road book tells us
that Croyland, as it was then, " was built on piles like Venice."*

a sturdy old Gothic structure over the Tees, near
Darlington. It was here that each succeeding
Bishop of Durham was met and presented with
the falchion (or short sword) that slew the Sockburn Worm, one of three mythical monsters that
terrorized Durham and Northumberland—" a
monstrous and poysonous
vermine or wyverne, aske or
werme which overthrew and
devoured many people in
fight." The monster met its
end—so the legend goes—at
the hands of Sir John Conyers, descended from Roger
de Conyers, Constable of
Durham Castle in the time
of William the Conqueror.

Bridges, even today, are
often the happy hunting
ground of beggars. It is not
difficult to inveigle alms
from those who pause, in
great content, to admire the
view or the bridge itself. In
the days gone by the beggars,
or hermits as they called
themselves, were often
licensed by the bishops. How
would a modern mendicant
care to swear such a declara-
tion as this before being

allowed to collect a copper? It was one
sworn in the Middle Ages in relation to
Maidenhead Bridge:

" In the name of God, Amen. I, Richard
Ludlow, before God and you my Lord
Bishop of Salisbury, and in the presence
of all these worshipful men here being
offer up my profession of hermit under
this form : that I, Richard, will be obedi-
ent to the Holy Church ; that I will lead
my life, to my life's end, in sobriety and
chastity ; will avoid all open spectacles,
taverns and other such places ; that I will
every day hear mass, and say every day
certain Paternosters and Aves : that I will
fast every Friday, the vigils of Pentecost
and All Hallows, on bread and water.
And the goods that I may get by free
gift of Christian people, or by bequest, or
testament, or by any reasonable and true
way, receiving only necessaries to my sus-
tenance, as in meat, drink, clothing and
fuel, I shall truly, without deceit, lay out
upon reparation and amending of the
bridge and of the common way belonging
to ye same town of Maidenhead."

Matcham's Bridge, spanning the little
river Wey, was the scene of a murder in
August, 1780. In fact, the bridge is named
after the crime, for the name of the murderer was
Gervase Matcham. His victim was a drummer
boy. Matcham had a spectacular career. At twelve
he was a jockey, and on one occasion was sent
to Russia. He served in the fleet, and on several
occasions joined the army, constantly deserting.

STEPHENSON

## A MEDIEVAL BRIDGE OVER THE MEDWAY

*This medieval structure is the only bridge between Maidstone and Rochester.
In 1331 a pontage grant was issued for a bridge here, and in 1370 the records
tell us that it " had always been repaired by the alms of those crossing."*

W. F. TAYLOR

### BRIDGE OF BATTLE

*This beautiful old bridge spanning the Forth at Stirling dates from 1400. It was at the Battle of Stirling Brig in 1297 that Wallace defeated the English forces under the Earl of Surrey. This encounter, however, probably took place by a wooden bridge of which no trace remains and may have been a mile upstream.*

EDGAR WARD

**A DELIGHTFUL BRIDGE OVER THE DART AT STAVERTON**

*Concerning the age of this bridge, a good deal of doubt exists, but it is probably early fifteenth century. An Indulgence of 1413 mentions it, and although another of twenty-three years later refers to Staverton " Brugge " as being of wood, another bridge is intended.    There is a similar arched bridge over the Fowey at Treverbyn.*

In 1780, when he was in the 49th Regiment, he was sent with a drummer boy from Huntingdon to Diddington to collect a sum of money—about £7—from an officer.   The boy, who was the son of a recruiting sergeant, took charge of the money, and on the return journey Matcham lured the lad to Matcham Bridge, attacked him and cut his throat, then made off with the cash.

Once again he joined the navy, but six years later he confessed his crime to a friend and begged to be handed over to justice.   He was tried at Huntingdon, found guilty and hanged in 1786.   The murder evidently inspired the *Dead Drummer*, one of Barham's *Ingoldsby Legends.*

The Sunderland Bridge, Croxdale, provides a quaint study in ancient and modern.   A picturesque old stone structure carries the bridge across the lazy river, while nearby the London expresses thunder over a viaduct.   In 1602, seven travellers were robbed and murdered at Sunderland Bridge, and a highwayman was subsequently hanged at the adjacent cross roads.   In 1822 a mail coach overturned there and two passengers were killed.

Small boys and girls, of course, love Tower Bridge and all opening and movable bridges. Many imagine such structures to be essentially modern.   Actually, they have been in use since quite early times.   A swing bridge was invented by Leonardo da Vinci in the fifteenth century.

Drawbridges were used for defence in medieval times, and old London Bridge had a draw span.

Suspension bridges, too, have a fascination for us.   The first one in England was erected in 1741, crossing the Tees near High Force, Middleton-in-Teesdale.   It was 70 feet long, though only 2 feet wide, and fell in 1802.   The first suspension bridge in England on a big scale was that over the Tweed, near Berwick, erected in 1820, 20 feet wide with a span of 440 feet.   It was blown down in a storm.   Clifton (Bristol) can claim the largest suspension bridge in the country.

### Grandeur and Romance

The pictures in these pages speak more eloquently than words of the grandeur and romance of our bridges.   Let the imagination drift, and you will hear the chant of the priests in the chantries ; you will hear the cries of old London on London Bridge ; see the pack-horse caravan winding its way across country streams.   So we may picture the workers in wood and stone, the medieval monks and forgotten masons.   We may dream of them hewing the rock and dressing the stones by some unsullied river, adding one stone to another with rare cunning and skill into a lasting masterpiece of graceful curves and enduring strength.   In the stones of these bridges there may be sermons, but there are also endless stories of charm and fascinating interest.

# GEORGIAN ENGLAND

## *by* G. BAKER

THE eighteenth and nineteenth centuries saw greater changes in England than the thousand years which had gone before them. Yet for the first sixty years of the period there was little indication of what was to come. As late as 1770 there was but one stage coach from Manchester to London, and that ran only once a week. Very few of the new turnpikes had yet been made : over all other roads, theoretically maintained by the parishes through which they ran, goods had to be carried on pack-horses. There were no canals ; water and wind were the only sources of power. Iron was smelted by wood, ships driven by sail, candles and oil lamps provided the only lighting. In many respects the English social and industrial scene had altered little since the Middle Ages.

While the country was thus marking time, the Jacobite risings of 1715 and 1745 took place. Seven miles south of Carlisle is Rose Castle, residence of the Bishops of Carlisle, which has associations with both insurrections. In 1715 when news came that the Highlanders under the Earl of Kenmure were advancing, it became the duty of Bishop Nicolson, as Commissioner of the Marches, to lead the Cumberland Militia whom he had called to arms. The Militia mustered, a few with shot-guns, the majority with scythes and pitchforks. The Bishop rode gallantly before them—in his coach and six. Near the beacon on Penrith Fell he drew up his men and prepared to resist the invaders. The mere sight of the Highlanders was enough for his levies, who bolted precipitously. From his coach the prelate tried to rally them. Preferring discretion to valour, his coachman whipped up his horses and followed the flying mob. Shouting from the carriage window for the man to stop, the bishop lost his wig. But the coachman ceased from his furious driving only when he and his master were safely back in the courtyard of Rose Castle.

In 1745 the rebels took Rose Castle by surprise. When they arrived, Bishop Fleming was christening his infant granddaughter. Captain Macdonald of the rebels presented the child with a white cockade, bade her grandfather go on with the ceremony, and gallantly marched his men away, leaving the castle unmolested.

As Rose Castle saw the comedy, so Carlisle Castle saw the tragedy of the Forty-five. After the failure of the insurrection, its keep was made the prison of many of the captured Jacobites, among them that Major Macdonald who was the Fergus MacIvor of Scott's *Waverley*. When these prisoners had been executed for high treason, their heads were exposed over the city's Scotch gate. One of these heads was that of a lad with long yellow hair. For some weeks, morning and evening, an unknown woman came and gazed at it. On the day when the woman came no more, the head was first seen to be missing from the gateway.

As poignant a figure as this unknown mother was the young wife of the last Earl of Derwentwater, one of the leaders of the Fifteen. Although he was head of the Ratcliffe family, in whom loyalty to the Stuarts was traditional, the Earl was reluctant to join in an enterprise which he feared would end in disaster. His wife is said

W. F. TAYLOR

### THE PANTILES, TUNBRIDGE WELLS
*From the days of Queen Anne this was a fashionable watering place. An old print of 1748 shows a number of celebrities gathered here. Among them are Dr. Johnson, Colley Cibber, Pitt, Beau Nash and David Garrick.*

VALENTINE

## A HALL OF TRAGEDY

*On rising ground above the Devil's Water near Hexham, Northumberland, stand the ruins of Dilston Hall. This was the home of the ill-fated Earl of Derwentwater, who, against his better judgment, it is said, joined the 1715 Rebellion. Taken prisoner at Preston, he was executed in 1716 and his estate was confiscated.*

W. F. TAYLOR

## HOME OF A FAMOUS GENERAL

*This statue in the centre of the picturesque Kentish village of Westerham commemorates General Wolfe who died at Quebec in 1759. Quebec House, nearby, where Wolfe spent his early years, was purchased by a Canadian and presented to the National Trust. Westerham, which lies between the North Downs and the green-sand ridge, and which has many attractive corners, also figures in Thackeray's "Virginians."*

to have called him coward and threatened herself to lead his tenants against the Hanoverian usurper. The Earl yielded, and rode south never to return to Dilston Hall, his ancient manor house, the ruins of which are still to be seen near Hexham, in Northumberland. A month later he, with 1,500 other Jacobites, became a prisoner in the hands of General Carpenter at Preston.

Derwentwater in the Lake District also has its associations with this story. From that lake the family took its title and on Lord's Isle was one of their seats.

After Lady Derwentwater heard of her husband's capture and of his being taken to the Tower of London to await trial for high treason she hastened to Keswick. There she evaded the Hanoverian troops lying in wait for her, reached the house on the island and gathered the family jewels and escaped over the hills. On the steep flanks of Walla Crag is Lady's Rake, up which she is said to have fled to avoid the soldiers.

To London she then hurried and in person pleaded with the king for her husband's life. But her tears availed not. George I was obdurate, and on February 24, 1716, the Earl was beheaded on Tower Hill. In the north that night there was an extraordinarily brilliant display of the Aurora Borealis which, even to this day, Northumbrian folk often refer to as " Lord Derwentwater's Lights."

The Jacobite rebellions were but eddies in the stream of the country's life. To the English countryman of that time his Mop Fair was of much more interest and importance than the question of the succession to the throne. To these Mop or Statute Fairs, held each Michaelmas Day in the market square or principal street of country towns and villages, came men and women who wished to be hired as servants for the coming year.

The market square of High Wycombe in Buckinghamshire, was one of these Georgian employment exchanges. Here, as at similar

EDGAR WARD

### BIRTHPLACE OF GAINSBOROUGH

*In the pleasant old-world town of Sudbury on the Suffolk Stour, may be seen this typical brick-built Georgian house. Here, in the year 1727, was born Thomas Gainsborough, the famous English portrait painter.*

fairs, the procedure was picturesque. Men who sought work wore the badge of their calling in their hatbands ; the shepherd's was a lock of wool, the cowman's a tuft of cow's hair, the carter's a wisp of horsehair, the clerk's an ink horn. Only women and boys were without such emblems. Masters and mistresses went from one to another, questioning them as to their experience and qualifications. With no testimonials asked for, the workers were engaged on the spot. Each was given a shilling to spend at the market booths or in the merrymaking which began when, at noon, the church bells rang to show that the hiring was over.

By the middle of the eighteenth century the Mop Fairs were becoming more crowded. With the extension of the enclosure system, strip ploughing was abolished ; the old open field principle in farming was ended by the planting

D. MCLEISH

## WHERE SAMUEL JOHNSON WAS BORN
*One of the most prominent literary figures of the eighteenth century was Dr. Johnson. In a room in this house at Lichfield he was born in 1709. Lichfield has several other mementoes of him.*

Palace, and such immense mansions as Seaton Delaval, in Northumberland, and Oulton Hall, in Cheshire. In the grandeur of its conception and the massiveness and solidity of its execution, Castle Howard is typical of both the style of the architect and the taste of the time.

Over 100 yards long, its south front has fluted Corinthian pilasters for its centre and above them a noble pediment. Wings of lower elevation give perfect balance to the whole. The north front, equally impressive in its Corinthian dignity, has the entrance to the Great Hall. This immense room, lit by a dome the top of which is 100 feet from the floor of the hall, has its walls and ceilings richly decorated with allegorical paintings. After his visit in 1772 Horace Walpole paid this lyrical tribute to Castle Howard: " Nobody had informed me that I should at one view see a palace, a town, a fortified city, temples on high places, the noblest lawn in the world fenced by half the horizon, and a mausoleum that would tempt me to be buried alive."

The smaller houses of the period, planned for comfort rather than display, show the Georgian architects at their best. As the result of disastrous fires in 1725 and 1731 respectively, which destroyed much of Buckingham and Blandford (Dorset), these two towns today are full of Georgian red brick buildings. Simple and unpretentious, they have dignity; above all they have line. The flat, sashed windows—sashes were first introduced in the eighteenth century—are admirably spaced; while often the substantial cornice gives a brim to the red-tiled roof.

Later the Adam brothers aimed at a unity of conception in architecture which should include not only the plan of the building but its finishing and decoration. Adam mantelpieces, sideboards and fire-irons, were as distinctive as Adam doorways with their fluted Doric columns and decorated fanlights above the door.

The symmetry and simplicity of eighteenth-century architecture were seen to even greater advantage in the unified planning of the streets and squares of the towns. Bath is the best example of a city whose street architecture is beautiful yet ordered.

The eighteenth-century renascence of Bath was due to three men—and to the stone in its own hills. Ralph Allen bought the unworked stone quarries on Combe Down, and induced John

of hedges; small farms were absorbed by large, and heaths and commons were enclosed. At the fairs ploughmen and shepherds found themselves in competition with smallholders and the poorer yeomen whom enclosures had robbed of their independence.

As the country workers grew impoverished, the rent rolls of the great landowners were correspondingly increased. No little of this wealth was used to erect the great country houses which are a feature of this period. The " Grand Tour," which at this time became fashionable among men of rank, directly influenced the architecture of these palaces—for palaces they were. Wealthy men came back from Italy full of admiration for the simplicity and balance of buildings, designed by Palladio, which they had seen in Rome and elsewhere.

One of the finest examples of these great houses is Castle Howard, fifteen miles north of York in the wooded country of the Derwent. Built for the Earl of Carlisle, it was the earliest masterpiece of Vanbrugh, who later designed Blenheim

W. F. TAYLOR

## A GEORGIAN BRIDGE

*From 1750 onwards there was a great revival of bridge building but use of these was usually subject to a toll. Local councils, companies, and landowners could obtain authority to levy a toll. Swinford Bridge which crosses the Thames at Eynsham, was built in 1770 and cars crossing it are still called upon for a fee.*

W. F. TAYLOR

## A TOWN REBUILT AFTER A DISASTROUS FIRE

*Blandford, the little market town in Dorset, which figures in Hardy's novels as " Shottsford Forum," suffered from a disastrous fire in 1731 when only forty buildings escaped the flames. In consequence it presents today an excellent illustration of eighteenth-century architecture. The photograph shows the Market Hall in the principal thoroughfare of the town. Blandford was the birthplace of the sculptor, Alfred Stevens.*

Wood the architect to come to Bath. In 1720 Wood began to build the series of streets, crescents and terraces, whose dignity of design has not been surpassed. In Queen Square, Gay Street, Pulteney Street and the Circus, particularly, he showed his genius in designing blocks of houses so that they gave the effect of a single palace. John Wood, junior, inheriting his father's gifts, was responsible for the noble symmetry of Royal Crescent with its magnificent sweep of houses designed in the Ionic style.

While Bath was being built in the stone to which time and weather add only mellow beauty, Beau Nash, " King of Bath " and famous Master of the Ceremonies, was providing it with the

Pope, Richardson and Fielding were friends of Ralph Allen, and visited him at Prior Park. Lord Chesterfield, who wrote many of the *Letters* to his son from his house in Pierrepont Street, lived next door to Elizabeth Linley, the famous singer and beauty with whom Sheridan eloped. Later Sheridan himself lived in Bath, and there wrote *The Rivals*.

Bath had its competitors. Tunbridge Wells with its chalybeate spring was the resort of monarchs, beaux and poets. Queen Anne may be dead elsewhere : in Tunbridge Wells she lives, because with the £100 she gave the town were bought the pan (i.e., hollow) tiles paving the celebrated Terrace Walk to which they give their name.

EDGAR WARD

### THE ROYAL CRESCENT, BATH

*This beautiful, dignified crescent built in 1769 is doubtless the best specimen in Britain of the architecture of the period. Of Bath in those days one writer remarked " two thirds of the company are attracted merely by amusement, society and dissipation ; in all of which it is only second to London."*

atmosphere and social attractions which for the fashionable made it the rival of London. Dandy and even mountebank though Nash was, he had personality enough to suppress duelling within the city, to reorganize the Pump Room, to secure the building of a new Assembly Room, to make both the dancing and the gaming more attractive.

Some of the most famous figures of the eighteenth and nineteenth centuries were associated with Bath. For some years William Pitt, afterwards Lord Chatham, was one of the city's parliamentary representatives. At his house, No. 7, The Circus, Pitt entertained General Wolfe on the eve of his departure as commander of the expedition to Quebec in 1759. A few doors away Clive lived during the illness which ended in his death in 1774.

Between 1760 and 1770, while he was waging his historic campaign on behalf of the freedom of the press, John Wilkes, the famous member for Middlesex, spent much of his time at Bath. From his house, 19, New King Street, Herschel the astronomer discovered the planet Uranus.

The literary associations of Bath are rich indeed.

In the mid-eighteenth century sea-bathing became a craze, and the day of the seaside town began. Margate—till that time a port for Holland—sprang into popularity. Weymouth flourished when George III paid frequent visits there. Fanny Burney records amusingly in her diary the mingled solemnity and trepidation with which bathing was viewed by many of her contemporaries. The king, who had prepared himself for the shock of immersion by first taking a series of warm sea-water baths in his bedroom, " had no sooner popped his royal head under water than a band of music struck up ' God save great George our king.' "

What his father had done for Weymouth, George IV did for Brighton. While Brighthelmstone—as it was then known—was still an obscure fishing village Dr. Richard Russell, of Lewes, made his home there. His fashionable patients followed him, and Brighthelmstone began to grow in size and popularity. George IV, then Prince of Wales, paid his first visit in 1783. In the following year he started to build the Royal Pavilion, a fantastic erection designed

W. F. TAYLOR

## A FANTASTIC GEORGIAN BUILDING AT BRIGHTON

*George IV, when Prince of Wales, built this pseudo-oriental Pavilion costing more than a million sterling.
One writer considered it satisfactory that durability had not been made subservient to beauty in the erection
of this " terrestrial paradise "—" the most original, unique and perhaps magnificent structure in Europe."*

STEPHENSON

## A CANAL IN THE PENNINES

*During the eighteenth and nineteenth centuries a great amount of capital was expended in the creation of canals
connecting various towns and forming links between the navigable rivers. In modern times many of these
works have become derelict and some are now quiet waterways often not without a placid charm. The
photograph shows the Leeds and Liverpool Canal where it passes through the Pennines near Skipton.*

FELTON

### A MOUNTING BLOCK AT THE VILLAGE INN
*Outside many an inn may be seen these reminders of other days. This inn at Cleeve Prior in Worcestershire still retains the stone steps used for mounting a horse as well as the chain by which the steed was tethered.*

that the cost of sending coal in panniers to Manchester only a few miles away exactly doubled its price. He decided to make a canal between the two, and employed James Brindley as his engineer. The undertaking, a triumph of Brindley's skill, was so successful that canal making became a mania in England : within forty years 2,000 miles of artificial waterways had been constructed in the country. Even Nature was thought to be canal-conscious. Thus, in the prospectus, dated 1776, of the Leeds and Liverpool Canal which in crossing the Pennines avails itself of the Aire Gap, this complacent statement is made : " It must be acceptable to the public to be informed that a person with great industry and application has discovered an opening betwixt the mountains of Yorkshire and Lancashire, which is the most eligible, if not the only one Nature has formed for this work."

in a hotchpotch of oriental styles. For thirty years building went on : domes, minarets and pinnacles were added, until in 1819 the bizarre pile stood much as it is today.

In pleasing contrast are Brighton's fine squares and terraces which in their dignity and their austere avoidance of mouldings and other ornamentation, are excellent examples of the Regency style at its best.

While the fashionable gamed and gossiped at Bath, or at Brighton joined in the extravagances of the " First Gentleman in Europe," at Bury and Blackburn, and Bolton and Birmingham, men of genius were quietly working on the inventions which were shortly to change the face of northern and midland England. The Industrial Revolution had begun.

The enormous quantities of machine-made goods, which the new factories poured out, at once created transport problems. The old stage-wagons were wholly inadequate to deal with the new traffic. Even so, the wear and tear on the badly kept roads were such that Arthur Young in his *Tours* tells of ruts 4 feet deep on the turnpike between Preston and Wigan, and of stage-wagons stuck so fast in the mud of Essex roads that it needed a team of forty horses to move them. In an attempt to meet the situation, laws were passed laying it down that stage-wagons were to be equipped with very wide wheels that they might assist in rolling the roads.

Pack-horses remained the chief means of transport, and the cost of carriage was in consequence excessive. Thus, in 1756, the Duke of Bridgewater, who owned coal mines at Worsley, found

STEPHENSON

### THE " STAR " AT ALFRISTON
*This delightful fifteenth-century inn was possibly a convenient rendezvous for the smugglers who flourished in Alfriston and other Sussex villages a century ago.*

FELTON

## A RELIC OF THE PACK-HORSE TRAINS

*During the eighteenth century, due to the inadequate and ill-kept roads which were often impassable for wheeled traffic, much of the commerce of the country had to be transported by trains of pack-horses. The majority of the old bridges were consequently only built of sufficient width to accommodate such traffic. A beautiful and typical example is this stone-arch bridge in the lovely village of Allerford in Somerset.*

A SMUGGLERS' COVE

FRITH

*At Cudden Point, the eastern boundary of Mount's Bay, is Prussia Cove, which gained its name from the notorious Cornish smuggler, John Carter, who made it his headquarters. Called by his comrades the King of Prussia, John Carter still lives in tales that are told of the smugglers and their audacious exploits.*

The transference of so much of the goods traffic to the canals left the roads freer for the transport of passengers and of the mails. At the beginning of the nineteenth century, every evening at eight o'clock the mail coaches could be seen setting out from the General Post Office in Lombard Street.

Year by year stage-coaches became faster and more numerous. To accommodate their passengers, all over England old inns were enlarged, and new inns erected—tall dignified buildings with sash windows, pillared porticoes, arched yard entrances and signs of very fine wrought ironwork.

Among these famous old coaching inns is the "Green Man" at Ashbourne, in Derbyshire. It was here that Boswell hired chaise and horses to go to Scotland, leaving Dr. Johnson with his friend Dr. Taylor.

In Lewes, the house of the Duke of Newcastle, Prime Minister in George II's time, became the White Hart Hotel. In one of its panelled rooms the Headstrong Club met, under the presidency of Tom Paine, author of the *Rights of Man*, to whom kings and dukes were alike abominable.

At Newark-on-Trent, Gladstone made the "Cheriton Arms" his political headquarters when at the outset of his career he fought the borough as a Conservative. From the balcony of the "Red Lion," High Wycombe, Gladstone's great opponent, Disraeli, made his first political speech. Newark and Wycombe each have a Guildhall designed by the brothers Adam, while Wycombe's queer octagonal Market House is also the work of those famous Georgian architects.

It was an inn, the "George and Dragon" in the Durham village of Yarm, near Stockton, that on February 12, 1820, was the scene of a momentous meeting at which were discussed plans for the Stockton and Darlington Railway. In five years the engineering genius of George Stephenson successfully carried the project through. When "Locomotive No. 1," now on view at Darlington station, made its first journey between the two towns, it was an evil day for both coaches and canals.

In conclusion, the eighteenth and nineteenth centuries saw the English landscape change most notably. Woods were thinned or obliterated, wild land was tilled, bogs and fens were drained. The system of enclosures brought the hedges which contribute much to the beauty of the English rural scene today; roads improved beyond recognition. With the coming of the railways men began to travel for pleasure, where formerly they had travelled only of necessity. Thus, at the close of the nineteenth century Englishmen were coming to know other towns besides their own and to have the delight of exploring their own island.

# THE RIVERS OF BRITAIN

## *by* I. O. EVANS

ISLANDS such as ours cannot produce mighty and awe-inspiring rivers, but small as are our streams they have played a tremendous part in the history and romance of our country.

Commerce has been influenced by our river heritage, for London and Liverpool, two of the six main ports of the world, have grown into importance largely through their position upon the banks of comparatively small water courses.

The development of our people has been bound up with our streams. The greatest need of man in his daily life, now and in the earliest days of history, is water both to sustain life and also to facilitate commerce.

Man first settled beside the river shore in order that he might live. He chose a position where the water could be forded so that he might travel from one side to the other with ease, whilst by means of the by-streams, and tributaries, the interlinking rivers developed his trade and solved his question of transport. Time has enlarged the human settlements into great cities, and flung bridges across the river banks, but the urge of commerce and the means of life remain just the same.

Of all the rivers of England that which is most dear, and also of most importance, is the Thames. At Thames Head, in the Cotswold Hills, one of the spots which claim to be the source of London's river, is an old Roman road, the Fosse Way, leading from Cirencester to Bath, and it may well be that many a weary legionary has blessed its waters as he stooped to quench his thirst.

Actually the source of the Thames is not easy

STEPHENSON

### A STREAM FROM THE MOORS
*The River Ure in Wensleydale receives many tributaries which come rushing headlong down the hillsides. Here is seen Hardraw Force which plunges 80 feet below.*

to determine. The spring at Thames Head is frequently dry; this supports the contention that the river actually rises at Seven Springs, near Cheltenham, some ten miles from Cirencester. For the first few miles the Thames follows a tortuous and winding course through peaceful agricultural country until its ever increasing size permits of navigation first by rowing boats and punts and then by larger craft.

The first city of any considerable size is Oxford, but before her grey walls are reached the river flows through Cricklade and Lechlade. Both these towns have a history extending back to Saxon times and speak of fords known in those days. At Kelmscott lived and is buried William Morris, who in *News from Nowhere* immortalized his vision of England as it might be. Farther downstream is Cumnor, the scene of the tragedy described in Scott's *Kenilworth*. Its Hall, now long vanished, was reputed to be haunted by an evil spirit which no exorcism could lay.

The meadows and the old stone bridges glide by, and soon Oxford appears, Oxford, not merely one of Britain's traditional homes of learning but a centre of sporting activity, a cathedral city, a town with over a thousand years of history—and, at the same time, a commercial centre with a flourishing industry. Above all, it is a city of unequalled architectural beauty. The view from Magdalen Bridge will linger long in the memory, and this is but the prelude to its colleges, its castle keep, its cathedral, and its "High."

Abingdon, formerly the site of a mighty abbey —at one time sacked by the townsmen and students

FOX PHOTOS

## RIVER OF BEAUTY AND ROMANCE

*The Wye is one of the most beautiful and most romantic rivers of Britain. From its source on bare Plynlimon it flows through mid-Wales and through the Marches by Hereford and Ross, by Tintern's lovely ruins and Chepstow's ancient Castle and so to the Bristol Channel. Here the river is seen at Symond's Yat.*

of Oxford—impresses the traveller by river or road with its quiet charm, its church, its gabled cottages, its bridge, and its chestnut-trees. Below are villages with old-world names, Nuneham Courtenay the home in 1710 of Simon Harcourt, Lord Chancellor of England; Long Wittenham, with its old " chepeing " or bargaining cross; Wittenham Clumps, the low, rounded hills crowned with beech trees forming a landmark to which the clumps of trees give their name; Clifton Hampden spanning the river with an old toll bridge and a modern red brick structure side by side, and Crowmarsh Gifford boasting a genuine Norman church. From Crowmarsh Gifford the ever widening river pursues its placid course through one of its most interesting geographical features. At this point it forms the dividing line between the counties of Oxfordshire and Berkshire, with Goring on one side and Streatley on the other.

On the Berkshire side the swelling slopes of the downs form an impressive range, while the Chiltern Hills rise on the Oxfordshire bank. The river, slipping along between them, runs through a V-shaped opening which is a landmark from many a hill-top, and so dividing the two ranges forms the beautifully picturesque Goring Gap. From here to Pangbourne is to be found one of the most lovely stretches of the Thames.

The very name strikes a romantic note, for it is here that the Pang bourne or stream, well known for its trout fishing, joins the parent river. The village itself is a little gem of architectural beauty, having preserved many fine examples of old English cottages.

At Reading the river becomes a little more industrialized, but Reading has had a past. The Danes established themselves in this old town, repulsing an attack by no less a warrior than Alfred the Great himself. Here, 600 years ago, an unknown poet, seated perhaps on the banks of the river itself, wrote the earliest English song, the well-known round, *Summer is icumen in.*

### Centre of English Tradition

Downstream from Reading the Thames is the paradise of rower and sailing man. Henley with its Regatta, Marlow, Cookham and Maidenhead lead on to Windsor, the seat of royalty, and the town which gave its name to England's ruling family. The mound on which it stands was seized upon by William the Conqueror as the right place at which to establish a castle which should form a western outpost of London. Today it is the centre of English tradition, the birthplace and burial vault of many a royal figure, a home of the reigning monarch, and almost a shrine of pilgrimage for visitors from all over the world.

Not far below Windsor lies the most famous spot in British constitutional history, the island of Magna Charta, where, according to popular belief, King John was forced by his barons to sign the Great Charter which has formed the basis of our political and industrial freedom. This island was supposed to form a neutral

EDGAR WARD

### THE THAMES AT PANGBOURNE
*" Ne'er saw I, never felt, a calm so deep!*
*The river glideth at his own sweet will."*—WORDSWORTH.

meeting ground for the king and his nobles who were camped on either side of the river, but there is no foundation for this story. In fact the Charter itself gives the signing place as "Runningmede" or Runnymede, a field lying between Egham and the river.

Now the Thames is flowing across the level stretch of fertile soil it has itself brought down from the hills. Here is Hampton Court, the princely residence of the ill-fated Cardinal Wolsey, with its Great Hall, its Haunted Gallery, its Gardens and its Maze. A little farther down the Thames becomes tidal; its course as a river is over, it is merging with the sea.

Here, too, its water becomes polluted, its banks dingy with warehouse and factory and wharf. Gleams of beauty enliven the drabness of the scene, Kew Gardens with its pagoda, the dome of St. Paul's Cathedral, the massive buildings of the New London which is rising before our eyes, the Tower which William the Conqueror built to overawe the city, docks and huge cranes, wharfs, a forest of masts without number, the greatest port in the world. So the river passes through that wide mouth where Viking longships sailed, whence explorers set out to the ends of the earth, where traffic is carried on with every nation in the world. "The Thames" said John Burns, "is liquid history"; and so indeed it is.

Of equal historic interest, and as dear to the heart of every Scot as is the Thames to a

EDGAR WARD

## MAPLEDURHAM MILL
*Probably few places on the Thames have been photographed and painted so much as this lovely old mill at Mapledurham on the Oxfordshire side of the river, upstream from Reading. Hereabouts is some of the most delightful scenery to be found on the Thames where richly wooded hills rise from the banks of the river.*

W. F. TAYLOR

## THE SEVERN AT BRIDGNORTH

*From the mountains of Wales the Severn, no mean rival of the Thames, winds its long course, leaving the land of its birth and pouring its silver flood across England, almost encircling ancient Shrewsbury, dividing Bridgnorth in half and lapping at the walls of Worcester and Gloucester before reaching its long, diverging estuary.*

Londoner, is the River Forth. Contrasting with the gentle smooth-flowing Thames is Scotland's chief river, which rises not among the low hills but on the slopes of the rugged mountains. Ben Lomond, famed in song and story, is its birthplace, and thence it flows eastwards ever through a country rich in historic and literary associations. This is the Walter Scott country, and the scene of *Waverley*; on the shores of Linn Menteith the tragic Mary Queen of Scots spent a part of her childhood. The scenery is as

robbers," by Sir Walter Scott, is now one of the main sources of water supply to Glasgow.

Framed in this lake is Ellen's Island, named after a heroine who defended it and the refugees upon its banks from marauding invaders. Opposite the island is the site of the Silver Strand, now submerged, and on the slope of the mountain is the Goblin's Cave, both famed in Scott's *The Lady of the Lake*.

Both valleys meet at the historic town of Stirling, where many a Scottish monarch held

PHOTOCHROM

### SILVER WINDINGS OF THE TAY NEAR PERTH

"'Behold the Tiber!' the vain Roman cried,
*Viewing the ample Tay from Baiglie's side ;*
*But where's the Scot that would the vaunt repay,*
*And hail the puny Tiber for the Tay.*"—SCOTT.

romantic as its history—lofty mountains, little inferior in grandeur to Ben Lomond itself, rise on either side, and, in the valley between, their crests are reflected in the waters of a chain of lakes.

A few miles to the north is another valley at once more beautiful and more known to fame. Here the hillsides are clothed with the mass of woodland, the silvery birches and darker oaks, that have given the region the name of " the bristly country," the Trossachs.

It is the setting of some of the most romantic and historic episodes of Scottish tradition. At Glengyle at the head of Loch Arklet, Rob Roy the cattle thief and outlaw was born, while Loch Katrine, named Lake Cateran, " the lake of the

his court in the grey castle overlooking the town from its perch of basalt crag. Some little distance from the town one of the most decisive battles in the history of Scotland was fought at Bannockburn.

Soon after leaving Stirling the river widens into an arm of the sea, but still its shores are rich in the memorials of the past. In Dunfermline Abbey lie the remains of Robert the Bruce ; and in the palace Charles I was born. As of old, the district still keeps its warlike associations, for on the shores of the Firth is Rosyth naval base. But " Queen of the Forth " is Edinburgh, the "Athens of the north," with its wonderful history, with its castle and its war memorial, Holyroodhouse and Arthur's Seat.

After Thames and Forth perhaps next in importance is the Severn, rising among the peat bogs of black Plynlimon in the range of hills between Cardigan and Montgomery. The district is one of the bleakest and most desolate, yet the Severn is closely associated with the stirring history of the land wherein it is born. Not far from its source is the Cefn Carnedd, an ancient stronghold where the Cymry organized their resistance to the Roman invader, whose station of Caersws is found not very far distant. Near Montgomery is Offa's Dyke, recalling the efforts of the Saxon kings to keep the wild mountaineers from raiding into the fertile plains of Mercia. The Long Mountain nearby is traditionally the site of the last battle for Welsh freedom, during which the insurgent Prince Madog ap Llewelyn was defeated.

Shrewsbury, almost ringed by the Severn and once the seat of the Princes of Powis, fell into Roman and Saxon hands and was many times plundered by the Welsh before Edward I made it the headquarters for his successful war of subjugation; and here the fiery Hotspur was defeated and slain. The Civil Wars also ravaged the Severn Valley; and Worcester, from its loyalty to the royal cause, earned its renown as the " ever faithful city."

Still more famous is the Severn's tributary, the Avon. It was near its source that the hopes

STEPHENSON

## A RUSHING TORRENT

*One of the headstreams of the River Aire emerges from beneath Malham Cove. Here another tributary is seen plunging down into the sublime rift of Gordale.*

PHOTOCHROM

## THE PEACEFUL EDEN

*In the Pennines on the edge of Yorkshire and Westmorland is born the River Eden which flows through the defile of Mallerstang and then across a wide plain by Kirkby Stephen and Appleby and on into Solway Firth. Here is a scene at Armathwaite, where the river flows through beautiful wooded and pastoral country.*

of the Royalists were shattered on the battlefield of Naseby in the Civil War. In its valley, at Lutterworth, lived John Wyclif, "morning star of the Reformation"; while overlooking its waters stands Warwick Castle, a well preserved example of fourteenth-century architecture, and one of the fortress-homes of the feudal nobility.

At Stratford is the birthplace of Shakespeare, one of the most famous of our sons. Here his house, Anne Hathaway's Cottage, and Holy Trinity Church, his place of burial, are preserved.

Below Tewkesbury, the scene of desperate

STEPHENSON

### RIVER OF THE PENNINES
*In the wild uplands dominated by that trinity of Pennine peaks, Whernside, Ingleborough and Penyghent rises the Ribble. From this bleak country it emerges in the softer country of Craven on its way to the sea.*

fighting and hideous slaughter in the Wars of the Roses, the Avon unites with the Severn in a mighty river sweeping on past Gloucester with its magnificent cathedral until, so long a Saxon stream, it returns to bathe the shores of the country from which it rose.

Our three "capital" rivers are only the beginning of Britain's waterways. Scotland is deeply pierced with innumerable glens drained by rivers no less beautiful and no less historic than the Forth itself. Greatest of these is the Clyde, best known to us for its clanging dockyards and its factories, and for Glasgow grim and forbidding beneath its pall of smoke. Yet the Clyde with its source among the heather hills and its lovely sea-lochs and its islands is a river of beauty and romance. Long ago its waters reflected the lurid glare of the Beltane beacons which blazed from Tinto, the "hill of fires."

In three magnificent falls the Upper Clyde leaps downwards; each roaring impressively

amidst the rocks and the bracken as at Cora Linn, one of the finest of Scotland's waterfalls.

Down the river from Glasgow is Dumbarton Castle, Dun-Breton, "the hill fort of the Britons." Here, so it is locally held, St. Patrick was born, and there is a legend that the great rock, 650 feet high, is a pebble hurled by the devil at the saint, in a fruitless endeavour to prevent his mission to Ireland.

Near Dumbarton the Clyde is joined by the Leven, which flows from the glorious island-flecked waters of Loch Lomond. These islets are a romance in themselves. Wordsworth was inspired by their beauty to write his ode to the "sweet Highland girl." The MacGregors, notorious cattle raiders, established their stronghold amongst the natural hiding places, and many a pious congregation gathered to hear a sermon preached from the summit of the huge Pulpit Rock.

Rich in memories of "old unhappy far-off things and battles long ago" is the country of the border rivers, the Tweed on the east and the lesser streams flowing into the Solway Firth on the west.

Teviotdale, especially, is rich in interest. At Abbotsford Sir Walter Scott was born and died, and it is the countryside of his earlier namesake, Michael Scott, who attained fame as a magician and wonder-worker and of whom we read in his *Lay of the Last Minstrel*. Here, too, on Eildon Hills another mystic figure, Thomas the Rhymer, met with his lover, the Queen of the Fairies, and was summoned away to join her by a hart and hind which entered the village street.

### Border Streams

Teviot flows into Tweed, a stream which though sluggish has witnessed scenes no less interesting than the more spectacular mountain torrents. At Wark Castle, so the discredited legend goes, Edward III founded the Order of the Garter, as he smilingly returned to the Countess of Salisbury the garter she had dropped. Coldstream not merely gave its name to the Guards regiment founded by General Monk, but at one time, like the more notorious Gretna Green, served as an informal registry office for runaway lovers. Berwick, at the mouth of the Tweed,

EDGAR WARD

## THE DERBYSHIRE DERWENT

*From its source on the bare heights of Bleaklow in the Peak District, the Derwent descends through moorland country, and in the neighbourhood of Matlock flows through a narrow ravine flanked with lofty crags of gleaming limestone.   Characteristic of this part of its course is the above view with the noble mass of High Tor soaring above the stream.   On the side of the glen opposite to the Tor rise the wooded Heights of Abraham.*

has the curious distinction of being for certain legal purposes neither in England nor in Scotland.

Among the more northerly of Scotland's streams is the Tay, on whose banks so improbable a person as Pontius Pilate is said to have been born. Though it rises on bare Rannoch Moor, it has several unusual associations with woodland and trees. The woods of Mithven sheltered William Wallace; at Dunkeld were planted the first larches to grow in Britain; the "Old Yew of Fortingall" is the oldest of its species in Europe; and Birnam Woods marching on Dunisane foreshadowed the overthrow of Macbeth.

F. BURFIELD DYER

### THE BURE AT COLTISHALL
*The Bure, perhaps the best known river of the Norfolk Broads rises near Melton Constable and with many a twist and turn, and often widening into lakes or "broads," it flows through the lowlands to join the Yare.*

Perth was formerly the capital of Scotland, and Dundee boasts a church steeple 156 feet high. Yet of all places on the banks of Tay, the most famous is surely Scone, in whose abbey, destroyed in 1559, the ancient kings of Scotland were crowned. The "Stone of Scone" upon which the kings were seated for their crowning was carried off to England by Edward I and now forms part of the Coronation Chair. It is said to be "Jacob's Pillow," upon which he rested his head and dreamed of the celestial ladder, and before it was brought to Scotland was the "Lai Fail" or Stone of Destiny of Ireland.

Natural features take little account of political boundaries, and the rivers of northern England have much in common with those of Scotland. Almost on the border itself rise the Coquet and the Northern Tyne, amidst scenes of bleak desolation, the peat bogs of the high hills. Yet even in these lonelinesses are found the memorials of those who ventured themselves among them, whether for reasons of military conquest or evangelical zeal. Roman milestones mark the paths where the legions trod; and the name of Holystone, still commemorates the spot where 3,000 Northumbrians were baptized.

Nor were the terrors of this bleak region purely physical. Two of the names given to the hill where South Tyne rises speak of the awe in which it was held, "Wizard's Fell," "Fiend's Fell"; its other name, "Cross Fell," speaks of the conquest of the powers of evil by the pious monks. The Romans felt these influences, too; for at their station at Chollerford was found the remains of the statue of the God of Tyne.

### Fierce Forays

To the harshness of nature and the fears of superstition were added the cruelties of man. We think of the "Border Country" as being the Scottish Lowlands, forgetting that England had its border likewise, and that there were raids from the north as well as from the south. In the river valleys stand the "Peel Towers" where the people might take refuge from the raids and forays of the fierce mosstroopers—strong-walled towers with a space below for the cattle and a room above for the women and children. So the sturdy north countrymen maintained themselves in a region which even the Romans had given up as hopeless, seeking not to conquer it but to keep its wild inhabitants at bay by the device of Hadrian's Wall.

There are other reasons for venturing into wild country than politics and religion. On the valley slopes of the northern hills are found Roman mine workings; and today the name "Tyne" suggests to us a grey industrial area similar to that of Glasgow. At this northern border point the Romans forded the Tyne and built a station known as Pons Aelii, but the foundation of the present city of Newcastle is due to the eldest son of William the Conqueror having built a castle at the same spot after one of his raids into Scotland. Two collections of shacks and shelters on the river's banks,

DIXON-SCOTT

## ESS NA LARAGH, GLENARIFF, CO. ANTRIM

*Glenariff, one of the far-famed " Nine Glens of Antrim," has two beautiful waterfalls.  Ess na Laragh (Fall of the Mares) and Ess na Crub (Fall of the Hoof).  Thackeray called this district " Switzerland in miniature," and Washington Irving hoped there to " dream quietly away the remnant of a troubled life."*

" shielings," as they were called, have given a name to North and South Shields. At Newcastle, too, Charles I was surrendered to the English Parliamentary forces.

Tees headwaters are noteworthy for the bleak lonely lake, curiously named " The Weel," and for their many beautiful falls, Caldron Snout and High Force. A picturesque medieval bridge and a few shattered ruins mark the spot where " Barnard Castle standeth stately on Tees." Here the name of a deep ravine, Thor's Gill, reminds us of the fierce Vikings who dwelt in this valley, while the remains of Egliston Abbey speak of their conversion by the pious monks.

Down the great valley between the Pennines and Cleveland hills flows the Yorkshire Ouse, gathering one by one many a noble tributary. First comes the Swale from the lonely hills, hurrying down its narrow vale and lapping the base of Richmond's mighty castle. Along the almost parallel valley, the wide green Wensleydale, flows the Ure, fed by lively streams leaping down the hill-sides and itself presenting a series of splendid falls at Aysgarth. Among the Pennine streams perhaps none offers more varied charm than the Wharfe, a bonny lively stream in a rich, romantic vale.

Farther south the streams are more placid from source to sea, yet still they traverse districts at once beautiful and famed in history or legend.

Derwent flows through the limestone regions, passing through caves where the glittering " Blue John " gleams, washes cliffs where the Romans dug for lead, or rises to the surface in a " petrifying spring " that deposits a thick chalky coating on every object immersed in its stream. It carves the rocks into dales no less lovely than those of Yorkshire — Miller's Dale, Tideswell Dale. Dovedale, the finest of all, is the work of the River Dove, in whose waters Izaak Walton fished. Instead of grim castles, palatial mansions stand beside the river banks, mansions like Chatsworth House which housed the unhappy Mary Stuart and her custodian, the Earl of Shrewsbury, no less than five times, and Haddon Hall, the home of Dorothy Vernon and the scene of her romantic elopement.

### Where Danes Ruled

On the banks of the Trent stands Gotham, about which is told the unenviable story of the " three wise men " who tried to capture a cuckoo by building a hedge round it. Nottingham, at one time the centre of Danish rule in England, was later divided into two separate boroughs, Norman and English, for the proud conquerors disliked too close an association with the " natives." Owen Glendower of Wales and David II of Scotland were imprisoned in its castle, where later Charles I unfurled his standard

W. F. TAYLOR

### HEMINGFORD GREY, HUNTINGDONSHIRE

*On the River Ouse, two miles from St. Ives. The church, dedicated to St. James, is an ancient edifice in the Norman and Early English styles, and possesses a register of baptisms dating from 1673. The Manor House, built about 1135, is one of the few Norman buildings of its kind, and the only one continuously inhabited.*

in the Civil War. At Gainsborough was moored the fleet of Sweyn, the invading Viking, for here the Trent is a stream of some size famous for its tidal wave, the "eagre."

### Hereward

Even more sluggish and more meandering are the waters of the fen country. Yet they win a place in history because of the refuge they afforded to the "last of the English," holding out under brave Hereward against the Norman conqueror behind the muddy streams and the marsh. From a river mouth in these low-lying regions went out another band of lovers of freedom, taking the name of their home town, Boston, half across the world. The streams of Norfolk and Suffolk combine to form those waters so beloved of sportsmen — the Broads; while it was the soft pastoral landscape of the Stour, so he declared, which made Constable a painter.

South of the

HUMPHREY AND VERA JOEL

**FAIR RIVER OF KENT**

*Rising in Ashdown Forest, the Medway here seen at Maidstone flows slowly and placidly through the hop fields by Tonbridge and Maidstone, and out by historic Rochester to the Thames estuary. Barges use the river as far as Maidstone.*

Thames, and joining it at Chatham, is a veritable gangster amongst rivers, the Medway. Its headwaters have cut their way eastwards into the soft sand and clays, and in doing so they have "captured" many small streams which at one time flowed direct to the Thames. The Medway forms an important adjunct to the Thames and is itself rich in historic and political interest. Chatham, used since the time of Henry VIII as a sea-going centre, is now one of the main naval and military stations of England.

On a hill overlooking the valley is the prehistoric Kit's Coty House, formed of three upright stones capped with a stone 11 feet in length. Legend says that it is the tomb of Katigern and Vortigern, who were killed in the battle with Hengist and Horsa.

The streams which flow from the South Downs, though small, have their historic import. Rye, one of the old Cinque Ports of Sussex, at one time stood at the mouth of its stream, but now, owing to the receding of the sea, finds itself inland. Here too may be seen the turreted Ypres Tower said to have been built in the twelfth century by William of Ypres, Earl of Kent. Arundel Castle beside the Arun was

STEPHENSON

### IN THE VALE OF THE USK
*Fairest of South Wales rivers and by some people considered a rival of the Wye, the Usk flows by the foot of Brecon Beacons, by Brecon and Crickhowell and down by Abergavenny and ancient Caerleon to the sea at Newport. Between Brecon and Crickhowell it provides many peaceful scenes such as the one above.*

originally built to defend the break made by that river through the chalky soil of the South Downs and has withstood more than one siege.

Longer and wilder in their scenery are the West Country rivers which rise on the Devonshire Moors, entering the sea by such tortuous waterways as Plymouth Sound. Of the Dart it is said that each year it claims a life, man one year and maid the next. Exe rises in the north, on heathery Exmoor, but flows southwards almost across the whole of the county.

Severn is not the only fine stream which Wales gives to England. The Wye is renowned for its scenery, for ruined Tintern Abbey and Symond's Yat; beside it Owen Glendower kept his stronghold, made his last stand. At " Wolf's Leap " the last wolf in Britain plunged into its waters. That a dragon should have haunted the vale has its parallel elsewhere, but what are we to think of the hill of Marcle (" miracle ") which moved across country with " a loud bellowing noise," doing much damage before it came to rest?

From Wales too we have the Dee, the "holy stream " of the Druids. In its valley, so the story goes, Arthur of Britain spent his early life. It flows through Llyn Tegid, " the lake beautiful," called by the Saxons Bala Lake or Pimblemere, and then eastwards to grey slaty Corwen, past the remains of Valle Crucis Abbey, " the

Valley of the Cross," to Llangollen whose bridge was reputed one of the Seven Wonders of Wales, and by the strange-shaped " Hill of Dinas Bran." So it reaches England and Chester, with its city walls and its ancient " Rows."

The list of Britain's rivers might go on, each with its own beauty, its own legend, its own place on history's page; Usk, with Brecon Castle deliberately destroyed by the townsfolk to avoid the horrors of a siege; Dovey, the bells of its lost city sounding faintly from beneath the wave. The streams of Lakeland, with the Rothay and the Brathay, the crystal Derwent flowing out of Borrowdale, and the lovely Duddon, Wordsworth's " Cradled nursling of the mountains," of these also much might be written.

By historic town and city, through the watermeadows in the wide vales, by many a dreamy village and on towards the narrowing hills, so we may follow these precious streams, dwindling in volume yet assuming a livelier motion as they tumble down the mountain sides.

The rivers of Britain keep the romance and the beauty they have ever held. Placid under the summer sun or whipped to fury by wind and rain, shrinking in drought or spread afar in the winter's flood, rushing bands of silver against the green of the fields or the shadow of the woods, they wind their devious ways to the sea.

# CURIOUS CUSTOMS AND CEREMONIES

## *by* I. O. EVANS

IN the soil of modern England we discover fragments of rock or remains of living creatures which speak to us of long-past ages. Among the countryfolk of Britain we equally find customs and ceremonies which recall to us the beliefs and ways of life of our ancestors of long ago. Many and varied are these old-time customs. Some are comparatively recent, derived at least in name from recorded historic events. Some are age-old, older than civilization, older perhaps than the tilling of the soil. Some have come down, almost un- changed, through countless centuries. Some, it is sad to say, have become vulgarized and spoiled. And some have adapted themselves to present conditions and have taken on in this modern age a vigorous new life of their own.

What is more important in the life of beast or man than water? Today, with our Water Boards and our mains, we often overlook its signifi- cance—until there comes a drought year to remind us that without water none can live. Our forefathers, with good reason, knew the value of water; the wells from which it came they regarded as sacred. To their waters they attributed a magic power, of healing, of bless- ing, of cursing. To the wells they resorted, and at the wells they performed solemn ceremonies, "dressing" them with floral decorations; and such ceremonies are still carried out even in our own time.

At Tissington, in Derby- shire, the wells are still dressed each year with im- pressive ceremony, and with special decorations which have come down from time immemorial. At this village are five wells of the purest

water, bubbling up from far below and keeping the same temperature all the year round: the Town Well, the Holy Well, the Coffin Well, Hand's Well, and Yew Tree Well. Each in turn is visited, every Holy Thursday after church, by clergy, choir and people. At each of the wells a short service is held, with the reading of appro- priate passages from the Bible—for are there not Waters of Healing in both the Old and New Testaments?—the chanting of psalms, and the singing of hymns.

TOPICAL

### THE TUTTIMEN AT HUNGERFORD

*The age-old ceremony of Hock Tide, a survival from the Middle Ages, is still carried out at Hungerford, Berks. This festival is the annual session of the Hock Tide Court. The two tithing men, or Tuttimen, parade the town demanding a coin of the realm from every male over the age of twelve and a kiss from every woman they meet. Tuttimen claiming their kisses.*

TOPICAL

A MAY DAY PROCESSION

*The annual May Festival is still celebrated in many places throughout the country.   Here a procession is seen on the way to the village green at Elstow, in Bedfordshire, where John Bunyan lived.   The May Queen, in her flower-bedecked carriage, accompanied by her charming retinue, is preceded in the procession by the May Pole.*

Meanwhile the wells have been decorated. Beds of moistened clay are prepared in wooden frames, and in these is worked a picture in a natural mosaic, white grains of rice, reds and blues from flower-petals and berries, greys from lichens and greens from mosses and buds.

### Villages of the Plague

This well-dressing is commonly explained as a thanksgiving service from deliverance from the Black Death, which ravaged the villages of Derbyshire, and from which the purity of its wells alone saved Tissington. Students of these matters, however, think it is far older than any medieval plague, though this may of course have revived it ; they consider that it goes back to very early days, that it is similar in idea to the many other customs, all over the world, by which springs and wells are regarded and treated as sacred places. Whatever its origin, the Tissington Well-dressing is a custom that none of us would like to see given up ; it speaks of days and methods of thought other than ours.

Elsewhere in Britain the customs associated with the wells are very different. Among the wishing wells is the Well of St. Keyne, in Cornwall, overshadowed by ash, elm and oak. Whoever, husband or wife, is the first to drink of this well, so the legend runs, will be master of the household for life ! A well-known verse by

a former poet-laureate tells of the competition for its waters which used to take place :
" I hastened as soon as the wedding was done,
        And left my wife in the porch-a,
But truly she had been wiser than me,
        For she'd taken a bottle to the church-a ! "

Man shares with the beast the need of water. But one of the earliest things to distinguish man from beast was surely the discovery of fire. To our primitive ancestors this was not, as it is to us, a mere household commodity : it was magic, it was an object of veneration, it was a means of overcoming the powers of darkness and strengthening the brightness of the sun. In our own islands the Bale-fires used to burn at the four seasons of the year, to mark the turning of the sun in the heavens. Today we still like the bright fire at Christmas, even if we have forgotten the Yule Log of tradition, and still we light fires all over the land in the autumn, at almost the time when they used to be lighted long ago. Nowadays we do it, we say, to commemorate Guy Fawkes. But the custom of lighting fires at this time of the year is much older than any Gunpowder Plot.

No period of the year is more impressive even to townsfolk than the spring. Still more is it significant to the countryman, who lives in the midst of burgeoning leaf and new-born lamb, and whose whole life is devoted to them. Spring festivals are known wherever the earth is tilled, and we find them likewise among ourselves. The time-honoured ceremonies of Maypole and Queen of the May seemed in danger of dying out, but now, fortunately, they are being revived. In one place we may see a Maypole erected, as it was in the days of old; in another a charming little girl is honoured as May Queen. At Minehead, in Somerset, the fishermen parade through the streets a gaily-decorated model of a ship. And at Oxford, ancient home of learning, a service is held to greet the dawn from the summit of Magdalen Tower.

At about the same season, though a few days later, is kept up another picturesque custom. The people of Helston, in Cornwall, one of the most westerly towns in England, deck themselves with flowers and branches and dance processionally through the town. The tune they dance to, like the dance itself, comes down from olden times; folk dancers know it well. Early in the morning the Furry Dance begins, and in and out through the houses, the doors of which are all left open, the merry dancers go. And as they dance they sing another song whose origin, like that of dance and dance tune, is lost in the mists of antiquity. It tells us of those heroes of olden time, Robin Hood and Little John, of going to the Merry Greenwood, " for to chase O,

to chase the buck and doe." It tells us of an ancient foe of Britain, " those Spaniards that make so great a boast O." It tells us, perhaps, of the real purpose of dance and song and tune, to banish the gloom of the winter and bring the summer home : " For we are up as soon as any day O, And for to fetch the summer home, The summer and the May O, The summer is a come O, The winter is a gone O."

Three paces and hop; one, two, three, hop. Round the streets and in and out the houses the merry dancers go. " With a hal-an-tow, jolly rumbelow ! " Just as they did long before the Saxons came to the shores of Britain, the Furry Dancers of Helston are bringing the summer home.

Robin Hood and Little John are our hunting heroes, and another custom recalls the days when hunting, and not corn-growing, gave mankind the staff of life. In Abbots Bromley, Staffs, each September may be seen a dance in which Robin Hood, astride on his Hobby Horse, and fair Maid Marian posture and caper with strange-garbed men who bear on their shoulders the antlers of the deer. The crossbow and arrow, those famous weapons of old, are brandished, and the fool, without whom no ancient function was complete, prances about. Moreover the deer represented are not the shy gentle creatures

TOPICAL

### HELSTON'S FURRY DANCE

*Each year in the ancient Cornish town of Helston homage is paid to the Goddess Flora, when the centuries-old Floral Dance is carried out by couples who dance through the town, in and out of the houses and shops and through the gardens. The photograph shows some of the dancers winding their way through the crowded streets.*

hunted and harried by "sportsmen" of today. They are a breed of deer unknown in a wild state in these islands since before the Norman Conquest—they are the great reindeer themselves. Modern savages, explorers tell us, have ceremonial dances in which they dress up as the animals they slay, no doubt to cast a magic spell upon them. So, it seems, did our ancestors of a thousand years and more ago, when they hunted the great antlered deer. The reindeer are gone, and hunting for food has gone—but the Horn

collect too. He travelled about the country inquiring about these ancient steps, these quaint costumes and simple haunting tunes. Some he learned just in time to save them from being forgotten; they had never been written down, the young people would not trouble to learn them, and the old folks who knew them were dying off. He had their steps codified, their music printed; he formed a special society to carry them on. That student was Cecil Sharp, and the movement he formed was the English Folk

FOX PHOTOS

### A WEIRD DANCE AT ABBOTS BROMLEY
*The dance of the Deermen is held at Abbots Bromley on " the first Monday after the Sunday nearest to September 4," when twelve Staffordshire yeomen each take a pair of deer's antlers from the parish church and, holding them aloft, dance through the district. The horns were originally used by the poor of the parish.*

Dance that our forefathers composed is still danced today. Nor is the dance entirely devoid of religious association, for the traditional garb of the dancers is stored in the tower of the church.

This is by no means the only dance which has come to us through the centuries. It is now nearly forty years since a student chanced to see in an Oxfordshire village one Boxing Day a procession of quaintly-dressed men. One of their number played on the concertina, and the others danced with strange old-world steps. This dance, the observer learned, was danced each year and had been so danced for ages, with the same steps and the same tune. And now it was to be danced as of yore.

The student was interested; already he had spent much time in collecting old folk-songs, and now, it seemed, there were folk-dances to

Dance Society; and thanks to him, and his movement, the ancient ceremonial dances have taken on a new lease of life.

These folk dances were no mere means of amusement, no mere social function. They were danced solemnly, with set ritual and to a set tune, as they are still danced in more than one Oxfordshire village. Dressed in white, girt with brightly-coloured ribbons on which tiny bells jingle, their heads covered with broad-brimmed or flower-decked hats, the Morris Dancers stamp and kick and bound, wave their handkerchiefs or clash their staves; the shrill strains of the fiddle mingle with the tinkling of the bells. So they danced long ago, it is said, to influence the corn and make it grow; no longer do we think that a dance is magic and can influence the crops, but the dance still goes on.

The Morris is not the only form of dance

FOX PHOTOS

### FOLK DANCING AT THAXTED

*The ancient timbered Town Hall of Thaxted, in Essex, makes a perfect background for these country dancers.*
*The local members of the Old English Folk Dance Society, which includes some of the hand weavers of Thaxted,*
*are here seen dancing in the main street to the strains of music supplied by a girl fiddler and a drummer.*

TOPICAL PRESS

## ANCIENT CUSTOM IN COTSWOLD VILLAGE

*Every Christmas at Marshfield, a village on the Cotswold Hills in Gloucestershire, this custom, stated to be eight hundred years old, is observed, having been revived after a lapse of some years. On Boxing Day the mummers, here seen setting out on their tour of the village, perform their traditional mumming play.*

the country people know. Elsewhere a Sword Dance is more common; the dancers brandish short blunted blades; they dance in a circle, grasp the swords of their neighbours and dance in a chain, leap over the swords, crouch under the swords, link the swords together in a complicated knot and hold it triumphantly on high. Most significant of all, they lay their swords to the neck of one of their number, as though they were about to take his life. Does this ceremony hark back, as certain students of these things tell us, to a time when human sacrifice prevailed, when selected members of the community were ceremonially slain, that their blood should give new life to the harvest, that buried like the corn they should spring again to life in the golden grain?

### Gathering Peascods

Morris and Sword Dances are for male teams; for men and women to join in are the Country Dances that we still enjoy. "Longways for as many as will" or in a circle the dancers assemble; they "set and turn single," bow to or "side with" or "arm" their partner; the accompanists go through the old familiar tunes. And so they dance what used to be a celebration of the corn-growing, to a melody that used to be played on the simplest of musical instruments, the tabor and pipe. Some of these dances are

associated with special places, and all, before they were taken up by the townsfolk, used to form an unvarying custom of the harvest home. Religious ideas now forgotten are recalled by some of their motions, for in the round dance of "Gathering Peascods," as the performers rush forward and clap their hands, they are said to be carrying out the old rite of "touching the sacred tree."

At Helston visitors and passers-by are apt to find themselves caught up and carried along in the dance. Still more strange is the experience of those who chance to pass through Hungerford, on the Bath Road, the second Tuesday after Easter. Then, at Hocktide as it is called, a picturesque ceremony takes place. An ancient horn is sounded by the Town Crier, who then parades through the streets in his uniform, summoning the Commoners to attend the Court House. The Hungerford Court of Feoffement is one of the few surviving examples of what used to be a very important feature of medieval life, the Manorial Court, which used to settle disputes arising among the commoners. This Court deals with fishing rights, which are of no small importance to the townsfolk, who find them a useful source of income. The Court itself is of interest to anyone who values the traditional and the picturesque; still more interesting is the outdoor part of the ceremony.

On Hocktide Tuesday two Tuttimen parade the streets of Hungerford. Each carries his ceremonial wand, which he has received from the Constable, a civic office which has come down from of old. The wand consists of a shoulder-high staff, topped with an orange and bedecked with flowers and streaming blue ribbons. By ancient law and custom the Tuttimen are entitled to claim a kiss from every girl they meet, or in default to demand a fine. They make their way through Hungerford, knocking at every door and demanding that all the girls out of the household come out to be kissed; they stop and kiss the girls that they meet. Very seldom, it is said, do the stalwart young Tuttimen have to content themselves with the fine! Meantime the Orange Scrambler, with befeathered hat, distributes gifts to the aged poor in the workhouse and to the children of the town.

Furry Dance and Tuttimen, Bale-fires and Well-dressing are perhaps older than Christianity. Yet the Christian festivals themselves are often celebrated locally with time-honoured rites. At Overton, Gloucestershire, and in other places, are found the Christmas Mummers, the only folk drama that has come down to us from the days of the ancient Mystery Plays. Costumes, words, acting, all are traditional; until recently the " book " of the play was never committed to print, but was passed down through the ages by word of mouth.

The characters of the Mummers vary in different villages and districts. In Wales a " Horse's Head " is sometimes found; an actor is of course concealed beneath it, and creates great merriment as he snaps its lower jaw open and shut. " Twing Twang " perhaps gets his name from the sound of a loosing bow-string, and " Little Johnnie Jack " from the burly henchman of Robin Hood; our Sherwood heroes are honoured everywhere throughout the land. The " Quack Doctor " has his astonishing pills and potions, fit to cure " the itch, the stitch, the palsy and the gout." " Father Christmas " introduces the Mummers and acts as " M.C.," and " King George " is the valiant knight who challenges all the world and overcomes the " Turks " and " Giants " with his wooden sword. In Cornwall there is a very fierce giant indeed :

" Here am I, old Hub-bub-bub
And in my hand I carries a club,
And on my back a frying-pan,
And am I not a valiant man? "

There is much horse-play and fooling about, but the central feature of the little drama is a duel between " King George " and the " Turkish Knight " who of course is left " lifeless " on the ground, only to be restored by the treatment given him by the " Quack Doctor." Here, it is said, is another vestige of the ancient custom of human sacrifice, taking us back to a pre-Christian age.

R. H. RAMSAY

## SPECTACULAR FESTIVAL OF VIKING ORIGIN

*At the annual festival of Up-Helli-Aa, at Lerwick in Shetland, which celebrates the close of the Yule festival, four hundred Guisers, headed by their chief Guiser Jarl, take part in a huge torchlight procession. A model of a Norse galley is drawn through the streets and burnt by the seashore. The Viking warriors in their galley.*

The Danes who ravaged our shores brought their old customs with them, and their ancient methods of honouring their dead leaders are still recalled in the Shetland Islands. In January the Up-Helli-Aa procession makes its way through Lerwick. By the light of the torches a number of armoured Vikings, with their round shields and their winged helmets, drag through the streets a model of an ancient Norse " long ship," with the traditional snake's head and tail at its prow and stern. Other Vikings man the galley, their oars projecting over its sides as though to beat the waves, the shields bearing the crests of the oarsmen being fastened above. High on its deck stands the Guiser Jarl, with his battle-axe and his coat of mail. The bands play the ancient Norse tunes, the rockets blaze overhead, the torches are held aloft ; the " long snake " moves forward on its platform, and a double line of flame follows behind.

### A Blazing Dragon Ship

The doomed ship moves through the town and reaches the sea front. The torch-bearers circle around, and the islanders, descendants of the ancient Vikings themselves, sing *The Norseman's Home.* The crew leave the ship, the bugles sound and the maroons crash aloft — and the torches are flung into the ship. So the " long-snake " perishes in a blaze of flame, as long

ago a blazing " dragon ship " was laden with the body of some fallen chief, to take him, as though he had been slain in battle, to Valhalla of the Gods.

In the Up-Helli-Aa of the Shetland Islands we find today a survival of the Scandinavian ceremonies of our Norse forefathers ; in the Tynwald of the Isle of Man we find, still as active and efficient as ever, one of their " Things," the folk-parliaments by which they governed their communal life. It is thus far older than the Westminster Parliament ; it is indeed the oldest legislative assembly our islands possess. Every July the Tynwald assembles to promulgate its laws. A service is held in the church, and then the Lieutenant-Governor of the Island leads a procession to the Tynwald Hill. At the summit of the hill he sits side by side with the bishop ; below him are the two dozen members of the Manx Parliament, the House of Keys, and below them the clergy and the officials. If the weather is wet, a tent is set up to cover the assembly ; if fine, the ceremony is performed in the open air. An unsheathed sword is held point upwards ; the wands of office are given in by the retiring coroners and handed to their successors ; the titles of the acts passed during their year are recited in English and Manx, and so they become the law of that tiny land. Thus, much as the Vikings of old settled their disputes and made

TOPICAL

### HISTORIC COMMON RIDING CELEBRATIONS
*Every June, Selkirk celebrates the granting to the Borough of the Confirmation Charter by James V. Led by the crowds a procession passes through High Street towards the River Ettrick, where the riders gallop away. Here we see the Standard Bearer, holding aloft the Selkirk flag, being welcomed at the Toll after the return.*

TOPICAL

## SHROVE TUESDAY FOOTBALL IN DERBYSHIRE
*The old-established Shrove Tuesday and Ash Wednesday football match is an event which draws crowds to the market town of Ashbourne, in the valley of the Dove. All the town join in the game and here a section of the crowd can be seen playing the ball in the river. Atherstone, Warwickshire, has a similar event.*

rules to govern their behaviour, the Manxmen receive their law.

In many villages it is still customary to perform the " Beating of the Bounds," the limits of the parish being solemnly traversed in time-honoured fashion. A similar tradition in the North Country has a grim event behind it. The Border Country is peaceable enough now, and the Scots and the English are fellow-countrymen who find it easy enough to live in common citizenship together. Yet it is not so many years since the Border was the scene of fierce fighting, of merciless outrages and vengeful forays and raids. Soon after their defeat at Flodden, the Scots of Hawick learned that some English raiders were encamped a few miles away. With grim delight they made an attack in the darkness, took the raiders by surprise, killed them or drove them panic-stricken away.

### Riding the Marches
So impressive was this victory, following on the crushing defeat of Flodden, that its annual celebration has been continued ever since. A banner, locally held to be that which was carried during the fight, is presented by the town Provost to the Cornet, or leader. Traditional songs are sung invoking the ancient Nordic gods, there is

a procession and a feast. Next morning the members of the ceremonial band rise in the night, as did the raiding party whose triumph they celebrate, and sing a hymn to the rising sun from the bank of the Moat. Another procession is held round the streets and up to the Common which the town received as a reward for the victory; and this is the " Riding of the Marches " which is observed as a festival and a holiday throughout the town.

Many other ceremonies could be described did space permit. The giving of the Dunmow Flitch to married couples who do not regret their marriage; the Midsummer Day sunrise-watching from Stonehenge itself; the Town Crier's contest in Wiltshire; the bottle-kicking at Hallaton in Leicestershire; the Forest Courts of Swainmote in the New Forest and at Speech House in the Forest of Dean; the distribution of oranges and lemons at St. Clements in the Strand—all flourish even in this hustling machine-using age. Such customs are not merely picturesque and quaint. They tell of manners of life and ways of thought other than ours but of manners and ways from which our own have sprung. They may enable us to understand our forefathers, and so they may enable us the better to understand ourselves.

E. SIMPSON

### THE GREATEST CAVERN IN BRITAIN
*The limestone plateau of Ingleborough, in Yorkshire, contains numerous caves, the greatest of which is Gaping Ghyll. This descends vertically and opens into an immense cavern, the floor of which is 365 feet below the ground level. Out of the impressive Main Hall, seen above, narrow winding passages lead into other caves.*

# THE SPLENDOUR
# OF UNDERGROUND BRITAIN

## by E. A. BAKER

THE appreciation of cave scenery ought to be regarded as a special branch of æsthetics. Not because it is to a certain extent an affair of natural curiosities, freaks, and marvels. But the whole basis of your science of beauty and grandeur is different and extraordinary: other senses than that of sight come into play; the sense of feel, in particular, is all-important, more even than when in the open air we contemplate the majesty of the Alps or the terrors of some great cataract.

In the upper world, under the open sky, we are often thrilled and fascinated by effects of light and darkness. Underground, it is not only the strange atmosphere and the strange surroundings, but the very inability to see, the great and essential element of darkness, which comes in everywhere and all the time, adding infinitely to the beauty and the suggestion of danger in the objects seen by the glimmer of a candle or the glare of an electric arc.

The unique characteristic of cave scenery is that so much of it is not visual at all. We are buried deep in the crust of the earth, with many hundreds of feet of solid rock overhead: we have an overpowering consciousness, not only of gloom, cold and damp, reinforced perhaps by the noise of tumbling waters somewhere in the distance, but also of potential danger, even if only of danger overcome. This is a subjective element that cannot be eliminated. It is, of course, the explorer into the unknown who feels it most. But even the ordinary sightseer proceeding from the cave mouth of Wookey Hole, for example, once the comfortable residence of prehistoric men, along the narrow, winding corridor in the rock to Hell Stair, leading down to the gloomy recesses and Styx-like pool of the Witch's Kitchen, is bound to experience the same sensations. That

gives the right word. Cave scenery is the most sensational of all scenery. And, as it happens, the caves of the British Isles can give you sensations as exciting as any, for we have one cavern as big as any on the Continent; and, though the immense underground labyrinths of North America are more extensive, by all accounts they lack those very elements of grandeur which are the most impressive of all.

Somerset, the Peak of Derbyshire, and the West Riding of Yorkshire are amongst the chief cave-regions of Britain, and there are groups of

E. A. BAKER

### A STRANGE CHAPEL

*Stump Cross Caverns, on Greenhow Hills in Yorkshire, extend for about six miles underground. The chamber seen above, with its curious stalactites and stalagmites, is for some reason known as " The Chapel."*

subterranean passages in parts of Ireland. Let us take Somerset first, where, but for a curious specimen in the Quantocks, the caves are all found in the Mendip Hills, within a short radius of Wells and Cheddar.

It is to the fact that they occur in mountain limestone, through the action of water in corroding and eroding this highly soluble rock, and dissolving out the carbonate of lime, which is then deposited in the form of stalactites and

PHOTOCHROM

## THE WITCH OF WOOKEY

*In the limestone of the Mendips, in Somerset, the River Axe has worn a series of fascinating caverns which provided shelter for prehistoric man. This curiously shaped boss of rock is known as the Witch of Wookey.*

We come out into the open with dazzled eyes, and ascend the gorge for a short distance to the other show cave, Gough's, the Great Cave of Cheddar. This is a much greater cavern, various natural cavities having been connected up by excavation or the natural tunnels enlarged to give comfortable access. There are some far-extending passages also which the ordinary visitor would find rather difficult ; even in Cox's Cave the part leading to the river is not accessible. Ranges of stalagmite pillars flank the main corridor which leads on to the pure white calcite basins called the Fonts, to the enormous mound of sculptured and fluted stalagmite known as the Organ Pipes, and the climax in Solomon's Temple, with its gigantic frozen fall of the same beautiful plastic material.

### Refuge of Britons

Gough's and Cox's are the two great public shows. But there are many other caves known to the explorer in the cliffs above and around. Gough's Old Cave contains some interesting curios. The Roman Cave is interesting as having been the refuge of ancient British fugitives after the withdrawal of their conquerors ; and its great arched mouth looking down on the village is picturesque from within or without. Then there is the Long Hole, and the rift known as the Slitters, with walls ascending high into the cliffs and descending far into the rock and easily accessible by a sort of rabbit-hole not far from the road.

There are caves in the Mendip Hills west of Cheddar, such as Denny's Hole on Crook's Peak and the Coral Cavern near Compton Bishop, the latter notable for the splash deposit like some beautiful submarine growth, arranged in symmetrical patterns by the rhythmic drip of water in ages long gone by. Legend tells of a mighty abyss hereabouts called the Gulf, discovered by the old lead-miners. A man was let down on a long rope, and at the extremity could see

stalagmites, that the special interest and beauty of these caves is due. Walk, for instance, into Cox's Cave at Cheddar, and it is as easy as walking into a church. Here you have in miniature but on a quite sufficient scale all the characteristics of underground scenery—exquisite translucent pendants hanging from a natural ceiling, walls draped with sheets and curtains of the same gleaming fabric, pools of clear water caught in the folds of the fantastic drapery, and most of this natural splendour a glistening white contrasting with dark rock and recesses of deep gloom. Here and there pendulous stalactites are coloured with bands of red and gold and violet, some thin and translucent, the colours exquisitely graded.

neither roof nor bottom. Its very position is now irretrievably lost.

Farther east, on the high plateau above Wells, and on the north side of Mendip, there are a number of caves, not a bit less wonderful, some open to the tourist, others only for the hardy and experienced explorer. Swildon's Hole and the great Eastwater Swallet are among the latter. It is a pity that Swildon's Hole is too wet and difficult except for those who do not mind hardship and a spice of danger. A stream descends gradually through passages and chambers that might have been carved out of purest marble. Then comes a waterfall, down which the caveman goes on a rope ladder, to find himself in a lower series of surpassing beauty. The final chamber, discovered some years ago, is unmatched anywhere in the British Isles; and it may prove not to be final, if the existing choke can only be cleared away.

Of course, there is the usual story of the dog that was lost down Swildon's Hole, and reappeared weeks later at Cheddar, with all his hair gone. In Ireland, it is a cow or a pig that goes through these tribulations.

Eastwater Swallet is a more formidable cave, and its descent calls for a strong party and a good deal of tackle, for there is pitch after pitch going down to a level some 700 feet below the surface. It is certainly one of those caves in which the darkness can be felt, and the accompanying sense of mystery is almost overpowering. There can be danger too. Years ago the present writer was penned down for many hours by a sudden flood, the tiny entrance at the surface being submerged under 10 feet of swirling water.

### Caves of Mendip

Lamb's Lair, some miles to the north of Eastwater, with its string of passages lined with dazzling white aragonite, a great chamber 110 feet high, adorned with incrustations and pendulous masses of calcite, superbly coloured, and the biggest stalagmite boss, the Beehive, in any English cavern, was found early in the eighteenth century, lost for one hundred and twenty years, then rediscovered, rendered inaccessible for years by the collapse of the deep entrance shaft, but is now made accessible again by a new shaft.

On the same side of Mendip, the Burrington caves vary in interest. Goatchurch yielded rich vestiges of prehistoric man, when explored by Boyd Dawkins, but is now simply a maze of passages in both the vertical and the horizontal planes. Aveline's Hole, where fifty skeletons

FRITH

### UNDERGROUND FAIRYLAND
*Cox's Cave, at Cheddar in Somerset, was accidentally discovered in 1837 and has since become one of the show places of the West Country. In its depths Nature has indeed produced some marvellous effects and wonderful architecture. Above is the fascinating corner known as " The Transformation Scene."*

were discovered, is now silted up.  Plumley's Den, a vertical hole, where a villager, probably more than half drunk, went down for a wager and had his neck broken in being hauled up, is blocked some 50 feet down.

### The Devil's Hole

Peak Cavern is the eponymous and the best known of the Derbyshire caves, best known formerly under the less respectable designation of the Devil's Hole.  The Speedwell runs horizontally, and a long way in bisects an enormous cross-fissure rising to a great height and descending into the Bottomless Pit.  The horizontal portion is traversed by a stream, ponded back by an artificial hatch above the Pit, which is by no means bottomless.  I have been on the steep rocks below when the hatch was inadvertently opened, and the rush of water and foam was like a tornado.

The Bagshawe Cavern is a lovely system of stalactite passages, rather like Swildon's Hole. It is much more complicated than the ordinary visitor would surmise, and once a friend and I spent some anxious hours hunting for two comrades who had gone astray.  The famous Blue John Cavern was opened up in mining, for fluorspar.  There are purple patches in many caves, but the Blue John is all purple, with shades of violet and pink.  Unfortunately, the vein of fluorspar is now worked out, and the tourist may possibly find the cave derelict.  A neighbouring cave, not recommended to the tourist, Elden Hole, still haunts my memory, as the scene of two narrow escapes.  It is a pot-hole without a stream ; 200 feet down is a lofty chamber.  But the scenery is not there.  It is its grim, ugly mouth, threatening danger, and very real danger too, that gives it a physiognomy never to be forgotten.  Giant's Hole, Ricklow Cavern, Manifold, and other Derbyshire caverns are small beer in comparison.

You must go to the Ingleborough region in Yorkshire to find pot-holes to beat Elden Hole. Gaping Ghyll is the most formidable, with its drop of 365 feet to the floor of the great chamber, the largest natural cavity in Britain.  For the mingled sensations of beauty, mystery, and terror, indicated above as the peculiar characteristic of cave scenery, the descent of Gaping Ghyll by wire rope and windlass is an experience hard to parallel.  Alum Pot, or Helln Pot, not far away, is equally as difficult, and Mere Ghyll, with its long succession of wet pitches descending to a depth of 450 feet, is a far harder nut to crack. But it was surely a unique feat of Martel the Frenchman, to make the first descent into Gaping Ghyll, and that by the arduous method of a rope ladder.

For grandeur, these Yorkshire pots, including

STEPHENSON

### A BLACK ABYSS

*On the bare hillside of Ingleborough, 1,250 feet above the sea, is the funnel-shaped mouth of Gaping Ghyll.
With a little caution one may approach the edge of the shaft, and lying flat on the rock, peer into the abyss
and see the walls of limestone fading into hidden depths from which cool moist air is wafted upwards.*

Hull Pot and Hunt Pot on Penyghent, Goyden Pot, Weathercote, which Turner thought worth painting, Gate Kirk, with its river running right through, and various others stand first among English caves. Those of Wales and the Welsh Border, the Tanyrogo Caves, near Abergele, the St. George Cavern, the Ogo, and one or two on the Ceiriog river, are strikingly picturesque, but on a minor scale and with one exception unattractive to the explorer. This very grandeur means the ordinary tourist had better give the Yorkshire Caves a wide berth, unless he has the advantage of expert guidance. He will have to content himself with the curios of Clapham Cave, the White Scar Caverns in Chapel-le-Dale, or the really beautiful Chapel, Bowling Alley and other show pieces in Stump Cross Cavern, near Pateley Bridge. Not for him, however, the nether regions, explored some years since by a friend of mine, who took a squad of undergrads, and had the Napoleonic idea of keeping them down till the job was finished. They could not escape; they did not know the way out. The result of a week's intensive effort under these conditions was that a very deep and very extensive series of passages and cavities were explored and mapped out, far more than doubling the known extent of the cavern.

H. E. WHITAKER

### EERIE, SUNLESS DEPTHS
*Near the hamlet of Selside, in Upper Ribblesdale, is the tree-fringed mouth of Alum Pot. The stream descending this shaft actually flows under the River Ribble and emerges on the far side.*

### Scene for Witch's Sabbath

Ireland has several cave districts, the most extensive of those open to visitors being the Mitchelstown Cave, in Co. Tipperary. Put the Cheddar and most of the other show caves of England end to end and you would not quite reach the quality and quantity represented by this vast horizontal labyrinth. Yet it is an easy cave to explore. Not so Desmond's Cavern, hard by, a terrible place, fit scene for a witch's sabbath, which yet has its beauties, although it was badly pillaged in the famine of 1847 by starving peasants.

The first descent of Noon's Hole, the exploration of the fantastic river caverns of Marble Arch, and other cave adventures near Enniskillen, would take up a chapter in themselves. Those of West Clare must accordingly end this account of our underground marvels. The biggest of them is Poulnagollum, near Lisdoonvarna; in fact it is by far the biggest of all British caverns, with its five miles of passages exactly

matching Bramabiau, the biggest in France, and perhaps on the Continent. The man who got to the end of it with me in 1925 has disappeared somewhere in Central Asia, and the lady who helped our third man to survey the main portion of the series met her death in a Dalmatian cavern.

Poulnagollum scenery is distinctly of the sort that can be felt, and is not recommended to the inexperienced. Better get a couple of boatmen and a curragh, and go as deep as you can into the wonderful sea caves that penetrate the limestone underneath the sheer grit of the incomparable Cliffs of Moher. That will make a perfect finish to your perambulation of the finest British caverns, that strange world of underground splendour where Nature has hidden some of her greatest marvels, and only as an afterthought providing access for venturesome man.

W. F. TAYLOR

## THE GIANT'S CAUSEWAY

*On the Antrim coast is the Giant's Causeway where a mass of once molten rock has cooled and solidified into innumerable columns of basalt, most of them of hexagonal shape. Fingal's Cave in the Isle of Staffa, presents a similar formation and legend claims both these outcrops as remnants of a bridge built by an Irish giant.*

# IRELAND—ISLE OF DESTINY

## by MARGARET MAGUIRE

" For, tread as you may on Irish soil
  From Antrim's coast to wild Cape Clear,
  From east to west no view is found
  Without its ruin, rath or mound
  To tell of times that were."

TO him who studies it with interest and attention, the face of Ireland reveals a woeful yet wondrous story—the romance of the Irish nation. Century has followed century into the tomb of time, each bearing its burden of " old unhappy far-off things " : but places and place-names, castles and abbeys, round tower and hallowed ruin — these with many other imprints of history remain

" Mute tongues that silent ever speak
  Of Ireland's past of grief and glory."

" Isle of Destiny " (Innisfail)—such was the name given it by the Milesians, a Scythian people reputed to have sailed the seas to find their promised land. Tradition, with unusual precision, holds that they first sighted the Irish coast on May 17, in the year 1029 B.C., and hailed it with joy as the island of which Moses had long previously prophesied to their famous ancestor, Gadelius—from whom they were known as the Gaels.

Having defeated, in epic battles, the inhabitants of the island (remnants of many preceding vague waves of colonization), the Milesians settled in Ireland and for more than 2,000 succeeding years their dynasty held sway. One of their monarchs, Ollamh Fodhla, the Solomon of Irish history, instituted (some 1,000 years B.C.) the great national legislative assembly summoned triennially at Tara Hill, in Meath. Tara was, until A.D. 563, the royal place of Ireland and the residence of the Ard-Ri or High King. Today, but a few raths and some grassy mounds and pillars mark the site of the once great heart of a nation. Christianity dawned on a world almost mastered by Rome. But to Irish soil the Roman Eagle never penetrated. Left to itself, the nation developed its own organization, legislation and institutions. The country was divided, as now, into four main provinces—Ulster, Munster, Leinster and Connacht, each having its provincial king as well as a host of princes of numerous clans.

In Ulster, two splendid palaces are known to ancient history—that at Emania, built in approximately 700 B.C., where now the Navan Fort, two miles west of Armagh, marks the spot ; and that at Aileach by the shores of Lough Swilly where the great ruin, now visited by thousands of tourists, comprises three ramparts of earth mixed with uncemented stones and enclosing a " Cashel " or stone rampart. Cashel, in Tipperary, where stands the " Rock " today, was, in its earliest beginnings, another such royal site.

To this pre-Christian era also belong such stone forts as the mighty Dun Aengus, cresting a sheer 300 feet cliff on Aran Island and Staigue Fort, in Kerry—the most perfect of its kind extant. All over the country there are hundreds of kindred relics—Raths (earthen structures), Cahers (stone structures), Duns (structures on high cliffs), Clochans (stone huts), Crannógs (lake dwellings) and Cairns, Stone Circles and Tumuli (sepulchral monuments).

Worth special mention among such pre-Christian remains are the Lia Fáil (Stone of Destiny) on Tara Hill ; the ancient and interesting group of clochans beside Slea Head, in Kerry ; the Pillar Stones bearing Ogham inscriptions in the old cemetery of Killeen Cormac, in Kildare,

BAINBRIDGE, BELFAST

### ST. PATRICK'S STONE

*The saint is supposed to have begun his missionary labours in this area, south-west of Carlingford Lough, which includes Downpatrick, where this granite slab is alleged, but on no good evidence, to mark his grave.*

W. F. TAYLOR

### THE WAVE-BEATEN COAST OF DONEGAL

*On the shores of Mulroy Bay stands this little hamlet of Carrigart, far away from the bustle and turmoil
of modern civilization. West of the village is the narrow neck of the Rosguill peninsula which thrusts
northwards between Mulroy Bay and Sheephaven. In the neighbourhood there are many historical features.*

and the Stone Circles at Carrowmore in Sligo,
by Lough Gur, in Limerick, and on the Lough-
crew Hills, a mausoleum in Meath.

### Beds of Diarmuid and Gráinne

In many parts of Ireland one stumbles across
" dolmens," more popularly called " cromlechs."
These impressive groupings of three or more
large unhewn stones supporting a huge flat
covering stone were once believed to have been
Druid altars, but are now recognized as sepulchral
erections dating from the Neolithic or Bronze
Age.

Splendid specimens of this feature of Pagan
Ireland may be seen at Kilternan, Co. Dublin,
the cap stone here measuring $23\frac{1}{2}$ feet by 17 feet,
and having six supports ; at Ballymacscanlon, in
Louth, where the massive structure is 12 feet
high ; at Carrowmore, in Sligo, where there is
quite a cluster of cromlechs ; and near Glanworth,
Cork, where one of huge proportions has given
its name—Labbacully, the old hag's bed—to the
surrounding district.

In romantic tradition they are known as
" Giant's Graves," and sometimes " Beds of
Diarmuid and Gráinne," those legendary lovers
who fled from Gráinne's betrothed husband,
Fionn MacCool, and were pursued all over
Ireland by a revengeful Fionn and his army of
Fenians.

The Fianna or Irish Militia headed by Fionn
reached the peak point of its glory in the third
century A.D. during the reign of Cormac MacArt.
Many and marvellous are the stories associated
with its fame. The Giant's Causeway at Antrim
is said to have been flung across the sea to Scotland by Fionn, to hasten his hostile encounter
with a fearsome Scottish rival. Cloughmore (Big
Stone) at Rostrevor, was hurled, it is said, by
the Scottish Giant at Fionn's head and just
missed it ! Fionn retaliated with the Isle of Man
which he pulled out of the space now occupied
by Lough Neagh. The dolmen at Howth, near
Dublin, is pointed out as the burial place of
Aideen, wife of Fionn's son Oisin, while Fionn's
two moated palaces were situated at the vantage
points of Moyvalley, in Offaly, and the Hill of
Allen, in Kildare. Scarce a spot in Ireland does
not treasure some legend of this renowned Irish
Giant.

Yet another great military order, but linked
up with the first century A.D. and confined for
the most part to Ulster, was the Red Branch
Knighthood of which Cuchullain was champion.
His name and doughty deeds re-echo in Rath-
croghan, where stood the royal palace of Ulster's
rival—Connacht, in Cooley, the venue of the
Cattle Raid by Maeve, the Amazonian Queen of
Connacht, on Slieve Gullion outside Dundalk,
where the hero captured the wild fairy steed of

Macha, and at Ardee (the Ford of Ferdia), where for three days Cuchullian was forced to fight his dear friend Ferdia. At Ratheddy, near Dundalk, one may view the " Leaning Stone " to which the champion bound himself that he might die standing. Only when his enemies saw the bird of prey alight on his shoulder did they dare approach. Today, in the General Post Office at Dublin, a beautiful bronze memorial by Oliver Shepherd depicts Cuchullian thus dying tied by his own mantle to the pillar.

The most famous royal burial ground of ancient Ireland was historic Brugh-na-Boinne along the River Boyne. Some of its vast Neolithic tumuli have been excavated, and that at Newgrange, which by its size and the elaborate ornamentation of its interior is one of the most remarkable monuments in Europe, deserves a visit.

In A.D. 432 St. Patrick brought Christianity to Ireland and won a speedy victory for his faith. Thenceforth the face of the nation took on new features readily distinguishable today in the large number of early Christian relics — oratories, churches, round towers, crosses and monastic settlements—which punctuate the countryside. Claims of a pre-Patrician Christian settlement by St. Declan at Ardmore, in Waterford (where there is a perfect round tower that still stands to this day), are supported by the presence there of some very ancient remains of the Oratory, Stone and Well of St. Declan.

All over Ireland there are footprints of Saint Patrick. On Slemish Mountain, when a slave boy, he tended the flocks of a Pagan chieftain. On Slane Hill he kindled the first Paschal fire in Ireland, thus incurring the wrath of the High King and the Druids who summoned him to their presence at Tara. In Cashel he baptized Angus, King of Munster ; Armagh he made the site of his cathedral ; Croagh Patrick and Lough Derg, to this day centres of unique and vigorous pilgrimages, were his places of penance and in Downpatrick a rough granite slab in the grounds of the cathedral marks his grave.

### Irish Missionaries

The seed sown by Patrick bore fruit a hundred-fold. From the sixth to the ninth century Ireland was the island of saints and scholars, a beacon light of faith and learning to a Europe engulfed in the aftermath of the great Roman collapse and inundated by the ensuing tidal wave of barbarism. In Ireland monastic establishments flourished everywhere, they were veritable Universities of Piety, Culture and Art. The Irish mission sent preachers and scholars to England and the Continent. Alfred the Great is said to have studied in the Irish schools, and the great Charlemagne summoned their teachers to direct his colleges.

At Glendalough, today a romantic beauty spot in Wicklow, St. Kevin in the sixth century

BAINBRIDGE, BELFAST

### SLEMISH MOUNTAIN

*Ireland's patron saint, Patrick, is supposed to have tended the herds of his master, Milchu, in the neighbour-hood of this mountain near Ballymena, Co. Antrim, and to have beheld visions which inflamed his imagination. A modern biographer states that the scene of his captivity was laid in Connaught, near Croagh Patrick.*

DIXON-SCOTT

## GLENDALOUGH, CO. WICKLOW: ROUND TOWER AND ST. KEVIN'S KITCHEN

*Here in the sixth century, St. Kevin founded the monastic city of Glendalough. The ruins of seven churches and an almost perfect round tower mark the site. Legend says that the poor Saint was continually tempted by a wileful maiden and to escape from her he took refuge in the cave now known as St. Kevin's Bed.*

I.T.A.

## THE "ROYAL AND SAINTLY ROCK" OF CASHEL

*The Rock of Cashel in Tipperary is one of Ireland's most ancient landmarks and on its crest are the remains of a number of beautiful medieval buildings. Here was the royal residence of the Kings of Munster and there are also ruins of a cathedral, the richly decorated twelfth-century Cormac's Chapel and a well-preserved Round Tower, 90 feet high. According to legend the rock was originally carried to this spot by the devil.*

founded his monastic city. Thousands of visitors climb each year the perpendicular rock overhanging the Upper Lake, to see his cave-bed in the cliff face. Seven churches, which may to this day be identified, grew up in this hallowed centre. The sixth century too, and the seventh, saw the setting up of many other famed schools and monasteries. St. Kieran founded Clonmacnois beside the Shannon—today a lovely and venerable ruin. St. Finian was the founder of Clonard in Meath, St. Colman of Kilmacduagh, in Galway, St. Brendan the Navigator of Clonfert, near Clonmacnois and St. Finbarr of lone Gougane Barra at the source of the River Lee. To this Golden Age belong, among many other jewels

above all, their greed and at this time round towers were erected to serve both as watch towers before and as places of refuge during a Norse raid.

These round towers, some of them sadly the worse for history's wear and tear, dot the whole countryside. Careful and studious research has assigned their origin to three distinct periods between A.D. 890 and 1238, and has divided them into four distinct classes, according to their style of masonry and their doorways. The towers range from 50 to 120 feet in height, and are all approximately 16 feet in diameter at the base. They comprise four to five storeys reached by interior ladders and having a doorway several

DIXON-SCOTT

## KILLINEY BAY AND THE WICKLOW MOUNTAINS

*Many writers have described in glowing words this beautiful bay near Dublin, comparing it favourably with that of Naples. On Killiney Hill, whence the picture was taken, Bernard Shaw wandered as a boy. In the distance is Bray Head, and behind it rise the Sugar Loaf and the hills and glens of the Wicklow Mountains.*

of art and architecture, the beautiful Book of Kells (now preserved in Trinity College, Dublin), lovely Gallerus Oratory on the side of Mount Brandon, in Kerry, and the noble High Cross of Monasterboice in County Louth.

The fearsome hordes of invaders known to Irish history as simply " The Danes," threw, towards the close of the eighth century, the first shadows of their fateful comings. In the beginning of their inroads they were mere pirates making intermittent but fierce attacks on various parts of the coast and landing to burn, pillage and plunder. Ecclesiastical settlements, being rich in sacred vessels of precious metals, attracted,

feet from the ground—out of reach of any battering ram, and allowing entrance by a ladder afterwards hauled in by the defenders.

Some seventy of these picturesque structures are now extant but not more than a dozen of them retain their original conical cap. Perhaps the best known to tourists are those at Glendalough (there are two here), Ardmore (in Waterford), Clondalkin (beside Dublin), Monasterboice (in Louth), Antrim (beside Lough Neagh), Devenish Island (on Lough Erne), Clonmacnois (beside the Shannon) and Cashel (upon the Royal Rock). Those at Cloyne (Cork), Killmallock (Limerick), Kildare and Kilkenny

DIXON-SCOTT

## CARRICKFERGUS CASTLE, CO. ANTRIM

*Probably the most interesting and perfect Norman fortification in Ireland, this castle was completed in the early thirteenth century and has been garrisoned continuously for over seven hundred years. It was for centuries the only castle held by the English in the north. Within recent years it has been completely restored.*

DIXON-SCOTT

## ST. PATRICK'S CATHEDRAL, DUBLIN

*This twelfth-century edifice, which is rich in historical associations, raises its smoke grimed head above the roofs of Dublin's poorest homes. From its pulpit Jonathan Swift, author of " Gulliver's Travels," preached in language as biting as his satires. He died in the deanery and was laid to rest in the cathedral near the woman he loved and may have married. Samuel Lover, the Irish novelist and poet is also buried here.*

carry a battlemented parapet erected to replace the conical cap after it had fallen down.

Later the Danish hordes began to come in fuller force and to settle down in sites favourable for maritime cities. So began modern Dublin, Drogheda, Waterford, Limerick and Wexford, whence the new settlers from time to time made marauding sallies into the interior of the country. About the year A.D. 840, a monster fleet under the fierce Thorgils sailed up the Shannon, sacked Clonmacnois and converted the cathedral into a pagan palace. Retribution was wrung from them by Malachy, Prince of Westmeath (he who " wore the collar of gold which he won from the proud invader "), and by Niall, then Ard-Ri of Ireland. But the decisive battle that crushed for ever the power of the Danes as a ruling force in Ireland was that fought at Clontarf outside Dublin on Good Friday, 1014, wherein Brian Boru, High King of Ireland defeated a combined Norse force of some 20,000 strong. Thenceforth the Danes continued to hold some maritime cities in the country, but never after did they aspire to its conquest.

### The Vikings

Danish footsteps have left many an imprint in Dublin, particularly in Christ Church Cathedral, a splendid erection founded by the Norse Settlers in 1038, and in St.

W. F. TAYLOR

MUCKROSS ABBEY, KILLARNEY

*Within these walls were buried two modern Gaelic writers: Egan O'Rahilly (died 1726), who wrote satires on the Cromwellian invasion; and Owen Roe O'Sullivan (died 1784), whose witty sayings are still current in Munster.*

Michan's Church whose vaults have always had curious preservative powers by virtue of which their dead remain undecayed. Reginald's Tower, in Waterford, commemorates these sea raiders too, while such places as Waterford, Wexford, Wicklow, Arklow, Strangford and Carlingford preserve in their names the story of their Scandinavian origin.

To the medieval chapter of Ireland's story date many well-known features of the countryside. Up to the middle of the twelfth century church architecture developed on very interesting lines, a style of elaborate ornamentation and decoration known as the Hiberno-Romanesque having come into use. Well proportioned columns with carved capitals and exquisitely moulded doorways are typical of such churches as Clonmacnois, Killeshin, Aghadoe (Killarney) and Freshford, while that gem of Irish architecture " Cormac's Chapel," on the Rock of Cashel, ascribed to 1127, shows, in its ruin, a richly-carved doorway, a steeply-pitched stone

BAINBRIDGE, BELFAST

### CASTLE OF THE BLARNEY STONE

*This castle at Blarney, Co. Cork, contains the magic " Blarney Stone." By the simple expedient of kissing the stone one is endowed with the ability to " speak with the tongue of men and of angels." The fortress was built by the MacCarthys, Princes of Desmond, and was at one time considered almost impregnable.*

roof and intricate external and internal ornament. But the latter half of the twelfth century witnessed a change to the large cruciform edifices in the pointed (transitional) style.

The establishment in Ireland, about this time, of the Cistercian Order resulted in the erection of many monastic structures, which even in their ruins today are very beautiful. Mellifont, sweet as its name, was the first such abbey, and owed its establishment, in 1142, to the bounty of Donagh O'Carroll, the Lord of Oriel. What splendour of scene attended its consecration in 1157! Among the royal guests were Tiernan O'Rourke, Prince of Breffni and his wife Devorgilla, whose abduction by Dermot McMurrough, the ill-famed King of Leinster, was the immediate cause of the Anglo-Norman invasion of Ireland. Almost forty years later, after much prayer and penance, this repentant queen returned to die and be buried within the walls of the monastery.

Bective Abbey, not far from Mellifont and very near to Tara, rose four years after the parent house and became an important centre, its abbot being a Lord of Parliament. Today it slumbers, grey-shrouded in peace by the banks of the historic Boyne. And Jerpoint beside the Nore, in Kilkenny, is another such beautiful group of ruins comprising a church, tower, cloisters and several monuments. Perhaps the most elaborate of these foundations was Holy Cross, near

Thurles—if one may judge from the wealth of detail and exquisite features noticeable in the ruin today. It was once a famed place of pilgrimage, for it enshrined a relic of the True Cross, now treasured in the Ursuline Convent in Cork. Hore Abbey, at the foot of the Rock of Cashel, and the cathedral, on the summit, are of this era, the latter being particularly beautiful and most historic.

### Loveliest of Irish Castles

The majority of Irish castles date from the Anglo-Norman span of history and range, in great variety, from the single and simple keep-tower of the invading chieftain to the defensive fortresses—now noticeable in the ruins at Trim, Maynooth, Bunratty, Roscommon and Limerick—and the modernized castles found liberally all over the country. Roscommon, known as " one of the largest and loveliest of Irish castles " was inhabited up to 1691 when it fell in the burnings that followed the Battle of Aughrim. A lovely specimen of the modernized castle is Lismore, overlooking the Blackwater River, in County Waterford. Today the Irish home of the Duke of Devonshire, it stands on a precipitous cliff amid a wealth of foliage that frames its majesty. Another such is storied Malahide Castle, the more than 700-year-old home of the Talbots; and again, Kilkenny, the castle of the Butlers of

Ormonde, on the banks of the " grey-watered " Nore, of which Spenser wrote. Dublin Castle, for more than seven centuries the hub of English rule in Ireland, was erected at the instructions of King John of England, and to this day remains a showplace of the city, although in strict truth, the only portion of the original building extant is the Bermingham Tower, which was used as a State Prison and has its own dread tale of suffering to record. St. Patrick's Cathedral, a very handsome building in the oldest part of the city dates from 1191, but has its chief associations with the eighteenth century.

Drogheda offers a good instance of Anglo-Norman town fortifications. Its walls were strengthened by twenty towers—portions of which still remain, and it was entered by ten gates, of which the only one extant is the impressive St. Lawrence's Gate. This consists of two lofty circular towers of four storeys, between them being a retiring wall pierced, like the towers, with loopholes. Other such fortifications may be identified in their remains at Limerick, Athlone, Drogheda, Clonmel and Waterford.

For place-names of Norman origin, perhaps the most interesting example is Buttevant—in Cork—a corruption of the war cry of the De Barrys—*Boutez-en-avant*—(push forward), in

their attacks and predatory raids around this district.

Tudor days left many a mark inscribed upon the face of Ireland. With the reign of Henry VIII came the dissolution of the monasteries and the confiscation of church lands. Thus were deserted Mellifont, Muckross (in Killarney), Timoleague, Clonmacnois, Durrow, Boyle and a host of other lovely settlements, some of which fell into decay through disuse, some of which were afterwards restored for a brief span and many of which were battered down when they were used as places of refuge and besieged during the numerous battles fought out on Irish soil between the supporters of the Royalist, Roundhead and Williamite sides in the English civil wars of the seventeenth century.

### Sir Walter Raleigh

Wars and rumours of wars on the part of " the rebellious Irish " fill the stretch of Elizabeth's reign in Ireland, and many grim landmarks enshrine their memories. Sir Walter Raleigh, who was given large estates in Munster, introduced the first potato and the first tobacco plants to Ireland. His name is echoed in Youghal, where at his house, Myrtle Grove, he entertained the poet Spenser. One can imagine the Lord Mayor of Youghal (Raleigh) and the Clerk to

BAINBRIDGE, BELFAST

### THE GAP OF DUNLOE, KILLARNEY

*Between Purple Mountain (2,737 feet) and Macgillicuddy's Reeks (3,414 feet), the highest range in Ireland, is this magnificent four-mile long defile. Visitors to Killarney often make the journey through the Gap on ponies. In a valley almost at right angles to it are the Three Lakes, connected by the Long Range Stream.*

the Council of Munster (Spenser) reading, in pleasant Elizabethan gardens by the sea, the manuscripts of *The Faerie Queene*, and perhaps of *Colin Clout's Come Home Again*, a work treasuring many references to Munster scenery. For Spenser spent eight years of his life at Kilcolman Castle, an old Desmond stronghold in Cork. It was sacked and burned over his head by the native Irish whom he hated as sincerely as he loved the natural beauty of their country.

In Dublin city, Elizabethan days are recalled by a lovely group of buildings comprising Trinity College, in the heart of the capital. A charter for the foundation of this university was obtained from the queen in 1591, and the lands of the old Augustinian monastery of All Hallows (established by Dermot McMurrough, in 1166, but suppressed in 1538), were granted by the Mayor and Corporation for the new institution. The original Elizabethan erections have alas, disappeared, the oldest surviving block (1722) being the red brick range on the east side of Library Square.

The queen's favourite, Essex, commanded for a time the queen's forces against the Irish chieftains, O'Neill and O'Donnell, but with disastrous results that led to his fateful breach with the queen and consequent death in the Tower of London. From Blarney Castle, just outside Cork City, and renowned for the " Stone of Eloquence " in its battlements, which many come to kiss

today, Elizabeth derived a new word to add to the English language. " Blarney," or soft talk, referred to the delays and delusive promises of surrender made by its owner, The McCarthy, to Sir George Carew.

Yet another famed Munster Castle was Dunboy, in the Berehaven Peninsula, on the outskirts of the Atlantic. This ancient seat of the O'Sullivans of Bere was almost shattered to pieces by Carew in one of the most obstinate sieges of history, in 1602. Only a portion of the walls now remain, while of the brave defenders not one survived.

### A Pirate Queen

In Western Ireland, in the late sixteenth century, the Corsair Queen, Grace O'Malley (Granuaile), sailed the seas in barques of plunder, a picturesque figure of rude beauty who once called upon Elizabeth's Court (1593) and met her sister queen with calmness and aplomb. Her castles are a feature of the west of Ireland today —strong square keeps of martial aspect. Clare Island was her home and Carrigahooley (Rock of the Fleet) the safe harbour of her pirate galleys.

Cromwell came to Ireland in 1649, to ravage with fire and the sword, the enemies of his dictatorship. For Ireland, with its ever fatal propensity of backing a losing side had, in espousing the Royalist cause, become the final stage of this civil struggle. The Protector's triumphant

BAINBRIDGE, BELFAST

CATHEDRAL OF ST. PATRICK, KILLARNEY

*This cathedral was built in the Gothic style after the design of A. W. N. Pugin. In the north transept is a brass to Bishop Moriarty and the three-light east window was a thank-offering from an Earl of Kenmare for the recovery of his only daughter. It is by far the most distinctive building in the town of Killarney.*

"tour" of Ireland left a tradition of cruelty which earned him undying hatred. His name became a household word of fear. In Drogheda, which he took by storm, with consequent ferocity, the ruins of the Abbey of St. Mary, as well as the once stout walls of the city, bear testimony to the power of his guns. In the Bull Ring, in Wexford Town, some three hundred civilians, mostly women, were slaughtered by the Ironsides. Several places connected with his cruel campaign carry his name today — Cromwell's Arch, in Youghal, Cromwell's Bridge, in Glengarriff (said to have been built, by his order, in an hour), and Cromwell's Rock, on the River Moy, in Mayo.

Cromwell, having broken the back of his Irish campaign, left it in the hands of his son-in-law, Ireton, and returned to England in 1650. In the subsequent successes of his followers, Limerick, Athlone and Galway were stormed and taken, while Ross Castle, a fourteenth-century stronghold of the O'Donoghue's of Kerry, surrendered in 1652—"the last place in Munster to yield." Today it is a handsome ruin fronting the waters of the Lower Lake. The almost perfect keep consists of a splendid square tower with a spiral staircase to the top.

BAINBRIDGE, BELFAST

THE CURFEW TOWER, CUSHENDALL
*From this tower, which stands in the centre of one of the most prettily situated towns in Ulster, the " curfew " is rung every night at seven o'clock. It was originally erected " as a place of confinement for rioters and idlers."*

All around there are places and things woven into the legends of storied Lough Leane and the exploits of the great O'Donoghue, "Donal of the Captives," who was the most famed of the Kerry chieftains. One can see the window in the castle, whence he leaped, charger and all, into the lake beneath, to arise every seventh year on the morning of May Day and, mounted on his white horse, ride over the Kingdom of Kerry. The boatmen of Killarney, rowing over Lough Leane, will point out the Island Library of The O'Donoghue, where shelves of rocks hold slabs of rocks, and his Prison Rock, whereto he chained delinquents and left them to starve— but always he saw to it there was plenty of water.

Many scenes of yet another war—that between Kings James and William—were set in Ireland, the decisive battle of this Stuart strife being fought at the Boyne Water on July 1, 1690. The ford where King William's army crossed to the south bank to close with the Jacobites is just outside Drogheda, and nearby is King William's Glen, a leafy place of memories. In this conflict, too, the city of Derry looms important for its historic siege (1689) which lasted one hundred and five days, and was at long last relieved by the Williamite forces who burst the blockade and rescued the exhausted city. The cathedral in Derry is filled with relics and trophies of that amazing and historical siege.

The last siege of this campaign was Limerick (1691) where on the Treaty Stone (in the town today) the famous Treaty of Limerick was signed. King John's Castle, dating from the early thirteenth century, bears some marks of Williamite guns, but the old and lovely cathedral (St. Mary's) remained intact and stands, a silent witness of eight troubled centuries of history.

Under the Georges, Dublin became a splendid city, ranking second in the Empire, next to London in population, extent and magnificence of buildings. The eighteenth century was her " glorious " age, and to those days date the wide streets and beautiful squares and houses so

years to complete. It suffered severely in the civil hostilities following the Anglo-Irish Treaty, but was restored, with little change in its external appearance.

Many visitors to Dublin regard the Customs House, near O'Connell Bridge, as the city's most beautiful building. It was begun in 1781 and took ten years to build. Leinster House, in Kildare Street, formerly the residence of the Dukes of Leinster and now the Dail or meeting place of the Irish Free State Parliament, was built in 1745 from designs by Cassels, while the Bank of Ireland—until the union in 1800 the Irish House of Parliament—dates from 1729, and

DIXON-SCOTT

THE FOUR COURTS, DUBLIN

*Erected at a cost of £200,000 during the closing years of the eighteenth century, it is one of Ireland's most impressive public buildings. During the Civil War of 1922 it was seized by the Republican leader, Rory O'Connor, and withstood a siege by the Free State forces under Michael Collins. It has since been restored.*

much admired in the Irish capital at the present day. Social gatherings of splendour assembled in the stately Georgian houses—Belvedere House (now a secondary school), Charlemont House (now the Municipal Gallery of Modern Art), and those of Merrion Square, Kildare Street, Stephen's Green, Fitzwilliam Square, Mountjoy Square and Parnell (then Rutland) Square. Many of their walls and ceilings were decorated by Angelica Kauffman.

The City Hall, beside Dublin Castle, was erected in 1769 as the " Royal Exchange." The Four Courts, which is one of Dublin's architectural masterpieces, dates from 1786. This beautiful pile cost £200,000 and took fourteen

is perhaps the proudest proof of eighteenth-century activity in the city. Its east front, with six lofty columns forms one of the most excellent specimens of Corinthian architecture to be seen anywhere.

St. Patrick's Cathedral, though of an earlier age, has eighteenth-century memories of Jonathan Swift its fiery dean " whom fierce indignation lacerated." Goldsmith and Burke are associated with Trinity College, and their statues (by Foley) stand within its railings. Addison lived in Glasnevin, where his house " Addison Lodge " is still to be seen. His favourite walk, along the Tolka Bank, is named " Addison's Walk "; now in the Botanic Gardens. Peg Woffington

DIXON-SCOTT

## THE GUILDHALL OF THE WALLED CITY OF LONDONDERRY

*Some of the stained-glass windows of this building were presented by the London Companies. It was in 1613 that a charter was granted to certain London trade guilds, grouped as the Irish Society, whereby they became owners of large tracts of Ulster, including Derry, which then added London to its ancient name.*

W. F. TAYLOR

### THE LOFTY CLIFFS OF MOHER
*These rugged cliffs in Co. Clare rise sheer out of the water to a height of 700 feet and extend for five miles. During rough weather the Atlantic waves, higher here than anywhere in the world except Cape Horn, present an enthralling spectacle as they thunder against the rocks. Moher is a veritable bird-lover's paradise.*

acted in Smock Alley theatre ; Handel played on the old organ in St. Michan's. The Royal Dublin Society was founded (1731) for the advancement of industry, agriculture, arts and crafts ; the Royal and Grand Canals were constructed and a service of mail packets introduced between Dublin and Holyhead. In effect, the main features of the plan and arrangement of modern Dublin may be said to begin from an Act of the Irish Parliament of 1757 appointing " Commissioners for making a wide and convenient street from the Essex Bridge to the Castle of Dublin." The ample accommodation built at the Docks is yet another testimony to the very far-seeing policy and sound judgment of the eighteenth-century town planners.

#### Fear of Invasion

To the eighteenth century also, when fear of French naval invasion was rife (and not without cause), belong the many Martello towers which one sees along the Irish coastline, particularly on the east front. Ugly and little-used structures, their purpose was to anticipate attack by fortifying the coast. Those standing at Sandycove, on Dalkey Island, and at Malahide are good examples of the type.

With the Act of Union, in 1800, Dublin ceased to be an independent capital, the seat of Government and the home of a resident aristocracy.

In the nineteenth century, cut off from the mainspring of government, industry and commerce, the city wilted into decay, amid the elegancies of its former independence. This decline was hastened by the opening up of outlying districts by rail and train in the nineteenth century, so that handsome suburbs grew up amid sea and mountains, but at the expense of the city. However, since the establishment of the Irish Free State as a separate political entity (1922) having its independent legislature, the city has thriven, and now bids fair to becoming as handsome and prosperous as, and a great deal more representative of its hinterland than the eighteenth-century capital.

Danes, Normans, English and the original Gaels—these have left most marks upon the face of Ireland today. One can read the story of her rough-hewn destiny in the many monuments of ancient times, and of medieval and modern centuries which are scattered in such rich profusion over her plains and mountains and in the heart of her deep-wooded glens. She has watched the battle smoke of many long centuries drift across the screen of troubled time. She has known trouble and distress and the bitterness of internecine strife. May she have at last emerged, triumphant if somewhat scathed, to reach, in quiet confidence, safe harbour, hard-won but long-enduring !

# BRITAIN OF THE NOVELISTS

## *by* E. A. BAKER

LANDSCAPE in fiction is a comparatively modern development. Fielding and Richardson, Jane Austen and Thackeray, had of course to describe the scenes in which their dramas were played out ; and their novels show what this country looked like in those days, especially in its human aspects, streets and buildings, towns and villages, roads and inns, and the variegated population to be found there. But it was not till the Romantic period that novelists employed landscape, not merely for stage scenery, but to provide a background having a vital function in the play itself.

People were beginning to appreciate the beauty and to feel the emotional power of external nature. It was the great era of the search for the picturesque. Novelists as well as poets perceived how the natural setting might be made to harmonize with the feeling dominant in a story ; it might be shown even that natural surroundings exercised a profound influence on the minds and actions of those whose lot is pitched in a certain spot, till eventually Thomas Hardy made the woodlands and wildernesses of his Wessex one of the dramatis personæ, the protagonist, or at any rate a principal character, in certain novels, not merely determining the material circumstances, but actually working upon and moulding the very souls of the woodlanders and the dwellers on Egdon Heath. Thus the novelists, better perhaps even than the poets, have produced a descriptive literature which is a graphic counterpart to the work of our great national painters in water colour or on canvas. We cannot go every day to a picture gallery ; but we can sit in an armchair and read our territorial novelists, and easily conjure up a vision of any part of Britain, as revealed by the observant and sensitive eye of an artist in words.

" Territorial " is the word, for a large number have applied themselves to the delineation of human life and incidentally of the visible surroundings in areas that they have annexed as their special provinces. Scott made a more

W. F. TAYLOR

## A DICKENS INN IN KENT

*Several miles from Rochester, and close to the great house that once was the seat of the Earls of Darnley, is the village of Cobham. Many relics of Dickens are to be found in the Leather Bottle Inn, for the great novelist put the house in his most famous book and, nearby, Mr. Pickwick found his wonderful inscribed stone.*

W F. TAYLOR

## LINK WITH A MEREDITH HEROINE

*George Meredith lived for many years at Flint Cottage, below Box Hill, in Surrey. The lovely Crossways Farm, near Abinger Hammer, suggested the title for his novel " Diana of the Crossways." Another great writer lived and died nearby for, on Wotton Hill stands the home of John Evelyn, the famous diarist.*

lasting conquest of his own land, including the Highlands, than his contemporary Napoleon did of Europe ; he was followed by Stevenson, Neil Munro, John Buchan, and many others, including William Black, who exploited the West Highlands and the Hebrides as a picturesque stage for his love tales, and " Fiona Macleod," who was really William Sharp, in his romances and visionary stories of the Western Isles.

### Lakeland Scenes

Galt set a similar example, though in a different spirit, in his novels and tales of the Lowlands, to be followed by Crockett, Ian Maclaren, and scores of others. Scott crossed the Border and invaded Northumberland, in *Redgauntlet* ; and, later on, R. H. Forster and J. H. Pease applied intensive culture to the same shire. Cumberland and the Lakes, still not without a lead from Sir Walter, have been the scenes for such an historical study as Collingwood's *Thorstein of the Mere*, for such a masterpiece of local characterization as Ollivant's *Owd Bob*, and for many of the social novels of Mrs. Humphry Ward.

Wales and the Welsh Marches served as a happy hunting-ground for Owen Rhoscomyl, Allen Raine, W. E. Tirebuck, Watts-Dunton, and Mary Webb. Down in " Wessex," Hardy was not a solitary potentate, for Baring-Gould and Eden Phillpotts, in a series of novels, made a conquest of Dartmoor, and Exmoor was subdued by Whyte Melville, in that fine novel *Katerfelto*, and by Blackmore in *Lorna Doone*. Baring-Gould forayed all over the west country, laying his plots in various definite localities from Devon and Cornwall even to the salt-marches of East Anglia ; whilst J. H. Harris and J. H. Pearce concentrated upon Cornwall, which was also the scene of memorable stories by the versatile " Q."

Yorkshire, especially the West Riding, has been the theatre of events in numerous novels and tales, from the time of the Brontës and Mrs. Gaskell to J. K. Snowden and Halliwell Sutcliffe, J. S. Fletcher and Mary Linskill, to name but a few. George Eliot with her " Dutch painting " left the finest gallery of pictures of the English midlands. Meredith enables us still to wander over the Surrey heaths and the woods and rich valleys of southern England, as they were before modernism invaded, though he was in no sense a territorial novelist.

Then, how many later novelists have depicted towns as well as countrysides, chief among them Arnold Bennett, with his *Five Towns*, and subsequently his admirable studies of life in London. Dickens was the first to portray the multitudinous life of that tremendous hive, and his pictures are unrivalled, though in his case idealism, sentimentalism, and sheer grotesquerie were at war with truth. Gissing and Bennett and innumerable others were to give different aspects, whilst for a Rembrandtesque vision there is nothing to compare with Conrad's *Secret Agent*. Ireland, also, has yielded a like harvest of native fiction, depicting every province and every county. Our territorial novelists have been followed by a host of Americans, as the names of Bret Harte, C. E. Craddock, Irving Bacheller, Mary Deland, Zona Gale, Mrs. Catherwood, etc., etc., remind us.

The French, on the other hand, gave us a lead, rather than the other way about ; Balzac, Maupassant, Daudet, and minor writers like Erckmann-Chatrian and André Theuriet, have profoundly influenced successively Dickens, Bennett, and many others who have concentrated upon certain places and certain tracts, with their human inhabitants only, unconsciously, yet none the less deeply, conditioned by the circumstances of time and place.

The grand original exemplar, for writers in English and for the foreigners, was Sir Walter Scott. He began it in his first novel, *Waverley*, which was primarily historical romance, but gave the Saxon reader an introduction to the jolly Lowland world centring in the Baron of Bradwardine's mansion of Tully-Veolan, took the same reader to the famous Holyrood ball, and on a trip into the rebellious Highlands. In the second, *Guy Mannering*, he was more intimate, more actual, and much more vivid. Who can ever forget who has once read it the entrancing account of the adventures in Galloway, quite apart from the fascinations of Dandie Dinmont, Dominie Sampson, and Meg Merrilies ; the romantic scenery of barren moorlands, dangerous coast, and ruined castles is rendered dramatic by the incidents with which it is indelibly associated? It is also the same with Forfarshire in *The Antiquary*, and with a broad stretch of the Lowlands in *Old Mortality*.

### To the Highlands

In *Rob Roy* Scott carries us on a fascinating journey into the Highlands round Aberfoyle and Loch Lomond, almost on the same trail as in *The Lady of the Lake*, which is often said to have introduced Highland scenery to the southron. It was not, however, by the magic of an evocative pen that Scott made descriptions of scenery

STEPHENSON

#### THE SCENE OF TOM BROWN'S CHILDHOOD
*The author of that great favourite of many boyhoods, " Tom Brown's Schooldays," spent his childhood at Uffington, in the Vale of the White Horse. Here, in the midst of this beauty, he made Squire Brown live and deal out justice in a rough way and beget sons and daughters and hunt the fox and grumble at the times.*

live. After all, his prose is lumbering and matter of fact. What made telling such episodes as the journey of Andrew Fairservice and the Bailie Nicol Jarvie into Rob Roy's country was a different sort of magic, that of canny personalities hobnobbing together, the incessant humour, and the contrast of town-bred respectability with the manners of the mountaineers, as yet untamed children of the wild. As the Bailie well knew, the proverb still held good then : " Forth bridles the wild Highlandman " ; and unfortunately for him he had to cross the Forth.

Never since I was a lad have I dipped into Scott's *Pirate*, one of his feeblest stories ; but the

pictures, pictures of places, and of persons identified with certain places for evermore. This is a far better policy than his set pieces, which sometimes seem to suggest that Scott did not fully appreciate the essence of the beauties that he is describing. Here is one, for instance, in which he seems to mean that the tame opulence of a Thames-side park is more than equal to the natural grandeur of Argyllshire. Scott hits the nail on the head, but it is the wrong nail.

> The carriage rolled rapidly onwards through fertile meadows, ornamented with splendid old oaks, and catching occasionally a glance of a broad and placid river. After passing through a pleasant village, the equipage stopped on a commanding eminence, where

STEPHENSON

### WHERE TRAGIC TESS WAS MARRIED

*The glorious stretch of country from Wareham to Dorchester is redolent of Thomas Hardy. In the little church of West Stafford, poor, tragic Tess of the D'Urbervilles married her Angel Clare. The wind-swept uplands of Purbeck and the grim, grand waste of Egdon Heath breathe the spirit of Hardy's Wessex.*

impressions it left of Orkney and Shetland scenery are still vivid, though I have not had a chance of comparing them with the originals. But as Scott says, in one of his most romantic tales, the *Legend of Montrose*, " those who journey in days of doubt and dread pay little attention to picturesque scenery." Accordingly, he talks trippingly of beautiful sheets of water, steep, precipitous acclivities, and broken paths overhung by fragments of huge rock ; but actually leaves images of wild and solemn grandeur imprinted on the mind by the simple expedient of combining the scene with the dramatic event. Hence *Redgauntlet*, *The Heart of Midlothian*, *St. Ronan's Well*, in fact every one of the Waverley novels is catalogued in our mind as a bundle of

the beauty of English landscape was displayed in its utmost luxuriance. Here the Duke alighted, and desired Jeanie to follow him. They paused for a moment on the brow of a hill, to gaze on the unrivalled landscape which it presented. A huge sea of verdure, with crossing and intersecting promontories of massive and tufted groves, was tenanted by numberless flocks and herds, which seemed to wander unrestrained through the rich pastures. The Thames, here turreted with villas and there garlanded with forest, moved on slowly and placidly, like the mighty monarch of the scene, to whom all its other beauties were but accessories, and bore on its bosom an hundred barks and skiffs, whose white sails and gaily fluttering pennons gave life to the whole.

The Duke, according to Scott, was familiar with the scene, but yet to a man of his taste it was always new. As he gazed on this " inimitable landscape " his thoughts turned to his

W. F. TAYLOR

## THE GREEN HEART OF EXMOOR

*Though Watersmeet, in the Doone Valley, has become almost a crowded beauty spot, nothing can destroy the magic of that wild glen. Within a stone's throw there are places like this, and the valley goes on mysteriously into the moor leaving the sweet woods of Lorna's love meetings for the savage haunts of Carver.*

R.B.—N

Highland home of Inveraray. "This is a fine scene," he said to his companion; "we have nothing like it in Scotland."

Jeanie was not prepared to agree with the Duke.

"It's braw rich feeding for the cows, and they have a fine breed o' cattle here," replied Jeanie; "but I like just as weel to look at the craigs of Arthur's Seat, and the sea coming in ayont them, as at a' thae muckle trees."

No, Scott fell flat in his formal description of scenery, and but for his drama the glamour of those wonderful peregrinations in glen and mountain would have been lost. A great story-teller and one of the very greatest creators of human character, he was singularly lacking in the literary arts by which a lesser artist such as Stevenson could make the reader, not only see a wild landscape, but also feel the wind blowing, and with it all the poetry and romance with which a quick and sensitive soul was thrilled.

John Galt, a few years later, drew Lowland life, especially in Ayrshire, with a vivid pen, but rarely turned an eye on the scenery. In one of his novels, however, *The Ayrshire Legatees*, his method was peripatetic, and it is amusing to quote a passage comparing a view of London with that of Edinburgh. The legatees, old Dr. Pringle and the son who keeps the diary have landed at Gravesend and approach the capital.

The old gentleman's admiration of the increasing signs of what he called civilization, as we approached

London, became quite eloquent; but the first view of the city from Blackheath (which, by the bye, is a fine common, surrounded with villas and handsome houses) overpowered his faculties and I shall never forget the impression it made on myself. The sun was declined towards the horizon; vast masses of dark low-hung clouds were mingled with the smoky canopy, and the dome of St. Paul's, like the enormous idol of some terrible deity, throned amidst the smoke of sacrifices and magnificence, darkness, and mystery, presented altogether an object of vast sublimity. I felt touched with reverence, as if I was indeed approaching the city of "The Human Powers."

The speaker goes on to say that, although the distant view of Edinburgh is picturesque and romantic, "it affects a lower class of our association." Compared to London, Edinburgh is what the poem of the *Seasons* is with respect to *Paradise Lost* or what the castellated descriptions of Scott are to the *Darkness* of Byron.

In the approach to Edinburgh, leisure and cheerfulness are on the road; large spaces of rural and pastoral nature are spread openly around, and mountains, and seas, and headlands, and vessels passing beyond them, going like those that die, we know not whither, while the sun is bright on their sails, and hope with them; but in coming to this Babylon, there is an eager haste and a hurrying on from all quarters, towards that stupendous pile of gloom, through which no eye can penetrate; an unceasing sound, like the enginery of an earthquake at work, rolls from the heart of that profound and indefinable obscurity—sometimes a faint and yellow beam of the sun strikes here and there on the vast expanse of edifices; and churches, and holy asylums, are dimly seen lifting up their countless steeples and spires, like so many lightning rods to avert the wrath of Heaven.

W. F. TAYLOR

### THE COUNTRY OF MARY WEBB

*Lord Baldwin has the credit for bringing Mary Webb's books to general notice but, to the few, her writing had long been known. The country of her books was the last western outposts of England where the hills of Wales lie grape-blue in the distance. This view from the Longmynd is typical of Mary Webb's Shropshire.*

STEPHENSON

### LOVELINESS BEWITCHED

*Harrison Ainsworth choose to place the scene of one of his most macabre novels, " The Lancashire Witches,"*
*in one of those beautiful stretches of Lancashire that rub shoulders today with gaunt industrialism. Downham,*
*in the lovely Ribble Valley, is the gem of that wide green dale, that stretches from Yorkshire to the sea.*

One must allow for the grandiloquence of the young Edinburgh reviewer, and also for the lapse of time which has washed the steeples clean and dissipated the smoke clouds, to make this tally with the view of London from Blackheath today.

When we think of Dickens's London, it is of an almost fabulous wilderness of streets, courts, alleys, grim old churches, mouldy old inns and taverns, cheerily lighted up at night, and sinister houses, such as Quilp's hideous lair, the appointed scenes for murder and villainy. Yet he too, like Scott, rarely indulged in set description : it is almost always the union of dramatic, or melodramatic, events with a certain spot that imprints

STEP IENSON

## IN THE BORDERLAND OF SCOTT

*Sir Walter Scott immortalized the Cheviots in prose and poetry, and Langleeford, under the shadow of the Cheviot (2,676 feet), remains peculiarly part of the Scott country. Through the countless narrow glens and over the hills above Langleeford, the writer's heroes strode, and gave romance to the wild and lovely places.*

the local features indelibly on our imagination. But here is half a page from *Barnaby Rudge* giving another entry into London; this time it is Gabriel Varden, who in spite of promises to his wife has just left a snug corner at the "Maypole," and is almost nodding in his dog sleep after putting down more than was good for him.

> And now he approached the great city which lay outstretched before him like a dark shadow on the ground, reddening the sluggish air with a deep dull light, that told of labyrinths of public ways and shops, and swarms of busy people. Approaching nearer and nearer yet, this halo began to fade, and the causes which produced it slowly to develop themselves. Long lines of poorly lighted streets might be faintly traced, with here and there a lighter spot, where lamps were clustered round a square or market, or round some great building; after a time these grew more distinct, and the lamps themselves were visible; slight yellow specks, that seemed to be rapidly snuffed out, one by one, as intervening obstacles hid them from the sight. Then sounds arose—the striking of church clocks, the distant bark of dogs, the hum of traffic in the streets; then outlines might be traced—tall steeples looming in the air, and piles of unequal roots oppressed by chimneys; then, the noise swelled into a louder sound, and forms grew more distinct and numerous still, and London—visible in the darkness by its own faint light, and not by that of Heaven—was at hand. The locksmith, however, all unconscious of its near vicinity, still jogged on, half sleeping and half waking, when a loud cry at no great distance ahead, roused him with a start.

Dickens too, you notice, cannot do without the incident, which gives magic to what already

has a glamour of its own. In another moment Gabriel comes upon the witling Barnaby, bending with a torch over the body of a man who has been stabbed and may be alive or dead. In *Nicholas Nickleby*, Dickens takes his hero on a long stage journey to Greta Bridge, Barnard Castle and Bowes. But, until we arrive at that mythical establishment of Mr. Squeers, Dotheboys Hall, almost the only thing we remember of the journey is the snowstorm at Grantham and the accident half-way to Newark when Nicholas feels the vehicle turning over and is relieved of all uncertainty whether it will do so or not by being flung into the road. And on the way back, the only thing we remember of Boroughbridge is that he could not get a bed there, and after a night in the corner of a barn he wakes up to find himself face to face with poor Smike.

But the classic pictures of those parts are of course to be found in the novels of the Brontë sisters. *Jane Eyre* and *Shirley* are so full of them that it is hard to choose; but Jane's walk over the hills from Thornfield to Hay, when she went slowly " to enjoy and analyse the species of pleasure brooding in the hour and situation " gives the very countenance of the West Riding.

> I was a mile from Thornfield, in a lane noted for wild roses in summer, for nuts and blackberries in autumn, and even now possessing a few coral treasures in hips and haws but whose best winter delight lay in

its utter solitude and leafless repose. If a breath of air stirred, it made no sound here; for there was not a holly, not an evergreen to rustle and the stripped hawthorn and hazel bushes were as still as the white, worn stones which causewayed the middle of the path.

It was freezing keenly as was attested by a sheet of ice covering the causeway where a little brook which was then frozen had overflowed after a thaw a few days previously. Jane, however, gathering her mantle about her, did not feel the cold.

From my seat I could look down on Thornfield: the grey and battlemented hall was the principal object in the vale below me; its woods and dark rookery rose against the west. I lingered till the sun went down amongst the trees, and sank crimson and clear behind them. I then turned eastward. On the hill-top above me sat the rising moon; pale yet as a cloud, but brightening momently: she looked over Hay, which, half lost in trees, sent up a blue smoke from its few chimneys; it was yet a mile distant, but in the absolute hush I could hear plainly its thin murmures of life. My ear too felt the flow of currents; in what dales and depths I could not tell: but there were many hills beyond Hay, and doubtless many becks threading their passes. That evening calm betrayed alike the tinkle of the nearest streams, the sough of the most remote.

That peaceful scene, touched with Wordsworthian beauty, is a contrast to the harsher prospects which Charlotte's sister, Emily Brontë, found most congenial, and amid which she placed her Wuthering Heights, the grim abode of Mr. Heathcliff — " Wuthering," as she explained,

" being a significant provincial adjective, descriptive of the atmospheric tumult to which its station is exposed in stormy weather."

Pure, bracing ventilation they must have up there at all times, indeed: one may guess the power of the north wind blowing over the edge, by the excessive slant of a few stunted firs at the end of the house; and by a range of gaunt thorns all stretching their limbs one way, as if craving alms of the sun. Happily, the architect had foresight to build it strong: the narrow windows are deeply set in the wall, and the corners defended with large jutting stones.

The cramped and gloomy interior, with its primitive, high-backed furniture, is a fit theatre for the most austere drama of love and hate in English fiction.

Another Romantic revival was beginning, and presently the two Kingsleys were to give the world such chronicles of adventure as *Westward Ho!* and *Ravenshoe*, and starting their young heroes on chequered careers from some port or other in the west country. Charles Kingsley's famous tale opens at Bideford, and the lineaments of the old town strike the right keynote.

All who have travelled through the delicious scenery of North Devon must needs know the little white town of Bideford, which slopes upwards from its broad tide-river paved with yellow sands, and many-arched old bridge where salmon wait for autumn floods, toward the pleasant upland on the west. Above the town the hills close in, cushioned with deep oak woods, through which juts here and there a crag of fern-fringed slate;

EDGAR WARD

### STEVENSON'S HOLIDAY HOME
*For a period of fourteen years, from 1867 till 1881, Robert Louis Stevenson went with his parents to the Pentland village of Swanston for his holidays each year. It is near Edinburgh and the soft Midlothian countryside saw the early promise of the frail genius who left his native land only to die on a Pacific isle.*

below they lower, and open more and more in softly-rounded knolls, and fertile squares of red and green, till they sink into the wide expanse of hazy flats, rich salt-marshes, and rolling sand-hills, where Torridge joins her sister Taw, and both together flow quietly toward the broad surges of the bar, and the everlasting thunder of the long Atlantic swell. Pleasantly the old town stands there, beneath its soft Italian sky, fanned day and night by the fresh ocean breeze, which forbids alike the keen winter frosts, and the fierce thunder heats of the midland; and pleasantly it has stood there for now, perhaps, eight hundred years, since the first Grenvil, cousin of the Conqueror, returning from the conquest of South Wales, drew round him trusty Saxon serfs, and free Norse rovers with their golden curls, and dark Silurian Britons from the Swansea shore, and all the mingled blood which still gives to the seaward folk of the next county their strength and intellect, and, even in these levelling days, their peculiar beauty of face and form.

Not less enchanting, though it is set in the moorlands and not by the sea, is Blackmore's farmstead above the meeting-place of the Bagworthy Water and the Lynn.

> Almost everybody knows, in our part of the world at least, how pleasant and soft the fall of the land is round about Plover's Barrow farm. All above it is strong dark mountain, spread with heath, and desolate, but near our house the valleys cove, and open warmth and shelter. Here are trees, and bright green grass, and orchards full of contentment, and a man may scarce espy the brook, although he hears it everywhere. And indeed a stout good piece of it comes through our farm-yard, and swells sometimes to a rush of waves, when the clouds are on the hill-tops. But all below, where the valley bends, and the Lynn stream goes along with

it, pretty meadows slope their breast, and the sun spreads on the water. And nearly all this is ours, till you come to Nicholas Snow's land.

It is a temptation to go on quoting, though there are passages in *Perlycross*, *Springhaven*, *Clara Vaughan* and *Christowell* that are just as challenging.

But all west country novelists are thrown into the shade by Thomas Hardy, by his sheer descriptive power as well as by the dramatic qualities of his work. *Under the Greenwood Tree*, *A Pair of Blue Eyes*, *Far from the Madding Crowd*, *The Return of the Native* and *The Woodlanders*, are the richest in poetic transcripts of scenery and their eloquent expression of the influence surroundings exert upon the mind of man. Hardy's rustics, through lifelong communion, become part and parcel of their natural environment. They may be unconscious of their intimacy, unless like Grace Melbury or Clym Yeobright they have been educated and refined beyond the ordinary range of the peasants. But Giles Winterborne lives so intensely with the seasons that he looks like Autumn's brother, and even stolid Gabriel Oak is roused to something like philosophic insight by the spectacle of a star-lit night. One could go on quoting for ever from the Wessex novels; but every one knows them, and a little vignette of the hamlet in which the action centres in *The Woodlanders* must suffice.

> Thus they rode on, and High-Stoy Hill grew larger ahead. At length could be discerned in the dusk,

A. A. MACGREGOR

BIRTHPLACE OF ROB ROY

*Here at the head of the lovely Loch Katrine we are back in the country of Sir Walter Scott. In Glen Gyle, seen above, was born Robert MacGregor or Campbell, the red-haired outlaw and cattle-thief, who is better known as the doughty Rob Roy in Scott's novel of that name. He died in 1734 and is buried at Balquhidder.*

A. A MACGREGOR

## BATTLEGROUND OF THE LITTLE WARS OF LORN

*Neil Munro's name is unforgettable in Scottish literature and here, in Glen Etive, he laid many scenes of his grand book " John Splendid." The tragic valley of Glencoe, too, comes into the story but it was here that the " seven broken men " retreated from the defeat at Inverlochy, ever harried by the pursuit of the Macdonalds.*

about half a mile to one side, gardens and orchards sunk in a concave, and, as it were, snipped out of the woodland. From this self-contained place rose in stealthy silence tall stems of smoke, which the eye of imagination could trace downward to their root in quiet hearthstones, festooned overhead with hams and flitches. It was one of those sequestered spots outside the gates of the world where may usually be found more meditation than action, and more listlessness than meditation ; where reasoning proceeds on narrow premises, and results in inferences wildly imaginative ; yet where, from time to time, dramas of a grandeur truly Sophoclean are enacted in the real, by virtue of the concentrated passions and closely-knit interdependence of the lives therein.

### Welsh Borderland

Mary Webb applied some small measure of the same vitalizing imagination in her histories of girls and lovers and wedded pairs, dwelling face to face with Nature, in Shropshire villages or in spots along the Welsh border. *Gone to Earth*, for instance, is the life story of a motherless child of the mountains ; and both *The House in Dormer Forest* and *Seven for a Secret*, not to mention the well-known *Precious Bane*, by arts akin to Hardy's, bring out the contrast between those calm souls who are in harmony with their everlasting neighbours, the woods and hills, and the sensual and brutal people, or those whose materialist religion shuts their minds to what are truly the things of the spirit. Even the most masterly descriptive pages would be mere rhetoric

and embellishment without this deeper meaning.

Hence, too, those who are attuned feel themselves in touch with something beyond mere romance when they read such pages as the flight in the heather, in Stevenson's *Kidnapped*, or John Splendid's adventures in the wilds of Glen Etive and Glencoe and on the fringes of the Muir of Rannoch, in that one of Neil Munro's Highland novels which most closely rivals Stevenson's. The same feeling is experienced in reading the Stevensonian, and more than Stevensonian, stories of him whom we still like to call John Buchan. As to the other Scots writers, those of the "Kail-yard School," the aim of Crockett, Ian Maclaren, and a dozen others, including the late Sir James Barrie, was not in the least romantic. They were of the family of John Galt and Susan Ferrier, and their object was to hit off idiosyncrasies of manners and temperament, with more kindness than malice, more sentiment than satire.

When they described a place, a house, a town, a village, it was simply like arranging the furniture for a tea-drinking or an evening party. This is not to deny that they are quotable ; but to quote would be never to stop, so racy and comic are the dialogue, narrative, and description, all in one. But they must assuredly not be overlooked in any study of the novelists as portrait-makers of the face of Britain as well as of Britons.

W. F. TAYLOR

## A WINDING ROAD OF THE DALES

*Many of our roads have adapted themselves to the lie of the land, following the valleys, seeking low places where it was necessary to cross the hills, and frequently making wide detours to avoid natural obstacles. Above, the road is seen winding through the valley of Milldale, in Derbyshire, curving gently with the line of the dale.*

# THE MAKING OF THE ROADS

## *by* GEORGE BAKER

THE study of the roads is a fascinating subject, and once our interest is roused we are led by it through the length and breadth of the land, not merely along the busy highways, but in narrow winding lanes and on downland tracks and half-forgotten paths and bridleways which once were very important thoroughfares.

"The road," says Hilaire Belloc, "is silent; it is the humblest and most subtle, but, as I have said, the greatest and the most original of the spells which we inherit from the earliest pioneers of our race. It was the most imperative and the first of our necessities. It is older than building and than wells; before we were quite men we knew it, for the animals still have it today; they seek their food and their drinking-places, and, as I believe, their assemblies, by known tracks which they have made."

The earliest inhabitants of Britain, the hunters of the Stone Age, doubtless had their trackways, not made roads, but paths trodden out by their naked feet. But these we cannot hope to trace. Neolithic men, we know, mined for flint at Cissbury Ring, in Sussex, and at Grimes Graves, in Norfolk, and it is likely that to and from these places there was a constant journeying of early traders.

In the Bronze Age there was evidently in addition to inland trading some measure of overseas commerce, and attempts have been made to trace within our shores the routes followed by these prehistoric traders. One line of attack has been to link up on the map the places at which

STEPHENSON

### WARDEN OF THE MARCHES
*On the line of the Border at Bloodybush in the Cheviots stands this landmark. It gives the distances to various places and the tolls on what is now a grass-grown road.*

certain objects such as Irish gold ornaments have been found. From evidence of this kind it has been assumed there was a prehistoric way from Anglesey to the Severn, down that valley, then over Salisbury Plain and by the Avon Valley to Christchurch on the south coast, where the traders crossed to the Continent.

With such reasoning it must be remembered that the travellers would not be using a metalled road, and, however well trodden, much of it must have disappeared in the intervening centuries. Therefore, all that can be assumed is a general line of movement and not an existing recognizable way.

On the chalk uplands, however, we are on safer ground, for they have a tendency to register with surprising permanence any disturbance of their surface and to yield to the observant traces of the movements and activities of the prehistoric denizens of the downs.

One track accepted as dating from the Bronze Age, if not from Neolithic times, is the Ridgeway, running along the Berkshire Downs from the Thames, at Streatley, and on to Avebury, in Wiltshire. For about forty out of the forty-five miles of its length, this ancient way is still a downland track with not a village and scarcely a house along its line. Round Barrows are frequent by the wayside, and there are also a number of important earthworks.

Across the Thames this route is continued along the Chilterns and on to the Wash, near Hunstanton, in Norfolk, while beyond Avebury are indications of an extension towards the coast.

STEPHENSON

### GREEN TRACKS OF PREHISTORIC MAN

*The earliest known roads are the trackways along the uplands. Probably one of the oldest of these is the Ridgeway which runs from the Thames at Streatley along the Berkshire and Wiltshire Downs to the prehistoric temple at Avebury. Above, the Ridgeway is seen, with the earthworks of Uffington Castle in the background.*

Avebury and Stonehenge and the innumerable burial mounds indicate that Salisbury Plain was the important centre of the times. The extensive chalk uplands made a desirable place of settlement and the radiating ridges above the forests and marshes were natural routes for the traveller, and so the Plain was the Bronze Age Rome of Britain to which all roads led.

Other ancient tracks, still traceable in places, link the region with the Mendips and the Cotswolds, and with Cornwall and the south-west. Southwards routes would lead to the prehistoric ports of the South Coast, eastwards ran the Harrow Way to Farnham, in Surrey, whence this line was extended along the North Downs through Surrey and Kent by the track now known as the Pilgrims' Way.

So along these converging routes, we may picture the passage of prehistoric folk down to this early mecca, as it has been termed, some for trading purposes, some for religious rites of an unknown nature, and some, it is safe to assume, conveniently combining religion and commerce.

Almost certainly it was the desire to trade direct with Scandinavia for supplies of amber that led to the making of the Fosse Way which runs northward from the south Devon coast towards Lincoln and the Humber. Parts of the trackway lay through marshlands and swamps, across which it was carried by wattles placed over faggots. Road-making, as such, had begun.

Among others of these prehistoric trade routes were the Icknield Way which can still be traced

from Wiltshire through Berkshire and so by way of Cambridgeshire to Suffolk and Norfolk, those lands of the ancient Iceni, from which, it is likely, the Icknield Way took its name.

### The Road to the North

A trackway led northward, fringing the fens, to the plain on which York now stands : on part of this the Romans laid Ermine Street. Peddars Way was probably a trackway of the Bronze and Iron Ages, before the Romans re-made it as a military road after the revolt of the Iceni under Boudicca. It ran through Suffolk and Norfolk to a harbour on the Wash which coastal erosion has now swept away. Very few traces remain of the tracks which in Celtic times must have provided cross communications between the villages of the Yorkshire Plain and those of Lancashire. One of these must have crossed the Pennines by the Aire Gap, but almost all indications of it have vanished as completely as the men who trod it.

Pedlars must have travelled by these trackways; for at points along them goods which they carried and which they buried in some emergency have been unearthed. Bronze axe-heads and spearheads, swords and bracelets, were among the goods which they bartered to the men of the villages. Chariot traffic, too, must have been considerable in the period immediately before the Roman era. From many of the round burial mounds found by the side of the trackways have been dug up the bones of warriors buried with the wheels of their chariots and the harness of their horses.

With the commencement of the Roman occupation of Britain in A.D. 43, a new epoch began in the history of the country's roads. Like Topsy, the trackways of the Celts had "just growed." There was nothing Topsy-like about the Roman roads whose making, in Hilaire Belloc's words, "was the one great initiative in the story of English communications."

With the Romans conquest and road-making went hand in hand. After every battle the men of the legions exchanged their short swords and javelins for shovels and picks. Each legionary was a trained road-maker, and every unit had its skilled engineers. The men first dug trenches on each side of the projected road, and then excavated the soil between until ground firm enough to make the foundations was reached. The road itself was built up in five or six layers : sand or fine earth made the first; quarried stones as big as a man's fist and rubble mixed with lime followed ; then came gravel, chalk and even broken earthenware ; more quarried stones and sandy earth completed the work, and the whole was made firm by ramming.

The road, when finished, was a causeway raised slightly above the level of the surrounding country, so that the troops using it might be less liable to attack. Its somewhat higher centre enabled water to drain into the ditches on either side. It was built as straight as possible to lessen the risk of ambushes, and to aid the progress of baggage wagons which, having no movable joint between the two pairs of wheels, could turn only with difficulty when loaded.

To achieve such straightness the Roman engineers had to build causeways over marshland, throw bridges over rivers, and drive cuttings through hill-crests. Even estuaries did not deter them. Thus, the Roman road in the north which followed the Lincolnshire ridge struck the Humber where it is a mile and a half wide, and continued on the farther bank, the troops being ferried across.

## Roman Highways

As the Roman hold on the country grew firmer, new roads were made or the old trackways taken over and remade, for the purpose of developing Britain's mineral resources. Silchester, forty-five miles from London, was a great road junction from which Roman highways led to the Mendips and their lead and copper mines, to Gloucester and South Wales and their iron, to Cornwall and its tin. Also passing through Silchester on its way to Winchester and Old Sarum, and so on to Dorchester and Exeter, was the Portway—probably one of the earlier of the Roman roads, since a brick found in its layers was marked with the stamp of Nero, Emperor from A.D. 54-68.

DIXON-SCOTT

### AS CROW FLIES AND ROMAN MARCHED
*The Fosse, second of the Four Ways made by our Roman conquerors, ran across England from Lincoln to Devon. In places, the character of the ancient road is still preserved and here is a section near Northleach, in Gloucestershire. Under Edward the Confessor, the Four Ways were protected by the " King's peace."*

FELTON

## MILESTONE TWO THOUSAND YEARS OLD

*This Roman milestone at Chesterholm, in Northumberland, stands on the Stanegate, a military road probably made by Agricola in the first century to link a chain of forts before the building of Hadrian's Wall. A number of other milestones have been found along this road, some bearing names of different emperors. Nearby is the Roman fort of Vindolanda, which was garrisoned by the Fourth Cohort of Gauls and was rebuilt about A.D. 370.*

STEPHENSON

## ROAD OF ROMAN LEGIONS

*On Wheeldale Moor, south-west of Whitby, the turf has been removed to reveal this Roman road which probably ran from York to the coast. The road is sixteen feet wide and raised above the surface of the ground and culverts and side gutter can be seen. The spaces between the stones were originally filled with gravel or earth. Locally the road is known as Wade's Causeway or Old Wife's Trod, and it may be of pre-Roman origin.*

Watling Street, begun earlier still, went from Dover to Wales, crossing the Thames at London, first by a ford and later by a wooden bridge; from Ermine Street, connecting London with Lincoln, York and Hadrian's Wall, Stane Street branched to Colchester, a prosperous port even before Roman times. Sarn Helen or Helen's Way ran through Wales from north to south, and on to Caerleon, the great legionary fortress of the west.

Along these great highways, which were maintained by the State, the Imperial mails were carried by relays of messengers, for whom the official posting-houses, built by the roadside,

Some road-making was done by the Saxons, for it was part of the work demanded by a thane from his peasants. But the roads made were local byways constructed unscientifically and without foundations. Knowledge of the use of mortar in holding stone together had gone with the Romans. In consequence, bridges became unsafe, and some of the usefulness of the splendidly durable Roman highways departed.

This deterioration continued throughout the troubled times of the Heptarchy. During the Danish invasion and the Norman Conquest, it was progressive. Bridges were frequently destroyed to check an invader or hamper an

EDGAR WARD

## AN EARLY BERKSHIRE CAUSEWAY
*Soon after the laborious metalling of roads began, attempts were made to avoid fords and bridges by a raised roadway called a causeway. They were often made for religious reasons by people desiring remission of sins, or to make a track for incessant pilgrimage. This one, at Steventon, Berkshire, runs between high trees.*

provided refreshment and changes of horses. Officials travelling on government business used light carriages drawn by a pair of horses or mules. Reckless driving of these was not uncommon and was punishable by a fine. Oxen drawing heavy wagons provided transport for goods and private travellers.

The excellence of the Roman roads served only to make the Saxon conquest of the country swifter and more easy. Most of the early Saxon settlements were made on river banks or estuaries, or in clearings in the forest off the Roman roads. On the latter, marauders were so many that in the late seventh century a law in both Kent and Wessex ran: " If a man from afar or a stranger travels through the wood off the highway and neither shouts nor blows a horn, he shall be assumed a thief and as such may be either slain or put to ransom."

enemy. The stones of the Roman highways subsided, and were not replaced.

It was a murder that revived road travelling— that of Becket, Archbishop of Canterbury, in 1170. In the following year the Canterbury Pilgrimage began. London pilgrims could hire a horse at Southwark for a few pence and on payment of a further shilling exchange it at Rochester for another on which the journey to Canterbury was completed. As the piety of some of the pilgrims was greater than their honesty, these horses were heavily branded by their owners to prevent their sale at the journey's end.

Although pilgrimages revived the habit of road travelling, little was done for the highways on which the pilgrims rode or trudged. By the beginning of the fourteenth century the roads were in so bad a state that travellers were looked upon as unfortunates whom the Church must assist. The monasteries undertook to repair the highways; any layman who contributed to the road repair funds was granted an indulgence. By the middle of the century hermits had begun to build themselves cells on the chief thoroughfares, and in return for their road repairing asked the passers-by for alms. In 1364 a decree of Edward III authorized "our well-beloved William Philippe the hermit" to set up a toll-bar on

landowners were to furnish wains or carts, each drawn by oxen or horses and each in charge of two men. Other householders, cottagers and labourers were to come equipped with the necessary tools and, either in person or by deputy, to work on the roads for four days—increased to six in Elizabeth's reign—under the direction of surveyors.

Although it effected some small improvement, the Act was not a success: the surveyors concentrated most of the labour on those parts of the roads which they themselves chiefly used; the rich evaded their obligations; the poor, resenting compulsory labour, did no more than two days' work in six.

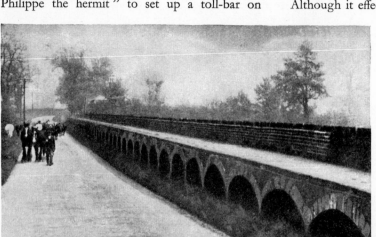

STEPHENSON

### CROSSING THE AVON DRYSHOD
*Maud Heath's Causeway, from Chippenham to Bremhill, dates from the fifteenth century and is named after its founder. It crosses the Avon Valley at Kellaways, its lowest point, on sixty-four beautifully-preserved arches.*

In Tudor times, as throughout the Middle Ages, men of all classes from kings to bagmen rode. The sick and infirm travelled in horse-borne litters. Children and occasionally adults were carried in the panniers of packhorses. Until the introduction of side saddles in the fourteenth century, women rode astride or pillion.

Medieval farm carts lumbered along on wheels cut out of solid wood. These wheels, like the shoes of the horses, were studded with big nails, to give them a grip on the mud. There were no vehicles to undertake transport for hire. According to Stowe, the long wains or stage-wagons which first provided such facilities came into use in about 1564. Covered and commodious, in its latest phase the stage-wagon could carry twenty passengers as well as goods. On its very broad wheels it was drawn at about three miles an hour by six, eight, or more horses. There were regular stage-wagon services between London, Canterbury, Ipswich, Norwich and Gloucester, among other towns.

Highgate Hill and to repair the road with the tolls imposed on "our people passing between Highgate and Smethfelde."

Yet travel conditions grew worse. By the end of the century chapels of ease were being built because congregations could not reach their parish churches; Parliament was adjourned after being summoned because members found the roads impassable; rural villages prepared for the winter as for a siege.

The first Road Act had been passed earlier—in 1285. It directed that on highways between market towns "there be neither dyke, tree nor bush whereby a man may lurk to do hurt within two hundred feet on either side of the way"—an interesting sidelight on the prevalence of robbery on the roads.

As few roads were fit for wagon traffic, goods were for the most part carried by pack-horses. These, with bales and panniers slung over their backs, had to pick their way along bridlepaths too narrow for two strings of horses to pass.

Little more was done by legislation until Queen Mary's reign. In 1555 an Act was passed which provided forced labour for the repair of roads leading to market towns. Each midsummer all

### Unwieldy Coaches

Like the stage-wagon the first private carriages were introduced into England about the middle of the sixteenth century. The "chariot drawn by six horses" in which Queen Mary rode at her coronation in 1553 aroused much curiosity. Like the coach presented by a Dutchman to Queen Elizabeth in 1565, it was but a glorified cart whose elaborate decorations did not compensate for its complete lack of springs. Nevertheless private coaches were soon in common use.

The first stage-coaches appeared in or about

1640. Carrying from four to eight inside passengers, they had neither springs nor windows. A huge basket for luggage was set over the axle, and in this two or three outside passengers could find places if they were content to sit on straw. It was not till later that either passengers or luggage were carried on the roof.

It was the competition of the hackney carriage rather than that of the stage-coach which met with strong opposition from the London watermen. The first twenty hackney carriages were licensed for hire in 1625, but these had to be hired at their stables. In 1634 they were allowed to ply the streets for hire, and near Somerset House the first public stand for four carriages and their liveried drivers was set up. Petitioning Charles I, the watermen said of their competitors : "They do carry sometimes three men for fourpence the man, or four men for twelvepence, to Westminster or back again, which doing of this doth undo the Company of Watermen."

All these innovations made it the more essential to improve the roads. In the Kentish Weald their condition was so vile that every autumn it was the custom to plough them up, and spread the surface mud in a half circle to dry. In other parts of the country, farmers were known to sow the roads as well as plough them. Thus, in 1660, Ralph Thoresby, the antiquary, found the Great North Road difficult to trace between Barnby Moor and Tuxford, and lost it completely at places between Doncaster and York. For the most part, seventeenth-century roads were without signposts or milestones; they had no drainage; many of them had ruts 4 feet deep. In this state they were used by ox-drawn farm wagons, and by the sledges in which timber was transported.

Early Stuart legislation sought to decrease traffic rather than to improve the roads. James I even went so far as to attempt—unsuccessfully—to make four-wheeled carts illegal. Acts of Charles I's reign prohibited any wagon or cart

STEPHENSON

**WHERE PACK-HORSES CROSSED**

*Almost until the end of the nineteenth century, and especially in rough country, the pack-horse still triumphed over the wagon for carrying goods. Hence many bridges were made only to take this traffic and many examples of these narrow, hump-backed bridges are in preservation. Above is Cam Beck Bridge in Ribblesdale.*

from being drawn by more than five horses, and limited the maximum load carried to a ton. Another statute forbade Sunday travelling.

In 1663 the first Turnpike Act was passed, establishing the principle that those who used the roads should pay for them. Three toll-gates were set up at Wadesmill, Caxton and Stilton, the tolls from which went to repair that part of the Great North Road which ran through Hertfordshire, Cambridgeshire and Huntingdonshire.

This system was extended only slowly, and against much opposition. By 1728 so many toll-gates and toll-houses had been either pulled down or burnt that an Act was passed making the penalty for such offences three months' imprisonment and a flogging at the market cross—a penalty later increased to seven years' transportation.

Riots occurred in many parts of the country. Although unreasoning prejudice prompted most of these, the rapidly extended turnpike system had grave defects. There were absurdities of administration—often a hundred commissioners were appointed to control fifteen miles of road; jobbery was common—frequently a road would be diverted merely that it might pass the house or the business place of one of the turnpike trustees. Nevertheless, the roads were improved, however uneconomically. Further, it was with money derived from turnpike tolls that two Scotchmen of genius, Thomas Telford and John

McAdam, in 1815, began the reconstruction work which revolutionized the English highways. Telford's method was to lay hard stones and gravel on a solid foundation of stone blocks; McAdam's was the setting, on a well-drained subsoil, of broken stones which the weight of the traffic bound into a comparatively waterproof surface.

### The Mail Coach

The coaches improved with the highways. Axles, wheels, hubs and springs were all of better construction; seats for outside passengers were installed on the curved roof; the wicker basket, known as the rumble-tumble, over the back axle, was replaced by a fore-and-aft boot. Some changes met with opposition: in 1805, when the coachman's box was fitted with springs, it was urged that the coachman would fall asleep, if no longer jolted.

Increased speeds came with the introduction of coaches called "flying machines." Whereas in 1712 the Edinburgh-London coach was advertised "to perform the whole journey in thirteen days without any stoppages (if God permits)," by 1830, the time taken was a mere forty hours. Mail coaches had much to do with the faster rate of travelling. Initiated by John Palmer of Bath in 1784, the first mail coach ran between London and Bristol, carried few inside

STEPHENSON

### A ROAD IN GREY GALLOWAY
*Roads in hill country and sparsely populated land, except where they were main arteries, grew slowly from prehistoric tracks, from cattle trails and pack-horse routes. Even today many of these byways receive little attention. Typical is this road leading to the farmsteads at the head of the lovely Glen Trool in Galloway.*

FELTON

### ANCIENT AND MODERN ROADS

*For centuries the Dover Road had diverged from the ancient line of Watling Street and passed through Gravesend. In 1924, however, this new road was made from Dartford to Rochester, and it reverts to the road of the Romans. Above, where the modern highway cuts through, the old Watling Street is seen on the left.*

and no outside passengers, was provided with fresh and first-rate horses at the end of each eight-mile stage, and took sixteen hours instead of twenty-seven for the journey. Its success led to the institution of a mail coach system throughout England, and for the first time since Henry VIII's reign post-boys and post-horses were no longer seen on the roads. The long distance mails were the first coaches to drive through the night, thus saving further time and forcing their competitors, the stage-coaches, to imitate them. It was the mail coaches, decorated with flowers, oak leaves and ribbons, that spread the news of such victories as Trafalgar and Waterloo through the countryside, to the triumphant sounding of the trumpets of their guards.

The coaching era reached its peak in 1836. There were then over 3,000 coaches on the road, half of them running to or from London. They made use of 150,000 horses, and gave employment to 30,000 coachmen, guards, horse-keepers and ostlers. They brought prosperity to hundreds of inns and hotels. From one London tavern alone eighty coaches set out daily for the north; from another, fifty coaches and as many wagons left for the west of England.

Within thirty years the competition of the railways had swept this prosperous industry out of existence. The first challenge came from the steam-carriage—a curious conveyance with its coke furnace, boiler, tubes and levers set over the back wheels—which appeared on the roads in the eighteen-twenties and which carried both inside and outside passengers. *Gurneys*, as they were sometimes called after their inventor, were killed by the heavy tolls which the turnpikes imposed upon them.

### The New Era

Few stage-coaches were left and the Turnpike Trusts were disappearing when steam-rollers and traction engines made their appearance in about 1862. These were unpopular, and called forth an extraordinary law by which any mechanically-propelled vehicle was forbidden to exceed four miles an hour, or to move at all unless preceded by a man with a red flag. This notorious measure remained in force until the year after the first motor car arrived in England in 1895.

To cope with these, with the motor coaches which have revived the prosperity of the old coaching inns, with the private cars and motor buses which have opened up the countryside to the townsman and created the weekly exodus into rural Britain, and also brought many of the town's amenities to the countryman's door—to cope with all these, the roads themselves have been reconstructed, straightened and widened at great cost.

Yet the cost is worth while. If Belloc exaggerates when he declares that " the road moves and controls all history," a country's roads are undeniably a criterion of its civilization; while the story of England's roads is less a time-saving by-pass in the study of English history than an epitome of that history itself.

D. MCLEISH

### PICTURESQUE HOUSES AT CANTERBURY

*These beautiful half-timbered dwellings, their walls washed by the gently-flowing waters of the Stour, were in the seventeenth century occupied by Walloon and Huguenot refugees who fled from religious persecution in France and the Netherlands. These immigrants introduced into Canterbury the art of weaving which is still carried on in these same houses, which today are one of the many pleasant features of this historic city.*

# THE DOVER ROAD

## *by* HAROLD SHELTON

FOR two thousand years the Dover Road has been a key road in the scheme of Britain's highways. The Romans recognized the need for a great artery connecting the coast with London and the north of England. Thus Watling Street came into existence of which the Dover Road is a small but significant part. At the vital points where the new road forded the only two considerable rivers it encountered, the Stour and the Medway, walled cities sprang up — the forerunners of the modern Canterbury and Rochester. It was the road which created these two great cities of Kent rather than the cities which created the need for the road.

The last Roman legions marched along it to their transports at Dover, recalled from the imperial outposts of Britain to repel the attacks of the heathen Goths upon the very centre of their empire. It was not long before the tribes of Teutonic invaders drove before them the Romanized citizens of the towns along the Dover Road and sacked their cities. Yet they could not destroy the strategic importance of the road. The paving which had resounded to the wheels of the Roman chariots and the clatter of their heavily-armed legionaries was repaired to carry the Norman knights and their mounted soldiers. Throughout the Middle Ages its use was unbroken. It carried the stage-coach in the dawn of the present era and harboured the highwaymen who conspired to make travel such an exciting adventure.

Even today the character of the road has not changed. Dover is still a vital port, still, as in the Roman days, a garrison town. Canterbury and Rochester still guard the bridges over the Stour and Medway where in Roman days they stood guard over the fords, whilst London has become the first city of the Empire. The Dover Road remains the great artery that it has always been, as important in the military life of the country as it is in its civil and commercial welfare.

It is a royal way which we follow from London to the coast. Almost every English monarch has travelled along it, and many of the foreign kings who have visited England. They had little alternative if they were to visit Canterbury or London before the modern network of motor roads had been constructed. The Roman emperors Severus and Constantius Chlorus marched along it on their way to York, destined both to die before they could retrace their steps. Ethelbert, King of the Saxon Kingdom of Kent, first of the Saxon kings to embrace the new Christianity, welcomed St. Augustine along it to his capital at Canterbury. William of Normandy made more than one pilgrimage along its whole course to inspect the work of the Constables whom he had set over the fortresses of Rochester and Canterbury. The illustrious Black Prince, victor of Poitiers with the French king captive, proceeded along it to the Holy Shrine. "Good" King Henry VIII met the Emperor Charles V at Dover before travelling with him to lay the most devout offerings at the shrine of the martyr. A few years later his troops marched from London to strip the shrine of all its riches—a sardonic sequence of events such as few other roads can have witnessed.

**SOUTHWARK'S FAMOUS COACHING INN**
*Situated on one of the oldest roads in England "The George" in the Borough High Street, London, is the last of the many ancient hostelries of Southwark.*

PHOTOCHROM

Queen Elizabeth, too, was a frequent traveller to Dover. If we may fairly judge by the number of hostelries which claim the honour of sheltering her royal person for the night, her journeys must have been of a surprising frequency and her taste in inns surprisingly capricious. But it has fallen to the lot of a great novelist, Charles Dickens, to immortalize the Dover Road in a way which no historic event could achieve. Dickens lived in Kent for most of his life ; he journeyed frequently along our road from his home to London. The *Pickwick Papers* reflect his love for it and its surroundings, the Leather Bottle Inn at Cobham, and Rochester in particular.

Like all the Roman roads the Dover Road is straight over most of its course. The scenic curse of modern development prevents its ever attaining the magnificent sweeps of a road like that which joins Cirencester with Gloucester. The views which it commands all too often include chimney stacks and massed dwelling houses. Between Rochester and Canterbury there is an irritating succession of straggling villages. Even so, it has not entirely lost its charm. Often we can see ahead of us for miles; and then the country-side opens out into the typical Kentish panorama of orchard, ploughed field and pasture land dotted with the inevitable oast houses.

### Where the Conqueror was Repulsed

From London Bridge our way is along the Old Kent Road, which perpetuates almost exactly the line of the Roman highway. Southwark, for all its unromantic appearance, is a place notable alike in history and in literature. Its name means " southern works " referring to the southern fortification of the old town of London. Its modern nickname " The Borough " reminds us that it was granted the status of borough among the earliest towns of England to receive that honour. It was here that William the Conqueror was repulsed when he first attacked the capital. Prior to that it was fortified by Ethelred, unjustly called Unready, when the Danish incursions were at their height. In later medieval times it was a great centre for travellers. The Tabard Inn is where the Pilgrims in Chaucer's *Canterbury Tales* set out on their journey.

DIXON-SCOTT

### BLACKHEATH, A HAUNT OF HIGHWAYMEN
*Standing high above the Thames this historic common, covering 267 acres, adjoins the Royal Park of Greenwich. Here in 1012 the Danes were encamped and it was used as headquarters by the Kentish rebels under Wat Tyler in 1381 and Jack Cade in 1450. Excavations revealed the location of a Roman town.*

DIXON-SCOTT

## ON THE MEDWAY AT ROCHESTER

*From the River Medway Rochester Cathedral and the ancient keep of the magnificent Norman stronghold
can here be seen silhouetted boldly against the skyline. Built in 1088 on an ancient site, the castle had a
stirring history. The cathedral is believed to occupy the site of a church founded by St. Augustine.*

The Old Kent Road takes us down to New
Cross Gate and into the ancient borough of
Deptford. Deptford Park was once the gardens
of Sayes Court where John Evelyn, the diarist,
lived, though he was by no means the greatest
of those who dwelt here; for it was the home
of the Duke of Sussex, famous in the reign of
Queen Elizabeth, and was honoured by the
presence of Peter the Great in 1698.

Blackheath, which modern excavation has
proved to have been a considerable town in
Roman days, is the next point of interest. The
Roman road crosses the heath and continues on
to Shooter's Hill (which will be well remembered
by readers of Dickens's *Tale of Two Cities*). In
the fourteenth and fifteenth centuries, for some
inscrutable reason, Blackheath seems to have
been the favourite place for revolutionaries to
gather their rebels. So in 1381 Wat Tyler
harangued his men on the heath and then led
them towards London. Jack Cade, too, the
other " glorious revolutionary " intimately associated with Kent, rallied his troops on the heath,
and it was here that the last fight of the so-called
Kentish Rebellion was decided.

As far as Dartford there is little left to please
the eye. But Dartford, itself, hides under a forbidding exterior a romantic past which almost
equals that of Rochester. Just as Rochester
guarded the wide ford over the Medway, so

Dartford was a Roman station guarding the
lesser ford over the Darent. The sixteenth-
century gateway, all but hidden by the factories,
was the entrance to a royal mansion which Henry
VIII converted from the abbey at the time of
the suppression. Here Anne of Cleves entertained her royal husband; here, later, Queen
Elizabeth lived among the splendid gardens which
are still partially preserved. But the palace is
now a factory. *Sic transit gloria mundi.*

### A Link with Elizabeth

The Dover Road of medieval times goes on
through Gravesend, but the modern by-pass
which avoids both Gravesend and Dartford,
reverts after Dartford Heath to the line of
Watling Street. On Dartford Heath itself a few
minutes' exploration will reveal the saucer-shaped
depressions which are the hollows scooped in
the ground by our ancestors of the New Stone
Age to give them protection from wind and rain,
and which perhaps they roofed with a rough
thatch to form the first dwelling-places of Britain.
Gravesend is yet another link with Elizabethan
England. It was the virgin queen who gave it
the standing of a borough in recognition of its
great services in the wars with the French.
The turbulent mood of Wat Tyler lives in its
streets, for here was the focal point of his
ill-conceived and ill-fated uprising.

STEPHENSON

## KENTISH OASTS
*The oast house is a characteristic feature of Kent, that fair land of orchards and hop fields, of broad green valleys and bare chalk downs. In the late summer the local farm workers are joined by a big army of hop-pickers from London and then the oast houses are busy day and night drying the flowers in the lofts.*

As we ascend the hill out of Gravesend, industrial England is spread before us cheek by jowl with this line of historic towns. The cement works border the river—one of the most thriving of the Thames-side industries. But we shall be unlucky if we do not see some red-sailed barge working its way up-stream in just the same way as the worthy citizens of Gravesend watched the Dutch fleet sailing up-river in 1667, destined to be the last hostile fleet which ever dared to sail so far up the reaches of the Thames.

### Land of Dickens
When we reach Cobham Park we are in the midst of the Dickens country, and though there is no view from the road of the Elizabethan manor house, our road gives us uninterrupted views over the famous parklands. It is when we are crossing Rochester Bridge, within sight of the square bulk of the castle keep, and the mean spire of the cathedral behind it, that our historic pilgrimage reaches its first and perhaps its most satisfying goal. If we pause and stroll

for ten minutes round the walled city we shall realize how nearly the past lives in its streets. First we enter the castle grounds, passing through the gateway in the outer wall and approaching the keep where we see the work of the great Bishop Corbeuil, first constable of the castle. The drum tower in the angle of the wall belongs to the thirteenth century, the two square towers on the eastern wall were added to give greater protection in the fourteenth century. Three times were the 12 feet thick walls of this stronghold besieged, in each case by a sovereign of England seeking vengeance upon a recalcitrant baron, before they suffered the usual fate of medieval castles and were dismantled by order of Cromwell.

Behind the castle the cathedral stands on the site of a church founded by St. Augustine, and of a Norman cathedral consecrated by Bishop Gundulph. We pass down the Pilgrims' Passage along which tradition related thousands of pilgrims came to the shrine of St. William of Perth, and so reach the High Street opposite

DIXON SCOTT

### DOVER CASTLE

*Covering an area of 35 acres, this castle is, after the Tower of London, the most extensive and magnificent fortification in Great Britain.   The date of its foundation can only be conjectured but, apart from the middle ward which was altered during the Napoleonic Wars, it is almost exactly as it was during the thirteenth century.*

Lloyds Bank, where a former residence sheltered King James II in his flight of 1688.   Along the High Street the gabled roof of Watt's Charity reminds us of Dickens's tale, *The Seven Poor Travellers*.   In Eagle Court we see the city walls with their Roman foundations and medieval upper brickwork.   Finally we go to the Bull Inn, which has the double distinction of having sheltered Queen Elizabeth, and being the scene of many episodes in the *Pickwick Papers*.

As we continue on our way through Ospringe, Key Street and Faversham, we are in the midst of the orchardland of Kent where we may notice the generous timbered barns of the farmsteads— the land of the Men of Kent who, so legend relates, went out to meet William the Conqueror and secured from him a continuance of their old privilege by which a man's land was divided on intestacy among his sons instead of passing to his eldest son according to the Norman custom. Thus arose the race of Kentish yeoman farmers, known for ever as the Men of Kent to distinguish them from Kentish Men, and of whom it was said in medieval song:

"A squire of Wales, a knight of Cales,
　　And a laird of the North Countree;
　A yeoman of Kent, with half a year's rent,
　　Can buy them out all three."

The entrance to Canterbury is one that befits a city taken from the annals of medieval England. The great bulk of the West Gate spans our road, part of the fortifications which made Canterbury an impregnable fortress in the Middle Ages. We cross the Stour where the quaint houses of the Flemish weavers overhang the river, we have a brief glimpse of the quiet beauty of the Cathedral Close, we traverse the narrow streets which have scarcely changed in the last four hundred years, except that more and more of the shop fronts are assuming the characteristic appearance of the twentieth century.   But that is the only discordant note in one of the most beautiful of Britain's cathedral cities.

### White Cliffs of Albion

Four miles on our way to Dover we pass Bishopsbourne, the village where Joseph Conrad passed the last five years of his life.   As we breast the downs on the last lap of our journey we have our first glimpse of the sea and the white cliffs of Albion.   Thus our road brings us to Dover with its great harbour and its castle perched high on the cliff, and its Saxon chapel hard by, and the Roman lighthouse, to find a parallel with which we should have to go to the Alexandrine shore.

EDGAR WARD

### BEAUTY AT THE DOCKYARD GATES

*Not all Portsmouth is a grim, grey naval dockyard, nor does every craft on its waters fly the White Ensign. The southern terminus of the Portsmouth Road does, in truth, exist because of the Navy, but, at the very entrance to the harbour, brown-sailed fishing boats ply their trade and the white wings of yachts flash in the Spithead sunshine.   It began its rise to fame as a port when sixteenth-century events required a strong navy.*

# THE PORTSMOUTH ROAD

## *by* TOM STEPHENSON

ALTHOUGH it eventually became an important thoroughfare leading to the famous dockyards, the Portsmouth Road cannot claim the antiquity of some of our other highways. It is true the Romans established a fortress at Portchester, at the head of Portsmouth Harbour, but its link with London was via Chichester and the Stane Street, now a forgotten grass-grown highway.

Not until the time of Henry VIII did the little town at the mouth of the harbour assume any importance, and, even with the establishing of the naval dockyard, there does not appear to have been any attempt at road-making.

Pepys, as an Admiralty official, frequently journeyed to Portsmouth, and from his diary may be gained some idea of the state of the highway in his days.

"Waked betimes," he writes, under August 6, 1668, "So over the water to Fox Hall (Vauxhall); and there my wife and Deb. took me up, and away to Gilford, losing our way for three or four miles about Cobham." At Guildford they dined and then "to coach again, and go to Liphook late over Hind-head, having an old man, a guide, in the coach with us; but got hither with great fear of being out of our way, it being ten at night. Here good honest people; and after supper to bed." On another occasion he mentions the need of a guide to take them to Havant "to avoid going through the forest."

If not among our oldest highways the Portsmouth Road can certainly claim a high place for its scenic interest, and it has few rivals which can claim an equal standard of sustained beauty.

From Wandsworth or Putney, Wimbledon Common is soon reached, the first of the many heaths and commons along the route and by no means the least attractive. Suddenly we seem to have left London behind, to have reached open country, a wide expanse of heath with little dells and hidden pools and slender, swaying birches.

Forward the road descends to the Beverley Brook in Kingston Vale. Here travellers of old were called upon for toll, for a turnpike stood at Robin Hood's Gate. Until the making of the by-pass the road ran through the busy streets of Kingston, which in Saxon days was the seat of a council or Witanagemot called by Egbert, and there is still preserved the famous stone on which, it is said, seven kings were crowned.

It was in Kingston that one of the last recorded instances of the use of the ducking stool occurred. A journal of April 27, 1745, records "Last week a woman that keeps the King's Head alehouse, Kingston, in Surrey, was ordered by the court to be ducked for scolding, and was accordingly placed in the chair and ducked in the river Thames in the presence of two or three thousand people."

STEPHENSON

### THE FAMOUS CLOCK OF GUILDFORD

*The mist-filled dip of Guildford High Street, the prominent clock on the ancient Town Hall, used both to be familiar sights on the old road. Nowadays a by-pass leaves them far on the left.*

DIXON-SCOTT

## LONDON'S LOVELIEST COMMON

*Wimbledon Common, with its birches, hawthorns and duck-haunted ponds, comes like an oasis in the Portsmouth Road as it mounts from Putney. For a stretch, the road follows the old turnpike over the hill and down to the Kingston Vale, where the first of the great by-pass roads takes the traveller as far as Esher.*

At Ditton Marsh the old and the modern roads converge. Just beyond this point, outside the " Orleans Arms " on the edge of Esher, there still stands a tall cylindrical eighteenth-century milestone which was known to the old coachmen as " The White Lady."

Esher, which has developed away from its village green, and protracted itself along the highway, has its place in history. By the banks of the Mole stands the ruined gateway of Wolsey's palace to which he retired after the Great Seal had been taken from him, and he was no longer in favour with Henry VIII.

By the Claremont Estate, where Queen Victoria once resided and where the French Louis Philippe found refuge after the 1848 Revolution, the road mounts to Esher Common. Open heath and tall dark pines fringe the road and then, after the straight stretch of the Fair Mile, we descend into Cobham or, more correctly, Street Cobham, where the " White Lion " marks the site of the fourth turnpike from London.

With its low-roofed houses and the trees on its broad green, Ripley is one of the prettiest villages on the road. It has, moreover, two fine old inns, the " Talbot " and the " Anchor." The " Talbot," a square-built inn with a red brick front boasts a fifteenth-century coffee-room. The " Anchor," which has a more ancient air, was for long a famous rendezvous of cyclists.

There they found welcome when elsewhere they were regarded as " cads on castors."

Another seven miles brings us to Guildford, with its famous High Street dipping steeply to the Wey. This has frequently been praised, and few towns in England have anything so distinctive to offer. The seventeenth-century Town Hall with its massive clock overhanging the road, the warm red brick of Abbot's Hospital, the Grammar School, the gabled houses with casements and latticed windows, despite their variety and differences in style, somehow blend into harmonious continuity.

### A King's Wine Cellar

Alfred mentioned Guildford in his will, and Mallory locates there the Astolat where the fair maid languished and died for love of Sir Lancelot.

A square keep is practically all that remains of the Norman Castle which appears to have had an uneventful history. The Royal Palace built by Henry II has completely disappeared, but there is evidence that it was long a favourite haunt of ruling monarchs. John kept Christmas there " with uncommon splendour and magnificence." Henry III made wine cellars of the caverns close by the castle, and Elizabeth travelled so frequently to and fro that the people of Surrey were roused to protest at the impositions for her horses and carriages.

Of the inns of Guildford John Aubrey said they were " the best perhaps in England." Pepys frequently stayed at the " Red Lion." There he " lay in the room that the king lately lay in." In the garden of the " Red Lion " with Mr. Creedy, he " played the fool a great while, trying who could best over the edge of an old fountain well ; and I won a quart of sack of him." The same evening at supper " my wife and I did talk high, she against and I for Mrs. Pierce (that she was a beauty) till we were both angry."

Most ancient looking of Guildford's inns is the "Angel" with its seventeenth-century clock and a beautifully panelled hall. The "Angel" also possesses two fourteenth-century vaulted crypts which have aroused much speculation. It has been suggested that they are the undercrofts of merchants' houses. Another theory is that they are the remains of a convent of White Friars, and that the "Angel" was originally the guest house of the friars.

Godalming, four miles from Guildford, is another ancient town with a delightful background of low wooded hills. Although endowed with some fine old buildings they are not displayed so effectively, nor has its High Street the grace and dignity of the one at Guildford.

In 1726 Godalming was very much in the lime-light owing to the supposed experience of one Mary Tofts, wife of a clothworker. According to her story, when working in a field she was startled by a rabbit, and in due course she presented her husband with a family of rabbits. Physicians debated the phenomenon with zeal and published their arguments for and against. Hogarth depicted the Wise Men of Godlyman, and rabbits fell out of favour at the table. At last Queen Caroline sent her doctor to investigate the marvel, with the result that Mary was sent to Bridewell.

### Surrey's Green Loveliness

Nowadays, both Guildford and Godalming are by-passed by a broad highway which mounts the Hog's Back, that upstanding chalk ridge between Guildford and Farnham.

From the summit, whence one may enjoy a wide prospect of Surrey's green loveliness from Leith Hill to Hindhead, the road sweeps down to the valley of the Wey. At Milford the old road is rejoined and there follows the long ascent of Hindhead, and five miles of heath and moor, of golden gorse, and sepia and silver pines, and all the glory of Surrey Commons at their best.

Half a mile west of this road lies the secluded hamlet of Thursley, which in its name commemorates some old Viking settlers in Surrey. In the churchyard there is a monument to an unknown sailor whose tragic end brought unenviable fame to Hindhead.

STEPHENSON

### A FAMOUS STOPPING-PLACE

*The Anchor Inn, like its companion at the other end of the village of Ripley has been a roadside rendezvous for many years. It was among the first inns to offer hospitality to cyclists when the new wheeling craze began and is a worthy link in the chain of refreshment houses that space the " rolling English road."*

DIXON-SCOTT

### DUTCH WILLIAM

*The town of Petersfield stands just north of the gap where the Portsmouth Road pierces the downs for the last descent. The equestrian statue stands in the market-place and represents William III.*

In September, 1786, this nameless unfortunate was walking from London to Portsmouth to seek a berth. At Esher he found three companions who travelled with him as far as the " Red Lion " at Thursley, eating, drinking and lodging at his expense. In that hostelry he was last seen alive.

#### *A Gruesome Sight*

Two cottagers found his corpse below the road over Hindhead, and his murderers were apprehended near Petersfield while trying to sell the dead man's clothes. On the highest point of Hindhead they were hanged in chains and for years their bodies swung over the coaches that passed along the road. So the spot gained its name of Gibbet Hill. Fortunately, no such gruesome relic remains, and instead of the gibbet, a cross now marks the summit of this famous landmark, and a brass plate indicates the features of the far-flung view extending across woodland and meadow, far over Surrey and Sussex, out to the Hog's Back and Leith Hill range, or across the widespreading weald to the South Downs and the dome of Chanctonbury Ring.

Beyond Hindhead the road descends over

Bramshott Common, entering Hampshire at the Seventhorns Inn and two miles beyond the boundary reaches Liphook. The Anchor Inn there, where Pepys stayed, has now blossomed into the Royal Anchor Hotel, perhaps an allusion to the sovereigns it has entertained.

Down the road which Nicholas Nickleby once followed with the pathetic Smike, on by Rake and its " Flying Bull," so we come to Petersfield.

This quiet little town Defoe describes as " eminent for little, but its being full of good inns and standing in the middle of a country still overgrown with a prodigious quantity of oak-timber."

In Castle House, formerly an inn, Charles II and his mother stayed when fleeing to France. Where once the old Market House stood, there is now an equestrian statue of Dutch William portrayed in lead as a Roman Emperor.

From Petersfield the South Downs are soon reached. Out of Sussex they extend in swinging curves by Harting Down to War Down and Butser Hill, between which the deep trench of Butser Cutting affords passage for the road.

Along the flanks of Windmill Hill, the windmill, now a decrepit and forlorn landmark, the road descends to Horndean and through the region of the ancient Forest of Bere, by Cowplain and Waterlooville, so we reach Portsdown, a ridge of downland ranging from Besthampton to Fareham. From this height we look down on Portsmouth Harbour and its many inlets, on the seemingly closely-huddled roofs of the town, and out across the gleaming Solent to the Isle of Wight.

On entering Portsmouth we no longer find the restrictions encountered by Defoe, " such as being examin'd at the gates, such as being obliged to keep garrison hours, and not be let out or let in after nine a clock at night and the like," but until as recently as 1925, beyond Cosham, the road passed over a moat and drawbridge and through a line of fortifications to enter the town.

So we reach journey's end—Portsmouth, with its many historic associations, where we may wander through its streets perhaps to note the church where Charles II married Katherine of Braganza, or the house where George Villiers, Duke of Buckingham, was assassinated. Some may seek the birthplace of Meredith or the house where Dickens was born, the home of Mr. Crummles of *Nicholas Nickleby*, or the room occupied by Nicholas and Smike.

The " Star and Garter," once frequented by Nelson, Hardy, Sir John Franklin and other heroes, the " George " where Nelson spent his last night in England ; the famous *Victory*, now restored to a semblance of its Trafalgar days, these are a few of the pointers to Portmouth's crowded and historic past and indications of one-time travellers down the Portsmouth Road.

# THE EXETER ROAD

## *by* I. O. EVANS

THERE seems little of romance about a modern road, yet in reality there are few things more romantic. The roads of Britain for the most part follow ways as old as civilization itself; where the early tribesmen blazed their lonely trails, where the legions tramped, where the heavy stage-coaches and farm wagons rumbled and the swift horsemen spurred, where the troops marched in time of war, today the modern traffic hastens, and there is scarcely a mile of the highway without its association with men and manners long since past.

Neither the longest nor the most frequented is the south-western road that links London with Exeter and leads the townsman to the moors and coastlands of the west, yet it is by no means the least rich in romantic memories. It leaves the Great West Road, the Bath Road, at Hounslow; and here, on Hounslow Heath, was the favourite resort of those "heroes" of romance, the highwaymen, of Dick Turpin and Claude Duval. It is easy to decry modern progress, but it has at least cleared the roads of parasites such as these; and though we dislike the sight of wayside advertisements, H. G. Wells reminds us that in an earlier age we might instead have seen the road embellished with the rotting skeletons of such malefactors hanging in chains.

At Staines our road crosses the Thames, and here, it is believed, the Romans had a garrison, *Ad Pontes*, "At the Bridges." On by Egham and within sight of historic Runnymede and soon the road skirts Windsor Great Park, and the traveller, after being charmed with the sight of a pleasant sheet of water, is astonished to see some ruined pillars, arranged in a fashion unknown to the archæologist. The pillars form an artificial ruin, set up to lend additional beauty to the park; the lakes which give Virginia Water its name are equally artificial, but they are no less charming for that.

An inn named the "Jolly Farmer" at Bagshot seems to suggest an age of agricultural prosperity. In former days it was known as the "Golden Farmer," and thereby hangs a tale. Bagshot Heath was once the haunt of a highwayman who would never take bank-notes, but only gold from his victims. At the same time there lived at Frimley a farmer who paid all his accounts in gold. At length farmer and highwayman were identified as one and the same person, and near the site of the inn the "golden farmer" swung in chains.

"DAILY HERALD"

**BEAUTY WITH GRIM MEMORIES**

*Near Basingstoke, on the Exeter Road, is the picturesque hamlet of Old Basing. Here are the slight remains of Basing House on the site of a medieval castle. This house was built by the first Marquess of Winchester in the sixteenth century and for two years withstood Cromwell's assaults before finally surrendering.*

Now through Hampshire we reach Basingstoke, with its memories of the Civil War. Basing House nearby was a stronghold of the Cavaliers; strong and well provisioned it resisted for over two years the attacks of the Parliament's armies, and was only stormed and pillaged when Cromwell himself gave the siege his personal attention and command.

The modern arterial road now follows the line of the prehistoric Harrow-way through the attractive little market town of Stockbridge and through Sutton Scotney. The traditional way south-westwards follows the Upper Test Valley, beloved of the angler, to Whitchurch and Andover. It is scarcely romantic, perhaps, but it is worthy of mention that at Laverstoke are the mills which by some secret process make the paper on which bank-notes are printed. Lovers of Cobbett will remember the curses he invoked on the place that the country-people named "Rag Hall."

Near Andover a sleepy village wakes to noisy life for a few days each year, for at Weyhill is held in October a great sheep fair, one of the few survivors of what in bygone days were the chief means by which the people traded their locally-made goods for wares brought from beyond the sea. Andover itself might easily have been the scene of a battle, for James I paused here while retreating before the advance of the invader William of Orange. Instead of fighting, however, he "debatailled" as the ancient phrase went; as we should say nowadays he went on retiring "according to plan."

### The Great Plain

Soon we are on Salisbury Plain, the centre of those chalk hills projecting north, south and east and spreading in radiating arms across England. It is a lonely region, even in these modern days. Travellers by the old stage-coaches must have dreaded and feared it, not only for its bleakness but for the footpads who used to infest it.

Amesbury, the last place of any size on the

STEPHENSON

#### THE VERY NAME OF ENGLAND

*Freefolk, at the head of the Test Valley, is English by name and looks. This beautiful little village is in the chalk stream country, the scene of the best southern trout fishing, and near the Bank of England papermill at Laverstoke. The association is not without point, for the fishing is exclusive and extremely expensive.*

FOX PHOTOS

## SALISBURY'S MEDIEVAL GATEWAY

*Salisbury, the grey old city by the Avon, is one of the most fascinating places on the Exeter Road. It is the successor of Old Sarum, the city on the hill nearby, which was abandoned at the beginning of the thirteenth century. The High Street Gate, seen above, was built of stones from the Norman castle at Old Sarum.*

EDGAR WARD

### PEACEFUL CHARM OF ILCHESTER
*The little market town of Ilchester lies on the most northerly of the three branches of the Exeter Road. Now lapped in the quiet of Somerset life, it was at one time an important Roman station at the crossing of the River Yeo, or Ivel, as it is often called, and from which the town is named.*

in Britain. Beyond, the chalk of Salisbury Plain stretches on, seemingly almost without end. The Plain is very appropriately an exercising ground for the army, and near Wilton may be seen the emblems that the troops cut into the turf when stationed here during the Great War. Emblazoned in gleaming white chalk are, among others, the maple leaf of the Canadians, the rising sun of the Australians, and the Maltese cross of the King's Royal Rifles.

### The Pretender
The ruins of Wardour Castle, near Shaftesbury, again recall the distresses of the Civil War. Another conflict, sooner ended but marked by equal horror, is recalled by the Monmouth Ash, where the ill-fated " Pretender," the Duke of Monmouth, was discovered and captured after his crushing defeat at Sedgemoor. He had been hiding in Cranborne Chase, at one time a great deer forest stretching from Salisbury to Shaftesbury and protected by game-laws of incredible ferocity.

Shaftesbury itself has more peaceful associations, for here a nunnery was founded by Alfred the Great, and here died King Canute. At Sherborne another of our national heroes is recalled, for its castle was in part built by Sir Walter Raleigh. This adventurer, it will be remembered, introduced tobacco to Britain ; and at the cross roads a little farther along, near the village of Henstridge, is the inn where one day he was sitting placidly smoking—until a servant who knew nothing of tobacco thought him to be on fire and " quenched " him by throwing a pot of ale over his head !

Sherborne today is quiet enough ; it is hard to realize that it was once the capital of part of the kingdom of Wessex and formed a stronghold against the onslaught of the Danes. Its abbey church was a Saxon cathedral a thousand years ago, and its prelates fought against the heathen invaders. Did they give its name to

way across the Plain, figures in Arthurian legend. When Guenevere heard that Arthur and all his knights were slain she " stole away and few ladies with her, and so she went to Almesbury ; and there she let make herself a nun, and wore white clothes and black, and great penance she took, as ever did sinful lady in this land."

Beyond Amesbury the road passes within sight of Stonehenge, on beyond the great earthworks of Yarnbury, once famous for its fair, and so down to the vale of the Wylye.

South of Amesbury lies Salisbury, the New Sarum, which will charm the traveller chiefly by its cathedral, seen from afar pointing its slender finger to heaven. Its spire, dating back 600 years, and more than 400 feet high, is the tallest

Babylon Hill, between the town and Yeovil?

In Yeovil there is another church of ancient foundation, erected in the finest "perpendicular" style. Not far away was the birthplace of that extraordinary genius, Roger Bacon, who foresaw, six hundred years before they were invented, the steamship, the motor, and the aeroplane itself, the use of the diving-suit and wars waged with poison gas.

### The Fosse Way

On Crewkerne Church are some curious carved figures, musicians playing on instruments whose very names are almost forgotten, St. George the English patron saint, and the dragon his mortal foe. Other carvings are to be found at Chard, the last town in Somerset. Here the High Street has been identified with the old Roman Fosse Way, and it has the curious distinction that the water from its gutters run on the one side to the south coast of Britain, on the other to the Bristol Channel.

Now we have reached Devon, and the villages on the road and the country which borders it have all the charm of the West Country, not the least delightful region of an island rich in scenic delight. The wayside cottages, and the inns, are not slow to inform us that here we can taste the renowned "Devonshire cream and cider." Honiton has earned its name through the lace it produces, a craft introduced into the westland by Dutch refugees. For a time the road follows the valley of the Otter, but soon this stream turns southward to reach the sea by way of Ottery St. Mary, whose church is, its people boast, the finest in all the county.

The route we have taken is not the only Exeter Road. From Salisbury an alternative way could be followed more to the south by way of Blandford Forum and Dorchester. Blandford has the distinction of having been several times burned, and the old parish pump is still preserved with a suitable inscription. Near Dorchester is a place that deserves to be remembered more than many a famous English site. Here six labourers, for the heinous crime of forming a trade union, were sentenced to transportation beyond the seas. This punishment aroused a widespread outcry, and in the long run helped to advance the cause of freedom; we owe much to the Tolpuddle Martyrs and the stand that they made for their rights.

W. F. TAYLOR

### A DORSET LANDSCAPE

*Another branch of the Exeter Road runs south from Salisbury by Dorchester and Bridport. Between these two towns the road runs through a pleasant rolling country of soft green hills and quiet hamlets. Typical is this view of Askerswell, an attractive little village which lies north of the road, about four miles east of Bridport.*

R.B.—O

W. F. TAYLOR

THE GUILDHALL, EXETER

*Teeming with historical associations is the beautiful old Guildhall of which Exeter is justly proud. It was rebuilt in 1330 and an Elizabethan portico was added two and a half centuries later.*

was not erected idly, but the events which led to its erection, as well as those that followed it, are largely unknown.

The sea coast is swinging inland to meet the road now, and on the shore is the Swannery of Abbotsbury, where the royal birds are protected and make countless nests. Bridport, however, is not too happily named, for it lies about two miles from the sea, a pleasant town formerly famous for the rope it produced; to be hanged was to be "stabbed with a Bridport dagger."

### Landing of Monmouth

The Dorsetshire coast is the happy hunting ground of the geologist, who finds in its cliffs abundant fossil remains, from tiny ammonites which can be polished and set in ornamental rings to the great reptiles that dominated the earth millions of years ago. Lyme Regis is famous because it was here that Monmouth landed, and because it figures in one of Jane Austen's novels, but it owes its chief fame to the remains of extinct animals it has given to the world. In its church is commemorated Mary Anning, the discoverer of the ichthyosaurus.

At Honiton the two roads join, and the straight line of the road is a reminder that we are on the Roman highway from Exeter to Bath. So at last Exeter is reached. To this city Queen Elizabeth gave the title of the "Ever Faithful." It is the "gateway to the west"; beyond it we find the wild desolation of Dartmoor, the numerous deep entries of the sea, and Cornwall where the old Celtic strain yet lingers. Exeter Cathedral is a building attractive enough; and in it, fit testimony to the seafaring prowess of its sons, among the regimental banners one is accustomed to find, is the sleigh flag borne by Captain Scott on his glorious dash to the South Pole.

Dorchester is of infamous memory for here was held the "Bloody Assize" at which the brutal Judge Jeffreys inflicted ferocious sentences on the unhappy supporters of Duke Monmouth. His chair is still on view in the Town Hall, and his lodgings are still pointed out. Yet the history of the town is far older than this. Almost within a stone's throw of the station is a Roman coliseum, the Maumbury Rings, for here was the Roman town of Durnovaria, and here is the Via Iceniana, as the Romans renamed the ancient track to the Chilterns known as the Icknield Way.

The Roman station, however, is modern compared with the great earthwork of Maiden Castle south-west of the town. The *Mai Dun* is one of the largest camps in the land, surrounded with wall after wall and trench after trench and covering over a hundred acres. Such a defence

Thus the Exeter Road leads back through history towards its very dawn. Early British earthworks, Roman camp and amphitheatre, Norman church, island of Runnymede, home of the sea-dogs of Devon, birthplace of trade unionism—all are found within a short distance of the way. Figuratively it leads to imperial Rome, to the "plantations" in the new world discovered beyond the Atlantic, or to the gallant band of heroes struggling among the Antarctic snows.

# THE BATH ROAD

## *by* MICHAEL GEELAN

THERE is a grace and an elegance and a charm about the Bath Road. It is an aristocrat among the highways. There steals along it a spirit of benevolent remembrance. Fashion and beauty have paved it with immortal memories. Along this highway, for all the hurrying traffic we may yet dream of the fragrance of lavender and roses and lace ; of the gallants and proud dames who rode down it in the more colourful years of old, lovely, lazy England.

And of all the ghosts that haunt the Bath Road there are two whose luminance is a steady and abiding glow of fascination. The first is Samuel Pepys, whose diary is an incomparable pageant of the times in which he lived, a delicious exposition of gossip and indiscretion as well as a valuable record of manners and customs. With his fashionable friends, and his suspicious wife, Pepys often took the Bath Road. Portraits of the diarist will be found hanging, to this day, in many of the old-time inns on and around it.

The second is Richard ("Beau") Nash—gambler and dandy, a Welshman who perfected the English manner; spendthrift and adventurer, yet a man with a subtle brain for business, who won for himself the title of "King of Bath." When he arrived there in 1705, Beau Nash gaily set about the task of making it a leading health resort, and the most fashionable town in the country. True, Bath had been steadily gaining in popularity among the rich and famous. As far back as 1667 there was a coach called the *Flying Machine* which carried passengers from London several times each week for a fare of twenty-five shillings, and it was advertised that " it performs the whole journey in Three Days (if

God permit) and sets forth at five o'clock in the morning."

Henrietta Maria, the unpopular wife of Charles I, had given the place fashionable publicity. Charles II, in the gay days of the Restoration, brought his entire Court to revel there. With the days of James II and, later Queen Anne, it had become the established mecca of royalty, nobility and the bright young people of the period, including young bloods who were a little too swift with both repartee and rapier.

But it was the Beau who, more than anyone else, perfected its reputation and appeal. He built a wonderful assembly hall, organized gambling and amusements, amazed everyone by putting a stop to duelling, and became the unquestioned social dictator. Moreover, he managed to raise by subscription a road fund of some £18,000. In 1717, possibly by his enterprise, the first daily coach ran from London, the passengers spending over forty hours on the journey. The trip was not accomplished in a single day until 1800.

The Bath Road has been one of the most casually developed of all our great highways. Like many of the idlers of luxury and rank whom it has served, it has taken its own time and gone its own way. The Romans began it, building a road from London that ran through Staines, Silchester, Newbury, Hungerford and Marlborough, but this did not apparently endure much beyond the Roman era. Next, in the Middle Ages, came the highway which was the father both of the coaching route and the modern trunk road we know today. This drove a more convenient path through Slough, Maidenhead and Reading, but over the Marlborough Downs

W. F. TAYLOR

**THE CLOTH HALL OF NEWBURY**
*Newbury, Berks, was a borough as early as 1187 and was at one time a centre of the prosperous wool trade. The industry declined early in the seventeenth century.*

the traveller took his choice, reaching Bath by way of Chippenham or else via Devizes and Trowbridge.

So now, hey-ho for the Bath Road! No coaches now with stamping horses and jingling accoutrement, no scented dandies in silk stockings and gaudy waistcoats, no ladies of fashion pouting prettily at the vexations of departure await us at the coaching houses. So in modern fashion we will leave from Hyde Park Corner, which in the eighteenth century was on the fringe of the open countryside.

was the greatest of all these desperadoes of the night, yet he was only twenty-seven years of age when he was captured and executed. Spectacular in his escapades, scorning violence and exercising a strange gallantry in the handling of his victims, young Duval on one famous occasion invited the pretty occupant of a held-up coach to join him in a dance on the heath. The lady accepted, and it is recorded that the highwayman " performed marvels ; the best masters in London, except those that are French, not being able to show such a footing as he did." He was a hero

W. F. TAYLOR

## MAIDENHEAD'S LOVELY BRIDGE

*Between Maidenhead and Reading, the Bath Road is never far from the Thames. It crosses the river at Maidenhead on a beautifully-designed bridge erected in 1772 and at which, until 1913, a toll was exacted. The view from the bridge up the straight of Maidenhead Reach is typical of the beauty of the Thames.*

After only seven miles we are at Brentford—deep in the realms of history. Here, in 54 B.C., Julius Cæsar crossed the Thames ford and shattered the forces of the Britons. King Offa of Mercia attended a Church Council there in A.D. 780, and in 1016 the English put Canute to flight across the river. A stone pillar at Brentford Ferry commemorates the Battle of Brentford between the armies of Charles I and Parliament.

Hounslow, a little farther on, is rich in memories of the great days of the open road. At one time it was astir day and night with horse traffic, and as many as 2,000 post-horses were kept in the town. Dick Turpin had more than one " hideout " here, and this, of course, brings us to Hounslow Heath, one of the happiest of all hunting grounds for highwaymen. Claude Duval

in his way, so much so that they buried him with not a little ceremony in St. Paul's, Covent Garden.

They were a strange company, these land-pirates of the mask and pistol, including an Old Etonian and renegade officers of the Services. Not all of them, however, showed the restraint of Duval, and their punishment was made to fit the crime. Round about 1800 " the road was lined with gibbets on which the carcases of malefactors hung in irons, blackening in the sun."

If one of these desperate characters could return today and thunder on his mount from the heath, along the old Bath Road into Colnbrook High Street he would find this little town almost unchanged. Time seems to have passed it by, and the modern divergence of the road has left

FELTON

### SAVERNAKE'S GRAND AVENUE

*Savernake was a royal forest and formed part of the jointure of Queen Eleanor.  " When the spring feeling is in the blood," wrote W. H. Hudson, " I think of all the places where I should like to be and one is Savernake; and thither in two successive seasons I have gone to ramble day after day forgetting the world and myself."*

it to return to its former quietude. At any moment you expect to hear the tantivy of the London mail coach. There are still local people who can tell you the legend of the Ostrich Inn, said to have been the scene of a series of ghastly murders. In one of the upstairs rooms—so the story goes—was a bed which operated over a trap door. In the dead of night the bed would tilt up and the occupant would be pitched through the trap door into a vat of scalding water! Then his money and belongings would be thieved, and his body disposed of. In yet earlier days King John is reputed to have stayed at Colnbrook on his way to Runney-mede to sign "Magna Charta."

The stretch of road between Colnbrook and Slough once knew the progress of royalty from Windsor Castle to St. James's. Salt Hill, near the Slough cross roads, was the halting-place of many of the crack coaches, and a sorry blow was dealt to its prosperity with the coming of the Great Western Railway to nearby Taplow.

W. F. TAYLOR

**ROYAL MEMORIES OF LONG AGO**
*As the Bath Road nears the Somerset border it reaches the twin villages of Corsham and Pickwick, the former of which was once the residence of Saxon kings.*

A diverting incident is associated with the coming of the railway to these parts. With the assistance of the Court, the heads of Eton College were successful in keeping it clear of both Windsor and Eton, and they were also successful in securing a ban on the erection of a station at Slough. But Slough was not despondent. Although a station was forbidden, trains stopped there from the very first. Two rooms were engaged at an inn near the present site of Slough Station, and here passengers waited and tickets were conveniently issued—strategy which even the brains and resources of the élite of Eton were unable to combat.

It was from Slough signal-box, incidentally, that a murderer was trapped in 1885 by means of a message sent by the startlingly new electric telegraph, a thrill repeated in history by the trapping of Dr. Crippen in the infancy of wireless.

The view from Maidenhead Bridge—where the toll-gate was thrown in triumph into the river only a year before the Great War, the toll having been abolished—is one of the most beautiful on the Bath Road, but for more tangible romance we must be on our way to Reading. Here are the ruins—regretfully, the very meagre ruins—of what was one of the greatest abbeys in England, the Abbot of Reading being exceeded in rank only by the Abbots of Westminster and Glaston-bury. In the days of its historic grandeur and significance sessions of Parliament were held here, royal marriages were celebrated, and kings and queens were buried there. The reverse of glory was the fate of Hugh Faringdon, the last abbot, however, for in 1539 he was hanged, drawn and quartered for falling foul of Henry VIII. The abbey was founded by Henry I in 1112 and conse-crated by Thomas à Becket in 1164.

In Reading will be found one of the most peculiar statues in England, and one of the few to be erected to a man during his own lifetime. It was put up to express the town's gratitude to Mr. George Palmer, one of its most notable citizens, and it was decided that he should be shown in life-like fashion. With the result that there he stands in a frock coat and trousers sagging at the knees, carrying a silk hat and an unfolded umbrella!

Theale is a charming, tree-shielded village, and Thatcham a market town that was renowned in the coaching days. Thatcham Chapel was actually bought by Lady Frances Winchcombe in 1707 for ten shillings, and presented to the Blue Coat School which she had founded.

### A Violent Siege

Newbury was the scene of two momentous battles between the king's men and the Parlia-ment forces in 1643 and 1644. The fighting was fierce, but the result, on both occasions, some-what indecisive. From the Bath Road, incident-ally, can be seen Donnington Castle, to which violent siege was laid during the Civil War. The Royalist governor put up an amazing resist-ance. Though attacked time and time again he held the fortress from August, 1644, until April, 1646, only surrendering in the end at the command of the king.

A notorious character who will for ever be associated with Newbury is the Rev. Thomas Stackhouse, Vicar of Beenham Vallance. The vicar was as fond of the bottle as he was con-scious of the Bible, and divided his time between the inn and the pulpit. However, drunk or sober, he contrived to write his *History of the Bible*, and, as he once told his critical bishop, " that's more than your Lordship could do."

On to Hungerford—and who has not heard of the famous " tuttimen " who, once a year, go round the town demanding kisses from the wives and daughters of the burgesses, and to each of them presenting an orange.

### Forest Splendour

Now the Bath Road passes through Savernake Forest and its outskirts, the most entrancingly lovely pageant of trees that the eye can behold, great battalions of beeches and oaks stretching for miles. From the forest the road descends the steep hill to Marlborough—a hill that brought disaster to many in the old coaching days.

The exceedingly broad High Street at Marlborough has still its pent-houses supported by pillars. It was down this very street that the Cavaliers of King Charles surged to attack the Roundheads of Cromwell. There are two fine old churches and, despite several great fires in the seventeenth century, some rare old houses.

The ruins of Marlborough Castle are eloquent with romance, for the castle had associations with the kings and queens of England from the time of William I to that of Henry VIII. Around the Castle Mound, a traditional resting place of the wizard Merlin, many Roman and prehistoric relics have been found. On over Marlborough Downs, and beyond West Kennet, we come to

Cherhill Downs with a White Horse carved out of the chalk.

The Bath Road takes us now to Calne, where St. Dunstan is reputed to have saved his life in A.D. 978 by hanging to the beam of a building that fell during an Anglo-Saxon Witan. Thence we come to Chippenham, on the outskirts of which is Maud Heath's Causeway, said to have been made in 1474 to enable country-folk to reach the market (the roads being impassable in winter) and paid for out of the life-savings of Maud, herself only a market-woman.

Past the little hamlet of Cross Keys, and we reach Pickwick, the name of which may or may not have impressed itself on the mind of Dickens when he passed through on his way to Bath. Pickwick is really a part of Corsham, once the residence of Saxon kings, and from here we pass to Box, a favourite country resort of the Romans. Box is renowned for its quarries, from which stone has been taken since Roman times.

A few miles more, and we are in Bath, at the end of the road. Bath, with its noble abbey and Roman baths. Bath, with its memories of Britain's greatest statesmen and warriors, artists and writers. Bath, where you still may fancy that you hear the scratching of Pepys's pen and the honeyed drawl of Beau Nash. The end of the Bath Road was the end of the road for the Beau, too. His power, health and looks gone, the fire of his personality burnt out, he lived his last years on a charitable pittance of £10 a month from the city whose prosperity he had inspired.

EDGAR WARD

### THE BEAUTIFUL CRATER OF BATH

*This panorama gives a splendid impression of the lovely situation of the city in the valley of the Avon. Inhabited by the early Britons, Bath was made permanent by the Romans and achieved the final beauty of its architecture in the eighteenth century with the dignified designs of the two John Woods, Ralph Allen and Richard Nash.*

EDGAR WARD

### "CITY OF THE RED ROOFS"

*Watling Street and Telford's road run through St. Albans, and here we glimpse the great Norman tower of the abbey looming above the uneven roofs of the Elizabethan houses. This Norman tower, said to be one of the finest in England, was built by Paul de Caen in 1077 of bricks and tiles from the old Roman city of Verulam. St. Alban was a Roman soldier who was executed for sheltering the priest who converted him to Christianity.*

# THE HOLYHEAD ROAD

## *by* G. BAKER

A DIRECT and forthright highway is the Holyhead Road. Take a glance at the maps and you see it striking diagonally across England and Wales. North-west from London it runs over the Chilterns and across the wide belt of the Midlands until it reaches the Severn; on through the mountains of Wales by the valleys of Dee and Conway, within sight of Snowdon and down to the narrows of the Menai Straits for its last lap across Anglesey to the rocky stacks of Holyhead.

Possibly our prehistoric forefathers traversed this route before the legions came. Speculative as that may be, there can be no doubt of its Roman days. Much of the present-day road follows the line of the ancient Watling Street, the road the Romans drove first from London to Dover and then right across country to their city of Uriconium by the Severn.

Beyond Shrewsbury it was not until modern days that the present Holyhead Road came into existence. The old coach road went round the coast by Conway and Penmaenmawr; and Macaulay gives a picture of this road near the end of the seventeenth century:

"The great route through Wales to Holyhead was in such a state that, in 1685, a viceroy, going to Ireland, was five hours in travelling fourteen miles, from St. Asaph to Conway. Between Conway and Beaumaris he was forced to walk a great part of the way; and his lady was carried in a litter. His coach was, with great difficulty, and by the help of many hands, brought after him entire. In general, carriages were taken to pieces at Conway, and borne on the shoulders of stout Welsh peasants to the Menai Straits."

At the beginning of the nineteenth century the old road was under the divided administration of no fewer than twenty-three separate Turnpike Trusts. That part of it under the control of the Welsh Trusts was, in particular, narrow and crooked and defectively drained; it climbed hills and crossed valleys without regard to gradients; it had no solid foundation,

much of it being little more than a covering of poor stones or gravel spread over unprepared soil; while it ran by the edge of dangerous precipices its fences were either weak or non-existent.

It was by this road that, after the Act for the Union of Great Britain and Ireland was passed in 1800, Irish Members of Parliament had to travel to Westminster. They made vigorous and persistent complaints about "the extreme inconvenience, difficulty and danger of travelling it."

DIXON-SCOTT

### MODERN STATUE IN MEDIEVAL HALL
*This lovely statue, which stands in the Great Hall of St. Mary's Hall, Coventry, commemorates Lady Godiva, wife of Leofric, Earl of Mercia, who founded a monastery in this city in 1043.*

PHOTOCHROM

### HEADQUARTERS OF THE GUNPOWDER PLOT

*Despite its position on a busy modern highway, Dunchurch, in Warwickshire, retains its rural air. The red brick houses grouped around the village green, the old parish stocks and lock-up, the village smithy and the setting of the parish church seen above, all combine to present a charming picture of an English village. Guy Fawkes and his fellow-conspirators used the village as a centre for an intended Roman Catholic rebellion.*

W. F. TAYLOR

### TWO FAMOUS COACHING INNS

*The " Cock " and the " Bull " the two Georgian inns at Stony Stratford, on the old coaching road to Holyhead, were famed for the gossip and rumours rife there during the Napoleonic wars. Such proportion did these stories assume that it gave rise to the expression " a cock and bull " story—a phrase still in use today. In days still farther away, Edward V was arrested in this Buckinghamshire town by Richard Crookback.*

In this they had the support of the Postmaster General who in 1808 found the highway actually unsafe for a mail coach, and indicted twenty-two parishes for leaving their sections of the road in a dangerous condition. Travellers who could afford it rode post-horses, changing their mounts at recognized stages. Wearing jackboots up to their hips and thick riding boots over their shoulders they were fortunate if they made the journey between London and Holyhead in six days, and still more fortunate if they avoided all falls in the numerous mud-filled pot-holes through which they had to splash their way.

Deciding that something must be done, in 1810 the Government commissioned Thomas Telford, the great Scottish engineer, to survey the road from end to end. Five years later, a first grant of £20,000 enabled him to start its reconstruction. Controlled by ten commissioners —the most active of whom was Sir Henry Parnell, one of the Irish Members—the work went on for fifteen years. In 1830 the road, completed at a cost of three-quarters of a million sterling, was regarded as a model of " the most perfect road-making that has ever been attempted in any country."

### Exits from London

Watling Street left London by the long straight line of Edgware Road. Telford's road, starting from the General Post Office, went by Islington and North Finchley to Barnet and thence by London Colney to St. Albans. The road of today avoids Barnet, but all three routes converge on St. Albans.

That little cathedral city by the Ver, *Verulamium* of the Romans, *Watlingceastre* of the Saxons, and today commemorating the soldier saint, Britain's first Christian martyr, this interesting town where history lies rich and deep would call for a chapter to itself, and some of its story is told elsewhere in this volume.

Two miles north of St. Albans, the Holyhead Road joins Watling Street and follows its course nearly all the way to Weedon. Redbourn village is reached with its fine Georgian inn, " The Bull," whose competitor in coaching days was the Mad Tom Inn opposite, with its picture sign showing " Mad Tom in Bedlam " on one side and " Tom at Liberty " on the other—a reference to the times when pauper lunatics, known popularly as " Mad Toms," were confined in Bethlem Hospital and, on recovering, were given a licence to beg along the roads.

Over the Bedfordshire border, where the Icknield Way crosses Watling Street, is Dunstable. Here Henry I not only built himself a house, used chiefly at Christmas time for riotous revels, but in 1131 founded the Augustinian priory, part of which, including the magnificent

Norman nave, is now the parish church.

Through a deep chalk cutting in the Dunstable Downs the road goes on to Hockliffe and Little Brickhill, whose houses, despite its name, are all of stone. Next comes Fenny Stratford with which several oddities of history are connected. In 1395 the town was fined half a mark for its failure to keep in repair the bridge by which

PHOTOCHROM
### A GATEWAY TO WALES
*The ancient city of Shrewsbury, county town of Shropshire, is rich in memories of her stirring past and has many quaint streets of which Butcher Row, seen above, is one of the finest examples.*

Watling Street was carried over the Ouse. In the church—rebuilt by Browne Willis, the antiquary, in 1726 and dedicated by him to St. Martin in memory of his father—are kept the six small cannon presented to the town by Willis that a salvo might be fired on every St. Martin's Day.

By way of Stony Stratford, Towcester—the Roman *Lactodorum*—is reached. Its " Pomfret Arms " was once the " Saracen's Head," unforgettable by reason of Pickwick's visit and the meeting of Slurk and Pott. On his journeys to Ireland, Swift would stop at the Talbot Inn, and the chair he used there is now kept in the Town Hall.

The road on to Weedon Beck is something of a switchback, although Telford cut down no fewer than seven of the hills and filled up many hollows. At Weedon the barracks and powder-mills were built during the Napoleonic Wars,

STEPHENSON

**A CASTLE OF THE MARCHES**

*In the Shropshire village of Whittington, only five miles from the border, the ruins of this old, moated castle stand on the roadside. Once a stronghold of the Peverils, the castle was maintained until the sixteenth century. In 1760 part of the structure fell into the moat. Some of the masonry was used for road repairs.*

when the invasion scare was at its height. So convinced were the military authorities that Bonaparte would invade the country that they erected a pavilion near the barracks in which George III was to take refuge when he fled from Windsor Castle.

At Weedon, Watling Street and Telford's road part company, but in recent years the Roman road has regained the ascendancy and is now listed as A5—the Holyhead Road.

By the tall, soaring masts of Rugby Wireless Station on along the borders of Leicestershire and Warwickshire, the modern and the Roman road are frequently one, running in long straight reaches until we come to High Cross. This was the Roman station of *Vennones*, where Watling Street crossed the Fosse Way. A monument on this spot once bore the following inscription:

" Traveller, if you seek the footsteps of the ancient Romans, here you may find them. Hence their most famous military ways, crossing one another, proceeded to the utmost limits of Britain. Here the Vennones had their settlement, and at the first mile along the street, Claudius,

the commander of a cohort, had his camp, and at the same distance along the Fosse, his tomb."

By Atherstone and within a few miles of Bosworth Field, and on across Staffordshire; by the edge of Cannock and into Shropshire, Watling Street continues until, in sight of the Wrekin, it is rejoined by Telford's road which runs by Daventry, Coventry and Birmingham.

### The Fifth of November

Daventry, with its conspicuous wireless masts was the Roman *Beneventa*, and some say it was the birthplace of St. Patrick.

In Dunchurch, with its Dun Cow Inn, parish stocks and ancient lock-up, still stands the house which, as the Lion Inn, was in 1605 the headquarters of the Gunpowder Plot conspirators. Had the plot been successful, the neighbouring Dunsmore Heath, through which the old road runs, was to have been the scene of the Roman Catholic rising planned to follow the blowing-up of the Houses of Parliament. When Guy Fawkes was discovered and arrested, his fellow conspirators, Rookwood and Winter, rode desperately from London to Dunsmore, covering the eighty-five miles in seven hours, and shouting, as they galloped through villages and towns, that they were carrying despatches from the king to Northampton.

Five miles from Dunchurch the road passes close to the socket of Knightlow Cross, at which on every St. Martin's Day, the " Wroth Money " due to the Duke of Buccleuch, as lord of the manor of Knightlow Hundred, is collected. At sunrise the representatives of twenty-eight villages deposit small sums totalling 9s. 3½d. in a hollow in the middle of the socket, and these are checked and taken away by the Duke's steward. Failure to pay carries a penalty of either a pound for each penny or, alternatively, " a white bull with pink nose and ears." How this ancient custom originated is not known.

Through Willenhall the road reaches Coventry, the " city of the three tall spires." At the corner of Hertford Street is the effigy of Peeping Tom, recalling the well-known legend of Lady Godiva who rode naked through the streets of Coventry in order to free the town from the oppressive taxation of her husband, Leofric, Earl of Mercia. The expression " to send to Coventry " is said to have originated in the Civil War, when the citizens of unwalled Birmingham sent Royalist prisoners to the then walled Coventry, that their escape would be less easy.

### The Centre of England

After Coventry, hub of England's motor car and cycle industries, comes the village of Meriden, the geographical hub of England. Its name is supposed to be derived, not from the fact that it is the centre of the country, but from the muddy valley or miry dene for which it was infamous among coachmen in Georgian days. Like the previous village of Allesley, Meriden gives evidence of the volume of the traffic carried by the Holyhead Road in the coaching era. In both villages most of the bigger houses, now privately occupied, were formerly inns or posting-houses.

At Stonebridge, one hundred miles from London, the Birmingham area begins. When, in 1547, Birmingham's Gild of the Holy Cross undertook as a work of charity the maintenance and repair of " two great stone bridges and diverse foul and dangerous highways," Birmingham was " one of the fairest and most profitable towns in all the shire." Birmingham is still profitable, but

W. F. TAYLOR

ONE OF THE SEVEN WONDERS OF WALES

*This beautiful old bridge spanning the Dee at Llangollen was originally built about the middle of the fourteenth century by Gobh Trevor, Bishop of St. Asaph, but was widened in 1873. When this work was in progress a stone was found with the initials W.S. and the date 1131 suggesting that an even earlier structure once existed.*

W. F. TAYLOR

### A LOVELY GLEN

*Close by Bettws-y-Coed, the River Conway winds its way through a lovely wooded glen—truly named the Fairy Glen. Here, beneath the trees, the stream leaps downwards to receive the tributary waters of the Lledr.*

hedges ") seems to celebrate. Just over the Shropshire border is the market town of Shifnal, which possesses a number of black and white timbered houses in which the country is so rich.

### The Wrekin

There follows a brief interlude of industrial districts and the mining district of Coalbrookdale and then we continue by Wellington and the Wrekin, Shropshire's famous landmark. The old toast " To friends all round the Wrekin " which Salopians in company seldom fail to drink, marks the local affection for this wooded hill.

From Wellington the road runs close by the ruins of Uriconium and over the Severn at Atcham Bridge. Here in fact there are two bridges side by side. One is a recent erection, the other dates from 1796. This replaced a structure built by Sir Rowland Hill, then Lord Mayor of London, in 1549-1550. But there was a bridge here in the thirteenth century, for there were complaints at the Assizes in 1221 of the Abbot of Lilleshall instituting a toll.

Today a by-pass avoids Shrewsbury, but the time saved can be no compensation for not visiting this fascinating old town, which is entered by the noble approach of Abbey Foregate with its fine trees and stately timbered houses. Through the precincts of the abbey ruins, impressive in their beauty of red sandstone, the road crosses the Severn by the English Bridge. Across the Welsh Bridge leading over the farther bend of the Severn loop in which Shrewsbury lies, the road becomes, in the language of the old chroniclers, " the reddie way to Wales."

Through the suburb of Frankwell with its wealth of " magpie " houses, the road climbs the steep rise on the crest of which is " The Mount." This fine old red-brick house was the birthplace of Charles Darwin in 1809. A little farther on, standing behind a one-time toll-house, is the

it is not fair. Nor are the typical Black Country towns—Wednesbury, Moxley, Bilston and Wolverhampton—through which the road next passes. Yet Wednesbury, built on the site of a Saxon town, is named after a god, the Saxon Woden; while the name of Wolverhampton preserves the memory of Wulfrun, the Saxon princess who in A.D. 994 founded its fine collegiate church of St. Peter, now the parish church.

With Wolverhampton the road leaves the Black Country behind—a fact which the oddly-named hamlet, the Wergs (meaning " the willow famous Shelton Oak under which, according to tradition, Owen Glendower watched the defeat and death of his ally Harry Percy (Hotspur) at the hands of the English under Henry IV at the Battle of Shrewsbury in 1403.

### The Hills of Wales

Beyond Shrewsbury the low hills of Breidden in Montgomeryshire, are a graceful landmark, for all their modest height presenting an attractive and dignified outline.

Whittington, a pleasing little hamlet with the ruins of a moated castle on the roadside, is next reached, and soon we descend to the vale of Ceiriog, and beyond that stream we step into Wales and mount the hill to Chirk with its castle dating from the eleventh century. Hereabouts the road cuts right through Offa's Dyke, the great earthwork made by the Saxon king of Mercia.

The Dee Valley is reached at Llangollen and for the next ten miles to Corwen Telford's highway affords many a lovely view of the river and its delightful vale. Beyond Corwen we begin to climb with the Berwyns behind us and moorlands ahead which we must cross on the way by Cerrig-y-Druidion and Pentre Voelas and down to the Vale of Conway.

Along this road came George Borrow on his way to Wild Wales, and with him we may journey to Bangor by Bettws-y-Coed and up the valley of the Llugwy and by the Swallow Falls where in the coaching days the Holyhead Mail would halt for five minutes so that travellers might admire the scene.

At Capel Curig, Borrow dined among fashionable company who surveyed him with supercilious disdain which, however, did not deprive him of his appetite.

Six miles west of Capel Curig the great horseshoe of Snowdon's peaks makes an eloquent appeal, but Telford's highway leaves them on one side and continues up the Llugwy Valley and on to Ogwen. Thence it runs between the boulderstrewn flanks of Tryfaen and the shores of Llyn Ogwen to the head of Nant Ffrancon. Here the road reaches its highest point 957 feet above sea level, and here too it attains its wildest grandeur. Over the stream plunging from Llyn Ogwen, Telford carried his highway on a single flying arch. From here we overlook the deep green vale of Ffrancon, down which may be seen the silver stream and the old track which was described in the year 1759 as "the most dreadful horsepath in Wales."

Borrow had a Welshman for company as he passed this way, but in between his gossip he noticed the valley down which the road ran, " having an enormous wall of rocks on the right and a precipitous hollow on the left, beyond which was a wall equally as high as the other one."

STEPHENSON

### "BY LAKES AND MOUNTAINS WILD"

*The wildest scenery on the Holyhead Road is found between Capel Curig and Bethesda where the road runs by the shores of Llyn Ogwen between the Carnedds and the Glyders. Here, Pennant, the eighteenth-century writer, said he saw the shepherds skipping from peak to peak, the point of contact being so small.*

JOURNEY'S END

W. F. TAYLOR

*Telford's famous highway reaches the end of its journeyings at Holyhead. South of the town is the rocky islet of South Stack with its famous lighthouse perched above the fine cliffs, the haunts of seagull and falcon.*

on the island is Llanfairpwll-gwyngyllgogerchwyndrob-wllltysiliogogogoch. To an Englishman its name suggests a stuttering sneezing, but for the Welshman it has the poetic meaning of "The church of St. Mary in the hollow of white hazel, near to the rapid whirlpool of St. Tysilio and a red cave."

### Dean Swift

On its final lap of twenty-one miles the road passes no fewer than five former toll-houses, at one of which the last toll was collected as late as November 1, 1895. A mile-long embankment connects Anglesey with Holy Isle on which Holyhead is built. Although an unlovely town, it is no longer " the scurvy, unprovided, comfortless place " which Swift described it to be in his *Journal* of 1727. But when Swift wrote, Stella lay dying in Ireland. To reach her bedside he had posted furiously along the Holyhead Road, only to find that because of wild weather, no ship would sail. For a week he waited, fretfully walking the beach, and raging against all things Welsh, even to the very dogs. "On my conscience," he wrote, "you may know a Welsh dog as well as a Welsh man or woman by its peevish, passionate way of barking."

So we have reached the end of Telford's great highway, in itself a magnificent engineering feat, and an historic event in the history of English roads. For the first time since the Romans had left Britain, national enterprise had undertaken the construction of a continuous piece of road, ordered and planned from end to end for the one purpose of making easy and quick travel between its two extremities. Even today it remains the most forthright and purposeful road in the country. It survived strongly against the first challenge of the railways that came so soon afterwards and now, with the rebirth of road transport, is coming once more into the birthright which workmanship and beauty deserve.

A little beyond Bethesda, where the slate quarries were mercifully hidden in darkness, and where he was informed the manners of the people were not so scriptural as the name, Borrow joined a market gardener and together they swung into Bangor at the goodly pace of six miles an hour. Bangor, whose diminutive cathedral is smaller than many English parish churches, now has a university college which was the huge " Penrhyn Arms " of coaching days.

The famous suspension bridge, 580 feet long, designed by Telford, carries the road at a height of 100 feet above high water over the Menai Straits to Anglesey. The second village reached

# THE GREAT NORTH ROAD

## *by* MICHAEL GEELAN

THE Great North Road, the A1 highway of Britain! The very name has the ring of romance. To those dwelling in the south country it offers a challenge and an invitation, an urge to traverse the length of Britain, a beckoning along its four hundred miles across the chequered counties by hamlet, town and city in varied succession, and at last over the border and on to Edinburgh's fair city.

Down through the centuries it has been a road of history. Its line has varied here and there with the changing times, but always it has served as the way to the north. Roman legionaries first forged its original course, perhaps utilizing existing trackways. For Saxons and Danes it was a ready-made highway. Along it Harold hastened to Stamford Bridge and back again on his way to his doom at Hastings. Along it the Norman Conqueror sent his armies to devastate the lands of the intractable Yorkshiremen.

Kings and nobles, pedlars and wandering minstrels, beggars and highwaymen have passed this way. Knights-at-arms on superb chargers, monks and merchants on slow, ambling mules and mares, and mountebanks on donkeys have travelled its length. The litter and palanquin, the post-chaise and the carrier's wagon, the stage-coach, the bone-shaker and the penny-farthing, the safety-bicycle and the steam-carriage—the Great North Road has known them all. It has been an avenue of travel and adventure for every phase of humanity.

For centuries it was a lonely and hazardous way. Its surface was broken and rough, due to neglect, which made many stretches of the road, particularly in mid-winter, quite impassable.

In 1282, for instance, Edward I summoned two Parliaments—one for the south and one for the north — because of travelling difficulties. When James VI of Scotland came to London to mount the English throne he took five weeks riding down the Great North Road. In 1634, when Charles I planned a trip to Scotland, a year's notice was given to the local authorities, so that the road might be prepared for his progress. During the Civil War, eight hundred soldiers of the king became mud-bound on the road, and were slaughtered by Cromwell's men.

STEPHENSON

### AN OLD BEDFORDSHIRE TOWN

*Forty miles north of London the Great North Road passes through Biggleswade, an ancient borough by prescription, and, at the time of Edward the Confessor, owned as a manor by Archbishop Stigand. Biggleswade is the centre of a great vegetable-growing district, but formerly it was extensively engaged in straw plaiting.*

PHOTOCHROM

## A GREY OLD TOWN

*Built almost entirely of grey limestone weathered by age, Stamford is probably the most picturesque town on the Great North Road.    A notable feature of the town is its beautiful churches, one of which, St. Martin's, is seen above.    In this edifice are several elaborate tombs including that of Lord Burleigh, Queen Elizabeth's Lord Treasurer.    In the fourteenth century seceding students made the town a rival to Oxford for a short time.*

The Great North Road of the coaching days, starting from what is now the General Post Office in St. Martins-le-Grand, proceeded through Islington with its market gardens to Highgate. It was from the top of Highgate Hill that Dick Whittington is said to have heard the peal of Bow bells entreating him to "turn again." Believe, if you please, that it is a fairy story, but there on Highgate Hill is the Whittington Stone which marks the spot where Dick meditated and rested with his cat and his bundle, his hopes and his dreams. It was on Highgate Hill, too, that Francis, Lord Bacon (the man who might have been Shakespeare!) caught his "death of cold," having ventured upon the very childish experiment of stuffing a fowl with snow.

At Finchley, with its wide stretch of common, the traveller looked to his purse and his pistols, for this spot was once a profitable territory for highwaymen. Dick Turpin was its most famous rascal, and a bullet-pocked oak tree is named after him to this day. Claude Duval came to Finchley sometimes when Hounslow was too hot to hold him, and Jack Sheppard was caught there by Bow Street runners, after having unwisely mixed drink with business. Many years after Dick Turpin had been well and truly hanged by the neck, the noble Earl of Minto declared, "I shall not trust my throat on Finchley Common in the dark."

### Swords for the Kingmaker

Whetstone, it has been suggested, owes its name to the fact that it was here that the soldiers whetted their swords before the Battle of Barnet. The hoary old stone is there, anyway. Pepys records that he found the road at Whetstone in a dreadful state. Apparently the natives were not entirely in favour of progress, for, in 1754 they drove the road-improvers out at the point of the pitch-fork.

It was at Barnet that Guy of Warwick made his last stand and was killed in 1471 during the Wars of the Roses. Of modern interest is Livingstone's house at Hadley Green, and the centuries-old Horse Fair held in September.

Hatfield, with its ancient manor house was once attached to Ely Abbey to which it was given by the Saxon King Edgar.

It was at Hatfield House that Queen Elizabeth, living in confinement, received the news of Mary Tudor's death and of her own accession. This old residence of the Marquess of Salisbury contains a valuable historical collection, including various mementoes of the young Elizabeth.

The hills of Highgate and the narrow streets of Barnet and Hatfield are avoided by the Great North Road today, for modern by-pass roads skirt these congested areas. North of Hatfield, however, the old road is rejoined and followed

TRUST HOUSES, LTD.

### ONCE A BISHOP'S PALACE

*In bygone days the Bishop of Lincoln had a palace at Buckden, Hunts., on the Great North Road. All vestiges have now gone save for the refectory, which is now part of the Lion Hotel, itself an ancient posting-house.*

through Welwyn to Stevenage, where six grassy mounds known as the "Six Hills" and thought to be prehistoric tumuli, can be seen beside the road. Here too at the Old Castle Inn is the coffin of a one-time landlord Henry Trigg, who made certain bequests in his will provided his body were committed "to the West end of my hovel." His executors placed the coffin among the rafters of his stable, where it remains to this day.

And so on to Baldock founded by the Knights Templars in the reign of Stephen. At the church of St. Mary is preserved a chalice which, filled with wine, was offered by the rector Mosias Byrd to the captive Charles I who passed through the town on his way from Newmarket to Windsor.

A few miles away lies Biggleswade, almost totally destroyed by a terrible fire in 1785, but now a flourishing agricultural centre. Sutton Park on the road just outside the town is said to have been the seat of John of Gaunt who gave it to the Burgoyne family. The grant is said to have been in the form of doggerel verse :

"I John of Gaunt
 Do give and do grant
 Unto Roger Burgoyne
 And the heirs of his loin
 Both Sutton and Potton
 Until the world's rotten."

Through the Bedfordshire levels the road follows a tortuous course and, after crossing the slow, unruffled Ouse, runs into the attractive village of Eaton Socon. This was doubtless the Eton Slocomb of *Nicholas Nickleby* where Dr. Squeers and his pupils broke their journey on the way to Dotheboys Hall.

Another few miles brings us to the village of Buckden in Huntingdonshire. Here in bygone days the Bishops of Lincoln had a splendid palace. A little north of this village, and lying off the road is Brampton, where may be seen the house where the father of Pepys lived and the garden where he buried his gold in fear of Dutch invaders.

At Alconbury Hill the road joins the older route which follows the line of the Roman Ermine Street through Ware, Royston and Huntingdon. At this point in 1786 was gibbeted one Gervase Matcham for a crime committed six years previously. Barham's *Ingoldsby Legends* in the *Dead Drummer* tells the story of the crime, of how Matcham murdered a drummer boy at the spot still known as Matcham's Bridge.

At Stilton they will tell you there is really no such thing as Stilton cheese. It originated at Melton Mowbray, but the landlord of the " Bell " at Stilton publicized and popularized it, and found it a profitable line at half a crown a pound.

Less than a mile away is Norman Cross, which during the Napoleonic Wars was the site of an internment camp for prisoners of war. Over 3,000 of the enemy remained in captivity there for something like ten years. Many died. Some went mad. Others escaped to the coast. The prison was demolished in 1816 and no trace of it remains. In 1914 a memorial was erected to the prisoners. Such is the irony of history.

### Grey Romantic Streets

At Sibson, as we near Stamford, you can still see at the roadside the old stocks and whipping-post of other days. Stamford itself, stately and . lovely, with narrow twisting streets and old houses of pearl grey stone, is rich in romance and tradition. Many centuries ago Stamford was the seat of a university. In 1260 a number of Oxford students who had quarrelled with the citizens of Oxford emigrated first to Northampton and later to Stamford. Several colleges were established, but eventually, owing to pressure from Oxford and Cambridge, Stamford University came to an inglorious end in 1463.

Stamford, too, has seen much fighting both during the Wars of the Roses and the Civil

W. F. TAYLOR

A LOVELY HOTEL FAÇADE

*Grantham, Lincs., can boast many evidences of its great age. The town is recorded as a borough in Domesday Book, there is a conduit dating from 1597 in the market-place and two ancient libraries in the church. The Angel and Royal Hotel, shown above, was built in the fifteenth century, but the gateway is even earlier.*

W  F. TAYLOR

### THE KEY OF THE NORTH

*Newark Castle, in Nottinghamshire, was founded by Egbert, King of the West Saxons, and was extensively altered and enlarged by the Normans, whose gate-house, tower and crypt remain.   The castle was known for centuries as  the Key of the North, and during the Civil War, endured three sieges for Charles I.*

DIXON SCOTT

### THE MARKET IN OLD DONCASTER

*This famous Yorkshire town, so largely associated with racing, has important railway and coal industries. Doncaster began its history as the manor of Earl Tostig.   A Charter granted in 1194 to hold fairs on the vigil, feast and morrow of the Annunciation was confirmed by Henry VII, and today the markets are still held under the charter.   The town, built to command the Don river crossing, is the true gate to Yorkshire.*

Wars. Here also may be found the grave of that strange figure Daniel Lambert, the fat man. His epitaph is: "In Remembrance of that Prodigy in Nature Daniel Lambert who was possessed of an exalted and convivial mind and in personal greatness had no Competitor. He measured three feet, one inch, round the leg, nine feet, four inches, round the body, and

DIXON-SCOTT

ST. JAMES'S SQUARE, BOROUGHBRIDGE
*When the line of the Great North Road was altered in the eleventh century, a bridge was erected over the River Ure and called Burgh Bridge. By it grew a village which gradually swelled into an important market town.*

weighed Fifty-two stone Eleven pounds." Daniel, who was only thirty-nine when he died in 1809, paid at least two visits to London, and his portly and benevolent form has figured in many an inn sign.

Onwards the undeviating line of the road speaks of the Roman surveyors, and reminds us we are now traversing Ermine Street. A few miles short of Grantham the little upland village of Great Ponton boasts a fine old Gothic church built in 1519, one of the most curious features of which is the violin weather vane on the pinnacle of the tower. The story goes that there once wandered into the village a poor fiddler, hungry and ill-clad. The villagers took pity on him, provided food and clothing, and paid him for playing at fairs and weddings and other such occasions. Eventually he was enabled by his savings to travel to America, where he amassed a fortune. In later years, when he revisited the village, he insisted upon repairing the decaying church, making the one condition that the weather-vane should take the shape of his old fiddle. So much for legend, but the precise historians give no credence to the tale.

Grantham, a few miles farther on, is one of the most famous coaching towns in history, boasting two ancient inns, the "Angel" and the "George." Both King John and King Richard III rested at the "Angel," while Dickens evokes memories of the "George" in his *Nicholas Nickleby*. Some idea of the vexations of travel along the Great North Road in the early nineteenth century is afforded by the words of Francis, Lord Jeffrey, presumably written in the "George": "Here we are ... toiling up through snow and darkness, with this shattered carcase and this half-desponding spirit. Tonight it snows and blows, and there is good hope of our being blocked up at Wytham Corner or Alconbury Hill, or some of these lonely retreats, for a week or so, or fairly stuck in the drift and obliged to wade our way to some such hovel as received poor Lear and his fool on some such season. Oh, dear, dear!" This was written on a Monday, and he added that he hoped to reach London before dark on the Wednesday.

It was near Grantham that Oliver Cromwell began to rise to fame when, in 1643, with only a handful of men, he defeated twice the number of Royal troops with ease. The battle took place at Gonerby Hill, which was immortalized by both Scott and Ainsworth. One of the most curious of the old customs at Grantham was the ceremony of "striking His Worship the Mayor." When his period of office had terminated, the Mayor was taken out in full view of the burgesses, his robes and his chain were removed, and he was then tapped on the head with a wooden mallet to indicate that his job was over.

### A Historic Stronghold

Newark is a name proud in historical associations. It was at Newark Castle that King John, one of the most disreputable of English sovereigns, died from over-eating—though it has been suggested that he was poisoned. The castle was also one of the last strongholds to remain faithful to Charles I. Besieged three times by the Cromwellian forces, it refused to yield until so commanded by the unfortunate king. Its ruins are a legacy of that final surrender. Newark is said to have at one time possessed half a hundred inns, and the market square was constantly agog with the arrival and departure of travellers. One of its most curious customs is the " Ringing for Gofer." Two hundred years ago, it appears, a merchant of that name was lost in the night in Sherwood Forest. At the mercy of the darkness and marauding bands of robbers, he had almost given up hope, when the bells of Newark rang out and piloted him to safety. To express his gratitude, Gofer bequeathed a sum of money for the bells to be tolled from the old parish church on six successive Sunday evenings before each Christmas.

At Grantham we left Ermine Street to continue its way to Lincoln and at Newark we cross the Fosse Way, another Roman road striking diagonally across England from Devonshire to Lincoln. As we proceed northwards, if the day be clear, we may gain a glimpse of the tall, upstanding towers of Lincoln Cathedral, a superb landmark nearly twenty miles away to the east.

Retford, on the Idle, is busy with various industries. It possesses many coaching relics and here they will tell you of the many redoubtable feats of John Blagg, a remarkable postboy, who once rode to York and back—a distance of one hundred and ten miles—in a day.

At Bawtry a saddler was once lynched for refusing the hospitable offer of a drink of ale. Here also there was once a sinister pond into which coaches in the pay of the highwaymen would be driven, and when the frightened travellers looked out of their windows they were confronted with the really ominous threat of " your money or your life."

### The Gate to Yorkshire

Now the Great North Road enters Yorkshire, the county of moors and fells, of lovely rivers and winding dales. The road, however, does not lead us through the choicest scenery, but follows the wide central vale offering little more than glimpses of the Cleveland and Hambleton Hills to the east and the Pennines in the west. In succession the road crosses the rivers of Aire, Wharfe, Nidd and Swale and finally over the Tees into Durham.

The road runs into Doncaster by the Town Moor, the famous racecourse where the St. Leger is run. Racing has been in progress there since 1600 and the St. Leger was founded in

EDGAR WARD

### VENERABLE DURHAM
*The River Wear at Durham loops round a rocky headland crowned with the castle and cathedral. The stately towers of the cathedral are seen in the background above. William the Conqueror founded the castle in 1089. Later it served as the residence of the Prince Bishops and now it is part of Durham University.*

W. F. TAYLOR

### CASTLE OF BORDER BALLAD

*Newcastle gained its name from the Norman stronghold built there in 1080. To the gates of the castle in 1388 came the Scots under the " doughty Douglas," a few days before the Battle of Otterburn, where Douglas was slain. Part of the Black Gate, seen above, now serves as a museum.*

road continues by Thirsk and Northallerton to Darlington.

The road of today keeps more to the west up to Wetherby and thence to Boroughbridge, an attractive little market town. Near here are the three standing stones known as the Devil's Arrows. Aldborough, a little to the south, now a quiet hamlet, was in Roman days of considerable importance and retains some relics of its former glory. Perhaps before the Romans it was a place of consequence, the capital of the fierce Brigantes. Queen of this intractable tribe was the fickle Cartimandua who, despite the advice of her husband, betrayed the brave Caratacus to the Romans. This action is said to have led to civil war and, in A.D. 69, the queen cast off her husband and married her standard bearer, Vellocatus. Her spouse, however, had the backing of his tribe and the queen was forced to flee to the Romans for protection.

### Agricola's Road

Northwards we are once more on a Roman road, the Dere Street which Agricola drove from York to Scotland.

Along the straight lengths of Leeming Lane by Catterick, once a Roman station and today an extensive army camp, and so we continue to Scotch Corner.

There we leave Agricola's Road, though a secondary road, often used today, follows much of his route across Weardale to the Tyne and on over the Cheviots and the border.

To continue by A1 we cross the Tees into Durham and on to Darlington, a town which sounded the knell of coaching days, for here, in 1825, the first steam locomotive line was opened. Yet the first train to run was drawn by a horse. Old coach bodies mounted on special wheels were drawn along as an experiment and human life was not entrusted to a locomotive for some months, when the speed was twelve miles an hour. The early carriages were all open topped.

1778. At one time the race meetings attracted a furtive and scheming element. Dickens, when he was there in 1857, records that he saw " a gathering of blackguards from all parts of the racing earth. Every bad face that had ever caught wickedness from an innocent horse had its representation in the streets."

From Doncaster the old North Road runs by Selby and over the Ouse toll-bridge to the grand old city of York, the city which more than any other in England retains the appearance of a walled town of the Middle Ages. Thence the

Stephenson's first engine, the "Locomotion" is today mounted on a pedestal at Darlington station.

Onwards the road leads to Neville's Cross, where the Scots were overwhelmed in 1346 and their king, David II, was taken prisoner. Here we are on the edge of Durham, a place of amazing contrasts, a town of dismal streets and huddled dwellings, and yet a city crowned with a superb cathedral unrivalled in Britain for its magnificent position. There, high above the contumacious town, it stands on a rocky promontory almost encircled by the River Wear. Close by, and now part of the University of Durham, is the ancient castle of the prince-bishops who once enjoyed temporal as well as spiritual authority, and who ruled with almost kingly power.

### A Link with Durham

Chester-le-Street, now a mining town, reveals in its name its Roman origin. There, in A.D. 883, after eight years of wandering, came the holy monks of Lindisfarne bearing with them "the incorruptible body" of St. Cuthbert. There the sacred relic remained for a century and more

until, in A.D. 995, it was taken to that eminence above the River Wear and over it was built the forerunner of Durham's stately cathedral.

Out of Durham we cross the Tyne into Northumberland at Newcastle. In this smoke-blackened city with its stone-cobbled streets and grim buildings there is a purposeful air, something of the dourness and determination of the canny Tynesiders. The castle from which the town takes its name was "new" as long ago as 1080, when it was built by the eldest son of the Conqueror on his return from a foray beyond the border. In Roman days the place was known as *Pons Aelii* from the bridge which was given the family name of the Emperor Hadrian, while in Saxon times it was named Monkchester.

Charles I was a prisoner in Newcastle for ten months in 1646 and from there he was delivered to Parliament by the Scots. During his captivity he attended the cathedral, a fourteenth-century edifice, then the parish church. The preacher announced the fifty-second psalm opening:
"Why dost thou, tyrant, boast abroad,
Thy wicked works to praise?"
Charles, not liking the personal reference, stood

FOX PHOTOS

### THE GATE OF HOTSPUR'S CASTLE
*Alnwick, the county town of Northumberland, scene of border forays for many a century, is dominated from the south bank of the Aln by the castle. Long held by the Percys, the castle has now largely lost its historic character through renovation. The Hotspur Tower, seen above, is a relic of the town's medieval fortifications.*

DIXON-SCOTT

## LINKING ENGLAND WITH SCOTLAND

*Berwick-on-Tweed dates its importance from the twelfth century when the River Tweed became the boundary between England and Scotland. Before the Royal Border railway bridge and the wider road bridge were erected, the Great North Road went into Scotland over this lovely old bridge which was completed in 1634.*

up and called instead for the fifty-sixth psalm :
> "Have mercy, Lord, on me, I pray,
>      For man would me devour."

The congregation sympathized with the king and his choice was sung.

Now through shaggy Northumberland the road approaches the border, passing through Morpeth and on to Alnwick. This grey old town, now a quiet place, has seen strife and excitement enough in the past. Scene of many a border clash, and the ancient home of the warlike Percys, it still retains hints of feudal days. Straddling our road is Hotspur's Tower, a fifteenth-century gateway, and a relic of Alnwick's medieval defences. Here Malcolm Canmore was slain in 1093. King John burnt the town down in 1216, and here three years later William the Lion, of Scotland, was taken prisoner. In the Wars of the Roses it was held first by Warwick, and then by Queen Margaret, just as in the Civil War it was held in turn by Royalists and Roundheads.

Now with distant glimpses of the Cheviot hills on the one hand and the grey waters of the North Sea on the other, and perhaps affording a view of Lindisfarne, Northumbria's Holy Isle, the road leads to the border town of Berwick.

In the thirteenth century Berwick, according to an ancient chronicler, was "a city so populous and of such trade that it might justly be called another Alexandria, whose riches were the sea and the waters its walls."

Three miles beyond Berwick the road enters Scotland at Lamberton Old Toll, which was once a goal for eloping couples, though lacking the fame of Gretna. Over the eastern end of the Lammermuir Hills, by Cockburnspath and down by Douglas Dene the road runs to Dunbar. This historic city was created a royal burgh by David II. In the Gaelic the name means "the fort on the point" and as early as A.D. 856 there is said to have been a castle on the cliffs. Today may be seen the ruins of the castle which in 1336 was successfully held against the English by the famed Black Agnes of Dunbar.

### The Hand of Cromwell

It was at Dunbar in 1650 that Cromwell overcame the Scots. As his troops advanced before dawn the Lord Protector was heard to remark "Now let God arise, and let his enemies be scattered."

Through the "red lands" of East Lothian, by Haddington with its ruined abbey, "the Lamp of Lothian," and on by Prestonpans with stirring memories of the '45, so at last we enter the Scottish capital of Edinburgh.

There at the end of the road as we behold Arthur's Seat and Calton Hill, and see the city "throned in crags" we may agree with the Scot who said "If Edinburgh can compare with the Eternal City in no other particular, she can do so in the eternal beauty of her site, which nothing that man's vandalism can inflict is able to impair."

# EDINBURGH TO JOHN O' GROAT'S

## by WALTER K. R. NEILSON

A VERY ancient highway indeed it is which leaves Edinburgh by the Queensferry Road and swings out westward above the estuary of the Forth. Modern developments and hurrying traffic cannot conceal the atmosphere of old romance which clings to the spare Scottish landscape along its course and the memorials of a stormy past which stud its length : the spreading tentacles of the Scots capital now reach out to Lauriston Castle, once the home of John Law, who, during a crowded and chequered career, founded the Bank of France ; a modern bridge has supplanted the old boo-backit brig across the Almond which served the traveller so faithfully for centuries, and a few miles farther on the beautiful 800-year-old Norman kirk of Dalmeny is worthy of more than passing notice.

The quaint red-tiled roofs of South Queensferry, with its ancient harbour, kirk and tollbooth, seem oddly at variance with the gigantic girder work of the Forth Bridge, for this little town is an ancient settlement. Malcolm Canmore's good Queen Margaret established the ferry and from the harbour Cromwell's industrious lieutenant, Monk, made his tiger-spring over into Fife.

Our road now leaves the shore and climbs up to Linlithgow with its vast Royal Palace and old St. Michael's Kirk where James IV received that miraculous warning which, if taken, would have prevented the disaster of Flodden. The palace was accidentally fired by General Hawley's dragoons during the '45, but the birthplace of Mary Queen of Scots, and the immense banqueting hall attest to its former importance.

Beyond Linlithgow our road traverses Scotland's narrow industrial belt. Falkirk's thriving iron foundries silence the voices of the past which whisper around this historic town, but the spire of the old, but very much restored, kirk may have witnessed the passage of Wallace and Bruce. North of Falkirk we begin to rise out of the midland valley and here and there we espy a suspicion of misty blue peaks ahead and we become dimly aware of crossing an invisible frontier. More than once this belt of country between Falkirk and Stirling has been the no-man's-land between Scotland's armed hosts and their foes. In 1297 Wallace's small army, its position and strength treacherously betrayed, was routed by the Welsh and Irish mercenaries of England's first Edward. In the wooded slopes north of the Carron Water, the cunningly contrived field fortifications of the Royalist, General Leslie, defied the might of Cromwell until the Ironside turned his flank by forcing the passage at Queensferry and so compelled that brilliant but unlucky strategist to fall back on Stirling.

A few miles short of Stirling our road traverses the straggling little townships of Bannockburn and St. Ninians between which, under the capable leadership of Robert Bruce, the Scots fought the most momentous battle of their long troubled history. The exact location of the armies is now a matter of dispute, time and the labours of the agriculturalist have long since effaced the surface evidence of the conflict, but on a slight eminence at St. Ninians may be seen the Borestone where the redoubtable Bruce planted his standard.

CHARLES REID

### "CROSSING THE INDIGNANT TAY"
*Aberfeldy Bridge is a fine example of work done by General Wade in opening up the country to enforce the Disarming Act of 1724. Nearby is the memorial to the first raising of that famous regiment, the Black Watch.*

FOX PHOTOS

THE GARRY RIVER AT KILLIECRANKIE

*Between Pitlochry and Blair Atholl is the thickly-wooded Pass of Killiecrankie, where the road runs by the side of the tumbling Garry. Here, near the present-day railway station, Bonnie Dundee brought his Jacobites to combat with General Mackay in 1689, led them to victory, only to be killed himself as the fight was won.*

FOX PHOTOS

### BIRTHPLACE OF THE QUEEN OF SCOTS

*Linlithgow Castle was built in the fifteenth century, a square and massive building doing duty as a fortress and palace. Mary Queen of Scots was born there in 1542, and from a little room known as Queen Margaret's Bower, it is said that the return of James IV from the stricken field of Flodden was watched for in vain.*

None of the ancient towns of Scotland wears its mantle of romance with a tighter fit than Stirling ; the embattled summit of its castle rock fairly dominates the country around, a pre-destined focus of military activity. The approach to the castle, up hilly streets with ancient arch-ways and narrow vennels tune the mind to the memorials of old Scotland which cluster around the Castlehill. There is a peculiar " Scottishness " in the austere simplicity of the ancient Kirk of the Holy Rood which closes the prospect at the head of the brae and in which the infant James VI was crowned. Its bell tower still bears the mark of Jacobite grape shot. Fronting the street, adjacent to the old kirkyard are the grey rubble walls of Mar's Wark built by the Earl of Mar, one of the ill-starred Regents of the Nation during the troubled minority of James VI.

A broad square fronts the aspiring pile of Stirling Castle. A modern drawbridge and door-way lead to the old gateway of James IV, inside which lies the courtyard flanked by the palace and the Parliament House. The former is believed to have been designed by Cochrane, the architect favourite of James III, who met an untimely death at the end of a rope over Lauder Bridge at the instance of the jealous nobles led by Archibald " Bell the Cat." Many other buildings of romantic associations crowd on the Castle Rock, the Chapel Royal, the Old Mint, the Douglas Room over the window of which the enraged James II cast the stabbed corpse of the Earl of Douglas after a hot dispute ; no other place in Scotland can offer so many objects of interest within so narrow a compass.

### Stricken Jacobite Hopes

Though now retired from active service, the old Stirling Bridge still spans the sluggish waters of the Forth close to the site of the timber structure around which William Wallace won his victory over a greatly superior English force. The great patriot is commemorated in the some-what pretentious Wallace Monument on the crags above the old bridge. Circling round the scarred shoulders of Dunmyat of the Ochils, our road traverses the fashionable spa of Bridge of Allan and touches history again at Dunblane. On the grassy wind-swept heaths east of the town was fought the Battle of Sheriffmuir which, although indecisive in itself, yet finished the '15 Rebellion and extinguished Jacobite hopes for thirty years until Prince Charlie again fanned the smouldering embers into flame.

The old Cathedral of Dunblane, with parts dating from the twelfth century, still raises its hoary tower above the swirling pools of the Allan Water. Inside the church a marble slab marks the tomb of the three Drummond sisters, one of whom was espoused to the young king,

A. BROWN

## TAY'S LOVELY CITY

*Beautifully situated on the River Tay, Perth is almost destitute of ancient relics, due to the firebrands who listened to John Knox in 1559, and to the work of energetic civic authorities early in the nineteenth century. In Curfew Row stands Simon Glover's House, the supposed home of Sir Walter Scott's heroine, " The Fair Maid of Perth."  A mile or two from the city was Scone Abbey, where Scotland's kings were once crowned.*

FRITH

## ON THE ALLAN WATER AT DUNBLANE

*Between its bonny wooded banks the Allan Water, here seen near Dunblane, flows through a pleasant country-side to join the Forth near Stirling.  Dunblane, on the north bank of the river, has a notable Gothic cathedral of the thirteenth century with a Norman tower, part of which belongs to the original church built in 1150. Allan Water is the scene of the soldier's betrayal of the " miller's lovely daughter, fairest of them all."*

James IV, to the displeasure of the Anglophile nobility who desired an English consort for their monarch. The times were not marked by a scrupulous niceness, the unfortunate sisters were poisoned and the way cleared for the accession of Margaret Tudor.

Our route from Dunblane passes up through the green fertility of Strathallan embosomed in the brown moorlands. On the left near Braco, old entrenchments whisper to us of a brief

both an injustice. Amid its thriving dye works, textile mills, cattle and railway yards, Perth has still preserved two memorials of its past in the Fair Maid's House and the ancient Church of St. John the Baptist where John Knox, in 1559, preached his fiery harangue and set alight the orgy of mob violence which destroyed all its religious establishments. Two miles farther up the road the modern Scone Palace has replaced the ancient residence of the Scots Royal House

R. M. ADAM

### GRACEFUL BIRCHES IN STRATHSPEY

*On the south side of the Spey, near Aviemore, is the beautifully situated Loch Pityoulish, one of the several lochs in the forest of Rothiemurchus, in the country of the famous " Wolf of Badenoch." Typical of the region are the slender birches, the great expanses of pine woods, and above them the massive Cairngorms.*

invasion by the Roman legions. The fruit nurseries around Auchterarder indicate few traces of its troublous past, of its burning by the Jacobites in 1715, of the dispute which led to the Disruption of the Kirk in 1843. Ahead lies the low haugh lands of Strathearn and Perth.

The old burgh of Perth is literally part of the texture of Scots history but now retains few relics of its days of ancient greatness. Its delightful situation astride the Tay and embosomed in well-timbered hills has evoked a comparison with Rome on the Tiber, an analogy which does

where Robert the Bruce was so precariously crowned.

The small town of Birnam has achieved immortality through its associations with Shakespeare's *Macbeth*, while its neighbour, Dunkeld, nestling below the wooded heights of Craig-y-Barns, is noteworthy for its old cathedral, part of which is still used for worship.

At Ballinluig we are but a short distance from Aberfeldy, which, in its graceful old bridge across the Tay, treasures the most impressive monument to the great roadmaker, General Wade. At Ballinluig also our highway forsakes the Tay and follows upwards the course of its tributary, the Garry, through the sophisticated little inland resort of Pitlochry and resumes its acquaintance with old romance on the green pastures of Urrard below the Pass of Killiecrankie where was fought the battle known to history by that name. The impetuous charge of the clansmen under " Bonnie Dundee " smashed the ranks of William's Dutch mercenaries, but in the height of the struggle their leader was shot and the Highlanders melted away into the mountains with their plunder.

We pass the hotels and villas of Blair Atholl

through its associations with Prince Charlie. Moy Hall is the seat of the chief of the Mac-Intoshes, a clan which rose in arms for the Young Chevalier at the bidding of " The Mac-Intosh Lady " or " Colonel Anne." Charles was entertained by the chief just before the final defeat and dispersal of his forces at Culloden Moor. The site of this, the last major clash of arms in the British Isles, is indicated by cairns marking the graves of the dead. Here it was, on a stormy day in April, 1746, that the charging waves of clansmen fell fighting before the concentrated musketry of the better equipped

. W. F. TAYLOR

### THE CAPITAL OF THE HIGHLANDS

*Inverness, town of river, firth and canal, is inseparably linked with many stirring events in Scottish history. Mary Queen of Scots lived there while seeking the country's support in 1562, and five miles away, on Culloden Moor, the gallant '45 came to a tragic end. The Northern Meeting, for Highland games, is held in the town.*

and Struan with its power station beyond which we emerge above the tree line and commence the traverse of about twenty miles of grandly desolate country around the summit of the road 1,500 feet above the sea at the Druimuachdar Pass, just past Dalnaspidal, the site of a mountain hospice in olden times. Thereafter our route lies down the valley of the Spey and at Kingussie we pass a memorial of old times in the mouldering ruins of the Ruthven Barracks, where a muster of the clansmen dispersed on learning of the disaster of Culloden.

From Aviemore, with its grand prospects of Cairngorm majesty, our road swings out westwards over outlying spurs of the Monadhliath Mountains traversing ground rendered immortal

Government forces. The Young Pretender escaped from the carnage. The epic of his wanderings, his breathless escapes and, above all, the loyalty of the countrymen who refused to betray him, have bequeathed a heritage of pride to the modern Gael.

Like most other old Scots towns, Inverness draws its romantic inspiration from the beauty of its situation rather than a living heritage of extant memorials. The castle which crowns the green bluff above the River Ness offers a commanding viewpoint, but it is a comparatively modern erection, and naught remains of the palace of the legendary Brude, King of the Picts, nor even of that castle which refused admission to Mary Queen of Scots, who is reputed to have

A. BROWN

## A SUTHERLAND FISHING VILLAGE

*On the road to John o' Groat's stands the Sutherland fishing village of Helmsdale. In the eighteenth century, when the Highland crofters were evicted from their glens, a number of them settled on this bleak coast, living on shell fish or whatever they could find, cultivating small plots of land and eventually turning to the sea for a living. In time, the settlement around the mouth of the Helmsdale River became an important fishing centre.*

A. BROWN

## THE LAST OUTPOSTS OF SCOTLAND

*The Land's End is to England what John o' Groat's is to Scotland. The latter is the longest distance from Cornwall, but Dunnet Head, nearby, is actually farther north. A room in the hotel perpetuates the legend that John de Groat built there an octagonal house with an octagonal table to avoid fraticidal strife over the question of precedence. Each claimant could enter by his own door and say that his was the place of honour.*

received entertainment in the old "Queen's House" in Bridge Street. The blue lozenge-shaped stone under the Town Cross is the Clach-na-Cudainn, the stone of the tubs on which the wives of the northern burgh used to rest their pails. It is claimed, however, to have been the coronation stone of the Lords of the Isles. Inverness is the centre for a number of enchanting tours, but bound for John o' Groat's we cross in succession the River Ness and the Caledonian Canal, and hug the coastline of the Beauly Firth till we reach the pleasant little spa which gives its name to that inlet of the sea. Beauly is the starting-point for the mountain

DIXON-SCOTT

**HERRING TOWN OF CAITHNESS**

*Wick, with a population of about 8,000, expands to over 12,000 in the herring season, and the beautiful old harbour is frantic with the activities of three hundred fishing vessels delivering the catch from the northern seas.*

wonderland of Glen Affric, and doubtless the long forgotten Carthusians who built the old Priory of Beauly, now partly restored, were not unconscious of the scenic grandeur of that hinterland.

From Beauly we cross the isthmus of the Black Isle, which is really a peninsula, and meet the sea again at the old market town of Dingwall. A pleasant journey of twenty-six miles farther on brings us to the historic town of Tain, where the Chapel of St. Duthus, now carefully restored, was of old a popular resort of the faithful. The queen of Robert Bruce was captured by the English on her way to this shrine, and James IV made it the subject of frequent pilgrimages and endowed it handsomely. Nearby the abbey of Fearn is an ancient fabric still used as a place of worship.

The County of Sutherland is entered at Bonar Bridge, and the town of Dornoch, with less than a thousand inhabitants, is yet the county town of Sutherland. The antiquity of this place is attested by its thirteenth-century cathedral and Bishop's Palace. The grave of the last witch burnt in Scotland is still pointed out in one of the local burial-grounds.

From Dornoch our road leads away north by the rocky coastline, past the town of Brora, which boasts a colliery, the only one in the Highlands, and through the little port of Helmsdale with its ruined keep on a high headland. Here and there are remains of these mysterious round towers, the Pictish Brochs, which have proved an insoluble enigma to the archæologist. Outside the crooked wynds of Wick the old castles of Sinclair and Girnigo whisper to us of the troublous times of old, of the feuds of the Caithness-shire clans; the Sinclairs, the Gunns and the Mackays.

Sixteen miles beyond Wick our long romantic journey from Edinburgh ceases at John o' Groat's. This name is reputed to be that of one of eight Dutchmen who settled on the Caithness coast in the reign of James IV. Mutual animosity over the question of precedence at the annual banquet threatened the welfare of their community until the worthy John constructed an octagonal house with an octagonal table and eight doors so that each of the jealous guests could consider himself at the head of the table if he so wished. Naught but a mound now remains to mark the site of this remarkable building. Even on this remote windswept plateau there is still something to remind us of the romance of old Scotland.

Just as, at the Land's End, the Scilly Isles lie dim on the horizon, so John o' Groat's commands a view of the Orkneys. The road may end in Caithness, but across the wild Pentland Firth are these outposts of Scotland, speaking with their place names of the Viking days of old. Till late in the fifteenth century, the Islands belonged to Norway and then were annexed to Scotland because Christiern I failed to pay the dowry of his daughter Margaret, who married James III. Land's End to John o' Groat's spells beginning and end by usage, but even beyond Orkney there is yet more of Scotland, the misty Isles of Shetland.

# THE ROAD TO THE ISLES

## *by* ALASDAIR ALPIN MacGREGOR

" It's the blue Islands that are pullin' me away,
    Their laughter puts the leap upon the lame,
It's the blue Islands from the Skerries to the
    Lews
Wi' heather honey taste upon each name."

*Kenneth MacLeod.*

FROM the viewpoint of natural beauty, history, romance, and legend, it matters not which of the recognized Roads to the Isles one adopts, since all of them are equally fascinating, and ultimately lead to a part of Britain that, in the main, still retains something of remoteness and old-worldness. Travel by Oban, the Charing Cross of the Highlands, to obtain a passing glimpse of the romantic shores of Loch Awe, and of the ancient MacGregor stronghold of Kilchurn with her towers, over-shadowed by the twin peaks of Cruachan. At Oban one is literally within shouting distance of the Isles themselves. Here, in the Lynn of Lorne, lie Lismore, or the " Great Garden," and Kerrera Isle, with that fine ruin, Gylen Castle, perched almost perilously on the edge of its southern cliffs, overlooking the Lynn itself and the peaks of Mull beyond. It was in the Horse Shoe Bay of Kerrera, situated only a few miles from Oban, that King Haco anchored his galleys of war, prior to his defeat at Largs in 1263. This countryside, in consequence, is rich in historical and legendary allusions to the Northmen who, up till this time, had dominated so much of Scotland for centuries.

At Oban, every lawful day, one may take ship for the Isles, circumnavigating the great Island of Mull and visiting Staffa and Iona while so doing. And thrice weekly, weather permitting, you may sail thence for the Outer Hebrides—for Barra, one of the most southerly of the Isles, and certainly one of the most historic and romantic. In making for Tobermory, the first port of call, the most important object of historical interest to arrest the attention is Duart Castle, situated on a rocky peninsula overlooking

that romantic tideway known as the Sound of Mull—the habitat of kelpies, and of the " Merry Men " of whom Robert Louis Stevenson wrote so fascinatingly. Duart is the ancestral seat of the warlike MacLeans of Duart ; and within its walls in 1936, and at the ripe age of ninety-nine, there passed away in the person of Sir Donald Fitzroy MacLean, chief of the MacLeans of Duart, the last surviving British officer who served in the Crimean War. In the castle itself one still may see the hooded cloak that the ancient chief wore when he went to the Crimea at the age of eighteen. On his nineteenth birthday Sir Donald received his Crimean medal at the hands of Queen Victoria. " Take my advice," said an old veteran, " and have a good hood put on your cloak, for you will have to lie a lot on the ground ! " The chief used to relate to those who visited him at Duart Castle how glad he was that he had taken the veteran's advice.

Tobermory, which one might describe as the capital of the Island of Mull, has many historical associations, but none more fascinating than those connected with the sinking in Tobermory Bay of the Spanish galleon, *Florida*, by the bellicose MacLeans of Duart in 1588. This vessel is believed to have been the pay-chest of the Great Armada ; and at varying intervals during the last three and a half centuries efforts have been made to recover the treasure from the sunken ship.

A. A. MACGREGOR

### A CRUSADER'S STRONGHOLD

*Kilchurn Castle, on Loch Awe, was built in 1440 by Sir John Campbell, a noted Crusader. The family used it as a residence till 1740, when the roof fell. Scott brought the castle into his " The MacGregor's Gathering."*

A. A. MACGREGOR

**AN ISLAND OUTPOST**

*On the Isle of Kerrera, which shelters Oban Harbour, stands the ruin of Gylen Castle. Dating from the grim days of war with the Norsemen, it became the stronghold of the MacDougalls of Lorn.*

pier at which are berthed all vessels visiting Barra, are the ruins of Kisimul Castle, for centuries the fortress of the dauntless chiefs of the MacNeils of Barra, many of whom were notorious in their day as pirates. Kisimul is surely one of the most picturesque ruins in all Britain ; and there can be few places round which cling so much legend, romance and song. Legends are still recounted in the Isles of how Kisimul came to be built ; and the folk-lore of Barra is rich in allusions to the Northmen— the Lochlannaich, as they are spoken of in the Western Isles.

### Cliff-bound Isles

Barra is the principal isle of the group known as the Barra Isles, which includes the cliff-bound islands of Mingulay and Berneray, or Barra Head, as it is referred to by mariners. Except for the lighthousemen on Barra Head, the more southerly of the Barra Isles are uninhabited by the human kind. Mingulay carried a fair fishing and crofting population during the nineteenth century. In 1881 it numbered one hundred and fifty souls, one hundred and forty-six of whom were Gaelic-speaking. Prolonged spells of inclement weather and inaccessibility during the frequent storms visiting the Outer Hebrides contributed toward making Mingulay increasingly uncongenial. Some twenty-five years ago, therefore, the island was evacuated in a manner not very dissimilar to that which was witnessed in 1930 in the case of St. Kilda, remotest of the habitable Hebrides. The gaunt cliffs of Mingulay and Berneray, like those of the St. Kilda group of islands, are the resort of numberless sea-fowl. Words fail completely when one attempts to describe the grandeur and magnitude of these stupendous cliffs, and the myriads of sea-birds that have their dwelling-place among them.

The more generally accepted Road to the Isles, of course, is that which crosses the lonely Moor of Rannoch, passes by Kingshouse Inn and through Glencoe, skirts the head of Loch Leven at Ballachulish, finds its way into Fort William, at the head of Loch Linnhe and in the shadow of Ben Nevis, and then meanders by loch and stream and sea, by woodland, moorland, and mountain, to the railway terminus and the wharfs at Mallaig, on the west coast of Inverness-shire. For many the Road to the Isles proper

Beyond Mull lie those happy isles of the Inner Hebrides, known as Coll and Tiree, the former rugged in aspect and noted for its black cattle and cheeses, the latter flat and low-lying, fertile and faery-haunted. The faery tales of Tiree would make a book in themselves ! Here, too, herds of " faery cattle " have come ashore from time to time ; and there are folks still living on this island who have heard the bark of the " faery dog," and who, on putting their ears to the green knowes, have heard the strains of faery music.

Perhaps the most compact, loveliest, and romantic of all the isles is Barra, with its wonderful, land-locked harbour of Castlebay, dominated by the heathery peaks of Heaval. Perched on a rocky islet in that harbour, quite close to the

A. A. MACGREGOR

## A CASTLE OF THE HEBRIDES

*Off the coast of Barra, one of the isles of the Outer Hebrides, on a little islet in the bay stands the ruined Kisimul Castle. Grey and forlorn amid the waves, it was once a stronghold of the MacNeils of Barra, many of whom gained notoriety as pirates. From this bay during the herring fishing a great fleet of fishing boats may be seen setting out to sea. Strange legends of far-off days still linger in this isle.*

A. A. MACGREGOR

## ON THE ROAD TO FORT WILLIAM

*This wintry scene on Loch Tulla shows the rounded peak of Stob Ghabhar, the peak of the goats, 3563 feet, at the head of the loch. This is one of the fine range of peaks seen from the road to Glencoe. Much planting of pine trees has been done in recent years in the district. Here in this desolate region the Gaelic poet-gamekeeper, Duncan Barr MacIntyre, the " Burns of the Highlands " was born in 1724.*

commences at Fort William, on the fringe of a territory so intimately connected with the deeds and misfortunes of " the 'forty-five " that, today, it often is spoken of as Prince Charlie's Country. This, to be sure, is one of the most storied parts of Britain.. Every clachan has its association with the hapless Prince—so much so, in truth, that the wanderer in these parts experiences little difficulty in coming into contact with people who speak of Prince Charlie as though they had known him intimately, and had actually assisted in sheltering him when there was a reward of thirty thousand pounds on his head. Was it not on the shore of that great arm of the

presence of a great assemblage of the Highland chiefs and their clansmen?

Today, on this very spot, stands the famous memorial, Prince Charlie's Monument, erected by MacDonald of Glenaladade, and commemorating the initial step in that arduous and fateful enterprise.

It was among the recesses of this intricate and beautiful countryside that the prince and his companions " skulked " until it was found possible to transfer them to the greater safety of the Outer Hebrides. The cave by the shore of Loch nan Uamh, not far from Beasdale, and in which tradition asserts the prince remained in hiding for

A. A. MACGREGOR

ON SCOTLAND'S GREATEST MOOR

*The Road to the Isles has its highest point on the Moor of Rannoch, where it runs round the shoulder of Beinn Chaorach at over a thousand feet. There it descends to Loch Ba and Lochan na-h-Achlaise, the latter being shown above. Through all this country, the scenery is grand and wild, like much of its ancient history.*

sea, Loch nan Uamh, the inmost creeks of which actually touch this very Road to the Isles at high tide, that Prince Charlie first set foot on the mainland of Scotland in his desperate attempt to regain a throne that admittedly was forfeited by the imprudence of his royal ancestors? Was it not at this self-same Highland loch that, after the rout of the Jacobites at Culloden in April, 1746, he actually embarked once more for the safety of France, accompanied by Lochiel and a few of his more intimate associates during the Rebellion? Was it not upon that flat stretch of ground at Glenfinnan, lying between this Road to the Isles and the waters of Loch Shiel, that in 1745 the Jacobite Standard was raised in the

some time, is one of the places of pilgrimage sought out by those who, in ever increasing numbers each year, visit this historic and romantic locality. Even more inaccessible is the cave in the hillside over by Loch Beoraid, where the Prince sheltered while in hiding among the mountain fastnesses of Morar.

Than the shore road passing on its way between the scattered township of Arisaig and Mallaig, there can be nothing in the world more beautiful. Out to sea lies that cluster of isles known as the Small Isles—an island parish, comprising Eigg, Rum, Canna, and Muck. From Mallaig these islands may be visited easily by the mail steamer plying between the mainland of Inverness and

FOX PHOTOS

## WINTER NEAR THE GLEN OF WEEPING

*The tragic defile of Glencoe is now laid open by a new motor road of doubtful welcome. Here is a scene where deep snow makes walking easier than driving. The silent mountains, cloaked in white made crystal by the sun, stand eternally across the path and, ahead of the car, is the peak known as "Watcher of the Moor."*

A. A. MACGREGOR

## THE LOCH OF THE CAVES

*As the road goes on towards Arisaig, there is a fine view over Loch nan Uamh, the rock-bound inlet to which Prince Charlie once came in a French frigate. After Culloden, other French ships came with arms to restore the Stuart cause and bitter fighting took place in the Loch when the British ships came upon them. From here the Prince escaped to the Hebrides where he lay in hiding until rescued by Flora Macdonald.*

the Outer Hebrides. Eigg is noted mainly for two things—that weird mountain of rock called the Scuir, and the cave in which, when on a punitive expedition in 1577, the MacLeods of Skye massacred the MacDonald inhabitants of Eigg. The Scuir is one of the most familiar landmarks, not merely on the Road to the Isles, but on the west coast of Scotland. The shores of Eigg, like those of Rum, are honeycombed with caves; but, mountainous as is Eigg, it cannot boast so fine an array of peaks as can Rum. Canna in olden times was one of the most prized possessions of the Lords of the Isles. In its beautiful, natural harbour, so well known to the Viking rievers, the chiefs of Clan Ranald used to anchor their birlinns or galleys in the days of the clan feuds. Muck is a fertile island and comparatively flat. It is full of legend and romance; and I myself know at least one native who is in the habit of hearing faery bagpipes when he places his ear to the green sward covering a certain knoll near his home.

The Road to the Isles beyond Mallaig and the Small Isles takes one westward to the Uists, to Benbecula, the ancient seat of the brave Clan Ranald, to the wild and remote places of Harris and Lewis, and to those legend-haunted islands situated in that turbulent tideway, the Sound of Harris. Among the waters surrounding the Isle of Berneray lived the Seal-folk of Hebridean

tradition, descendants of the Clan MacCodrum of the Seals. Hereabouts, too, dwelt the Clan Andy of the Widgeons—so called because a sept of them is believed to have forfeited human form for that of the *lach* or widgeon. From this isle came Sir Norman MacLeod, one of the most illustrious of the MacLeods of Berneray. Sir Norman was knighted by King Charles after the Battle of Worcester, in 1651. In the Isles the old folks still repeat the language of the Widgeon Clan, said to have been reduced to writing by this distinguished cavalier, when he returned to his Hebridean home after the wars. At the " Town " of Berneray, among the clover-fields of the " Town " farm, may be seen an old building, now used as a barn, which, in times less peaceful, was the gunnery of the MacLeods of Berneray. Placed above its entrance is a marble slab bearing the Latin inscription, *Hic natus est illustris ille Normannus MacLeod de Berneray, eques auratus.*

### A Helpful Brownie

The home of the MacLeods of Berneray shared with so many other Highland and Island homes the distinction of having a family guardian in the person of a brownie. To this day, the story is told in the Isles of the occasion upon which Sir Norman and a guest were playing at " the tables " (backgammon), hour after hour, without

A. A. MACGREGOR

### THE ISLE OF EIGG
*The curiously named isles of Eigg, Muck and Rum, it has been said, suggest some strangely conceived cocktail. Above is a view from Muck of the Isle of Eigg, with its upstanding Scuir, a great mass of volcanic rock with shafts of basalt, which makes Eigg a prominent feature both from the mainland and from the adjacent isles.*

A. A. MACGREGOR

### DUSK IN THE OUTER ISLES

*A picture taken among the mountains of Harris. The rock-face in the centre is that of Ullaval, one of the heights in the northern fringe of the Forest of Harris. It overlooks Loch Resort, a narrow arm of the sea that forms part of the boundary between Lewis and Harris and between the counties of Inverness and Ross.*

either of them making any headway against his opponent. Eventually a retainer, standing near at hand, indicated to Sir Norman the move that would ensure his winning the game. As time was dragging on, it was agreed that the retainer's advice should be taken. Consequently Sir Norman won.

After the guest had departed, he took his retainer quietly aside, and asked him whether he had had any experience of the game. Imagine Sir Norman's interest when the retainer informed him that he never had played it in his life, but that he had noticed the brownie alight for a brief moment on the square into which Sir Norman should move his piece, if he expected to win!

### Tombs of Island Chiefs

Than Rodil, in the very south of Harris, there can be few spots more lovely in the world. Here, among the mools at the ancient Church of St. Clement, are buried several chiefs of the MacLeods of Harris and Skye, who are not to be confused with the luckless MacLeods of Lewis, nineteen of whose chiefs lie in the old kirkyard of Aignish, at Eye, not far from Stornoway. On the south side of the chancel of St. Clement's is the beautifully-carved tomb which the chief known as Alasdair Crotach prepared

for himself in 1528—nineteen years before he died. This tomb is one of the loveliest specimens of ancient art in the country.

Northward from Rodil swings the island road to Lewis, and to its farthest extremity at the Butt, passing between mountains and skirting some of the most exquisite shore-lands. Far across a promontory of grass and sand lies Luskentyre, where, as recently as the middle of last century, a herd of faery cows came ashore! Over the shoulder of the Clisham climbs the road, before it descends to Lewis and the shores of Loch Seaforth. In olden days this territory was the patrimony of the fearless Chiefs of the Lewis MacLeods.

Today not a vestige is to be seen of the ancient stronghold occupied by these chiefs. Its site lies somewhere beneath the piers of the Hebridean port of Stornoway. Their dynasty came to an end when, acting ostensibly on behalf of the Crown authorities, MacKenzie of Kintail (Seaforth, as he was called) displaced them early in the seventeenth century, and when Neil MacLeod, the last and bravest of them, who meanwhile had adopted the life of a pirate on Berisay Isle, in wild Loch Roag, went to his execution in 1613, and in a manner described by Sir Thomas Hamilton, the Lord Advocate, as " verey christianlie."

EDGAR WARD

## WHITE WALLS OF ZUMMERZET

*Many West Country villages have cottages of brilliant white, capped with stubbly thatch. Often, too, the village street runs uphill as with this one at Minehead. Hills shut it in on the north and west and, once again, the church tower which, in this case, was once used as a lighthouse, takes a prominent place in the picture.*

# THE VILLAGE AND ITS STORY

## *by* RUSSELL PAGE

OF all the factors that go towards the making of the English scene the village is not the least important. The red roofs of cottages clustered round a church beyond the water meadows, a ribbon of stone-tiled houses climbing a Cotswold hillside, the bright simplicity of whitewash and slate lightening the bareness of a northern moor—our villages invest our varying landscape with a human element, and now perhaps only in the villages can we clearly trace the slow change in the patterns of our daily life during the last 2,000 years.

To find the first evidences of the English village we must go back a long way. Our earlier ancestors, the Celts, lived as shepherds on the bare downs and hills which rose like islands above the thickly-forested lowlands and the swamps of the undrained river valleys. Little beyond a few names and well-worn tracks where the daisies still grow thickest remains to tell us of these people except in the west, where in Cornwall and parts of Wales the countryside is peppered with many tiny hamlets showing that these were a people who lived in much smaller groups than the Saxons.

The village was based on an economic necessity. Settlers stopped at a place which offered them a favourable opportunity of gathering their livelihood from the very earth around them. It is hard to imagine trying to make a life with only such things as you could grow. Bread, meat, milk, beer and wool from field and grassland, timber from the forest for furniture, and clay from the river bank for pots and dishes.

As a result the beauty of our villages is a great deal more than skin deep. Implicit in their buildings, their bridges, their mills and fords, their field tracks and their common lands is the accumulated experience of generations of sturdy men working their lands for daily bread and accumulating a deep knowledge of the hard necessities of life.

In the fifth and sixth centuries the Anglo-Saxons came in bands to conquer the Celts or drive them into the far west. They pushed their way up the river valleys in their long boats.

These people were agriculturists rather than shepherds—the bare wolds and hill-tops were less useful to them. They needed well drained land for growing wheat, rye and barley, water meadows for their cattle, good water, and woodlands for fuel and pigs. By the very pattern and placing of most of our villages in the middle of their open fields we can still see how the Saxons and Danes instituted in England the idea of a larger communal agricultural life quite different from the smaller grouping and tiny enclosures of their Celtic predecessors.

By the time the Domesday Book came to be written in 1086, many villagers, owing to successive small waves of invasion, had given up their freedom in return for protection from a local lord, and from this usage grew the "manorial" system on which medieval village life was based. The manor house and the church became the two social centres of the village.

Very soon the village ceased to be a collection of primitive dwelling-places where men and their cattle shared a common roof. The church and the manor linked the village directly to a national life. Under the feudal system the village was a link in the chain that connected the lord of the manor through his overlord to the king and to the idea of central government.

STEPHENSON

### A DALE OF ITS OWN

*Dent, near the western border of Yorkshire, has a dale to itself and is an example of the stone-built villages that nestle so beautifully in the north country.*

The feudal system is reflected to this day in the thousands of villages which cluster round the tower or steeple of the village church, and the manor house. In many places only the manor and church remain close together—the village has grown away towards a road. In other places cottages may have encroached on the manor field and only a dried-up moat or a piece of finely-cut stone incorporated into a barn remain to tell us that here was the great house.

The next great change in village life was due partly to the Black Death, and partly to improved methods of weaving on the Continent. The first was a plague which towards the end of the fourteenth century decimated the population of England. Whole villages were deserted, land fell out of cultivation and by accident of disease the feudal system of land tenure fell into jeopardy. About this time, too, came the increasing demand for fine wool. The English uplands produced the best wool obtainable and landowners were quick to buy up small farms and enclose the common lands to form huge sheep runs. By the reign of Henry VII whole villages had disappeared, rents went up, small tenants unable to pay lost their farms, and the system of large farmers employing landless men as labourers began.

This new system brought into being a new kind of village, the most characteristic of which still exist almost complete in the Cotswolds. These limestone hills made the best sheep-walks and fine grass and plentiful water made good wool. The same hills were quarried for limestone to build in lasting material such exquisite villages, some large enough to call themselves towns, as Chipping Campden, Broadway and Stanway, Burford and Bourton, Stow and the Swells. Noble architecture in the rigid perpendicular manner reflected the riches of the new kind of landowner and set a new standard.

### Birth of England's Hedges

In the eighteenth century the rising price of wheat led to a new revival of arable farming and the great enclosures began.

These Enclosure Acts had enormously important economic reactions on the village, but they are chiefly interesting to us because the present setting of most of our villages dates from this period.

The endlessly shifting shapes of grass and ploughland changing in texture and colour through the seasons, enclosed by quickthorn hedge, punctuated by lines of hedgerow trees—in fact the whole network of field and hedgerow patterned like stained glass in its leading, dates from the late eighteenth century.

One hundred years ago the railway took the traffic off the roads—the factories and towns

HUMPHREY AND VERA JOEL

### A PERFECT COTSWOLD VILLAGE

*William Morris considered that Bibury, Gloucestershire, was the most beautiful village in England. It is difficult to disagree, for the stone cottages cluster round a meadow and the crystal-clear Coln flows through, a mirror to the beauty on its banks. Paths, walls and cottages seem to grow as if a part of the hills themselves.*

STEPHENSON

### A VILLAGE OF THE DOWNS

*The main street of Alfriston, in the Cuckmere Valley, not far from Eastbourne, is beautified by the timbered Star Inn and the stone pillar that remains from the old market cross. The Star Inn, a sixteenth-century building is, like the nearby Market Cross Inn, noted for its associations with the old-time smugglers.*

tempted the people from the villages. Food came across the sea. Our villages became static for nearly a century and changed scarcely in detail.

Now the roads are alive again, but with the new life flowing through the countryside there goes attendant disease. We want to live, perhaps, in a village because we appreciate its beauties, and so we go to the country and with us take electrified railways, petrol stations, main drainage, the " grid," arterial roads and the vast mechanical necessities which we have invented. Until now these elements have seemingly worked only destructively. Can the positive sides of our civilization be used constructively, not only to preserve but to add new life and beauty to our older heritage?

Our villages have been conditioned as well by geography as by history. The hills, the forests, the open river valleys have each produced a special form of living and so a special kind of village. The use of local materials has made the villages seem always part of their immediate setting.

The Wiltshire village built of cob walling and thatched and covered with creepers is directly related to its surroundings, and the stone roofed, whitewashed village in a Yorkshire dale repeats and accentuates the austerity and strength of its background.

In the woodland village of the Sussex Weald

the cottages will be framed in oak shaped as it grew in the surrounding woods. The old weather-boarded houses of a south coast fishing village repeat the construction of the boats by which their owners gained a living, and the enchantingly decorative flintwork of many villages on the Norfolk coast is there because flint was easily available for building.

### The Stone of the Country

The most remarkable results of geological control over the villages of earlier Englishmen are to be seen in the villages which lie in the great Oolite Belt, that band of limestone which runs half over England from Dorset to Lincolnshire and on into Yorkshire.

Here every village is almost completely stone, yet each a little different, and you can see how slight variations in the quality of the stone have affected the local architecture. On the ridge which runs from Lincoln to Grantham the stone is coarse and hard to work and there are no strata which produce stone roofing slates, so the houses are built of a coarse, uncut stone and roofed in pantiles. In Rutland and Northampton such villages as Ketton, with its superb thirteenth-century church; Geddington, which has an Eleanor Cross; and Colley Weston, famous for its stone roofing slates, reflect in their architecture the fine-textured stone of this district. So again in the Cotswolds, where the roofing stone is of even finer quality, you will see much more play made with gables and a steeper roof pitch.

In districts which were once or still are heavily wooded, villages appear scattered; since, though the woods may have gone, little clusters of houses tell of ancient clearings in the trees. In open areas villages have tended to cluster together and present a solid face to the winds and rains.

A main road would make the village into a wide street. Broadway, one of the noblest and best-known villages in the Cotswolds, is such a street village.

towards the growth of the village: man's necessities, the slow processes of change and growth, and the physical potentialities of the site.

We can make happy voyages of discovery through the villages of England, our pleasure enriched by understanding something of their growth. There is so much to see on such a voyage that it is difficult to know where to begin.

Since we are exploring an island, perhaps the coast will make a good starting-point. In the south especially, few coast villages have managed to remain as such. Now there is a seemingly endless belt of houses along the shore but just

STEPHENSON

IN HARDY'S WESSEX

*Tolpuddle, in the heart of Hardy's Wessex, has other claims to fame than its association with the " Martyrs."*
*It is typical of the Dorset villages that hug the road running west through Dorchester to Bridport and Exeter.*
*Trees, thatch, whitewash and local stone are blended into charming cottages that straggle along the roads.*

Water supplies have affected the shape and appearance of our villages. In broken, hilly country with many springs one or two cottages would be built round each well. In a wide country where water might be rarer a whole village would grow round one source of supply. It is possibly for the same reason that one sees that most charming of village compositions, a row of cottages parallel to an open stream.

In the Fens every village seems huddled close, a small oasis of large trees and houses in a wide landscape where land and sky melt into each other on the horizon. Here formerly, as on Romney Marsh, only occasional islands of higher ground rising from miles of mere and swamp allowed a safe site for a village.

Such are some of the elements that have gone

inland we can find unspoilt villages still with a salty atmosphere. On Romney Marsh, in Kent, Dymchurch is already bungalow ridden, but fine old churches with clusters of houses set on mounds in the marsh, such as Brenzett with its alabaster figures, are worth a visit.

Winchelsea, although strictly a town (was it not one of the Cinque Ports?) and now no longer by the sea, we may regard as a village. A place of weather-boarded painted houses nobly situated on a green hill above the marshes, and still entered by a medieval gate, Winchelsea is, indeed, one of the most fascinating of the many treasures of Sussex.

In a fold of the downs lies Alfriston, not a sea village but yet of the sea, for the men of Alfriston were daring smugglers landing their

DIXON-SCOTT

## THE CATHEDRAL OF THE MOOR

*Widecombe-in-the-Moor, Devon, lies in one of the greener hollows of the great Dartmoor uplands and the church spire rises perfectly from among the old cottages. This is the scene of the famous fair and the song about Tom Pearce's grey mare which is sung in every corner of the world where English and Devon men meet. Owing to its high and remote situation, the village is sometimes jocularly referred to as " Widecombe-in-the-Moon."*

W. F. TAYLOR

## A VILLAGE OF GREY PENWITH

*High on the Penwith moors, near St. Ives, Cornwall, Zennor's sombre beauty is rarely seen by the casual tourist. The moor granite has been used for the cottages and it crops up immovably in garden and road. The district is reputed to be so barren that there is a local saying: " Zennor, where the cat ate the bell-rope."*

cargoes at Cuckmere Haven and carrying them inland by devious ways to baffle the excisemen.

Alfriston today consists chiefly of a single street of attractive houses including the ancient timbered building of the Star Hill, which was once within the jurisdiction of Battle Abbey and a place of sanctuary for fugitives from justice.

Beaulieu, lost in the New Forest, should be approached by river from the sea. The atmosphere of a great monastery still clings to it, and on the way we pass Buckler's Hard, designed to be a shipbuilding centre in the eighteenth century, but ships ceased to be of timber and Buckler's Hard remains a village of little, formal red brick houses between the slow moving river and the forest.

Now we are nearly into Dorsetshire and, since we may not come this way again, we must go inland a few miles behind Studland to see Corfe Castle, where stone-tiled houses cluster round the ruin-covered mound of the great castle, set dramatically in a sudden gap in the Purbeck Hills.

Once we stray into Dorset we are tempted to wander from one village to the next for here lies many a hamlet of thatched cottages in the neighbourhood of a grey old church, sometimes with a clear little rivulet flowing down the street. Hardy gave fame to some, others may have furbished and bedecked themselves to attract tourists from the holiday resorts, but many remain plain and unadorned and attractive in their simplicity.

Sydling St. Nicholas, for instance, is as charming as its name, with thatched cottages and a duckpond, and a background of smooth green hills. Also in a hollow in the hills is Cerne Abbas, more famed for the giant, but worthy of note if only for that charming street leading to the church and the abbey gate-house with its beautiful two-storeyed oriel window. Nearer the coast are such places as Upwey, nestling in a soft green valley, and Burton Radstock, a picturesque stone-built hamlet where artists congregate.

### Glorious Devon

In Devonshire we come to the land of cream and roses, of colour-washed houses, fuchsia hedges and clusters of blue hydrangeas at almost every cottage door. Dittisham, where the Dart meets the sea, is as good a Devon village as any that slope down to the sea between Exmouth and Plymouth. The upper portion of the village is finely placed on the neck of Gurrow Point above the tidal waters of the River Dart and overlooking its tree-hung banks.

Beyond St. Germains, which seems almost too good to be called a village, the country changes and we are in Cornwall, a county of violent contrast, treeless and wind-swept on the high ground where hundreds of small villages merge with the stone-walled fields, and almost tropical in the sheltered coves on its southern coast. Though there is little of architectural interest these Cornish villages are extremely attractive, and many have odd and often beautiful names.

One of the quaintest of Cornish fishing villages is Polperro, with its little natural harbour round which the houses are irregularly grouped one above the other in picturesque confusion.

I suppose Clovelly is one of the most famous of English villages, though it is always written about as being exactly like Italy. Actually it is like nowhere else. You have to go to realize how intimate it is and how exactly " right " is the cobbled street that tumbles between two rows of cottages stepped one above the other to the smallest harbour possible. The whole place has been exquisitely cared for. It remains a real and a live village, singularly free from unsightly development.

Where Exmoor falls sharply to the sea Lynmouth has grouped its houses most effectively against the steep hillside, and inland from here the hamlets of Brendon and Oare have blended themselves with the valley and the confining hills.

Porlock, attractive as it is in itself, suffers perhaps in comparison with Bossington, a lovely old-time hamlet with soft-tinted cottages, luxuriant gardens and great spreading walnut trees. Bossington in turn must yield homage to Selworthy. Among the trees at the foot of its Beacon, Selworthy's thatched houses, whitewashed church and sixteenth-century cross make a splendid harmony.

### The East Anglian Flats

Devon and Cornwall still have a coast dotted with beautiful and unspoilt villages. Their steep geography presents problems beyond the speculative builder's power. Other coasts have been less lucky.

There are, however, in Norfolk a series of coastal villages joined to the sea by tidal creeks winding slowly through the salt marshes to the North Sea. Shifting sands and a new economy have lost them their prosperity, but since they are not actually on the sea they have never grown into seaside resorts.

Farthest east of these, Wells has fine though melancholy deserted wharves; Holkham is famous

EDGAR WARD

### A WEST COUNTRY GEM

*Dunster is built in a green Somerset valley and the street rises sharply at both ends. On one hill stands the Elizabethan castle, the other being crowned by a tower built two hundred years later. The octagonal Yarn Market comes beautifully into the picture, a quaint and gabled relic of the old town's medieval wealth.*

for a great house and the agricultural experiments of Coke of Norfolk which changed all English farming in the eighteenth century. The Burnhams—Burnham Deepdale, Burnham Overy, Burnham Market and the rest—are all exquisitely simple villages of darkest red brick and flint, often roofed with glazed Dutch pantiles, and remarkable for the brilliance of their flower gardens where all sorts of plants grow that one expects only in Devon or Cornwall.

The flat lands of the Fens—South Lincolnshire, Cambridge and parts of Norfolk, Suffolk and Essex—are full of unexplored villages, since the uneventful landscape and the lack of large towns do not encourage tourists.

There is no stone. Houses are almost entirely of plain red brick with pantiled roofs except in Essex where there is a good deal of half timber. The simplicity of these villages is no small part of their charm, and many have beautiful churches.

Castle Acre and Castle Rising, though not in the Fens are specially interesting. The first has its Norman keep and an almshouse for old ladies who still wear a dress styled in the sixteenth century, while Castle Rising is built among the ruins of a castle and great church.

### Sole Relic of the Fens

Wicken, in Cambridgeshire, is a typical Fen village, with two greens, a duckpond, an old mill, and hard by it the only remaining patch of original Fen, swamps and meres full of birds and wild flowers. In all this part of the country the valuable agricultural land washes right up to the village. There seems no gentle transition from village to open country where one ends and the other begins.

If you like fine woodwork, whitewash and thatch go to Suffolk and Essex where signposts marked with pleasant medieval names will lead you to quiet, pale villages with wide goose greens set in an uneventful countryside.

STEPHENSON

### THE BELL-CROWNED TOWER OF CAVENDISH

*Suffolk's pleasant levels are rich in beautiful villages. Cavendish, near the Essex border, is a large one, centred round an extensive green. At one end are the picturesque thatched cottages, shown in the picture, with the church tower rising behind them in a perfect composition. The tower carries a turret, a bell sling and flagstaff.*

STEPHENSON

### TILE-HUNG WALLS OF WITLEY

*Surrey claims many beautiful villages, especially in the Dorking and Guildford districts. None is lovelier than Witley, where the presence of tile clay made the use of tiles so cheap that the village has an architecture all its own. Combined with half-timbering, it has weathered with great beauty as this old house shows.*

STEPHENSON

### WILTSHIRE STONE AND TIMBER

*Lacock, on the River Avon, near Chippenham, in Wiltshire, has buildings with an unusual combination of stone and timber and brick. The result is a blend of mellow colour and great dignity. Picturesque streets ring the inner buildings so that their gardens are all in a central space and the streets come back to the starting point.*

HUMPHREY AND VERA JOEL

### AN OXFORDSHIRE IDYLL

*Wroxton, on the Banbury Road, has idyllic corners. It is largely built of tawny stone and thatch, and possesses a beautiful specimen of that ancient village pride, the duckpond. The Abbey, standing in beautiful woods, was founded as an Augustinian priory in the eleventh century by a nephew of the founder of Trinity College, Oxford.*

Leaving the levels of East Anglia it will be pleasant to explore the river valleys and the wooded districts.

Albury, Shere and Abinger Hammer, near Guildford, are three typical valley villages. At Abinger Hammer red brick and tile-hung cottages, with their gardens reaching to the road, face the village green through which ripples the Tillingbourne. Overhanging the road is a picturesque clock with the effigy of a village blacksmith to strike the hours.

Shere has an ancient air and the grey shingled spire of its old church stands high above the old timbered cottages. Here too the Tillingbourne adds to the picture, flowing through the village under a little brick-built bridge, its banks lined with graceful drooping trees.

The Weald of Kent, Surrey and Sussex is also full of interest for the village lover and presents many quiet little hamlets with unpretentious but satisfying features.

In Hampshire the valley of the Test is full of thatched and whitewashed villages pleasantly set in water-meadows and backed by the grey-green ridges of chalky hills. Laverstoke and Wherewell are two of the best. Heytesbury is a typical large Wiltshire village on the Avon, and hard by Stonehenge, on Salisbury Plain, is Amesbury, another river village.

Those villages at the gates of a large house often have a special dignity and an air of unity and distinction. Such a one is the pretty village of Penshurst, in Kent, by the historic home of the Sidneys. Not far from here is Chiddingstone, surely one of the loveliest of Tudor villages remaining in England.

#### Villages of the Road

Ripley, near Harrogate, is a beautiful stone-built village in the Nidd Valley. Castle and village are here closely connected by a common pride in looking their best. Though the houses are mostly without front gardens, window boxes and creepers seem to have a special brilliance against the hard stone of this Yorkshire village.

West Wycombe, in the Chilterns, now safe from decay and spoliation, is in any case a fine example of a roadside village, but it would lose much were it not for the fine park behind it and the romantic eighteenth-century church and mausoleum which loom above the village street.

The villages which owe their importance to road traffic can be found along all the old coaching roads out of London. The weight of eighteenth-century traffic can almost be judged by their frequency and the size of the old inns.

Wansford, near Stamford, now by-passed, has a superb late seventeenth-century inn, a gothic bridge and beyond it the church with an early fourteenth-century spire. Only the few stone houses that are there are needed to complete one of the most satisfying village pictures it is possible to find.

Trumpington and Harston on the Cambridge Road are road villages in a different medium of whitewash and thatch.

Burford is another road village, and since it calls itself the Gateway of the Cotswolds it must be an introduction to those fine stone villages which lie along the limestone belt between Bath and Lincoln. Before we turn north there are places we must not miss in the basin of the Upper Thames, such as Fairford with its famous church, and Lechlade. On the Windrush, like Burford, is North Leach, and nearer Oxford the charming hamlet of Minster Lovel.

The Cotswolds are so full of enchantment that it is difficult to select. Stow-on-the-Wold typifies the hill-top village, Stanway lies under the carp of the hills on the way to Tewkesbury, Broadway has its magnificently wide street of fine architecture. Lower Slaughter and Bourton-on-the-Water both lie by the River Windrush, and in both of them stone cottages and water fall into the happiest compositions. Further south, between Burford and Cirencester, is Bibury. Here is a famous line of cottages called Arlington Row.

Let us follow these stone villages into Oxfordshire. Hidden away in the forest of Wychwood

are Shipton-under-Wychwood and Charlbury in the valley of the Evenlode.

Aynho (just into Northamptonshire) on the Banbury-Bicester Road is considered one of the most beautiful villages in the country. It is beautifully kept and one feels its close connection with the great house. Enormous pride is taken in its appearance and plantings of red roses and apricot trees make it unique.

### Gems of the Midlands

Off the line into Buckinghamshire is Weston Underwood, a beautiful secluded stone village where Cowper lived. Beyond Kettering and Wellingborough we suddenly come again into an area compact of good stone villages. Rockingham has a wide street uphill from the Welland Valley to Rockingham Castle, once King John's hunting lodge.

Where Rutland, Northamptonshire and Lincolnshire meet, there are many interesting villages. Duddington and Colley Weston are close together on a ridge above the Welland, near Stamford. From Colley Weston came the stone slates so widely used in past times. A little to the north, in Rutland, is Ketton with the most exquisite of Early English church spires, own brother, surely, to the famous spire of St. Mary's, Stamford, only four miles away.

N. A. CALL

### IN THE CATTLE AND CIDER COUNTRY
*Weobley, in Herefordshire, is largely composed of black-and-white houses, many using paint where no timber exists. One house is noted as the home of a Mr. Tomkins who achieved fame not only as the father of thirty-two children but also as the originator of the white-faced cattle known the world over as Herefords.*

STEPHENSON

### A SECLUDED YORKSHIRE HAMLET

*In the pleasant green vale of the Hodder, a tributary of the Ribble, lies the quiet little village of Slaidburn. During the winter months the curfew is still rung from the church tower. In the fifteenth century the village parson led his flock in driving out a monk who dared to come and collect tithes for the Abbot of Whalley.*

STEPHENSON

### A GREY OLD WHARFEDALE VILLAGE

*Conistone, in the lovely valley of the Wharfe, in Yorkshire, has that indefinable beauty that springs from a combination of age and the use of local stone for building both cottages and field walls. The lichen-roofed cottages nestle against the bare hills, there is a tiny green, and a maypole stands at the meeting of the roads.*

Going north through Grantham towards Lincoln, only Furbeck perhaps deserves to be called a beautiful village, but if we make a wide detour past Heckington towards Boston, we come to Tattershall, a splendid group—brick castle, stone church and low cottages in dead flat country between river and wold.

Perhaps it is such a charming patchwork of different materials as this which has created the average English village, and all over the country where geological limitations are not too severe are villages where half timber, red brick and stone are happily mixed. Elmley Castle, by Bredon Hill, in Worcestershire, is such a village. Worcestershire, Hereford, Warwickshire are full of good composite architecture. In Shropshire black and white work becomes more frequent. Pott Shrigley, although it has an unattractive name, is a charming village between Cheshire and Derbyshire. Sudbury, between Uttoxeter and Derby, is a wonderful village, seeming more remarkable among rather dull neighbours.

### The Dales

In the dale country of the West Riding the stone villages reappear, but without the architectural niceties of the Cotswold villages. Here utility rather than grace has been sought. The houses are solidly built to withstand northern blasts. Constructed of local gritstone, walls, floors and roofs of the same material, they present an air of permanence and lasting strength.

Built as they are of local materials, cottage and church, farm buildings, garden walls and the bounding walls of the field, all harmonize with the landscape and often have been woven into a singularly successful pattern.

Many of these northern villages indeed have an appreciable charm. Whether spread round a spacious green as at Reeth in Swaledale, at Bainbridge in Wensleydale, or Arncliffe in the narrow confines of Littondale, or closely huddled like grey sheep in a storm as in the quaint hamlet of Dent, they appear at one with their surroundings.

One of the loveliest of the dale villages is Burnsall, in Wharfedale, a few miles upstream from Bolton Abbey. Seen from the hillside, with the lively river rippling beneath a substantial bridge, and with the square tower of the old church rising above trim soundly-built

W. F. TAYLOR

A WESTMORLAND MARKET CROSS

*The village of Brough is divided into secular and religious departments, one end being called Market Brough and the other Church Brough. Ancient and important fairs are held at the Cross on September 30 and October 1.*

cottages, Burnsall, indeed presents an aspect of permanence and imperturbable calm.

Wensleydale contains a number of villages of distinction including Bainbridge, still retaining the stocks on the green, Aysgarth, with its wide street and rose-covered cottages, and Wensley where a venerable elm still shades the green. Best of all perhaps is Castle Bolton on the northern flanks of the dale, a wide street of stone cottages dwarfed by the massive

W. F. TAYLOR

IN A NORTHERN VALLEY
*Near the source of the Derwent, on the borders of Northumberland and Durham, is the village of Blanchland,
grouped beautifully round the church and framed against wooded hills. The traveller comes upon the village
after crossing the moorland, in whose rough heart it gleams like a jewel of grey and green and brown.*

walls of the castle, the feudal stronghold of the
Scropes.

In Swaledale the little village of Muker lies
at the foot of the domed Kisdon Fell with the
road running between the houses and the little
moorland beck. Here again one sees a happy
blending of bridge and church and cottages with
the green hillside patterned with stone walls for
a background.

### The Northern Counties

The east side of Yorkshire also presents some
villages of note including Coxwold where a wide
street flanked with green between the houses
leads up to the church where the author of
*Tristram Shandy* once ministered. Bishop Burton,
between York and Beverley, is said to be the
prettiest of Yorkshire villages, and it is indeed
a delightful place. It possesses a large crescent-
shaped pond and a chestnut shaded green, and
its houses instead of being in a row are dotted
about in a most pleasing style.

In the Lake District men seem to have been
content with, or even awed by the landscape—
the villages offer no competition. Lowther, near
Askham, is an exception, since it is an almost
unique example of an eighteenth-century planned
village. The cottages and the bailiff's house are
placed as part of the whole and carried out, all
alike in stone with Westmorland slate roofs.

Among the villages of Northumberland I would
give Blanchland first place. It is securely hidden
in the wooded valley of the Derwent above which
rises the bare brown moorlands. The village
has grown on the site of the abbey which was
founded in 1175, and now occupies what was
the outer court of the monastery. The houses
and the village inn are arranged round the sides
of the quadrangle which is entered on the north
through a battlemented gateway. Whether
approached by this entrance, or by the bridge
which spans the Derwent, one is immediately
conscious that here is a village of rare and
distinctive beauty.

After giving the palm to Blanchland I remember Bywell on the Tyne. This is a sequestered
little hamlet boasting two churches, relics of the
days when Bywell consisted of two parishes, for
of old it was a busy place, its inhabitants being
employed in the ironwork making horse-trappings
for the border folk.

Then there is Bamburgh dominated by its
mighty castle but there is no end to our quest of
beautiful villages.

There are, I am told, 13,000 villages in England.
Each has its special qualities, its attractions and
charms for someone. All of us have special ties
with one or more of them and no two men
would agree in their choice of, say, the twelve
prettiest villages in the land.

# THE DEVIL'S LEGACY

## *by* TOM STEPHENSON

A THOUSAND years hence an antiquarian delving into the past might well conclude that at some time in its history Britain had been peopled by a race of devil-worshippers. If, by any chance, a complete set of our Ordnance Survey maps survived so long, then the evidence for such a conclusion would seem incontrovertible.

All over those maps from Kent to Caithness the devil's name is freely sprinkled. On them you will find Devil's Dens and Caves, Devil's Elbows, Mouths and Throats, at least a dozen Devil's Dykes and as many Devil's Bridges. Devil's Causeways, Chairs and Cauldrons there are, and Devil's Punchbowls, sufficient to suggest he was an inveterate toper.

Natural features such as headlands, bays and glens, masses of rock and pools in the rivers have been named after him. Standing stones and other prehistoric relics, trackways and Roman roads have taken his name, and it would need a lengthy list to enumerate all the devil features in the land.

The prevalence of the name need cause no great surprise if we remember that until recent times the devil was considered a very real person, ever stalking the land and seeking to trap the unwary. Seventeenth-century Scottish theologians believed that the devil's cunning increased with his advancing years, and one writer refers to him " as now almost of 6,000 years and of great wilyness and experience."

After all, it is less than two and a half centuries since our forefathers were burning old women for the crime of witchcraft. Some of these women, in fact, confessed to having sold themselves to the devil. In 1752 an old woman at Longmarston, in Northants, died as a result of having been ducked as a witch. Even nowadays cases occasionally come to light of women being suspected of witchcraft.

In all probability the devil has in many instances usurped the giants and deities of our pagan ancestors, for it frequently happens that when a new religion is adopted, the gods of the old beliefs become the devils of the new one. This would account for many of the prehistoric features, which hitherto had been considered homes or temples of forgotten gods, later being regarded as works of the devil. Canute had to proscribe the worship of stones and doubtless the early Christian priests sought to exterminate such practices by instilling fear of the devil.

" Old Nick " is another name for the devil, and this, it is thought, may be derived from *Nikr*, a Scandinavian water-demon. " Owd Scratch " is another name prevalent in the north of England, and this may perpetuate the Norse demon, *Skratti*.

In many parts of the country there was formerly some reluctance to make direct reference to the devil and we find various euphemisms such as " The Evil One," the " Old Man " or " Old Lad." In Sussex there appears to have been an element of pity for the oft-thwarted demon, and he was referred to as " The Poor Man " and the Devil's Dyke, near Brighton, was known as " The Poor Man's Wall."

For all his supposed accumulated wisdom the devil is usually represented in the old legends as a gullible person. In many instances he makes a bargain only to be outwitted by some simple trick.

Typical is the story of the Devil's Bridge at Kirkby Lonsdale. A woman of the village found one day that her cow had strayed across the River Lune and had not returned with the town herd at milking time. Meanwhile the river had risen, and to make matters worse, her husband was also on the wrong side of the water.

W. F. TAYLOR

### THE DEVIL'S CAUSEWAY

*Many prehistoric tracks and Roman roads were in bygone days ascribed to the Devil. The Roman highway running across Shropshire to the town of Uriconium, near the Wrekin, is known as the Devil's Causeway. Here it is seen near Acton Burnell.*

The devil appeared to the distressed woman and offered to build a bridge by nightfall if she would promise him the first living thing that crossed the bridge. To this she agreed, and on returning in the evening she found a handsome stone structure over the flooded stream, and on the far side was the builder waiting for his reward.

Obviously the devil expected the old woman or her husband as his prey. The good wife, however, had brought her dog and a piece of meat. The morsel she threw across the bridge

in the tale. That night Ralph spent in merry mood with the porter at Fountains and the devil was forgotten.

Next day, however, as he climbed out of Nidderdale, the cobbler fell to thinking of his dream and could not get the devil out of mind. On reaching the River Dibb he waded the stream and while replacing his shoes and stockings he burst into song, singing of none other than " Old Nick " himself.

Greatly to his astonishment he heard a rich deep bass joining in the chorus, and on looking

STEPHENSON

THE DEVIL'S BEAUTIFUL BRIDGE

*Spanning the River Lune at Kirkby Lonsdale is this graceful old bridge now preserved as an ancient monument. Apart from its vague satanic connection, it possesses beauty that entitles it to be called the finest bridge in the north of England. Its great age is shown by the first grant of pontage which was in the year 1275.*

and after it sprang the dog, the devil's unexpected fee. With a howl of rage the baffled fiend fled, leaving his stone neck collar beneath the bridge.

At a Yorkshire bridge the devil appears to have built in good fellowship rather than in a huckstering mood. There lived at the hidden village of Thorpe, in Wharfedale, one Ralph Calvert, a merry cobbler fond of a drink and a song. At intervals Ralph travelled over the moors to Nidderdale and on to Fountains Abbey with shoes for the monks.

On one of these journeys he had a sleep by the wayside, and dreamt the devil had him by the throat and was thrusting him into a sack. With a yell of terror the cobbler jumped to his feet, probably to find the strings of his own bag tightened round his neck—but that is not

round there was his satanic majesty, robed in black, complete with horns and tail and cloven hoofs.

Perhaps, feeling there could be little harm in one who sang so heartily, Ralph offered the stranger a bite and a sup—worthy fare, no doubt from Fountains. So for some time they ate and drank, and followed on with glees and ballads and an exchange of gossip and scandal, and the latest tittle-tattle from the abbey kitchen.

When the devil rose to depart, the emboldened cobbler remarked, " If tha be t'devil or not, tha bees a merry chap, but if tha be, bigg us a brig over this river." " It shall be there in three days " replied Nick, and in two strides he was on top of the hill. There he disappeared in a swirling black cloud which sent a flood of water

VALENTINE

## A NATURAL DEVIL'S BRIDGE

*Another of the bridges ascribed to the Devil is the De'il's Brig, on Holborn Head, in Caithness. Here, the sea has worn through the underpart of a tremendous cliff, but the level strata have held fast above leaving a narrow gorge, loud with sea music, and bridged by a massive, laminated slab of rock on the seaward side.*

down the stream. Meditating on this lively encounter the cobbler walked slowly home. Three days later Dibbles Bridge appeared and it stands today on the Pateley Bridge road from Hebden.

Fountains Abbey also reminds us of the devil in another mood. On the Great North Road six miles eastwards of the abbey is Borough-bridge. There, a little west of the town, may be seen three great monoliths, the tallest of which is 22½ feet high and 18 feet in circumference.

STEPHENSON

**THE SHAFTS OF SATAN**
*Near Boroughbridge, Yorkshire, there are three pillars of millstone grit, the smallest of which is 18 feet high, called the Devil's Arrows, from their likeness to enormous shafts sunk deep in the earth.*

These are the Devil's Arrows. In Leland's day there were four of these stones, but one was later broken up to make the foundations of a bridge.

South-east of Boroughbridge is the village of Aldborough, once a Roman station and before that the capital of the Brigantes. Against this place the devil had some unspecified grudge and one day he endeavoured to destroy the town.

From a hill near Fountains he loosed his ponderous bolts crying—
     " Borobrigg, keep out o't'way
     For Audboro' town
     I will ding down."

Perhaps it was the day after the devil's carousal with the cobbler of Thorpe, for his aim was bad and there his arrows stand today a good mile short of their mark.

Northumberland is another county once fre-quented by the devil. Near Hexham is the Devil's Water, but that is not of true parentage and probably takes its name from the ancient family of D'Eivill.

To the north of Hexham, however, the North Tyne claims the unique distinction of having drowned the devil. Near Birtley Holy Well is a mass of rock about 12 feet high, known as the Devil's Rock. In a rash moment the demon endeavoured to spring from this point to the far side of the Tyne, more than a mile away. His jump was short, and down he went headlong into Leap Crag Pool, the deepest spot in the whole course of the river. The Devil's Rock still bears the footprints he made in that fatal leap.

Many old roads and trackways are ascribed to the devil, and Northumberland has a Devil's Causeway, the relics of a Roman road which ran from Hadrian's Wall to Long Framlington. Similarly in Hampshire there is a Devil's High-way making a beeline, in true Roman fashion, for Silchester, the *Calleva Atrebatum* of the legions.

### Dykes of the Arch-fiend

Devil's Dykes are other mementoes of common occurrence. Sometimes these are natural features such as the outcrop of volcanic rock in the isle of Great Cumbrae in Buteshire. The Devil's Dyke running from Loch Ryan, in Wigtown-shire, across Galloway to the Solway Firth is a long earthwork possibly of Roman origin.

Probably the best known of the Devil's Dykes is the one on the South Downs, near Brighton. Overlooking the blue expanse of the Weald, that extensive view attracts many who give no thought to his " Infernal Majesty." Yet here legend credits the devil with attempting a great engineering feat which, of course, like many of his ventures was never fulfilled.

Annoyed at the building of so many churches along the foot of the Downs, the devil decided to let in the sea and drown the weald. For this purpose he started to cut a trench through the hill, beginning at the top and working downwards. Such an evil plan could only be executed in the dark hours and here as elsewhere the " Stupid Beast," as Pope Gregory dubbed him, was foiled. An old woman, hearing strange noises, came out to see what was happening. She carried a sieve in front of her candle to shield it from the wind, and the devil, seeing a round disc of light, thought it was the rising sun. Thereupon he fled with his work unfinished, and leaving his footprints as evidence of his visit.

STEPHENSON

### ON A YORKSHIRE MOOR

*Near the old inn at Saltersgate, on the moorland road from Pickering to Whitby, is the Hole of Horcum, a deep hollow in the hills. According to legend it was formed by the Devil, or the mythical Giant Wade, who, when pursuing a witch, took up a handful of earth and flung it at her. He missed his mark. The witch escaped and the mass of earth made the hill of Blakey Topping, two miles away on Pickering Moor.*

W. F. TAYLOR

### A FAMOUS SUSSEX VIEWPOINT

*Well known from its proximity to Brighton, the Devil's Dyke, a vast hollow in the South Downs is familiar to most people. The entrenchment in the picture is of ancient British origin. On the crest of the hill above there is a hotel from which there is a magnificent view over the whole of the Weald from the village of Poynings, at the foot of the Downs to the pine-clad ridges of Surrey in the blue northern distance.*

W. F. TAYLOR

## THE BRIDGE OF THE EVIL ONE

*Twelve miles from Aberystwyth, the Rheidol River joins the Mynach and they plunge together through a rocky chasm.  Three bridges span the abyss, a modern one of iron, a stone bridge dating from 1753 and, lastly, the Devil's Bridge.  Though traditionally the work of the Devil, it was probably erected by the Knights Hospitallers.*

Down in Dorset we find another instance of the devil in destructive mood. Crowning a low hill about a mile from Studland there is a mass of rock known as the Agglestone. This, although weighing about 400 tons, was but a pebble in the devil's hands. According to one legend he picked up this stone in the Isle of Wight and threw it at Corfe Castle. Another version says he was on his way to drop the boulder on Salisbury Cathedral when he let it fall in its present position.

In Cornwall, as would be expected, the devil is well in evidence. Asparagus Island at Kynance Cove has the Devil's Letter Box and Bellows where the sea is driven through the clefts in the

The parson of St. Breward in those days was a noted wizard, and at the request of the distressed farmer he recalled the spirit of Tregeagle from the underworld.

Jan, or at least his ghost, duly appeared and, so says the story, he even attended the assizes to testify in favour of the farmer.

By his good deed, however, Jan had imperilled his soul, and the devil and all his fiends were waiting to drag him away. Only by constantly labouring at some impossible task could Tregeagle escape them, and so he was set to bale dry the bottomless pool of Dozemary. There for ever sits the forlorn spirit seeking to empty the pool with a limpet shell, and even that small ladle is

W. F. TAYLOR

AMID THE HILLS OF DUMFRIES

*Deep in the grand, lonely hills of Dumfries, at the foot of Hartfell, is the gigantic hollow known as the Devil's Beef Tub. Any legend connected with the name appears to have been lost, but cattle raiders are reputed to have used the Beef Tub to hide their ill-gotten gains in the bad old Border days of long ago.*

rock with tremendous force. Here also is the Devil's Mouth, a great hole into which one may peer down on the water flowing in the hollows of the rock.

Dozemary Pool, famed for its Arthurian associations, also has a legend of an unfortunate soul ever seeking to escape the clutches of the devil.

In the moorland parish of St. Breward, Jan Tregeagle was steward to the Lord of the Manor. After Jan's death some dispute arose as to whether a certain farmer had paid his rent. The farmer contended he had paid Tregeagle although he could not produce a receipt.

pierced with a hole. Round him hovers the devil eternally watching for the unfortunate to cease from his labour so that he may be carried off to hell.

There are other versions of Tregeagle and his impossible tasks, and we hear of him again at Helston and Padstow, and sometimes of him spinning ropes of sand on the seashore.

In the Lamorna Valley there is a prehistoric underground passage, or fogou, locally known as the Fogie Hole. One day Squire Lovel of Trewoofe was out shooting when his dogs put up a hare and chased it into this hole with the squire in hot pursuit. Some hours later the

STEPHENSON

### A GRIM WELSH PRECIPICE
*Not far from the Holyhead Road where it runs between the mountains of Snowdonia is the Devil's Kitchen. Through the impressive cleft one may peer down to Llyn Idwal. No bird, it is said, will cross that lake since Prince Idwal was drowned in its waters. In the background, on the right, is the bold peak of Tryfaen. This mountain (3,010 feet) rises steeply from the shores of Llyn Ogwen, seen in the distance on the left.*

dogs came to the surface in sorry plight, with their tongues protruding and their bodies lathered with foam.

The hare, it seems, was a witch in disguise on her way to a gathering of witches at which the devil also was present. When the squire discovered them the hags were dancing wildly with their master, and on hearing the squire's voice witches and devil turned upon him so that he had to flee for his life. Not until after midnight did the squire reach the open, and then he was sadly demented and persisted in singing some devilish refrain.

affright a man." This was the Devil's Cheesering or Devil's Knife. There Mother Meldrum sheltered in the winter " which added greatly to her fame, because all else for miles around were afraid to go near it after dark or on a gloomy day."

So we might continue in the steps of the devil for the list is by no means exhausted. Perthshire has its Devil's Cauldron and Devil's Mill. In the heart of the Cairngorms the great hulk of Cairntoul has its Devil's Point. High in the Cairngorms too, is the Devil's Elbow. Out of Glencoe runs the Devil's Staircase by which the

VALENTINE

A DEVILISH ROAD FEATURE

*Many people who have motored in Scotland know the famous stretch of road between Alyth and Braemar where it crosses the shoulder of the Cairnwell. Here the road drops 200 feet in half a mile, and the first of two tremendous hairpin bends is known as the Devil's Elbow. It is well shown in the picture.*

Near Penzance is the Devil's Leap, its surface marked with some slight resemblance of a fishing net. One day Satan stole the nets of the Newlyn fishermen with which to take a shoal of pilchards he had seen in Mount's Bay. As he was on his way, the choir of St. Peter's Church, seeing him overhead, began to chant the psalms. The spell worked, for the devil dropped his burden and hastened away, but the fishermen were none the better off, for the nets were turned to stone.

Devonshire among other diabolical features has a Devil's Cheesering, near Lynton. When Girt Jan Ridd went to visit Mother Meldrum, it will be remembered, he went through the Valley of Rocks at Lynton to " a queer old pile of rocks bold behind one another and quite enough to

two young sons of the chief of the Macdonalds escaped when their clan was massacred.

Ireland has a Devil's Glen in the Wicklow Hills and the Devil's Mother is a mountain in Connemara. In Tipperary there is the Devil's Bit, a mountain near Templemore, so named from a gap in its skyline. This was made by the devil who took a bite out of the ridge to annoy a local saint. The holy man, however, had no fear of the fiend, and mounting his mule he followed the encumbered demon into the valley. There in the stream is the Devil's Island, the chunk of earth and rock taken from the top of the mountain. A variant of this tale says the devil did not drop his burden until he was farther south and there it formed the Rock of Cashel.

W. F. TAYLOR

## THE DEVIL'S PUNCHBOWL

*There are many natural hollows named Devil's Punchbowl. Above is seen the famous example on the Portsmouth Road at Hindhead, where the highway runs round the lip of the bowl or valley head. The Devil is also in evidence at Thursley a mile or two away where three conical hills are known as the Devil's Jumps.*

Of the many Punchbowls the most impressive is that on Mangerton Mountain, near Killarney, more than 2,000 feet above the sea. Here is a tarn of dark cold water from which flows the Devil's Stream to form the Torc Waterfall. Nearby is " The Cliff of the Demon." Killarney, in fact, may be said to sup with the devil, for this mountain tarn is the source of its water supply.

### The Devil's Throne

For the throne of the devil we must turn to the Stiperstones, in Shropshire, on the borderland of Wales. There, on top of the hill, is the upstanding mass of the Devil's Chair. Here the devil rested one day when carrying an apronful of stones with which he proposed filling Hell Gutter, a ravine in the hill-side. When he rose his apron string broke and the stones were scattered in their present position. Another tale has it that if the Stiperstones ever sink in the earth, then England will be lost. To the devil, apparently, that is a consummation devoutly to be wished, and he spends his idle moments sitting on the chair in the hope that his weight will crush the stones into the earth.

Mary Webb made dramatic use of the Devil's Chair, and in her novel *The Golden Arrow* she described it as " a mass of quartzite, blackened and hardened by uncountable ages. In the plain

this pile of rock and the rise on which it stood above the rest of the hill-tops would have constituted a hill in itself. The scattered rocks, the ragged holly-brakes on the lower slopes were like small carved lions beside the black marble steps of a stupendous throne. Nothing ever altered its look. Dawn quickened over it in pearl and emerald ; summer sent the armies of heather to its very foot ; snow rested there as doves nest in cliffs. It remained inviolable, taciturn, evil. It glowered darkly on the dawn ; it came through the snow like jagged bones through flesh ; before its hardness even the venturesome cranberries were discouraged.

" For miles around," continued the authoress, " in the plains, the valleys, the mountain dwellings it was feared. It drew the thunder, people said. Storms broke round it suddenly out of a clear sky ; it seemed almost as if it created storm. No one cared to cross the range near it after dark."

That last touch, which might be taken for artist's licence, I found true enough only a year or two ago. A villager with whom I talked and who had never even heard of Mary Webb, although she had lived for a time in a neighbouring village, assured me that the local people would not go by the place in the dark.

While such feelings linger, the devil obviously is not dead.

# COMMONS AND VILLAGE GREENS

## *by* SIR LAWRENCE CHUBB

COMPARATIVELY few people realize that, dotted up and down the countryside of England and Wales, there still exist some 1,600,000 acres of common lands and village greens which, for the most part, are free to the public for air, exercise and recreation. That area is so vast that it is difficult for the mind to grasp exactly what it means. But put in another way it is more comprehensible. If the whole of the commons could be brought together they would provide a National Park two hundred and fifty miles in length and ten miles in width.

Although the commons are, on the whole, widely distributed, the bulk of them lie in the wild parts of the country: thus they occur in richest profusion in the fells and dales of Yorkshire and the Lake District and in parts of Wales.

It is interesting to note that the largest unbroken stretches of common land still remaining are, or were, Royal Forests—the New Forest and the Forest of Dean still belong to the Crown and Dartmoor to the Duchy of Cornwall. The Crown sold its rights in the once vast forest of Waltham, of which Epping Forest is the remaining shred, and the bulk of that area soon disappeared. It is to the fact that the Crown retained its rights over the other forests referred to that we can largely attribute the survival of those beautiful resorts.

The origin of Royal Forests in England is lost in antiquity. Many of them undoubtedly existed in Saxon times. Others were created in later ages. Thus it was the Norman Conqueror who created the New Forest. Domesday shows that King William I found in Hampshire 75,000 acres of land practically uninhabited. He turned this land into a forest: the chase thus formed was insufficient in size, so the king is recorded to have annexed to it a further huge area by clearing off the whole population of some five hundred families. All the forest area was subordinated to the hunting fever of the king of whom it was written in 1087: " He laid laws that he who slew hart or hind, that man should blind him: so sooth he loved the high deer, as though he were their father." The forest laws

were indeed harsh and oppressive in the extreme: but we must not forget that it was largely due to them and to their effect that what is perhaps the noblest common in the country still remains.

The open parts of the New Forest extend to nearly ninety square miles. Spacious heaths are there where the commoners' ponies and cattle can graze: other portions consist of groves of ancient oak and beech of outstanding beauty. Mark Ash is, perhaps, almost the loveliest of them all. Here the venerable trees are of great size and it is interesting to note how all around the wood natural regeneration is gradually taking place, wherever seed finds a safe spot for germination sheltered by holly or hawthorn in early years from browsing deer.

The Forestry Commissioners have statutory

A RELIC OF MERRY ENGLAND

DIXON-SCOTT

*On the village green at Offham, in Kent, stands this quintain or tilting post. If the lancer was not sufficiently skilful he was liable to receive a blow when the horizontal bar swung round.*

power to keep enclosed for the growth of timber at any time 18,000 acres of the wastes of the New Forest. Much criticism has been evoked in the past by the policy (now happily modified) which insisted upon replacing the stately oak, indigenous in Hampshire, by sombre plantations of conifers, alien to the region. The dull uniformity of an artificial plantation of pines, unrelieved by any break, in contrast to the wild beauty of nature, has to be seen to be believed.

The former area is wild, rugged and in parts has almost forbidding grandeur and aloofness. By way of contrast the New Forest has a smiling face : again, the latter region is thickly wooded while on Dartmoor the only tract of primeval woodland to be found is the weird collection of gnarled and dwarfed oaks, known as Wistman's Wood, near Two Bridges. Yet Dartmoor, like the New Forest, is technically a " forest." The explanation is that a " forest " in a legal sense

DIXON-SCOTT

SILVER BIRCHES ON WIMBLEDON COMMON

*No city in England has a finer heritage of commons and open spaces than London. Wimbledon Common is the fairest of them all. In 1865 this beautiful area was in danger of enclosure. Fortunately the threat produced an outburst of public feeling and by Parliamentary action, this and other commons were saved.*

But what a mecca is the New Forest to the nature student and rambler ! Bramshaw and Denny Woods and Bratley convey an adequate idea of what a real forest is like when unspoilt by the hand of man. Their groves and glades are open to the walker who, if wise, will arm himself with an official permit to camp unless he prefers to seek accommodation in Beaulieu or Lyndhurst, in Brockenhurst or Ringwood or some other old-world village with an equally delectable name.

Dartmoor is one of the other Royal Forests which has also retained its character as a common and is worthy of inclusion in any short list of areas sufficiently striking and important for preservation as National Parks. It is strange to couple Dartmoor and the New Forest together.

does not necessarily imply the existence of woodland : trees *may* be there : but on the other hand may be almost unknown. The definition of a forest as given by Manwood in 1717 is " a certain territory of woody grounds and fruitful pastures, privileged for wild beasts and fowls of frest, chase and warren, to rest and abide there in the safe protection of the King for his delight and pleasure."

Dartmoor once embraced 130,000 acres of unfenced lands : now, alas, that area has shrunk in consequence of the policy of putting convicts at Princetown to work upon the reclamation of the moorland. Moreover, many large enclosures were made early last century of land which is still known as the Newtakes. The moor is a common and forms part of the estates of the

Duchy of Cornwall. The commoners have interesting rights. They come from most of the parishes which surround the moor, and their rights, peculiar to Dartmoor, are known as "Venville" or "Fen-field" rights which enable them to depasture their beasts not always only on the moor itself but also on the commons in all the "Venville" parishes.

The tors of Dartmoor are its most notable feature. The loftiest is Yes Tor, near Okehampton, which rises to 2,050 feet: other famous summits, which command marvellous views, include Cawsand Beacon, Brent Tor, Rippon Tor and Hound Tor, all of which are freely accessible. But it is not only the tors that have made Dartmoor popular. The little streams, the spacious stretches of heather-clad moors, the deeply-cut valleys and the early British hut circles, avenues and earthworks, all serve as magnets.

The future of Dartmoor has often been discussed: it is certain that sooner or later the moor

STEPHENSON

### A WINDMILL CHURCH

*Reigate, an old Surrey town at the foot of the North Downs has an extensively sandy heath enlivened with gorse and pines. The picturesque windmill on the hill in the background now serves as a place of worship.*

must become a National Park to be conserved as the most noble example of ancient Britain still remaining in the West Country.

Commons are not all on the heroic scale and the value of many of them depends not so much upon their size as upon the extent to which they can contribute to the health and well-being of

A. L. SIMPSON

### A VILLAGE GREEN IN SURREY

*In the south-west corner of Surrey, in the area known as "The Fold Country," there are a number of quiet little hamlets such as Alford, Chiddingfold and Dunsfold, each of them consisting of a sprinkling of houses, a church, an inn and a village green. Typical is the village green and common of Dunsfold, which is seen above.*

the whole community. What, for instance, would Harrogate be without its Stray, Newcastle without its Town Moor, Tunbridge Wells without its common and Toad Rock, or Wimbledon, without its fine open space? Again, what would Surrey be like as a dormitory for London without its commons?

Hindhead and the Devil's Punchbowl, the crowning glory of the county's western hills, are typical of these scenes of national beauty. They look down over a veritable network of lesser open spaces, some richly wooded, others, such as Witley and Frensham Commons, typical

absorbed into private parks or fields. Like so many other good things, commons are taken for granted. " They have always existed and will always remain because they are common property," expresses the popular view.

It is true that, in consequence of years of struggle in Parliament and in the Law Courts, most commons are now fairly safe and likely to remain playgrounds for the community ; but that safety does not necessarily prove that the commons belong to the people. They may have been bought by, or given to, a local authority or otherwise dedicated to the public, but as a

EDGAR WARD

### A LOVELY COMMON NEAR ROYAL RICHMOND

*Near Richmond, in Surrey, is East Sheen Common, seen in this photograph, a beautiful link in that belt of open spaces on the edge of London which includes R chmond Park, Wimbledon Common, Putney Heath and Barnes Common. Here is a typical scene of green bracken and golden gorse, and graceful silver birches.*

heaths. Large or small these commons give to Surrey 20,000 acres of its most beautiful natural features and provide its residents, as well as Londoners, with splendid open country. Why is it that Surrey has so large an area of commons whereas other counties—such as Lincolnshire—can scarcely boast of a single acre? The reason is that the soil of the surviving commons in Surrey and elsewhere was too sterile to justify the expense of fencing it in during the hey-day of the inclosure movement.

It is not often that people pause to ask themselves why these commons have remained unfenced when all the surrounding land has given place to bricks and mortar, or has been

matter of fact most commons are still private property. They are a relic of a very ancient and widespread system of land tenure, as old as the time when men began to settle down into village communities and evolved a method of land cultivation suited to their needs. Thus in the East, China, India and Chaldea all have had their commons of different types for as far back as authentic history extends.

In our own country, when the Norman conqueror reached England, fences were few and far between outside the towns and villages. Even the arable land was unenclosed. The grazing grounds of each hamlet were also open, and became known as the " Waste of the Manor "

A. L. SIMPSON

### STOCKS ON THE GREEN

*Usually the village green was the place selected for punishment of local offenders, and in many places remains of the stocks are still to be seen on the green. In this picture at Roydon, in Essex, in addition to the stocks we see the village lock-up which, despite stout padlocks, would offer little resistance to a modern gaol breaker.*

STEPHENSON

### IN A YORKSHIRE VILLAGE

*The pretty Yorkshire village of Bolton by Bowland has a wide green fringed by a row of stately trees and with the dignified parish church in the background. At Bolton Hall Henry VI lay in hiding for some months, after fleeing from the Battle of Hexham. Here also lived William Pudsey, a godson of Elizabeth, who was banished for mining silver, which was then a royal prerogative, and also for forging coins from the metal.*

and subsequently as common land. This waste land was essential to provide the grazing required by the local flocks and herds, the fuel needed for heating and cooking, litter for bedding, livestock, and materials necessary for the repair of buildings, walls and paths.

### Rights of Common

The custom to use the wastes in these ways gradually became crystallized into rights known as rights of common, and it is the existence of these rights, enjoyed, as lawyers say, in common, that marks land as a common, and it is those rights that have saved the commons. The commoners do not own the common itself but merely rights exercisable over it. In theory, when a manor was given by the Conqueror to one of his barons the gift included the waste; but the new owner soon found that he could not ignore the needs of the inhabitants of his manor, or trample upon their old customs without giving rise to bitter opposition. The Statute of Merton, one of the early Acts of Parliament, passed by the barons in 1235, when the people were unrepresented in Parliament, was accordingly designed to give the barons, or lords of the manor, as they came to be called, power to override the rights and customs of the ancient copyholders and largely to ignore those of the freeholders. The Statute of Merton, in a modified form, still remains unrepealed.

From that day to this the fight for commons has gone on; sometimes, as in the time of the Tudor Agrarian Rebellion, dissatisfaction about the enclosure of commons has flared up into bitter rioting which has shaken the whole country

and given rise to a sense of injustice which found expression in the lines :
" We punish swift the man or woman
   Who steals the goose from off the common,
   But let the greater villain loose
   Who steals the common from the goose ! "

Subsequently over five millions of acres of commons were authorized by Parliament to be partitioned under Inclosure Acts. These measures often inflicted extreme hardships upon the smaller commoners because the common had always been the poor man's farm. The little farmer or yeoman ceased to exist because when his holding was under crop he had no other land on which to feed his few animals, which hitherto had been grazed on the common.

The excuse for the enclosure of commons under the 4,719 Inclosure Acts which found their way to the Statute Book between the years 1710 and 1869 was that the land was needed for agriculture ; but much of it, though fenced in, has been worthless to produce anything but rabbits and gorse.

It was not until 1865 that a feeling of uneasiness against the gradual loss of many of the people's traditional playgrounds came to a head. National sentiment was outraged by a series of attacks on the commons of London. Amongst the threatened spaces were Wimbledon Common and Putney Heath, which together form a magnificent area. A bill was introduced into Parliament which sought to authorize the enclosure of the Heath and large parts of the Common. An outburst of indignation arose and a Select Committee was appointed to consider the scheme. The committee heard evidence, and promptly reported

HUMPHREY AND VERA JOEL

### COTSWOLD CHARM

*At the foot of the Cotswolds lies Broadway, one of the prettiest villages in England. Broadway is famed for its beautiful Elizabethan houses gabled and dormered, and weathered into mellowed gold and grey. It owes no small measure of its charm, however, to its wide green, which is carefully tended and looked after.*

that not an inch of Wimbledon or Putney Heath could be spared by the public. They went even further and strongly recommended that steps should be taken to protect against enclosure all the commons in and around London.

The Select Committee's report led to the formation of a non-political body known as the Commons and Footpaths Preservation Society, in order to organize efforts to preserve commons for the public use. From that day to this the society has had its hands full of work.

### Village Greens

Many fights were organized in the Law Courts and others in Parliament with almost uniform success, and commons are now fairly free from the risk of attack.

Village greens, too, need safeguarding. These small open spaces are often of the utmost importance. They generally lie in the heart of the village and, where large enough, are invaluable for recreation.

It has to be remembered that the demand for land for recreation is of relatively modern growth. Indeed, the first attempt at statutory interest in the subject aimed not at saving land as open spaces but at repressing the national instinct of healthy human beings of all ages to employ their leisure hours in health - giving exercise. For instance, in the Archery Act of 1541, passed to rescue archery from " sore decay," the parish officers were directed to provide butts, and the Act forbade the playing in public places of " tennis, bowls, closh or cloysh, shove-groat (the father of shove halfpenny !) coyting, logating or any other unlawful games."

The public had to wait until the days when Puritanism had spent its main force before it was held by the judges that " it was necessary for the inhabitants to have their recreation." It was nevertheless the exercise of these rights of recreation that has kept safe our village greens. It is not enough to be able to say that a piece of land has always been known as a village green. What is necessary is to be able to prove that the inhabitants of the " vill " or parish have enjoyed some special or exclusive right or custom to resort to the green for dancing around the Maypole or to play an annual game, or to enjoy some other right in such a manner as to signify that

A. L. SIMPSON

### THE BRACKEN HARVESTER

*Rights of common included grazing of flocks and herds, and the gathering of fuel and bedding for the cattle. Here we see a Surrey villager exercising his rights by taking bracken for his livestock.*

the green is subject to a local custom. Many greens have been lost because of the impossibility of establishing some definite custom, or of showing that the land has been controlled or cared for by the Parish Council or other local authority.

The commons and village greens are indeed a romantic feature of our heritage and should remain for all time free and open to the people. Some 600,000 acres are now so preserved. There remains, however, another million acres. They also are worth saving. They are, it is true, largely in the wildest and most remote parts of the country, but after all, they represent all that is best of unspoiled primeval scenery ; they give us a large measure of access to mountains and they must form the basis of every National Park scheme. Their preservation is a duty not only to this generation but to posterity.

DIXON SCOTT

## THE VALLEY OF LORNA DOONE
*A large tract of lovely country in the heart of Exmoor, including Watersmeet and the Falls of Lyn, passed to the nation in 1936 after great efforts. It covers a large stretch of the right bank of the East Lyn River from Woodside to Rockford, as well as the beautiful Barton Wood on the other side of this grand valley.*

# THE NATIONAL HERITAGE

## *by* TOM STEPHENSON

IN the preceding pages we have seen some-thing of Britain's romantic beauty and its amazing legacy of the past. We have glanced at its natural features, its long and varied coast, its rivers winding from the hills to the sea, its forests, its downs and moors and mountains. The relics of our prehistoric ancestors, clues to Roman days and the troubled times of Saxon and Norsemen have been reviewed. Scenes of legend, castles of song and story, the monastic ruins and the splendour of the cathedrals, the mellow glory of the medieval towns, the charm of the villages and the story of age-old tracks and roads from Roman to modern highways; all these have been presented, and so we have realized how great is our heritage.

With all this in mind we may feel with Emerson that Britain " is stuffed full in all corners and crevices with towns, towers, churches, villas, palaces, hospitals and charity houses. In the history of art it is a long way from a cromlech to York Minster ; yet all the steps may still be traced in this all-preserving island."

We must confess though that our worthy endowment is by no means what it might have been. We have to admit that much has been lost irrevocably, and many a lovely scene and many noble monuments of other days have been sacrificed in the past.

The venerable beauty of the English scene has not saved it from the vandals and despoilers who have ruthlessly hacked and marred, and often entirely effaced, some of its finest features. The long protracted working of natural forces which gave the land shape, and the labours of forgotten generations who added the finishing graces have roused little veneration in the nation as a whole. Man, with all his destructive potentiality is seldom stayed by æsthetic considerations in his quest for wealth and power.

One man's profit or the gain of a few has been accepted as sufficient justification for the destruction of beauty which is the rightful heritage of all. Ownership of a piece of land has been thought to confer the right, not only to desecrate one's own estate, but also the liberty to foul the air and pollute the streams, and blight the surrounding countryside by obtrusive hideousness.

Over the earliest ravages of the Philistines we cannot at this date pretend any deep emotion. Time and nature have softened the effects of their depredations but the fragments which have endured may rouse regret for what has been lost.

From our Saxon forefathers, on plunder bent, one could scarcely expect historical appreciation of the civilization they found in existence. When they overthrew the walled cities, and burned the

WALTER SCOTT BRADFORD

### LIMESTONE CLIFFS OF CHEDDAR
*One of the glories of Somerset, Cheddar Gorge was acquired for the people over a period of years, and the grand cliffs, threatened by quarry workings and unmatched for grandeur in southern England, are permanently saved.*

temples and the villas, they could not foresee that centuries later men would be digging and sifting the soil for minute relics of Roman days. Sometimes, however, and doubtless without a thought for posterity, they did preserve for us some interesting fragment.

At Corbridge-on-Tyne, for instance, a Saxon town grew close by the Roman *Corstopitium*. There when the seventh-century St. Wilfred raised his church the stones dressed and tooled by the forgotten Roman masons were ready at hand. Thus was preserved a second-century Roman arch, which was removed stone by stone, and rebuilt in the porch of the early church. Through the succeeding centuries Corbridge continued to grow at the expense of Corstopitium, and even comparatively modern houses display in their walls stones which were chiselled in the days of Hadrian and Severus.

Corbridge may also serve as a reminder of those other invaders not a whit less destructive than the Saxons. Like many another place it suffered from the ruthless Vikings who sacked the monasteries at Lindisfarne, Jarrow and Whitby, and who burnt and plundered wherever they went.

Those pre-Norman monasteries, however, were but modest forerunners of the splendid

magnificence. Stained glass windows, skilful work of early craftsmen, were ruthlessly shattered. Often the buildings themselves served as quarries for the neighbourhood. Many a cottage and farmhouse today contains stones that were once part of an adjacent monastery. What was once an altar stone in an abbey church may be found serving as a hearthstone or as a shelf in a kitchen or dairy.

Strangely enough in those days which witnessed the desecration of so many fine pieces of architecture we find one of the earliest expressions of regard for the face of the land.

STEPHENSON

### MIRRORED GLADES OF HAMPSHIRE

*Bought in 1919 as a memorial to the late Sir Robert Hunter, first Chairman of the Executive Committee of the National Trust, the estate of Waggoners Wells, near Hindhead, was increased by gifts of Kingswood Firs and Croaker's Patch. With it went Summerden House, now a Youth Hostel, and eighty-seven acres.*

establishments which arose after the Conquest. They had none of the grandeur or noble beauty of Fountains or Furness or Tintern.

Those great abbeys, built by medieval masons, grew and flourished until the Reformation, and then they in turn were sacrificed, not in the blind fury of war, but to fill the coffers of Henry VIII. There is many a sorry tale of the dismantling of the abbeys. After the Dissolution those noble edifices were hurried to ruin. Roofs were removed for the sake of the lead, and chancel and cloister were left to crumble and decay. A chapter house might be turned into a barn, and an austere refectory serve as a cowshed, and one may read of men being paid a few pence per yard for the dismantling of architectural

We who are familiar with the verdant loveliness of modern Sussex can scarcely visualize it as England's " Black Country." Yet such it was and for centuries it was busy with the mining, smelting and working of iron. To serve as fuel for the furnaces, the forest of Anderida of the Romans, the Andresweald of the Saxons, was laid bare.

In the days of Henry VIII attention was drawn to the rate of destruction and enactments were gradually introduced for the preservation of timber. Camden and Fuller later commented on the way the woods were being sacrificed and Michael Drayton lamented as one might do today. " These iron times," he wrote, " breed none that mind posterity."

STEPHEN-ON

## THE FAMOUS TOWER OF SURREY

*Leith Hill, near Dorking, is the highest point in south-east England, and commands a great area of pine and heather country.   The tower on the summit has been a familiar landmark for many years.   All around, the National Trust has been enriched by presentations of beautiful country covering nearly three hundred acres.*

STEPHENSON

## AN ANCIENT MONUMENT BENEATH THE DOWNS

*At the foot of the North Downs, near Wrotham, in Kent, are the prehistoric Coldrum Stones, the remains of a Long Barrow or a Neolithic burial mound.   The site was presented to the Trust as a fitting memorial to the late Benjamin Harrison, the village grocer of Ightham who became world famous as an archæologist.   The great stones seen above formed the burial chamber, and between them a number of Neolithic skeletons were found.*

" Jove's oak, the warlike ash, veined elm, the
      softer beech,
Short hazel, maple plain, light asp, the bending
      wych,
Tough holly, and smooth birch, must altogether
      burn ;
What should the builder serve, supplies the
      forger's turn,
When under public good, base private gain
      takes hold,
And we, poor woeful woods, to ruin lastly
      sold."

It was also Henry VIII, the despoiler of the
monasteries, who made John Leland King's
Antiquary, and sent him on a tour of England
and Wales.  In the same century Camden and
others founded a society for the preservation of
national antiquities.

Neither Camden nor Leland, however, appears
to have heard of the great megalithic temple at
Avebury.  Although this is the oldest monument
in the land there is no mention of it prior to
1663 when John Aubrey, himself a Wiltshire
man, showed it to Charles II, and by command
wrote an account of the royal visit.

The present village of Avebury has grown at
the expense of the temple and of the five hundred
huge stones that had been so laboriously erected
in the circles and avenues only about a score
remain today.  In the eighteenth century a notorious Tom Robinson was active here.  He broke
up many of the great monoliths, one of which
was said to have provided twenty cartloads of
stone.  So disappeared much of this " once
hallowed sanctuary, the supposed parent of
Stonehenge."

### Threat to Hadrian's Wall

Lest this sacrilege should rouse in us any
unwarranted superiority let it not be forgotten
that so recently as 1931 there was a serious
proposal to quarry the basalt of the Whin Sill,
in Northumberland, at a point which would have
meant the destruction of one of the remaining
portions of the Roman wall.  Only by the
intervention of His Majesty's Office of Works
was this prevented.

For all the irreparable damage that was done
in preceding centuries we have to admit that the
greatest depredations have been committed within
the last hundred years.  A century ago industrialism had not blighted any considerable area

DIXON-SCOTT

### THE KNOTTED LIMES OF ASHRIDGE

*Ashridge Park, the mansion of which is now a political college, is famous as the place of Princess Elizabeth's
arrest when her sister, Mary Tudor, came to the throne.  The famous lime avenue is in the park.  Around
it are Trust properties covering 2,600 acres of down and heath and woodland including Berkhamsted Common.*

STEPHENSON

## THE LOVELIEST PART OF LANCASHIRE

*The Lake District is the stronghold of the National Trust and friends of this beautiful part of England have subscribed from all over the world for its preservation; Tarn Hows, near Coniston, is the gem of the property known as Monk Coniston, which covers 2,770 acres of superb country and adjoins other Trust properties.*

of the land, our towns had not developed into dense congestions with sprawling tentacles spreading through the countryside.

The machine age, which developed regardless of the men and women it broke at the wheel, could not be expected to show any consideration for inanimate beauty. A crystal stream from the hills was a heaven-sent water supply and at the same time a natural conduit for industrial effluvia. What mattered it if a factory, uglier than any prison, sprouted in a verdant meadow and with the outpourings of its tall chimney blackened the countryside for miles round? Who was to complain if mines and furnaces left their refuse piled high across the land?

In 1844 Wordsworth cried :

" Is there no nook of English ground secure
  From rash assault ? "

William Morris, Ruskin and others denounced the thoughtless and unplanned development which was rapidly eating up the beauty of Britain. Gradually it was realized, by some at least, that a growing population need not devour the countryside like locusts, that natural beauty and historic monuments were worthy of preservation and that it was really possible to achieve this by means of sensible planning and control.

In 1895, mainly through the efforts of Sir Robert Hunter, Miss Octavia Hill and Canon Rawnsley, there was founded the National Trust for Places of Historic Interest or Natural Beauty. After twelve years of slow but steady progress this body was incorporated by the National Trust Act for the purpose " of promoting the permanent preservation for the benefit of the nation of lands and tenements (including buildings) of beauty and historic interest, and as regards lands for the preservation (so far as practicable) of their natural aspect, features, and animal and plant life."

### A National Estate

Today most people have heard of the National Trust, and thousands of holiday makers are familiar with its notice boards proclaiming that some historic site or beauty spot is owned by the Trust, and so is preserved for all time for the nation.

The Trust is, in fact, now the possessor of a great estate and owns some of the finest features of the land. Mountains, moorlands, downs and woodlands are so preserved. Among its many properties are also included notable landmarks,

STEPHENSON

## THE FAMOUS CRAG OF DERWENTWATER

*Perhaps the most photographed view in the Lake District, and worthy of it, Friar's Crag, near Keswick, was bought by the public in 1921 in memory of the Lakeland writer, Canon Rawnsley. Other beautiful tracts nearby were added by gift or purchase in 1925 and 1929 so that beautiful Derwentwater is ringed by National property. In the background, on the left, is Causey Pike, while Grisedale Pike is to be seen through the trees.*

STEPHENSON

## LOOKING ACROSS BUTTERMERE TO HONISTER PASS

*The three lakes of the beautiful Buttermere Valley, Cumberland, are actually owned by the National Trust, and the whole is linked up with the grand Ennerdale property by land under preservation covenants. The area has a varied charm, as it includes the lakes of Buttermere, Crummock and Loweswater, the peaks of Red Pike, High Stile, High Crag, etc., the waterfall of Scale Force, and the woods of Burtness and Hassness.*

prehistoric monuments, ancient bridges, medieval castles and Tudor houses and even an old English village.

Nowhere in England is the Trust so well established as in the Lake District, and nowhere is there greater need for its protecting influence, or scenery so worthy of preservation. Between the Trust and this incomparable region of mountains, lakes and dales there is indeed a close affinity if not a mutual indebtedness. The late Canon Rawnsley, already mentioned as one of the founders of the Trust, was for many years Vicar of Crosthwaite, near Keswick, and in this

properties round Derwentwater have either been purchased by, or presented to the Trust, so that more than half of the shores of that lovely lake are now national property. Friar's Crag, that little jutting promontory on the east side of the lake, one of the most popular view-points in the district, was bought as a memorial to Canon Rawnsley.

Also included in the Derwentwater properties is Castle Head, overlooking the lake, and commanding one of the grandest prospects in Britain. From its summit one may view the full length of Derwentwater, the long line of Walla Crag rising sheer above the road, and the seemingly knife-like

STEPHENSON

### GREAT GABLE'S MASSIVE BROW

*Great Gable, here viewed from the path to Esk Hause, is probably the noblest of Lakeland mountains. It is the centre-piece of the grandest and wildest of the possessions of the Trust, 3,000 acres of mountain summits above the 1,500-feet contour, and presented by the Fell and Rock Climbing Club in memory of their war dead.*

and many other ways he worked assiduously for the preservation of Lakeland.

Largely at his instigation the Trust, whilst still in its infancy, launched a public appeal for £7,000 for the purchase of its first large acquisition. With some anxiety the committee undertook this venture, but Canon Rawnsley was a determined worker, and, even in those days, the "Lakes" had many admirers. In 1902 the desired sum had been collected and the Trust purchased one hundred and eight acres of woodland at Brandelhow on the shores of Derwentwater.

Since that first bold venture a number of other

ridge of the Cat Bells swelling upwards to Maiden Moor, whilst beyond the head of the lake, Borrowdale leads into the very heart of the hills, to Glaramara, Great Gable, and Scafell Pike, the highest of them all. These also are the property of the National Trust.

Another early acquisition was seven hundred and fifty acres on Gowbarrow Fell overlooking Ullswater and including a mile of the shore of that delightful lake, the shore where Wordsworth saw :

" A host of golden daffodils ;
    Beside the lake, beneath the trees,
    Fluttering and dancing in the breeze."

To this was added in later years Glencoin Wood, but Ullswater, although equal to, if not outrivalling Derwentwater in the beauty of its setting, has not been so effectively secured against possible depredation.

One of the Trust's greatest achievements in Lakeland was the acquiring of the Buttermere Valley. This alluring dale, with the three lakes of Buttermere, Crummock and Loweswater, is now saved from undesirable development, and those serene lakes and brooding hills will be handed down the generations with their charms unmolested.

When we leave the dales for the hills we again discover how active the Trust and its friends

Climbing Club who were killed in the Great War. The tablet also bears a relief map of the surrounding mountains which were bought by the club and presented to the Trust. Look around and you will see the magnificence of this gift, Gable itself and its neighbouring Green Gable and the outlying spurs of Base Brown and Brandreth are included, as is Kirk Fell rearing above Ennerdale. Glaramara and Allen Crags are part of the gift and so are the sheer black crags of Great End, and the boulder strewn Broad Crag and the heights of Lingmell sweeping down to the green floor of Wastdale.

This is the club's memorial, inspired in its conception and meriting the everlasting gratitude

L. C. RUTHERFURD

### THE HILLS ABOVE WALTON'S RIVER

*Magnificent peaks rise above Dovedale, the Derbyshire ravine beloved of Izaak Walton. Bostern Nab and Bayley Hill were presented to the Trust in 1936, and at the same time, protective covenants were secured over a further two hundred and fifty acres of farm lands, a magnificent addition to other properties here.*

have been. Let us start from the head of Borrowdale. As we walk up to Seathwaite we have the steep craggy slopes of Glaramara on our left. That mountain of rugged crests is Trust property and only one of a noble group. When we reach Sty Head we are roughly in the centre of one of the most magnificent of all the possessions of the National Trust. The surrounding mountains are, moreover, the most sublime war memorial to be found in Britain, but the better to appreciate this splendour we must climb to the crest of Great Gable.

There by the summit cairn is a bronze tablet in memory of members of the Fell and Rock

of all who love the hills, for, to quote the words of Geoffrey Winthrop Young at the unveiling of the memorial, " That which hills only can give their children the disciplining of strength in freedom, the freeing of the spirit through generous service, these free hills shall give again, and for all time."

The summits included in this gift are not, however, the whole of the Trust's properties hereabouts. Ennerdale, the most desolate of Lakeland valleys, is now held by the Forestry Commissioners. From this body the Trust secured on a five hundred years' lease more than 3,000 acres including Pillar Mountain, with its

DIXON-SCOTT

### GRANDEUR OF A WELSH GORGE

*The magnificent Pass of Aberglaslyn, on the road from Caernarvon to Portmadoc was largely preserved for posterity in 1936. Some three hundred acres passed anonymously to the Trust, and a further two hundred were protected. The land includes some of the finest mountain and river scenery in North Wales.*

famous rock tower, and the adjacent heights of Steeple and Haycock. Southwards from Great Gable we see the great cairn on the crest of Scafell Pike, England's highest mountain. That summit is also held by the Trust, in memory of Lakeland men who fell in the war. Across the gap of Mickledore from Scafell Pike are the soaring crags of Scafell, and that mountain down to the 2,000 feet contour is also Trust property.

### Snowdonia

While so much has been achieved in Lakeland, the Trust has not neglected its opportunities elsewhere. Among its more recent acquisitions may be mentioned the property in the famed Pass of Aberglaslyn in Caernarvonshire, 300 acres of land near Pont Aberglaslyn. This is a good beginning in Snowdonia, and it is hoped that before many years have passed much more of that mountainous region will be in the hands of the Trust, if in the meantime it has not been made a National Park, an even more desirable end.

One property of the Trust does in itself constitute a miniature National Park. The shaggy upland of Dunkery Beacon, in Somerset, the Trust's largest single holding, includes something like 10,000 acres. Almost the whole of this wide sweep of moorland is thus preserved, from near Porlock to Dunkery Hill Gate, and from Brockwell to Alderman's Barrow on the edge of Exmoor.

From Dunkery's topmost point the beacon flares of old spread the alarm. In *Lorna Doone*, the author pictures the place on such an occasion. "The Beacon was rushing up in a fiery storm to heaven, and the form of its flame came and went in the folds, and the heavy sky was hovering. All around it was hung with red, deep in twisted columns, and then a giant beard of flame streamed throughout the darkness. The sullen hills were flanked with light and the valleys chined with shadow, and all the sombrous moors awoke in furrowed anger."

By the great cairn on Robin How, by the

STEPHENSON

### RELIC OF ANCIENT TRANSPORT

*A picturesque reminder of the old days before the general use of wheeled vehicles is this single-arched bridge spanning the River Ribble at Stainforth, near Settle. It lies on the old route followed by the pack-horse trains between York and Lancaster. At least two hundred years old, some authorities say it is even older.*

hearths of the ancient beacons, we may overlook fifteen counties from the Malvern Hills, in Worcestershire, to the heights above Plymouth, from the moors of Cornwall to the hills of Wales beyond the Severn Sea.

Except for the great seaports the coast of Britain has seen little industrial development. Yet we have to confess that in many places it has suffered serious ravages, and many a one-time delightful place has had its beauty sadly dimmed, if not obliterated, by ugly building developments, by the spread of houses, ill conceived and completely out of harmony with the surroundings, rearing their unsightliness in most obtrusive fashion.

Only in recent years, and only after much damage has been done, have some of the seaside resorts realized the importance of preserving their scenic attractions unimpaired.

As far as its means and circumstances permit, the National Trust has striven to secure attractive coastal scenes and preserve them from spoliation. In fact, the first property it acquired was four and a half acres of cliff-land overlooking Cardigan Bay, near Barmouth. Another early acquisition was Barras Head at Tintagel in King Arthur's fabled haunts.

Round the coast of Cornwall the Trust now holds about a score of properties. Among them are Pentire Head, a bold promontory jutting out into the Atlantic near Padstow, a range of cliffs which has been described "as beyond comparison the finest in all Cornwall." Another beautiful property is Pendarres Point, affording splendid views over the famous Bedruthan Steps.

Between Sennen and Land's End the Mayon and Trevescan Cliffs are now National Trust property. This site possesses a ghost, for it is told "Long before the days of lifeboat or rocket, a ship sailing from Ireland was wrecked in a terrible gale off the rock now called the Irish Lady. All were drowned except one—a lady of great beauty, who managed to clamber to the top of the rock and cling there. Desperate efforts were made to save her. The storm raged and she clung there for three days. Those who watched from the cliff top saw that she had a rose in her mouth. At last, exhausted, she slid into the sea. Now in times of tempest she can

still be seen, a rose between her lips by day, a lantern in her hand by night, watching from the rock that bears her name."

Logan Rock, the well-known rocking stone, and the wild headland of Treen Cliff Castle, was presented to the Trust in 1933. A naval officer in a foolish prank dislodged the Logan Rock in 1824, and was, for his pains, compelled to restore

DIXON-SCOTT

## IRON WALLS OF CORNWALL

*All who know the wild Lizard Peninsula rejoiced when the magnificent cliffs from Mullion to Predannack, with the lovely moor behind them, had been acquired for the people. The Trust also owns land at Kynance Cove.*

it to its original position, at great expense to himself.

Across Mount's Bay, in the Lizard Peninsula, the Trust owns four properties, including control of the cliffs extending from Mullion Cliffs at Porth Pyg to the northern end of Predannack Head. Adjoining the rugged Kynance Cove, the seventy acres of Lizard Downs are also vested in the Trust.

### Devon Beauty

In Devonshire the Trust also holds several properties along the coast, most notable of which is the fine group between Salcombe and Hope, and including Bolberry Down, Bolt Head and Bolt Tail. There one may walk for five miles along an unspoiled stretch of coast almost entirely national property. For the rest of our shores, however, little has been done. In the Isle of Wight, between Ventnor and Shanklin, St. Boniface and Bonchurch Down are preserved, and so is Tennyson Down with its splendid chalk cliffs between Freshwater and the Needles. Along the South Coast, however, from Sidmouth, in Devon, to Beachy Head, in Sussex, the Trust

WALTER SCOTT, BRADFORD

A BEAUTIFUL YORK INTERIOR

*Work of the thirteenth century is still to be seen in the basement of the Treasurer's House, York, but the building was mainly carried out four hundred years later. This picture shows the beauty of the timbered walls.*

Saltwick Nab at Whitby represents the only Yorkshire site. In Northumberland at Sea Houses there is one and a half miles of sandy shore owned by the Trust and a little further north are the Farne Isles, also held for the nation.

Thus it will be seen that except for these few possessions, and except where local authorities have had the sagacity to impose restrictions, the coast of Britain is not assured of security from the despoiler.

### Roman Relics

Among the prehistoric relics held by the Trust may be mentioned the great earthwork of Cissbury Ring on the South Downs, near Worthing, and the Druid's Circle, near Keswick. Roman times are represented by several properties including the ruins of the villa at Chedworth, in the Cotswolds, and the remains at Housesteads, in Northumberland. This latter property includes in addition to the fort of Borcovicium, one of the milecastles of the Romans, and three-quarters of a mile of Hadrian's Wall. It is, in fact, one of the most visited places in the wall, and probably affords a clearer conception of the magnitude of that immense work than is to be gained at any other point along its course from the east coast to the Solway.

So far we have said nothing of the architectural possessions of the Trust, of its castles and mansions, villages and inns, and various monuments. Probably the most popular of all its treasures is the lovely Bodiam Castle, in Sussex. In the valley of the Rother, its stately walls and towers rise in splendid majesty from its surrounding moat and it would hardly surprise one, as Lord Curzon remarked, if a train of richly-clad knights with falcons on their wrists, and their ladies in gaily caparisoned palfreys were suddenly to emerge from the barbican gate.

Not so imposing as Bodiam, and yet a picturesque and interesting ruin is Tattershall Castle, Lincolnshire. The dominant feature here is the

can only boast one possession. This is the Crowlink Estate, near Eastbourne, which includes two of the Seven Sisters, those great chalk cliffs where the sea has cut across the hills leaving the abrupt white gable ends, dipping into little green valleys which also end suddenly at the edge of the cliffs.

If we continue coastwise round the North Foreland, not until we reach the Norfolk shores do we find the Trust again established. Blakeney Point, west of Cromer, is a shingle spit of 1,100 acres kept as a sanctuary for sea birds. Scolt Head, between Wells and Hunstanton, consists of about 1,200 acres of sand-dunes, salt marsh and shingle and this also serves as a nesting place for bird life.

EDGAR WARD

## A PERFECT ENGLISH STREET

*West Wycombe, on the London-Oxford Road, in Buckinghamshire, contains many beautiful examples of sixteenth- and seventeenth-century houses. The greater part of this picturesque village in the Chilterns was acquired in 1934 from the Royal Society of Arts, who had carried out much careful restoration. This work was completed by the National Trust and the hill behind the village was presented a year later.*

EDGAR WARD

## AN OLD PRIEST'S HOUSE

*This almost perfect example of a small fourteenth-century house is at Muchelney, in Somerset. It has been most carefully restored and, standing as it does, with the ancient cross in front of it, shows unchanged a lovely corner of the England of the Middle Ages which is now kept in trust for the nation for all time.*

WALTER SCOTT, BRADFORD

### AN OLD DARTMOOR BUILDING

*The fifteenth-century Church House at Widecombe-in-the-Moor, Devonshire, became national property in 1932. It is the gem of the little moorland village famous for its association with Uncle Tom Cobley and his friends.*

was described as "ruinous and decayed time out of mind." Today all its inner buildings have gone, but its great circular keep rising from the centre of the court is still a dominant landmark in the valley.

Of the many picturesque old houses held by the Trust we may mention that of Paycockes at Coggeshall, in Essex, a beautiful specimen of a merchant's house richly decorated and carved, and probably dating from 1500. At Long Crendon, in Buckinghamshire, is preserved an old building known as the Courthouse. This was probably built in the fifteenth century as a wool store or Staple Hall. Because of its size the manorial courts were held there from the days of Henry V down to the present century.

Also in Buckinghamshire, in a fold of the Chilterns, is the attractive little village of West Wycombe. This place, with its picturesque seventeenth and eighteenth-century cottages was acquired by the National Trust from the Royal Society of Arts, and has been carefully reconditioned to present the original appearance of an unspoiled and typical English village.

At Aylesbury the Trust owns the "King's Head," an interesting old inn dating in parts from the fifteenth century. In Southwark a recent acquisition is the George Inn, built in 1677, which still retains fragments of the original work. In the yard of this inn plays were performed in bygone days and later it became a famous coaching inn.

We have only been able to glance at a few of the gems the Trust has succeeded in saving for the nation. It has many other valued possessions, some of which are depicted in the accompanying illustrations. There remains, however, many a fair scene and many an historic feature yet unprotected. If we are wise in our generation we shall not continue to repeat the sins of our forefathers. Instead, we shall bestir ourselves to save the comely face of Britain that it may indeed be a joy for ever.

great square tower, or keep, built of brick. This four-storeyed structure dates from the fifteenth century when Ralf Cromwell, Treasurer of England, rebuilt the castle. The first floor was the Great Hall, and on the second storey was the great chamber. All four floors have beautifully sculptured fireplaces carved with foliage and the shields of former owners. These fireplaces would now be in America had not Lord Curzon bought them back before they were shipped.

Skenfrith, in Monmouthshire, another castle held by the Trust, takes us back to Norman times. With Grosmont and Whitecastle it was administered as a royal fortress by Henry II. With them also it was granted by Henry III to his son Edmund of Lancaster. In Tudor times the castle

W. F. TAYLOR

### THE RED TOWERS OF TATTERSHALL

*Lincolnshire can boast one of the finest examples of early English brickwork in Tattershall Castle, between Sleaford and Horncastle. Bequeathed by the Marquess Curzon of Kedleston, it was built about 1440, and remains an almost perfect specimen of the English fortified dwelling. It was rebuilt by Henry VI's Lord High Treasurer, Baron Cromwell. Parts of an earlier structure built in the thirteenth century may also be seen.*

# INDEX

References to pictures are printed in *italic* type